Contents
Page

Contents   Page

Contents   Page

Contents   Page

Contents | Page

Contents | Page

Contents	**Page**

Contents   Page

Tables

Contents

Exhibits

Figures

To:

Linda for her enduring support that made this project possible;
Eddie, Al and Sid for their school of life wisdom and knowledge.

About the Author

James M. Yokley, Ph.D., is a Clinical Psychologist on the medical staff in the Department of Psychiatry at MetroHealth Medical Center in Cleveland, Ohio as well as an Assistant Professor at Case Western Reserve University School of Medicine and Department of Psychological Sciences. Dr. Yokley has expertise in the cognitive-behavioral treatment of multiple forms of unhealthy, harmful behavior and has been a regular conference speaker on Social Responsibility Therapy for unhealthy, harmful behavior treatment. He has authored five books/workbooks and more than 50 research publications, book chapters, and professional presentations. He has over 20 years of experience in training, teaching and supervising psychiatry residents, psychology and counseling graduate students, social workers, nursing staff and substance abuse treatment providers along with over 10 years experience training foster parents on managing unhealthy, harmful behavior. Dr. Yokley also has over 20 years program development and implementation experience in behavioral health treatment programs for unhealthy, harmful eating, substance use and sexual behavior. He is the current Behavioral Health Director of the MetroHealth Weight Loss Surgery and Weight Management Center where he provides staff consultation, supervision and direct services to patients with unhealthy, harmful eating behavior in need of lifestyle change. For the past 20 years, Dr. Yokley has also been the consulting psychologist at CommQuest Recovery and Prevention Services, a community treatment program providing substance abuse treatment on a full continuum of care.

Acknowledgements

I would like to thank Stephen Kerestes, LPCC-S, LICDC for his careful copy editing, important contributions related to substance abuse treatment and for adding gambling problem examples.

Finally, I would like to thank the many staff, students, clients and caretakers whose invaluable feedback was a key contribution to the development of Social Responsibility Therapy over the years.

Cover by Stephen Yokley, M.S.

Preface

Social Responsibility Therapy (SRT) was designed to help develop social responsibility in clients with multiple forms of unhealthy, harmful behavior from multiple cultural backgrounds, whose level of social responsibility will not only determine their future but will ultimately determine the quality of living in our society.

The Clinician's Guide to SRT begins with an introduction to SRT in Chapter 1 that summarizes the SRT treatment manual (Yokley, 2008) for those who may not be familiar with this treatment approach. Chapter 2 covers helping clients clarify their healthy lifestyle goals and prepare for the challenges of change. The SRT multicultural treatment approach and Multimethod-Multipath Behavior Therapy Model is covered in Chapter 3. This treatment model combines internal control, external control and social learning procedures to address the highly resistant, self-reinforcing nature of many unhealthy, harmful behaviors. Relapse prevention, emotional regulation, decisional balance and social problem solving are made user friendly for a wide range of clients and easy for clinicians to implement with instructions on how to "Avoid trouble, Calm down, Think it through and Solve the problem." Each of these four SRT "Healthy Behavior Success Skills" selected to help clients let go of unhealthy, harmful behaviors and pull themselves towards positive change (internal control) are described in chapters 4- 7. Chapter 8 covers setting up clients to succeed with structured, reinforced rules and appropriate consequences that provide the structure needed to help push clients towards positive change (external control). Helping clients develop "Healthy Relationship Success Skills" with PRAISE participation motivation and group unity skills is described in Chapter 9. PRAISE skills provide the positive modeling needed to redirect clients away from old unhealthy behaviors during stressful times and motivate them towards positive change (social learning). Finally, Chapters 10, 11 and 12 cover helping clients understand how they acquired, maintained and generalized their unhealthy, harmful behavior to other problem areas through The Problem Development Triad" along with clinician support for using the Social Responsibility Therapy workbooks.

All clinical intervention chapters begin with "straight to the point, goals and objectives" for clinician treatment planning and include both practical application examples and treatment exercises. In order to make this clinician's guide user friendly, whenever possible the research support for each treatment approach, method or procedure discussed has been moved to a text box at the end of each section. This maintains the clinical guide focus for practitioners in direct service settings while providing scientist-practitioners in academic settings with the background information needed for their teaching and research.

Clinicians who are familiar with the Social Responsibility Therapy workbooks but not the treatment manual may want to overview of this treatment approach by reading Chapter 1 first. Clinicians who want further information on the specific intervention skills used in Social Responsibility Therapy to address unhealthy, harmful behavior should read...

- Chapter 4 first if relapse prevention is their focus;
- Chapter 5 first if emotional regulation is their focus;
- Chapter 6 first if decisional balance (responsible decision-making) is their focus;
- Chapter 7 first if social problem solving is their focus.

"First we make our habits, and then our habits make us"-- John Dryden (1631- 1700)

Chapter 1
Introduction to Social Responsibility Therapy
for Unhealthy, Harmful Behavior

"You cannot hope to build a better world without improving the individuals. To that end each of us must work for his own improvement, and at the same time share a general responsibility for all humanity, our particular duty being to aid those to whom we think we can be most useful"
-- Marie Curie (1867-1934)

Social Responsibility Problem, Definition, Theory and Therapy

Problem: The lack of social responsibility exhibited by multiple forms of unhealthy, harmful behavior consistently on display in the news media tears the moral fabric of our society, threatens our safety and security, violates our civil rights, overcrowds our jails, overloads our health and human services system and prevents achievement of our life goals.

Definition- Social responsibility suggests an ethical obligation for organizations and individuals to act for the benefit of society by avoiding socially harmful acts or performing socially helpful ones.

Theory- Social responsibility theory originated in the 1940's during World War-II to address the responsibility of the news media. At that time the Commission on Freedom of the Press was established to address widespread public criticism of powerful publishers engaged in selfish politics for profit motive without concern for the rights or interests of the people. Social responsibility theory proposed that if the news media did not assume the responsibility of considering the overall needs of society, the public would demand government regulation of the media. Social responsibility theory was supported when the Commission noted that continued misuse of press power would necessitate regulation. Similar public criticism has occurred regarding corporations engaging in selfish business practices for profit motive without concern for the rights or interests of the people. This resulted in environmental protection laws and application of social responsibility theory to corporations who now self-regulate with Corporate Social Responsibility policies that avoid the need for government regulation.

Therapy- Social Responsibility Therapy (SRT) is a skills-based treatment aimed at developing the multicultural prosocial values, beliefs and behaviors needed for a socially responsible lifestyle free of unhealthy, harmful behaviors. SRT aims to increase socially responsible behavior, decrease unhealthy, harmful behavior and address contemporary issues in harmful behavior-specific treatment. SRT interventions promote positive personal as well as community adjustment by directly targeting unhealthy, harmful behavior. In SRT, unhealthy, harmful behavior relates to a lack of social responsibility, which is the result of a pathological level of social immaturity (i.e., serious problems with honesty, trust, loyalty, concern, and responsibility) in conjunction with a pathological level of emotional immaturity (i.e., serious problems with self-awareness, self-efficacy, and self-control). The strength-based aspect of SRT develops social maturity and emotional maturity as competing factors to unhealthy, harmful behavior. SRT utilizes evidence-based[1] interventions to target multiple forms of unhealthy, harmful behavior and develop the multicultural prosocial values needed for positive lifestyle change. Targeting multiple forms of unhealthy harmful behavior helps prevent shifting from one unhealthy, harmful behavior to another during treatment. It also allows a broader view of unhealthy, harmful behavior as part of a human nature spectrum of maladaptive coping responses. This view avoids stigmatizing and alienating clients, which can decrease denial and increase client acceptance of treatment. SRT combines research-supported interventions that use different methods and pathways to increase intervention intensity and therapeutic pressure towards positive change. Initial outcome data is encouraging (Yokley, 2010a) and SRT development projects exhibit strong social validity (i.e., social significance/importance of project treatment goals/outcomes and social acceptability of procedures, Foster & Mash, 1999). In order to maintain a healthy economy, relationship, culture, and community, we have to establish and maintain a human development infrastructure with particular emphasis on behavioral health programs such as SRT that develop social-emotional maturity characteristics as competing factors to unhealthy, harmful behavior.

Social Responsibility Therapy Development
"Necessity is the mother of invention"--(Plato circa 369AD in The Republic, Book II)

SRT was originally designed to help develop social responsibility in young people with multiple forms of unhealthy, harmful, behavior, from multiple cultural backgrounds, whose level of social responsibility will not only determine their future but will also ultimately determine the quality of living in our society. SRT was developed as a "clinic therapy" in a clinic setting with high problem severity heterogeneous clinic referrals. This development path was almost the mirror image opposite of the typical university-based "research therapy" development approach that often begins with recruitment of low problem severity homogeneous samples (Weisz, Weiss, and Donenberg, 1992). SRT began its development in a multicounty detention center for the treatment of youth who were removed from their homes for sexually abusive behavior. Almost immediately it was apparent that the referral behavior was not their only problem behavior in need of treatment. Co-occurring behavior problems threatened removal of youth referred for sexual behavior problems from their post-release foster home placements as 59% exhibiting all 5 types of unhealthy, harmful behavior measured at admission (i.e., sexual, abuse, physical abuse, property abuse, substance abuse and trust abuse) and the average client exhibiting 4.5 types of unhealthy, harmful behavior (Yokley and Boettner, 2002). This finding is consistent with research revealing the referral unhealthy, harmful behavior is not usually the only problem behavior in need of treatment, particularly with substance abuse which is a relatively prevalent co-occurring problem across unhealthy, harmful behaviors including sexual abuse, physical abuse, property abuse/gambling and food abuse/overeating (Basu, Paltiel & Pollack, 2008; Greenfield,et. al. 2010; Klostermann et. al. 2010; Levenson, 2016; Okunna et. al. 2016). It is obviously too time and cost prohibitive to treat multiple co-occurring unhealthy, harmful behaviors consecutively. Fortunately, research suggests treating these problems concurrently with similar treatment strategies (Zmuda, 2014). Sexual behavior problem relapse was rare and relapse was much more frequent with other forms of unhealthy, harmful behavior and required program modification to address multiple forms of unhealthy, harmful behavior. This made SRT useful with other referral populations paving the way for SRT to be applied to substance abuse and weight management clients.

The content and process of the interventions employed in SRT were selected to be:

1. **Effective-** by putting together an essential evidence-based treatment toolbox that is necessary and sufficient to address unhealthy, harmful behavior;[2]
2. **Engaging-** with communication that holds the participant's emotional attention, learning experiences that are personally relevant and a Structured Discovery insight/understanding development approach that is *structured* to help participants *discover* important motives for their unhealthy, harmful behavior;[3]
3. **Portable-** making transfer of training from sessions to the community inherently easy through repetition of key concepts, user friendly, relevant mnemonic devices, acronyms and behavioral adages that are found in a variety of community settings. In addition, multicultural prosocial values that enable client navigation across cultures and intervention training that is useful across problem areas are reinforced.[4]

In SRT, unhealthy harmful behaviors are summarized in five basic categories: trust abuse (e.g., lying, relationship cheating, fraud, harmful behavior cover up tactics); substance abuse (e.g., drugs, alcohol, cigarettes, overeating); physical abuse (e.g., domestic violence, school bullying), property abuse (e.g., theft, vandalism), and sexual abuse (e.g., harassment, molestation, rape). Some unhealthy, harmful behaviors are fairly equally harmful to both self and others (e.g., substance abuse liver damage to self and impaired driving collisions into others). However, behaviors that are primarily harmful to others (e.g., sexual or physical abuse) can do secondary harm to self (e.g., incarceration for abusive behavior). Likewise, and behaviors that are primarily harmful to self (e.g., unhealthy eating/obesity) can do secondary harm to others (e.g., emotional and financial stress on relatives providing for loved ones with weight-related health problems). SRT addresses harmful behavior along a two axis Harmful Behavior Continuum of behavior severity and primary area of impact target (See Table 1.1)[5]

Harmful behavior-specific Twelve-Step programs span the Harmful Behavior Continuum from Food Addicts Anonymous to Sex-Addicts Anonymous. Likewise, abuse-specific treatments limiting referrals to sexual abuse, domestic violence (physical abuse), substance abuse and obesity (food abuse) are numerous. Many if not most of these programs focus heavily in eliminating socially irresponsible, negative, harmful behavior. A focus on developing socially responsible, positive, helpful behavior is typically lacking. In addition, harmful behavior-specific programs by nature have a number of treatment issues and barriers that can interfere with lasting behavior change. SRT maintains a strong focus on developing socially responsible behavior while addressing the following key treatment issues and barriers to positive behavior change in unhealthy, harmful behavior-specific treatment.

1. *Harmful behavior comorbidity,* i.e., the referral unhealthy, harmful behavior is not usually the only harmful behavior.
2. *Comorbidity adverse impact,* i.e., one harmful behavior can trigger others.
3. *Harmful behavior migration,* i.e., unhealthy, harmful behavior can migrate to another harmful behavior during treatment when it is being observed and shift back afterwards;
4. *Negative social influence,* i.e., peer, parent or partner modeling or encouraging unhealthy, harmful behavior.

5. *The need for increased intervention intensity* to address treatment resistance due to the combined effects of negative social influence, comorbidity adverse impact and harmful behavior migration.
6. *The need for comprehensive harmful behavior conceptualization* covering harmful behavior acquisition, maintenance and generalization due to unhealthy, harmful behavior comorbidity and treatment resistance.
7. *The need for multicultural recognition in treatment program design* since unhealthy, harmful behavior occurs across cultures and minority treatment problems include high dropout rates, infrequent session use and poor level of functioning at the end of treatment.

Note: Research support for harmful behavior-specific treatment barriers is provided in Chapter 3.

Table 1.1   The Harmful Behavior Continuum: Selected Behavior Examples

Primary Area of Impact ⟶

	Harmful to Self	**Harmful to Self and Others**	**Harmful to Others**
B **e** **h** **a** **v** **i** **o** **r** **S** **e** **v** **e** **r** **i** **t** **y**	**Unhealthy Eating** (Overeat/binge/purge/starve) **Medication Non-compliance** **Nicotine Abusers** (Deviant masturbation, porno) (Single shopaholics) (Single alcohol and drug abusers) Source: Condensed with permission from Table 1.1 in Yokley (2008) 4	**Sexual Compulsives** (Unprotected sex, affairs, prostitution) **Money Abusers** (Gamblers with partners/family) **Substance Abusers** (Alcohol and drug abusers with partners/family)	(Embezzlers, Credit card fraud) (Drunk drivers, Drug dealers) **Verbal/Power Abusers** (employee harassment) **Property Abusers** (theft, fraud, vandalism, arson) **Physical Abusers** (bullying, assault, child abuse) **Sexual Abusers** (rape, child molestation) **Contract Killers** **Lust Murderers, Serial Killers** **School/Active Shooters**

SRT addresses harmful behavior comorbidity by targeting multiple forms of unhealthy, harmful behavior which in turn prevents comorbidity adverse impact and harmful behavior migration. The SRT focus on development and reinforcement of multicultural prosocial values through positive staff and peer modeling addresses negative social influence and the need for multicultural recognition in treatment program design. Finally, while many unhealthy, harmful behavior treatment programs focus on understanding and breaking the behavior maintenance cycle, SRT utilizes a Problem Development Triad to help clients understand how they acquired their problem behavior, what maintained it and how it spread to other life problem areas.

The ART of Social Responsibility Therapy

In SRT interventions that are aimed at avoiding relapse and achieving life goals involve: Awareness training on what clients need to know; Responsibility training on the tools clients need to learn and; Tolerance training on how to tolerate feedback, unwanted feelings, change and setbacks. Successful implementation of SRT methods and procedures relies on these basic components. Awareness training in SRT involves developing awareness of thoughts, feelings and motivations (i.e., "where you are coming from")[6] associated with actions. Staff review of the daily Situation Response Analysis log helps clients become aware of the connections between their thoughts, feelings and behaviors.[7] Awareness of the antecedents (triggers) and consequences of unhealthy, harmful behavior is developed along with awareness of self-defeating habits (e.g., ruminating, procrastination and giving up) and needs (e.g., exaggerated for attention, acceptance or excitement).[8] These awareness building blocks are important in helping the client develop awareness of their Problem Development Triad which involves understanding: 1) how they acquired their unhealthy, harmful behavior through the Risk Factor Chain; 2) how their unhealthy, harmful behavior was maintained by the Stress-Relapse Cycle and; 3) how their unhealthy, harmful behavior generalized to other problem areas.[9] Key Awareness Training advances that SRT clients need to be able to demonstrate at the end of their treatment center around the question… "What do you need to become aware of and 'Keep up front' in order to maintain your recovery and get what you want in life?" Example pre and post treatment SRT Awareness Training questions are provided in Appendix A, "Life Long Recovery Skills" and "Knowledge about how you developed your problem" sections.

Responsibility Training in SRT involves helping clients take responsibility for replacing their unhealthy, harmful behavior with healthy, prosocial behavior. Examples include learning healthy behavior success skills for: relapse prevention (i.e., how to avoid and escape high-risk situations for relapse); emotional regulation (i.e., how to dissipate unwanted feelings and accommodate to them), decisional balance (i.e., how to make responsible snap decisions and weigh out important life decisions) and; social problem solving (i.e., how to meet healthy lifestyle goals by generating solutions to overcome barriers). Developing multicultural prosocial values as competing factors to unhealthy, harmful behavior is also an important aspect of responsibility training in SRT where our number one responsibility is self-control.[10] Think about it, even in the top 20 cities with the highest number of police there are only 4- 7 officers for every 1,000 citizens.[11] This means that if you issued mass e-mail, Facebook, twitter and automated cell phone messages declaring this Saturday as "One free item day" at a specific department store and everyone responded, that specific department store would be put out of business in your city because there simply is not enough law enforcement personnel or jail space to prevent large scale looting. The bottom line is that our community is counting on our self-control which is strongly influenced by how much we value honesty, trust, loyalty, concern and responsibility. Key Responsibility Training advances that SRT clients need to be able to demonstrate at the end of their treatment center around the question… "What do you need to be responsible for learning to help you maintain your recovery and get what you want in life?" Example pre and post treatment SRT Responsibility Training questions are provided in Appendix A, "Healthy Relationship Success Skills" and "Healthy Behavior Success Skills" sections.

In addition to traditional diversity tolerance, Tolerance Training in SRT includes developing feedback tolerance, frustration tolerance, need tolerance and distress tolerance. For example, in relapse prevention, clients learn to tolerate feedback about their behavior patterns and harmful behavior triggers in order to become aware of how their problem starts. In emotional regulation, clients learn to tolerate frustration and other unwanted feelings to prevent from continuing to act them out. In decisional balance, clients learn to tolerate change after weighing out the benefits and drawbacks of their decisions so they will be able to maintain their decisions to change. In social problem solving, clients learn to tolerate setbacks after implementing solutions so they will be able to keep trying other options until they meet their goals.

Developing feedback tolerance is particularly important in resisting having the last word in conflict situations by accepting that "When your words are no better than silence, silence is far better than words." Frustration tolerance includes learning to manage problems with low frustration tolerance and stopping self from "feeding the PIG", (i.e., the Problem of Immediate Gratification)[12] through immature "King Baby" fits that occur when frustrated because needs are not being immediately gratified (Cunningham, 1992). Need tolerance involves learning to avoid compromising yourself (i.e., your values and what you believe is right or wrong) for attention, acceptance or excitement.[13] Finally, developing distress tolerance is focused on decreasing emotional reactivity[14] and not justifying unhealthy, harmful actions based on unwanted feelings.[15] Key Tolerance Training advances that SRT clients need to be able to demonstrate at the end of their treatment center around the question… "What do you need to learn to tolerate in order to maintain your recovery and get what you want in life?"

Tolerance Training History and Research Support: Tolerance training, a term coined by George DeLeon was defined as low tolerance for discomfort of any sort. Low discomfort tolerance was posited as both a cause and a consequence of chemical abuse by DeLeon (1990-91). Tolerance training in the residential Therapeutic Community for substance abuse takes a social learning path toward the development of frustration tolerance. In the Therapeutic Community, social learning procedures are aimed at delaying gratification of urges to act out feelings from interpersonal conflicts and other stressors incurred during activities of daily living which would be expected to trigger substance relapse (See "If you can't deny the feeling, delay the action", p.16). This social learning method of tolerance training was implemented as an inoculation method against later relapse cravings due to expected life stressors after treatment. While this social learning path towards developing discomfort tolerance was probably the first frustration/distress tolerance method used in the Therapeutic Community clinical setting since the late 1950's, the first internal control path towards frustration/distress tolerance was probably the ABC model used in Rational Emotive Behavior Therapy developed by Albert Ellis (Ellis, 2002; Ziegler & Leslie, 2003) which provided the foundation for addiction treatment alternatives to the 12-step model (Bishop, 1996). More recently, Dialectical Behavior Therapy originally developed by Marsha Linehan for chronically suicidal women with borderline personality disorder integrated distress tolerance with several other internal control skills to successfully target self-harm and substance use problems (Dimeff et. al., 2000).

The negative reinforcement model of addiction posits that substance use provides perceived and/or actual relief from negative affective states, which reinforces it and increases the likelihood of substance use in the future (Baker et al., 2004). This is consistent with research that shows depressive symptoms can predict alcohol relapse (e.g., Kodi et. al. 2008) and indicates that ability to tolerate distress can determine the ability to avoid relapse. There is some evidence that individuals with high levels of depression and low levels of distress tolerance exhibit greater substance abuse problems (Ali, Seitz-Brown, & Daughters, 2015; Gorka, Ali & Daughters, 2012). In addition, lower psychological distress tolerance predicts a higher dropout rate of smokers before completing their first session and predicts early residential substance abuse treatment dropout (Daughters et. al. 2005; Mc Pherson et. al. 2008).

Finally, as expected distress tolerance treatments can have a positive impact on the treatment of individuals with substance use disorders (Bornovalova et. al. 2012). Regarding unhealthy, harmful "comfort eating", distress tolerance difficulty and the belief that eating will relieve negative affect has been linked with bulimic symptoms (e.g., Kozak & Fought, 2011; Lavender et. al., 2015). Low distress tolerance is present in some individuals whose behaviors are harmful to others, violate the law (e.g., sexual abuse/harassment, physical abuse/assault, property abuse/theft,) and involve trust abuse/deceit,/lying without concern/remorse or a sense of responsibility. Specifically, individuals with antisocial personality disorder evidence low distress tolerance with inability to persist in goal-directed behavior during an aversive situation (e.g., Daughters et. al. 2008; Sargeant et. al. 2011). It should be noted that this finding does not apply to the psychopathic subset of antisocial personalities (about 25%) whose characteristic emotional detachment and absence of startle response to threatening stimuli provides them with a higher distress tolerance.

In summary, SRT has Awareness Training, Responsibility Training and Tolerance Training (ART) components in all aspects of the treatment model. One outcome measure of clients who successfully complete treatment is their ability to state what they need to: be Aware of about their harmful behavior; take Responsibility for the management of their harmful behavior and; learn to Tolerate unwanted feelings and setbacks in order to maintain their harmful behavior recovery. Further information on the basic ART of SRT is provided in Yokley, 2008.

Developing Socially Responsible Behavior
"Our prime purpose in this life is to help others.
And if you can't help them, at least don't hurt them" -- Dalai Lama

In SRT unhealthy, harmful behavior is considered to be the primary symptom of a social-emotional maturity deficit and increasing social responsibility involves developing social-emotional maturity. Social maturity is defined in SRT as having adequate multicultural prosocial values (i.e., honesty, trust, loyalty, concern, and responsibility) while emotional maturity involves adequate self-awareness, self-efficacy, and self-control. The strength-based aspect of SRT develops social maturity and emotional maturity as competing factors to unhealthy, harmful behavior.

Social Maturity Development
In SRT social maturity is defined as having multicultural prosocial values (i.e., honesty, trust, loyalty, concern, and responsibility)[16] that are strong enough to compete against or block unhealthy, harmful behavior thoughts and feelings (i.e., including cravings/urges) in order to enable socially responsible behavior. Thus, a central SRT treatment focus is on developing social maturity with "Healthy Relationship Success Skills" which involves actualizing multicultural prosocial values (Frankl, 1963). Putting honesty, trust, loyalty, concern and responsibility into action is a competing response to multiple forms of unhealthy, harmful behavior (i.e., sexual abuse, physical abuse, property abuse, substance abuse and trust abuse). These social maturity values were selected based on existing research support[16] and are consistent with multicultural values theory.[17] Honesty, trust, loyalty, concern, and responsibility are a subset of the 19 distinctive traits identified through content analysis that many people may consider to be characteristic of a moral person (Aquino & Reed, 2002) and were included in the descriptors of what was considered to be a highly moral person after data reduction techniques in a study of moral maturity (Walker & Pitts, 1998). Since multicultural prosocial values and behavior are not compatible with unhealthy, harmful behavior increasing one can act to inhibit or block the other

as outlined in Table 1.2. Simply stated, it is not possible to be a dishonest, irresponsible drug abuser while being honest and responsible and it is not possible to be a physically abusive cheating boyfriend while being concerned and loyal. Thus, the rationale behind reinforcing multicultural prosocial values is to develop healthy relationship success skills while inhibiting unhealthy, harmful behavior.

Table 1.2. Social Maturity Development (i.e., honesty, trust, loyalty, concern & responsibility) as Competing Responses to Unhealthy, Harmful Behavior

Social Maturity Development	Unhealthy, Harmful Behavior
Getting <u>honest</u> in treatment about...	• sexual abuse fantasies (e.g., child sex or date rape); • physical abuse urges (e.g., domestic violence, bullying); • property abuse plans (e.g., shoplifting, vandalism, gambling, overspending); • substance abuse cravings (e.g., alcohol/drugs, tobacco, food) • trust abuse thoughts (e.g., lying, partner cheating, fraud).
and developing <u>trust</u> by disclosing past unhealthy, harmful behavior patterns and situations that are high risk for...	• coercing a child into sex or forcing a date into sex; • physically assaulting a partner; • shoplifting; vandalism, gambling, overspending; • drinking, drugging, smoking, overeating; • lying to cover-up, cheating on a partner, conning someone.
while developing <u>loyalty</u> and <u>concern</u> for yourself/others (e.g., empathy training) and taking <u>responsibility</u> to make relapse prevention plans that will prevent another episode of...	• sexual abuse; • physical abuse; • property abuse; • substance abuse; • trust abuse.
are competing responses to...	• making plans to molest a child or rape a dating partner; • justifying domestic violence, bullying; • rationalizing shoplifting, vandalism, gambling, over-spending; • excusing drinking/drug use, smoking or overeating; • minimizing lying, cheating/infidelity or conning someone.

The theoretical foundation for reinforcing prosocial values and behaviors as competing responses to unhealthy, harmful behavior can be traced back to differential reinforcement and reciprocal inhibition. Differential reinforcement of alternative behavior (DRA) is used to increase appropriate behavior while decreasing inappropriate behavior by withholding reinforcement during inappropriate behavior and giving reinforcers when appropriate behavior is observed. DRA is one of the most common applied behavior analysis interventions used to decrease unwanted behavior. DRA has been successful with a range of problem behavior particularly in children and is well established for treating destructive behavior of those with developmental disabilities (e.g., Petscher et. al., 2009). This approach can be especially effective with pre-teaching discussions of the alternative behavior desired to replace the unwanted behavior (e.g., LeGray et. al. 2013).

Reciprocal inhibition is a behavior therapy technique based on the principle that different physiological responses are incompatible and mutually inhibit each other. Reciprocal inhibition was originally developed in the 1950's by Joseph Wolpe for the treatment of anxiety and associated muscle tension with the competing response of progressive muscle relaxation.

Teaching competing responses to unwanted feelings has been successful in the treatment of anxiety (e.g., Wolpe, 1958, 1995) and anger reactions (e.g., Hearn and Evans, 1972) along with deviant sexual behavior (e.g., Lowenstein, 1973). Empathy development research provides another important building block in the foundation of developing prosocial values and behaviors as competing responses to unhealthy, harmful behavior. Empathy development facilitates prosocial behavior, a competing response that helps prevent aggressive behavior (e.g., Eisenberg and Miller, 1987; Foubert and Newberry, 2006; Miller and Eisenberg, 1988; Sams and Truscott, 2004; Swick, 2005; Vaziri & Azimi, 2012) and acts as a protective factor against serious offending for males and females (e.g., Broidy et al., 2003; Wastell, Cairns & Haywood, 2009).

When teaching competing responses is accomplished by withholding reinforcement during inappropriate behavior and rewarding behavior that is incompatible with the problem behavior, the procedure is known as differential reinforcement of incompatible behavior (DRI). In applied behavior analysis, DRI is the intervention of first choice for reduction of high-rate challenging behaviors (Jones & Baker, 1990). Problem behavior can remain controlled when restitution is added to DRI (e.g., de Zubicaray & Clair, 1998). Restitution is an alternative to punishment of aggressive behavior. Restitution educates the individual to assume responsibility for the disruption caused by their behavior by requiring the situation to be amended. Key features of restitution outlined by Foxx and Azrin (1972) are that the restitution should be: directly related to the problem behavior; conducted immediately following the act; extended in duration and; the individual should be required to actively perform the restitution. In SRT, individuals with behavior problems that are harmful to others receive Emotional Restitution Training to prepare them for therapist supervised meetings when requested by the survivors of their harmful behavior. Emotional Restitution Training is described in Chapter 3 of Yokley (2008).

In SRT, the healthy relationship success skills exercise on "What do we want in others" is an example of pre-teaching the desired prosocial behavior in preparation for DRA. Developing prosocial values and behaviors as competing responses to unhealthy, harmful behavior involves: 1) consistent "Responsible reinforcement" of honesty, trust, loyalty, concern and responsibility (i.e., DRI) throughout treatment while; 2) implementing healthy behavior success skills to inhibit unhealthy, harmful behavior with emotional restitution when needed after behavior slips.

Social Maturity Research Support Summary: Probably the most established evidence base for developing social maturity (i.e., prosocial values and behaviors) as competing factors to unhealthy, harmful behavior comes from the Therapeutic Community (TC) model. This model implements DRI by teaching the prosocial values of "Right Living", i.e., Honesty, Responsible concern, Work ethic and Learning for personal growth (DeLeon, 2000) as competing responses to the unhealthy, harmful behavior exhibited by the criminal addict population in TC residential treatment. Ongoing restitution interventions in this model are referred to as "learning experiences." Research support for this treatment approach is extensive including meta-analytic research support in the community and corrections-based settings (Lees, Manning, and Rawlings, 2004; Pearson and Lipton, 1999) and has been successfully applied to the treatment with multiple forms of unhealthy, harmful behavior often associated with the criminal addict lifestyle but also involving the homeless, mentally ill, antisocial personality disordered, and sex offenders. Successful therapeutic community applications include the ability to address self-harm (HIV risk behavior such as sex with high-risk people, unprotected sex, or needle sharing), sexual abuse/offense (including prostitution and promiscuity), physical abuse (violent crime), property abuse (property crime), substance abuse (including drug trafficking), and trust abuse through honesty development (e.g., Boswell and Wedge, 2003; Clarke, 2002; Cooperman, Falkin, and Cleland, 2005; DeLeon, 2000; De Leon et al., 2000;

Jainchill, Hawke, and Messina, 2005; Messina et al., 2002). Other established treatments that utilize prosocial values development to support positive behavior change are Dialectical Behavior Therapy (e.g., Cameron, Palm Reed & Gaudino, 2014), Acceptance and Commitment Therapy (Robb (2007) and Logotherapy (Sharp et. al., 2004).

Social Maturity Development Summary
In summary, social maturity is developed in SRT with "Healthy Relationship Success Skills" which involves putting the multicultural prosocial values of honesty, trust, loyalty, concern and responsibility into action (Frankel, 1963) as competing responses to multiple forms of unhealthy, harmful behavior. Developing prosocial values and behaviors as competing responses to unhealthy, harmful behavior has a strong theoretical and research evidence base. Honesty, trust, loyalty, concern and responsibility are what we want from peers, partners, parents and employers who also want these characteristics from us. The value of these characteristics cannot be underestimated. They are the commodities needed to develop the relationships we want, avoid the harmful behavior we don't want and establish the self-esteem we need to succeed in life.

Emotional Maturity Development
Emotional maturity development is necessary in order to manage unhealthy, harmful behavior. In SRT emotional maturity is defined as *self-awareness, self-efficacy and self-control*. Developing emotional maturity is critical in SRT because in order to successfully manage unhealthy, harmful behavior, it is necessary to have: enough *self-awareness* to identify thoughts, feelings, motivations, and situations that can trigger the harmful behavior; enough *self-efficacy* (confidence) to try solutions and substitute new alternative responses, behaviors, and activities for old negative, harmful ones; and enough *self-control* to delay gratification of urges, postpone emotional decisions and consider consequences and in order to do the right thing.

Self-Awareness
"What is necessary to change a person is to change his awareness of himself" -- Abraham Maslow (1908- 1970)

SRT develops self-awareness of high-risk situations for relapse including trigger emotions, irresponsible thinking and impulsive decisions along with stress buildup from daily living problems. Developing self-awareness is critical for client relapse prevention planning. In general, processes that reduce self-awareness (e.g., narrowing awareness to focus on expected benefits only or blocking awareness by ruminating on cravings/urges) are needed to continue the harmful behavior while treatment interventions that increase self-awareness (e.g., identification of relapse triggers and harmful behavior consequences) are needed to stop the harmful behavior. Clients relapse by playing their harmful behavior tape through in their head from the beginning when they first get the urge/craving to the middle where they are receiving the expected/desired benefits. Ruminating on the craving/urge and expected benefits of indulging builds up the desire to go through with the harmful behavior and stops the tape at that point. Not playing the tape through to the end blocks out awareness of possible consequences and clears the way for relapse.

Increasing self-awareness of the feelings and situations that start the harmful behavior empowers clients to avoid justifying unhealthy actions based on unwanted feelings and avoid situations that put them at high-risk for relapse. Increasing self-awareness of the irresponsible thoughts that justify decisions to do (or continue) the behavior provides clients with the chance to escape the high-risk situations that they find themselves in and escape falling back into their relapse cycle. Finally increasing self-awareness of the harmful consequences to self and others makes it more difficult for clients to justify entering high-risk situations for relapse, start or continue, unhealthy, harmful behavior.

Self-awareness development includes learning to use the "Mirror Concept". The goal of the Mirror Concept is to master using other people's feedback as a mirror to better see yourself. This requires focusing on what is being said, not how it is being said or who is saying it. Teaching the Mirror Concept allows client self-awareness training received in group and individual therapy to generalize beyond treatment sessions and into the community. Given that most if not all unhealthy, harmful behaviors can be initiated by unwanted emotions (i.e., justifying actions based on feelings), emotional awareness training is an important aspect of self-awareness development. Regularly stopping what you are saying to clients and asking "Right now, what am I thinking and how do I feel?" can help clients begin their emotional awareness training in a less threatening manner by looking at others as practice to prepare them to begin looking at themselves.

Self-awareness of certain coping strategies is also important in relapse prevention. Developing an action-oriented lifestyle with an emphasis on doing to avoid feeling contributes to self-awareness problems. Individuals with biological risk factors including a family history of depression or traumatic risk factors such as child abuse, can experience a manic defense against depression. This chronic hypomania involves going through life at 100mph in the 10mph zone, a rate which precludes feeling. Individuals with this coping style need to learn to "slow down and let yourself feel" in order to be able to identify, label and channel their unwanted emotions to avoid racing into relapse. Others adopt being over-active when it comes to doing for others which blocks out awareness of own needs and caring for self. This creates resentment because they do not get back what they put in and like depression, resentment can also trigger relapse.

Individuals from dysfunctional families (including street gangs and negative peers) where emotional expression results in harsh ridicule can develop hypersensitivity to criticism, "a fear of being put down" (Yochelson & Samenow, 1976) and bottle up feelings. This sets the occasion for acting feelings out. In dysfunctional surroundings, the ability to develop self-awareness with the "Mirror Concept" using honest, concerned, responsible feedback from others is blocked by a "closed channel"[1] defense against the expectation of harsh ridicule, devaluation, derogatory remarks or verbal assault. Self-awareness development in those from dysfunctional surroundings requires accepting that it is not possible to get responsible, constructive feedback from irresponsible, destructive people and getting help from mental health professionals.

Practical Application Example- After three times in drug and alcohol treatment 19-year-old Brandon, remained unaware of the connection between his marijuana amotivational syndrome, chronic school truancy and repeated job loss for theft. Whenever his high-risk situations for relapse were pointed out, he would feel attacked, snap back, "You don't know me!" (which really meant "You should agree with me") and shut down. As a result, he was unable to recognize that whenever he became upset, he would fall back into his stress-relapse cycle and get high again. He also did not realize that he managed stress much better when around people who supported him and held him accountable. Instead, he believed that they were against him and were holding him back. Brandon needed learn to use others feedback to develop self-awareness of his emotional triggers and avoid relapse. In addition, he needed to accept the benefits of support and accountability in order to stop holding himself back in treatment.

Self-Awareness Research Support Summary: Self-awareness has been considered to be a critical ingredient for effective counseling and psychotherapy (Pieterse et. al., 2013). Emotional awareness is prerequisite to emotional regulation and self-control of unhealthy, harmful behavior. Low levels of emotional awareness and emotional regulation ability have been identified in individuals with unhealthy, harmful behavior including: sex offenders (e.g., Gery et. al., 2009); alcohol substance dependent clients (e.g., Carton et. al., 2010; Stasiewicz et. al., 2012); pathological gamblers (e.g., Williams et. al., 2012) and; obesity/emotional eaters (e.g., Da Ros et. al., 2011; Rommel et. al., 2012). Increasing self-awareness can help fight self-control failure by preventing the depletion of cognitive resources needed for self-control (e.g., Alberts, Martijn & de Vries, 2011). Negative emotions are high-risk situations for triggering unhealthy, harmful behavior and are a relapse prevention target in the treatment of: sex offenders (e.g., Jeglic, Mercado & Levenson, 2012; Steen, 1995); batterers (e.g., Dinwiddie, 1992); alcohol/drug addicts (Bradizza & Stasiewicz, 2003; El Sheikh & Bashir, 2004; Ross et. al., 1994); criminal behavior among forensic clients (e.g., Day, 2009); binge eating (Carano et. al., 2012) and; exercise relapse (Stetson et. al. 2005).

The literature on cognitive distortions that set the occasion for or maintain unhealthy, harmful behavior and unwanted mood states is fairly comprehensive. Published sets of cognitive distortions include: Irrational beliefs (Ellis, 1994), originally developed in Rational Emotive Behavior Therapy for depression, anxiety and self-depreciation (later applied to substance abuse and personality disorders); Automatic thoughts (Burns, 1980; Beck et. al. 1979), originally developed in Cognitive Therapy for depression (later applied to anxiety, substance abuse and personality disorders); Thinking errors (Yochelson & Samenow, 1976, Ch. 5). Originally developed for criminal personality; Cognitive distortions in aggression (Bandura, 1973), developed for social learning theory of aggression; Schemas in personality disorders (Young, 1990; McGinn & Young, 1996), developed for personality disorders; Cognitive distortions that impede social problem solving (D'Zurilla & Netzu, 2007), developed for social problem solving therapy and; Irresponsible thinking (Yokley, 2008; 2010a), developed in Social Responsibility Therapy on externalizing population with a history of internalizing issues (abusers with a typical history of being abused).

Self-Efficacy

"People who have a sense of self-efficacy bounce back from failure; they approach things in terms of how to handle them rather than worrying about what can go wrong" -- Albert Bandura

Self-efficacy involves core goal attainment ability beliefs and judgements of "how well one can execute courses of action required to deal with prospective situations" (p. 122, Bandura, 1982; 1977). This "can do" belief in the power to produce the desired effect impacts emotional well-being, stress/depression vulnerability and tenacity in the face of goal frustration. According to Bandura, "The capacity to exercise control over the nature and quality of one's life is the essence of humanness" (p. 1, Bandura, 2001). Self-efficacy can apply to many behaviors and "recovery self-efficacy pertains to beliefs about one's ability to resume a behavior after a setback" (Luszczynska et. al. 2007). In order to manage unhealthy, harmful behavior, it is necessary for clients to develop enough recovery self-efficacy (i.e., belief in ability to succeed in recovery) to try new solutions to old unhealthy, harmful habits. This involves substituting new alternative responses, behavior, and activities for old negative, harmful ones. In SRT, recovery self-efficacy is developed through knowledge of when to act and what to do to avoid relapse. Knowing when to act requires awareness of high-risk situations for relapse. Learning what to do requires reinforced practice of ACTS skills for unhealthy, harmful behavior management.

Pastorelli et al. (2001), reminds us that self-efficacy (i.e., judgments of personal capability) is often used interchangeably with self-esteem (i.e., judgments of self-worth) and confused with locus of control (i.e., judgment that one's fate is determined by self or external forces). This is particularly true with a considerable proportion of those with unhealthy, harmful behavior with adverse historical risk factors. The abuse and neglect experienced in a rejecting environment of helplessness have left these individuals with low general self-efficacy, low self-esteem and an external locus of control. Put another way, their adverse historical risk factors left them feeling inadequate, lacking confidence to change and attributing any changes that do occur in their lives to forces outside of themselves (e.g., bad luck, the system, etc.) which further reinforces helplessness. For clinical purposes, "low self-efficacy" with the SRT unhealthy, harmful behavior population is used to describe the "I can't attitude" about ability to change that is supported by a low self-esteem and an external locus of control. In summary, self-efficacy problems in individuals with unhealthy, harmful behavior problems often relate to adverse historical risk factors that were not in their control resulting in a form of learned helplessness with reactive depression, anxiety and anger reactions.

When it comes to confidence in ability to change, self-efficacy is for SRT treatment purposes, the opposite of the sense of helplessness and powerlessness created by historical risk factors such as traumatic, inescapable abuse. It is important to remember that severely traumatic historical risk factors are not the only contributors to low self-efficacy. According to Pastorelli et al. (2001), the first three sources of efficacy information are family, peers and school where positive, responsive significant others can set the occasion for success experiences that can build a sense of personal efficacy or failure experiences related to dysfunctional parenting, negative peer influence and an unhealthy school environment that can undermine self-efficacy. Thus, dysfunctional families with constant criticism from harsh, perfectionist parents can impact self-efficacy leaving children feeling inadequate and helpless to win acceptance from others because they believe "I can never do anything right." In this respect, low self-efficacy can directly impact achievement motivation.

Just like there can be unhealthy, negative forms of self-awareness (e.g., hypervigilance reflecting paranoia), there may also be unhealthy, negative forms of self-efficacy. Yochelson & Samenow (1976) describe a "criminal pride" which appears to reflect criminal behavior self-efficacy complete with grandiosity in "super-optimism" thinking about ability to get away with anything.

Practical application example- Diego, a 20-year-old who continued to get in trouble with the law finally confided to thinking, "I don't have to plan ahead because I can talk my way out of anything." His problem was being overly confident in his ability to manipulate others (i.e., grandiosity or negative self-efficacy). He needed to be talked though this grandiose thinking by reviewing the statistics of all of his favorite sports team players in order to accept that even the best of the best can't succeed 100% of the time. Then he needed to discuss and consider the Abraham Lincoln quote that "You can fool all the people some of the time, and some of the people all the time, but you cannot fool all the people all the time" in order to accept that his grandiose thinking (negative self-efficacy) was putting him at risk for serious consequences and jeopardizing his freedom. Helping clients question their confidence in the negative things they are good at (i.e., challenge grandiosity beliefs) and build their confidence in the positive things they are not good at or have never had the courage to try (i.e., reinforce prosocial behavior attempts) is an important challenge to meet in self-efficacy development.

In summary, historical risk factors involving situations where client responses to problem situations consistently had no effect inhibits the development of self-efficacy and contributes to a learned helplessness "I can't attitude" that prevents trying new responses or solutions to social problems. In addition, negative expectations associated with low self-efficacy can interfere with incoming positive feedback.

Practical application example- Reinecke (1995) presents a 17-year-old youth with abusive behavior (i.e., property abuse, trust abuse and substance abuse) and comorbid depression who stated "it's really hard for me to accept positive things from people... from therapists, my mother, anybody... Whenever I'd do something right, or someone would say something good about me... I'd ignore it, then I'd purposefully go and get in trouble again" (p. 317). Helping the client become aware of the connection between their adverse historical risk factors and their low self-efficacy (i.e., helpless, "I can't attitude" and consequent lack of effort to change), is an important first step towards getting them to try new prosocial coping responses.

Low self-efficacy involving feelings of helpless, hopeless incompetence to cope with life problems is linked to low self-esteem and is a social-emotional risk factor which decreases resistance to pressures and temptations. For example, youth with sexually abusive behavior and low self-esteem are at higher risk for acting that inferior state out sexually (e.g., Smith, Wampler et al., 2005) and men who are physically abusive to their partners with low self-esteem appear to vent that inferior state through a higher use of intimidation and threats (Schwartz, Waldo & Daniel, 2005). This increases the risk of relapse back into harmful behavior that temporarily provides relief or distraction from those life problems. Simply put, feeling one down as a result of historical risk factors can gravitate individuals towards situational risk factors where they feel one up. For example, perceived incompetence can gravitate a person towards high-risk situations such as involvement with deviant/negative peers as a way to feel more competent by comparison and contrast (e.g., Wills & Hirky, 1996).

Practical application example- Jason the foremost running back on his high school football team suffered a back injury his second year and was unable to recover well enough to play first string again. As a result of his perceived incompetence, he quit football entirely, began hanging out with negative peers, smoking marijuana and dealing drugs. He rose to the top again in his high school, this time as the foremost drug dealer. When finally apprehended and placed in residential SRT treatment, his negative self-efficacy explanation was, "If I can't be the best of the best, I'll be the best of the worst."

On the other hand, positive self-efficacy and perceived control empower persons to be more resistant to pressures or temptations for harmful behavior including unhealthy eating, smoking, drinking, drugs and sexual offense (e.g., Dolan et. al. 2008; Hays & Ellickson, 1990; Kuusisto et. al. 2011; Lee et. al. 1999; Pollock, 1996) making the development of self-efficacy important to harmful behavior relapse prevention. For example, self-efficacy is considered important in the probability of transitioning to the recovery phase of the substance abuse cycle (Scott, Dennis & Foss, 2005) as efficacy beliefs are involved in forming and maintaining the social relationships needed for recovery support as well as to resist peer pressure to engage in harmful activities (Bandura, 1993).

Self-Efficacy Research Support Summary: Individuals with multiple forms of unhealthy, harmful behavior report similar histories of adverse historical risk factors that instill helplessness and foster the development of low self-efficacy. For example, sexual offenders have been sexually abused as children significantly more often than the non-sexual offenders (e.g., Dudeck et. al. 2007). One study of youth sex offenders found that 55% identified feelings of helplessness as an offense trigger (McMackin et. al. 2002) and another study revealed that youth sex offenders were not significantly different from female sexual abuse victims on measures of powerlessness (Edwards & Hendrix, 2001). Physical violence against adult partners has been directly related to childhood physical abuse (e.g., Edwards et. al. 2014; Lawson, 2008) which can also predict later physical abuse of children (e.g., Merrill et. al. 2005). Problem gamblers have established histories of childhood abuse/trauma and family dysfunction (e.g., Black et. al. 2012; Hayatbakhsh et. al. 2013; McCormick et. al. 2012). Multiple substance-related unhealthy, harmful behaviors including exchanging sex for cocaine and heroin, arrests for prostitution and engaging in unprotected sex with a casual partner have been connected with childhood sexual abuse (e.g., Baldacci et. al. 2014) and family dysfunction has been linked to later drug and alcohol addiction (e.g., Pardeck et. al. 1991; Pinheiro et. al. 2006). In addition, adult obesity has been associated with childhood abuse (e.g., Salwen et. al. 2014; Williamson et. al. 2002).

Perceived self-efficacy to control one's behavior in high-risk relapse situations for relapse has been linked to positive behavior change with a number unhealthy, harmful behaviors including:

- substance abuse abstinence (e.g., Carbonari & DiClemente, 2000; Dolan, Martin & Rohsenow, 2008; Rychtarik, Prue, Rapp, & King, 1992; Stephens, Wertz, & Roffman, 1995) with lower self-efficacy predicting earlier relapse (e.g., Kuusisto, Knuuttila & Saarnio, 2011; Tate et. al. 2008);
- less heavy alcohol use and abstinence (e.g., Stein, Zane & Grella, 2012; Witkiewitz, Donavan & Hartzler, 2012);
- smoking cessation (e.g., Schnoll et. al. 2011);
- gambling abstinence (e.g., Hodgins, Peden & Makarchuk, 2004; May et. al. 2003; Weinstock et. al. 2009);
- diet and exercise associated with weight loss (e.g., Byrne, Barry & Petry, 2012; Warziski et. al. 2008) with lower self-efficacy being associated with obesity treatment dropout (e.g., Mitchell & Stuart, 1984) and specific self-efficacy for temptations, as opposed to motivation and global self-efficacy, was predictive of subsequent weight loss (Armitage et. al. 2014).

Self-Control

"The power of man has grown in every sphere, except over himself"
--Sir Winston Churchill (1874- 1965)

The number one responsibility in Social Responsibility Therapy is self-control. Self-control is defined as control over one's feelings or actions, which requires exercising restraint over one's impulses, emotions or desires. Behavioral researchers operationally define self-control by measuring impulsive choice-making and the ability to delay gratification from a choice option that is immediately available in favor of an option that is more advantageous but typically delayed (McKeel & Dixon, 2014). Since too much spontaneity leads to impulsiveness and too much delay leads to procrastination, healthy self-control requires a responsible balance between spontaneity and restraint. Self-control also involves goal-directed behavior which can be helpful or harmful to self or others. In this respect, the social-psychological definition of self-control is overriding or inhibiting behaviors, urges or desires that interfere with goal directed behavior (Baumeister, et. al. 1998). The SRT definition of self-control combines the ability to delay gratification of unhealthy, harmful choices with a focus on healthy, responsible goal behavior.

In SRT, self-control is simply the ability to stop yourself from doing the unhealthy, harmful behavior that you want to do and get yourself to do the healthy, responsible behavior that you don't always want to do. In other words, self-control in SRT is when clients with unhealthy, harmful behavior problems avoid relapse and "Do the right thing." In order to manage unhealthy, harmful behavior, it is necessary for clients to develop enough *self-control* to delay acting on unhealthy, harmful thoughts and feelings long enough to consider the consequences. Self-control requires considering: actions and learning the tools to support acting responsibility; feelings and learning the tools to support regulating feelings; decisions and learning the tools to support responsible decision-making; problems and learning the tools to support responsible problem-solving. In SRT, self-control skills are taught for relapse prevention. These skills include escape and avoidance of high-risk situations, regulation of trigger emotions, responsible thinking and decision making along with solving life problems that contribute to stress buildup.

Self-control Theory

Developing self-control is critical for managing unhealthy, harmful behavior habits. Without self-control, individuals would continue to gratify immediate wants/needs and be unable to override urges/cravings that interfere with goal directed behavior or carry a risk of long-term consequences. The original "Self-Control Theory" put forth by Gottfredson and Hirschi (1990) focused on research relating low trait self-control to criminal behavior which is typically harmful to others. The results of this line of research consistently revealed that low levels of self-control increases the risk of a range of antisocial and criminal behaviors (e.g., Baron, 2003; Polakowski, 1994; Pratt & Cullen, 2000). Self-control theory was later expanded to non-criminal behavior typically harmful to self (e.g., unhealthy eating, drinking, drug use, smoking, gambling and risky sexual behavior) which like criminal behavior also carries a risk of consequences (Marshall & Enzmann, 2012). In addition, there is some evidence for inherited weaknesses in self-control (e.g., Connolly & Beaver, 2014; Yancey et. al 2013). Finally, a "Self-control strength model" was developed by Baumeister, Heatherton & Tice (1994) and has been applied to multiple forms of unhealthy, harmful behavior.

Multicultural support for Self-Control Theory has been provided by a number of studies. For example, comparative analysis by race between African American and Caucasian adolescents provided cross-cultural validity through evidence of similarity in the importance of self-control particularly for male adolescents (Vazsonyi & Crosswhite, 2004). Regarding eastern vs western culture, with the exception of alcohol use, the low self-control and deviance relationship was preserved across Japanese and U.S. late adolescents (Vazsonyi et al., 2004). An evaluation of large, representative adolescent samples from four different countries (Hungary, the Netherlands, Switzerland, and the U.S.) revealed that developmental processes involving self-control and criminally deviant behavior are largely invariant by national context (Vazsonyi et al., 2001).

The Self-control Strength Model

The self-control strength model advances self-control theory with findings that both low trait or low state self-control increases the risk of unhealthy, harmful behavior (e.g., Gailliot et. al. 2012). According to the self-control strength model, individuals have a limited amount of self-control strength to use for resisting various temptations. In this model, inhibiting an urge, emotion, thought, or behavior draws on the limited reservoir of energy (i.e., self-control strength) that is necessary for successful self-control of emotions or behavior (Baumeister et al., 1994). Drained strength from one self-control effort sets the occasion for poor self-control performance on any task requiring self-control effort that follows shortly thereafter. In this respect, self-control is like a muscle that gets depleted by prior use (Muraven & Baumeister, 2000; Shmueli & Prochaska, 2009). When applied to addictive behavior, self-control facilitates quitting unhealthy, harmful behaviors and relapse risk is increased when self-control is depleted (Baumeister & Vonasch, 2014).

Self-control Depletion

"You're getting on my last nerve"- The self-control strength model is easy to understand. Just like strength depletion and muscle fatigue from strenuous exercise, self-control depletion also occurs after heavy use. Since stress is cumulative, having your self-control strength worn down from heavy use is a common experience. If you have ever found yourself, saying "You're getting on my last nerve", "I just can't take this anymore", "I've had enough of this" or "I'm getting fed up with this", you have experienced your self-control strength being worn down. Since using self-control (including trying to stay calm, ignore cravings, distractions or being stressed by making decisions) depletes this resource for a short time and sets the occasion for poor performance on back-to-back tasks that require self-control (e.g., Muraven & Baumeister, 2000; Vohs et. al. 2014), self-control depletion sets the occasion for unhealthy, harmful behavior relapse.

Practical application example- Darrell was in his mid-teens with a history of physical and sexual aggression that got him removed from the community and placed in long term community-based residential care with SRT. His self-disappointment over not being able to keep up in school made him hypersensitive to teacher feedback triggering ongoing arguments about what he needed to do. This resulted in coming back to his group home each day with depleted self-control that he described as being "pre-pissed." As a result, Darrell would typically get into a fight with the first group home resident who made a comment that he found upsetting. To make matters worse, these regular fights had resulted in Darrell's bed being moved to outside the staff office where he could receive constant supervision in a small time out area taped off on the floor around his bed. This arrangement allowed his instigating peers to drop insults on him on their way to and from the staff office in the morning depleting his self-control before school and setting the occasion for further conflicts during school. Struggling not to completely lose control during school depleted his self-control resulting in him coming home "pre-pissed" and at risk for another afternoon peer fight.

Darrell's situation illustrates the need to provide unhealthy, harmful behavior clients with a "stress decompression" activity after self-control is taxed that will allow it time to restore. An example of a stress decompression activity after self-control depletion is when forensic foster parents in SRT programs schedule Sunday night movies at the theater (not home DVD's) to allow teens from dysfunctional homes a positive transition time with their forensic foster parents where there is no conversation and associated risk of argument. With adults, going to the gym or running could serve the same stress decompression purpose. In Darrell's case, staff were able to help him get an after school job that he liked which acted as his stress decompression time before coming back to his group home and provided a small but reinforcing paycheck.

"One thing at a time"- In order to prevent the stress overload that depletes self-control, "One thing at a time" needs to be added to the recovery adage "one day at a time." In addition to using up self-control energy by resisting temptations, there is some research evidence that making many choices and decisions also depletes self-control (e.g., Vohs et. al. 2014). Thus, advising clients to do "one thing at a time" is recommended to support self-control maintenance and avoid relapse. This involves teaching clients to "act as if" they are laboratory researchers conducting social stress experiments on themselves. Using the experiential method involves holding everything constant and changing "one thing at a time" while carefully watching the effects on themselves.

Practical application example- Paul was a mid-30's professional with a growing weight-management and unhealthy eating problem who decided to change his job, start dating an old girlfriend, get his next Judo belt and rehabilitate his guitar skills to the point where he could play with a band again all at the same time. The decision on where to work, how to effectively distance himself from his current partner without alienating his son, whether he should get back surgery before or after his next judo belt and how to set aside the very little time he had left to practice guitar used up all of his self-control energy. These multiple life change decisions depleted the self-control that he needed to lose weight and his vegetarian diet crashed within a week. Since doing everything at once is not possible, keeping the focus on everything and refusing to compromise the desire to do it all created feelings of helplessness and depression which triggered emotional eating. Paul needed to take one thing at a time by making one decision while watching his eating behavior very carefully and only going on to the next life change decision after a period of stable healthy eating.

"If you can't deny the feeling, delay the action"- The tolerance training utilized in the Therapeutic Community social learning model for unhealthy, harmful, addictive behavior utilizes encounter groups to help residents learn to tolerate behavior feedback. In this model, a delay of gratification feedback slip system is used to help residents wait until the right place at the right time to express their feelings (DeLeon, George, 1990-91). In the Therapeutic Community, residents are taught that "All feelings are valid" since they are a real part of your experience that you can't deny. Although you can't deny your emotional experience, what you can do is to delay acting on it. This is done by expressing those feelings in encounter groups as opposed to immediately acting them out on the person who triggered them. Dr. Roy Baumeister[18] points out that telling yourself "not now, but later," can decrease the temptation to do something you are trying to avoid (e.g., eating, drinking, drugging, smoking, spending, sex, aggression). Telling yourself, "I can always (eat, drink, drug, spend, smoke, sleep with or slap them) tomorrow, there's no state law that says I must do it today" doesn't deny the feeling but gives the option of delaying the action which helps with the Problem of Immediate Gratification referred to as "Feeding the PIG" by G. Alan Marlatt (1989).

"Sleep on it" is good advice and it is definitely true that you can always do the unhealthy, harmful behavior tomorrow. Unfortunately, delaying gratification typically results in ruminating about doing those things. Disturbing, intrusive, ruminating thoughts can ruin a perfectly decent day by pulling attention away from the moment and into past events that triggered the feelings or future thoughts about venting those feelings. This creates a distraction that causes mistakes. If intensified, ruminating may also set the occasion for acting on the thoughts associated with the unwanted feelings because they typically don't go away. On the positive side, there is some laboratory research that indicates making a plan can eliminate the ruminating thoughts that result from unfulfilled goals/desires (Masicampo & Baumeister, 2011). In the Therapeutic Community social learning model for the criminal addict population, this plan involves residents accepting that there is no state law requiring that venting feelings, gratifying needs (feeding the PIG) or getting revenge must be done today. In the Therapeutic Community, residents are taught not to "react on the floor" (i.e., during their daily job function) but to exercise self-control by writing it down and making a plan to deal with it later. The act of "Dropping a slip" by filling out an encounter slip which puts them in an encounter group with the person that triggered their unwanted feelings, acts is a delay of gratification plan. When intrusive ruminating thoughts occur, being able to remind themselves that they can always vent their feelings on the person who irritated them today in an encounter group tomorrow (i.e., a plan to take action but at a later time) is in fact a delay of gratification exercise. Telling self "not now but later" can help delay gratification and maintain self-control if a plan is in place.

One really important part of delaying action on any unhealthy harmful behavior that is driven by emotions is that feelings and urges are like waves, they rise, fall and pass but the consequences of emotion-based decisions are permanent. Put another way, if you plan to put off an unhealthy, harmful behavior until tomorrow, when tomorrow comes that feeling/urge may have subsided to the point where you change your mind and retract your plan to do it. However, if you don't "sleep on it" and act on those feelings right away, the unhealthy, harmful behavior along with whatever consequences result cannot be retracted. Since feelings pass but the consequences of decisions stay, when it comes to developing self-control of unhealthy, harmful behavior that is driven by emotions is "If you can't deny the feeling, plan to delay the action." This advice was first published in an 1899 New York Newspaper[19] as "Always put off until tomorrow any evil you can do today."

Practical application example- Jamar was an early 20's male with a residential treatment parole mandate from state prison where he was sentenced for interstate narcotics trafficking and third-degree murder during a drug-related shoot out. Upon seeing his charges, peer intake worker Tim, a late teen marijuana smoker who was referred by his middle class parents went on a self-appointed mission to get Jamar to lose self-control, run away from treatment which would violate his parole and get him sent back to prison "where he belonged." Tim regularly had Jamar repeat cleaning jobs that were already done properly and wrote incident reports for every minor infraction he could find. All of the self-control energy that Jamar was pouring into resisting the urge to hospitalize Tim distracted him from his work resulting in mistakes. These mistakes were regularly written up on incident reports by Tim creating further reprimands for Jamar, which increased his preoccupation with injustice and revenge. Jamar could not deny the feeling that he wanted to seriously injure Tim but knew that if he did it now, even though he would make sure that there were no witnesses including Tim by knocking him out from behind, all of those incident reports coming to light during the investigation might be enough documentation to violate his parole for treatment non-compliance. He could not deny the feeling but had to delay the action. Jamar made a plan to delay his retaliation against Tim until he was promoted for a track record of positive performance. Who would suspect him of hospitalizing Tim on the day he was celebrating his promotion? Months went by and Jamar was promoted to the maintenance crew. Since he and his family were all good carpenters, he developed a track record of excellent job performance. Unable to find any work problems to write up on Jamar, Tim moved on to harassing Marcus, an inner city gangbanger who also made Tim feel threatened. Somehow, delaying his desire to seriously injure Tim and feeling good that he was being appreciated for his carpentry skills on the maintenance crew made it less important for Jamar to get even with Tim. He no longer really cared and had already let it go before Marcus busted Tim up in the downstairs bathroom. According to Jamar, "What comes around goes around" and since humans are creatures of habit, if you continue to resist letting them "push your buttons", you will eventually get "ring side seats to watching someone else mop the floor up with their face." Jamar's experience teaches us that if our clients can't deny the feeling but can take the first step of delaying the action, the need to do the harmful behavior will fade with time.

Prosocial values can block harmful behavior during self-control depletion- Gino et. al. (2011) describe self-control as working much like a house thermostat that is constantly comparing the room temperature to the desired temperature set by the owner and heats or cools the house to meet the set/goal temperature. Specifically, when self-control is active people are comparing their actions to their goals (or standards) and exert conscious self-control to bring their actions in line with their goals. While these authors found that self-control depletion resulted in increased unethical behavior (i.e., trust abuse by cheating on a problem solving task), they also found that when moral identity (i.e., identifying with being Caring, Compassionate, Fair, Friendly, Generous, Helpful, Hardworking, Honest, and Kind) was high, self-control depletion did not influence unethical behavior (i.e., cheating on a problem-solving task). Thus, one important way to inoculate clients against unhealthy, harmful behavior relapse from self-control depletion and help them with self-control development is to reinforce prosocial values. As mentioned before, SRT reinforces honesty, trust, loyalty, concern and responsibility as competing responses against unhealthy, harmful behavior.

In summary, self-control depletion occurs after back-to-back events that challenge self-control without time out to recuperate. The take away message here is that is the importance of helping clients avoid depleting their self-control by: 1) learning to take one stressful thing at a time, putting a HALT on stress buildup (i.e., don't get to Hungry, Angry, Lonely or Tired); 2) helping them delay plans to take action during when experiencing strong feelings that they can't deny and 3) Reinforcing honesty, trust, loyalty, concern and responsibility to inoculate against harmful behavior relapse during periods of self-control depletion.

Self-Control Development

Self-awareness is an important component of self-control development. Clients who are not aware of the internal motivations (thoughts and feelings) and external motivations (social and situational) that are triggering the urge to act, are less likely to be able to control their actions. Self-awareness of certain problem coping strategies is also important in self-control development. An action-oriented style with an emphasis on doing without thinking contributes to self-control problems in some clients who need to learn to slow down and let themselves think, particularly about behavior consequences. Fatalism as a coping strategy reflected by statements like "it just happened" is a key barrier to self-control development which requires accepting

responsibility for decisions. Awareness of our responsibility for decisions can be illustrated with clients using the analogy of driving a car which involves decisions on whether to: text or talk on the cell phone; stay a safe distance behind the car in front of you or; continue through the intersection on a yellow light. Most clients accept that decisions about these high-risk situations determine whether a harmful auto accident is likely to occur and the translation to high-risk decisions for unhealthy eating, substance use or sexual behavior is fairly easy for them to grasp. The more aware clients are of their high-risk situations (i.e., people, places, things, thoughts and feelings), the more opportunities they have to practice ACTS skills for self-control development.
"The more we know, the more we can grow"

Recovery self-efficacy is also an important component of self-control. Recovery self-efficacy requires knowing when to act and what to do to prevent relapse. If clients are aware of their thoughts and feelings but don't believe in their ability to manage the situation, even with behavior management knowledge, they are unlikely to succeed in re-directing their unhealthy thoughts and unwanted feelings. This is because the "I got this" belief in ability to handle barriers to recovery (i.e., recovery self-efficacy) is needed for a 100% effort or sometimes even for giving a behavior change skill a fair try. The self-defeating, "It won't work but I'll try it because I said I would" statement is the opposite of the "I got this" self-efficacy belief that is needed to succeed. Self-efficacy or belief in the ability to change increases attempts to change which increases the probability of succeeding at change. In other words, "Insight gives you confidence but practice gives you competence." Succeeding at making one small change builds confidence in the ability to succeed at making another small change which provides further motivation to avoid relapse triggers. This is what is meant by "Nothing succeeds like success."
"The more we believe, the more we can achieve"

Self-control requires having the tools to manage out of control thoughts, feelings and people. Self-awareness and self-efficacy provide the foundation for self-control. Self-awareness of high-risk situations for relapse and self-efficacy in ability to use ACTS skills to deal with those situations develops self-control of unhealthy, harmful behavior. Self-control development involves learning to tolerate frustration, feelings and feedback which has been an important aspect of the Therapeutic Community Model (DeLeon 1990-91). Dr. Albert Ellis was probably the first psychologist to declare low frustration tolerance a key component of addictive behavior from his rational-emotive Rational Emotive Behavior Therapy (REBT) perspective (DiGiuseppe, R., & McInerney, 1990). The ABC's of letting feelings go (see pg. 83) which are the core of REBT helps dissipate frustration to improve self-control development. Likewise, Mindfulness-Based Relapse Prevention (Bowen, Chawla & Marlatt, 2011) and the mindfulness-based distress tolerance techniques implemented in Dialectical Behavior Therapy developed by Dr. Marsha Linehan, helps individuals with unhealthy, harmful behavior accommodate to unwanted feelings (see pg. 101) which improves self-control. The stress overreaction effect in individuals with historical risk factors and resulting negative emotional state along with a setback in self-awareness and self-efficacy is illustrated in Figure 1.1.
"Self-control is not doing what you want to do and doing what you need to do"

Figure 1.1.
Impact of Self-Awareness and Self-Efficacy on Self-Control: The Fulcrum Analogy

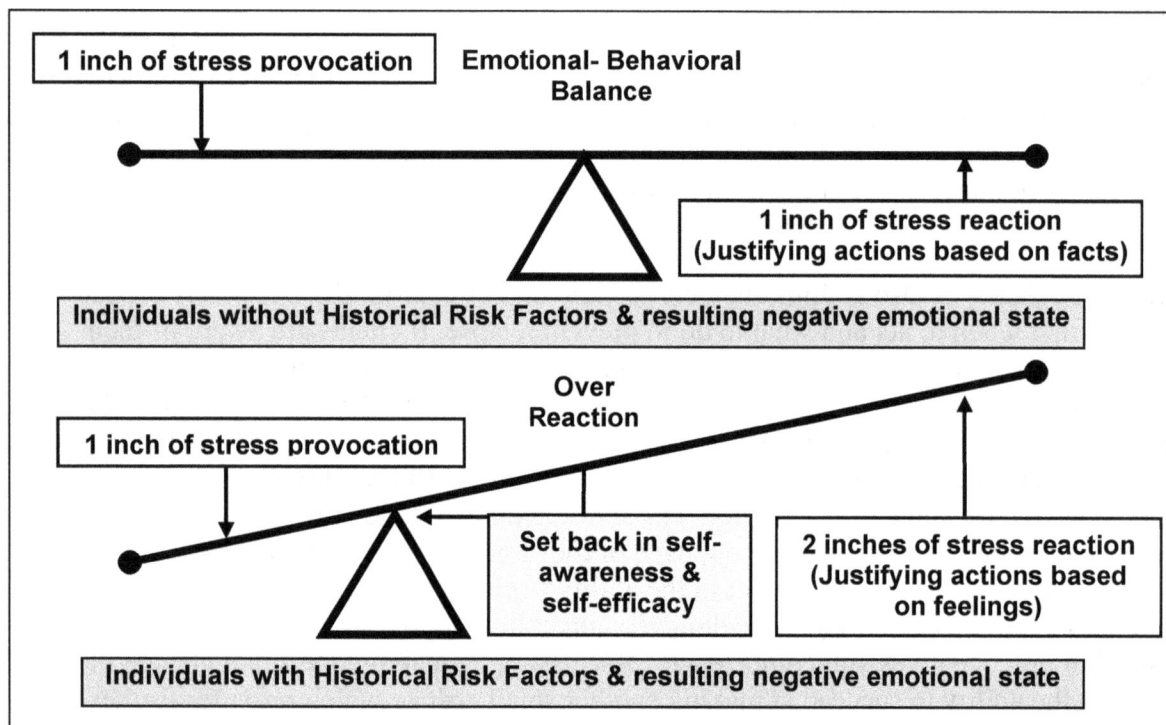

| 1 inch of stress provocation | Emotional- Behavioral Balance |

1 inch of stress reaction (Justifying actions based on facts)

Individuals without Historical Risk Factors & resulting negative emotional state

Over Reaction

1 inch of stress provocation

Set back in self-awareness & self-efficacy

2 inches of stress reaction (Justifying actions based on feelings)

Individuals with Historical Risk Factors & resulting negative emotional state

Note: Historical Risk factors can include a family and personal history of mood instability

Learning to develop enough frustration tolerance to let go of emotions by channeling them to the right place and the right time is a key component in developing self-control (see Chapter 5 section on "The ABC's of Developing Emotional Control: Letting Go"). Learning to delay gratification of venting emotions until the place and right time is a second important component in developing self-control (see "Earning the right to complain" in Chapter 5 section on "Learn use & teach the Reality Scales"). Exaggerated needs for attention, acceptance and excitement also have a direct impact on *self-control* of unhealthy, harmful behaviors (See Chapter 4, Component 10, "Self-Defeating Habits" section).

On the issue of *Self-Control*, learning to develop enough frustration tolerance to hold on to emotions until the right place and the right time is a key component in developing self-control (see Chapter 5 section on "The ABC's of Developing Emotional Control: Holding On" and "Earning the right to complain"). Learning to become aware of and contain exaggerated needs for attention, acceptance and excitement are also important in the *self-control* of unhealthy, harmful behavior (See "Self-Defeating Habits" section, Chapter 12, Component 10). According to self-control theory, effective self-control (or self-regulation) involves: 1) standards (i.e., goals that drive behavior or rules that govern what the individual deems to be appropriate) that are often determined by cultural norms; 2) monitoring (i.e., tracking the actions individuals want to regulate so that they can achieve their goals or adhere to their standards) and; capacity to change through self-control strength which is also known as willpower (Baumeister, 2013). In

SRT, "Planning power beats willpower" and self-control of unhealthy, harmful behavior is developed by learning to implement the basic relapse prevention, emotional regulation, decisional balance and social problem solving skills needed to: 1) manage high-risk situations for relapse; 2) manage feelings including urges/cravings; 3) consider consequences when making decisions and; 4) solve problems that are barriers to harmful behavior recovery and life goals.

Planning power beats willpower- While there may be a genetic predisposition limiting the amount of self-control energy available to resist temptations in some individuals, a meta-analysis by de Ridder et. al. (2011) concluded that trait self-control may involve establishing effective habits and routines more than resisting single temptations. In other words, people with good self-control may avoid temptations rather than resisting them as revealed in a study by Ent et. al. (2015) where people high in trait self-control reported engaging in behaviors thought to minimize or avoid temptation to a greater extent than people low in trait self-control. Since avoidance of high-risk situations for unhealthy, harmful behavior requires planning, when it comes to self-control development, in SRT "Planning power beats willpower" for relapse prevention, maintaining recovery and achieving life goals.

The reason that planning power beats willpower when it comes to dealing with temptation is simple. It is far easier to avoid trouble than escape it once it starts. Think about it. Once a person in treatment for unhealthy, harmful behavior enters a high-risk situation for relapse, they are flooded with thoughts and feelings associated with their unhealthy, harmful behavior urges or cravings. Thus, in SRT, planning power is developed through high-risk situation avoidance and escape plans (See Chapter 4).

Practical application example- Linda was an early 50's health professional whose chronic alcoholism resulted in liver damage and job loss, leaving her at home with an alcoholic husband. She reported a drinking relapse after her weekly outpatient treatment on her drive home which went directly past a brightly lit liquor store. All of the attractive bottles and advertisements in the window triggered an urge to pull in and she found herself buying a bottle of vodka on automatic pilot mode as she had done many times before. Her treatment group recommended that she plan her way around that visual trigger but Linda had resisted changing her driving route, stating that the route past the liquor store was shorter plus she "should" be able to just drive by the liquor store and resist the urge to stop in. The following week on the same route home, she called her husband just to ask if there was anything he needed. This resulted in buying a bottle of vodka for him that she ended up drinking with him. Linda was able to accept that her Foresight Deficit Decision, i.e., making a decision without using "foresight" by looking ahead to consider the consequences (see Chapter 6) to call her alcoholic husband on the way home to see if he needed anything provided her with the excuse she needed to stop in the liquor store. The third week in group she was able to accept the need to plan a route that did not pass the liquor store. She got home that week without buying alcohol because "planning power beats willpower".

Self-Control Research Support Summary: Low self-control is associated with a broad range of criminal and noncriminal risk-taking activities (Chapple & Hope, 2003) and Self-Control Theory research has been applied to a broad band of harmful behavior including reckless driving, risky sex, academic dishonesty, pathological gambling and drug use (Jones & Quisenberry, 2004; Sorenson & Brownfield, 1995). With respect to the age range, low self-control has been significantly related to both criminal and imprudent self-reported offending activity through age fifty (Burton et al., 1999). While opportunity always plays a part, low self-control has been related to multiple forms of unhealthy harmful behavior, for example...

- Sexual abuse- Rapists have exhibited lower self-control along with higher post-treatment relapse and criminal versatility (i.e., likelihood of committing other crimes as well) than other sex offenders (Symbaluk, 1998). Juvenile sexual assault offenders lowest in self-restraint had significantly higher recidivism at long term follow up (Tinklenberg et. al., 1996).
- Physical abuse- Juvenile physical assault offenders lowest in self-restraint had significantly higher recidivism at long term follow up (Tinklenberg et. al., 1996). Low levels of self-control and exposure to criminal opportunities are significantly associated with engaging in dating violence and gang violence (Chapple, 1999; Chapple & Hope, 2003).
- Property abuse- A study of juvenile and adult drug-using offenders revealed that property crimes were more frequent among offenders with lower self-control and higher opportunity (Longshore, 1998). There also appears to be a self-control connection with college student software piracy (Higgins, 2005) and employee theft (Langton, Piquero & Hollinger, 2006).
- Substance abuse- In a representative sample of U.S. high school seniors, low self-control is a correct and certain predictor of deviant behaviors including cigarette smoking, and the use of alcohol and marijuana (Stylianou, 2002). The results of a large scale study on drinking and driving support the existence of a relationship between low self-control and driving under the influence of alcohol for both male and female drivers (Keane, Maxim & Teevan, 1993). On days that underage social drinkers experienced more self-control demands than average, they were more likely to violate their self-imposed drinking limit (Muraven et. al. 2005). With respect to unhealthy eating, individuals with high dispositional self-control ate fewer calories, exercised more, and lost more weight during a weight loss program than individuals with low dispositional self-control (Crescioni et al., 2011).
- Trust abuse- When 17 forms of dishonesty were evaluated in a sample of undergraduate students, qualified support was found for the association between levels of self-control and involvement in academic dishonesty (Cochran et al., 1998). Trait self-control and self-control depletion predict cheating on activities where students have the opportunity (Gino et. al. 2011; Muraven, Pogarsky & Shmueli, 2006). Poor self-regulation has been associated with infidelity (McIntyre, Barlow, & Hayward, 2014).

Emotional Maturity Development Summary

Self-awareness, self-efficacy and self-control support each other. The more aware you are of the connections between your thoughts and feelings, the more confidence you have in being able to challenge those thoughts which maintains self-control by lowering feelings below the threshold of acting on them. The more you practice self-control, the more you stay on track towards achieving positive life goals. "Good things happen to people who keep doing good".

"Every man must decide whether he will walk in the light of creative altruism
or in the darkness of destructive selfishness"
-- Martin Luther King, Jr. (1929- 1968)

Recommended Readings

Chapter 1 in Yokley, J. (2008). *Social Responsibility Therapy for Adolescents & Young Adults: A Multicultural Treatment Manual for Harmful Behavior*, New York, NY, US: Routledge/Taylor & Francis Group. **ISBN:** 978-0-7890-3121-1, 357 pp.

Yokley, J. (2010). Social Responsibility Therapy for Harmful, Abusive Behavior, *Journal of Contemporary Psychotherapy,* 40(2), p. 105- 113. DOI 10.1007/s10879-009-9131-7.

Chapter 2
The ART of Positive Change:
Helping Clients Get What They Want in Life

"You never truly need what you want. That is the main and thoroughgoing key to serenity"
-- Albert Ellis (1913- 2007)

Like other aspects of Social Responsibility Therapy the ART of Positive Change and helping clients what they want in life involves Awareness training, Responsibility training and Tolerance Training. Getting what we want in life involves learning to master the ART of Positive Change by developing Awareness of exactly what we want, taking Responsibility to go after it and learning to Tolerate setbacks. This requires ongoing practice of the skills needed to set and achieve life goals, solve old problems and avoid new ones.

Life Goal Awareness Training: Helping Clients Clarify What They Want in Life
"Give me liberty or give me death"—Patrick Henry [1]

Throughout history, humans have fought for their freedom and been willing to die for it. Since freedom is the most valuable right in human existence, it stands to reason that imprisonment is the strongest human punishment. There is more than one type of prison for humans. Traditional prisons with concrete walls and bars prevent many humans from achieving their positive life goals. This is often the result of violating the rights of others. However, many more humans are imprisoned by their unhealthy, harmful behavior, which spans the Harmful Behavior Continuum (See Table 1.1)[2] from behaviors that are primarily harmful to self (e.g., overeating) to behaviors that are harmful to self and others (e.g., drunk driving) to behaviors that are primarily harmful to others (e.g., physical and sexual abuse). Overeaters are serving time in body prison where their morbid obesity prevents them from doing what they want, when they want due to metabolic syndrome complications including type 2 diabetes, sleep apnea, high blood pressure, high cholesterol, knee, joint and back pain. Alcoholics and addicts are imprisoned by their full time compulsive pursuit of pleasure or avoidance of pain leaving no time to consider anything else or anyone else. Physical and sexual abusers are imprisoned by their full time compulsive power, control and deviant sexual urges that violate the rights of others, which eventually brings on traditional imprisonment. Being imprisoned in an endless stress-relapse cycle of unhealthy, harmful behavior prevents humans from getting what they want in life.

Clients can't get what they want in life until they know what they want in life. This requires figuring out what they want for themselves and their future. Helping clients get what they want in life involves helping them look beyond recovery from unhealthy, harmful behavior and thinking about exactly what they want in life if they were free of their imprisonment in their ongoing stress-relapse cycle. Many individuals that experience some form of unhealthy, harmful behavior have been so caught up in the struggle, that they have never given any thought to what they want after they learn to manage their eating, drinking, drugging, smoking, physical aggression or sexual behavior. They have been completely preoccupied with managing their unwanted feelings/cravings and unwanted thoughts/urges along with covering up their unhealthy, harmful behavior and worrying about consequences. Being stuck in that daily struggle has side tracked them from thinking about what they want in life and making plans to get it. This is particularly important in light of the clinical observation by Dr. Albert Ellis that those individuals who find an all-consuming life goal that is more important to them than their unhealthy, harmful need gratification are much more likely to maintain long term successful recovery. In summary, long-term successful recovery from unhealthy, harmful behavior requires individuals with unhealthy harmful behavior problems to "Keep your eyes on the prize"[3] of what they want in life. Clients can't keep their eyes on the prize of getting what they want in life unless they know what they want in life. One way to help clients think beyond their unhealthy, harmful behavior struggle and clarify what they want in life is the Five-Year Future Introduction.

Treatment Exercise: The Five-Year Future Introduction
Give your clients the "Fantasy Fast Forward" assignment of imagining that they are well on their way to getting what they want in life. Ask them to imagine that it is five years in the future, that everything has gone right for them and that they have achieved their life direction goals. Instruct them write out their introduction beginning like this...

"Hi, my name is [_____], I'm (add 5 years to their current age) [___] years old and things have been going very well for me over the past 5 years."

Have them continue their introduction by plugging in their ideal life if everything went the way it was supposed to over the past five years. They need to put in all of the details including health, relationships, life direction, activity schedule, where they live, what they are doing, if taking the first step towards getting what you want in life was successful. Answering the following questions will help. What will life be like after recovery from unhealthy, harmful eating, drinking, drugging, smoking, spending, gambling or sex? What will your day look like? What will you be doing? Who will you be with? How will you feel? If everything goes the way you want it in life, what is the best thing that could happen to you? What do you want most in life?

After helping your clients clarify what they want in their life, it is important to help them clarify what they need to get what they want and keep it once they get it. Put another way, clients in treatment for unhealthy, harmful behavior need awareness training clarifying what they want in life followed an understanding of the basic needs that have to be met to get what they want.

You can't get what you want until you get what you need
Explain to your clients that... What you need is to take care of yourself. If you don't take care of your car, it won't go. If you don't take care of your garden, it won't grow and of you don't take care of your body you won't get everything you want out of life. Unfortunately, humans often take better care of our cars and gardens than our bodies. According to Dr. Abraham Maslow, humans have a hierarchy of needs that must be met before we can focus on getting what we want. Taking care of yourself begins with treating your body right, includes having healthy relationships and developing a healthy life direction. According to Dr. Maslow's hierarchy of needs, we can want anything in the world but what we need for positive growth is:

1. **A healthy body, behaviors and safe environment**- that meets our basic physical needs (i.e., a drug/alcohol/food addiction-free healthy body and a behavioral addiction-free healthy mind). We don't really care about psychological needs for companionship or acceptance if we're hungry, tired or afraid of others, afraid of our impulses or stuck in a cycle of unhealthy or harmful behavior. What we need first is a healthy body, mind and environment that meets our basic physical needs for healthy food and safe, healthy behaviors that do not threaten our freedom (i.e., are not illegal and cannot result in incarceration) are not unhealthy or harmful to self or others (e.g., unhealthy harmful eating, drinking, drugging, smoking spending/gambling, physically or sexually abusive behavior) in a safe environment. People with healthy bodies in safe positive environments are happier.

2. **Healthy positive relationships**- that meet our psychological needs. We don't really care about self-fulfillment needs to achieve our full potential if we feel lonely, rejected, worthless and have too many barriers to grow. After developing a track record of meeting our basic physical healthy life needs, we need positive, healthy relationships that meet our psychological needs for companionship, acceptance and feeling valued to provide the support to maintain our recovery from unhealthy harmful behavior and develop a positive, healthy life direction that meets our self-fulfillment needs to "be all we can be." People with healthy relationships are happier.

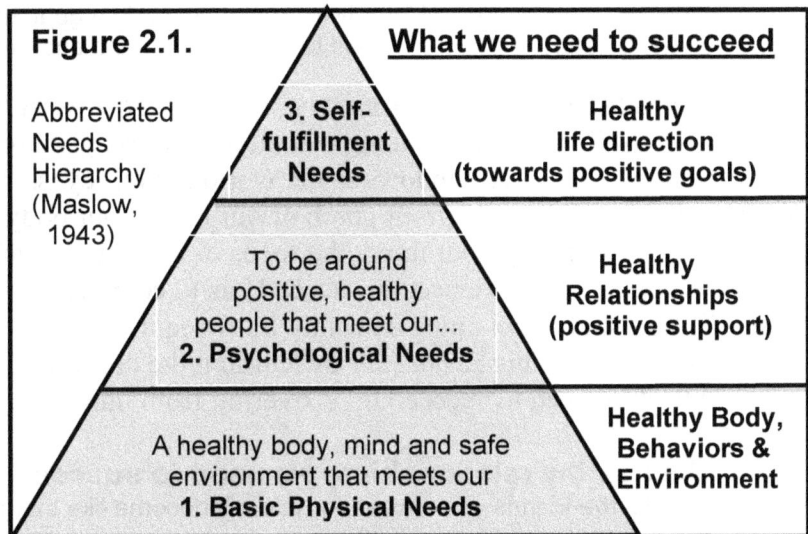

Figure 2.1.

Abbreviated Needs Hierarchy (Maslow, 1943)

What we need to succeed

3. Self-fulfillment Needs

To be around positive, healthy people that meet our...
2. Psychological Needs

A healthy body, mind and safe environment that meets our
1. Basic Physical Needs

Healthy life direction (towards positive goals)

Healthy Relationships (positive support)

Healthy Body, Behaviors & Environment

3. **A healthy positive life direction**- that meets our self-fulfillment needs to "be all we can be" After our basic positive healthy physical life and psychological relationship needs are met, we are able to focus on achieving our full potential. This requires finding a place where you can follow your healthy life direction dream and be all you can be (Figure 2.1). A healthy positive life direction develops our skills which is important because "When you have no skills, you look for thrills." "Happy people have something to look forward to" and a healthy positive life direction gives you something to look forward to each day. People with healthy positive life directions are happier.

"The good life is a process, not a state of being. It is a direction not a destination"
-- Carl Rogers (1902- 1987)

Helping Clients Change their Lifestyles by Fulfilling Healthy Need Goals

Recovery in SRT goes beyond developing a track record of not engaging in unhealthy, harmful behavior to reinventing themselves through the development of a healthy positive lifestyle. This involves: healthy behaviors in a healthy environment; healthy relationships and; a healthy life direction. In order for clients with a history of unhealthy, harmful behavior to change their lifestyles, a shift from gratifying unhealthy needs to developing healthy life goals is required. This often means a shift from the past and other people's behavior to the present and their behavior. Reinventing self requires clients to make careful step-by-step healthy life goals. This means not trying to make up for lost time and not using a recovery identity as part of the reinvented self. Dr. Alan Rochlin cautions individuals in the process of putting their lives back together after drug and alcohol treatment to "be a professional, not a professional addict." Helping clients reinvent themselves in order to get what they want in life involves having them use "Fantasy Fast Forward", think ahead and imagine their life after developing a track record of long-term recovery. They need to take time to think outside the recovery box by imagining they are looking at their life through a camera. They need to zoom out to see the big picture of what they need to succeed in developing a positive, healthy life that goes beyond managing their unhealthy, harmful behavior. This means making healthy life goals involving where they live, who they associate with and what they do in their life. The following is a brief explanation of the rationale behind these life success goals.

"Happiness is experienced largely in striving towards a goal, not in having attained things, because our nature is always to want to go on to the next endeavor" -- Albert Ellis (1913- 2007)

Getting the healthy body, behaviors and environment we need to succeed

Where do we live? If you are thinking of a street address you are wrong. We live in our body. Our body is our house; our windows to the world are our eyes. "Everywhere we go there we are" looking at the world from the front porch of our house, our body. Since we live in our body and interpret the world through our mind, the focus of healthy life goal #1 is really on *where we live*. Getting the healthy body we need to succeed has to come first. We can't get ahead if we're sick or dead. Getting and maintaining a healthy body requires developing healthy behaviors and a healthy environment. This has to start by learning the "Healthy Behavior Success Skills" (See Table 3.1) that we need to succeed in recovering from unhealthy, harmful behavior habits.

Getting the healthy relationships, we need to succeed

"Be careful the friends you choose for you will become like them"
-- W. Clement Stone (1902- 2002)

This doesn't have to involve romance, it can involve good friendships and good family relationships. Since healthy relationships can support healthy eating and activity, the life focus of healthy life goal #2 is on *who we associate with*. Getting the healthy relationships that we need to succeed has to start by clarifying what we want in others and what others want in us (See "Healthy Relationship Success Skills", See Table 9.2). Humans often spend much more effort trying to change the negative habits of those we are close to then we spend on developing new relationships with positive people. At some point we have to accept that, "If you can't change the people around you, change the people around you".

Getting the healthy life direction we need to succeed

After our basic physical needs (for a healthy body) and psychological needs for (healthy relationships) are met we are able to focus on developing a healthy life direction that meets our self-fulfillment needs to achieve our full potential. In human growth terms this means finding a place where you can follow your dream, achieve as much as you can and to quote the Army slogan "Be all you can be." A healthy life direction is "Something to do that's positive for you."

A healthy life direction doesn't have to involve making money from a job you like but it does have to instill a meaningful sense of purpose, hold your positive emotional attention and keep you active. It can be things you do for free such as a volunteer activity or teaching a skill to others. The point is to become engaged in something interesting and positive that you like to do. The positive state of engagement that people report when they are intensely involved in something that they like to do is known as "flow." In the Positive Psychology movement started by Martin Seligman, the five pillars needed for The Good Life are Positive emotion, Engagement, Meaning and Accomplishment (Rich, 2013). Developing a healthy life direction in SRT is consistent with the flow theory that a good life includes complete absorption and Engagement in "something to do that's positive for you".

The best life direction is the one that meets your healthy needs best. This doesn't just mean your basic physical needs for financial stability. This means your psychological and self-fulfillment needs. Your life direction can be a job but doesn't have to be. What it does have to be is interesting enough to completely absorb you. If what you are doing during the day is not interesting, it's a boring emotional burden. If you are rich but bored, you are at risk for doing unhealthy things for excitement. The focus of healthy life goal #3 is on *what you do with your life*. Getting the healthy life direction that we need to succeed has to start with The Five-Year Future Introduction Exercise. Humans are creatures of habit and easily fall into routines of acting and thinking. Thinking about the healthy life direction we want is the first step.

"Let the beauty of what you love be what you do"-- Rumi (1207- 1273)

Healthy Life Direction Treatment Exercise: What's in it for me?

Structure a discussion to help clients discover the following benefits of a healthy life direction.

1. Happiness- "Happy people have something to look forward to." Since your life direction is something positive that you like to do and look forward to doing, people with a positive life direction are happier. The opposite side of this coin is that people who do not have a life goal guiding their direction everyday are likely to get bored every day because they are not working on (or using) any life skills that interest them. The problem with boredom is simple. The more bored you are, the more likely you are to fall into unhealthy eating, drinking, smoking, spending or sex to break that boredom. In short, "If you're not working on skills, you look for thrills." In addition to this problem, "If you're bored, you're boring." This is true because it means you are not putting any effort into developing positive interests and having positive interests builds positive relationships because it makes you interesting to others who share those positive interests. Discuss some examples of how sharing positive interests can build positive relationships.

2. Improved self-efficacy- Developing skills whether it's people skills (e.g., parenting, teaching, counseling), technical skills (e.g., carpenter, mechanic, electrician), mental skills (e.g., college study skills, social problem-solving skills) or physical skills (e.g., sports, dance, acting) builds self-efficacy. Efficacy means being effective and self-efficacy means feeling effective, like you can get something done if you really try. Some people view self-efficacy as the confidence that you can do something you set out to do. The more you get yourself involved in "something to do that's positive for you", the better you will get at it and the more you will feel you are effective in that area (i.e., self-efficacy). Discuss some examples of how developing a skill makes you feel more confident.

3. <u>A sense of purpose</u>- Having a positive life direction helps you get through hard times because you have a positive purpose to look forward to. Since (according to the Greek philosopher Aristotle), "You are what you repeatedly do", if you repeatedly strive towards a positive life direction, you become a positive life force that receives positive gratitude and respect from those in your community. If you want to feel good you have to do good. Doing something positive that matters to you gives you a sense of purpose beyond just trying to get more money to buy more things. Discuss the age-old question, "Can money buy you happiness?" Is it better to have more money and less sincere friends or more real friends and less money?

In summary, Awareness Training on achieving healthy life goals involves helping clients clarify what they really want in life through Fantasy Fast Forward five years into the future along with the needs that have to be met to get what they want. Awareness Training on helping clients get what they want in life involves helping them set goals that focus on where they live (i.e., in their body- getting the healthy body that they need to succeed), who they live around/with (i.e., family/social network- getting the healthy relationships that they need to succeed) and what they do with their life (i.e., a positive goal and purpose that they value- getting the healthy life direction that they need to succeed). Getting a healthy body has to be goal #1 because it affects everything else. Think about it, you can't fully enjoy relationships, activities or even wealth if you don't have your health. Finally, those who maintain long term recovery have an all-consuming life goal and purpose that they are striving to achieve that is more important to them than the gratification they received from their past unhealthy, harmful behavior.

Life Goal Responsibility Training: Helping Clients Achieve Life Goals
"Growth occurs when individuals confront problems, struggle to master them,
and through that struggle develop new aspects of their skills,
capacities, views about life."-- Carl Rogers (1902- 1987)

Responsibility training involves helping clients accept responsibility to learn the skills they need to get what they want (i.e., accept that in life "You don't get what you want, you get what you work for") and take responsibility to implement those skills. This involves learning important Healthy Behavior Success Skills drawn from the evidence-based recovery areas of relapse prevention, emotional regulation, decisional balance and social problem solving. Clients need to accept responsibility to learn and implement these skills to help them overcome recovery barriers and stay on target towards achieving their life goals. Taking responsibility to become proficient at Healthy Behavior Success Skills is particularly in high-risk situations for relapse in order to avoid falling back into the stress-relapse cycle of unhealthy, harmful behavior.

Healthy Behavior Success Skills are tools that clients with unhealthy, harmful behavior habits need to learn in order to achieve healthy life goals. These tools enable clients to get what they want in life by doing the right thing at the right time for the right reason while others continue to do what they want, when they want for the reason they want and fall, fail or go to jail. These skills include developing multicultural prosocial values from the evidence-based Therapeutic Community social learning model of lifestyle change along with behavior management tools drawn from the evidence-based behavior change areas of relapse prevention, emotional regulation, decisional balance and social problem solving. It takes drills to develop these skills in clients. Drills involve having clients go over and over these healthy relationship and behavior success skills in group and individual therapy sessions until they become automatic responses in a crisis situation that is high risk for unhealthy, harmful behavior relapse.

It is obvious that clients who are able to reinvent themselves by developing a healthy body, healthy relationships and a healthy life direction will be happier than those who are sick, alone and bored with no life goals to inspire their souls. However, there will always be barriers to achieving healthy life goals. When trouble comes to interfere with life goal achievement, clients need to remember that, "Your ACTS speak louder than your words" and take positive action to overcome the negative situation. The specific "ACTS" skills that clinicians need to develop in their clients in order to get past life barriers and get what they want in life are: Avoid trouble (with relapse prevention); Calm down (with emotional regulation); Think it through (with decisional balance) and; Solve the problem (with SET social problem solving). Those clients who successfully learn to use these skills to overcome the problems that interfere with their healthy life goals, have developed the internal control needed to get what they want in life. These skills are explained in detail along with a case example in Chapters 4- 7.

Getting what you want in life requires developing your social-emotional maturity. A person with social maturity has honesty, trust, loyalty, concern, and responsibility. This allows them to be respected as a good friend, loved by family and trusted by employers. A person with emotional maturity has self-awareness, self-efficacy, and self-control. In order to manage harmful, addictive behavior that blocks getting what you want in life, you have to have enough:
1. self-awareness to identify thoughts, feelings, motivations and situations that can trigger the harmful, addictive behavior;
2. self-efficacy (confidence) to try solutions and substitute new alternative responses, behaviors, and activities for old negative, harmful ones and;
3. self-control to delay gratification of urges, consider consequences of impulsive thoughts, postpone emotional decisions, do the right thing at the right time, and keep it up. To help develop all three, every night have clients review, "Three things that went right today and how I made that happen".

Life Goal Issue #1:
"You don't get what you want, you get what you work for"- Unless clients have specific short and long term life goals, they have no life direction. Without life direction they have no motivation. Without motivation, they can't achieve life goals.

Practical application example- Cindy was a mid-20's single parent group member under considerable financial stress with an ex-partner who continued to make empty promises to pay child support after leaving her to raise the children by herself. She reported that he spent his day driving around trying to get in an auto accident so that he could file a disability claim for a neck injury. She pointed out that he could probably put in 20 job applications per day during all of his driving around. He said that he didn't need a job because he was going to win the lottery. She shook her head as she told her group that he wouldn't even buy a lottery ticket.

Treatment goal exercise 1: Have your clients review their Five-Year Future Introduction and use what they wrote to make life goals to get what they need (i.e., the healthy body-behavior-environment; healthy relationship and; healthy long-term life direction goals) in order to stay on the path towards getting what they want in life. Start with, "What do you want most in life?" Then have them set five month goals as a first step towards getting what they want in life. Start with "What do you want now?" Finally, have clients write out specific steps that they need to accomplish to get what they want in life in each of the three important human need categories (i.e., 1. healthy body/behavior/environment, 2. healthy relationships and 3. healthy life direction). Regarding healthy relationships, have them list everyone they can count on to help them achieve their life goals.

Life Goal Issue #2:
"You can't get something without giving something away"

Helping clients get what want in life means helping them let go of the things that hold them back. This means letting go of the unhealthy habits that: hurt their body (e.g., unhealthy eating, drinking, drugging); kept them in unhealthy relationships (e.g., depending on undependable people, exaggerated needs for attention, acceptance or excitement) and; side-tracked them from following their dreams to develop a healthy, body, relationships and "something to do that's positive for you." Getting something by giving something away also involves "Each one teach one" which is the social responsibility to help others achieve positive life goals. The social responsibility to help others recover from their unhealthy, harmful behavior is the final step in 12-step programs. Giving away recovery knowledge requires clients to teach which improves treatment concept learning. This has research support in what is known as "the protégé effect" where students who teach others score higher on tests than those who are learning only for themselves (Chase et. al. 2009). For over two thousand years, humans have known that if you want someone to really learn something, have them teach it to someone else. "While we teach, we learn", Seneca (54- 39BC).

Treatment goal exercise 2: "Each one teach one"- Have your clients write a story of the most important learning experience that helped them achieve their longest period of recovery from their unhealthy, harmful behavior and then teach this to their treatment group. Discuss how they can help others struggling with the same issues after they have achieved their positive life goals.

Life Goal Issue #3:
"If you forget where you came from, you're doomed to return there"-

Means that we have to "keep our problem up front" (i.e., stay aware of it) in order to avoid slipping into high-risk situations for triggering relapse into unhealthy, harmful behavior. An important step in keeping our problem up front is to get honest about our unhealthy, harmful, behavior and the problems it has created.

Treatment goal exercise 3- In order to keep their problem up front, have your clients need to make a detailed list of "What I don't want to go through ever again and how to avoid it." Have them write what caused things to go wrong in the past. Then have your clients list the opposite positive things they need to do to keep you from having to ever go through those negative situations again and process this in their treatment sessions. Remind clients to include events or situations that were harmful to their body, relationships or life direction. Point out that we do not live on a desert island so if you do something harmful to others, the consequences can be harmful to your relationships and your life direction. Likewise, if you do something unhealthy to yourself it can harm those who care about you. Cover the following information…

The Consequences of Unhealthy, Harmful Behavior- Have clients show how their unhealthy, harmful behavior went from bad to worse by dating their harmful events. Focus on the last 5- 10 years. Include the symptoms and the negative consequences of unhealthy, harmful behavior. Have clients tell how parents, partners, friends, children and bosses were hurt by their behavior. Although hanging with negative peers did result in other people encouraging them to do the wrong thing, try to focus on their part on the problem. Use the language of responsibility and stay away from "it happened." Auto accidents "just happen" and we can catch a cold if someone sneezes on us but we cannot catch a case without breaking the law. "I caught a case" for drunk driving is really, "I was driving after drinking" and got arrested. Have clients list the consequences of unhealthy, harmful behavior their health, relationships and life direction. Use guided discovery to help them get honest about the negative consequences of their behavior on getting the healthy body, healthy relationships and the healthy life direction they want.

Life Goal Tolerance Training: The Facts About Tolerating Change
Achieving life goals require change. You can't achieve life goals without being willing to make changes in your life. Tolerance training in SRT involves helping clients learn to: Tolerate change; Tolerate and value the feedback needed to help them grow to their maximum potential (using the "Mirror Concept") and; Tolerate frustration from life problems and other barriers to life goal attainment without giving up (using "the ABC's of letting feelings go").

Clinical Teaching Points on Tolerating Change
Acknowledge that change is difficult. Humans strive for comfort and avoid uncomfortable change. Acknowledge that we are creatures of habit, that old habits die hard and that a number of basic facts about change have to be accepted in order to tolerate change well enough to achieve life goals.

Behavior Change Fact #1: "Nothing is constant but change"-
This teaching point helps prepare clients for the real road to recovery, which is not typically a direct straight line but does typically involve learning to reestablish goals after setbacks. Recovery from unhealthy, harmful behavior is often said to involve two steps up, one back, two up and so on until the recovery goal is reached. The same process applies to the bigger picture of getting what we want in life. Achieving life goals involves dealing with change and adapting to setbacks. Since we do our best when we are prepared and our worst when we are caught off guard, it is important for clients to have a "Plan B" path to their goals.

Treatment fact exercise 1: "Plan B"- Review Treatment goal exercise 1 (under Life Goal Issue #1) on making short term and long-term goals and have your clients write a "Plan B" alternative path to reaching their short and long-term goals or actual "Plan B" goals that they would also find acceptable and meaningful to them.

Behavior Change Fact #2: "You have to keep your eyes on the prize"-
This means that in order to maintain lasting positive change, while keeping their problem up

front to avoid slipping backwards, clients have to continue to stay focused on their life goals. In order to help stay focused on positive life goals, clients need to write out exactly "What I want in Life and Steps Towards Getting It" and process this in their treatment sessions.

Treatment fact exercise 2- Have your clients write about their longest period of recovery, how they were able to achieve it (i.e., what they learned about what they need to succeed, what supported their recovery, who they were with, what they were doing) and what they will do to extend turn their recovery into a permanent positive lifestyle.

Behavior Change Fact #3:
"You have to go to the opposite extreme to meet the median"- This fact about
achieving lasting change has been referred to as "The Pendulum Concept" and reflects the archery fact that "If you would hit the mark, you must aim a little above it" (Henry Wadsworth Longfellow, 1807-1882). The following example is a typical explanation of the pendulum concept to clients.

> **"The Pendulum Concept"-** Another important step in getting what you want in life is to use the pendulum concept which states that you need to swing your self-control pendulum way over to the very high side during treatment to balance out letting your self-control swing way over to the very low side before treatment. Going to the opposite self-control extreme and doing what you should, when you should for the reason you should is needed to develop enough positive lifestyle practice to be able to meet community standards after treatment when self-control naturally swings back towards the median. In summary, using the pendulum concept in treatment to help you get what you want in life means practicing: 1) protecting your healthy body recovery by doing the opposite of what you used to do that was harmful to your body; 2) protecting your healthy relationship recovery by doing the opposite of what you used to do that was harmful to your relationships and; 3) protecting your healthy life direction recovery by doing the opposite of what you used to do that was harmful to your positive life direction.

Further information on this behavioral "overcorrection" approach is provided on p. 137- 139 & 161 in Yokley (2008) and a good summary of this historical Therapeutic Community best practice approach for harmful behavior treatment is provided on p. 13- 15 in Yokley (2012).

Treatment Fact Exercise 3: Recovery Sabotage- Getting what we want in life requires becoming aware of life goals barriers in order to plan around those barriers. Humans don't always know how to plan a perfectly good day but we sure know how to plan a perfectly bad one. The same is true for planning to get what we want in life. Have your clients list what they would have to do to make sure that they absolutely DID NOT get what they want in life. Get them to discuss what caused things to go wrong in the past. Then have them write down a point-by-point matching list of how they can go to the opposite extreme to make sure they do not go back through that again and that they get what they want in life.

Behavior Change Fact #4: Maintenance is Progress During Hard Times
During times when things are not working out and there is stress overload from too much

external pressure (e.g., problem people) or internal pressure (e.g., unwanted feelings or unhealthy thoughts), not falling back into unhealthy, harmful behavior and maintaining gains is progress.

Practical application examples- Denise, a late 30s African-American female in Intensive Outpatient treatment was expecting probation for passing bad checks to support her drug addiction but received a Federal Prison sentence instead. To make matters worse, her sentence was not to start for 3 months and she was only clean and sober for half that time. She left her house because she felt those calling and encouraging her to stay clean and sober were just reminding her about using. On top of that she ran into her nephew who offered her drugs. Denise used "the 3 G's" to Avoid Trouble (see Table 4.6). She Got out, Got honest with herself "I knew I would use if I stayed" and Got responsible by calling her sponsor. Denise ran away from her recovery support. What she took with her was her ACTS Healthy Behavior Success skills. Maintaining her sobriety during this difficult time was definitely progress for Denise.

Shirley, an early 40's Euro-American female in weight management group was struggling with maintaining her weight during a period of single parenting stress, partner drinking/aggression stress, physical illness stress and stress over having Thanksgiving dinner with relatives. This dinner typically starts around 2pm where everyone brings a dish for an appetizer buffet. the eat and talk goes until around 6pm so by the time everyone has sat down for dinner they have already eaten a meal. At the table there is usually turkey and gravy, mashed potatoes and gravy, stuffing and gravy, real fresh baked rolls with real butter and a host of other fattening foods not to mention people serving you when you finish your plate and ongoing beer or wine refills. Around 8pm someone always turns on a college football game and everyone crawls into the family room where pumpkin pie with whipped cream, apple pie with vanilla ice cream or pecan pie is served with coffee so that people will not pass out from a food coma. In short, on top of all of her other life stressors, Sheila was facing a 6 hour eat-a-thon during a time that she was at high risk for emotional overeating.. She accepted that "Planning power beats willpower", took her digital camera, made herself the family photographer taking pictures the whole time, waited on others, was the last to sit down and the first up again to clear and do dishes. As a result, although she did have a little of everything, she didn't overdo anything and her weight in at group after Thanksgiving showed the same weight as the week before. Her weight maintenance was progress during this difficult time.

Treatment fact exercise 4- Have your clients write about a time when things were not working out, they were overloaded with people problems, unwanted feelings and unhealthy thoughts) but did not fall back into unhealthy, harmful behavior. Have them discuss how they were able to succeed and use that information to make a success plan for the next tough time in their life.

Behavior Change Fact #5: Lifestyle change takes time
Long-term unhealthy, harmful behavior patterns result in lifestyles that center around those behaviors. Individuals who have struggled with unhealthy, harmful behaviors for some time can get understandably anxious to be relieved of the consequences of those behaviors. However, present behavior consequences can't be relieved until the unhealthy, harmful behavior patterns that result in those consequences are changed. In addition, future consequences can't be avoided

until a track record of healthy, prosocial behavior is developed and extended into a healthy, positive lifestyle. This takes time.

While some individuals in residential Therapeutic Community treatment have been known to "do a flip" (i.e., go directly from their unhealthy, harmful behavior pattern to consistently practicing healthy, prosocial behavior), most individuals who have developed an unhealthy, harmful behavior pattern achieve their lifestyle change in stages. The five stages of change in terminating an unhealthy, harmful behavior described by the Transtheoretical Stages of Change Model (Prochaska & DiClemente, 2005) are: precontemplation (not aware of the unhealthy, harmful behavior problem or not disturbed by it); contemplation (considering changing the harmful behavior but not committed); preparation (thinking about change and beginning to take action); action (committed to and actively working on changing the harmful behavior); and maintenance (has changed behavior and is now working on relapse prevention). Advancing through these stages to achieve lifestyle change takes time.

Wanting to be relieved of unhealthy, harmful behavior lifestyle consequences is a common desire among client referrals across the harmful behavior continuum (See Table 1.1). Those who have been referred for behaviors considered primarily harmful to others (e.g., sexually or physically abusive behavior) typically resulting in jail sentences followed by mandated sex offender or domestic violence treatment want to get out of treatment and get off probation/parole right away. Their initial focus during treatment is often on regaining their freedom and autonomy as opposed to learning to understand and manage the factors that led to the loss of their freedom and autonomy (i.e., the precontemplation stage of change). Greg, a young man referred for sex offender treatment said it this way; "I'm just here to get outta here."

Practical Application- It is fairly typical of clients facing incarceration to make a plea for treatment in lieu of incarceration. After admission to treatment these clients often experience the same "flight into health" that patients who wake up in the psychiatric hospital experience after a behavior episode that warrants involuntary hospitalization. This involves saying "I'm fine," stating that their problems are over now and adopting a "that was then, this is now attitude." This attitude supports feelings that others are holding them back from getting on with their lives, that they can make it on their own and would do fine if you just discharged them from treatment. This "closed channel" (Yochelson & Sanenow, 1976) blocks acceptance of the need to learn the healthy relationship and behavior success skills that it takes for lifestyle change. The first step towards helping clients develop an "open channel" towards change is to have them "Act as if" they believe that they could relapse if they don't learn these treatment skills and to practice these skills simply to show treatment providers that they know how to use them if they ever need to use them. Shifting the focus from accepting the treatment skills to practicing the skills can help providers "Roll with the resistance" (Miller and Rollnick, 1991) and can help clients because "Old habits die hard, new habits take practice".

Clients referred for behavior that is both harmful to both self and others like substance abuse which often results in treatment referral by local courts or concerned family sometimes hold a belief that their life can't begin until treatment ends. Some hold an "I need to catch up" attitude focuses on developing relationships, completing school, getting a job and other life areas where they fell behind as a result of their unhealthy, harmful behavior lifestyle. This attitude pulls the treatment focus away from learning the skills to stay sober and get the healthy body needed to succeed in all other areas of their life. Others want things quickly, become frustrated about the recovery process and get a "they're holding me back" attitude. This irresponsible thinking results in "doing time instead of doing treatment" and counting the days left in treatment as opposed to focusing on "keeping your problem up front" and working on the factors that resulted in the referral for treatment. As a result of the "I need to catch up" or a "they're holding me back" attitude, they miss important steps in their recovery learning, don't get promoted in treatment (which is based on skill development, not time served), get angry and give up on themselves (i.e., drop out or relapse). Wanting to move on too quickly also relates to having "no concept of track record" (Yochelson & Samenow, 1976) and not understanding that there is a big difference between just learning a treatment skill and practicing it long enough to develop a track record of making it an automatic positive reaction to a negative situation. Both the "I need to catch up" and a "they're holding me back" attitude reflect the precontemplation stage of change.

Practical Application- SRT addresses the "I need to catch up" and "You're holding me back" attitude by teaching, "What we need to succeed" (See Figure 2.1). This includes getting the relationships and healthy life direction that clients with this attitude are focused on but clarifying that you can't get these needs met without first getting a healthy body, developing healthy behaviors and being in a healthy environment (See Figure 2.1). The client problem to address here is that developing a track record of healthy body habits, healthy behavior success skills and "weeding your relationship garden" to transition to a healthy environment with positive peers takes time. Having no concept of track record involving the belief that because they have entered a high-risk situation for relapse to unhealthy, harmful behavior and did not fall back into problem eating, drinking, drugging, smoking, physical aggression or sexual behavior that because they have done it right once, they have changed (Yochelson & Samenow, 1976). Hold a discussion with clients on the concept of track record and guide them to discover that while doing it right once means that you can change, only doing it right consistently over time means that you have changed. Emphasizing that each time you enter a high-risk situation for relapse there is another chance that you could relapse and the more chances there are, the higher the probability of falling back into unhealthy, harmful behavior. Clients need to understand that even if they are doing well, the more lottery tickets for trouble they buy the higher the chances of hitting the trouble lottery. Help clients put things into perspective. Point out that if they ran into the staff on the street corner five years from now and were asked "Exactly how many days were you in treatment?" they would have to say "How should I know, that was five years ago".

Individuals referred for behaviors considered primarily harmful to self, such as unhealthy eating resulting in morbid obesity and weight-related health problems (e.g., type 2 diabetes, sleep apnea, high blood pressure, high cholesterol, knee pain) and body image depression are walking around in their own body prison. Their autonomy and freedom is diminished by metabolic syndrome consequences such as being able to climb stairs, perform household chores or walk without pain. Their self-esteem is diminished by inability to enter amusement park rides, sit down on a crowded bus, finding clothes that fit and results in weight-related fines such as having to purchase two airline seats or larger first class seats. As a result, they want to lose their weight to get out of their body prison right away. Their body image related low self-esteem sets them up to compromise themselves to be accepted by others. Over-extending themselves to gain appreciation and acceptance acts as compensation to boost their low self-esteem. Their food abuse/addiction can result in getting addicted to doing things for others to receive the acceptance they crave. Maria, a late-30's client in weight loss treatment put it this way, "It feels good to help people and you think you should so you don't want to stop." Always doing for others pulls the focus off of taking care of self and gets others dependent on the client. If clients stop doing for others and refocus their attention on their weight loss treatment, they are likely to experience guilt and self-esteem withdrawal symptoms from the loss of appreciation/acceptance they were getting out of doing things for others. In addition, others who have become dependent on the client's help are likely to go through withdrawal symptoms when having to learn to do things for themselves. This results in negative social pressure to relapse by others nagging the client to go back to doing things for them, which in the past left little time for the client to work on their own treatment. Thus one reason that lifestyle change takes time is because human motivation for change is impacted by social influence resulting in advances with support group encouragement and regression related to negative peer influence.

Case Example- After years of unsuccessful dieting, Joann a mid-40's client began to experience both metabolic syndrome and self-esteem consequences of morbid obesity. As a result, she signed herself up for bariatric surgery and began attending weight loss surgery support groups to find out more about that treatment option. Regular attendance to qualify as a candidate was required and Joann fell behind on two occasions first to attend a high school reunion as a result of old friends wanting her to go with them and second "because they need me at work" because she had consistently helped others with their responsibilities causing them to become dependent on her. Although signing herself up for weight loss surgery support groups shows an initial preparation stage of change, compromising her lifestyle change eating/weight goals for acceptance from high school peers and work associates reveals a lack of commitment that reflects regression back into the contemplation stage of change. Lifestyle change takes time because becoming aware of the self-defeating habits and needs (see page 2) that hold clients back takes time and learning the tools to overcome those and other barriers to change takes time. The important shift that needs to be made with clients who distract themselves from the treatment of their problems by taking on the problems of others and always doing for them is to clarify that self-care isn't selfish and you don't have to go all the way from one extreme attitude (e.g., "Do unto others as you would have others do unto you" 24 hours/day, 7 days/week) to another extreme attitude (e.g., "You have to look out for number one" 24/7). What needs to happen is finding a balance but making sure that lifestyle change treatment comes first (i.e., "You're number one but there are other numbers").

Lifestyle change takes time because the referral harmful behavior is not usually the only harmful behavior, some harmful behaviors are more severe than others and some have a broader impact or are more frequent than others. This means that positive change has to occur in all of these ways for lifestyle change, which of course takes time. Probably the most common example of how unhealthy, harmful behavior change occurs that everyone is familiar with is decreased frequency. This is most typical with smokers who go from 2 backs of cigarettes/day to one pack to one half back and so on down to zero. Harmful behavior can also decrease in impact across the harmful behavior continuum (See Table 1.1). Individuals whose behavior is harmful to both self and others can decrease to behavior that is harmful to self. For example, an alcohol abuser referred for driving under the influence on the way home from a bar and causing an accident that injured another motorist can engage in harm reduction and limit their drinking to home.

Case Example- Jerry, a late 60's male referred for driving under the influence went through the stages of responsibility acceptance from blaming the police speed trap to blaming friends who kept buying him drinks to admitting that he should have got a ride from someone or called a cab. He remained angry for some time stating, "I'm a grown man, I have a right to drink, it's just not right to drink and drive" and telling his providers that he would drink at home after he got off of probation. After an extended period of sobriety during treatment, he came to realize that life without alcohol was in some ways better than life with alcohol and decided that there was no real need for him to drink at home.

Unhealthy, harmful behavior types can decrease over time. For example, alcoholics who smoke and overeat but are referred for drunk driving may successfully quit drinking (i.e., a drop from 3 types of harmful behavior to 2) which results in increased smoking that then needs to be addressed. Quitting smoking (i.e., a drop from 2 types of harmful behavior to 1) which results in increased unhealthy eating then needs to be addressed in order to develop the healthy body clients need to succeed in their other healthy lifestyle goals. This transition is not always an easy one for clients. Frank, a mid-40's male referred for weight management said, "First I quit drinking, then I quit smoking, now you guys want me to quit junk food, what do I have left?" Finally, harmful behavior can also decrease in severity across the harmful behavior continuum (See Table 1.1). For example, clients referred for sex offender treatment may shift behavior from putting their hands on other people without their permission to putting their hands on other people's property without their permission (i.e., from sexual abuse to property abuse). Another example would be young clients referred for fighting shifting venting their anger through physically abusive behavior to venting their anger through vandalism. These behavior changes represent a severity decrease in severity on the harmful behavior continuum from personal crimes of violence to property crimes.

Stages of Change Research Support Summary: The finding that clients go through stages of change described by the Transtheoretical Model has been documented in the research literature on a number of unhealthy, harmful behaviors (e.g., Nigg et. al. 1999; Prochaska, Velicer et. al. 1994). For example, the stages of change described by the Transtheoretical Model has been successfully applied to; sexual abuse risky and sexual behavior (e.g., Tierney & McCabe, 2004; Velasquez et al 2009); physical abuse, e.g., male and female perpetrators of physical abuse (Babcock et al., 2005; Eckhardt, Babcock & Homack, 2004) and women ending partner violence (e.g., Anderson, 2003; Burke et al., 2001); property abuse by general criminal offenders along with problem spending, debt and gambling in (e.g., Soberay et. al. 2014; Yong et. al. 2015; Xiao et. al. 2004); substance abuse including smoking and unhealthy eating (e.g., Prochaska, Velicer et. al. 1994) and; addressing family trust abuse by mobilizing support for victims (Corcoran, 2002).

Change Fact #6: Sometimes you have to start over
Since "Old habits die hard" (Delude, 2005), individuals with a history of unhealthy, harmful behavior are unlikely to successfully quit on their first attempt. According to the Transtheoretical Stages of Change Model, termination of harmful behavior involves progression through five stages of change (described in Change Fact #5 above) and "individuals typically recycle through

these stages several times before termination of the addiction" (p. 63, Prochaska, DiClemente & Norcross, 2003).

Clients who have serious problems letting go of their unhealthy, harmful behavior and fall back onto that behavior during treatment or relapse afterwards, need to repeat treatment. Those with a probation or parole officer are likely to be ordered by the court to do so. Becoming demoralized after giving up on healthy life goals can result in a "closed channel" (Yochelson & Samenow, 1976) attitude towards starting over preventing the client from picking up what they missed before because they "have been there and done that" and "already heard this before." In a mixed group where some clients have had considerable past treatment, are starting over and thus at risk for blocking information out, it is important to implement the wood block learning experience.

Treatment fact exercise 6: The wood block learning experience- was designed to answer the question, "How do you learn from treatment if you have already been in treatment?" Get a length of 2" X 2" lumber (which will typically measure 1.5" X 1.5" (used wood with knots and nail holes are best) and cut off 1.5" sections so that you have a pile of wood blocks that are 1.5" on each side. Don't bother to sand them. Just bring them into your group and hand out one to each of your group members. Start out by asking how many group members have been in treatment before with a show of hands. Then instruct everyone to look at their wood block and say "I have a wood block, what do you have?" After each member says "A wood block", say "OK, let's do this again." Then look at the block you are holding and add something. For example, "I have a wood block with a knot on one side, what do you have?" The next member might say, "I have a wood block with a chip on one side." Go around until each member has added a new observation to their wood block, then say "OK let's do this one last time", look at the block you are holding and add something again. For example, I have a wood block with a knot on one side and a nail hole on the other, what do you have?" Go around until each member has added a second woodblock observation. Then say, "Even when looking at a simple wood block, each time we looked closer, we say something new. How does this apply to treatment?" Then facilitate the discussion until the group concludes that each time they cover the same treatment concept or issue, if they look a little closer, they will see something new. Conclude with "Looking closer is the difference between doing time and doing treatment".

"It does not matter how slowly you go as long as you do not stop" -- Confucius (551- 479BC)

Achieving Life Goals Theoretical Background Summary: The SRT treatment approach of helping clients get the healthy positive life they need to succeed is consistent with Abraham Maslow's human needs hierarchy (e.g., Kenrick et.al., 2010; Taormina & Gao, 2013) and the behavioral intervention method of reciprocal inhibition (i.e., decreasing unwanted emotions by providing competing responses to those emotions, see Heriot & Pritchard, 2004) by reinforcing multicultural prosocial values as competing factors to unhealthy, harmful behavior. The ART of achieving life goals in SRT is consistent with the evidence-based Therapeutic Community Model that has promoted the "Right Living" values of honesty, responsible concern and work ethic in unhealthy substance use treatment since the 1950's (DeLeon, 2000). This approach is also consistent with the Good Lives Model focus on developing the core values and skills needed for a "good life" plan that reduces the risk of reoffending in the treatment of harmful physical and sexual behavior (e.g., Ward & Fortune, 2013).

Chapter 3
Helping Clients Manage their Unhealthy, Harmful Behavior

Multicultural Recognition in Treatment Program Design
"We are like islands in the sea, separate on the surface but connected in the deep"
-- William James (1842- 1910)

Introduction

Continuing the path to optimize impact of mental health services for ethnic minorities requires parallel processing of multiple barriers. The limited services, large number of groups in need and problems with the dominant therapy model create a call for a dramatic change in our research and practice (Kazdin, 2008). These challenges have divided researchers on the issue of whether or not to continue the population-based solution path of attempting to optimize treatment impact for ethnic minorities by adapting each evidence-based treatment to each ethnic group for each diagnostic condition (e.g., Kazdin, 2008; Miranda, Nakamura & Bernal, 2003; Sue (2003). While this debate continues, one area of agreement by some is a call for multicultural theoretical research that focuses less on populations and more on psychological phenomena (e.g., Miranda, Nakamura & Bernal, 2003; Sue, 2003).

The treatment research path for ethnic minorities continues to require a concerted effort on resolving problems with high dropout rates after one treatment session, infrequent session use and poor level of functioning at the end of treatment (Maramba and Hall, 2002). In addition to advances in adapting evidence-based treatments to improve treatment outcome for ethnic minorities, important advances have been made in the area of cultural sensitivity training for therapists. While cultural sensitivity training can address one aspect of the client-therapist relationship, it does not address therapist values or incompatible aspects of the therapy being offered. This is important since clinical practice "arises from a Euro-American framework, many culturally different groups claim that counseling and therapy are culture-bound, that the values of the helping professions are antagonistic to their values" (p. 80, Bingham et al., 2002). For example, Latino-focused psychologist Elizabeth Fraga points out that Latino cultures tend to value a family's health over that of individual family members and may view a psychologist's suggestions for self-care, such as taking a short vacation alone as selfish while psychologist Patricia Arredondo adds that therapists from a society that highly values individualism, may not think to include the family or to interview family members (Dingfelder, 2005). This finding suggests that any minority client therapeutic relationship improvements obtained from client-therapist ethnic matching could be negated by training in the dominant therapy model. Minority therapist training in culture-bound procedures that convey dominant culture values may serve to explain why meta-analytic evaluation from the past twenty years has revealed "that ethnic match is not a significant clinical predictor of decreasing dropout after the first session or increasing number of sessions attended" (p. 290, Maramba and Hall, 2002). Overcoming this barrier requires research and treatment to move beyond cultural sensitivity training and client-therapist ethnic matching into multicultural recognition in treatment program design through attempts to develop treatment approaches that are not culture bound or antagonistic to minority values. Three straightforward multicultural behavior therapy approaches to this goal are to: 1) examine cross-cultural research in search of common, multicultural prosocial values that can be utilized in behavior therapy; 2) include multicultural group therapy in a social learning treatment protocol with multicultural members and a structure that assures mutual client identification/support is present while negative peer influence is absent and; 3) implement the existing cognitive-behavioral interventions that have a known multicultural evidence base.

Multicultural Values Theory

The theory that certain human values have basic universal, multicultural content (Schwartz & Bilsky, 1987) has been tested in a study of values in Australia, Finland, Hong Kong, Spain and the United States revealing similar value priorities in all western cultures. The finding of basic multicultural human values has been replicated and extended to Africans and Italians (Schwartz, Melech, Lehmann, et. al. 2001). Although more differences are typically found between eastern and western cultures (e.g., Schwartz & Bilsky, 1990) than within western cultures, there appear to be at least some global multicultural prosocial values. For example, a study of cross-cultural similarities and differences in values of American and Japanese college students revealed largely similar overall value priority ratings (Akiba & Klug, 1999). More specifically, a 21-culture study of eastern values and a 9-culture study of western values revealed common values of self-restraint and discipline in both (Bond, 1988). These findings tend to indicate that self-control is viable multicultural prosocial value that may span eastern and western cultures. In addition, a study of US and Japanese nurses revealed common values including competence, patient respect, responsibility, relationship and connection, family importance, caring, truth-telling and understanding the patient/situation (Wros, Doutrich & Izumi, 2004). Taken together, these data tend to indicate that honesty, concern and responsibility (including self-control) are multicultural prosocial values accepted by many culturally different groups that span both eastern and western cultures.

Multicultural Prosocial Values

Social Responsibility Therapy (SRT) was originally developed on a multicultural population of youth and young adults exhibiting harmful, abusive behavior (Yokley, 2008). SRT takes another path towards addressing the culture-bound treatment issue by attempting to answer the call for theory-driven multicultural research on psychological constructs that apply to different cultural groups and interventions effective across cultural belief systems (Miranda, Nakamura, and Bernal, 2003; Sue, 2003). SRT adopts the theoretical approach of trying to identify "least common denominators" in basic human values that are multicultural in nature. SRT attempts to preserve the individuality of cultural groups while seeking unity through a treatment platform that will support multicultural intervention by taking an approach that all humans adopt when they actually want to make a new friend- looking for similarities. SRT respects diversity but seeks unity through common, multicultural values, a position referred to as "diversity within unity" (Etzioni, 2001; 2004; 2006). Respect for the whole and respect for all is at the essence of "Diversity within unity" which "presumes that all members of a given society will fully respect and adhere to those basic values and institutions that are considered part of the basic shared framework of the society. At the same time, every group in society is free to maintain its distinct subculture-those policies, habits, and institutions that do not conflict with the shared core-and a strong measure of loyalty to its country of origin".[1]

Social maturity development in SRT draws on multicultural values theory (e.g., Akiba and Klug, 1999; Schwartz and Bilsky, 1987, 1990; Schwartz et al., 2001) to select basic prosocial values accepted by multiple cultural groups. Specifically, the social maturity focus of SRT involves developing the multicultural prosocial values of honesty, trust, loyalty, concern, and responsibility as "Healthy Relationship Success Skills" (See Chapter 9) and competing factors to unhealthy, harmful behavior. Research support for the selection of these specific multicultural prosocial values in SRT multicultural intervention has been published (Described on p. 31- 39 in Yokley, 2008). Consumer report of the multicultural prosocial values utilized in SRT continues to be validated through structured clinical exercise surveys of multicultural population youth, their caretakers and clinical staff (Described on p. 171- 174 in Yokley, 2008).

Multicultural Group Therapy

The SRT protocol which includes group therapy with a diverse population of individuals exhibiting harmful behavior, provides ample opportunity for multicultural therapeutic interaction, along with strong reinforcement of multicultural prosocial values and behaviors that are incompatible with the presenting unhealthy, harmful behaviors. This is accomplished with a set of PRAISE multicultural group unity and participation motivation skills involving: Pulling people in; Responsible reinforcement; Acknowledgement; Instant identification; Social mathematics and; Enabling responsibility (See Chapter 9). In adolescent groups, written accomplishment awards for client modeling of multicultural prosocial values and behaviors are provided while incident reports on behaviors reflecting multicultural values problems are targeted for change. Tolerance training in SRT expands beyond emotional tolerance training with emotional regulation skills to include social tolerance training with role reversal and perspective-taking skills. The culturally diverse SRT group develops multicultural interaction self-efficacy for clients and addresses client needs to practice multicultural navigation skills in a safe, therapeutic setting.

Multicultural Behavior Therapy Interventions

Evidence-based interventions and procedures are combined in SRT to develop awareness and actualization of multicultural prosocial values. The behavior therapy interventions combined in SRT (e.g., cognitive-behavioral therapy, operant conditioning, contingency management, social learning procedures utilized in the therapeutic community model, token economy systems, rational emotive behavior therapy and cognitive therapy) have a known multicultural evidence base. The SRT "Healthy Behavior Success Skills" involve basic skills from the evidence-based areas of relapse prevention, emotional regulation, decisional balance and social problem solving to help clients Avoid trouble, Calm Down, Think it through and Solve the problem in stressful situations that threaten their recovery from unhealthy, harmful behavior problems (See Table 3.2).

The utility of these interventions is repeatedly demonstrated in multiple cultural settings year after year at the World Congress of Behavioral and Cognitive Therapies by its umbrella organizations, the Association for Advancement of Behavior Therapy (USA), International Association for Cognitive Psychotherapy, The Australian Association for Cognitive and Behaviour Therapy, the Japanese Association for Behavior Therapy, Association Latinoamericana de Analisis y Modificacion del Comportamiento, Southern African Association for Behavior Therapy and the European Association for Behavioural and Cognitive Therapies. The irrational beliefs central to Rational Emotive Behavior Therapy have been evaluated in multicultural studies involving Colombia, Costa Rica, El Salvador, Spain and the USA with respect to a violence index and acculturation along with selected medical conditions, opening new multicultural directions for REBT (Lega & Ellis, 2001).

The utility of the multicultural social learning approach adopted by SRT involving social learning experiences implemented by rational authority and supported by socially responsible peer role models in a functional family setting has been demonstrated throughout the world with multicultural therapeutic community research spanning back almost 20 years (e.g., Biase & Sullivan, 1986). With respect to substance abuse, the Therapeutic Community approach used in SRT has been referred to as "The predominant residential modality for treating addictions from Chile to China" (Waters, Fazio, Hernandez & Segarra, 2002). Multicultural research on therapeutic community social learning treatment procedures has been implemented to improve treatment retention of both African Americans and Native Americans in the United States (e.g., DeLeon, Melnick, Schoket & Jainchill, 1993; Fisher, Lankford & Galea, 1996). Although the basic behavioral principles and procedures used in SRT are applicable in multiple cultural settings, since cross-cultural interactions are prone to interpersonal misunderstanding which can impair the impact of cross-cultural behavior therapy (Seiden, 1999), multicultural competence is important in behavioral intervention with multicultural clients (Hayes & Toarmino, 1995) and implementing PRAISE multicultural skills is strongly recommended to develop group unity and motivate participation. A summary of research support for the contingency management and social learning procedures used in SRT is provided in Chapter 4 of Yokley (2008).

Summary and Conclusion

SRT exhibits strong social validity with a social maturity focus on multicultural prosocial values that: 1) benefit the client and community; 2) are competing factors to unhealthy, harmful, behavior and; 3) are necessary to achieve success in a democratic society where social responsibility is prerequisite to successful community adjustment. Since the diverse SRT group mirrors our multicultural society and focuses on the development of multicultural prosocial values, it has the potential be an optimal training environment for positive multicultural interaction. SRT employs cognitive-behavioral interventions and social learning procedures that enjoy a multicultural evidence base. SRT respects diversity but seeks unity by developing common, multicultural values, a position referred to as "diversity within unity" (Etzioni, 2001; 2004; 2006). The diversity within unity approach of SRT may provide a more inclusive path for multicultural recognition in unhealthy, harmful behavior treatment by identifying cultural similarities to celebrate in addition to the traditional approach of developing awareness of cultural differences to respect.[2]

In conclusion, with respect to tolerance training, SRT adds social tolerance to the traditional emotional tolerance training skills. With respect to awareness training, SRT adds awareness training on cultural similarities to celebrate to the traditional awareness training on cultural differences to respect. The SRT approach to multicultural recognition in treatment program design is one prescription for decreasing the culture clash discomfort that exacerbates client stress, increases treatment drop out, decreases outcome and can inhibit clients from pursuing any desired goals, which may exist outside of their familiar cultural environment. Further information is provided in "Multicultural intervention approach, rationale and content" (p. 25-46, Yokley, 2008).

The SRT Multimethod-Multipath Behavior Therapy Model
"Strong Medicine for Strong Problems"

SRT utilizes a Multimethod-Multipath Behavior Therapy treatment model with multiple intervention methods across multiple intervention pathways for the treatment of unhealthy, harmful behaviors that are often highly resistant to change. In SRT intervention pathways are categorized as primarily utilizing internal control, external control and social learning. Each intervention pathway involves a number of methods and procedures capable of targeting multiple forms of unhealthy, harmful behavior.

The multiple intervention pathways utilized in the SRT Multimethod-Multipath Behavior Therapy model are similar to the biopsychosocial medical model which acknowledged that medical treatment involves multiple paths of healing and patient care. This revolution in medical thinking resulted in the biomedical model evolving to include the psychosocial dimensions (e.g., personal, emotional, family, community) of patient healing and care (Smith, 2002). Internal control methods and procedures in Multimethod-Multipath Behavior Therapy are implemented by clients and involve relapse prevention, emotional regulation, decisional balance and social problem solving referred to as Healthy Behavior Success Skills in SRT. These internal control methods and procedures are similar to the psychological healthcare aspect of the biopsychosocial model.

External control methods and procedures in Multimethod-Multipath Behavior Therapy are implemented by agents of change (e.g., mental health professionals, physicians, probation officers, parents, partners and peers) and involve operant conditioning procedures providing reinforcement, consequences and behavior monitoring. Examples of external control methods and procedures include: relapse risk assessment; behavior modification; behavior monitoring; physiological/electronic monitoring and; medication prescriptions. External control methods and procedures involving medication prescription and physiological monitoring are similar to the biological healthcare aspect of the biopsychosocial model.

Social learning methods and procedures in Multimethod-Multipath Behavior Therapy are implemented by those in close contact with the client (e.g., peers, partners, parents, treatment group members, therapists) and involve observational learning and modeling procedures focused on multicultural prosocial values and associated healthy behaviors referred to as Healthy Relationship Success Skills. These social learning methods and procedures are similar to the social healthcare aspect of the biopsychosocial model. A summary of the evidence base for the type of internal control, external control and social learning procedures employed in SRT is provided in "Intervention evidence base: The toolbox for multiple forms of harmful behavior" (p.18- 24, Yokley, 2008).

Multimethod-Multipath Behavior Therapy Overview

In order to maximize the probability of behavior change and minimize the risk of harmful behavior impact, resistant unhealthy behaviors that are harmful to self and others require multiple intervention methods and behavior change pathways. Multimethod-Multipath Behavior Therapy acts to:

1. Push individuals with harmful behavior toward positive change with external control procedures (e.g., contingency management, Reinforcement, consequences, behavior contracts, etc.).

2. Pull them toward positive change through internal control procedures (e.g., healthy behavior success skills)- cognitive interventions, mainstream CBT.

Figure 3.1.
The SRT Multimethod-Multipath Behavior Therapy Model

Healthy Behavior Success Skills [2]

External Control [1] → Unhealthy, Harmful, Behavior → Internal Control [2] → Positive Behavior Change

Social Learning [3]

1. **Pushes** clients toward positive change (reinforcement and consequences)
2. **Pulls** clients towards positive change (cognitive interventions)
3. **Redirects/Motivates** clients towards positive change (social modeling/influence)

Healthy Relationship Success Skills (honesty, trust, loyalty, concern & responsibility- Facilitated by PRAISE participation motivation and group unity skills)

3. Redirect/motivate them towards change with social learning procedures (e.g., modeling healthy relationship success skills). See Figure 3.1.

The self-reinforcing aspect of many unhealthy, harmful behaviors has resulted in increasing acceptance of their addictive nature along with similarities in general symptoms, consequences and underlying brain neurotransmitter systems.[3] These similarities lay the foundation for the SRT Multimethod-Multipath Behavior Therapy model that targets primary contributing factors to multiple forms of unhealthy, harmful behavior.

"The common ground is greater and more enduring than the differences that divide" -- Nelson Mandella

Multimethod-Multipath Behavior Therapy Background

Many unhealthy, harmful behaviors are highly resistant to change because they are self-reinforcing. For example, sexual abuse can be reinforced by the pursuit of pleasure (i.e., sexual gratification or "sensation seeking"- see Scully & Marolla, 2003), avoidance of pain (e.g., internet pornography use and loneliness- see Yoder, Virden & Amin, 2005) or control and power need gratification (e.g., Wood, Wilson & Thorne, 2015). Physical abuse can be reinforced by sensation seeking (e.g., during bullying- see Lovegrove, Henry & Slater, 2012) or control and power need gratification (e.g., during domestic violence- see Wagers, 2015). Property abuse can be reinforced by stolen money (or value of the stolen property), the pursuit of pleasure (e.g., sensation seeking, thrill crime shoplifting- see Turner & Cashdan, 1988), the avoidance of pain (e.g., distraction from unwanted feelings- See Coid, 1984) or control and power need gratification as in extortion, blackmail or in some cases rape as a bonus thrill to burglary or robbery (e.g., Scully & Marolla, 2003). Substance abuse can be reinforced by the pursuit of pleasure (i.e., the substance induced "high") or the avoidance of pain (i.e., taking power over and controlling mood to avoid unwanted feelings or "self-medicating"- see Bolton, Robinson & Sareen, 2009). In a related substance use area, it goes without saying that the delicious taste of unhealthy food makes unhealthy eating self-reinforcing. Trust abuse can be reinforced by the pursuit of pleasure (e.g., infidelity as a desire for sexual excitement- See Blow & Hartnett, 2005 or a test "cheaters high"- See Reudy et. al. 2013) or the avoidance of pain (e.g., lying about harmful behavior to avoid social or legal consequences).

Cognitive-behavioral therapy (CBT) over the past three decades has centered on internal control/cognitive intervention by challenging cognitive distortions that support unwanted feelings and unhealthy, harmful behavior. This approach has overshadowed the more external control/behavioral approaches, until a pivotal study by Jacobson et. al. (1996) revealed that the behavioral components in CBT for depression to be just as effective as the cognitive components and meta-analysis confirmed that finding (Ekers et. al., 2008). This finding supports adding external control/behavioral interventions to the treatment plan for unhealthy, harmful behaviors which often present with co-occurring depression and are typically self-reinforcing making them highly resistant to change. Freeman et. al. (2004) point out that in general the more severe the pathology and intellectual limitations, the greater the emphasis need to be on behavioral (external control) strategies. In addition, many unhealthy, harmful behaviors are reinforced by social learning factors and the social influence model predicts that as a social influence group increases in size, its impact increases (Tanford & Penrod, 1984). Put another way, the number of people modeling healthy or harmful behavior in the client's social network can help predict harmful behavior recovery or relapse. SRT Multimethod-Multipath Behavior Therapy matches intervention intensity to problem severity. This is achieved with a

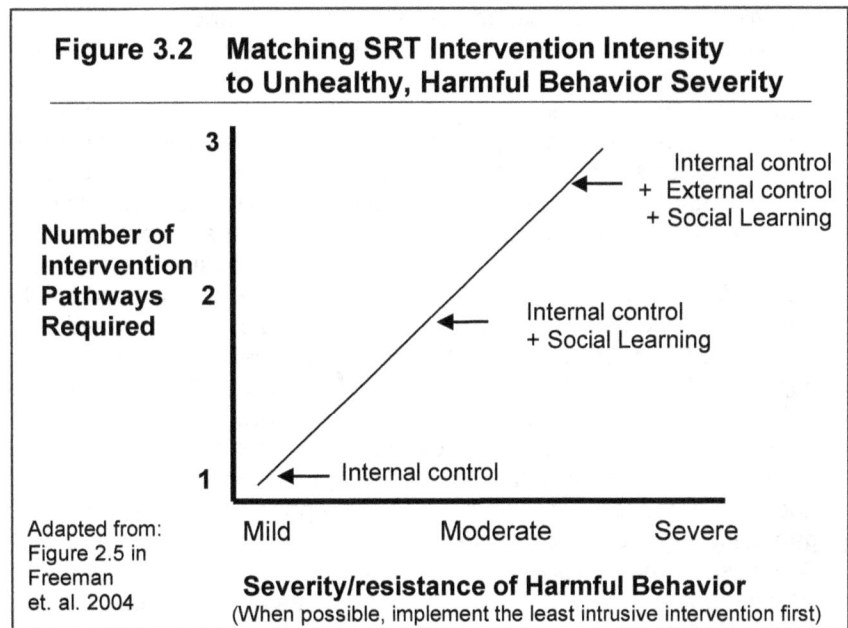

Figure 3.2 Matching SRT Intervention Intensity to Unhealthy, Harmful Behavior Severity

combination of internal control, external control and social learning interventions (Figure 3.2). In summary, unhealthy, harmful behaviors often present with co-occurring problems and are typically self-reinforced making them highly resistant to change. More severe, self-reinforced, resistant unhealthy, harmful behavior problems particularly in clients with co-occurring disorders (e.g., depression or other unhealthy harmful behaviors) require more intervention pathways.

Key treatment issues and barriers to positive behavior change in unhealthy, harmful behavior-specific treatment (see p. 3- 4) make a strong case for Multimethod-Multipath Behavior Therapy. Specifically, unhealthy, harmful behavior treatment needs to address the facts that: 1) the referral harmful behavior is not usually the only harmful behavior; 2) one harmful behavior can set the occasion for or trigger others; 3) the target harmful behavior can migrate to another harmful behavior during treatment when it is being observed and shift back afterwards and; 4) peer, parent or partner models support/encourage harmful behavior. Since the referral harmful behavior is not usually the only harmful behavior,[1] best practice in harmful behavior treatment requires targeting the primary contributing factors that support multiple forms of harmful behavior to prevent one harmful behavior from triggering another,[2] stop harmful behavior migration[3] from blocking self-control development and keep negative social influence[4] from supporting/encouraging unhealthy, harmful behavior. The Internal control, External control and Social learning components of Multimethod-Multipath Behavior Therapy provides the *increased intervention intensity* (p. 4 #5) needed to address unhealthy, harmful behaviors and three structured workbooks address *the need for comprehensive harmful behavior conceptualization* (p. 4 #6) issue by helping clients understand how they acquired, maintained and generalized their harmful behavior (Yokley, 2010b; 2011a; 2012)

Harmful Behavior-Specific Treatment Barriers: Research Support Summary

1. ***Harmful behavior comorbidity-*** Substance abuse is a comorbid problem across harmful behaviors including sexual abuse, physical abuse, property abuse and food abuse/overeating (See summary in Yokley, 2010a). Despite being referred for a specific harmful behavior, youth sex offenders commit significantly more physical abuse (felony assault) and property abuse (felony theft & damage) than nonsexual youth offenders (Burton, 2008). Males in batterer intervention programs exhibit a higher percentage of problem gambling, were more likely to be hazardous drinkers and engage in sexual aggression (Brasfield et. al. 2012). Gambling has significant association with smoking and drinking (Griffiths et. al., 2011) and problem gamblers are significantly more likely to binge drink, use hard drugs, pay for sex and engage in illegal activity for profit (Hall et. al. 2000; Walker, Clark & Folk, 2010). Pathological gambling is associated with obesity, chronic medical conditions, poor lifestyle choices, worse quality of life and costly medical care. (Black et. al., 2013). A summary of co-occurring harmful behaviors in youth referred for sexually abusive is provided in Chapter 54 of Yokley (2011b).

2. ***Comorbidity adverse impact-*** Youth sex offenders who used alcohol had a higher number of victims than those who didn't and those who reported alcohol increased their arousal had the most victims (Becker & Stein, 1991). There is a strong association between alcohol abuse and physical abuse supported by seven meta-analytic studies (Exum, 2006). Research revealing that 64% of the men in batterer programs were alcoholic and 59% in alcohol programs used relationship violence (Stith, Crossman, & Bischof, 1991) tends to indicate that some men beat their partners, feel guilty, then get drunk while others get drunk, lose control, then beat their partners. 65% of severe problem gamblers and 20% of moderate problem gamblers reported that their criminal activity was the result of their gambling, e.g., to pay off yesterday's debts or to support today's gambling (Turner et. al., 2009). Bulimics are more likely to binge and purge after drinking alcohol (Abraham & Beumont, 1982; Williamson, 1990) and 34% of smoking lapses are triggered by eating or drinking (Shiffman et. al., 1996). Bottom line- "The superego is soluble in alcohol and evaporates with narcotics." Continued smoking appears to place abstinent alcohol and drug abusers at elevated risk for relapse (Satre, Kohn & Weisner, 2007) with a dose response finding that even decreases in smoking over time significantly decreased the likelihood of alcohol relapse (Friend & Pagano, 2005).

3. ***Harmful behavior migration-*** Problem gamblers, drinkers, or both shift these behavior patterns regularly (Shaffer and Hall, 2002).

4. ***Negative social influence-*** See " Negative Social Influence Research Support: Selected Problem Examples" on p. 208. See also "The negative social influence problem" p. 16 in Yokley (2008).

Internal Control: Healthy Behavior Success Skills- Avoid trouble; Calm down; Think it through and Solve the Problem

"When we know better, we do better"-- Maya Angelou (1928- 2014)

SRT utilizes internal control procedures to address barriers to positive behavior change in unhealthy, harmful behavior-specific treatment (e.g., harmful behavior comorbidity, comorbidity adverse impact and, harmful behavior migration). These cognitive interventions are referred to as Healthy Behavior Success Skills in SRT. They are implemented by clients to overcome recovery threats and life goal barriers. In other words, they help clients pull themselves towards positive change (See Figure 3.1). These skills were drawn from the research-supported areas of Relapse Prevention; Emotional Regulation; Decisional Balance and; Social Problem Solving. Two relapse prevention skills are taught to help clients "Avoid Trouble." Two emotional regulation skills are taught to help clients "Calm down." Clients learn a decision-making Reality Check and three Reality Scales to weigh out the benefits and drawbacks of decisions to "Think it through" before taking action. Finally, a three-step social problem skills is taught to help clients "Solve the problem" when it comes to issues that are barriers to their recovery or life goals.

These Healthy Behavior Success Skills are easily remembered with the acronym "**ACTS**" by most clients who have been told that " your **ACTS** speak louder than your words" in the past. A summary of the ACTS Healthy Behavior Success Skills that will be covered in this section is provided in Table 3.1. If teaching internal control

Table 3.1. Healthy Behavior Success Skills Overview		
Evidence-based Intervention Area	**ACTS Skill Area**	**Specific ACTS Skills**
Relapse Prevention	**A**void trouble	1) High-risk situation Avoidance 2) High-risk situation Escape
Emotional Regulation	**C**alm down	1) ABC's of letting feelings go 2) ABC's of holding on to feelings
Decisional Balance	**T**hink it through	1) Reality check 2) The 3 reality scales
Social Problem Solving	**S**olve the problem	The 3 step SET social problem solving skill

is successful, the client's automatic response in an emotional or crisis situation will be to: **A**void trouble, **C**alm down, **T**hink it through and **S**olve the problem. Assess the clients self-management knowledge base and skill set by administering the SRT Learning Experience Questionnaire (Appendix A). Chapters 4 through 7 cover each of the four ACTS Healthy Behavior Success Skills listed in the SRT Learning Experience Questionnaire.

Healthy Behavior Success Skills Agenda- "Avoid trouble, Calm down, Think it though and Solve the problem." In the next four chapters, the emphasis will be on teaching patients one key intervention skill in each of the four evidence-based healthy behavior success skill areas listed in the overall intervention goal below.

Overall Goal- If intervention is successful, the patient's automatic thought in an emotional or crisis situation will be four important goals, "Avoid trouble, Calm down, Think it though and Solve the problem".

1. Avoid trouble (through Relapse Prevention and Positive Planning)
2. Calm down (through Emotional Regulation and Self-Control)
3. Think it through (with Decisional Balance and Responsible Decision-making)
4. Solve the problem (with Social Problem Solving) and summary of ACTS Healthy Behavior Success Skills

Make an ACTS skills card like the one shown in Table 3.2 below for clients to keep with them at all times before, during and after learning to use the SRT Healthy Behavior Success Skills as a pocket reminder to, "Avoid trouble, Calm down, Think it though and Solve the problem".

Table 3.2   ACTS Healthy Behavior Success Skills Card

Keep your Skill Cards with you at all times
"There are two basic types of knowledge in life... Knowing it or knowing where to get it" [a]

Social Responsibility Therapy- ACTS Healthy <u>Behavior</u> Success Skills [b]
Getting what we want in life involves learning to...

Avoid trouble (relapse prevention)- Use "the 3 G's" (i.e., the three-step responsibility plan):
  Get out (Remove yourself)- "You need to be laughing and leaving, not staying and stewing";
  Get honest (Block the thought)- Tell yourself the truth, feelings change but actions can't be changed. If you can't deny the thought, delay it. Tell yourself "I can always do this tomorrow" and weigh your decisions before taking action (see "Think it through" below).
  Get Responsible (Substitute a more responsible thought). Do the responsible thing. "Act as if" you are the person you want to be and go to the opposite healthy, helpful extreme.

Calm down (emotional regulation)- Use the ABC's of letting feelings go:
  "A" is the **A**ction that occurred;
  "B" is the **B**elief problem, i.e., the word "should" or "must" that is triggering the feeling;
  "C" is **C**hallenging the Belief problem in order to stop working yourself up, prevent following feelings and let it go.[c]

Think it through (decisional balance)- Do a Reality Check, ask yourself- "Is what I'm considering helpful or harmful to myself and others?" [c] If possibly harmful or unhealthy use "the 3 S's" (i.e., the three decisional balance Reality Scales)
      (0- 10 scale, 0= not necessary/important/severe, 10= highly necessary/important/severe):
  Survival scale- How necessary for my survival is it for me to... ? ("Do I need to do this to survive?")
  Success scale- How important for my success is it for me to...?
  Severity scale (Bad or Awful scale)- How severe would the consequences be if I...?

Solve the problem (social problem solving)- Get <u>SET</u> for solving problems:
  Set your goal;
  Evaluate your progress and options;
  Take responsible action. Do the right thing for yourself and others.

---

a. Adapted from "Knowledge is of two kinds. We know a subject ourselves, or we know where we can find information upon it." - Samuel Johnson (1709- 1784).
b. SRT early stage recovery skills to help prevent unhealthy harmful behavior relapse (Yokley, 2010b).
c. See Ellis & Bernard (2006); Ellis & Velten (1992) for ABC,s in Rational Emotive Behavior Therapy.

Chapter 4
Internal Control- Healthy Behavior Success Skill #1:
Helping Clients "Avoid Trouble" with Relapse Prevention

Helping Clients "Avoid Trouble" with Relapse Prevention
"We gain the strength of the temptation we resist"-- Ralph Waldo Emerson (1803- 1882)

Relapse Prevention involves interventions that decrease the risk of relapsing back into unhealthy, harmful behavior. In SRT, the ART of Relapse Prevention involves Awareness Training on high-risk situations for relapse, Responsibility Training on two basic relapse prevention skills and Tolerance Training on learning to tolerate behavior feedback needed to accept behavior problem issues, succeed in recovery and achieve life goals. In order for health lifestyle change to occur, the ART of Relapse Prevention is applied to all three basic areas of healthy lifestyle development, i.e., developing a healthy body/behavior/environment, healthy relationships and healthy life direction.

Relapse Prevention: "Straight to the Point"
The point of this section is to help clients: become aware of what they need to know; develop the skills they need to use and; the tolerance they need to have to prevent unhealthy, harmful behavior relapse.

Relapse Prevention Goals and Objectives
Awareness Training Goal: Increase client awareness of high-risk situations for unhealthy, harmful behavior relapse.
   Objectives: Clients will be able to identify and discuss examples of high risk people, places, thoughts and feelings that set the occasion for or trigger relapse.
Responsibility Training Goal: Develop responsible relapse prevention strategies.
   Objectives: Clients will be able to explain their high-risk situation avoidance plan and be able to use "The 3 G's" to escape high-risk situations for relapse, i.e., <u>Get out</u> (Remove yourself)- "You need to be laughing and leaving, not staying and stewing"; <u>Get honest</u> (Block the thought)- Tell yourself the truth, feelings change but actions can't be changed; <u>Get Responsible</u> (Substitute a more responsible thought)
Tolerance Training Goal: Develop the feedback tolerance needed to increase awareness of high-risk situations for relapse and increase acceptance of behavior problem issues.
   Objectives: Clients will be able to explain how the "Mirror Concept" develops feedback tolerance.

Treatment Exercise: Relapse Prevention Benefits
It is important for clients to make the connection between their unhealthy, harmful behavior and getting what they need to succeed by learning relapse prevention skills. Individuals referred for unhealthy, harmful behavior need to take a camera lens perspective and "zoom out" to look at the broader picture of their life. They need to expand their perspective and view the unhealthy, harmful behavior in terms of what it prevents them from getting in the long run not just what it provides in the short run or the consequences of the behavior. Desire to achieve long term life goal benefits can provide motivation for learning relapse prevention skills. Have clients write and discuss how relapse back into unhealthy, harmful behavior can prevent them from developing the healthy body/behavior/environment, healthy relationships and healthy life direction that they need to succeed in life.

The ART of Relapse Prevention

"High-risk situations" are situational factors that put clients at risk for relapse. High-risk situations involve people, places, circumstances, thoughts or feelings that can trigger falling back into unhealthy, harmful behavior. High-risk situations provide a motive or opportunity for relapse. Clients who are not aware of high-risk situations that can or have triggered relapse back into unhealthy harmful behavior can't plan to avoid those situations. This is unfortunate since "Planning power beats willpower", clients who are unaware of their high-risk situations for relapse are left to rely on willpower which is easily overcome by both

Awareness Training

If you're not **A**ware of how the problem starts, you can't do anything to stop it.

Responsibility Training

If you don't take **R**esponsibility for learning how to treat it, you can't expect it to change.

Figure 4.1. The ART of Relapse Prevention

Tolerance Training

If you can't **T**olerate feedback, you won't become aware of how the problem starts.

internal and external triggers. External relapse trigger examples include <u>people</u> who model, enable or encourage the problem behavior and <u>places</u> where the behavior often occurred in the past, where there is access to the behavior or where it is not likely to be noticed or result in consequences (e.g., being alone). Internal trigger examples include, <u>things</u> such as unwanted emotions/feelings (including physical pain) or irresponsible thinking (e.g., rumination on wanting to do it or justification to do it) that set the occasion for relapse. Unwanted feelings and trigger thoughts interact often by justifying actions based on feelings.

The **ART** of avoiding trouble involves: <u>A</u>wareness training on identifying high-risk situations for unhealthy, harmful behavior; <u>R</u>esponsibility training on learning high-risk situation avoidance and escape skills and; <u>T</u>olerance training on learning to tolerate behavior feedback particularly on relapse triggers and barriers to success (Figure 4.1).

Awareness Training in Relapse Prevention:
Becoming Aware of High-risk situations
If you're not Aware of how the problem starts, you can't do anything to stop it.

Awareness Training Goal: Increase client awareness of high-risk situations for unhealthy, harmful behavior relapse.
   Objectives: Clients will be able to identify and discuss examples of high risk people, places, thoughts and feelings that set the occasion for or trigger relapse.

High-Risk People and Places- Helping clients identify high risk (trigger) people is fairly easy unless it's someone they want to protect like a family member or a peer they don't want to implicate. For example, youth who drink or drug with parents may risk removal from the home if they disclose this information or peers may not want to give up the social aspect of the relationship with individuals involved in the same unhealthy, harmful behavior. High risk places

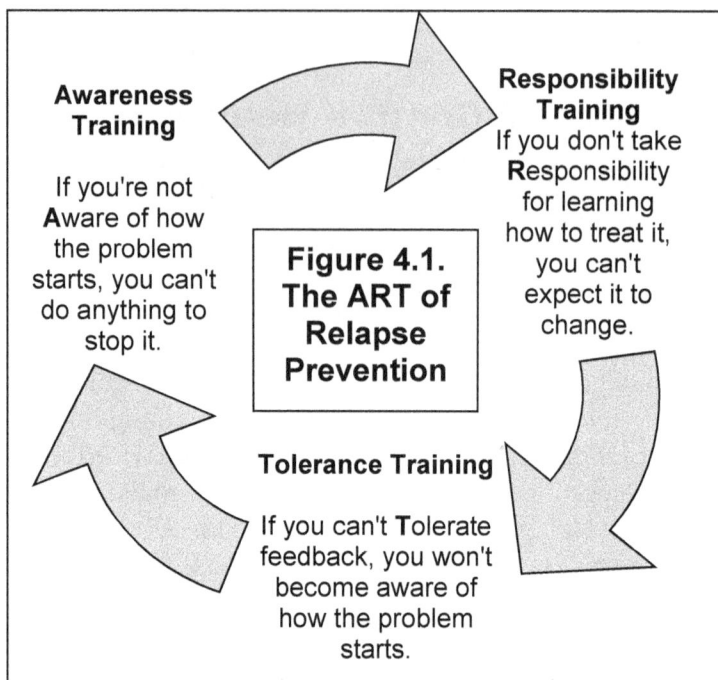

where the harmful behavior has occurred in the past include trigger objects, sights and smells.

Case Examples- Bennie was an older adolescent referred for youth sex offender treatment with a history of putting his hands on other people (sexual imposition) and their property (shoplifting) without their permission. He was removed from the custody of his mother as a result of her sexual advances towards him while they were in a homeless shelter. He had managed to develop a track record of abstinence from making sexual advances towards younger children but it was not forthcoming about his criminal relationship with his father. Benny would push his father through department stores in a wheel chair putting shoplifted electronics in the storage area under the wheel chair and then push his father out of the store with the stolen items. Having lost contact with his mother, disclosure of his criminal activity with his father risked losing visitation from his father as well. A high risk person and place for Bennie to relapse on shoplifting would be visiting his father and going to a department store.

Diana, was a 43-year-old obese female in weight-management treatment. During a discussion of high risk people she announced, "I guess I have to give up the food gang" and went on to discuss her regular Friday night eat-a-thon with 4 other women. They would all go to a new restaurant (or an old favorite) and each order a different appetizer, main course and dessert off of the menu. Everyone would then try some of everything. She was quite close to these ladies and was having to face missing the social aspect of her "food gang." High risk people and places for unhealthy eating by Diana would be at restaurants (trigger sights, smells) with the "food gang".

High Risk Thoughts and Feelings- Helping clients identify high risk (trigger) thoughts and feelings that set the occasion for unhealthy, harmful behavior may require more structure to help them discover these internal triggers. Since what we say to ourselves can increase (or decrease) our emotional reaction to a given situation, start with Awareness Training on high risk, irresponsible thinking.

Irresponsible Thinking ("Trigger thoughts")

Irresponsible Thinking has played a central role as a cognitive risk factor for relapse over time. In the ART of avoiding trouble, clients that are not aware of the Irresponsible Thinking that enables their contact with high risk people, places, things or increased unwanted feelings that trigger unhealthy, harmful behavior can't do anything to stop it. Awareness training focuses on identifying the Irresponsible Thinking that sets the occasion for relapse. SRT develops client awareness of twenty

Table 4.1
Summary of Irresponsible Thinking and Characteristics Targeted in SRT

1. Deception	11. Image problems
2. Double standards	12. Need problems
3. Irresponsible loyalty	13. Planning problems
4. Don't care attitude	14. Boundary problems
5. Responsibility issues	15. Victim view
6. Blind ambition	16. Justifying actions
7. Motivational blindness	17. Extremism
8. "I can't" belief	18. Minimizing
9. Grandiosity	19. Magnifying
10. Control issues	20. Assuming

Reproduced with author permission from Table 2.1 in Yokley (2008).

specific types of irresponsible thinking and characteristics that set the occasion for unhealthy, harmful behavior. These cognitive relapse triggers were developed on the SRT treatment population of clients with multiple forms of unhealthy, harmful behavior. The twenty specific types of Irresponsible Thinking and characteristics that set the occasion for unhealthy, harmful behavior are listed in Table 4.1. Detailed descriptions of these forms of Irresponsible Thinking along with examples of corresponding socially responsible alternatives needed for cognitive restructuring are provided in "Types of Irresponsible Thinking and Responsible Alternatives", in Social Responsibility Therapy Workbook 1 "How did I get this problem?", Workbook 2 "Why do I keep doing this?" and Workbook 3 "How did my problem spread?" (Appendix C in Yokley, 2010b; 2011a; 2012).

Four basic types of Irresponsible Thinking that increase the risk of unhealthy, harmful behavior are Minimizing, The Victim View/Blaming, Justifying Actions and Magnifying. Minimizing allows clients to play down the seriousness of their problem or a trigger situation which gives them unrealistic expectations and the false confidence needed to enter high-risk situations for relapse. Justifying provides the excuses needed to enter high-risk situations for relapse. Irrational Beliefs support most of the twenty types of Irresponsible Thinking by providing the client with a rationale and encouragement for taking an irresponsible action. Extremism provides the "all or nothing" thinking that fuels giving up on recovery after a minor mistake, magnifying a problem until it is unbearable and taking an extreme action based on a gross overgeneralization.

These four basic types of Irresponsible Thinking that contribute to relapse risk can be identified by key words. Specifically, minimizing a problem or situation that allows clients to enter a high-risk situation for relapse can be identified from their use of the words "just" or "only." Client excuses, avoiding responsibility, taking the victim view, blaming others and not holding themselves accountable for unhealthy, harmful behavior can be identified from their use of the words "but" or "because." Client use of Irrational Beliefs supporting negative emotions and justifying actions has been well documented with multiple forms of unhealthy, harmful behavior in Rational Emotive Behavior Therapy (See also research summary, p. 20- 21 in Yokley, 2008). Clients increasing their risk of relapse through the use of Irrational Beliefs about a problem or situation can be identified by their use of the words" should" or "must." Finally, client "all or nothing", extremism, and over-generalizing problems or situations which put them at risk for relapse can be identified by their use of "always" or "never." Teaching clients to identify the four basic types of Irresponsible Thinking described above by their key words can be remembered with the acronym "**JOBS MAN"** as follows...

"**J**ust" and "**O**nly" helps clients become aware of when they are minimizing a behavior or issue, e.g., "It's OK, I'll *just* do it a little or *only* do it once"
"**B**ut" (or "Because") helps clients recognize excuses involving responsibility issues, victim view, blaming and "I can't belief", e.g., "I know it's wrong… *but* I can't help it, they got me upset. *But* they started it. I did it *because* they deserved it. I did it *because* I was upset. It wasn't my fault *because*..."
"**S**hould" and "**M**ust" helps clients recognize irrational beliefs that can justify actions, e.g., "They got it for me so I *should* take a [drink/bite]", "I *must* smack their insulting mouth shut."
"**A**lways" and "**N**ever" helps clients be aware of "all or nothing", magnifying that blows things out of proportion, supports giving up and relapse after a slip through recovery perfectionism, e.g., Since I slipped and messed up, I'll always be a failure and will never make it so I give up!"

Irresponsible thinking can be used before the unhealthy, harmful behavior to enable clients to engage in the behavior, during the unhealthy, harmful behavior to allow clients to continue the behavior once started and after the unhealthy, harmful behavior to excuse the behavior and alleviate regret or emotional upset about doing it. Table 4.2 provides examples of basic forms of Irresponsible Thinking that can enable or trigger relapse into unhealthy harmful behavior.

Table 4.2
Basic Types of Irresponsible Thinking That Enable or Set the Occasion for Unhealthy, Harmful Behavior Relapse: Selected Examples

Basic Types of Irresponsible Thinking	Selected Unhealthy, Harmful Behavior Examples		
	Unhealthy, Harmful Eating	Unhealthy, Harmful Drug/Alcohol Use	Unhealthy, Harmful Sexual Behavior
Minimizing- Use of "Just" or "Only"	"I'll only have one small bite of cake after dinner for dessert"	"I'll just stop at the party to say hello, will only have one drink and then leave"	"I'm only going to look at porno, not rape someone"
Victim View & Blaming- Use of "But" (or "Because")	"It wasn't my fault, I ate the pizza because they didn't have anything else I liked"	"I want to quit but I can't because every time I try one of my friends comes over and gets me high"	"I thought about stopping but since she came on to me, I kept going because she started it"
Justifying Actions- Use of "Should" or "Must" in irrational beliefs	"They made this cheesecake from scratch for me so I should at least taste it"	"I should be able to party with friends and not drink so I must keep going until I learn to handle it"	"I'm not supposed to be around children but, I must go to the playground to walk my dog".
Extremism- Use of "All" or "Never"	"I always have to make my weekly weight goal or I quit, it's either reach the top or flop"	"Since I slipped and got high, I'll always be a druggie and will never be able to stop using so I quit"	"Girls never really mean no when they say it, they just don't want to look trashy"

For further examples of how Irresponsible Thinking can support and maintain multiple forms of unhealthy, harmful behavior by excusing it afterwards, see Table 2.3 of the SRT treatment manual (p. 94 in Yokley, 2008).

Research Development Summary of Irresponsible Thinking Types and Characteristics- Clinical observation and client self-report on an "Awareness and Honesty Exam" covering thirty-three "automatic errors of thinking" (i.e., thinking errors that contribute to criminal behavior and treatment resistance) found in the harmful, abusive criminal population (Samenow, 1996, 2001; Yochelson and Samenow, 1976), six common cognitive distortions from the social learning theory of aggression (Bandura, 1973), and the ten most prevalent cognitive distortions in depression (Beck et al., 1979; Burns, 1980) along with social responsibility items (i.e., honesty, trust, loyalty, concern, and responsibility, Yokley, 2008) were selected for clinical observation in the SRT treatment development population. Clinical observation over time led to the integrated set of twenty socially irresponsible thinking types and characteristics that act as cognitive risk factors setting the occasion for or triggering multiple forms of unhealthy, harmful behavior described in Appendix C of SRT Workbook 1, 2 and 3 (Yokley, 2010b; 2011a; 2012).

Unwanted Emotions ("Trigger feelings")

When it comes to trigger feelings begin with awareness of three basic emotions: depression; anxiety and; anger. Discuss the concept that emotions are on a continuum. Give basic examples using depression, anxiety and anger. For example: depression ranges from mild sadness to moderate depression to suicidal despair; anxiety ranges from mild discomfort to moderate anxiety to severe panic attacks and anger ranges from mild annoyance to moderate anger to homicidal rage. Point out that anger can be a protective reaction when we feel afraid, attacked, hurt, rejected, disrespected, offended or frustrated. Ask your clients what they say to themselves that increases these emotions and what they can say to themselves to decrease these emotions. Then transition into the connection between unwanted (high risk/trigger) feelings, irresponsible (high risk/trigger) thinking, high risk people, high risk places and unhealthy, harmful behavior as indicated in Table 4.3.

Table 4.3.
Connections Between High Risk People, Places, Thoughts and Relapse

High Risk People or Places	Trigger Feeling	Trigger Thoughts	Unhealthy, Harmful Behavior Relapse
All you can eat buffet	Depressed	"That dessert bar looks so good, I'll just have a little"	Unhealthy overeating relapse
Outlet mall	Depressed	"I deserve it after the day I had"	Over-spending relapse
Smoke filled party	Boredom	"I need a cigarette"	Cigarette relapse
Bar with boss	Anxious	"I'll just have one drink to relax"	Alcohol relapse
Party with using friends	Happy	"It's just weed, no big deal"	Marijuana relapse
Person insulting you	Anger	"I can't take that crap!"	Violence relapse
Intoxicated party girl	Arousal	"Go ahead, she wants it!"	Sexual assault relapse

Treatment Exercise: Awareness of High-risk situations for Relapse

Everyone in treatment has people, places and things/situations that put them at risk for relapse back into their past form of unhealthy, harmful behavior but for each person, some of these situations are more of a risk than others. Some people have strong people needs and are more likely to relapse due to negative peer influence. Others are more emotional in nature making relapse more likely for them when emotionally upset. Still others are more intellectual making it more likely for them to relapse when bombarded by rationalizations to do it "just a little" or "only one more time." Hold a discussion with clients having them list their high risk people, places, thoughts and feelings and then rating their relapse risk level in each of those high-risk situations (0- 10 with 10 being very high risk of relapse). As clients speak put their risky situation on a dry erase board or flip chart to illustrate that different situations result in different risk levels for different people. Conclude with the point that each person needs to develop awareness of the people, places, feelings and thoughts that put them at highest risk for relapse in order to develop a successful relapse prevention plan that protects their recovery. In other words the first step in relapse prevention is developing awareness of those situations that pose the highest risk for relapse in order to make a plan to avoid them.

Responsibility Training in Relapse Prevention:
Two Basic Relapse Prevention Skills
If you don't take **R**esponsibility for learning how to treat it, you can't expect it to change.

Responsibility Training Goal: Develop responsible relapse prevention strategies.
   Objectives: Clients will be able to explain two relapse prevention skills and demonstrate how they plan to avoid and escape high-risk situations for relapse.

Basic SRT Relapse Prevention Skill #1: High-risk situation Avoidance
"Planning power beats willpower"

In Social Responsibility Therapy, our number one responsibility is self-control. Self-control is maintained by avoiding and escaping high-risk situations. The easiest way to maintain self-control of unhealthy, harmful behavior is to learn how to avoid high-risk situations because it is far easier to avoid harmful behavior than to stop it once you get started. This rule can be traced back to the early Roman philosophers…

It is easier to exclude harmful passions than to rule them, and to deny them admittance than to control them after they have been admitted-- Seneca (5 BC - 65 AD)

The conclusion to be drawn from this age-old insight is that successful self-control and management of unhealthy, harmful behavior (e.g., overeating, drinking, smoking, spending, physical or sexual abuse) depends more on developing planning power than inheriting willpower. Two important Relapse Prevention assumptions are:
1. It is much easier to avoid trouble than escape it once it starts and;
2. The sooner you correct a slip (lapse) the less likely you are to take a fall (relapse).

These assumptions call for client development of a high-risk situation avoidance skill to help them identify and avoid high-risk situations them along with a high-risk situation escape skill to help clients to get out of high-risk situations right away that they didn't plan for or expect.

Since "We do our best when we are prepared and our worst when we are caught off guard" it is easier to avoid trouble than escape it once it starts. In other words "planning power beats willpower." Thus, the first place that relapse prevention skills need to be developed is identifying high-risk situations for relapse and making relapse prevention plans to avoid those situations. Clients can't avoid situations that they are not aware of so Awareness Training in relapse prevention involves having clients identify the high-risk situations that set the occasion for falling back into unhealthy, harmful behavior. High-risk situations typically involve people, places and things (objects, thoughts, feelings) that trigger harmful behavior. Three common high-risk situations for multiple forms of harmful behavior that require positive planning to avoid are trigger places (including access), trigger feelings and trigger thoughts which are referred to as negative social influence if they are verbalized by others. Some basic examples are provided in Table 4.4.

Develop a Relapse Prevention Plan- Have your clients discuss these categories while you list them on a black board or flip chart. Use guided discovery to help them formulate their relapse prevention plan by making their high-risk situation list with a positive plan to avoid each trigger situation that they list. Help clients develop an accurate list of high-risk situations for relapse including both external triggers (e.g., people and places like individuals who are involved with, enable or encourage the unhealthy, harmful behavior or access to engage in the harmful behavior) and internal triggers, (e.g., things such as unwanted trigger emotions or enabling, irresponsible trigger thoughts). Further examples are provided on p.66- 67 of Yokley (2008).

Have clients discuss their relapse prevention plan with their treatment provider or group and take notes for the assignment of writing an individual relapse prevention plan. Make sure to emphasize the responsibility for planning, i.e., "If you fail to plan, you plan to fail" and for

Table 4.4
High-risk situations for Selected Unhealthy, Harmful Behaviors

Unhealthy, Harmful Behavior	Trigger Places (Access)	Trigger Feelings	Trigger Thoughts or People (Negative Social Influence)
Trust abuse- cheating	Singles bar	Arousal	"They're flirting with me so it's OK to ask them out"
Substance abuse- Unhealthy eating	All you can eat buffet	Depressed	"You have to try this"
Substance abuse- Smoking	Smoke filled party	Boredom	"You look like you could use a smoke, have one"
Substance abuse- Drinking	Bar	Anxious	"I'll just have one drink to calm myself"
Money abuse/gambling	Casino	Excitement	"You're due for a win"
Property abuse/theft	Outlet mall	Depressed	"It's not fair, I deserve it"
Physical abuse	Person insulting you	Anger	"Are you going to take that crap?"
Sexual abuse	Intoxicated party girl	Arousal	"Go ahead, she wants it"

controlling harmful behavior by "Keeping your problem up front" (e.g., carry a relapse prevention plan pocket card). Since we do our best when we are prepared and our worst when we are caught off guard or warn out remind clients to HALT their relapse by not letting themselves get to Hungry, Angry, Lonely or Tired. Have clients rate their risk of relapse in the high-risk situations that they list as low, moderate or high risk making sure that they rate situations that they have relapsed in the past as high risk.

Case Examples- Diana was the 43-year-old weight management emotional eater who hung out with "foodie" friends that she would overeat with regularly. Brad was a 22-year-old college student drop out in outpatient alcohol treatment with motivation to get off probation and get driver's license back so he could enlist in military. Keith was 16 when he was removed from the home and placed in forensic foster care for youth sex offender treatment after being charged for sexual imposition against his younger sister. Client ratings of their high-risk situations are listed in Table 4.5.

A discussion with notes approach for developing a written relapse prevention plan typically works well with higher functioning outpatient clients meeting weekly. However, clients whose sessions are scheduled farther apart, clients with higher needs for direction or those in higher levels of care (e.g., intensive outpatient programs, treatment foster care, corrections/forensic settings or community residential treatment) may require a more structured written explanation or a written between session reminder to help them develop their relapse prevention plan. For those clients, detailed Structured Discovery workbook exercises structured to help them discover and plan to avoid their high-risk situations are provided in the SRT Workbook "How did I get this problem?" If needed, see chapter entitled "Link #3- Situational Risk Factors: High-risk situations for Harmful Behavior" (p. 41- 52, Yokley, 2010b).

Treatment Exercise: Relapse Avoidance- Have your clients write out examples of statements that they said to themselves before their unhealthy, harmful referral behavior that

Table 4.5
High-risk situation Ratings for Selected Unhealthy, Harmful Behavior Cases

Trigger Case Example	People	Places	Things (thoughts, feelings)
Diana- Unhealthy, Harmful Eating	Talking to her "food gang" of restaurant dining friends. Relapse Risk Level- **Moderate**	Being in new restaurants that she had never been to before. Relapse Risk Level- **High**	Feeling down and in need of comfort. Relapse Risk Level- **High**
Brad- Unhealthy, Harmful Drinking	Old girlfriend and drinking buddy comes over with 6 pack and overnight bag. Relapse Risk Level- **High**	Bars where favorite martial arts sports are on TV Relapse Risk Level- **High**	Ruminating on past mistakes and having to drop out of school Relapse Risk Level- **Moderate**
Keith- Unhealthy, Harmful Sexual Behavior	Being around his sisters elementary school friends who looked up to him. Relapse Risk Level- **High**	Being alone with any of his sister's younger friends. Relapse Risk Level- **High**	Telling himself "Other people did it to me so it's OK to do to others". Relapse Risk Level- **High**

included the JOBS MAN words Just, Only, But, Because, Should, Must, Always or Never. Have them explain how those self-statements led to relapse. If your client's self-statements before relapse do not include any JOBS MAN relapse triggers, pull from the list of 20 types of Irresponsible Thinking listed in Table 4.1 and described in SRT Workbook 1, 2 and 3 (Appendix C of Yokley, 2010b; 2011a; 2012). After clients have identified the Irresponsible Thinking that triggered their unhealthy, harmful behavior, have them generate opposite responsible thoughts that would have prevented that harmful behavior. Have them journal this discovery under the heading "Relapse Prevention Plan for Trigger Thoughts" and discuss it in session.

Higher functioning outpatient clients should be able to manage this cognitive risk factor and restructuring exercise easily. Clients who need more structure or those in higher levels of care (e.g., intensive outpatient programs, treatment foster care, corrections/forensic settings or community residential treatment) may require more step-by-step guidance. For those clients, a brief Structured Discovery exercise is provided on p. 19 of SRT Workbook 3 (Yokley, 2012) and a detailed Structured Discovery exercise is provided in the SRT Workbook 1 chapter "The Risk Factor Chain: Link #4- Cognitive Risk Factors" (Yokley, 2010b).

Basic SRT Relapse Prevention Skill #2: High-risk situation Escape
"Get out, Get honest and Get responsible"

Unfortunately, no matter how well trained clients are in avoiding falling into trouble by avoiding high-risk situations, this cannot prevent trouble from finding them. For example...

- Derek, a teenage client in youth sex offender treatment client avoids a high-risk situation by turning down a neighbor's offer to pay him to watch her children after he gets out of school every day until she gets home from work. The client is caught completely off guard when his neighbor calls him stating she has a doctor's appointment in the afternoon, can't find anyone to watch her children and is counting on him to get the key from under the doormat, let the kids in after school and make them a sandwich.

- Bill, a mid-30's client in alcohol treatment likes to bowl but <u>avoids</u> the company bowling league where the boss pays the bar bill and regularly brings drinks to all of her employees. The client is caught off guard by a surprise birthday party where a champagne glass is thrust into their hands during a toast to the boss's health and happiness.
- Laticia, an early-30's weight management client in treatment for unhealthy eating <u>avoids</u> going to a wedding reception that has several open buffets and dessert bars by presenting the bride and groom with their present after the ceremony and leaving before the reception. She is caught off guard when the doorbell rings and two of her friends are there with several large catering boxes containing portions of all of the entrees and desserts stating "We know how much you loved this food so thought we'd bring you some of everything since you had to leave".

In each of these situations, although the client <u>avoided</u> high-risk situation trouble, the trouble came to them. Thus in addition to developing high-risk situation avoidance skills, clients need to develop a high-risk situation escape skill to get them out of high-risk situations they didn't plan for or expect right away, without delay. SRT teaches clients "If you can't avoid, escape" and utilizes a three step plan to help clients maintain their social responsibility to escape leave high-risk situations for harmful behavior. Since our number one responsibility is self-control, the "three-step responsibility plan" involves teaching clients to take time out in order to maintain self-control by making responsible decisions. This plan is often referred to by clients as using "the 3 G's", i.e., Get out, Get honest and Get responsible. The three steps basically involve helping clients learn to "remove yourself, block the harmful thoughts (harmful urge, irresponsible thinking), and substitute more responsible thoughts" as described in the client instructions below.

"The 3 G's" of High-risk Situation Escape (Three-Step Responsibility Plan Instructions)

Get out (Remove yourself). Get out of the high-risk situation for relapse by leaving without hesitation. Don't wait, don't think, "Just do it." Accept that "hesitation kills recovery" and the longer you stay in high-risk situations for relapse, the higher the risk of relapse. No one thinks clearly in emotional situations. "You need to be laughing and leaving, not staying and stewing." Since "we do our best when we're prepared and our worst when we're caught off guard", get out of high-risk situations immediately to give yourself a chance to think. The longer you stay in the problem situation, the higher the risk of acting irresponsible. Stay aware of your high-risk situations for relapse and escape them immediately to give yourself time to think before you act. Be prepared to escape trouble by developing "concrete face saving mechanisms" (excuses to leave high-risk situations that will work) to have ready if needed. A good concrete face saving mechanism to escape an unexpected high-risk situation where you are hit with trigger sights, sounds or people is to "Get out" by excusing yourself to use the bath room to give yourself time to think. No one will tell you that you can't use the bathroom. When peer pressure is involved, don't fall for the "should" word by telling yourself either "I should be able to hangout out here without a problem" or "Why should I remove myself, why shouldn't they leave?" Remember that "why" questions are often angry questions, it's really "Why shouldn't they leave, damn it!" Set your pride aside in these situations and Get out.

Get honest (Block irresponsible thoughts by getting honest with yourself). Get honest about the increased chance of relapse if you return to the high-risk situation and block the irresponsible thoughts that set the occasion for returning (e.g., "I need to go back and handle this, it's no big deal" or "I don't need to leave for long, nothing will happen if I go back after my urge passes", etc.). Also get honest about what will happen to your positive life goals and feelings about yourself if you act on the unhealthy, harmful thoughts that get triggered by the high-risk situation. Use "Fantasy fast forward" to play the story through to the real end consequences of your actions. Include both possible consequences to self and others. Ask yourself, "If I do this, how will it affect myself or others?" Get honest with yourself about past consequences and the fact that with using, "Feeling good now means feeling bad later." Get honest with yourself about the fact that urges, cravings and feelings can change with time but once you have done something, that can't be changed. Use dealing by delaying. If you can't deny the feeling, delay the action by telling yourself "I do not need to do this right now, I can always do this tomorrow." Our adolescent clients like to substitute "Get Real" for "Get Honest" here.

Get responsible (Substitute more responsible thoughts and do the right thing). Replace the irresponsible thoughts that were triggered by the high-risk situation with responsible thoughts that are helpful or at least not harmful to self and others (i.e., do not enable unhealthy, harmful behavior) and do the right thing (get responsible). Begin by asking yourself, "How will doing this really help me? "How is me doing the wrong thing going to get them to do the right thing?" or "Why should I hurt me just because other people or other things hurt me?" Then substitute responsible thoughts. For example, "I need to stay out of that situation", "It's not worth the risk", "I need to put my recovery first", "I need to put my freedom before my feelings" and escape trouble.

Over the years many different acronyms and mnemonic devices have been used to help clients remember the three-step high-risk situation escape plan before arriving on "Get out, Get honest and Get responsible" as typically accepted by most (although our teenaged clients often use "Get out, Get Real, Get responsible"). Since different individuals may prefer different ways to remember these the three-step escape plan, a number of alternatives are provided on p. 155 in Yokley (2008). Whatever they decide to call it, the important thing is that clients learn, practice and master the three steps to escaping high-risk situations in order to avoid unhealthy, harmful behavior relapse as illustrated in Table 4.6.

In both group and individual sessions clients need to be reminded that "You are only limited by your creativity" when dealing with life problems but whenever they become aware of a high-risk situation, they need to immediately use "the 3 G's" to: Get out (remove yourself from the situation); Get honest (by telling yourself the truth about what could happen if you do the harmful behavior) and; Get responsible (substitute a responsible thought that will keep them out of the high-risk situation and act to avoid relapse). Get out is the critical step because "We do our best when we're prepared and our worst when we're caught off guard" so when caught off guard by a relapse trigger, it is critical to get out in order to remove the alarm of being caught off guard and clear the path for creative ways to "Get responsible".

Note: In SRT, Emotional regulation, Decisional balance and Social problem-solving skills are integrated into this simple three-step relapse prevention framework.

Table 4.6
High-risk situation Escape with "The 3 G's": Selected Examples

	Get out (Remove yourself)	Get Honest (Block the thought)	Get Responsible (Substitute a more responsible thought)
Unhealthy, Harmful Eating (Weight management treatment referral)	High-risk situation- The phone rings and you are invited to a family birthday party where family has prepared some of your favorite foods. Get out- Without hesitation say "I need to call you right back"	Get honest- about the trigger thought that, "I'll go but just try one bite of my favorites, that won't hurt"	Substitute- "I've never just had one bite of anything." Don't call back until you come up with a relapse prevention plan (e.g., wait on others, volunteer to be the birthday photographer)
Unhealthy, Harmful Drinking (Substance abuse treatment referral)	High-risk situation- Acting on an invitation to an old friends house, there is a party going on and an they pour you a drink. Get out- Without hesitation ask where the bathroom is and excuse yourself	Get honest- about the trigger thought that, "I'll just have this one drink and then go home"	Substitute- "It's never just one" and "One drink will trigger another." Pour it out and call your sponsor to come and get you.
Unhealthy, Harmful Sexual Behavior (Sex offender treatment referral)	High-risk situation- Your ride to a party arrives very late and when you get there, several underage females are obviously too high to say no to the guys who are hitting on them. Your ride says, "let's get in on this." Get out- Tell your ride you need to go out for a smoke first.	Get honest- about the trigger thoughts that, "These girls are too high to care so why should I?", "They won't know", "What you don't know won't hurt you"	Substitute- "It's a probation violation just to be present during a felony, so I've got to get out of here and come up with a way to get the authorities to break up this party before someone gets hurt, maybe a noise complaint."

Treatment Exercise: Relapse Escape with "The 3 G's"- Have your clients write out a high-risk situation for relapse back into their unhealthy, harmful referral behavior that they didn't expect and caught them off guard. For example...

- Unhealthy eating/weight management referral- A date picks your client up for dinner and takes her to the Cheesecake Factory, not knowing that she just enrolled in your weight management program.
- Substance abuse referral- Teen friends come over with marijuana not knowing that your client just got put on probation with random urinalysis testing.
- Sex offender referral- Your client is on probation with an ankle bracelet and can't leave his home so several friends decide to bring the party to him. They come over with several females all drinking and definitely look underage. They don't know that your client is in court ordered treatment for sexual imposition as a result of dating an underage girl.

Have your clients journal how they would "Get out" of this situation where they weren't looking for trouble but it came to them. Then have them journal how they would "Get honest" by writing out the JOBS MAN Irresponsible Thinking (or Irresponsible Thinking from the list on Table 4.1) that the situation triggered. Finally, have them write out how they would "Get responsible" by substituting a responsible thought and following that thought into responsible action and relapse escape. Higher functioning outpatient clients should be able to manage this high-risk situation escape exercise easily. Clients who need more structure or those in higher levels of care (e.g., intensive outpatient programs, treatment foster care, corrections/forensic settings or community residential treatment) may require more step-by-step guidance. For those clients, a more structured, "High-risk situation Escape" exercise is provided on p. 20- 21 of SRT Workbook 3 (Yokley, 2012) and for those who need help generating responsible alternative thinking Responsible Alternatives are described in SRT Workbook 1, 2 and 3 (Appendix C of Yokley, 2010b; 2011a; 2012).

Relapse Prevention Skills Practice: The Situation Response Analysis Log

Have clients journal their progress in avoiding and escaping high-risk situations for relapse in a Situation Response Analysis log that documents their high-risk situations, their response to those situations and their analysis of their response. This is accomplished by having clients complete a simple daily log with three columns labeled "Situation", "Response" and "Analysis" to be discussed in their group or individual treatment sessions. Daily log completion and discussion is important for Awareness Training on the connection between the situation and their thoughts, feelings and behaviors. These logs are also important in Responsibility Training on holding themselves accountable by analyzing their responses to situations, identifying positive and negative coping along with developing positive planning in situations that can result in relapse. Basic client log instructions are listed in Table 4.7. Each evening have clients include "Three things that went right today and how I made that happen" on the back of their log.

Table 4.7 Situation Response Analysis Log Instructions		
Situation	**Response**	**Analysis**
Date & Description (What actually happened)	**My Thoughts, Feelings and Behavior**	1. Was my response positive/helpful or negative/harmful? 2. What do I need to do in this situation next time?
Date and what actually happened in the situation (the facts). People, places, things, sights, sounds, smells or other experiences that triggered relapse thoughts, feelings, cravings or urges.	Your response to the situation. What you said to yourself (thoughts), what you were feeling (emotions) and what you did (behavior- What you said to others and what actions you took).	**1. Positive vs Negative Coping?** **2. Positive Planning** What you need to say to yourself (or do) next time to improve your response to the situation.

There is more than one way to construct a Situation Response Analysis Log and different log formats with varying levels of detail may be preferred by different clinicians for different clients. Several Situation Response Analysis Log formats are provided in Appendix B.

While most outpatient clients can manage completing their Situation Response Analysis logs with the basic instructions provided in Table 4.7, further client instructions for those with higher needs for direction or in higher levels of care are provided in SRT workbook 1, 2 and 3 (Appendix D of Yokley, 2010b; 2011a; 2012). Table 4.8. provides log completion examples.

Table 4.8
Situation Response Analysis Log Examples

Situation	Response	Analysis
Date & Description (What actually happened)	**My Thoughts, Feelings and Behavior**	1. Was my response healthy/helpful or unhealthy/harmful? 2. What do I need to do next time?
Unhealthy eating client- Ted (40-year-old male) Monday, 9/2- "I was invited to a family birthday party where I knew they were having my favorite foods."	**Thoughts-** Told myself, "I'll just try one bite of my favorites " **Feelings-** Feeling nervous because I knew I shouldn't be around my favorite foods. **Behavior-** Got honest with myself and admitted- "It's never just one" and "One bite will just lead to another." Then used "the 3 G's" to avoid trouble.	**Thoughts:** __Positive Coping; _X_ Negative Coping **Feelings:** __Tolerable; _X_ Stressful; __Unbearable **Behavior:** _X_ Healthy/helpful; __Unhealthy/harmful **My positive plan for next time is...** Use positive planning, think ahead and bring my own dish next time.
Substance abuse client- Ray (35-year-old male). Friday, 4/20- "I was invited to an old girlfriend's house, there was a party going on with drugs and alcohol."	**Thoughts-** Started thinking about how we used to get high, have sex and watch TV. Told myself, "I really want to do this." **Feelings-** Excited to see her again **Behavior-** Got honest with myself and admitted- "Since I'm on random urinalysis, doing this is freedom suicide." Then used "the 3 G's" to avoid trouble.	**Thoughts:** __Positive Coping; _X_ Negative Coping **Feelings:** __Tolerable; _X_ Stressful; __Unbearable **Behavior:** _X_ Healthy/helpful; __Unhealthy/harmful **My positive plan for next time is...** Don't compromise myself to be accepted by entering a high-risk situation. Invite her out for coffee.
Sex offender client- Dan (16-year-old male). Saturday 9/11- "I received a porno exchange e-mail address from another member of my sex offender group"	**Thoughts-** Telling myself "it's only pictures not people." **Feelings-** Feeling aroused thinking about taking them up on it. **Behavior-** Got honest with myself and admitted- "If I let myself get started, I won't be able to stop." Then used "the 3 G's" to avoid trouble.	**Thoughts:** __Positive Coping; _X_ Negative Coping **Feelings:** __Tolerable; _X_ Stressful; __Unbearable **Behavior:** _X_ Healthy/helpful; __Unhealthy/harmful **My positive plan for next time is...** Give this guy a choice to hold himself accountable before I tell our staff.

Tolerance Training in Relapse Prevention
Helping Clients Tolerate Feedback with the "The Mirror Concept"
If you can't Tolerate feedback, you won't become aware of how the problem starts.

Tolerance Training Goal: Develop the feedback tolerance needed to increase awareness of high-risk situations for relapse and increase acceptance of behavior problem issues.
Objectives: Clients will be able to explain how the "Mirror Concept" develops feedback tolerance.

An important aspect of Tolerance Training involves learning to tolerate feedback from others. Clients who can't tolerate feedback will continue to block out what others have to say about their high-risk situations for relapse and won't become aware of how their problem starts. In order to tolerate feedback, clients have to let go of their "closed channel"[1] and learn to value feedback. In order to value feedback instead of just reacting to it and blocking it out, clients need to see a benefit from it. This is where the Mirror Concept can help. The "Mirror Concept" helps develop self-awareness by learning to tolerate, accept, use and eventually value feedback. The goal of the Mirror Concept is to help clients avoid minimizing or blocking out valuable feedback from others and to master using other people's feedback as a mirror to better see themselves. The Mirror Concept holds that when it comes to behavior observations, "Other people can see you better than you see yourself" and learning to use the feedback of responsible others provides clients with a mirror to better see themselves.

Barriers to being able to use the Mirror Concept to develop self-awareness include a view of awareness that is limited to self-knowledge as demonstrated by defensive responses to feedback like, "You don't know me!" This defensive response is based on the client's knowledge that there are things that they know about themselves that others can't see. Start addressing feedback defensiveness by teaching Johari Window construct of self-awareness. Agree that we all are aware of things about ourselves that others don't but point out that this is just one of the four window panes of awareness (See Table 9.4). Bring up the fact that there are things that are known by both ourselves and others such as smoking or stuttering and things that neither of us may know like why we smoke or stutter. Finally, point out that that there are things that others are aware of about us that we do not always see. Give a simple concrete example. Ask clients to think about coming back to class or work from lunch and not noticing food on our face or smeared makeup. Point out that since we can't see ourselves while talking to others, we wouldn't be aware if this unless someone was kind enough to tell us so that we can take care of it. Point that since we don't walk through life looking at ourselves, when we get caught up in something that is bothering us, we may not be aware that we are frowning with sadness or scowling with anger. Point out that, "We do our best when we're prepared and our worst when we are caught off guard" and unexpected feedback can catch us off guard. In order to avoid automatically dismissing feedback, clients need to practice the open channel feedback response of "I'll have to look at that" and reserve judgment for later.

Another barrier to being able to use the Mirror Concept is emotional hypersensitivity. This can come from dysfunctional family feedback like, "you'll never amount to anything" or a history of being around people who "build themselves up by putting others down." A closed channel response style can result where constructive criticism is viewed as destructive verbal assault and feedback is blocked out. Hypersensitive clients may need to accept that what is being said is not always what they hear. They may need to learn to look at what they hear as a text message, just focusing on what is being said, not who is saying it or how it is being said. In order to avoid dismissing important information, they may need to actually turn the feedback into a text message by writing it down word for word and processing it with "responsible" others at a later time. Questions are less likely to elicit hypersensitive shut down reactions than statements and therapist Socratic questioning (See Overholser, 1993) to help clients examine their thoughts and feelings provides the non-threatening feedback from "responsible" others that allows clients to better see themselves. In the course of processing feedback with others, it is important that clients become aware of their human needs for acceptance and not defensively respond to unexpected feedback with "You don't understand!" when what they really mean is "You should agree!" Clients need to accept that others may understand but also disagree. In order to benefit most from what applies, clients need to accept the feedback consensus saying that "If ten people say you're a horse, you're a horse."

A final barrier to using the Mirror Concept is viewing an expert witness as a hypocrite. This results in dismissing the feedback of others with statements like, "You can't talk to me about that because you do the same thing yourself!" Using the Mirror Concept involves accepting that "It takes one to know one." In other words, if someone has the same problem or made the same mistake that they are making the client aware of they are not a hypocrite because they have done the same thing. The fact that they have done it themselves makes them an expert witness at seeing it. Accepting feedback from others with similar problems as expert witness testimony helps clients keep the focus on the present and their behavior, not the past and others.

Learning to tolerate feedback can be difficult for some and reassurance that humans can develop a tolerance to cigarettes, alcohol, food, feelings and feedback may be needed. Tolerating feedback means being able to encounter the thoughts, feelings and opinions of others without blocking them out. Since "the truth hurts", tolerating feedback often involves tolerating unwanted feelings. When you see someone at a funeral really sobbing over the loss of a loved one, you can see their belly heaving in and out with emotion. Just like practicing pull-ups on the high bar develops calloused hands that can tolerate heavy exercise, helping clients practice pulling themselves up to the level of others awareness by accepting feedback will "develop a callous on your belly" that allows them to emotionally tolerate responsible feedback and make positive change.

In summary, the Mirror Concept helps clients reframe their negative view of feedback from others as a valuable tool that can help them see things about themselves that they would not be able to see without a feedback mirror from responsible others. In order to successfully use the Mirror Concept, when clients are made aware of a mistake, they need to view the other person's feedback as a mirror and use it to better see themselves as opposed to playing it down or blowing it off. The Mirror Concept shifts the focus to looking at what needs to be done to correct the problem and away from trying to correct the person. Clients need to use the feedback of responsible others to improve their self-awareness, relapse prevention plan and behavior change promise letter. A behavioral indicator of successful application the Mirror Concept is when clients are able to let go of the defensive closed channel response to feedback and give a proper open channel response such as "Thank you I'll take care of that" when in their opinion the feedback is accurate and "I'll have to look at that" when they are not sure if the feedback is accurate.

Helping Clients Provide Feedback
The flip side if using the "Mirror Concept" to develop self-awareness is using "Confrontation with Concern" to help develop the awareness of others. Confrontation with Concern is structured to help clients discover the connection between their behavior and the possible consequences. This is important when clients see something others are doing that could lead to: unhealthy, harmful behavior relapse; relationship damage or; life direction problems. In the Therapeutic Community model "confrontation and responsible concern... is closely akin to the notion 'I am

my brother's keeper.' It instructs residents to show responsible concern by confronting others whose behavior and attitudes are not… consistent with the goal of rehabilitation" (p. 1547, DeLeon, 1990-91).

Teach clients the social responsibility to "be their brother's keeper" and help develop the awareness of fellow treatment members with "Pull-ups". A Pull-Up is a brief constructive criticism which pulls the other person up to your level of awareness. Pull-ups can be considered part of responsible assertiveness because they reinforce speaking up for self when upset by others. However, pull-ups are to be given by assuming that the other party is not aware of their problem behavior or has not carefully considered the consequences as opposed to assuming that they did it on purpose and don't care about the consequences. Pull-ups start with "Excuse me, I need to make you aware that… [describe the problem behavior/attitude]." It may not always be appropriate to follow Pull-ups made to fellow treatment members in passing with concern about the possible consequences of their behavior. However, it is important to always follow confrontation in group therapy with concern about the possible behavior consequences, not just expression of the feelings that were triggered as a result of the problem behavior/attitude. In Social Responsibility Therapy, client progress is evaluated on both helping self by accepting pull-ups (e.g., "Thank you, I'll take care of that") and helping others by giving pull-ups.

It is important to note that in the group therapy setting confrontation does not help clients develop self-awareness, self-efficacy and self-control unless the confrontation clarifies the: 1) behavior problem or pattern; 2) attitude triggering/supporting the behavior and; 3) intervention to change the attitude in order to stop future behavior problems. "If you give feedback, get feedback." Don't assume what you say is instantly understood. After important feedback state, "Tell me what you think I said so I know I said it right." Further description and research literature support on Confrontation with Concern can be found on p. 147- 152 in Yokley (2008). In summary, since "people don't appreciate anything they don't ask for" particularly when it comes to feedback, it is important to balance confrontation with concern.

The SRT "Kite Analogy" of Confrontation with Concern

In SRT, therapists and clients use the "Kite Analogy" of Confrontation with Concern. Problems with feedback tolerance can occur if a cold steel confrontation approach is applied to individuals with a history of being abused who may need a warm support to form a therapeutic bond. Likewise, there are problems with applying the warm supportive approach to clients with a history of abusing others who are initially unable to bond and likely to view supportive kindness as weakness. Thus, feedback tools for both populations are needed. Put another way…

- "If your only tool is a hammer, all of your clients will look like nails" (Fritz Perls) and
- "If your only tool is glue, all of your clients will look like they can bond" (SRT Maxim)

In "the Kite Analogy" of Confrontation with Concern, if you yank too hard on the kite string (i.e., provide too much confrontation and not enough concern), it breaks and you lose the kite (i.e., therapeutic relationship). If you give in, go the direction the kite is pulling or run after the kite (i.e., provide too much concern and not enough confrontation, AKA "enabling"), the kite crashes. If you stand still and don't pull against it but also don't give in (i.e., fail to provide any more structure than was received in the past), the kite maintains its present level and does not climb higher. If you provide appropriate, positive resistance and consistently pull against the kite (i.e., provide a consistent client needs-based balance of confrontation with concern), it rises to its maximum potential. Balancing confrontation with concern prevents stigmatizing and enabling.

Treatment Exercise: Feedback Tolerance - Hold a discussion on how to tell when humans are in "closed channel"[1] mode and unable to accept or tolerate feedback. Have clients identify verbal signs (e.g., "You don't understand", "You don't know me", "Yes but...", "Whatever!" or changing the subject), emotional signs (e.g., defensive raised voice) and body language (e.g., crossed arms, hands on hips, no eye contact). Discuss ways to hold the emotional attention of others so that they will receive important feedback including eye contact, intonation, humor, relevant examples and expression of concern. Then discuss how the Mirror Concept can help people tolerate feedback beginning with ways that behavior feedback can benefit a person. Finally, have clients practice giving pull-ups to others from the standpoint that others are not aware of the problem behavior or attitude and balancing confrontation with concern so that others can tolerate the feedback and be successfully pulled up to the clients level of awareness.

Important Relapse Prevention Issues
Relapse Prevention Issue #1: Slip (lapse) vs Fall (relapse)

A slip is a lapse, slight error or mistake which can be corrected before a fall or relapse into complete loss of self-control (Maisto & Connors, 2006; Marlatt & Gordan,1985). While there are problems with arriving at a single operational definition of relapse, conceptually (Brownell et. al., 1986), relapse is a recurrence of problem symptoms after a period of remission, i.e., a fall back into self-control loss after a period of self-control maintenance. Multiple forms of unhealthy, harmful behavior share a common relapse/recovery pattern. Relapse and recovery typically involves a series of slips (lapses) and falls (relapses) with two steps up, one back, two up, one back and so on until a track record of successful behavior management (self-control) has been achieved.

On the continuum of unhealthy harmful behavior (See Table 1.1), entering a high-risk situation for relapse on very severe behavior considered primarily harmful to others such as violent rape can be far more serious than entering a high-risk situation for less severe behavior considered primarily harmful to self, such as overeating. For example, a binge drinker can tell their probation officer that they slipped, went to a bar and had a drink but left and didn't continue their lapse into another drinking binge relapse. However, if a child sex offender tells their probation officer that they went to a playground enticed a child to get into their van, slipped and fondled them but didn't continue their fondling lapse into a penetration relapse, they will be arrested for sexual offense relapse. Self-control slips on behaviors that are considered unhealthy or harmful to self (e.g., alcoholic taking a sip of beer or overeater having a bite of cake) involve starting to engage in the unhealthy, harmful behavior while self-control slips on behaviors considered unhealthy or harmful to others (e.g., domestic violence client follows partner into next room during argument to have the last word or child sex offender client accepts a babysitting offer) involve just entering a high-risk situation for relapse. Thus, as we move up the harmful behavior severity continuum, the definition of a slip must become much more restrictive.

Setting the bar higher when there is an imminent danger to others- Social responsibility in a democratic society dictates that definition of slip/lapse in unhealthy, harmful behavior has to be more stringent in cases where a slip poses an imminent danger to others and a fall/relapse would be more harmful to others than to self. In these cases simply entering a high-risk situation for relapse is considered a slip/lapse. Examples are provided in Table 4.9 below and further information is provided in the section on "Types of slips or lapses", p. 83- 86 in Yokley (2008).

In summary, what is considered a slip/lapse in less severe behavior that is primarily harmful to self involves starting that behavior (e.g., taking a drink) a while a fall/relapse involves continuing that behavior (e.g., getting drunk). However, with more severe behavior that is considered primarily harmful to others (e.g., child molestation), just entering a high-risk situation for that behavior is considered a slip/lapse and a fall/relapse occurs when the harmful behavior is started (i.e., isolating the child) even if it is not continued.

Table 4.9.
SRT Slip (lapse) vs Fall (relapse) examples

Type of Unhealthy, Harmful Behavior	Slip/lapse vs Fall/relapse
Trust abuse- Starting to cheat on income tax return but erasing the false claim.	This would be a trust abuse **Slip/lapse**
Substance abuse- Starting to drink alcohol, use drugs or eat unhealthy food but stopping.	This would be a substance abuse **Slip/lapse**
Money abuse/Gambling- Starting to take money out of the ATM for poker but stopping.	This would be a money abuse/gambling **Slip/lapse**
Property abuse- Starting to shoplift something but putting it back instead of walking out with it.	This would be a property abuse **Slip/lapse**
Physical abuse- Starting to beat up a partner but leaving after slapping them in the face.	This would be a physical abuse **Fall/relapse.** A slip/lapse would be entering a high-risk situation for relapse, e.g., client on probation for domestic violence raises voice and gets into an argument with a partner.
Sexual abuse- Starting to penetrate a child but stopping after holding them down and fondling them.	This would be a sexual abuse **Fall/relapse.** A slip/lapse would be entering a high-risk situation for relapse, e.g., client on parole for sexual imposition is alone with a child.

Relapse Prevention Issue #2: Harmful Behavior Migration

Harmful behavior migration is an important barrier to the development of the self-control needed for harmful behavior management that clients need to understand. Harmful behavior migration involves the target (referral) behavior migrating to another (often co-occurring) problem during treatment, then returning afterwards. Successful elimination of the target behavior through self-control development cannot occur when the client's harmful behavior has simply migrated to another harmful behavior in the client's response repertoire. The presence of comorbid harmful behavior allows shifting back and forth from one form of harmful behavior to another which enables the client to avoid developing and practicing self-control. Harmful behavior migration has often been observed in drug and alcohol treatment by marijuana users receiving broad band urine toxicology screening to monitor their substance use during probation. Since marijuana is detectable in frequent users for about 10 days (i.e., through traditional urine testing, blood test or breathalyzer) but alcohol is only detectable for 10- 24 hours, it is common for marijuana use to migrate to alcohol use during probation and migrate back afterwards when monitoring stops.

Case Example- Devin was an 18-year-old male on parole from the state department of youth services. As a result of his gross sexual imposition charge involving fondling his younger sister he was placed in Forensic Foster Care. His initial assessment revealed a co-occurring history of smoking marijuana and shoplifting. Devin would put his hands on other people and other people's property, sell shoplifted items and buy marijuana. After passing his urine

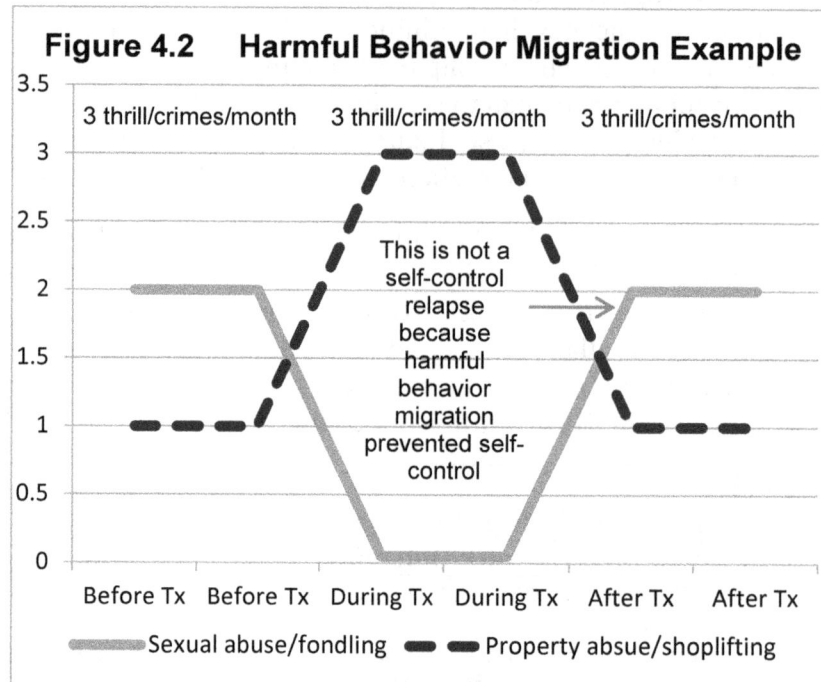

Figure 4.2   Harmful Behavior Migration Example

screens for marijuana and a polygraph exam on sexual imposition during treatment, Devin had earned the trust of his parole officer. His community observation and monitoring were discontinued in his last month of treatment and shortly thereafter, he lost his after-school mall job for shoplifting. This triggered contact with his employer which revealed that in the past month he had started to spend too much time talking to younger girls in the store. His harmful behavior migration shifting from putting his hands on other people without their permission to putting his hands on other people's property had maintained his excitement-related criminal behavior. This in turn blocked his self-control development resulting in slipping back towards sexual imposition when parole monitoring was discontinued. Since Devin had already lapsed by entering high-risk situations (i.e., conversations with age inappropriate females), relapse was considered likely if Devin had managed to complete treatment get off parole and move out on his own (See Figure 4.2).

Harmful behavior migration bears some resemblance to the psychodynamic concept of symptom substitution. In symptom substitution, successful elimination of the presenting symptom without treating the underlying factor results in the appearance of a new symptom supported by the underlying factor (Kazdin, 1982). Both harmful behavior migration and symptom substitution initially involve substituting one problem for another. However, in harmful behavior migration the client's behavior migrates back to the original behavior problem after treatment, probation or another external observation of the original behavior problem is discontinued. The definition of relapse requires a period of self-control which harmful behavior migration prevents by shifting to another out of control behavior during treatment and then back afterwards. Thus, in the treatment of multiple forms of unhealthy, harmful behavior the issue of harmful behavior migration prevention has to be addressed in relapse prevention. This can be done by assessing multiple forms of unhealthy, harmful behavior at intake, targeting those co-occurring behaviors and teaching clients to use the ACTS Health Behavior Success skills that are effective with multiple forms of unhealthy, harmful behavior.

Relapse Prevention Issue #3: Recovery Perfectionism

The Abstinence Violation Effect, Goal Violation Effect and Rule Violation Effect can be considered forms of "recovery perfectionism" where violating self-imposed target behavior abstinence (e.g., smoking, alcohol, drugs), self-imposed goals (e.g., diet, exercise) or other-imposed rules (e.g., probation, parole) through a harmful behavior, interacts with low self-efficacy to trigger all or nothing recovery perfectionism thinking. This recovery perfectionism results in the individual completely giving up their commitment to behavior abstinence, goal maintenance or rule compliance by escalating as opposed to correcting the harmful behavior.

In general, older more socially-emotionally mature clients tend to exhibit more instances of the Abstinence or Goal Violation Effect related to problems complying with self-imposed rules. On the other hand, younger particularly adolescent clients tend to exhibit more instances of the Rule Violation Effect due to stronger authority problems and difficulty complying with other-imposed rules. With adolescents, the Rule Violation Effect often occurs after violating treatment or house rules which results in giving up on self-control, giving up on treatment and running away returning to unhealthy, harmful behavior when unsupervised out on their own.

Technically, the terms Abstinence Violation Effect or Goal Violation Effect should be used by clients to describe their maladaptive reactions to self-imposed abstinence or goal violations while the term Rule Violation Effect should be used by them to describe their maladaptive reactions to violations of other-imposed rules. However, in clinical practice is simpler to refer to giving up on self-control after the violation of any rule (i.e., either self-imposed or other-imposed) as the Rule Violation Effect. Thus, The Rule Violation Effect became the Recovery Perfectionism term of choice for youth in Social Responsibility Therapy.

In Social Responsibility Therapy, use of the term Rule Violation Effect has become more broad and encompassing than just referring to giving up on self-control after violation of a rule imposed by others and includes all three forms of "Recovery Perfectionism" after violation of either a self-imposed or other-imposed rule. In SRT, the Rule Violation Effect is used to describe: 1) abstinence violation by individuals whose harmful behavior treatment outcome must be abstinence, e.g., substance abuse clients who must abstain from drinking/drugs or sex offenders who must abstain from non-consenting sex; 2) goal violation by individuals whose goals are to bring the harmful behavior within normal limits, e.g., binge eating clients whose goal is moderation management and; 3) rule violation by individuals with goals of maintaining appropriate social behavior and compliance with laws, parole, probation, treatment and house rules governing multiple forms of harmful behavior.

"The Slip Give-up Trigger"- is often used with clients when discussing the Rule Violation Effect because it provides a straightforward, concrete description of the Recovery Perfectionism mechanism involved in the Rule Violation Effect and explains this treatment concept without technical language. The Slip Give-Up road to relapse begins with "all or nothing" perfectionism thinking about recovery and self-control. When combined with low self-efficacy conclusions and

Irresponsible Thinking, the result is giving up after making a single mistake during a period of self-control success. An individual with this "Recovery Perfectionism" attitude feels that their rule violation (Slip) has completely "blown it" for them making it impossible for them to continue their perfect self-control track record or regain self-control. The way they reduce internal conflict over their Slip is with low self-efficacy conclusions that redefine self as hopeless or powerless. Finally, thinking that since they "must" start all over, why not indulge themselves first excuses giving up and allowing their behavior to go "out of control" (Marlatt, 1985). While there may be more than one conceptualization of the underlying process, the Slip Give-Up Trigger involves an interaction of a rule violation (Slip), Recovery Perfectionism and Irresponsible Thinking influenced by Low Self-Efficacy conclusions (Give-Up) in the following basic steps:

- A Rule Violation (Slip)- Making a mistake
- Recovery Perfectionism- "All or nothing" thinking about recovery and negative rumination about the Slip.
- Irresponsible Thinking influenced by low self-efficacy conclusions (Give-Up)- Justifying giving up on self-control. Expecting failure. Telling self that treatment doesn't work, they can't change or they must start over and feeling helpless or disappointed in self and adopting an "I can't attitude." For example, "Because I must not drink again and I did what I must not do, it's hopeless, I'll always be a drunk and never be able to stop drinking", (p.74, Ellis et al., 1988). This excuses taking the next step into doing an unhealthy, harmful behavior or continuing the harmful behavior if already started.

Case example- Jake was a late 30's forensic patient with a long criminal record for robbery, a short temper and good sense of humor who liked to refer to his electroconvulsive therapy as "Edison Medicine." Jake reported that he was driving on the freeway when he noticed the flashing lights of a police car in his rear view mirror. Glancing down at his speedometer, he realized that he was going 90 in the 60 mile an hour zone (Slip). He thought that since he never gets a break, he would surely get a ticket that would require a court appearance and violate his parole. He told himself that since his parole was already blown and he was going back to prison anyway, he might as well just take off (i.e., Give up entirely on parole rule compliance). He floored it, cutting between the guard rail and a semi-tractor trailer truck with inches to spare. Glancing back he saw the police car being slammed by the tractor trailer and flipping over the guard rail. Jake fled the state, driving across the country committing armed robberies whenever he needed money until finally apprehended and charged with multiple robberies.

In order to effectively block the Slip Give-Up Trigger, it is necessary to help clients learn to let go of the Recovery Perfectionism that is the first step towards giving up after a Slip and to correct their Slip to avoid taking a harmful behavior Fall. In short they need to learn, "If you can't make it better, don't make it worse."

Examples of the Rule Violation Effect or "Slip Give-Up Trigger" in categories that span the continuum of unhealthy, harmful behavior (Table 1.1) are provided in Table 4.10. For further examples of the Rule Violation Effect or "Slip Give-Up Trigger" across multiple forms of unhealthy, harmful behavior, see Table 22, p. 88 in Yokley (2008) and Table 15, p. 76 in Yokley (2011a) or Table 12, p. 105 in Yokley (2012).

Letting go of Recovery Perfectionism: The Engineer and the Physicist
Story telling is a non-directive approach that can help clients let go of their Recovery Perfectionism. The story of the contest between the engineer and the physicist illustrates how perfectionism can prevent progress. In some clients it is important to first let them know that engineers are the practical builders of things. Their job is to get things done. A physicist on the other hand is scientist who uses mathematics to figure out how things work.

In the contest, between the engineer and the physicist, both were positioned at the one yard line of a football field. The winning Powerball multistate 100 million dollar lotto ticket was at the other end of the field 100 yards away. The ticket would be given to the first one to get there using the following method. The contest moderator explained that when the starter pistol was fired, each was to pace off half the distance of the field (50 yards). They were then to take the remaining distance, divide it by two and pace off that distance (25 more yards), then take the remaining distance divide it by two (12.5 yards) pace it off and so on until reaching the other end

Table 4.10 "Slip Give-up Trigger" Examples Across Harmful Behavior Categories			
	Rule Violation or "Slip"	Recovery Perfectionism	Irresponsible Thinking
Unhealthy, Harmful Behavior Category	**Since I already slipped and...**	**I blew it so I might as well just...**	**Besides, if I stop now, I will...**
Trust Abuse a. Relationships b. Teen AWOL	a. went out with someone, b. stayed out too late,	a. cheat [**give up** on staying true] b. just not come back [**give up** on following the rules]	a. have to lie to my partner anyway b. get consequences anyway
Substance Abuse a. Alcoholics Anonymous b. Cocaine or Narcotics Anonymous c. Smoke enders d. Overeaters Anonymous	a. had a drink b. did some coke, pills, weed c. smoked a cigarette d. had a piece of candy	a. finish the bottle [**give up** on AA] b. keep going [**give up** on CA, NA] c. finish the pack [**give up** on Smoke-Enders] d. finish the box **give up** on OA]	a. still have to start my recovery program over b. still fail my urinalysis tomorrow c. still smell like smoke and have to lie about it d. have to start my diet all over tomorrow anyway
Property Abuse a. theft b. vandalism c. arson d. gambling	a. put it in my pocket b. been seen tagging (spray painting) c. started playing with matches d. used my maxed out credit card	a. leave the store with it [**give up** on probation] b. bomb it (do the whole wall) c. make a little fire d. make a bet to try and get the money back	a. just get caught putting it back b. still get in trouble so I might as well go big c. still have to cover up the smell of gasoline d. have to pay big overdraft fees
Physical Abuse	got angry and told them to shut up	punch them out [**give up** on anger management]	look like I'm afraid of them
Sexual Abuse	Pushed her down on the bed	Take what I want [**give up** on sex offender treatment]	still get arrested

of the field. When the pistol was fired the engineer immediately paced off 50 yards while the physicist took out his pad and an pencil and began to make some calculations. After about a minute, the physicist approached the moderator and said "Excuse me but it is not technically possible to reach the end of this football field using your method because in the system of real numbers there is always another number that you can divide by two." Meanwhile the engineer can be seen running off in the distance with the winning lotto ticket because he got close enough for all practical purposes.

Have a structured discussion of this contest to help clients discover that they don't have to recover perfectly to function well with others in the world, they just have to get close enough for all practical purposes. Discuss examples of how being less than perfect doesn't mean that you won't succeed at getting what you want in life. For example, Walt Disney was fired from the Kansas City Star because his editor felt he "lacked imagination and had no good ideas." Oprah Winfrey was publicly fired from her first television job as an anchor in Baltimore for getting "too emotionally invested in her stories." Steven Spielberg was rejected by the University of Southern California School of Cinematic Arts multiple times. Colonel Harland David Sanders was fired from dozens of jobs before founding a fried chicken empire.

Recovery Perfectionism Research Support Summary- When a Fall relates to the Rule Violation Effect, *Unhealthy Perfectionism, Low Self-Efficacy* and *Irresponsible Thinking* interact to trigger relapse. The Rule Violation Effect in Social Responsibility Therapy is a form of "recovery perfectionism" that occurs in multiple forms of unhealthy, harmful behavior (Yokley, 2008). This occurs in a manner similar to that described by the Abstinence Violation Effect in the relapse prevention model (Larimer, Palmer & Marlatt, 1999; Marlatt, 1985) that was originally designed to address the post treatment relapse problem in smoking (Curry, Marlatt & Gordon, 1987). The Abstinence Violation Effect was later modified to address multiple forms of unhealthy, harmful behavior (e.g., Physical abuse- King & Polaschek, 2003; Substance abuse including tobacco- Shiffman, Hickcox et. al. 1997, alcohol- Collins & Lapp, 1991, Muraven et al., 2005, marijuana- Stephens, Curtin et. al. 1994, binge eating/dieting- Grilo & Shiffman, 1994, Johnson, Schlundt et. al. 1995, Mooney, Burling et. al. 1992, Ward, Hudson & Bulik, 1993; Sexual abuse- Carich & Stone, 2001; Hudson, Ward & France, 1992, Hudson, Ward & Marshall, 1992; Ward, Hudson & Marshall, 1994). The Abstinence Violation Effect is referred to as the Goal Violation Effect, when the goal of treatment is not abstinence (Larimer & Marlatt, 1990). The Abstinence Violation Effect is hypothesized to occur following a Lapse (Slip) in response to recognizing that a commitment to abstinence has been violated and the individuals response to that violation determines whether they Fall into a full-blown relapse which is mediated by locus of the perceived cause (i.e., internal or external) and controllability (i.e., their belief about whether the individual can exert control) over the cause (Wheeler, George & Marlatt, 2006). The Abstinence Violation Effect is an important concept to understand in the treatment of unhealthy, harmful behavior and a clear illustration in substance abuse treatment is provided in Wheeler, George & Marlatt (p. 236, 2006). Use of the Abstinence Violation Effect to enhance sex offender risk perception and initiate coping responses has been recommended for some 20 years (Russell et. al. 1989).

Correcting a Slip to Avoid a Fall: The Olympic Ice Skater Analogy

In Olympic Ice Skating, a slip doesn't become a fall unless the skater hesitates in correcting it. When these athletes land from a spinning jump but slip, they automatically extend their opposite arm, their fall turns into a graceful swoop narrowly touching the ice and recovering for the next jump. Only the judges know they slipped, the rest of us view it as a graceful swoop. Olympic Ice skaters make immediate moves to recover from slips as they are happening, they don't hesitate and as a result they rarely take a fall. The point here is simple, "Hesitation kills recovery"- If you hesitate in correcting a slip, you take a fall.

Discuss the Ice Skating analogy with your clients and the importance of becoming a Recovery Ice Skater by automatically correcting Slips to avoid the Fall. Just like professional ice-skaters extend their opposite arm to correct a slip and avoid a fall, Recovery Ice-Skaters need to do the opposite healthy, helpful behavior from the unhealthy, harmful behavior that they were slipping into. "You are only limited by your creativity" in coming up with ways to go to the opposite extreme to correct an unhealthy, harmful behavior slip and avoid taking a fall. Any Healthy Behavior Success Skill that addresses a harmful behavior slip and fits the situation should be applied but "the 3 G's" beginning with Getting out of the high-risk situation and going in the opposite direction of trouble should always be the first move that clients make. Summarize the bottom line from these two relapse prevention issues. Underscore that if you want to get what you want in life you need to become a recovery engineer and a recovery ice skater. This means just letting go of paralyzing perfectionism, start pacing towards your goal, work on getting close enough for all practical purposes and correct each slip before it becomes a fall.

Relapse Prevention Issue #4: One harmful behavior can trigger another

Since committing one type of harmful behavior can trigger another, it is important to look at other forms of unhealthy, harmful behavior as possible relapse triggers. In addition, violating one healthy life goal can trigger violating another. Some examples of how one harmful behavior can trigger another and block healthy body, relationship and life direction goals are listed in the following Table 4.11. Review the Table 4.11 examples with your clients and discuss the types of

Table 4.11 One harmful behavior can trigger another: Selected examples		
Referral Problem	**Trigger Behavior**	**Connection between trigger behavior and referral problem relapse** (How one harmful behavior triggers another)
Food abuse- Unhealthy eating (Healthy Body Goal)	Spending (Money abuse)	"I'm feeling really nervous about maxing out my credit cards at the mall, am really craving chocolate and <u>must</u> go to the Food Court.
Substance abuse (Healthy Body Goal)	Fighting (Physical abuse)	"Anybody else would get totally wasted after what they said to me but I'm <u>just</u> going to use enough to calm down and keep from choking them".
Trust abuse- cheating (Healthy Relationship Goal)	Substance abuse-Cocaine	"I already did coke with them <u>but</u> it's OK if I have sex <u>because</u> I'm not actually married to my fiancé yet"
Sexual Abuse (Healthy Relationship Goal)	Drinking (Alcohol abuse)	"I know I'm not supposed to be drinking, particularly with an underage girl <u>but</u> she started it so I might as well have sex"
Trust abuse- (Healthy Life Direction Goal)	Stealing (Property abuse)	"This store item was not on the inventory and will <u>never</u> be missed so I might as well take it"
Responsibility neglect (Healthy Life Direction Goal)	Substance abuse-Marijuana	"Since I got high and called in late, I <u>should</u> just blow off the rest of the day"

irresponsible thinking involved in the harmful behavior relapse examples listed (See Table 4.2).

Positive Lifestyle Change Plan: Relapse Prevention

The first step towards developing the healthy body/behavior/environment, healthy relationships and healthy life direction that clients need to succeed is to help them "Avoid Trouble." This involves making effective relapse prevention plans for high-risk situations that can block or interfere with their healthy lifestyle goals. The second step is helping clients "Approach Success." This involves plans to "Go to the opposite extreme" from who they are and where they are in life to who they want to be and where they want to go in life.

Help your clients write their own Positive Lifestyle Change plans for Avoiding Trouble and Approaching Success. Make sure they list their own specific examples of how they will use their Relapse Prevention Skills to develop: 1) a healthy body/behavior/environment; 2) healthy, positive relationships and; 3) a healthy, positive life direction. Don't forget to reinforce the need to correct a slip before it becomes a fall and have clients give their own examples of how the recovery perfectionism involved in the rule violation effect or "Slip Give-up Trigger" can result in relationship and life direction trouble as described in Table 4.12 below.

Table 4.12 "Slip Give Up Trigger" Examples with Healthy Relationship and Life Direction Goals		
	Healthy Relationships	**Healthy Life Direction**
Since I already slipped and...	had the last word with them in front of friends	might be late for my job interview because I got up late
I blew it so I might as well just...	get all the rest of my feelings off my chest	stay home
Besides, if I stop now, I will...	still have to get grief about this tomorrow	have to apologize and make up an excuse

Have your clients write their Positive Lifestyle Change plans as if they were writing a story using who, what, when, where, why and how for their healthy body, relationship and life direction goals as follows...

- Who they should avoid and escape from along with who they should approach and hang around.
- What they should say to themselves to avoid trouble (relapse) and what they should say to themselves to approach success.
- When they are most likely to have problems with unhealthy, harmful behavior, relationships or life direction issues and will need to use their relapse prevention skills.
- Where they should avoid and escape from along with where they should spend their time.
- Why to leave a stressful situation that could trigger trouble without hesitation.
- How to use "the 3 G's" when experiencing increasing unwanted feelings, cravings or urges or any other situation that could trigger trouble.

The outline in Table 4.13 provides basic areas to cover in helping clients use relapse prevention skills in their positive lifestyle change plan.

Table 4.13
Positive Lifestyle Change Plan: Relapse Prevention

Healthy Lifestyle Change Steps	Positive Lifestyle Goal		
	Healthy Body, Behavior, Environment	**Healthy Relationships**	**Healthy Life Direction**
1. Avoid Trouble Have clients write a plan to use their high-risk situation avoidance and escape (i.e., "the 3 G's") skills.	**High-risk situations for Unhealthy, Harmful Behavior-** Have clients list and discuss the high-risk situations that can trigger their unhealthy, harmful behavior and what they need to avoid. Have clients write out specific examples of how they will use "the 3 G's" to escape their high-risk situations for unhealthy, harmful behavior relapse.[1]	**High-risk situations for Relationship problems-** Have clients list their relationship problems including those related to their unhealthy, harmful behavior along with the high-risk situations that can trigger relationship problems or block healthy relationship development. Have clients write out specific examples of how they plan to avoid and escape situations that put them at risk for relationship problems.	**High-risk situations for Life Direction problems-** Have clients review their healthy life direction goals (Chapter 2), then list and discuss examples of the high-risk situations that can block those goals. Have clients write out specific examples of how they plan to avoid and escape high-risk situations that can block their healthy life direction goals.
2. Approach Success Have clients write a plan to "Go to the opposite extreme" of their high-risk situations.	Have clients list and discuss the people, places and things (thoughts & feelings) that will support their healthy, helpful behavior goals.	Have clients list and discuss what they need to do to develop healthy relationships beginning with how they are doing with their honesty, trust, loyalty and concern.	Have clients list and discuss the specific steps needed to achieve their healthy life direction goals along with the people and changes that will help them.[2]

1. See Table 4.4 for examples of relapse trigger people, places, and things (thoughts and feelings) across 7 types of unhealthy, harmful behavior. See Table 4.5 for high-risk situations to avoid for case examples of harmful eating, drinking and sexual behavior. See Table 4.6 for examples of using "the 3 G's" to escape these situations.
2. Don't forget examples of how: 1) planning before; 2) excuses during and; 3) covering up after their unhealthy harmful behavior created problems with honesty, trust, loyalty, concern and responsibility which in turn created relationship problems. If your clients didn't cover their behavior up, start with the negative associates that enabled it or were doing the same thing. Then help them make high risk person avoidance and escape plans.

Relapse Prevention Research Support Summary- Relapse prevention which was originally developed for the post-treatment relapse problem in addictive behaviors has a clinical and research literature base dating back 30 years (e.g., Marlatt & Gordon, 1985). Relapse Prevention has evolved to address a wide variety of unhealthy, harmful behaviors and symptoms including problem eating, drinking, smoking, drug use, gambling, intimate partner violence and sexual offending (e.g., Echeburúa, Fernández-Montalvo & Báez, 2000; Gilbert, et.al. 2006; Hendershot, Marlatt & George, 2009; Marlatt & Donovan, 2005; Witkiewitz & Marlatt, 2007 & 2009; Yates & Ward, 2007). Meta-analysis of relapse prevention with offenders has revealed moderate mean reductions in recidivism (Dowden, Antonowicz & Andrews, 2003). Overviews of the Relapse Prevention model are provided in Larimer, Palmer & Marlatt (1999) and Newring et. al. (2008). Summaries of the evidence base for Relapse Prevention are provided in Witkiewitz & Marlatt, (2007) and Hendershot, Marlatt & George (2009).

Relapse Prevention Summary

In summary, SRT employs two basic strategies for relapse prevention: 1) high-risk situation avoidance and; 2) high-risk situation escape. High-risk situation avoidance involves Awareness Training on people, places and things (e.g., thoughts and feelings) that can set the occasion for or trigger relapse. High-risk situation escape involves Responsibility Training on the "Three-Step Responsibility Plan" or "the 3 G's" of escaping high-risk situations for relapse (i.e., Get out, Get honest and Get responsible).

Important issues in relapse prevention include: 1) Identifying and replacing Irresponsible Thinking that sets the occasion for unhealthy, harmful behavior (e.g., JOBS MAN- just, only, but, should, must, always, never); 2) Distinguishing between a slip/lapse and a fall/relapse for individuals whose behavior is more harmful to others than to self; 3) Harmful behavior migration which defeats self-control practice by simply shifting to another harmful behavior during treatment and back to the target harmful behavior afterwards; 4) Recovery perfectionism involving having an "all or nothing" perfectionist view of recovery and giving up on self-control after a minor slip has tarnished an otherwise perfect record; 5) The need to target multiple co-occurring unhealthy, harmful behaviors because the referral behavior problem is not usually the only behavior problem and one harmful behavior can trigger another. Since tolerating feedback is necessary for developing awareness of high-risk situations, Tolerance Training in SRT includes helping clients tolerate feedback with the "The Mirror Concept" involving learning to use other's feedback as a mirror to better see yourself.

"It's not what happens to you, but how you react to it that matters"
-- Epictetus (55- 135AD)

Chapter 5
Internal Control- Healthy Behavior Success Skill #2:
Helping Clients "Calm Down" with Emotional Regulation

Helping Clients "Calm Down" with Emotional Regulation
"Problems are not the problem; coping is the problem"-- Virginia Satir (1916- 1988)

Emotional regulation in SRT addresses "justifying actions based on feelings." Multiple forms of unhealthy, harmful behavior can be triggered by emotions that are activated by high-risk situations. Emotional Regulation in unhealthy, harmful behavior treatment involves interventions that help clients regulate their emotions to keep them below the threshold of acting those emotions out through unhealthy, harmful behavior and avoid justifying unhealthy, harmful actions based on unwanted feelings.

Emotional Regulation: "Straight to the Point"
The point of this section is to help clients regulate the unwanted emotions, cravings and urges that trigger unhealthy, harmful behavior, create relationship problems & interfere with life goals.
Emotional Regulation Goals and Objectives
Awareness Training Goal: Increase client awareness of basic human emotions and high-risk situations that can trigger acting out feelings through unhealthy, harmful behavior.
   Objectives: Clients will be able to identify and discuss examples of basic human emotions and triggers for acting out feelings.
Responsibility Training Goal: Develop responsible emotional regulation strategies.
   Objectives: Clients will be able to explain two emotional regulation skills: emotional accommodation to hold on to their feelings and emotional dissipation with the ABC's of letting feelings go: the Action that occurred; the Belief problem that triggers the feeling; "Challenging the Belief problem to let the feeling go.
Tolerance Training Goal: Improve tolerance for emotional distress and frustration.
   Objectives: Clients will be able to explain when to use the ABC's of holding on to feelings and when to use the ABC's of letting feelings go.

Treatment Exercise: Emotional Regulation Benefits
Three basic assumptions about emotional triggers of unhealthy, harmful behavior are:
1. There can be no comfort eating, drinking, smoking spending, sex, etc., without discomfort and;
2. You can't justify unhealthy, harmful actions based on unwanted feelings, without unwanted feelings.
3. It is therefore important to learn emotional regulation skills to deal with discomfort and unwanted feelings.

Desire to achieve long term life goal benefits can provide motivation for learning emotional regulation skills. Have clients write and discuss how emotional episodes, following their feelings and/or justifying their actions based on their feelings has: 1) resulted in unhealthy, harmful behavior (i.e., interfered with healthy body/behavior/environment goals); 2) created relationship problems (i.e., interfered with healthy relationship goals) and; 3) got in the way of the healthy life direction that they need to succeed.

The ART of Emotional Regulation

In SRT, The ART of Emotional Regulation involves lowering the intensity of trigger feelings below the threshold of acting out. "Acting out" means acting feelings out by doing unhealthy, harmful behaviors. This involves becoming overwhelmed with feelings and justifying actions based on feelings. Unwanted feelings usually go in only two directions either: in on the client (e.g., eating, drinking, drugging, smoking, cutting) or; out on others (e.g., hitting, stealing, dealing, cheating, fondling). If unwanted feelings become too powerful, humans will become overwhelmed and give up. Three basic ways humans give up on when they are overwhelmed with feelings

Awareness Training
If you're not **A**ware of your feelings, you can't do anything to change them.

Responsibility Training
If you don't take **R**esponsibility for learning how to let feelings go, you can expect them to stay.

Figure 5.1 The ART of Emotional Regulation

Tolerance Training
If you don't learn to **T**olerate feelings, you will continue to act them out.

are to: 1) give up on life and start thinking about killing themselves; 2) give up on dealing with feelings, i.e., "I don't want to kill myself but I definitely want to kill these feelings" so they drink, drug, smoke, eat, spend, have sex to distract themselves from unwanted feelings and/or; 3) give up on the situation, i.e., "I don't want to give up on life or dealing with my feelings but definitely want to get rid of this situation" (job, relationship, etc.). While there are many feelings that can set the occasion for unhealthy, harmful behavior (e.g., greed, envy, jealousy), it is important for clients to be able to identify the basic human emotions that can motivate acting out feelings through behavior that is harmful to self or others (See Table 4.3).

The **ART** of calming down (Emotional Regulation) involves: Awareness training on basic human emotions and high-risk situations that can trigger acting out feelings through unhealthy, harmful behavior; Responsibility training on developing emotional dissipation and accommodation skills to regulation emotions and; Tolerance training on learning to tolerate frustration and emotional distress (Figure 5.1).

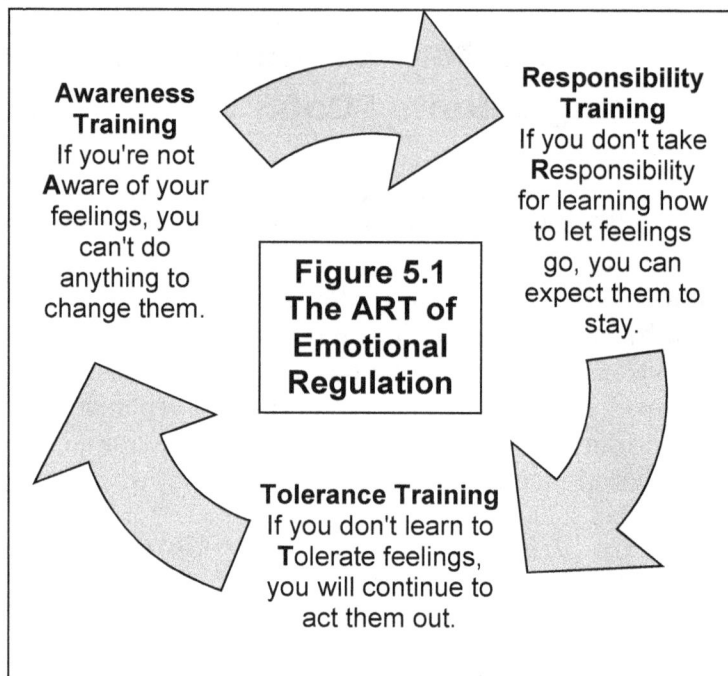

Awareness Training in Emotional Regulation:
Awareness of Basic Emotions, Urges, Cravings and Mediating Thoughts
"If you're not Aware of your feelings, you can't do anything to change them"

Awareness Training Goal: Increase client awareness of basic human emotions and high-risk situations that can trigger acting feelings out through unhealthy, harmful behavior.
 Objectives: Clients will be able to identify and discuss examples of basic human emotions and triggers for acting out feelings.

Basic Feelings 101

Three basic types of unwanted feelings that clients need to be able to identify and regulate to keep below the threshold of acting out are anger, anxiety and depression. Basic emotional awareness training needs to include the following. Human emotions range in severity from mild to severe and may begin during the stressful event or may be delayed until much later in time. Anger can range from a mild annoyance to moderate angry cursing to severe assaultive rage and may include continuous rumination on perceived injustices and revenge thoughts. Anxiety can range from mild social discomfort to a moderate anxiety (fear) to a severe panic attack and may include continuous thoughts about the worst happening. Depression can range from a mild sadness to moderate feeling of depression (including feeling helpless) to suicidal despair (including feeling hopeless) and may include continuous thoughts about giving up.

Treatment Exercise: Picking up on Feelings- Awareness of feelings is prerequisite to regulating feelings. Practice picking up on the feelings of others begins with clients becoming more aware of their own feelings and learning to label those feelings. A good practice exercise to sensitize clients to become aware of others feelings is simply to stop in the middle of your sentence and ask them, "Right now, What am I thinking and how do I feel?" Ask clients to take their best guess about your feelings and validate accurate answers. As a comparison and contrast social experiment, if you try this with your colleagues, you may be surprised to find that while colleagues are able to generate responses based on what your last words were (i.e., the emotional aspect of what you just said), your facial expression, tone of voice, posture, etc., often times your clients do not even have a clue as to what you might be thinking or feeling. Thus, to help clients learn to pick up on the feelings of others, you may have to select television shows that provide exaggerated expressions of various feelings and pause the DVD to have clients label feelings that are easily identifiable. Some cases may require handing out and discussing a feelings list such as the one listed in Table 5.1 below to help develop awareness of feelings.

Table 5.1
Feelings that Humans Experience

Angry	Embarrassed	Humiliated	Misunderstood	Relaxed
Anxious	Envious	Hungry	Neglected	Resentful
Aroused	Excited	Inadequate	Nervous	Revengeful
Bored	Exhausted	Insecure	Overwhelmed	Sad
Confident	Frustrated	Irritated	Passionate	Tense
Criticized	Guilty	Jealous	Paranoid	Tired
Depressed	Grieving	Lonely	Physical pain	Worried
Deprived	Happy	Miserable	Pressured	

With younger or special needs clients a facial expression chart may be needed. There are many of these charts available on line by searching "feelings faces chart." Clients who need more structure or those in higher levels of care (e.g., intensive outpatient programs, treatment foster care, corrections/forensic settings or community residential treatment) may require more step-by-step guidance on identifying emotions and making awareness connections between thinking, feeling and doing. For those clients, Structured Discovery exercises are provided on p. 43-49 of SRT Workbook 1 (Yokley, 2012).

Treatment Exercise: Trigger Feelings Risk Level Card Sort

Make a set of index cards from the list above with one feeling on each card. Then make three large cards with the low risk, moderate risk and high-risk category headings printed on them. Have your clients sort the trigger feelings that you checked above into the three columns above that indicate how likely they are to relapse when they experience each feeling. Then have them make a list of their low, moderate and high risk for relapse feelings as defined in Table 5.2.

Table 5.2 Low, Moderate and High-Risk Feelings		
Low Risk of falling back into my (list referral unhealthy, harmful behavior here*) when I get this feeling.	**Moderate Risk** of falling back into my (list referral unhealthy, harmful behavior here*) when I get this feeling.	**High Risk** of falling back into my (list referral unhealthy, harmful behavior here*) when I get this feeling.
* e.g. eating, drinking, drugs, gambling, spending, physical violence, sexual behavior problems		

Have a group discussion of client high risk feelings with examples of the situations that have triggered those feelings in the past. Make sure that clients use their high risk feelings in the emotional regulation examples that are provided in this section. In situations that trigger feelings, clients need to become aware that what they tell themselves can influence what feeling they will experience. Review some basic examples with clients of how thoughts can influence feelings after a trigger situation (See Table 5.3).

Table 5.3	Thoughts Influence Feelings after a Trigger Situation "You mainly feel the way you think" -- Albert Ellis (1913- 2007)	
Trigger Situation	**Client Self-statements (thoughts)**	**Resulting Feeling**
Client loses their best friend and roommate in auto accident.	"I miss them so much, life's not worth living without them" can result in feelings of...	Depression
	"I don't know what I will do without them, I can't pay the bills on my own" can result in feelings of...	Anxiety
	"Why did they refuse a ride home, they should have let me drive them" can result in feelings of...	Anger

Urges and Cravings are Feelings too

Many feelings get easily attached to motivations and are easily vented through behaviors. For example, depression can motivate the desire to give up on life (e.g., suicide ideation). Anxiety can motivate the desire to give up on dealing with feelings (e.g., drinking or drugging to block out the mood). Anger can motivate the desire to give up on dealing with the situation (e.g., quitting a job or breaking up with a relationship partner). Cravings are feelings that get easily attached to motivations (i.e., the desire to approach pleasure or avoid pain) and are easily vented through unhealthy, harmful behavior.

Have your clients consider the following. When you get an <u>urge and crave</u> ice-cream, alcohol, weed, gambling or sex you tell yourself... "<u>I feel like</u> having some ice-cream", "<u>I feel like</u>

having a drink", "I feel like smoking a blunt", "I feel like going to the casino" or "I feel like having sex." Since the stronger the urge is, the higher the chances are that clients will relapse back into the unhealthy harmful behavior they are carving, it is important for clients to be able to rate their urges/cravings on a 1- 10 scale (i.e., where 1= low risk of relapse by caving into the craving and; 10= high risk of relapse). Clients can tell how strong cravings/urges they are by listening to what they are saying to themselves which indicates their actual beliefs (See Figure 5.2). For example, clients who decide to tell themselves...

- "I could" (or want to) do the unhealthy, harmful behavior, give themselves complete choice which only generates a mild craving (1- 3).
- "I should" (or need to) do the unhealthy, harmful behavior, take away some choice which generates a moderate craving (4- 6).
- "I must" (or have to) do the unhealthy, harmful behavior, give themselves no choice which leaves them with a severe craving (7- 10).

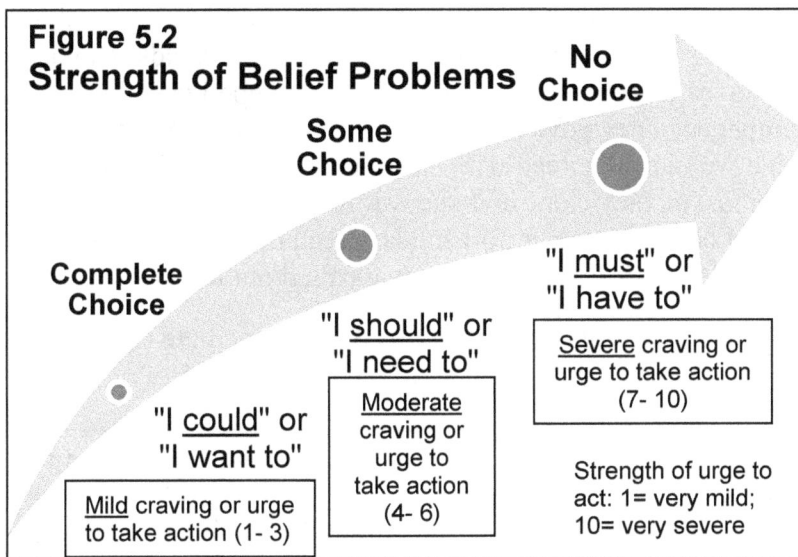

Figure 5.2 Strength of Belief Problems

Cognitive Mediation 101

"The greatest weapon against stress is our ability to choose one thought over another"
-- William James (1842- 1910)

Cognitive mediators are thoughts or self-statements that occur after a trigger situation and before an action that mediate or bring about a compromise between justifying actions based on feelings and justifying actions based on facts. Clients need to become aware that what they tell themselves can mediate and thus regulate their emotions. Put another way, self-statements can determine whether clients calm themselves down or work themselves up emotionally. This in turn determines how likely they are to act on the urge to vent their feelings. Help clients understand the following unhealthy eating, substance abuse and sexual behavior examples of how the urge to vent their feelings can be mediated or regulated by what they say to themselves.

Practical Application Example: Unhealthy Eating

Laticia is an early-30's client in weight management treatment for morbid obesity with depression problems that are compounded by a strong sense of responsibility and doing much more for others than she does for herself. Her kind heart has resulted in involvement in a number of "take-a-holic" relationships with men she has supported financially and who have not helped support her three children after they left. Her symptoms of depression included increased eating and decreased activity. Her overwhelming single parenting and financial responsibilities are now being complicated by serious health problems including type-II diabetes, sleep apnea, high blood pressure, high cholesterol, lower back and knee pain. These physical problems along with relationship loneliness have increased her depression, which in turn is making it extremely difficult for her to avoid emotional comfort eating.

On the positive side, Laticia got through her best friend's wedding ceremony today without self-pity loneliness tears. She used her relapse prevention positive planning skills by skipping the wedding reception where she knew she would be at high risk for loneliness comfort eating. Unfortunately for her, later that day two of her friends who had planned the reception dropped by with boxes of delicious wedding reception appetizers, pasta and desserts along with a bottle of champagne. They gave her a hug, said they knew she must have not been feeling well to miss such a wonderful spread with all of her favorites dishes so they brought everything to her. They left as fast as they came and she was alone again with her sad loneliness and massive quantities of all of her favorite comfort foods spread out on her kitchen table. The room was filled with all the smells of her favorite dishes that called out to her.

Examples of self-statement options that can mediate (i.e., increase or decrease) Laticia's feelings, urges and consequent behavior are listed Table 5.4.

Table 5.4 Self-statement options that can mediate Laticia's feelings, urges and resulting behavior	Resulting Feeling & Urge Severity (0 = no urge at all; 10 = overwhelming urge to act)	Resulting Behavior
"I <u>could</u> stay here and eat something that's not too rich but I skipped the reception because I knew I couldn't stay without having some of everything. If I go, my urge will go. If I stay my urge will stay. I need to fill my loneliness up with people, not pasta."	Mild loneliness and sadness. Urge to overeat = 2	Leaving immediately for the local homeless shelter and bringing back a staff member to take everything to the homeless. Not acting on sadness or urge to overeat (avoiding unhealthy eating)
"I <u>should</u> try just one bite of everything because I know I will be asked what I liked best and I need to be able to tell them. Besides, seeing all those couples at the wedding was depressing and I need some comfort."	Moderate loneliness and depression. Urge to overeat = 5	Eating some pasta, then going to the gym to walk on the treadmill and think about what to do. Inviting family over for dinner to avoid throwing food out. Acting on depression but correcting the slip (food abuse slip/lapse)
"I <u>have to</u> eat everything because they brought it just for me and it's wrong to waste food. No matter how much I do for others, I can't count on anyone to do for me. It's so depressing to know that food is the only comfort I can ever count on so I might as well give up on trying to control it."	Severe loneliness and depression. Urge to overeat = 8	Staying in the house and eating everything. Then feeling sick with indigestion and self-disappointment. Becoming overwhelmed by loneliness, depression and urge to comfort eat (food abuse fall/relapse)

Practical Application Example: Unhealthy, Harmful Substance use- Karen is a late 40's, unemployed nurse with anxiety attacks. After an auto accident she received a pain medication prescription (Percocet) and was much calmer on the job. As a result, she continued her Percocet use, developing a tolerance and addiction which resulted in losing her job and nursing license. Her anxiety increased, she received a Xanax prescription from her primary care physician and started drinking a lot more with her husband. Her liver function tests revealed her problem to her primary care physician, her request to refill her Xanax prescription was denied and she was referred for alcohol treatment.

On her way home she started to feel uneasy while driving. When she pulled over and got out of the car to get some air, her eyes locked on the corner bar. Examples of self-statement options that can mediate (i.e., increase or decrease) Karen's feelings, urges and consequent behavior are listed 5.5.

Table 5.5 Self-statement options that can mediate Karen's feelings, urges and resulting behavior	Resulting Feeling & Urge Severity (0 = no urge; 10 = overwhelming urge)	Resulting Behavior
"I want to go in and have a drink to steady my nerves but I know that my anxiety will pass and it's never just one drink".	Mild anxiety. Urge to drink = 3	Not going into the corner bar. Not acting on anxiety or urge to drink (avoiding substance abuse)
"I should go in and have a drink to calm my nerves and help me let go of my anxiety."	Moderate anxiety. Urge to drink = 6	Having a drink but calling their AA sponsor to come and get them. Acting on anxiety but correcting their slip (substance abuse slip/lapse)
"I can't stand this awful anxiety and must drink until it goes away".	Severe anxiety. Urge to drink = 9	Getting drunk and arrested on the way home for driving under the influence. Becoming overwhelmed by anxiety and urge to drink (substance abuse relapse)

Practical Application Example: Harmful Sexual Behavior- Jack is an early 20's, single, truck driver with anger management problems in sex offender treatment for aggressive sexual advances towards several "stuck up" female dispatchers (Table 5.6). He receives an unexpected insult by Gina, an attractive young woman who lives across the hall. He believes that Gina has been flirting with him for some time. He has had a number of sexual fantasies about her and hopes that she will someday respond to his ongoing invitations to come over and join him for a drink. Gina had just returned from a bar, and bumped into him in the hallway. When he took her by the arm and offered to help her inside she blurted out "get your ugly, stupid ass off of me and get out of my f#*king way." She then stumbled into her apartment fell on the floor passed out with the door still open. Examples of self-statement options that can mediate (i.e., increase or decrease) Jack's feelings, urges and consequent behavior are listed in Table 5.6.

Table 5.6 Self-statement options that can mediate Jack's feelings, urges and resulting behavior	Resulting Feeling & Urge Severity (0 = no urge; 10 = overwhelming urge)	Resulting Behavior
"I <u>could</u> do her and get away with it but I've said a lot of insulting things when drinking so I guess what comes around, goes around".	Mild annoyance. Urge to take sex = 1	Pulling Gina's door shut and leaving. Not acting feelings or urges out on defenseless victim (avoiding sexual abuse)
"I <u>should</u> do her for what she said. Besides, what she don't know won't hurt her."	Moderate anger. Urge to take sex = 5	Cursing back at Gina, slamming her door & leaving the situation (anger slip/lapse)
"I can't stand this disrespect and <u>have to</u> give this stuck up b#%*h what she deserves.	Severe anger and sexually assaultive rage. Urge to take sex = 10	Pulling Gina into her apartment locking the door and raping her. Acting anger and sexual urges out on defenseless victim (sexual abuse fall/relapse)

Responsibility Training in Emotional Regulation
"If you don't take Responsibility for learning how to let feelings go, you can expect them to stay"

Responsibility Training Goal: Develop a responsible emotional dissipation strategy.
Objectives: Clients will be able to describe and use "The ABC's of letting feelings go".

Responsibility training in emotional regulation involves accepting responsibility for challenging irresponsible thinking that triggers unwanted feelings because "Feelings don't kill you, telling yourself I can't stand these feelings kills you" and "If you blame other people for your feelings you give them control over your life." Emotional responsibility training also involves using socially responsible assertiveness to avoid stress buildup that can trigger relapse by: holding self and others accountable to (i.e., "The truth will set you free"); not taking on too much; not compromising self to be accepted, to get attention or for excitement. Socially responsible assertiveness requires practicing refusal skills and concrete face saving mechanisms (i.e., positive excuses to avoid following negative feelings and negative peers). The key Responsibility Training skill for clients to develop in emotional regulation training is emotional dissipation through "The ABC's of letting feelings go".

Client Instructions for Combining Emotional Regulation with Relapse Prevention

Always start with Relapse Prevention. Use "the 3 G's" to escape high-risk situations first...
1. **Get out** (Remove yourself)- Since "Hesitation (to leave high-risk situations) kills recovery", leave without hesitation. "You need to be laughing and leaving, not staying and stewing." Clients need to get out of high-risk situations immediately to keep from following feelings.
2. **Get honest** (Block the thought)- Tell yourself the truth, "I can't get what I want by doing what I want" or "It's never just one last time."
3. **Get Responsible** (Substitute a more responsible thought)- Go to the opposite extreme, a place you can't act on the thought. Then use the ABC's of emotional regulation.

- If you can identify the emotional trigger and know why you're upset, use the ABC's of letting feelings go (Emotional Dissipation- See below) to calm down and act responsibly.
- If you can't identify the emotional trigger and don't know why you're upset, use the ABC's of accepting and holding on to feelings (Emotional Accommodation- See below) until you get used to them and can act responsibly.

Basic Emotional Dissipation

The healthy behavior success skills needed to "Calm down" involves emotional control skills often referred to as "emotional regulation" in treatment manuals. Many unhealthy, harmful acts are justified based on feelings while ignoring facts. Given the human tendency to justify unhealthy, harmful actions based on unwanted feelings, it is important for individuals in treatment for unhealthy, harmful behaviors to learn emotional regulation skills to deal with the distress of unwanted feelings. The core of acting feelings out is justifying actions based on feelings and the cure for acting feelings out is emotional regulation. If your client was standing next to you (or a highly responsible best friend) when a problem situation hit, you (or their responsible) friend would talk them down, not work them up. Unfortunately, clients are not usually standing next to their therapist or a responsible best friend when problems hit. In most life situations, clients need to learn to talk themselves down, not work themselves up.

Responsibility training in emotional regulation to "Calm down" involves clients learning emotional dissipation to let feelings go and emotional accommodation to accept and adjust to feelings. In SRT, emotional dissipation involves learning the ABC's of letting feelings go by challenging the irresponsible thinking that enables unhealthy, harmful behavior. The ABC's used in SRT were condensed from the Rational Emotive Behavior Therapy (REBT) developed by Dr. Albert Ellis.[1] The basic goal of ABC's of letting feelings go is to learn to justify actions based on facts not feelings. Emotional dissipation is typically the intervention of choice when clients are upset, need to calm down and know what triggered their feelings.

Emotional Dissipation: The ABC's of letting feelings go

Emotional dissipation through the ABC's of letting feelings go involves clients accepting responsibility for challenging the irresponsible thinking that gets them worked up emotionally to the point of justifying unhealthy, harmful behavior based on overwhelming feelings. Challenging irresponsible thinking that triggers unwanted feelings is important because...

"Feelings don't kill you, telling yourself 'I can't stand these feelings' kills you and
"Cravings don't trigger relapse, telling yourself 'I can't stand these cravings' triggers relapse"

The ABC's of letting feelings go was adapted from the well-established Rational-Emotive Behavior Therapy (REBT) method of disputing irrational beliefs developed by Dr. Albert Ellis. This alphabetical step method begins by having the client identify the: Activating event, irrational Beliefs about that event, upsetting emotional Consequences that the irrational belief triggered and then; Dispute the irrational belief followed by substituting an Effective response.

REBT training- The advantages of integrating REBT into harmful behavior treatment are well worth the time spent in training at the Albert Ellis Institute. Primary, advanced, fellowship and supervisory certification training information with continuing education approved by the American Psychological Association is available online at www. rebt.org.

Emotional dissipation involves clients learning to let go of belief problems that are working them up. The ABC's of letting feelings go are as follows...

"A" is the <u>Action that occurred</u> (the problem situation or event);

"B" is the <u>Belief problem</u>, trigger. This is what clients say to themselves about that Action (problem, situation or event) that occurred that works them up to the point of triggering or activating unwanted feelings and urges to act on those feelings (i.e., gets them to justify their actions based on feelings). This has been well documented in Rational Emotive Behavior Therapy as often containing the word "should" or "must".[1] Having a mild (could) belief about the action that occurred is not enough to get them going, it takes a moderate (should) or severe (must) belief to justify acting on feelings (See Figure 5.2).

"C" is <u>Challenging the Belief problem</u> about the Action that is triggering/activating the problem feelings and/or harmful urge. Challenging beliefs/thoughts that trigger the problem feeling is needed in order to decrease the feeling, stop following the feeling and let it go. This is accomplished with any straightforward Who, What, When, Where, Why and How question that challenges the validity of the Belief that is motivating the emotional response to that belief.

Ways to Challenge Belief Problems (Who, what, when, where, why and how)
- "Who could prove that?" or "I can't prove that" (Validity challenge).
- "What if the worst happens?" (Preparation challenge).
- "When/why should I have known better?" (Self-criticism challenge).
- "<u>Where is the evidence that...?</u>" (Objective challenge) START WITH THIS FIRST-
- "Why does it follow that...?" (Philosophical challenge).
- "How likely is it that the negative outcome will occur?" (Probability challenge) or
- "How likely is it that me doing the wrong thing will get them to do the right thing?"

Start with the objective challenge, "Where is the evidence that..." first. Make this the "go to" challenge as it helps work on finding facts, not following feelings. Review appropriate examples with your clients and discuss other ways that the belief problems described could be challenged in order to dissipate the feelings that can trigger unhealthy, harmful behavior.

Using the ABC's of letting feelings go:
Unhealthy eating, substance use and harmful sexual behavior examples

Practical Application Example: Obesity treatment referral- Ted
Letting go of food cravings

Ted was a 40-year-old Euro-American outpatient weight-management referral who was doing very well in his program and was also saving some money by avoiding his old pizza parlor poker buddies. After the third Friday night of Ted calling to say he couldn't make it to the poker game, the doorbell rang. He opened the door and five guys burst in with a poker table, an extra-large pizza and several bottles of soda pop. Before he could say hello, the table was up, six chairs were positioned, the chips and cards were out and the pizza was opened on his kitchen counter. It was then that he realized it was his night to host the game and he forgot to call off. It was too late; the smell of a Papa John's pizza with all of Ted's favorite toppings filled the room. He was overwhelmed by cravings and excuses to smash down some delicious pizza.

Ted had to use "the 3 G's" to prevent relapse: Get out (without hesitation, he excused himself and went to the bathroom to give himself a chance to think); Get honest (Ted admitted, "The smell of that pizza is going to kill my diet if I go back out there without a plan") and; Get Responsible (by telling himself, *Since I know what triggered this craving, I need to use the ABC's of letting cravings go*). He talked himself through the ABC's of letting cravings go as follows...

- Action that occurred- "After I forgot to call off poker night, my pizza eating poker buddies showed up with my favorite pizza to play cards which triggered my pizza cravings."

- Belief problem- "I told myself that I *must* eat one piece because they brought it just for me but I know that having one piece will result in thinking that since I already broke my diet rules and have to start all over tomorrow, I might as well eat what I want tonight" (See Recovery Perfectionism, p.67).

- Challenging the Belief problem- "Where Is the evidence that I must eat some pizza even if they did bring it just for me? All I need to do is come up with a positive excuse to let them eat it and then I can play cards without blowing my diet."

Ted left the bathroom, was offered some pizza said no thanks and dumped all of the trash cans into a trash bag so that he could get out of the apartment for the few minutes that it would take his buddies to kill off the rest of the pizza. When he returned, the pizza was gone and his cravings focus was soon replaced by his focus on the game.

Practical Application Example: Substance abuse treatment referral- Ray
Letting go of alcohol cravings

Ray was a 35-year-old, African-American single male referred for residential drug and alcohol treatment as a result of out of control drinking since age 17 along with regular marijuana smoking and later crack cocaine use since age 25. After one month in his 90-day program, Gina an old girlfriend who was still interested in him invited him to shoot some pool with her on Sunday during visiting hours and home pass time when he was usually alone. She picked him up around 2pm and drove him to a local bar where they used to meet, drink, shoot pool into the late hours and then go home together. Gina ordered a beer, racked up the balls and flipped a coin to see who would take the first break shot. She was flirting with him and just like old times, said that if he won maybe he'd get lucky. He won the coin toss around the time her beer came in a tall frosty mug. His drinking cravings came on full force. Ray knew he was in trouble when he found himself staring more at the beer than Gina. He was overwhelmed by grandiose thoughts that he could handle shooting pool in his old hangout and would have just one drink.

Ray had to use "the 3 G's" to prevent relapse: Get out (without hesitation, he excused himself to have a cigarette and went out to the back patio to give himself a chance to think); Get honest (Ray admitted, "The excuses to drink are going to get the best of me I go back in there without a plan") and; Get Responsible (by telling himself, *Since I know what triggered this craving, I need to use the ABC's of letting cravings go*). He talked himself through the ABC's of letting cravings go as follows...

- Action that occurred- "Gina invited me to shoot pool and I was so excited to get out of rehab on Sundays when everybody gets visits but me that I didn't even consider that she might take me to our old hang out where we used to drink, shoot pool and then spend the night together."

- Belief problem- "I started setting myself up to fail by "musturbating and shoulding all over myself".[2] I told myself that "I *must* just have one drink so she won't have to drink alone" and since I've stayed clean and sober for 30 days, I *should* be able to fight the urge to drink for one night and just shoot pool."

- Challenging the Belief problem- "Where Is the evidence that just because I have been able to stay sober in rehab where alcohol is not allowed, that I should be able to stay sober in a bar?" and "Why would I even think about having just one drink when I know with me it's never just one?"

Ray knew what he had to do. He walked back in the bar and got honest with Gina. He told her that he could not stay and shoot pool, his craving to drink was too much for him and he needed to get out of there right now. She apologized, said that she just assumed that he would want to go where they always went and asked him what she could do to help. He invited her to go to an AA meeting with him. After the meeting, his craving had passed. He felt calm and relieved as he asked Gina to go for coffee at a local Starbucks. She thanked him for getting honest with her and they shared things with each other that would have never come to light around a noisy pool table in a dark bar. The next day, he told his group about using the ABC's of letting his cravings go. He also disclosed that Gina went to an AA meeting with him and thanked him for being honest with her about his problem and for an evening of getting to know each other again at Starbucks. He was open about his realization that without the focus of pool, loud music, dim lighting or beer to hide behind, he actually enjoyed spending time with Gina. Finally, he shared that she appeared to feel the same way as she asked him if they could get together next Sunday. Ray received strong applause from his group for avoiding relapse and for getting in touch with the fact that he didn't need alcohol to enjoy being with Gina.

Practical Application Example: Sex offender treatment referral- Dan
Letting go of harmful sexual urges

Dan was a 16-year-old Euro-American male discharged from secure residential treatment to community-based residential treatment for sexually abusive behavior after being arrested for repeatedly molesting his stepsister, Kyla over a 2 year period. On his first home pass, Dan stayed out past his probation curfew to avoid the unpredictable temper of his alcoholic step-father Willie. Unfortunately, Willie caught him sneaking back in and gave him another under the influence beating. As in the past, this beating triggered an overwhelming urge to take his feelings out on Willie's little girl Kyla by molesting her again.

In therapy, Dan had become aware of the connection between feeling totally helpless at the hands of Willie during his beatings and relieving that helplessness by taking sexual power and control over Kyla. He used to tell himself, "It's better to be an offender than a victim" and that molesting Kyla was all about getting even with Willie. In reality, Dan knew that he was using Willie as an excuse to keep molesting Kyla and that most of the reason he kept doing it was his own pent up sexual needs because he was too shy to approach girls his own age. He knew it was wrong but just like in the past, Dan got completely caught up in justifying sexual assault based on feelings of anger and wanting to vent the helplessness he felt at the hands of Willie by re-offending against his daughter. He found himself dwelling on feeling helpless, angry and starting to get aroused by thinking about what he had done to Kyla in the past. He sat on his bed starring at the floor hurt, angry and aroused. After a while, he looked up and saw that Willie forgot to shut the door and turn the door alarm on after he shoved Dan to the floor his room and stormed out cursing. This wasn't the only thing Willie forgot. The red light on the baby monitor was off giving Dan the green light to leave his room without being heard to molest Kyla again. Dan couldn't ignore his sexually aggressive feelings, found himself falling back into re-offense planning by justifying molesting Kyla based on his anger at Willie. He was going over and over what he had done to Kyla in the past. Dan was working his sexual arousal up to an overwhelming urge by thinking about what he could do to Kyla as soon as Willie passed out and started snoring.

Dan had to use "the 3 G's" to prevent relapse: Get out (he got out of his high-risk situation for relapse by turning the door alarm on and shutting the door); Get honest (Dan admitted, "Molesting Kyla to get even with Willie isn't right. It's just an excuse to get my sexual urges off" and; Get Responsible (Dan told telling himself, *"Since I know what triggered this urge, I need to use the ABC's of letting urges go"*). He talked himself through the ABC's of letting urges go as follows...

- Action that occurred- "I was trying to avoid another conflict with my step-father by staying out of the house until he drank himself to sleep but got caught and took another beating which triggered urges to take my feelings out by re-offending against his daughter."
- Belief problem- "I started thinking, "I *should* do what I want to Kyla because Willie did what he wanted to me. Besides, it's better to be an offender than a victim" and I *must* teach Willie a lesson for hurting me by hurting his daughter."
- Challenging the Belief problem- "Where is the evidence that I *should* do what I want to Kyla because Willie did what he wanted to me? Two wrongs don't make a right. "Where it the evidence that it's better to be an offender than a victim? I want to be respected but no one respects people that build themselves up by putting others down or taking advantage of them. "Where is the evidence that taking my sexual urges out on Kyla will teach Willie a lesson for beating me? If I want Willie to learn a lesson, I have to ignore his threats stand up to him and call the police.

Dan picked up his cell phone, called his caseworker and told her the whole story. She called his probation officer who arrived at the house with Emergency Medical Services. At the hospital he was examined, his bruises photographed and he was interviewed by Child Protective Services who obtained a warrant for Willie's arrest on assault and battery charges. Dan had finally succeeded in venting his feelings in the right way. His urge was gone and he felt relieved.

Using the ABC's of letting feelings go:
Other Unhealthy, harmful behavior examples

Practical Application Example: Property abuse/Gambling- Gary

Action that occurred- Gary, a late night, bored 30-year-old clerk at the family convenience store, takes a $2 scratch off lottery ticket without paying for it, scratches it off and wins $5

Belief problem- "I *must* (or have to) keep playing because I'm on a winning streak"

Challenging the Belief problem- "Where is the evidence that because I won, I will keep winning? I was just lucky I didn't lose and have to put $2 of my own money in the cash register."

Practical Application Example: Physical abuse treatment referral- Darrell

- Action that occurred- Darrell, a 20-year-old anger management client gets in an argument with his date who embarrasses him at a party and storms off. He sees people staring and laughing at him. One thug friend says, "I would slap the crap out of that b#$*h if she said that to me."
- Belief problem- "I *should* slap some sense into her for disrespecting me in front of my friends" (triggers further embarrassment along with justifying harmful actions based on angry feelings)
- Challenging the Belief problem- "How likely is it that slapping an angry woman will make her sensible? Angry people can't be sensible. I need to give her time to calm down. There's no state law that says I must deal with this right now."

Using the ABC's of letting feelings go: Healthy life goal examples
"Strong feelings are fine; it's the overreactions that mess us up" -- Albert Ellis (1913- 2007)

Practical Application Example: Healthy body development example

- Action that occurred- Went to first day of aerobics class and couldn't keep up.
- Belief problem- "They must be staring and talking about how I look so I can never go back."- triggers self-conscious worrying.
- Challenging the Belief problem- "Where Is the evidence that I'm being talked about, the music is too loud to hear. They can't stare if I go to the back of the class. Why should I hurt me, by quitting just because other people hurt me by staring?" (dissipates self-consciousness)

Practical Application Example: Healthy relationship development example

- Action that occurred- Partner, parent or close friend gets suspicious about you falling back into your past problem behavior use and asks where you have been.
- Belief problem- "They *should* know me enough by now to trust me" (triggers anger and justifying yelling based on anger over not being trusted).
- Challenging the Belief problem- "Who said that someone who cares about me shouldn't get worried about me and start asking questions? I need to just answer them straight up and not get so defensive."

Practical Application Example: Healthy life direction development example

- Action that occurred- Applied for a job, got an interview but they didn't call back.
- Belief problem- "There *must* be something wrong with me, I'll never get what I want in life" (triggers self-disappointment and justifying giving up based on feelings)
- Challenging the Belief problem- "Where is the evidence that I'll never get what I want in life if I keep trying? If I give up, I guarantee that I won't get what I want. I need to double my efforts."

Other examples of "Relieving high-risk emotions: The ABC's of letting feelings go" are provided in Table 14, p. 73 in Yokley (2011a).

Treatment Exercise: The ABC's of letting feelings go

"Save your sadness for the real tragedies, Save your anger for the real injustices and Save your fear for the real threats"-- SRT Maxim

Review the following brief summary of the ABC's of letting feelings go with your clients and have them write an example of their own using a recent event that triggered a feeling that put them at high risk for relapse on the unhealthy, harmful behavior that resulted in their referral for treatment. Emotional dissipation involves letting go of belief problems that are working you up. The ABC's of letting feelings go are as follows: **"A"** is the <u>Action that occurred</u> (the problem situation or event); **"B"** is the <u>Belief problem</u>, about the action that works you up and triggers problem feelings or urges (i.e., often contains the word "should" or "must"); **"C"** is <u>Challenging the Belief problem</u> about the action in order to stop following the feeling and let it go.[1]

Then, review the unhealthy, harmful behavior examples or life goal examples listed above that relate to the client. Have them apply the ABC's of letting feelings go to a real life example of a recent event that triggered one of their high risk feelings. Have them write answers to the following questions. What got you upset? What was the <u>A</u>ction that occurred? What were you thinking? What did you say to yourself about the action that occurred? What was the <u>B</u>elief problem? (Hint: The statement you said to yourself that had the word "should" or "must" in it). Now <u>C</u>hallenge the belief problem (Hint: Try starting with "Where is the evidence that..." and fill in the rest.)

Treatment Exercise: Letting go of helplessness

There are only two things in life that you can't change; the past and other people's behavior. Since these things are out of our control, the more we focus on them, the more out of control and helpless we feel. This is reflected by the saying, "If you blame other people for your behavior, you give them control over your life." Letting go of helplessness involves consistently re-directing our focus from what we can't change (i.e., the past and other people's behavior) to what we can change (i.e., the present and our behavior). The more we focus on the present and our behavior, the more effective and in control we feel. Have your clients list a few things they want to change that relates to the past and other people's behavior. Then have them explain how to use the ABC's of letting feelings go with those issues in order to let go of the helplessness that is kicked up by ruminating on the past or other people's behavior.

Emotional Dissipation Skills Practice: The Situation Response Analysis Log

Have your clients use a Situation Response Analysis Log (Appendix B) to begin documenting emotionally upsetting situations where they used the ABC's of letting feelings go to avoid relapse by justifying unhealthy, harmful actions based on unwanted feelings (See Table 4.7 for instructions and Table 4.8 for examples). If cravings/urges are involved have clients look carefully at what they said to themselves and rate their cravings (See figure 5.2). Help clients estimate their 1- 10 craving severity ratings by what they said to themselves. For example. telling themselves: "<u>I want to</u>" (or could) use, gives them complete choice creating only a mild craving (1- 3). Telling themselves, "<u>I need to</u>" (or should) use, gives them less choice creating a moderate craving (4- 6) but telling themselves, "<u>I have to</u>" (or must) use, gives them no choice making the craving severe (7- 10).

Emotional Dissipation (REBT) Research Support Summary: Emotional dissipation has a clinical and research literature base in Rational Emotive Behavior Therapy (REBT) dating back over 50 years (Ellis & Harper, 1961). The Rational Emotive Behavior Therapy approach for dissipation of unwanted emotions through challenging or disputing irrational beliefs is supported by several meta-analytic studies (Engels et al., 1993; Gonzalez et al., 2004; Lyons and Woods, 1991). This emotional dissipation approach has been utilized to treat a wide range of unhealthy, harmful behaviors including sexual abuse, physical abuse, property abuse/gambling, substance abuse, and trust abuse/infidelity (e.g., Angelillo, 2001; Bishop, 2000; DiGiuseppe, & Kelter, 2006; Whitford & Parr, 1995; Solomon & Ray, 1984; Stoop, 2012). For further information, see Rational Emotive Behavior Therapy: Theories of Psychotherapy (Ellis & Ellis, 2011).

Tolerance Training in Emotional Regulation
"If you don't take Responsibility for learning how to hold on to feelings, you will continue to follow them "

Tolerance Training Goal: Develop a responsible emotional accommodation strategy.
  Objectives: Clients will be able to describe and use "The ABC's of holding on to feelings".

Tolerance Training in SRT Emotional Regulation involves: 1) learning to tolerate feedback; 2) learning to tolerate frustration and delay of gratification along with; 3) learning emotional accommodation to tolerate unwanted feelings, urges and cravings through "The ABC's of holding on to feelings".

Treatment Exercise: Tolerating Feedback
Hold a discussion on learning to tolerate feedback. Begin by discussing human nature, the fact that, "People don't appreciate anything they don't ask for" and when we receive unrequested or unwanted feedback, this triggers the urge to have the last word. Apply "the 3 G's" to this problem recommending that clients Get out "Excuse me, I'll be right back", head to the rest room sit down and Get honest, "If I have the last word, that will trigger them to throw some more words at me and we will go back and forth on insult ping pong until someone starts throwing fists instead of words." Then, Get responsible, looking at it like a text message, just focusing on what is being said, not who is saying it or how it is being said. If the feedback is being given by an authority figure (e.g., instructor, supervisor, police officer, judge, etc.), discuss the need for accepting that the only proper response to authority is, "Thank you I'll take care of that" which allows you to Get out of a conflict so you can Get honest with yourself about the possible consequences and Get responsible by not putting yourself in an authority conflict situation.

Treatment Exercise: Tolerating Frustration
Hold second discussion on learning to tolerate frustration and delay the gratification you would receive by saying or doing what would feel good without considering the consequences. Using "Fantasy Fast Forward" and getting clients to ask themselves, "Will I even remember this event as a significant turning point in my life 5 years from now?" can help. Having clients look for the "should" or "must" thoughts they are having that fuel frustration and using the ABC's of letting feelings go to deal with frustration can also help. Being asked to do a responsibility when it is not your turn is a frustrating event that is best managed by "Earning the right to complain" (i.e., doing the assigned responsibility before complaining about the injustice, "save your anger for the real injustices"). This demonstrates the level of self-control, responsibility and maturity that avoids authority conflicts and results in conflict resolution.

Emotional Accommodation: The ABC's of holding on to feelings

Learning accommodation to feelings is like the bathwater example where after drawing a hot bath you get yourself used to it by making yourself step in (stay, don't leave) accepting the initial uncomfortable feelings of the high temperature and staying there while you notice your body accommodating to that situation. Emotional accommodation can be viewed as thought stopping to achieve thoughtless peace through distraction therapy focusing on sensations. This creates a sort of "Time out" from the thinking that fuels emotions. Learning emotional accommodation is particularly important for clients who have voiced that "Ignoring it doesn't work." Emotional accommodation involves a mindfulness approach to emotional regulation which includes acceptance and accommodation to unwanted feelings.

Emotional accommodation in SRT involves the ABC's of holding on to feelings involves staying with unwanted feelings until clients accommodate to them and the feeling intensity drops to the point where the feeling is no longer a relapse trigger risk. This is the mindfulness approach to emotional regulation which involves acceptance and accommodation to unwanted feelings. Emotional accommodation is typically the intervention of choice when clients are upset, need to calm down but <u>don't know what triggered their feelings.</u>

Using Mindfulness Meditation for Distress Tolerance

Mindfulness "has been described as a kind of non-elaborative, nonjudgmental, present-centered awareness in which each thought, feeling, or sensation that arises in the attentional field is acknowledged and accepted as it is" (Bishop et.al. 2004). Mindfulness of emotions and sensations has been around for centuries as an essential part of eastern religious (particularly Buddhist) practice. Developing mindfulness is gradually developed with daily practice using meditation involving moment to moment awareness of one's subjective conscious experience from a first-person perspective. Mindfulness has been adopted in the west as a method to regulate emotions beginning with the development of Mindfulness-Based Stress Reduction in 1979 at the University of Massachusetts Medical school by Jon Kabat-Zinn.

Mindfulness training- There are many books, training courses and descriptions of this awareness training procedure involving clients "paying attention in a particular way, on purpose, in the present and non-judgmentally" (Jon Kabat-Zinn) in order to help clients answer the questions, "What do I notice right now?" or "How do I need to respond or be with this situation?" (e.g., "8 keys to practicing mindfulness: Practical strategies for emotional health and well-being" Mischke-Reeds, 2015). Mindfulness meditation typically involves daily short 10- 15 minute practice sessions where clients learn to sit and notice their body sensations keeping attention on the breath and body sensations, noticing wandering thoughts and gently redirecting the focus back to their body sensations (particularly breath). Although mindfulness meditation scripts are widely available at no cost on the internet, a recommended treatment approach to help clients with unhealthy, harmful behavior problems develop mindfulness is Mindfulness-Based Relapse Prevention for Addictive Behaviors. This treatment has a well-documented clinician's guide (Bowen, Chawla & Marlatt, 2011) and professional staff trainings are offered on the program website. While some clients prefer to have mindfulness script recordings made by their therapists for their daily practice, a good brief (12 minute) and longer (25 minute) guided mindfulness meditation exercise along with training information is available at no charge on Mindfulness-Based Relapse Prevention website (www.mindfulrp.com).

A Google or YouTube search on "Meditation scripts" will produce many demonstrations of mindfulness and a free 8-week self-guided course can be found at palousemindfulness.com. Three useful mindfulness interventions in emotional accommodation are: Mindful Breathing (i.e., SOBER breathing; Mindful breathing; Urge Surfing and; Mindfulness Meditation. Summaries of these interventions are provided in Appendix C.

Interpersonal Mindfulness

Mindfulness meditation has a strong focus on developing awareness of internal event responses (e.g., thoughts, feelings, sensations) generated by the environment (e.g., sensations from sitting in a chair, sounds in the room, wandering thoughts) all of which form a key first step toward managing unhealthy, harmful behaviors triggered by internal event responses. Before the 1979 introduction of mindfulness meditation awareness training with its intrapersonal approach to emotional regulation, Gestalt therapy was developed by Fritz Perls, Laura Perls and Paul Goodman in the 1940s and 1950s (Perls, Hefferline & Goodman, 1965). Gestalt therapy utilizes a similar but more interpersonal awareness training approach. Gestalt therapy assists the individual to become more self-responsible by becoming more self-aware which enables taking responsibility for emotions, becoming comfortable with self and accepting others (Resnick, 1974). Gestalt interpersonal interaction awareness trainings and books have been incorporated into Therapeutic Community addiction treatment programs since the early 1970's (e.g., Stevens, 1971).

Like mindfulness, Gestalt therapy awareness training also focuses upon the individual's experience in the present moment but pays careful attention to the bodily sensations that accompany strong emotions and expands awareness to relationship interactions. In short, Gestalt awareness training goes beyond being mindful of our internal event responses and into being mindful of how we interact with others, particularly in response to emotions triggered during our interactions with others (Latner, 2000; Wheeler & Axelsson, 2015). A more complete picture of the Gestalt interpersonal mindfulness approach along with training information is available online at The Gestalt Institute of Cleveland website (www.gestaltcleveland.org).

Since unhealthy, harmful behavior often can involve unhealthy, harmful interaction with others, being mindful of interactions with others is a key component of healthy lifestyle development. In fact, one of the criticisms of cognitive-behavioral therapy that can also be applied to traditional mindfulness meditation is the limitation in developing interpersonal awareness (Jacobson, 1987). However, mindfulness does appear to be expanding into interpersonal areas. For example, "lying mindfulness" has been a focus in adolescents with behavior problems (Wisner & Starzec, 2015). Expanding awareness training to social interactions enables examination of motivations or "where we are coming from" in terms of why we said or did something. An 8-week psychoeducational program integrating mindfulness and transactional analysis theory into mindfulness-based transactional analysis has been developed (Žvelc, Černetič & Košak, 2011) and in keeping with the Gestalt attention to the bodily sensations that accompany strong emotions, the view of the body as a manifest expression of the Child mode has resulted in sensory stimulation techniques (e.g., breathing, grounding) being utilized (e.g., Gowell, 1975).

Transactional Analysis was probably one of the first and certainly the most user-friendly approach to interpersonal awareness training. This awareness training approach was developed by psychiatrist Eric Berne in the late 1950's popularized by his bestselling book "Games People Play" (Berne, 1964) and described in a very user friendly form by psychiatrist Thomas Anthony Harris in his 1969 self-help book "I'm OK, You're OK" which became one of the best-selling self-help books in history. One important aspect of Transactional Analysis interpersonal awareness training that is similar to Gestalt therapy awareness training is the focus on responsibility. Specifically, in Transactional Analysis individuals are considered responsible for what happens in the future, no matter what has happened in the past. Since what we say or do to others elicits a response from others, our communication involves a transaction or exchange between people.

In Transactional Analysis, awareness training involves being mindful of where we are coming from (i.e., our position, stance, mode or ego state) when communicating with others. Careful attention is paid to three basic modes or ego states (i.e., the entire system of thoughts, feelings, and behaviors from which we interact with one another) that humans consistently use: the Parent, the Adult and; the Child. In the Parent mode, people behave, feel, and think like parents (or other parental figures). For example, a person may find themselves, advising, nurturing, criticizing or ordering others as they learned from an influential childhood figure. In the Child mode, people behave, feel, and think similarly to how they did in childhood. For example a person faced with faced with criticism, a challenge or disappointment may find themselves crying, sulking, being afraid. Likewise, an "inner child" reaction to an unexpected reward may result in joyful gestures of gratitude.

The goal of Transaction Analysis is to strengthen the Adult mode involving objective, rational, problem solving, fact finding, questioning, analyzing, helping, cooperating and positive planning. This is accomplished by awareness training on being mindful of and analyzing interactions with others. In Transactional Analysis, client self-efficacy is built through understanding of "where they are coming from" in their interactions with others. The above brief summary of Transactional Analysis was highly simplified and abbreviated. A more complete picture of the Transactional Analysis interpersonal mindfulness approach along with training information is available online at The International Transactional Analysis Association website (www.itaaworld.org).

Emotional Accommodation and The ABC's of holding on to feelings

Physical accommodation or adaptation is the hot tub example where you get used to the uncomfortable temperature by making yourself stay in the tub until your body gets used to it (i.e., accommodation). Typically your thoughts stop and all your focus is on the hot water sensation along with the cool air around you. Emotional accommodation is where you get used to or adapt to the uncomfortable feeling by staying with it until you get used to it. Being mindful or focusing on your body sensations and the environment around helps stop the thoughts that are fueling the unwanted feeling. Facing unwanted feelings in this manner is similar to the cotton candy experience where it's big, it's blue and it's in your face right up until you take a bite out of it and realize there wasn't that much to it. The ABC's of holding on to feelings is structured to help clients discover "the cotton candy effect" of facing unwanted feelings, accepting them and letting themselves accommodate to them. Remember urges and cravings are feelings too!

Mindfulness and the ABC's of holding on to feelings

Accepting and holding on to feelings (including urges or cravings), does not mean holding them inside and ruminating on them like holding a grudge. Holding on to feelings means accepting them and being mindful of them, not fighting them but staying with them and using mindfulness. This acceptance and accommodation to feelings helps prevent them from becoming overwhelming to the point where clients justify unhealthy, harmful actions based on unwanted feelings. Put another way, the ABC's of holding on to feelings involves using mindfulness to sit with the sensations until the emotion has been accommodated and lost its power to activate unhealthy, harmful behavior. Blending mindfulness into the ABC's of holding on to feelings in SRT involves the following three structured steps to help clients discover their ability to stay in the moment with sensation awareness until the thoughts fueling emotions (and the associated urge to act them out) have stopped and the emotion has been accommodated.[3]

Emotional Accommodation: The ABC's of holding on to feelings

Emotional accommodation in SRT involves three structured steps to help clients discover their ability to stay in the moment with sensation awareness until the thoughts fueling emotional impact (and associated urge to act them out) have stopped

"A" Accept the distressing feeling (urge or craving). Accept that distress and discomfort are a real part of everyone's life that we need to accommodate. Accept the trigger situation. Don't deny the distress. Receive the feeling. Don't avoid it. Don't distract yourself with activity, slow down and let yourself feel.

"B" Begin getting used to the feeling (urge or craving). Allow yourself to accommodate and adapt to it. Give yourself permission to have the feeling. Stay with the feeling. Don't fight it. Visualize easing into a very hot tub, being uncomfortable at first but getting used to it as you stay with it (accommodating). Get honest with yourself and admit there is no "fight or flight" survival need to protect yourself from the feeling you are experiencing. Accept the fact that feelings can't hurt you, but telling yourself "I can't stand it" triggers reactions that can hurt you. Tell yourself, "I dislike this feeling but I can deal with it and don't have to act it out" or "This feeling is disturbing and disappointing but not dangerous so there is no need to take action." Then politely tell yourself that you have decided to hold on to the feeling until you get used to it as opposed to venting it an a harmful manner.

"C" Channel the feelings (urges or cravings) to the right place at the right time. Give yourself time to channel feelings to the right place. Tell yourself, "I can always act on my feelings tomorrow." Continue sensory awareness. Find a breathing space where you can sit and be mindful of your sensations. For example, if you are in the mall, find a bench near a water feature where you can hear the relaxing noise of the babbling water. If you are in a noisy grocery, go outside and sit on one of the benches in front of the store. Use mindful awareness of your breathing to stay centered and balanced (see description In Appendix C, p.266 on Mindful Breathing).

Since moods and urges are like ocean waves that start small, swell build to a crest and then subsides and slides into the sand, imagine that you are mood and urge surfer. You see a mood ocean swell and paddle out to it, you catch the mood wave and ride the wave, which usually lasts only for several minutes until the wave subsides and slides into the sand. While you are riding your mood or wave, stay on top of your feelings by focusing on your surroundings, your sensations and your breath. Stay balanced, observing the flow of your feelings throughout your body so you don't fall into the ocean of mood triggering thoughts (See Appendix C, p.267). Use your wise, responsible mind to channel your feelings with mindfulness meditation (See Appendix C, p.268). Continue to be aware of your surroundings and the body sensations associated with the feeling, just notice them, don't attach any thoughts to them, don't fight or struggle with them, just be aware of the sensations, let them be and allow thoughtless peace right now. Stay in the moment. When thoughts that trigger feelings and urges come up, tell them "not now." Think of the Chinese finger trap, stop struggling and pulling against the feeling, just let it be so you can get free.

Treatment Exercise: Emotional Acceptance and Accommodation
The Chinese finger trap is used by Dr. Steven Hayes in Acceptance and Commitment Therapy to provide an example of what happens when we struggle against unwanted feelings as opposed to sitting with our sensations, accepting our feelings and letting ourselves accommodate to them. Pass out Chinese finger traps to your clients and have them push the finger trap on to both of their index fingers. Ask them to try to get out of the trap by fighting it (i.e., pulling both index fingers away from each other hard). Then ask them to try and get out of the trap by accepting it, not fighting it, moving towards it and going with it. Have your clients alternate between fighting it and accepting it until they get in touch with the need to stop struggling and "let it be so you can get free." Have your clients discuss the analogy of fighting against unwanted feelings (or trying to ignore them) and facing unwanted feelings, accepting them and letting themselves accommodate to those feelings until we are used to them and they subside. Then take the problem issue to the right place.

Using the ABC's of holding on to feelings:
Unhealthy eating, substance use and harmful sexual behavior examples

Practical Application Example: Obesity treatment referral- Ted
Accepting/Holding on to food cravings
Ted, a 40-year-old Euro-American outpatient weight-management referral was unaware that his decision to enter the mall to buy a pair of walking shoes through the food court entrance was the source of his powerful food cravings. He stated, "I was fighting an awful craving for pizza and the urge to have some before I left the mall. I don't know where it came from. It just hit me and then I couldn't get it out of my mind."

Ted had to use "the 3 G's" to prevent relapse: Get out (without hesitation, he went to the mall bathroom and washed his face with cold water, tried to ignore the cravings and figure out where they came from); Get honest ("I can't ignore these cravings and I don't know what triggered them") and; Get Responsible (by telling himself, *"Since I don't know what triggered this craving, I need to use the ABC's of holding on to cravings to keep from acting on them"*). He talked himself through the ABC's of accepting and holding on to cravings go as follows...

- <u>Accept the distressing feeling (urge or craving)</u>- and the situation triggering it. Receive the feeling. Don't drift into dwelling on the problem (emotional rumination).

     Ted was frustrated as he could usually identify what triggered his cravings. He started thinking, "I'm stupid and weak, I can't stand this feeling and don't even know where it came from. I need to eat something to get rid of it." He has to remind himself to accept the feeling. "I need to stop putting myself down and working myself up. I need to slow down and just let myself feel."

- <u>Begin getting used to the feeling (urge or craving)</u>- Give yourself permission to have the feelings and not fight it. Be honest about it.

     Ted got honest with himself and admitted, "Cravings won't kill me, but telling myself I can't stand these cravings will kill my diet. This craving is disturbing but not dangerous so the only action I need to take is to go to a calm place like the mall waterfall, then sit with my sensations and feelings until I get used to them. I need to think of my pizza cravings like the Chinese finger trap, stop struggling and pulling against it and just let it be so I can get free."

- <u>Channel the feeling (urge or craving) to the right place at the right time</u>- Continue sensory awareness. Stay in the moment and surf the mood or urge until it subsides. Then take the problem issue to the right place (See Appendix C).

     Ted sat down in front of the mall waterfall and started his mindfulness meditation. He became aware of the calming sounds of the babbling waterfall echoing off of the high mall ceiling and store walls. The water sounds helped him imagine himself on a surfboard, staying on top of his wave of feelings while being very aware of his breath, his sensations and surroundings. His eyes drifted into a blur as he noted the sounds of hard soled shoes and high heels clacking on the mall tile floor. He felt the cool surface of the granite slab he was sitting on and noticed himself smiling as his craving subsided and he realized that they hit right after he walked through the food court. He took one final deep breath, got up and decided to take his problem to the right place by going to the mall map an looking up an alternative exit from the mall that was nearest to the shoe store and out of sight from the food court where he entered. Walking around the outside of the mall would give him a chance to try out his new walking shoes.

Practical Application Example: Substance abuse treatment referral- Ray Accepting/Holding on to alcohol cravings

Three months after his graduation from residential drug and alcohol treatment, Ray a 35-year-old regular AA member was doing great. He had regained his weight in rehab, looked healthy again, felt much better, got his old job as a luxury auto detailer back and was receiving constant positive feedback for his excellent work. Things were going so well in his relationship with Gina that they were discussing moving back in together. He invited Gina to his boss's Saturday afternoon office birthday party where his promotion to assistant manager was announced. On the way back, Gina suggested going out that evening and celebrating his promotion. They were in the middle of a discussion of nice restaurants when Ray got slammed by cravings to drink. This was the really frustrating part for Ray. Everything was going good including being able to identify and avoid or escape his drinking triggers but this seemed to come out of nowhere and he was starting to think about restaurants that had great bars.

Ray had to use "the 3 G's" to prevent relapse: Get out (without hesitation, he had to escape his high-risk situation, change it up, get out of the celebration conversation, get out of the car and get to a safe place where he was not likely to act on his cravings); Get honest (He told Gina that he just got hit out of nowhere with strong cravings to drink, was starting think of celebration restaurants with good bars and needed to get to a safe place where he could not to act on his cravings until he figures out how to handle it) and; Get Responsible (by telling himself, *"Since I don't know what triggered this craving, I need to use the ABC's of holding on to cravings to keep from acting on them until they pass"*). He talked himself through the ABC's of accepting and holding on to cravings go as follows...

- Accept the distressing feeling (urge or craving)- and the situation triggering it. Receive the feeling. Don't drift into dwelling on the problem (emotional rumination).
    Ray admitted, "Getting hit hard by cravings to drink when everything was going so well totally caught me off guard and I'm frustrated that I don't know what triggered these cravings. I guess I thought that after treatment cravings would only come during tough times when expected. I need to accept that cravings to drink are just part of having a history of alcoholism and stop dwelling on the need to always be able to figure out what triggers these cravings."
- Begin getting used to the feeling (urge or craving)- Give yourself permission to have the feelings and not fight it. Be honest about it.
    Ray told himself, "It's OK for me to have cravings to drink as long as I face those cravings and don't just get rid of them by drinking again. The important thing isn't whether you ever get cravings again after treatment, it's what you have learned to do with your cravings that counts. Instead of going to a restaurant with a good bar where I can drink to get rid of my craving, I need to go someplace that is peaceful and impossible to drink so I can let the craving run its course."
- Channel the feeling (urge or craving) to the right place at the right time- Continue sensory awareness. Stay in the moment and surf the mood or urge until it subsides. Then take the problem issue to the right place (See Appendix C).

Ray told Gina about his craving to drink and his need to go somewhere peaceful to sit in silence and let it pass. She drove to the local park where they sat on a picnic bench together in the warm sun. Ray started his mindfulness meditation beginning by focusing on his breath and allowing himself to stay in the moment with his sensations. He imagined himself far away out on the ocean surfing his urge, keeping his balance on his surfboard to stay with his urge wave until it washes out onto the warm sandy beach. He felt the gentle touch of Gina's hand on his and the comforting warm heat of the sun on his body as he drifted into the soft sound of leaves rustling in the warm breeze. He focused on his breath and the warm air coming into his nostrils, noticed the top of the picnic table supporting his back, the feel of his feet on the ground and the nearby sound of chirping birds in the trees above him and the distant sound of children playing on the swing set. His craving had passed. He felt calm and relieved as he asked Gina to walk the park trail with him. They walked and talked and sat at benches along the several mile trail.

Ray took his craving problem to the right place at the right time. He and Gina went to an AA meeting that evening where he shared all of the good things that had happened in his life since he became sober. He laughed as he told the group about his unrealistic expectation that rehab would somehow give him crystal ball insight into all of his cravings. He ended by telling the group about his promotion and using the ABC's of holding onto cravings to keep from acting on them. His meeting members gave him a round of applause for his his sober accomplishments.

Practical Application Example: Sex offender treatment referral- Dan
Accepting/Holding on to harmful sexual urges
Dan a 16-year-old Euro-American male in sex-offender treatment was promoted to the re-entry phase of his community residential treatment. The good news was that Dan was doing well and ready for transition from online school back into public high school. The bad news was that Dan was shy, didn't know anyone in this new school and was getting nervous as his first day approached. It was finally here. Dan stepped off the bus and toward the front doors where everyone was heading. He entered the building and was bombarded by emotional reactions including: happiness to be back in school followed by fear of failure; excitement from seeing many attractive girls followed by shyness and social anxiety about meeting new people and; feeling inadequate and fear of being put down followed by the need to act tough to cover it. He got through it, got back on the bus, got back to his treatment facility, got dinner and got through the homework he received. Despite emotional overload, Dan's science lab partner Lisa was really cute, actually easy to talk to, seemed interested in him and had given him her number to discuss their first project. That night as he lay in bed thinking about his cute lab partner, his romantic fantasy of Lisa was interrupted by unwanted sexual thoughts of his victim Kyla. Dan had been in treatment long enough to know that it was definitely wrong to allow his past sexually aggressive urges that he had for Kyla get mixed in with romantic thoughts of Lisa. He was afraid of his impulses and had no idea what triggered his past sexually aggressive urges. What he did know was that he had to stop this or it would likely lead to targeting Lisa as a victim of his sexual aggression.

Dan had to use "the 3 G's" to prevent relapse: Get out (without hesitation, he had to escape this high-risk situation, get out of bed, get out of his room and get out of the isolation that enables deviant sexual fantasy/urges); Get honest (He admitted that he needed to get to a safe place where he could not continue his deviant sexual fantasy/urge until he figures out how to handle it) and; Get Responsible (by telling himself, *"Since I don't know what triggered this urge, I need to use the ABC's of holding on to urges until they pass"*). He talked himself through the ABC's of accepting and holding on to urges go as follows...

- Accept the distressing feeling (urge or craving)- and the situation triggering it. Receive the feeling. Don't drift into dwelling on the problem (emotional rumination).

Dan said "I know how to let an urge go when I can identify what triggered it but I'm afraid of my impulses when an urge comes on and I don't know where it came from. I need to stop hating myself for having these thoughts and start accepting them as part of my sexual behavior problem that I need to manage."

- <u>Begin getting used to the feeling (urge or craving)</u>- Give yourself permission to have the feelings and not fight it. Be honest about it.

Dan went through what he had learned in his sex offender treatment. He told himself, "Having sexual feelings is part of human nature. There's no need to fight healthy sexual urges about romantic relationships with consenting girls that are my age like Lisa. But I need to get honest with myself when deviant sexual urges hit and I don't know what triggered them, I need to get to a place where I can't act on that urge and use my ABC's of holding on until my urge passes."

- <u>Channel the feeling (urge or craving) to the right place at the right time</u>- Continue sensory awareness. Stay in the moment and with the mood or urge until it subsides. Then take the problem issue to the right place (See Appendix C).

Dan went out on the front porch and sat on one of the big deck chairs facing the street and started his mindfulness medication. It was late, dark and the streetlights were on. He closed his eyes, focused on his breathing, noticed the warm summer air coming in his nostrils, felt his arms being supported by the soft armchair and his feet on the wood porch. He could hear the crickets chirping between the occasional passing swish of a car. He felt completely relaxed, took in one last deep breath and opened his eyes. His urge had subsided. He got up, went back to his room and took his urge to the right place by journaling his experience in his Situation Response Analysis Log to discuss in tomorrow's treatment group (See Table 5.7).

Table 5.7	Situation Response Analysis Log- Dan	
Situation	**Response**	**Analysis**
Date & Description (What actually happened)	**My Thoughts, Feelings and Behavior**	1. Was my response positive/helpful or negative/harmful? 2. What do I need to do next time?
5/30, 11pm - It was my first day back at high school where I met Lisa. She was cute, easy to talk to and seemed interested in me. That night my romantic fantasy of Lisa was crashed by thoughts of my past victim Kyla. I had no idea what triggered those thoughts. I was afraid that I would start having sexually aggressive urges about Lisa and ruin everything.	**Thoughts-** I don't know what triggered these sexually aggressive thoughts and can't let them get mixed in with my romantic feelings about Lisa. **Feelings-** Sexually aroused thinking about Lisa, upset when images of what I did to my victim Kyla popped up and took over. Afraid of my past impulses might come out on Lisa. **Behavior-** Left my isolated high-risk situation, went to a safe place where I couldn't continue deviant sexual fantasy and used my ABC's of holding on until my urge passed.	**Thoughts:** _X_Positive Coping; __Negative Coping **Feelings:** __Tolerable; _X_Stressful; __Unbearable **Behavior:** _X_Healthy/helpful; __Unhealthy/harmful **My positive plan for next time is...** Continue to use "the 3 G's" to prevent relapse. Use the ABC's of letting go when I know what triggered the urge and use the ABC's of holding on when I don't know what triggered the urge. Continue to talk with my staff and group about how I am doing with Lisa.

Using the ABC's of holding on to feelings:
Other Unhealthy, harmful behavior examples

Practical Application Example:
Accommodating to unwanted feelings from infidelity
Examples of using the "ABC's of holding on to feelings" to accommodate to feelings of depression, anxiety and anger after a relationship break up due to infidelity are described in Table 5.8.

Table 5.8 **The ABC's of Holding on to Feelings- Relationship cheating & break up**		
Accept the feeling- and the situation triggering it. Receive the feeling. Don't drift into…	**Begin getting used to it-** Give yourself permission to have an emotion and not fight it. Be honest about it.	**Channel the feeling at the right time-** Continue sensory awareness. Stay in the moment. Surf the mood/urge until it subsides. Then take the problem to the right place.
Depressive thinking that the break up is too awful to live through.	I feel depressed but it's OK. Feelings can't kill me, telling myself "I can't stand it" is what will kill me.	Let your thoughts stop. Notice your breathing, the feeling of your head in your hands, hear the clock on the wall tick. Let it be as it is, let yourself accommodate.
Anxious thinking that you will never find anyone else	It's OK to feel anxious. Anxiety is disturbing, not dangerous.	Enter thoughtless peace. Notice how your abdomen rises and falls as you breathe. Feel the chair against your back. Just be there.
Angry thinking about getting even for cheating	It's OK feel angry. Anger doesn't hurt people, angry decisions do.	Let thinking go. Just sit with your sensations. Notice your nostrils as you breath in and out. Feel your feet on the floor, stay in the moment

Practical Application Example:
Accommodating to unwanted feelings from bereavement
Examples of three family members using the "ABC's of holding on to feelings" to accommodate to feelings of depression, anxiety and anger after a vehicular homicide are described in Table 5.9 below.

Table 5.9 **The ABC's of Holding on to Feelings (Father killed by drunk driver)**		
Accept the feeling- and the situation triggering it. Receive the feeling. Don't drift into…	**Begin getting used to it-** Give yourself permission to have an emotion and not fight it. Be honest about it.	**Channel the feeling at the right time-** Continue sensory awareness. Stay in the moment. Surf the mood/urge until it subsides. Then take the problem to the right place.
Depressive thinking that the loss is too awful to live through. **(Wife)**	I feel depressed but it's OK. Feelings can't kill me, telling myself "I can't stand it" is what will kill me.	Let your thoughts stop. Notice your breathing, the feeling of your head in your hands, hear the clock on the wall tick. Let it be as it is, let yourself accommodate .
Anxious thinking about what will happen to the family **(Daughter)**	It's OK to feel anxious. Anxiety is disturbing, not dangerous.	Enter thoughtless peace. Notice how your abdomen rises and falls as you breathe. Feel the chair against your back. Just be there.
Angry thinking about getting the person who did it **(Son)**	It's OK feel angry. Anger doesn't hurt people, angry decisions do.	Let thinking go, Just sit with your sensations. Notice your nostrils as you breath in and out. Feel your feet on the floor, stay in the moment

Treatment Exercise: The ABC's of holding on to feelings

If you are familiar with basic mindfulness meditation (see "Mindfulness training", p. 95), have your clients practice mindfulness meditation daily. If urges and cravings are present, have your clients also practice Urge Surfing (Appendix C). Using a therapy session script that matches an audio homework script mindfulness meditation or Urge Surfing that clients can listen to each day on their own should help increase the frequency of recommended daily practice. After your clients are proficient with basic mindfulness meditation, review the brief summaries of the ABC's of holding on to feelings (See Table 5.6 and 5.7) and explain the ABC format to your clients. Then have them discuss an example of their own using a recent event that was emotionally distressing and triggered a feeling that put them at risk for relapse on the unhealthy, harmful behavior that resulted in their referral for treatment. Guide them through the ABC's with their example providing the same mindfulness narrative you have been using in sessions and for daily practice during the "Continue body sensation awareness" portion. After mindfulness meditation, ask the client for a right place or a positive direction to take their trigger issue.

Integrate Emotional Regulation into the Relapse Prevention Plan

In high risk situations for relapse first Avoid Trouble with the "3 G's".
1. Get out (Remove yourself);
2. Get honest (Block the thought)- Challenge, "I must vent (get rid of) this feeling right here and now." Tell yourself "It's probably best if I take time to manage this feeling, rather than just vent it."
3. Get Responsible (Substitute a more responsible thought)- Go to a non-stressful place and use Emotional Regulation, (i.e., the ABC's of letting feelings go or the ABC's of holding on to feelings) to calm down, manage the feeling and avoid acting on it.
    − Note: Emotional Regulation is not a subset of Relapse Prevention, it's a separate skill that supports Relapse Prevention and is best used after leaving stressful situations.

Emotional Accommodation Skills Practice: The Situation Response Analysis Log

Have clients journal their progress in regulating their emotions to avoid relapse using the ABC's of Letting Feelings Go and The ABC's of Holding On to Feelings in a Situation Response Analysis log. These daily logs that document their high-risk situations, their response to those situations and their analysis of their response need to be reviewed and discussed in each treatment session. Basic client log instructions are listed in Table 4.7 on p. 61 and several Situation Response Analysis Log formats are presented in Appendix B, p. 263.

Emotional Accommodation (Mindfulness) Research Support Summary:
Emotional accommodation has clinical roots in mindfulness popularized by Dialectical Behavior Therapy (DBT) dating back over 20 years (Linehan, 1987). Emotional accommodation in DBT has strong empirical support as evidenced by seven well-controlled randomized clinical trials from four independent research teams and has been effectively adapted to address a number of conditions involving harmful behavior beginning with borderline personality disorder treatment and including substance abuse, suicidal adolescents, eating disorder patients and correctional setting inmates (Robins & Chapman, 2004; Lynch et al., 2006). For further information, see the DBT Skills Training Manual, Second Edition (Linehan, 2015) and Mindfulness-based Cognitive Therapy: Distinctive features (Crane, 2009).

Research support for the use of mindfulness in emotional regulation through acceptance and accommodation has been established in a number of treatment programs. The targeted mindfulness practices in Mindfulness-Based Relapse Prevention appears to support have strengthened client ability to monitor and cope with craving or negative affect discomfort. This has resulted in an added benefit over cognitive behavioral relapse prevention and treatment as usual (12 step programming and psychoeducation) in reducing drug use and heavy drinking at 12-month follow-up (Bowen et. al., 2014). Mindfulness-Based Stress Reduction originally developed and published by Jon Kabat-Zinn (1991) at the University of Massachusetts has been established as an effective in reducing stress, depression, anxiety, emotional distress and improving the quality of life of healthy individuals (Khoury et. al. 2015). The Acceptance and Commitment Therapy approach of using acceptance and mindfulness may be as effective in treating anxiety disorders, depression, addiction, and somatic health problems as established psychological interventions and appears to be a promising intervention for substance use disorders (e.g., A-Tjak et. al., 2015; Lee et.al. 2015). The core mindfulness exercises, emotional observation and acceptance approach used in Dialectical Behavior Therapy developed by Dr. Marsha Linehan originally designed to address unhealthy, self harmful behaviors in borderline personality disorder has had a positive impact on controlling the self-destructive behavior of clients with borderline personality disorder symptoms and in decreasing unhealthy eating episodes in clients with eating disorders (e.g., Lenz et. al., 2014; Panos et. al., 2014). The Mindfulness-Based Cognitive Therapy approach of helping depressed clients step away from their automatic depressing thoughts by expanding their awareness to all incoming thoughts and feelings, accepting them and just observing them, not reacting to them has been established as effective in the treatment of depression (Galante, Iribarren & Pearce, 2013).

Mindfulness meditation has been applied to the treatment of multiple forms of unhealthy, harmful behavior including: sexually abusive behavior (e.g., Jennings et. al. 2013); physically abusive behavior (e.g., Shorey, Larson & Cornelius, 2014); problem gambling (e.g., Toneatto, Pillai & Courtice, 2014); substance abuse (e.g., Witkiewitz et. al. 2014) and; trust abuse/lying mindfulness (e.g., Wisner & Starzec, 2015).

Emotional Regulation Summary

In summary, SRT employs two basic strategies for emotional regulation: 1) Emotional dissipation (i.e., helping clients let go of unwanted feelings) and; 2) Emotional accommodation (i.e., helping clients accept and hold onto unwanted feelings until they subside). SRT adopts a Rational Emotive Behavior Therapy approach to emotional dissipation with "The ABC's of letting feelings go" to challenge thoughts that fuel emotional distress in order to dissipate it below the threshold of harmful acting out. SRT employs a mindfulness-based approach to emotional accommodation with "The ABC's of holding on to feelings" to help clients accept and accommodate to emotional distress to avoid acting it out. Emotional dissipation (i.e., an REBT approach with ABC's of letting feelings go) is typically the intervention of choice when clients are upset, need to calm down and know what triggered their feelings. Emotional accommodation (i.e., a mindfulness-based approach like ABC's of holding on to feelings) is typically the intervention of choice when clients are upset, need to calm down but don't know what triggered their feelings.

Since many clinicians are familiar with cognitive-behavioral therapy, cognitive restructuring for emotional dissipation of unhealthy, harmful behavior requires little if any new training for them. However, it is important to note that emotional accommodation can be quite useful when the client cannot identify the trigger thought needed in cognitive restructuring to dissipate their distress. In SRT, emotional regulation involves knowing when to accept, hold on to and accommodate to feelings and when to dispute the irresponsible thoughts needed to let go of unwanted feelings.

"You gotta know when to hold 'em and know when to fold 'em"- Kenny Rogers

Helping clients "Think it Through" with Decisional Balance
"It's choice, not chance that determines your destiny"-- Jean Nidetch (1923- 2015)

Every time we do something, we have made a decision to do it. If you were ever asked "What were you thinking?", chances are that you didn't think your decision through before you took action. Thinking it though by balancing the benefits against the drawbacks before making the decision is referred to as "decisional balance" in treatment manuals. Responsible decisions protect recovery from unhealthy, harmful behavior while irresponsible decisions set the occasion for relapse back into unhealthy harmful behavior. Decisional balance in SRT involves making responsible decisions by balancing the benefits and drawbacks of choices before taking action. Like playing checkers, Decisional Balance is a foresight (thinking ahead) development skill that involves asking yourself, "If I make this move, what could happen?" Decisional Balance was originally developed to help clients through their stages of change in letting go of unhealthy, harmful behavior. Decisional balance can be applied to stopping harmful behaviors (e.g., smoking, unhealthy eating, drug use, delinquent behavior) as well as starting healthy behaviors (e.g., exercising, safer sex, condom use, sunscreen use).[1] A version of decisional balance referred to as "triage" (French for "to sort") is routinely used by emergency room physicians to weigh out the benefits and drawbacks of who should get treatment next.

Decisional Balance: "Straight to the Point"
The point of this section is to help clients: become aware of what they need to know; develop the skills they need to use and; the tolerance they need in order to make responsible decisions. How to balance the benefits against the drawbacks of important decisions that can result in relapse, create relationship problems and interfere with life goals will be covered. For short term, time limited treatment, focus on Responsibility Training in Section 1, Decisional Balance: Thinking it Through, p. 114.
Decisional Balance Goals and Objectives
Awareness Training Goal: Increase client awareness of the primary contributing factors to responsible decisions.
   Objectives: Clients will be able to identify the primary contributors to irresponsible decisions that can result in relapse, create relationship problems and/or interfere with life goals
Responsibility Training Goal: Develop responsible decision-making skills and strategies.
   Objectives: Clients will be able to use the "Reality Check" for on the spot decisions 3 Reality Scales to weight out decisions, i.e., "the 3 S's" Survival scale- How necessary for my survival is it? Success scale- How important for my success is it? Severity scale- How severe would the consequences be?
Tolerance Training Goal: Improve tolerance for positive change.
   Objectives: Clients will apply decisional balance skills to help them tolerate making important positive changes in their lives.

Decisional Balance is required for responsible decision-making and involves thinking through important decisions by balancing the benefits against the drawbacks of taking an action that is being considered prior to taking action.

Treatment Exercise: Decisional Balance Benefits

Balancing the benefits against the drawbacks before taking an action in emotionally charged or other high-risk situations for relapse:

- Takes some time which allows emotions cool down and delays impulsive responses;
- Activates rational thinking which helps prevent justifying actions based on feelings;
- Requires considering consequences to self and others, which develops foresight and role reversal ability.

Desire to avoid consequences can provide initial motivation for learning decisional balance skills. Have your clients write and discuss examples of relapse back into unhealthy, harmful behavior as a result of acting on impulses, justifying actions based on feelings or not considering consequences. Reinforce getting honest about the consequences to self and others.

The ART of Decisional Balance

The ART of Decisional Balance involves: Awareness training on the impact of client decisions to self and others; Responsibility training on learning decisional balance tools to weigh the benefits and drawbacks of important decisions and; Tolerance training on learning to tolerate change in order to maintain positive, healthy decisions (Figure 6.1). Decisional Balance is needed to make responsible decisions that avoid unhealthy, harmful behavior relapse. In addition, by helping clients "Think it through", Decisional Balance develops the foresight needed to achieve healthy recovery, healthy relationship and healthy career goals. In order for healthy, positive lifestyle change to occur, the ART of Decisional Balance needs to be applied to developing: a healthy body; healthy relationships and; a healthy life direction (See Figure 2.1).

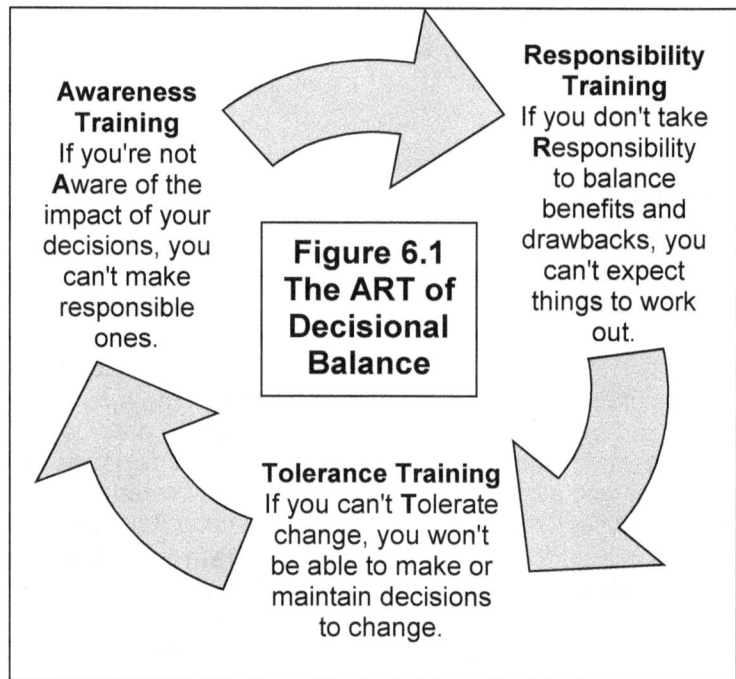

Awareness Training — If you're not Aware of the impact of your decisions, you can't make responsible ones.

Responsibility Training — If you don't take Responsibility to balance benefits and drawbacks, you can't expect things to work out.

Tolerance Training — If you can't Tolerate change, you won't be able to make or maintain decisions to change.

Figure 6.1 The ART of Decisional Balance

Awareness Training in Decisional Balance and Other Responsible Decision Factors

"If you're not Aware of the impact of your decisions, you can't make responsible ones"

Awareness Training Goal: Increase client awareness of the primary contributing factors to responsible decisions.

Objectives: Clients will be able to identify the primary contributors to irresponsible decisions that can result in relapse, create relationship problems and/or interfere with life goals

In order to learn the responsible decision-making that protects recovery clients need to be aware of the primary contributing factors to the irresponsible decisions that set the occasion for relapse and jeopardize recovery from unhealthy, harmful behavior.

Primary Contributing Factors to Irresponsible Decisions include...

1. Not considering consequences or thinking it through (Decisional Balance deficit)
2. Making "Foresight Deficit Decisions"
3. Not being aware of irresponsible thinking
4. Irrational or unrealistic hope
5. Problem priorities
6. Exaggerated needs

Awareness Training in Decisional Balance

1. Not Considering Consequences or Thinking it through (Decisional Balance deficit)

Not considering consequences or thinking it through results in irresponsible decisions that set the occasion for unhealthy, harmful behavior. Not taking the time to weigh out the benefits and drawbacks of decisions can result in severe consequences to health, relationships, success and depending on the type of unhealthy, harmful behavior on survival. In addition to resulting in consequences that clients don't want, not thinking decisions through can prevent clients from getting what they want in life.

Bottom line: Failing to consider consequences usually results in consequences. "What the hell was I thinking" is by far the most frequent expression of self-disappointment uttered by clients who relapsed as a result of making important decisions without thinking their decisions through and considering the consequences before taking action. Put another way, "Nobody ever did, or ever will, escape the consequences of his choices"-- Alfred Montapert (1906- 1997).

Not considering consequences or thinking it through: A Case Example

Hope was a 32-year-old never married female on probation after losing her job due to physical complications of morbid obesity. This resulted in a 9-month downward spiral of "couch surfing" with various weed smoking friends ending in drug and prostitution charges as a result of getting pulled into Internet dating of what she referred to as "chubby chasers." At her first court ordered AA meeting she met Geno who volunteered to give her a ride back to the homeless shelter after the meeting. After several rides back to the shelter, Geno asked her to stop for coffee with him. After several "coffee and conversation" stops on the way back to the shelter, Geno asked her if she wanted to move in with him. Although Hope knew that Geno was court ordered to AA for drunk and disorderly after being divorced for domestic violence, she only focused on getting out of the shelter. She didn't weight the benefits of staying at the shelter until she finished her vocational training, found a job and got her own place against the drawbacks of moving in with someone who was divorced for drinking and anger issues.

As a result of not thinking it through, Hope left the shelter before completing her cosmetology training making her totally dependent on Geno for food and shelter. Spending as much time as possible with her old weed smoking friends just to get out of the house and away from Genos violent nature resulted in a return to smoking marijuana. Regular marijuana smoking stimulated her appetite and triggered a return to unhealthy eating which resulted in regaining 50 of the 75lbs she lost. Feeling bad about her weight gain while being high resulted in getting involved in Internet dating again to get complements and boost her self-esteem. Finally, failing multiple urine toxicology screenings resulted receiving an upcoming court date for probation violation and Hope has been asking herself, "What was I thinking? Why didn't I stay at the shelter, finish cosmetology school, get a job and move into my own place?"

Treatment Exercise: Not considering consequences or thinking it through

Hold a discussion with your clients about times when they made bad choices as a result of not thinking it through or considering consequences. Have them write out, read and discuss "the worst decision I ever made" along with the consequences they experienced as a result of not thinking their decision through before taking action. File this in their chart to be used later.

Awareness Training in Other Irresponsible Decision Factors

2. Foresight Deficit Decisions
"The road to hell is paved with good intentions"
-- John Ray circa 1670

Foresight Deficit Decisions are foresight slips that often lead clients into high-risk situations for relapse due to a lack of foresight or not looking ahead. The decision to enter a high-risk situation for relapse is often the result of thinking that is not apparently relevant or seemingly important to falling into a relapse. Thus, these foresight slips are also known as Apparently Irrelevant Decisions, Seemingly Irrelevant Decisions or Seemingly Unimportant Decisions because if you just look at the decision itself and not at what could come afterwards, the decision does not appear to be or seem to be related to relapse. These foresight slips have been observed and described in the literature for over 25 years (e.g., Jenkins-Hall & Marlatt, 1989; NIDA Archives, 1998; Yokley, 2008).

Nowhere is the importance of developing self-awareness and using foresight as clear as in the case of Foresight Deficit Decisions. Foresight Deficit Decisions are decisions made without using foresight or thinking ahead and without awareness of potential high-risk situations. These decisions pave the road to unhealthy, harmful behavior relapse often beginning with good intentions. Foresight Deficit Decisions or foresight slips can lead to relapse in many of not most forms of unhealthy, harmful behavior. The following example illustrates that the key to maintaining recovery from harmful behavior is developing enough self-awareness to avoid the foresight slips that lead to relapse.

A Foresight Deficit Decision case example:
Multiple forms of unhealthy, harmful behavior

Overweight, over the top football fan Shane was on parole for statutory rape (sexual intercourse with an underage female), assault of a police officer and drug trafficking (possession of a large amount of marijuana) all while under the influence of alcohol. On game day, his equally over the top football fan and past cellmate Billy came in all excited about stealing club box seat tickets to the game. Billy went on and on about how club box seat tickets were the best seats in the house and included full meal catering, an open bar, really hot waitresses and there was always floating half time parties between club boxes. Shane couldn't stop screaming "Oh hell yes!" when Billy asked him if he wanted to go.

Shane was totally focused on the game. He began reciting his team's history against the opposing team and announced his good intentions to be the designated driver and keep Billy out of trouble. Shane told himself that he was *only* going to see the game, he would *just* drink non-alcoholic beer and he *must* be there to look after Billy because Billy had his back when they were cellmates. He thought that since he hadn't been in trouble since he was released on parole 3 months ago, he could easily handle himself and watch over Billy. He told himself that football was the only exciting thing left for him in life now that drinking, smoking weed and sexual acting out were on his parole rules and off the table. He was completely aware that his need for excitement was ramped up by this football road trip and partially aware of his need for acceptance by Billy who had watched his back in the past.

Shane was doing well, drinking O'Doul's non-alcoholic beer, eating a few peanuts and cheering on his team without yelling profanity up until half time when an out of control party from another club box spilled over into their club box. He was completely caught off guard when an attractive, young, intoxicated, female wearing the same jersey as Shane walked in and locked eyes with him. They exchanged smiles and he waved her over. She made her way through the crowd, plopped down in his lap like they were lifelong partners and introduced herself as Sherry. Since the label of his non-alcoholic beer was facing away from her, Sherry had no idea that Shane was not really drinking and signaled to the waitress who brought two tall draft beers in ice-cold frosty mugs. He was definitely interested in Sherry, knew he shouldn't drink on parole or as the designated driver but told himself he would order a full meal to counter the alcohol. That worked until Sherry started ordering shots after which Shane basically said, "Screw it, I blew it" and got totally trashed.

Unfortunately, after half time when the game resumed one couple from an opposing team club box remained behind and began cheering loudly for their team. Sherry went off on them screaming "Get the f@#k out of here!" When the guy stepped up in Sherry's face, Shane got pissed and punched him out. Security arrived, the incident was written up, everyone's tickets were checked and Shane told himself that his statement that "My best friend gave this ticket to me" wasn't actually lying. The visiting couple declined to press charges and were escorted back to their club box. This prompted an even wilder celebration during which both Shane and Sherry were going over the top with their making out. The next morning, Shane was awakened by Sherry shaking him and yelling "Get up, get up, I need a ride home, my parents are going to kill me!" On the plus side, it turns out that Sherry was 19 years old. On the minus side she was too young to drink and too intoxicated to give consent. In summary, the Foresight Deficit Decision to go a football game as the designated driver for Billy resulted in relapse on multiple unhealthy, harmful behaviors and parole violation.

Treatment Exercise: Identifying Foresight Slips

Read Shane's Foresight Deficit Decision case example to clients. Then hold a discussion and see how many foresight slips clients can identify. Use the language that you and your clients are familiar with to describe the problems that Shane has encountered. Don't forget to have clients list the expected short and long term consequences to Shane. Basic slips/relapses are marked in the Treatment Exercise on p. 123. Note that only the basic problem issues are marked and accept any rational thinking that clients have to offer. Then hold a second discussion on the many ways that Shane could have prevented relapse on any of his unhealthy, harmful behaviors.

3. Not being aware of Irresponsible Thinking

Irresponsible thinking sets the occasion for the irresponsible decisions that result in unhealthy, harmful behavior. The specific purpose of developing awareness of the irresponsible thinking that sets the occasion for relapse is to "go to the opposite extreme" and substitute responsible thinking that protects recovery. Irresponsible thinking is only one type of cognitive distortion. Others include: automatic thoughts; false assumptions; irrational beliefs; negative attitudes; misattributions; misperceptions; schemas, core beliefs; thinking errors, unrealistic expectations and; unwarranted justifications. The cognitive distortions outlined by Bandura, (1973), Beck et al (1979), Burns, (1980), D'Zurilla and Netzu (2007); Ellis (1994) as well as Yochelson & Samenow (1976), Young (1990) Young, 1990; McGinn & Young, 1996 and Yokley (2008) for problems with aggressions, depression, unhealthy, harmful behavior, criminal behavior and personality disorders are listed in Table 6.1.

Table 6.1
Cognitive Distortions that can Set the Occasion for Unhealthy, Harmful Behavior

Internalizing conditions, victim population:
1. Irrational beliefs (Ellis, 1994). 11 items. Originally developed in Rational Emotive Behavior Therapy for depression, anxiety and self-depreciation (later applied to substance abuse and personality disorders)
2. Automatic thoughts (Burns, 1980 & Beck, 1979). 10 items. Originally developed in Cognitive Therapy for depression (later applied to anxiety, substance abuse and personality disorders)

Externalizing conditions, offender or personality disorder population:
3. Thinking errors (Yochelson & Samenow, 1976). 33 items. Originally developed for criminal personality;
4. Cognitive distortions in aggression (Bandura, 1973). 6 items. Developed for social learning theory of aggression
5. Schemas in personality disorders (Young, 1990; McGinn & Young, 1996). 18 schema categories. Developed for personality disorders

Both Internalizing and Externalizing Conditions
6. Cognitive distortions that impede social problem solving (D'Zurilla & Netzu, 2007). 5 items. Developed for social problem solving therapy.
7. Irresponsible thinking in unhealthy, harmful behavior (Yokley, 2008). 20 items. Developed in Social Responsibility Therapy on externalizing population with history of internalizing issues (being abused).

Similar to the specific purpose of identifying irresponsible thinking, the general purpose of identifying other types of cognitive distortions is also positive self-statement substitution. As mentioned earlier, a brief summary of the types of cognitive distortions published in the literature is listed in Table 6.1.

Cognitive distortions originally identified in internalizing conditions- In Rational Emotive Behavior Therapy, Ellis (1994) identified eleven irrational beliefs that people often hold.

Irrational belief self-statements are often identified by the words "should" or "must." Ellis also highlights the human tendency to take unreasonably exaggerated viewpoints, referring to overly pessimistic rumination as "awfulizing." According to Beck et al. (1979), in his classic psychotherapy text "Cognitive Therapy of Depression", seven cognitive distortions (automatic distorted or dysfunctional thoughts) cause many if not all of a person's depressed states. Dr. David Burns (1980) presented Beck's theoretical ideas in an easy to read popular book, entitled "Feeling Good" which presents the illogical, pessimistic attitudes that play a central role in the development and continuation of depressive and thoughts that maintain feeling lethargic and inadequate. The ten most prevalent cognitive distortions are summarized in Burns (1980).

Cognitive distortions originally identified in externalizing conditions- In their three volume work "The Criminal Personality", Yochelson & Samenow (1976) establish their theory that crime is not the outcome of intrapsychic conflict, organic problems or external forces but is directly related to a certain view of life and certain thinking errors. These authors focus on correcting 17 basic "Thinking Errors" in criminal behavior and 16 Tactics which obstruct effective corrective teaching. Cognitive distortions (i.e., attitudes, attributions, thoughts and irrational beliefs) that mediate emotional arousal and behavior choices is one of the most widely accepted factors in partner aggression (Feldman & Ridley, 1995). Six cognitive components from the Social Learning Theory of aggression that set the occasion for abuse are proposed by Bandura (1973). Personality disorders are thought to have their origins in adverse developmental experiences that form schemas which are enduring core beliefs that are shaped in childhood by life experience including parent teaching, modeling, school education, peer influence/experiences, tramatic experiences, successes and failures. CBT for personality disorders (Young, 1990; McGinn & Young, 1996) focuses on 18 schemas (referred to by Beck as "core beliefs"), which are the global organizing beliefs (often absolute rules) that guide behavior, dysfunctional interpersonal strategies and environmental influences in five adverse developmental experience domains.

Cognitive distortions identified in both internalizing and externalizing conditions- With respect to social problem solving D'Zurilla & Netzu (2007) propose five common distortions that can impede accurate problem definition. A set of twenty specific types of Irresponsible Thinking (and responsible alternatives) was constructed from an "Awareness and Honesty Exam" covering cognitive distortions commonly exhibited by individuals with internalizing and externalizing conditions. Many of the internalizing cognitive distortions that were included have been described by Beck et al. (1979), Burns (1980), and Ellis et al. (1988) in individuals with negative affective state problems (e.g., depression, anxiety, obsessive rumination). Many of the externalizing cognitive distortions that were included have been described by Bandura (1973), Yochelson & Samenow (1976), and Samenow (1996, 2001) relating to social learning of aggressive and criminal behavior. Items tapping problems with social responsibility (i.e., honesty, trust, loyalty, concern, and responsibility) were also included (Yokley, 2008).

The twenty specific types of Irresponsible Thinking and characteristics that set the occasion for unhealthy, harmful behavior are listed in Table 4.1. When similarities across the seven cognitive distortion category lists in Table 6.1 were examined, the set of 20 types of Irresponsible Thinking (Table 6.2) had the largest item overlap across types of internalizing and externalizing lists. This was expected given the development population had a large proportion of offenders who were themselves victims and given that the "Awareness and Honesty Exam" used to develop the item set was an aggregate of almost all of the types of cognitive distortions listed in Table 4.1.

Becoming Aware of Irresponsible Thinking: Key Words to Look for

In order to avoid and correct the Irresponsible Thinking that enables relapse, clients have to be able to identify that thinking. Fortunately, there are a number of key words that can help. When helping clients become aware of self-statements that can identify their Irresponsible Thinking, it is important to remember that there is a continuum of Irresponsible Thinking strength from mild to strong that is benchmarked by the words "I could", "I want to", "I should", "I need to" and "I have to" or "I must" (See Figure 5.2). Table 6.2 below provides some brief examples of self-statements that can identify or enable Irresponsible Thinking.

Table 6.2
Self-Statement Examples that can Identify or Enable Irresponsible Thinking

Irresponsible Thinking Self-statements that can Identify or Enable this Thinking

1. Deception	"I can't stand getting in trouble.", "I need to get out of this (or cover it up)"
2. Double standards	"They *should* level with me but they don't need to know my opinion", "They *should* trust me but they're not trustworthy"
3. Irresponsible loyalty	"I know they have problems *but* if I just stick with them, they'll change", "I *must* cover for them, they're my friends"
4. Don't care attitude	"Who cares", "So what", "Whatever", "I don't give a damn" or "Screw it"
5. Responsibility issues	"I don't need to, "I don't want to", "It's not my job/problem", "I forgot",
6. Blind ambition	"I will do whatever it takes to succeed", "I *must* get what I want"
7. Motivational blindness	"I don't know", "I have no idea" or "It just happened"
8. "I can't" belief	"I can't do it", "I quit" or "I already tried that"
9. Grandiosity	"I can handle anything", "I can get out of anything" or "This doesn't apply"
10. Control issues	"I can't stand being bossed" or "I need to or *must* be in control"
11. Image problems	"I can't let myself look bad", "I need to or *must* look good/tough/cool"
12. Need problems	"I want to or *must* be liked, exciting, entertaining or interesting and fit in"
13. Planning problems	Not planning ahead- "I'll do it later", "I lost track of time", "I didn't think about it"
14. Boundary problems	"I can't stand not hearing from them", "I feel suffocated", "I *must* help them", "They *should* know how I feel", "What's mine is mine and yours is mine"
15. Victim view	Using, "But" or "Because", "But... it wasn't my fault/ they got it started/they didn't give me a chance", "That wasn't fair/right/I couldn't help it Because...", dwelling on the past and other people's behavior.
16. Justifying actions	Using, "I Should", "I Must", "I have to" (often based on feelings)
17. Extremism	"You're either a winner or loser/with or against me/100% perfect or quit"
18. Minimizing	Using, "Just or "Only"- "I'll just/only do it this one last time"
19. Magnifying	Using, "Always" or "Never"- "I always fail (or never succeed) so why try?"
20. Assuming	"I just know that..." or "I know what's going on" and not checking it out

---

Complete descriptions of these twenty specific "Types of Irresponsible Thinking..." are provided for clients in the SRT Therapy Understanding Harmful Behavior Workbooks 1, 2 and 3 (Appendix C of Yokley 2010b; 2011a; 2012). The utility of the Irrational Beliefs described by Dr. Albert Ellis in his Rational Emotive Behavior Therapy (Item 1 in Table 6.1) can be seen in the ability to apply the "should" and "must" self-statements that identify Irrational Beliefs to a number of other types of cognitive distortions in addition to justifying actions (See Table 6.2).

Irresponsible Thinking Short Form
An abbreviated version of the 20 types of Irresponsible Thinking, covers the following six cognitive distortions that appear across the majority of the cognitive distortion lists described on Table 6.1 (i.e., that are found on 4 or more of the 7 lists):

1. Minimizing (Item 18)- Just or Only
2. Victim view (Item15)- But (or because)
3. Justifying actions (Item 16)- Should or Must
4. Magnifying (Item 19)- Always or Never
5. Assuming (Item 20)
6. Control issues (Item 10)

The first four on the short form are identified by the key words listed above which make up the JOBS MAN acronym described on p. 52. Statement examples of the first three on the short form are provided on Table 2.3 in Yokley (2008).

Treatment Exercise: Identifying Irresponsible Thinking that enables relapse
Review the Irresponsible Thinking short form item examples on p. 52, Tables 4.2 and 6.2. Then conduct a client Awareness Training discussion on the key words in their statements to self or others that signal they are using one of the first four types of Irresponsible Thinking on the short form list above. Use the "JOBS MAN" acronym to help clients remember the key words that identify the first four of these six types of Irresponsible Thinking and have each client write out and read examples of how this thinking has resulted in a past relapse or can set the occasion for relapse. File this in their chart for use later.

4. Irrational or unrealistic hope
Many client decisions to enter high-risk situations on purpose are based on irrational or unrealistic hope. This can be from: grandiosity/overconfidence; the need to test self-control (i.e., "I need to see if I can handle this"); denial and not wanting to admit the risk to self or; unhealthy pride and not wanting to have to admit the risk to others (i.e., exaggerated need for acceptance). All except the first have to do with the client's need to prove they are in control and do not have an unhealthy or harmful behavior problem. In this respect, it is important to remind clients that everyone has problem issues so having problems isn't the problem. Problems don't make us less than others, they make us human like others. Clients need to accept that being aware of their problem issues and being able to manage them is the only thing they need to do to achieve their healthy lifestyle goals. In short, it is unrealistic to hope that long term problems will get resolved through short term treatment but it is realistic to expect to be able to learn the healthy behavior and relationship success skills needed to build the track record of long term behavior management that will evolve into a healthy lifestyle.

5. Problem Priorities
Until a track record of long term behavior management is established, staying focused on managing unhealthy, harmful behavior, avoiding relapse and staying on track with healthy lifestyle goals has to be the client's daily priority. Problem Priorities or "triage trouble" work together with Foresight Deficit Decisions to set the occasion for relapse. As mentioned earlier, triage is from the French trier "to sort" and refers to emergency room sorting of battle and disaster victims in a system of priorities designed to maximize the number of survivors. Problem

priorities involves not keeping the focus on the most important problem. Like Foresight Deficit Decisions, this often relates to good intentions, putting other people or tasks first, forgetting about self and letting priorities slip. In summary, Problem Priorities involve putting other people, projects and daily living activities before recovery (from unhealthy, harmful behavior).

Before treatment, Problem Priorities can interfere with clients getting help. For example, a client saying, "I know I should get help for drinking but I can't take the time, I need to take care of the kids." Before treatment, Problem Priorities can come from putting own selfish needs over others. Examples include eating to the point where weight gain results in impairment or inability to complete personal or family responsibilities. Drinking or drugging to the point where chemical dependency results in impairment or inability to complete personal or family responsibilities. Venting feelings of anger to the point where the safety and security of others is jeopardized. Following feelings of sexual excitement or control and power needs to the point where the rights of others are violated.

During treatment, Problem Priorities can interfere with clients completing it in a timely manner and can result in repeating treatment. Problem Priorities often come from putting other people or tasks first, forgetting about self and letting recovery priorities slip. This can occur from assuming that good intentions can be substituted for good foresight (i.e., thinking ahead) and planning. For example, a client saying, "I know I should go to my outpatient treatment group but I have a chance to work a second shift and need to catch up on my bills." During treatment is where clients are supposed to get their priorities straight. Think about taking an airline trip. Just before departure the staff make an announcement that, "In the event of a sudden loss of cabin pressure, the oxygen masks will drop down. Please put your mask on before you put one on your children." The reason for this announcement is obvious. You can't help your kids if you pass out from lack of oxygen. This is true of life in general. You can't take good care of others if you don't take good care of yourself. Self-care is not selfish as long as you remember that, "You're number one but there are other numbers."

After treatment, Problem Priorities involve clients not "keeping their problem up front" and letting recovery take a back seat to other life endeavors. Problem Priorities can return over time through "Priority Drift." Priority Drift is like Program Drift. In Program Drift, staff adherence to treatment program policies slowly become lax over time until an accident occurs. This typically triggers a state audit followed by a policy revival and mandatory staff retraining. In Priority Drift, client adherence to relapse prevention plans for unhealthy, harmful behavior slowly become lax over time until a relapse occurs. In many cases, this triggers a chain of events that eventually results in client readmission.

At any time, fatigue can result in letting awareness drop to the point where automatic processes (old habit thinking and behavior) take over guidance and steer clients back toward trouble. In short, "not keeping your problem up front" is most likely when clients get tired, lax, distracted, or preoccupied and drifts from manual relapse prevention planning to maladaptive behavior auto-pilot which steers you into a high-risk situation.

In summary, healthy lifestyle development priorities have to stay in order or decisions can become irresponsible. Healthy body (i.e., staying clean and sober, eating right, sleeping right, staying active) has to come first. Healthy relationships (i.e., positive support absent of any form of abuse, balanced with equal social exchange, not putting in more or taking more than you get from others) have to be developed and maintained. Finally, a healthy life direction (i.e., "Something to do that's positive for you", balanced and absent of blind ambition or work encapsulated "projects over people") is needed that is more important to clients than their unhealthy, harmful behavior. "Put first things first" -- AA Recovery Slogan

6. Exaggerated Needs

Exaggerated needs for attention, acceptance or excitement can result in irresponsible decisions. Clients need to be aware that a past history of being ignored can set them up for making risky decisions that get attention. For example, some young people with a past history of family neglect or lack of positive peer attention can fall into compromising themselves for attention by posting dangerous stunts or challenges on YouTube or Facebook which get reinforced by viewers or accepting unhealthy, harmful behavior dares that can result in serious consequences.

A past history of rejection can set clients up for compromising themselves to be accepted by others. For example, an individual with a past history of rejection or feeling inadequate can fall into compromising themselves to be accepted by "players" who "love bomb" them with insincere flattery and phony compliments to get what they want. Another example would be a client in alcohol recovery with an exaggerated need for acceptance stemming from dysfunctional family rejection being at risk for compromising what they know is right and going to an office party at a bar to be accepted by co-workers. Clients from dysfunctional families with a past history of rejection and physical abuse can become preoccupied with perceived injustices and have an exaggerated need for respect. They can mistake fear for respect and react to perceived disrespect with aggression "to teach them some respect". This situation calls for a role reversal challenge, "How many people that you fear to you respect?

Emotional double jeopardy. The hurt and betrayal experienced as a result of some Historical Risk factors, particularly sexual abuse by a relative or close family member can result in strong exaggerated needs for acceptance and comfort combined with distrust of others. This can result in clients meeting their exaggerated needs by comforting themselves with food, drugs/alcohol or sex (i.e., mistaking intensity for intimacy). Develop client awareness of this emotional injustice by giving a simple double jeopardy analogy.

Ask your female clients to imagine standing at a bus stop (or waiting for a cab) after work in front of a bank with two close friends when they are sexually harassed by a passerby who makes abusive propositions to all. In response one of them picks up a loose sidewalk brick, hurls it at the abuser who ducks and then runs after the brick smashes the bank front window. When the police arrive, none of the friends admit who threw the brick so all three are arrested, tried and sentenced. After serving their sentence while standing at their usual bus stop the officer who arrested them was driving by, recognized them and got out of his squad car screaming about how the hours spent on trying to get them to talk along with paper work caused him to miss his anniversary flight to the Bahamas. If he told you the sentence you got wasn't nearly enough and arrested you again for what occurred in the past, you would be screaming double jeopardy and calling your lawyer because in the United States you can't be punished for the same crime twice.

Next point out that every time you use comfort eating, drinking or sex to relieve unwanted feelings left over from past hurt and abuse, you are committing emotional double jeopardy. Since you have already been punished once by unwanted feelings, punishing yourself again by breaking your diet with comfort food, breaking your sobriety with drugs/alcohol or justifying a sexual addiction relapse based on unwanted feelings, is effectively being punished twice. Hold clients accountable to stop emotional double jeopardy during emotion-triggered relapse thoughts by asking themselves, "Why should I hurt me just because other people or other things hurt me?"
Note: The double jeopardy example is easily adjusted for male clients by removing the sexual harassment trigger for throwing the brick and substituting taking a dare.

It is also important for clients to be aware that an exaggerated need for excitement and low boredom tolerance can lead to risky decisions involving exciting things. For example, take the case of the sexually compulsive client with an exaggerated need for excitement with nothing to do. Being bored to tears puts them at risk for saying "yes" to a dangerously exciting ex-partner who asks them out again despite getting too far into thrill sex and thrill crimes with them in the past. Bottom line: "Idle hands are the devil's workshop" in clients with an exaggerated need for excitement who need to stay busy with something positive that is challenging or interesting to them.

Treatment Exercise:
Awareness of Primary Contributing Factors to Irresponsible Decisions
Conduct individual and/or group treatment session discussions covering the six primary contributing factors to irresponsible decisions that result in relapse until these factors are completely understood. Then have clients discuss their own examples of how these factors interacted and combined to result in irresponsible decisions that led to relapse. Don't forget to have clients discuss the consequences of their irresponsible decisions.

Responsibility Training in Decisional Balance
and Other Responsible Decision Skills
"If you don't take Responsibility to balance benefits and drawbacks, you can't expect things to work out"

> **Responsibility Training Goal:** Develop responsible decision-making skills and strategies.
> **Objectives:** Clients will be able to apply the "Reality Check" to on the spot decisions and use the decisional balance Reality Scales to make responsible decisions and avoid unhealthy, harmful behavior.

In reality, no matter how good our intentions are decisions determine our destiny. In order to maintain the responsible decision-making that protects recovery clients need to: weigh out possible consequences; think ahead; think responsibly; avoid unrealistic hope; stay grounded; maintain recovery priorities and; gratify their needs in a healthy manner. Otherwise Murphy's Law will kick in, "whatever can go wrong, will go wrong" and our clients will fall back into their Stress-Relapse Cycle of unhealthy, harmful behavior. Just like irresponsible decisions set the occasion for relapse and jeopardize recovery from unhealthy, harmful behavior, responsible decisions prevent relapse and protect client recovery.

Primary Contributing Factors to Responsible Decisions include...
1. Decisional Balance: Thinking it through
2. Using "Fantasy Fast Forward"
3. Responsible thinking
4. Staying Grounded
5. Maintaining priorities
6. Healthy need gratification

| Responsibility Training in Decisional Balance |

"Man is fully responsible for his nature and his choices"-- Jean-Paul Sartre (1905- 1980)

1. Decisional Balance: Thinking it through

Clients struggling with unhealthy harmful behavior habits are faced with ongoing life decisions. Their choices determine whether they stay on target or get set back in developing the healthy body, relationships and life direction needed to get what they want in life. As mentioned earlier, responsible decisions protect recovery and irresponsible decisions set the occasion for relapse. In order for clients to learn to make responsible decisions that protect their recovery and avoid relapse, they need to learn to "Think it through" and balance the benefits against the drawbacks of their decisions before taking action.

When clients go through a stressful, emotionally upsetting experience, rumination or brooding over the possible reasons or perceived injustice of the situation makes it worse. Rumination blows the problem out of proportion, which increases unwanted feelings (e.g., depression, anxiety, anger, frustration, helplessness). Unwanted emotional distress and discomfort sets the occasion for comfort eating, drinking, smoking, spending, sex or other unhealthy, harmful behavior that can act to make the client feel better or more in control. The reality scales can help clients with "Thinking it through" to put things back into perspective, not "make a mountain out of a mole hill" and avoid justifying unhealthy, harmful actions based on unwanted feelings.

An important part of "Thinking it through" for clients is learning to talk to themselves like their own best friend. Fake friends who just want to be popular with everyone or who just want to stir up trouble, are often referred to as "enablers" because they tell us what we <u>want to hear</u>. They enable unhealthy, harmful behavior by minimizing it using the words "just" and "only" (e.g., "It's a <u>only</u> little thing, no big deal" or "We'll <u>just</u> do it this one time"). They work us up by justifying unhealthy, harmful actions saying, "You <u>should/must/have to</u>."

Real friends are honest, concerned and responsible. They tell us what we <u>need to hear</u>, not what we want to hear. If our best true friend in the whole world is a real friend, then when we get hit with temptation to do something we shouldn't, they will give us a Reality Check. Our best friend would tell us that in reality, it's <u>only</u> a little thing if no harm could come to self or others and it's never <u>just</u> once. Since best friends can't always be there to give clients a Reality Check when they need one, they have to learn to do this for themselves. The *Reality Check, Reality Scales* and *Decisional Balance Sheet* described below will help clients weigh things out during difficult decisions, think it through and guide themselves into responsible action.

The "Reality Check"

On the spot or "snap" decisions can be risky and are for individuals with a lot of experience or very good judgment. This rules out most children and adolescents with limited experience or all adults whose social-emotional immaturity impairs sound judgment. Unfortunately, in life sometimes things pop off fast and since quick decisions can be unsafe, it is important for clients with unhealthy, harmful behavior problems to stop and take a "Reality Check" when a quick decision needs to be made.

Client Instructions: Use the Reality Check during on the spot "snap" decisions by asking yourself "Is what I'm thinking about doing helpful or harmful to myself or others?" Decisions that could be unhealthy or harmful need to be weighted out on a Decisional Balance tool.

The Fork in the Road "Pros and Cons" List
"To do or not to do: that is the question"-- Jeff Rich

The simplest form of Decisional Balance is weighing out the benefits and drawbacks of a decision with a "Pros and Cons" list. Just about every clinician has done this at one point in their lives so it should be relatively easy to discuss with clients. The instructions are simple. Just have clients fold a sheet of paper in half, label the left half "Pros", the right half "Cons" and fill in as many benefits and drawbacks as they can on each side of the list. When the list is done, clients need to talk to partners, parents and peers to gather as much pro and con information as they can before discussing this with their therapist or clinical staff.

Typically, comparing the "Pros" side to the "Cons" side can provide a fairly good indicator of which way to go. However, in terms of considering consequences and developing foresight, it is important for clients to add "What could happen if..." to their both sides of their decision. Although this simple procedure is by and large self-explanatory, a brief case example follows.

The Fork in the Road "Pros and Cons" Decision List Case Example- Craig was a 56-year-old male on parole for gross sexual imposition against his teenage daughter who he states he "fell in love with." He began his sexual imposition during a period of marital conflict with his wife, which he discussed in detail with his sympathetic daughter. He told his treatment group that he was overcome with guilt and his only focus now was to make sure that the family did not lose their home as a result of mortgage foreclosure. His staff thought that saving the house might be part of a long-term plan to move back in with his family. Although Craig was an experienced electronic technician, criminal records checks resulted in being turned down for job after job. The good news was that he finally got a job as a TV repairman. The bad news was that it was an in-home service where he would drive the company van to the house and make repairs on site. Craig's Fork in the Road "Pros and Cons" Decision List appears in Table 6.3. With serious decisions, it is important for clients to further weigh out their choices on the "Reality Scales" before taking action. Bottom line: "When in doubt, weigh it out".

Thinking it through with the "Reality Scales"
"Each man must reach his own verdict, by weighing all the relevant evidence"-- Leonard Peikoff

In SRT decision-making, the reality scales are used to make responsible decisions. Using the reality scales involves weighing out the benefits and drawbacks of an action on three 10-point

Table 6.3
Craig's Fork in the Road "Pros and Cons" Decision List

Pros Benefits of taking the home service job	Cons Drawbacks to taking the home service job
• Helping the family keep the house • Other financial support for the family • Feeling a part of the family again • Relieving guilt	• Jeopardizing his freedom- TV repair in a home where children are present is a parole violation • Increasing anxiety • Less desirable working conditions than at the shop • Lots of driving involved • Longer hours than TV shop work

The Fork in the Road: What could happen if...
<u>I take the job?</u>   <u>I don't take it?</u>

Violate conditions of parole   Family could lose home

Go back to prison if caught   I won't violate parole

Feel less guilt but more anxiety   Feel more guilt but less anxiety

Craig's decision fork in the road

rating scales: the Survival Scale (i.e., How much it is needed for survival); 2) the Success Scale (i.e., How much it is needed to succeed in life); and; 3) the Severity Scale (i.e., How severe will the consequences of taking the action be on self/others). Clients often refer to these scales as "the 3 S's".

The Survival Scale evaluates <u>how necessary for actual survival</u> it is to do the behavior being considered on a scale of zero (not necessary at all) to ten (absolutely necessary to save my life). Ask yourself, "On a scale of 0 to 10, how necessary for my survival is it for me to do what I am considering?" (Client needs to explain why it is necessary) "What will happen to my survival if I don't act?" (Client needs to explain what will happen if they don't act)

The Success Scale evaluates <u>how important for success</u> in life doing the responsible thing or failing to do it would be on a scale of zero (not important at all) to ten (so important that it could change the entire course of my life). Ask yourself, "On a scale of 0 to 10, how important is it to my success in life for me to do what I am considering?" (Client needs to explain why it is important for success in life) "Do I have to do this in order to succeed in life?" Is this something you will look back on 10 years from now and say, "That decision changed the course of my life?" (Client needs to explain). On the other hand, "What will happen to my life success goals if I don't do this?" (Client needs to explain).

The Severity Scale ("Bad Scale" for young children) evaluates <u>how severe the consequences of doing the responsible thing or failing to do it</u> will be on a scale of zero (not severe, awful or bad at all) to ten (so severe that I can't hardly stand it, must avoid it and need help to get through it).

On one side of this scale is the reality of what will likely happen <u>if the unhealthy, harmful behavior is committed</u>. For example...

- <u>With trust abuse</u>, "In the worst case, on a scale of 0 to 10, how severe could the consequences be (to self and others) if I lied to, cheated on, manipulated or conned this person and why do I need to avoid these consequences?" (Client needs to give reasons);
- <u>With substance abuse</u> (including food), "In the worst case, on a scale of 0 to 10, how severe could the consequences be (to self and others) if I ate, drank, smoked or took this and why do I need to avoid these consequences?" (Client needs to give reasons);
- <u>With property abuse</u> (including money), "In the worst case, on a scale of 0 to 10, how severe could the consequences be (to self and others) if I bought, bet on, took or smashed this and why do I need to avoid these consequences?" (Client needs to give reasons);
- <u>With physical abuse</u>, "In the worst case, on a scale of 0 to 10, how severe could the consequences be (to self and others) if I smacked, slugged or choked this person and why do I need to avoid these consequences?" (Client needs to give reasons) or;
- <u>With sexual abuse</u>, "In the worst case, on a scale of 0 to 10, how severe could the consequences be (to self and others) if I fondled or penetrated this person and why do I need to avoid these consequences?" (Client needs to give reasons).

On the other side of this scale is the reality of what will likely happen <u>if the unhealthy, harmful behavior is not committed</u>. "On a scale of 0 to 10, how severe would the consequences be (to self and others) if I do the right thing and decide <u>not to do this</u>?" (Client needs to give reasons). In cases of trust abuse, substance abuse, property abuse, physical abuse or sexual abuse, "Could I handle these consequences?" In summary, the severity scale is used to help clients show concern for themselves and others by weighing out the severity of the consequences to self and others on a 0 to 10 scale and making the best choice based on responsible reasons before taking action.

Client Reality Scale Instructions

Tell clients that the Reality Scales will help them clarify the "reality" of how much their decision will likely affect their survival, their success and the severity of consequences that may occur. Always have clients start with the survival scale first because few situations in day-to-day life threaten our survival. Have clients use the success scale second because not many situations in daily life can result in absolute life failure. Save the severity scale until last because clients with extremism thinking tend exaggerate the severity of not doing the unhealthy, harmful behavior and/or minimize the severity of doing it. Be sure to anchor the three Reality Scales with examples of what would be considered a "0" and a "10" to help clients avoid "all or nothing" thinking" extremism thinking.

Walk the client through how to use the Reality Scales with a problem that they recently experienced. In the case of the residential substance abuse youth who is furious about not getting a privilege request approved as a result of unruly behavior and is becoming unruly, you would walk them through the following steps.
1. "Rate the impact of not getting your privilege approved on the survival scale where "0" means that it doesn't threaten your survival at all and "10" means that it will stop your heart and breathing." Point out that not getting a privilege would be a "0" on the survival scale because it doesn't threaten your survival and does not require you to fight for your life.
2. "Rate the impact of not getting your privilege approved on the success scale where "0" means that it doesn't interfere with your success in life at all and "10" means that it will stop

you from ever achieving your life goals." Point out that not getting a privilege would be a "0" on the success scale because it doesn't interfere with your success in life and will have no impact on your future goals to graduate high school and go to college.

3. "Rate the impact of not getting your privilege approved on the severity scale where "0" means that the consequences will not be severe at all and "10" means that the consequences will be so severe that you will not be able to endure it without professional help. Point out that not getting a privilege is about a "3" on the severity scale because it is disturbing but not dangerous, inconvenient but not permanent.

After You Weigh it, Delay it
"Quick decisions are unsafe decisions"-- Sophocles (496BC- 406 BC)

In most cases with anything less than a "10" you don't have to immediately take action to avoid trouble, trauma or drama. Thus, whenever possible, "sleep on it" before you take action. While taking time to use the Reality Scales is important in delaying action on unhealthy, harmful behavior, it is also important in developing tolerance of others (i.e., delaying opinions until all of the facts are found). Finally, taking time to use the Reality Scales improve work relationships (i.e., delaying expression of feelings about work assignment mistakes and "earning the right to complain" by completing work assignments before complaining about them).

Since "We do our best when we are prepared and our worst when we are caught off guard" always tell clients to first remove self from the immediate situation to think for a minute. Weighing out important decisions on the Reality Scales requires time to weight things out. Thus, a good habit for clients to get into is telling self "I need to weight this out" and telling others "I need to get back to you on that." This buys the time needed to weight out their decision on the Reality Scales, make a responsible decision and if possible sleep on it.

Practical application examples
Food abuse/Overeating- An example of using the Reality Scales to weigh out the decision to overeat is provided in Table 6.4 below. The client was in Overeaters Anonymous recovery after completing hospital-based weight management treatment and losing 50lbs.

Table 6.4 Using the Reality Scales to "Think Through" the Decision to Overeat			
Behavior (History of overeating and obesity)	**Reality Scales** 0 = not at all necessary or important/no impact; 10= absolutely necessary or important/very severe impact		
	Survival Scale How necessary for my survival is it for me to...	**Success Scale** How important for my success is it for me to...	**Severity Scale** How severe could the consequences be if I...
Food Abuse-Overeat	...have a second portion and dessert? **0- not necessary for survival** (only wanted for urge gratification)	...have a second portion and dessert? **0- not important for success** (will actually impair weight management)	...have a second portion and dessert? **8- severe** (will trigger regret & self-loathing, could trigger a binge, may get self sick)

Substance abuse/alcohol- An example of using the Reality Scales to weigh out the decision to attend an office party with an open bar is provided Table 6.5 below. The client is on probation and attending Alcoholics Anonymous after completing residential treatment.

Table 6.5 Using the Reality Scales to "Think Through" the Decision to have a Drink			
Behavior (History of alcohol abuse, drunk & disorderly, driving under the influence)	**Reality Scales** 0 = not at all necessary or important/no impact; 10= absolutely necessary or important/very severe impact		
	Survival Scale How necessary for my survival is it for me to...	**Success Scale** How important for my success is it for me to...	**Severity Scale** How severe could the consequences be if I...
Substance Abuse (client with alcohol/anxiety problem goes to office party)	...attend the open bar office party? **0- not needed for survival** (only wanted to socialize)	...attend the open bar office party? **4- somewhat important for success** (provides the opportunity to network with supervisors)	...attend the open bar office party? **9- severe** (open bar is a high-risk situation for relapse, probation violation & another DUI or assault charge)

Sexually abusive behavior- An example of using the Reality Scales to weigh out the decision to babysit for a neighbor is provided in Table 6.6 below. The client was out of work client, behind on his rent and on parole. The neighbor was unaware of the client's child sexual imposition conviction.

Table 6.6 Using the Reality Scales to "Think Through" the Decision to Babysit a Child			
Behavior (History of sexual imposition against a minor)	**Reality Scales** 0 = not at all necessary or important/no impact; 10= absolutely necessary or important/very severe impact		
	Survival Scale How necessary for my survival is it for me to...	**Success Scale** How important for my success is it for me to...	**Severity Scale** How severe could the consequences be if I...
Sexual Abuse (Out of work client convicted of sexual imposition is offered a babysitting job)	...take this babysitting job? **0- not necessary for survival** (only wanted to pay bills and avoid homeless shelter)	...take this babysitting job? **2- not important for success** (money helps but one babysitting job won't open the doors to success)	...take this babysitting job? **10- severe** (could result in re-offense, parole violation and jail sentence, the homeless shelter is better than jail)

In cases involving life decisions that could have a long term serious impact on self or others or that are likely to result in major life changes, having clients use a Decisional Balance Sheet to evaluate both the benefits and drawbacks on both sides of their decision is important.

The Decisional Balance Sheet

A decisional balance sheet combines both the benefits and drawbacks of continuing or quitting any unhealthy, harmful behavior on a simple 2 X 2 matrix. Benefits/Pros and Drawbacks/Cons are recorded in the two columns and whether to Keep or Quit doing the unhealthy, harmful behavior is recorded in the two rows. Have clients discuss and write the tangible benefits and drawbacks of what they are considering or doing in terms of goods and money along with other physical, social or emotional rewards that are received.

The Decisional Balance Sheet: A Case Example

As a result of not thinking her decision through by weighting out the pros and cons before moving in with Geno, Hope is now facing some fairly serious consequences (see case example on p. 105). Hope now needs to consider important: healthy body decisions (i.e., about smoking marijuana and overeating); healthy relationship decisions (i.e., about continuing to live with Geno and hang out with her old weed smoking friends) and; healthy life direction decisions (i.e., about returning to Vocational Rehabilitation to complete her cosmetology training and get a job). Given her upcoming court date for substance abuse relapse, smoking marijuana was her most pressing issue. Hope had to make a decision about her marijuana use, i.e., "Should I keep smoking weed and just try to lie and get a prescription to do it legally? or Should I quit?" After discussing the benefits and drawbacks with her staff, Hope constructed the following Decisional Balance Sheet on her substance use decision (See Table 6.7).

Table 6.7 Hope's Decisional Balance Sheet on Smoking Marijuana		
	Benefits	**Drawbacks**
Keep Smoking weed	"Helps me calm down after Geno's violent blow ups."	"I'll get another probation violation, go to jail, gain the rest of my weight back and feel even worse about myself."
Quit Smoking weed	"I won't have to worry about going to jail for failed urines or gaining more weight from the marijuana munchies."	"I won't get withdrawal symptoms from quitting weed but I will have to find another way to deal with Geno's violent blow ups."

In Summary: Hope's benefits of quitting and drawbacks of continuing to smoke marijuana look to be more stronger for her than the Benefits of continuing and the Drawbacks of quitting.

Bottom line: Hope's Decisional Balance sheet indicates a need to quit smoking marijuana.

Validity Note: It should be noted that the validity of all Decisional Balance sheet results depend entirely on clients being honest with themselves and others when developing their benefits and drawbacks list. The validity of a decisional balance sheet is only as strong as the clients honesty.

Adding "Reality Scales" to the Decisional Balance Sheet

With serious life decisions where: 1) there is a need to "Do the Math" and actually weigh out tangible, measurable benefits and drawbacks on a scale or; 2) the regular decisional balance sheet results in a tie and clients are on the fence about what to do, adding Reality Scale ratings to the Decisional Balance Sheet can help. To do this, clients need to rate the benefits and drawbacks that they came up with on the three Reality Scales (i.e., the Survival scale, the Success scale and the Severity scale) in the four decisional balance sheet sections as follows. Have clients ask themselves...

1. "How necessary for my survival is it for me to quit doing it?" and rate the benefits of quitting what they are doing on the survival scale from zero (Don't need to quit to survive) to ten (Really need to quit to survive, lot bad could happen if I don't quit).

2. "How severe could the consequences be if I keep doing it? and rate the consequences of continuing what they are doing on the severity scale from zero (Not that severe, nothing could happen) to ten (So severe that I couldn't stand it, Serious consequences could occur).

3. "How important for my life success is it for me to keep doing it?" and rate the benefits of continuing what they are doing on the success scale from zero (don't need it at all for success) to ten (Can't succeed without it).

4. "How severe could the consequences be if I quit doing it?" and rate the consequences of quitting what they are doing on the severity scale from zero (Not that severe, nothing could happen) to ten (So severe that I couldn't stand it, Serious consequences could occur).

Adding the Reality Scales to a Decisional Balance Sheet: A Case Example
A case example of how to add the Reality Scales to a Decisional Balance sheet is provided in Table 6.8 below.

Table 6.8 Adding the Reality Scales to Hope's Decisional Balance Sheet on Smoking Marijuana		
	Benefits & Reality Scale Rating	**Drawbacks & Reality Scale Rating**
Keep Smoking weed	"Helps me calm down after Geno's violent blow ups." 3) How important for my life success is it for me to keep smoking weed? Success scale rating 0→ Not important for success won't help me finish cosmetology school.	"I'll get another probation violation, go to jail, gain the rest of my weight back and feel even worse about myself." 2) How severe could the consequences be if I keep smoking weed? Severity scale rating 10→ Severe consequences.
Quit Smoking weed	"I won't have to worry about going to jail for failed urines or gaining more weight from the marijuana munchies." 1) How necessary for my survival is it for me to quit smoking weed? Survival scale rating is? (0- 10). 9→ Necessary for survival of freedom (to avoid jail).	"I won't get withdrawal symptoms from quitting weed but will have to find another way to calm down up after Geno's violent blow ups." 4) How severe will the consequences be if I quit smoking weed? Severity scale rating is? (0- 10). 3→ Minor consequences.

Hope's Reality Scale Summary

1) <u>9</u> (Benefit of quitting)
    Necessary for freedom
+ 2) <u>10</u> (Drawbacks of keeping it up)
    Severe consequences
= <u>**19**</u> **Need to quit score**

3) <u>0</u> (Benefit of continuing)
    Not important for success
+ 4) <u>3</u> (Drawbacks of quitting)
    Minor consequences
= <u>**3**</u> **OK to continue score**

Reality Scale Results: Hope's "Need to quit" ratings outweighs her "OK to continue" ratings.

In Summary: Hope's Reality Scale ratings emphasize her need to quit smoking marijuana.

Bottom line: Both Hope's Decisional Balance sheet and her Reality Scale ratings indicate a need to quit smoking marijuana.

What if... The Reality Scales don't confirm or support the Decisional Balance Sheet? Causes for the Reality Scale ratings not matching the Decisional Balance conclusion include:
1. Dishonesty with self- Denial about the severity or possible consequences of the behavior.
2. Dishonesty with others- Unhealthy pride and not wanting others to know the severity of the problem (Maximizing benefits of continuing or drawbacks to quitting);
3. Resistance to change- Wanting to continue and have things remain the same can result in leaving out, skipping over or Minimizing drawbacks to continuing or benefits of quitting.

What to do if... The Decisional Balance Sheet and Reality Scale Ratings do not match, agree or support the same conclusion. Review the Decisional Balance Sheet benefits, drawbacks and the Reality Scale ratings with the client asking for explanations of their reasons and their ratings. During this discussion pay special attention to the JOBS MAN Irresponsible Thinking, particularly key words that can identify minimizing and maximizing. Help the client identify and modify any Irresponsible Thinking that is preventing accurate disclosure of benefits, drawbacks or Reality Scale ratings. The feedback of others in group treatment for the same unhealthy, harmful behavior can be very beneficial in terms of "Confrontation with Concern" on Irresponsible Thinking if the treatment group has advanced to the point of holding self and others accountable. It may also be helpful to review other case examples with clients. Specific Decisional Balance case examples that "Do the Math" and actually weigh out tangible, measurable benefits and drawbacks for unhealthy eating, drug dealing, smoking and sexually abusive behavior are provided in SRT Workbook 3 (Appendix H, p. 221- 226 in Yokley, 2012).

Treatment Exercise: Thinking it through with Decisional Balance

Review the three Decisional Balance tools with your clients, i.e., The Fork in the Road Pros and Cons List, The Reality Scales, and The Decisional Balance Sheet. Then, review the Treatment Exercise "Not considering consequences or thinking it through" (p. 109) with your clients. Have them re-read their assignment on "the worst decision I ever made" along with the consequences they experienced as a result of not thinking their decision through before taking action. Then have them discuss how using the Reality Scales could have helped them make a better decision and avoid the consequences they experienced. Give your clients a "do-over" fantasy assignment. Have them re-write their worst decision using any of the Decisional Balance tools to make it their best decision. Hold a discussion on "making responsible decisions" using decisional balance tools.

Responsibility Training in Other Important Decision Skills
"You have to go to the opposite extreme in order to meet the median" – TC Maxim

In addition to Decisional Balance with the reality scales, in SRT Fantasy Fast-Forward, Responsible Thinking, Staying Grounded, Maintaining Priorities and Healthy Need Gratification are also used to help clients make responsible decisions. Foresight Deficit Decisions can be avoided by using "Fantasy Fast Forward." These skills and healthy living habits are the opposite extreme of the six primary contributing factors discussed earlier and need to be regularly implemented during treatment in order to meet the community median afterwards.

2. Using Fantasy Fast Forward- Foresight is the ability to look ahead and anticipate problems. Fantasy Fast Forward is a foresight development tool. In Fantasy Fast Forward helps clients avoid the "Foresight Deficit Decisions" that enable entering or remaining in high-risk situations for relapse. This is accomplished by teaching clients play the mental tape of an action being considered all the way through to its end in order to consider the possible outcomes. In short, Fantasy Fast Forward involves learning to "Think ahead and plan ahead to get ahead."

Client Instructions- In Fantasy Fast Forward you need to view the situation you are considering (including a favor or something that involves good intentions) like a movie with you as the main character. Run it through your mind and fast forward to think ahead. Play the movie through to the very end in your mind, stop at each decision step and ask yourself, "What is the worst thing that could happen if I take this step?" Use a Reality Check (p. 120) to consider the consequences and determine whether to go ahead or tell yourself "I'm not falling into that" and change your course.

Treatment Exercise:
Mapping the Connection between Foresight Slips and Relapse
The first step in developing foresight is to become aware of the foresight slips that lead to relapse. These are all of the decision junctions where clients took action without thinking ahead. Have your clients write out the story of a Foresight Deficit Decision they made that resulted in relapse back into their unhealthy, harmful behavior. It needs to be detailed with a beginning, middle and end including all of the thoughts and feelings they experienced along the way. Then help them break it down to develop awareness of each foresight slip they made on their road to relapse. Help your clients label each type of foresight slip they made.

Foresight Slip Mapping Case Example- Here's how you would map the foresight slips in the earlier example of Shane (p. 110), the overweight, over the top football fan on parole as a result of sexual abuse, physical abuse and substance abuse.
1. On game day, Billy came in all excited about stealing club box seat tickets to the game. Shane couldn't stop screaming "Oh hell yes!" when Billy asked him to go (**slip #1,** not considering consequences of going to an open bar game with stolen tickets while on parole).
2. Shane was totally focused on the game and announced his good intentions to be the

designated driver and keep Billy out of trouble (**slip #2,** diversion away from "keeping your problem up front" by good intentions).

3. Shane told himself that he was *only* going to see the game, he would *just* drink non-alcoholic beer and he *must* be there to look after Billy because Billy had his back when they were cellmates (**slip #3**, irresponsible thinking).

4. He thought that since he hadn't been in trouble since he was released on parole 3 months ago, he could easily handle himself and watch over Billy (**slip #4,** unrealistic expectations).

5. He told himself that football was the only exciting thing left for him in life now that drinking, smoking weed and sexual acting out were on his parole rules and off the table (**slip #5,** Problem Priorities).

6. He was aware that his need for excitement was definitely ramped up by this football road trip and partially aware of his need for acceptance by Billy who had watched his back in the past (**slip #6,** exaggerated needs).

7. He was definitely interested in Sherry, knew he shouldn't drink on parole or as the designated driver but told himself he would order a full meal to counter the alcohol (**slip #7,** compromising self to be accepted).

8. That worked until Sherry started ordering shots after which Shane basically said, "Screw it, I blew it" and got totally trashed (**relapse #1,** falling into the Rule Violation Effect and getting drunk).

9. When a opposing team fan got in Sherry's face, Shane got pissed and punched him out (**relapse #2,** justifying actions based on feelings and assaulting another fan).

10. Security arrived and Shane lied about the stolen tickets (**relapse #3,** trust abuse by deception).

11. The next morning, Shane was awakened by Sherry shaking him and yelling "Get up, get up, I need a ride home, my parents are going to kill me!" On the plus side, it turns out that Sherry was 19 years old. On the minus side she was too young to drink and too intoxicated to give consent (**relapse #4,** sexual intercourse with an intoxicated female and drinking with an underage female).

Thus, the Foresight Deficit Decision to go a football game with Billy as designated driver to look after him and "just drink non-alcoholic beer", triggered a chain of events which resulted in relapse on multiple unhealthy, harmful behaviors and four parole violations.

"The road to hell is paved by good intentions"-- John Ray, circa 1670

Other case examples Foresight Deficit Decision where the foresight slips are mapped in specific cases of trust abuse (cheating, overspending), food abuse (overeating), smoking, substance abuse (marijuana), gambling, property abuse (theft), physical abuse (domestic violence) and sexual abuse are provided in all three SRT workbooks (Appendix B in Yokley, 2010b; 2011a; 2012).

Treatment Exercise: Developing Foresight with "Fantasy Fast Forward"

Have your clients review the exercise they completed on "Mapping the Connection between Foresight Slips and Relapse." Then have them describe how they could use Fantasy Fast Forward to avoid the same unhealthy, harmful behavior relapse in the future. Clients who are less insightful may have to start at the end with the unhealthy, harmful behavior they fell back into and be prompted to work their way back step by step (e.g., "OK then what happened before that?" What were you thinking, feeling or doing?).

Like insight and self-awareness, foresight does not come overnight. While foresight is difficult for some more action-oriented clients to develop, practicing Fantasy Fast Forward is a good first step. Many individuals with unhealthy, harmful behavior are very good at playing their fantasy tape from the beginning (urge) to the middle (gratifying their urge through unhealthy, harmful behavior) but that's where their imagination stops. They stay stuck on their euphoric recall of the feel good event and don't continue the tape to the very end which include all consequences that are likely to occur (or that have occurred in the past). Thus, in order to keep from inadvertently reinforcing the gratification of unhealthy, harmful cravings and urges during Fantasy Fast Forward, it is very important for clients to play their fantasy tape past the middle all the way to the end where realization of the consequences to self and others occurs.

To get your clients in the habit of thinking ahead, every week, have them write their weekend plans no later than Wednesday. Have your clients talk about their upcoming plans for the weekend using Fantasy Fast Forward. At each activity decision have them stop and consider the possible unintended consequences or what could go wrong with a "Reality Check" and correct their plans as needed.

Treatment Exercise: Developing Foresight with "Consequence Checkers"

Have a discussion of all of the consequences from relapse expected from the type of unhealthy, harmful behavior treatment that you are providing and list them on a flip chart. Follow this in your next session with a discussion of all of the treatment recovery benefits from stopping the type of unhealthy, harmful behavior that you are providing treatment for and list those benefits on a flip chart. Get a set of checkers. Put some white round stickers or some masking tape on the bottom of all of the checkers so that you can write on them. Write the important expected consequences listed on your flip chart on the bottoms of the red checkers. Then write the important expected benefits on the bottoms of the black checkers. In individual therapy, give your clients the red checkers so that every time they use foresight, jump one of your checkers and turn it over they are reminded of the benefits of learning to think ahead in treatment. You take the black checkers so that every time your client does use foresight and you jump their checker and turn it over, they are reminded of a possible consequence of not thinking ahead. Have a brief discussion of how they could think ahead in real life and avoid the consequence written on the red checker before continuing the next move.

"While we are free to choose our actions,
we are not free to choose the consequences of our actions" -- Stephen R. Covey

3. Responsible Thinking- Responsible thinking involves substituting responsible thoughts that protect recovery for irresponsible thoughts that enable relapse. This cognitive re-structuring process is also known as responsible self-statement substitution. The first step in Responsible Thinking is to teach clients to listen to themselves and pick up on the "JOBS MAN" words in their self-statements that identify their Irresponsible Thinking. The second step is to teach clients to label their negative Irresponsible Thinking and come up with an opposite, positive Responsible Alternative self-statement. The third step involves clients learning to protect their recovery by substituting their Responsible Alternative thinking for the Irresponsible thinking that enables relapse. Table 6.9 provides some brief examples of the Responsible Alternatives that can be substituted for the 20 types of Irresponsible Thinking listed in Table 4.1 and 6.1. Complete descriptions of these twenty specific "Types of Irresponsible Thinking and Responsible Alternatives" are provided for clients in all three of the SRT Understanding Harmful Behavior Workbooks (Appendix C of Yokley 2010b; 2011a; 2012).

Table 6.9
Summary of Responsible Alternatives for Irresponsible Thinking

Irresponsible Thinking Responsible Alternative, "Helpful Opposite"

1. Deception — **Get honest.** If you can't make it better, don't make it worse by lying. Weight out the consequences of deception on the reality scales.

2. Double standards — **Treat others the way you want to be treated.** Accept that to get honesty, trust, loyalty, concern and responsibility, you have to give it.

3. Irresponsible loyalty — **Be loyal to those who earn it** by being honest, trustworthy, loyal, concerned and responsible with you.

4. Don't care attitude — **Show the courage to care, share and try.** Push past fears of rejection or failure and start working on the problem. Take a first small step.

5. Responsibility issues — **Accept responsibility.** Hold yourself & others accountable. Do the right thing, when you're supposed to, for the reason you're supposed to do it.

6. Blind ambition — **Show Socially Responsible Achievement.** Weigh what will take to succeed against consequences to others. Look for "win, win" situations.

7. Motivational blindness — **Develop your Awareness and Insight.** Use other's feedback. Look at what triggered your feelings to determine the motive for your actions.

8. "I can't" belief — **Build your self-confidence.** Accept that "I can't" is really "I won't" if you don't get up the courage to try. Lose the excuses and put in the effort.

9. Grandiosity — **Be Realistic.** Don't over-estimate your self-control ability. Accept that staying in high-risk situations is likely to trigger relapse.

10. Control issues — **Work on controlling yourself, not others.** Stop using anger to win by intimidation. Admit that underneath anger is a fear of not being in control.

11. Image problems — **Drop your image.** Don't let needs to be accepted make you act like you think others want. Be honest, trustworthy, loyal, concerned, responsible.

12. Need problems — **Get a grip on your needs.** Don't compromise yourself to be accepted, act out for attention or endanger yourself for excitement.

13. Planning problems — **Use Positive planning, "Think ahead, plan ahead, get ahead."** Each night list what you have to do tomorrow with responsibilities first. Be proactive.

14. Boundary problems — **Show Respect.** Treat people like they deserve to be treated. Respect others personal space, privacy, personal property, feelings and opinions.

15. Victim view — **Hold yourself Accountable.** Shift your from dwelling on the past and other people's behavior ("But they...") to the present and your behavior.

16. Justifying actions — **Follow facts not feelings.** Use the ABC's of letting feelings go to challenge "I should/must", calm down, don't act on it and move on

17. Extremism — **"Take a Balanced View.** Let go of "all or nothing thinking." Accept that you don't have to be #1 to succeed, you just have to finish what you start.

18. Minimizing — **Call it like it is.** When a mistake has been called to your attention don't minimize it by using, "I Just or "I Only." Use others feedback for change.

19. Magnifying — **Reel it in.** Use the Reality Scales to weigh out the real seriousness of injustices, criticism or conflicts, don't magnify it with "Always" & "Never."

20. Assuming — **Verify.** Since things are not always the way they appear before acting on unverified information, check it out. Get the facts and other opinions first.

Knowing and correcting the set of 20 types of Irresponsible Thinking and characteristics (Table 6.2) is an important part of responsible decision making in SRT. In order to keep from overwhelming clients with too much information at once, begin developing Responsible Thinking by using the short six-item form (i.e., Minimizing, Victim view, Justifying, Magnifying, Assuming and Control issues). Use the JOBS MAN acronym to help clients identify the first four types of the short form with the following key words: **J**ust or **O**nly (Minimizing); **B**ut or because (Victim view/blaming); **S**hould or **M**ust (Justifying actions); **A**lways or **N**ever (Magnifying).

Treatment Exercise: Changing Irresponsible Thinking that enables relapse
Review the basic Irresponsible Thinking examples on Table 4.2 and self-statements that can identify Irresponsible Thinking on Table 6.2. Then review the "Identifying Irresponsible Thinking that enables relapse" treatment exercise that clients wrote earlier (p. 115) that identified and labeled their irresponsible thinking. Finally, conduct a client Responsibility Training discussion on coming up with responsible alternatives (helpful opposites) to substitute for their irresponsible thinking and have them record a responsible alternative to each type of irresponsible thinking that they identified. With some types if Irresponsible Thinking, using REBT self-challenging statements such as, "Where is the evidence that..." can be helpful in guiding clients to construct responsible alternatives. See "Ways to Challenge Belief Problems" (p. 88). For further information, see "Challenging Irresponsible Thinking", p. 190- 191 in Yokley (2008).

4. Staying Grounded- "When in doubt, check it out." The best way for clients to avoid unrealistic hope is to stay grounded by bouncing their thoughts off a responsible other before making important decisions. Clients need to obtain trusted second opinions from responsible others to inoculate against irrational or unrealistic hope which can result in entering high-risk situations on purpose to test self-control. If no trusted, responsible second opinion is available, clients need to use the reality scales to make a responsible decision. Staying grounded means showing Social Maturity and asking self, "Is what I am considering honest, trustworthy, loyal, concerned and responsible?"

5. Maintaining Priorities- Maintaining priorities means instructing clients to "keep your problem up front" by making recovery from unhealthy, harmful behavior their #1 priority. Maintaining priorities for clients means protecting their: 1) healthy body recovery by staying aware of unhealthy, harmful behavior relapse triggers; 2) healthy relationship recovery by staying aware of their social maturity (i.e., honesty, trust, loyalty, concern and responsibility) and; 3) healthy life direction recovery by staying on target (i.e., "Keep your eyes on the prize") and moving towards achieving positive life goals to get what they want in life (i.e., "Something to do that's positive for you"). "Not keeping your problem up front", slipping into automatic pilot and falling into old habits often occurs when clients are fatigued or upset. Thus, clients need to maintain priorities and HALT relapse by not getting too Hungry, Angry (upset), Lonely or Tired.

6. Healthy Need Gratification- Healthy need gratification involves accepting human needs for attention, acceptance or excitement and finding a positive outlet for those needs to prevent irresponsible decisions based on those needs. Clients with a past history of being ignored, need to find a present positive activity that meets healthy needs for attention (e.g., volunteer work, internet blogging, studying hard for good grades, working hard for a raise, promotion or award).

Those with a past history of rejection are advised to get involved in a regular positive activity that meets needs for acceptance (e.g., AA fellowship, clubs, team sports). Clients with a low boredom tolerance and high stimulation threshold need to get involved in a positive activity that is exciting and does not jeopardize their recovery or freedom (e.g., action sports such sky diving, skiing, surfing). In summary, healthy need gratification means getting involved with a positive activity that meets needs for positive attention, acceptance or excitement and being careful not to compromise values to meet exaggerated needs.

Treatment Exercise: Meeting Healthy Needs
Have your clients write out and discuss any past history of being ignored, rejected or bored. Then facilitate a discussion on how strong they feel their needs are for attention, acceptance and excitement. Ask for specific examples of irresponsible decisions they made in the past that fulfilled their needs for attention, acceptance or excitement and any consequences that resulted. Finally have your clients discuss positive activities that could meet healthy needs for attention, acceptance or excitement.

Responsible Decision Summary... In order for clients to learn responsible decision making that protects their recovery, they need to "Go to the opposite extreme" of past irresponsible decision-making that can result in relapse in the key areas listed in Table 6.10 below.

Table 6.10 Summary of Contributing Factors to Irresponsible and Responsible Decisions	
Irresponsible Decisions are supported by...	**Responsible Decisions are supported by...**
1. Not considering consequences	1. Thinking it Through with the "Reality Scales"
2. Making "Foresight Deficit Decisions"	2. Using "Fantasy Fast Forward"
3. Not being aware of irresponsible thinking	3. Socially Responsible thinking
4. Irrational or unrealistic hope	4. Staying Grounded
5. Problem priorities	5. Maintaining priorities
6. Exaggerated needs	6. Healthy need gratification

Treatment Exercise: Responsible Decision Skills that Protect Recovery
Conduct individual and/or group treatment session discussions covering the six responsible decision making skills that protect recovery until these skills are completely understood. Then have clients discuss their own examples of how they could use these skills to prevent the last relapse they had or a relapse that created problems in their life.

Avoid Trouble: Try not to use Decisional Balance in Stressful Situations
First escape the stressful situation with the "3 G's."
1. Get out (Remove yourself);
2. Get honest (Block the thought)- Challenge, "I must make this decision right here and now." Tell yourself "It's probably best if I take time to 'Think it Through' first."
3. Get Responsible (Substitute a more responsible thought)- Go to a non-stressful place and at a non-stressful time use the use the Reality Scales to weigh out the benefits and drawbacks.
   Note: Decisional Balance is not a subset of Relapse Prevention, it's a separate skill that is best used after leaving stressful situations.

Decisional Balance Skills Practice: The Situation Response Analysis Log
Have clients journal their progress in making responsible decisions using any of the three Decisional Balance tools that they learned (i.e., The Fork in the road Pros and Cons List, The Reality Scales or The Decisional Balance Sheet) on their Situation Response Analysis log. These daily logs that document their high-risk situations, their response to those situations and their analysis of their response need to be reviewed and discussed in each treatment session. Basic client log instructions are listed in Table 4.7 on p. 61 and several Situation Response Analysis Log formats are presented in Appendix B, p. 263.

**Tolerance Training in Decisional Balance
and Other Important Responsible Decision Skills**
"If you can't Tolerate change, you won't be able to make or maintain decisions to change"

> **Tolerance Training Goal:** Improve tolerance for positive change.
>   **Objectives:** Clients will apply decisional balance skills to help them tolerate making important positive changes in their lives.

Tolerating Change
Human beings strive for comfort and have problems tolerating change. On the Social Readjustment Rating Scale (Holmes & Rahe, 1967), a change score over 300 puts humans at greatly increased risk of stress-related illness. For example...

- Divorce- 73 stress points
- Marriage- 50 points
- Death of a close family member- 63 points
- Gaining new family member (birth/adoption/in law)- 39 points
- Beginning or ceasing formal schooling- 26 points
- Revision of personal habits (e.g., quitting smoking)- 24 points

Explain to clients that the concept of "addiction" is not limited to problem drug and alcohol use and can apply to a wide range of other excessive, compulsive "behavioral addictions" including gambling, video game playing, eating disorders, sports and physical exercise, internet/phone use, sex addiction, pathological working and compulsive criminal behavior (e.g., Alavi et. al. (2012). Help clients understand that humans are creatures of habit capable of becoming addicted to any behavior routine that creates comfort. Use concrete examples in story form. For example, if you slipped a $100 bill under your neighbors door the first of every month, within 6 months they would have developed a tolerance, become used to having an extra $100/month and have regularly scheduled activities that consumed that money (e.g., regularly scheduled manicure, massage, movie and dining out night, etc.). Then at month 7 if you suddenly stopped, your neighbor would go through financial withdrawal as a result of you taking away something that they were using to make their life more comfortable. The bottom line here is that humans strive for comfort and avoid/resist discomfort. Thus, even without chemically induced withdrawal symptoms, humans can become psychologically addicted to comfortable, rewarding behaviors or routines, develop a tolerance to those behaviors or routines and have trouble tolerating behavior change.

Just like the Decisional Balance tools can be used to weigh out decisions and support stopping unhealthy, harmful behavior, they can also be used to weigh out decisions and support starting healthy, helpful behavior, help tolerate positive behavior change, address procrastination and resistance to healthy behavior change. For example, starting- Drug treatment, Alcoholics Anonymous, Smoke enders, Weight Watchers diet, Yoga, Weight training, Walking/jogging, Couples counseling, Medication, Psychotherapy, Credit counseling or an engagement to be married.

One of our most important decisions in life is whether to change an unhealthy, harmful, addictive behavior. In changing unhealthy eating, drinking, smoking, spending, etc., change typically occurs in five basic stages, i.e., precontemplation, contemplation, preparation, action and maintenance (see p. 36). Decisional balance by weighing the pros and cons of changing on the Reality Scales can help clients move towards positive change from precontemplation or contemplating change to taking positive action. The flip side of deciding not to do something unhealthy/harmful like drinking at a party is deciding to do something healthy/helpful like tolerating positive change like the discomfort of avoiding drinking at a party where alcohol is being served. Facilitate a discussion about the important healthy changes clients need to make in the healthy lifestyle goal areas of healthy body, healthy relationships and healthy life direction.

Tolerating Change is Required to Make and Maintain Healthy Lifestyle Decisions

Unhealthy Eating Example- Making and maintaining healthy lifestyle decisions require tolerating biopsychosocial changes. For example, biologically, the decision to start and continue a weight management program means eating healthier foods and changing your metabolism through healthy exercise. This involves tolerating change in food types, tastes and portion sizes along with tolerating a change in activity level. The two basic things our female weight-management clients have come to accept are that, "If the food tastes good it's not healthy and if the shoes look good they hurt." Unfortunately too many are willing to accept the pain of the shoes for fashion but are unwilling to accept the taste of the food for health. Psychologically, it is clear that, "There can be no comfort eating without discomfort."

Psychological change in weight management involves tolerating counseling for emotional coping skills development, awareness of eating triggers and the loss of letting go of food as a source of emotional comfort. Weight-related emotions need to be tolerated to avoid emotional eating. For example anger at self for allowing weight gain to go this far, anxiety or depression about the consequences (e.g., type 2 diabetes, sleep apnea, high blood pressure, high cholesterol, knee and back pain). Letting go of the desire to try another "All you can eat" diet to avoid having to part with an unhealthy food habit needs to be tolerated. This has to begin by clients accepting that "There is no recipe solution for a self-control problem." Weight management expert, Eileen Seeholzer, M.D. put it this way, "If we were feeding you, you would lose weight. The problem is that you are feeding you." Accepting medical treatment and counseling for depression and anxiety to help let go of "eating feelings" means setting unhealthy pride aside and learning to tolerate asking for help. Socially, clients have to tolerate change in who they associate with and where they go.

Tolerating social changes from eating with friends at fast food or all you can eat buffet restaurants to health food restaurants or inviting them over for a healthy meal involves a change in the way food is viewed. After listening to a discussion about the power of social influence environmental triggers on unhealthy eating, one of our weight-management clients said, "Well I guess this means I'll have to quit my food gang" and went on to explain how every Friday night, five of her friends would get together to try a new restaurant. Each would order a different appetizer, main course and dessert. Then everyone would try some of everything in what might be described as a food taste orgy. Food is supposed to be fuel that runs our bodies from dawn to dusk, not a social pastime or the source of entertainment that television food networks have created. Since these were long term close friends, deciding to enter weight-management required tolerating a difficult change in her social network.

"It's easy to make good decisions when there are no bad options"-- Robert Half (1918- 2001)

Unhealthy, Harmful Substance Use Example- Biopsychosocial changes also need to be tolerated for individuals to make and maintain their recovery decisions in drug and alcohol treatment. The clients decision to start drug and alcohol treatment begins with having to tolerate biological changes that in many cases involve physical withdrawal symptoms from their drug of choice. Those drugs that do not have pronounced physical withdrawal symptoms often have psychological withdrawal symptoms. This is particularly true with clients that have used the drug to calm down or comfort themselves. Depending on the symptoms, client problems tolerating their biological adjustment to sobriety may require medical treatment. While some individuals do admit themselves for treatment, difficulty tolerating physical or psychological withdrawal symptoms often prevents clients from starting drug and alcohol treatment on their own. Since "the superego is soluble in alcohol and evaporates with narcotics", continued drug and alcohol use typically results in impaired decisions that trigger involuntary treatment (i.e., court mandate or family pressure admission).

Psychologically, clients who admitted themselves to treatment have often experienced feelings of desperation after significant resource loss forcing them to accept that their habit became uncontrollable and their lives became unmanageable. In traditional drug and alcohol treatment this has been referred to as "hitting rock bottom" and a recent study has found that resource loss is a predictor of treatment completion (Gruszczyńska et. al. 2016). As a result, of accepting their addiction, self-referred clients have to tolerate great self-disappointment along with possible guilt or shame about their present and past behavior. Clients do not have to be self-referred or "hit rock bottom" to benefit from treatment. However, in order to make the decision that a healthy, clean and sober lifestyle is needed, clients who are involuntary admitted need to tolerate change and overcome resentment towards the authority who mandated or pressured them into treatment. Group therapy can help clients let go of their irrational beliefs that they could make it on their own if only the program was not holding them back. Tolerating this authority issue has been successfully managed in Therapeutic Communities by helping residents accept that, "You alone must do it but you can't do it alone." Substance-related emotions need to be tolerated to prevent "pity-party" using. For example anger at self for allowing drug/alcohol use to get out of control, anxiety or depression about the consequences (e.g., legal charges, relationship loss, debt/credit loss, house/car loss). Accepting treatment for anger, anxiety or depression to prevent using drugs and alcohol to cope with those unwanted feelings means getting honest about feelings and learning to tolerate asking for help.

Socially, clients making a decision to enter drug and alcohol treatment have to tolerate a level of care recommendation for outpatient (weekly meetings), intensive outpatient (3- 5 half day meetings/week) or residential treatment which changes their social activity schedule, who they associate with and where they go. Given the well-established power of social pressure to use drugs and alcohol, clients with substance use problems have to tolerate the discomfort of making decisions on who to eliminate from their social network. They also have to tolerate the discomfort of developing a new sober support network. Finally, to avoid high-risk situation relapse triggers, they have to tolerate limitations on where they can go.

"When we are no longer able to change a situation ,
we are challenged to change ourselves"-- Viktor Frankl (1905- 1997)

Harmful Sexual Behavior Example- Tolerating biopsychosocial changes are also needed to make and maintain healthy lifestyle decisions by individuals in treatment for sexual behavior problems. Tolerating the recommendation for antidepressant or antiandrogen treatment of biological sexual drive is an issue that some sex offender clients have to face. Probation and parole rules which prohibit alcohol use due to the combination of impaired judgment and biological disinhibition of sexual behavior also have to be tolerated.

Clients attending Sex Addicts Anonymous for excessive, compulsive, possibly risky but not abusive sexual behavior may be self-referred. However, most clients with harmful, abusive sexual behavior problems (e.g., child molestation or adult rape) are mandated to treatment by the courts and registered as sex offenders with the local police. Psychologically, these mandated clients have to tolerate great self-disappointment along with public embarrassment and shame about their behavior. Sexual behavior-related emotions need to be tolerated to prevent giving up on trying to change or using alcohol/drugs to cope. Examples include: anger at self for allowing sexual behavior to get out of control; anxiety about the consequences (e.g., legal charges, offender registration, stigma, debt); depression about relationship loss, job loss and having to move out of the neighborhood. Learning to tolerate stigma can be assisted in group therapy with a focus on adopting prosocial values and practicing prosocial behavior, e.g., "You may be able to call me a sex offender but you can't call me a liar because I don't do that anymore."

Socially, clients convicted of child molestation typically have probation, parole or treatment program rules limiting them to contact with adults and receive social skills training needed to help them develop age appropriate relationships. Those convicted of adult rape often have anger management requirements to help them tolerate their control and power obsession. Close community supervision is part of their treatment and constant surveillance has to be tolerated. They have to tolerate change involving probation, parole and treatment rule limitations on who they can associate with, where they can go and what they can do.

"Right actions in the future are the best apologies for bad actions in the past"-- Tyron Edwards

In summary, basic changes and issues that need to be tolerated in order to make and maintain healthy lifestyle decisions for clients with unhealthy, harmful behavior problems include:
- Physical rules on what clients can eat, drink or smoke along with medical treatment recommendations;
- Unhealthy, harmful behavior-related emotions need to be tolerated to prevent giving up on

trying to change. For example, guilt, shame or anger at self for allowing the problem to get out of control along with anxiety or depression about physical health complications, legal complications and/or social/relationship complications;

- Social development of a new support network, limitations on who clients associate with, where they can go and what they can do need to be tolerated in order to avoid high-risk situation relapse triggers.

Decisional Balance Tolerance Training: Three Basic Tools to Use

Three basic tools clients can use to tolerate the change needed to make and maintain positive lifestyle decisions are: Positive Change Accommodation; Decisional Dissipation and; Change Impact Analysis.

Positive Change Accommodation: "Do the Opposite"

In Positive Change Accommodation, clients accommodate to unwanted feelings, urges or cravings by going beyond delay of gratification and actually doing the opposite positive change behavior. In residential care this "The Pendulum Concept" practice has helped Therapeutic Community clients swing their lifestyle pendulum way over to the very positive, healthy, helpful side during treatment in order to counter-balance the very negative, unhealthy, harmful behavior habits they developed before treatment (De Leon, 1990-91). In behavior therapy this approach has been referred to as "overcorrection" and is summarized by the Therapeutic Community maxim, "You have to go to the opposite extreme to meet the median".[2] In outpatient care, Dialectical Behavior Therapy (DBT) has a similar positive change approach. In DBT, clients who justify unhealthy/harmful behavior based on unwanted feelings are instructed to identify the feeling and action that goes with it. Then they are told to "do the opposite action all the way" by not only acting opposite of the feeling/urge but thinking opposite as well (Linehan, 1993).

Positive Change Accommodation involves practicing going to the opposite extreme of the negative thinking that enables irresponsible decisions to engage in unhealthy, harmful behavior. This allows clients to accommodate enough to positive lifestyle change to be able to meet community standards after treatment when self-control naturally swings back towards the median. Examples of Positive Change Accommodation by practicing opposite positive responsible thinking and decisions are provided in Table 6.11.

Treatment Exercise: Positive Change Accommodation

Facilitate individual and/or group treatment session discussions with clients on how they could "Go to the opposite extreme" with the negative thinking and irresponsible decisions that were involved in their unhealthy, harmful behavior. Discuss the importance of practicing positive, healthy thinking and decisions in order to develop a positive, healthy lifestyle.

Decisional Dissipation

Decisional Dissipation involves adding the 3 S's (Decisional Balance Reality Scales) to Emotional Dissipation (described in Chapter 5) to help dissipate the irresponsible thinking that enables acting on feelings, cravings or urges. This process involves adding the Reality Scales (3 S's) in the third "C" step of the ABC's of letting feelings go to help clients "Challenge" irrational

	Negative, Irresponsible, Unhealthy/Harmful Thoughts	**Opposite Positive, Responsible Thoughts/Decisions**
Table 6.11 **Positive Change Accommodation Examples Across Unhealthy, Harmful Behaviors**		
Sexual Abuse	"It's <u>only</u> a drinking game, not rape"	"Drunk people can't consent. I'm putting a stop to this and making some coffee."
Physical Abuse	"I <u>must</u> smack some sense into them, they disrespected me"	"How is me doing the wrong thing going to get them to do the right thing? I'm getting out of here."
Property Abuse	"It's OK for me to take a few bucks from them, they <u>always</u> borrow from me and <u>never</u> pay me back."	"Borrowing without asking is stealing. I'm not doing this."
Substance Abuse	"I'll <u>just</u> have one drink and then leave." "I'll <u>just</u> try one bite to see how it tastes."	"It's never just one. I'm getting out before I start something that I can't stop."
Money Abuse	"I <u>shouldn't</u> go to the Casino but I got a raise so luck is on my side"	"I make my own luck, I worked for my raise and I'm not risking it at the Casino"
Trust Abuse	"I <u>should</u> get even with my girlfriend for flirting by cheating on her"	"How is doing worse than she did going to make things better? I'm going to talk to her about this."

Note: Key words that identify the irresponsible thinking that enables unhealthy, harmful behavior are underlined. See Table 4.2.

beliefs that enable unhealthy, harmful decisions. Practical examples for unhealthy, harmful eating, substance use and sexual behavior are summarized below.

Practical Application Example: Unhealthy Eating

Consider the weight management case of Ted (p. 88) who was caught off guard when his poker buddies brought over his favorite pizza.

- <u>Action that occurred</u>- Ted's pizza eating poker buddies showed up with his favorite pizza. The sight and smell triggered his pizza cravings.
- <u>Belief problem</u>- Ted tells himself, "I *must* eat one piece because they brought it just for me" to justify acting on pizza cravings.
- <u>Challenging the Belief problem</u>- "Why must I eat pizza with the guys?" Then add the 3 S's...
  1. <u>Survival scale</u>- How necessary for my survival it is for me to eat pizza with the guys? Rating (0- 10) is <u>0</u>→ Not necessary for my survival at all.
  2. <u>Success scale</u>- How important for my life success is it for me to eat pizza with the guys? Rating (0- 10) is <u>0</u>→ Not important for my success at all.
  3. <u>Severity scale</u>- How severe will the consequences be for me to eat pizza with the guys? Rating (0- 10) is <u>7</u>→ Moderate consequences. "Eating one piece will trigger the goal violation effect, I'll go on another pizza binge and feel really bad about myself."

Ted's Conclusion: "Eating pizza with the guys is not necessary for my survival or important for my success and there are unwanted consequences. It's not worth doing."

Practical Application Example: Unhealthy, Harmful Substance use
Take the substance abuse case of Ray (p. 89) whose old girlfriend Gina took him to a bar they used to hang out at on a day pass from his residential drug and alcohol treatment program.
- Action that occurred- Gina took Ray to their old hang out bar where they used to get drunk, shoot pool and then spend the night together. People drinking triggered his alcohol cravings.
- Belief problem- Ray thought, "I *must* have just one drink so she won't have to drink alone" to make himself feel better about caving into his cravings.
- Challenging the Belief problem- "Why must I have a drink with Gina?" Then add the 3 S's…
  1. Survival scale- How necessary for my survival it is for me to have a drink with Gina? Rating (0- 10) is 0→ Not necessary for my survival at all.
  2. Success scale- How important for my life success is it for me to have a drink with Gina? Rating (0- 10) is 0→ Not important for my success at all.
  3. Severity scale- How severe will the consequences be if I have a drink with Gina? Rating (0- 10) is 9→ Severe consequences. "Having a drink with Gina will violate my program and probation rules."

Ray's Conclusion: "Having a drink with Gina is not necessary for my survival or important for my success and there are severe consequences. The drawbacks far outweigh the benefits."

Practical Application Example: Harmful Sexual Behavior
Process the sex offender case of Dan (p. 90) who was in treatment for molesting his step-sister Kyla which he told himself was justified because her alcoholic father Willie would beat him.
- Action that occurred- Dan was caught sneaking back in after trying to avoid Willie by staying out of the house until he was asleep and received another drunken beating from Willie. This triggered his anger, revenge thinking and sexual re-offense urge.
- Belief problem- Dan told himself, "I *should* do what I want to Kyla because Willie did what he wanted to me" to justify venting his anger and sexual urges on Kyla.
- Challenging the Belief problem- Why should I do what I want to Kyla? Then add the 3 S's…
  1. Survival scale- How necessary for my survival it is for me to do what I want to Kyla? Rating (0- 10) is 0→ Not necessary for my survival at all.
  2. Success scale- How important for my life success is it for me to do what I want to Kyla? Rating (0- 10) is 0→ Not important for my success at all.
  3. Severity scale- How severe will the consequences be if I do what I want to Kyla? Rating (0- 10) is 10→ Severe consequences. "Doing what I want to Kyla will hurt her as much or more than I was hurt and will hurt me by violating my probation rules."

Dan's Conclusion: "Doing what I want to Kyla is not necessary for my survival or important for my success and there are severe consequences. I'm not using Willie as an excuse to relapse."

Treatment Exercise: Decisional Dissipation
Conduct a flip chart or dry erase board discussion with clients on adding the Reality Scales to the ABC's of letting feelings, cravings and urges go that were involved in their unhealthy, harmful behavior. Start by putting up examples of the "Action that occurred" and the "Belief problem" with typical examples like those listed above in order to focus clients on how they would use the

Reality Scales to help them Challenge their Belief Problem. Then have clients write and discuss their own specific Decisional Dissipation examples.

Change Impact Analysis

In reality, change kicks up unwanted feelings and unwanted feelings kick up resistance to change. More specifically, humans tend to be creatures of habit that strive for comfort and avoid change because change disrupts their habits, which makes them uncomfortable. Unfortunately for humans in life, "Nothing is constant but change." Since making positive changes can be difficult to tolerate, humans create ways to resist or avoid change. Three common ways that humans avoid having to tolerate change are: 1) Procrastination, i.e., tell themselves, "No need to change today, I can always make this decision tomorrow"; 2) Distortion- Either minimize, i.e., tell themselves, "It's not so bad and it will get better" (no need to change) or maximize, i.e., tell themselves, "I won't be able to stand the consequences of doing it" (too stressful to change) and; 3) Pessimism, i.e., tell themselves, "I can't do anything about it" or "It won't help so why even try" (There is no sense trying). Rating the expected impact of change on the Reality Scales can help humans break through procrastination, distortion and pessimism. Getting honest about change impact with the Reality Scales can help make the decision to tolerate change and move forward towards positive lifestyle goals.

"Not to make a decision, is to make a decision" [3]

Practical Application Example: Starting Weight Management

Although Laticia (p. 83) and Ted (p. 88 & above) have a different, age, sex, race and socioeconomic background, they have three things in common. First of all they both are experiencing ongoing negative social influence from overeating friends who enable relapse. Secondly, they are both very self-conscious about their weight and third, they both need to start Overeaters Anonymous to develop a positive support network that will help them stay on track with their healthy body goals. The logic here is simple: more positive modeling, less relapse. Specifically, spending more time with healthy eaters who redirect them when they slip and spending less time with unhealthy eaters who enable them to overeat will help them with their weight management. Rating the expected impact of avoiding change on the Reality Scales can help them move from resistance to change and avoiding getting help, e.g., "I should be able to do this on my own" to acceptance of change and help, e.g., the Therapeutic Community maxim, "You alone must do it but you can't do it alone."

Rating the Expected Impact of Change

- Survival scale- How much of a threat to my survival it is for me to get help at Overeaters Anonymous (accept change)? Rating (0- 10) is 0→ No survival threat to at all. No one dies from attending Overeaters Anonymous.
- Success scale- How important for my life goal success is it for me to get help at Overeaters Anonymous (accept change)? Rating (0- 10) is 8→ Very important for healthy body goal success and somewhat important in relationships (i.e., less weight, less self-consciousness around others).
- Severity scale- How severe will the consequences be for me if I get help at Overeaters Anonymous (accept change)? Rating (0- 10) is 2→ Minor consequences. Getting help at OA

involves letting go of unhealthy pride and getting on the scale in front of others but will actually help let go of the negative social influence that enables unhealthy eating.

Conclusion: "Accepting Overeaters Anonymous: poses no threat to survival; is important for healthy body goal success, only minor social discomfort consequences and is well worth doing."

Practical Application Example: Returning to Alcoholics Anonymous
Grace was a 49-year-old female referred to hospital-based drug and alcohol treatment after her nursing license was suspended. Her referral occurred as a result of prescription opiate use at work subsequent to a motor vehicle accident, which left her in chronic pain. Her nursing license suspension was to be reviewed after treatment completion and Grace had discontinued her pain medications in order to pass random urine toxicology screenings. With much time on her hands and increased contact with her alcoholic husband, she developed an alcohol problem that required further treatment followed by regular Alcoholics Anonymous support. For several years she did quite well maintaining her sobriety and actually becoming a sponsor to others in AA. Unfortunately, when her request for license reinstatement was denied, she was so hurt and angry that her recovery progress was not recognized by the board that she returned to drinking with a self-destructive vengeance. Her drinking was so severe that she was hospitalized several times. Grace knows that she needs to return to AA for additional support between her weekly hospital-based treatment sessions but is ashamed to face her old sponsor and does not want those that she sponsored when they entered AA to know that she relapsed.

Rating the Expected Impact of Change
- Survival scale- How much of a threat to my survival it is for me to return to Alcoholics Anonymous (accept change)? Rating (0- 10) is 0→ No threat to my survival at all. "Attending Alcoholics Anonymous didn't kill me in the past, it only killed my excuses to drink."
- Success scale- How important for my life success is it for me to return to Alcoholics Anonymous (accept change)? Rating (0- 10) is 10→ Extremely important for my healthy body goal of remaining clean and sober, preventing further liver damage and for my healthy life direction goal of returning to work.
- Severity scale- How severe will the consequences be if I return to Alcoholics Anonymous (accept change)? Rating (0- 10) is 3→ Minor consequences. Returning to AA means no longer covering up my relapse from old AA members and people I sponsored and blowing my image by holding myself accountable and starting over.

Conclusion: "Returning to AA: poses no threat to my survival; is extremely or important for my success, has only minor social discomfort consequences and needs to start now."

Practical Application Example: Getting Sexual Behavior Problem Aftercare
Ron was an early 30's junior executive in a mid-sized company started by his father. As a result of taking advantage of his position, Ron's sexual harassment of attractive female employees finally made it over the company policy wall and into the office of the local prosecutor. This in turn resulted in a court ordered referral for psychological evaluation and treatment of his sexual behavior. He reluctantly completed his court requirements and retained his job. However, the public disclosure of his sexual behavior problem put retaining his marriage in question and he

was in need of staying aware of his high-risk situations in order to avoid relapse. To address those issues, he was offered an aftercare referral for marriage counseling with an experienced sexual behavior problem treatment provider and a referral to Sex Addicts Anonymous

Rating the Expected Impact of Change

- Survival scale- How much of a threat to my survival it is for me to accept marriage counseling and aftercare support at Sex Addicts Anonymous (accept change)? Rating (0- 10) is 0→ No threat to my survival at all. No one dies as a result of attending marriage counseling or Sex Addicts Anonymous.
- Success scale- How important for my life success is it for me to accept marriage counseling and aftercare support at Sex Addicts Anonymous (accept change)? Rating (0- 10) is 8→ Very important to maintaining my healthy relationship goals and in staying aware of high-risk situations for relapse.
- Severity scale- How severe will the consequences be for me if I accept marriage counseling and aftercare support at Sex Addicts Anonymous (accept change)? Rating (0- 10) is 3→ Minor consequences. If I enter marriage counseling, I will probably to have to go over the embarrassing details of my problem in front of my wife and I don't want my wife to always view me as a sex addict.

Conclusion: "Accepting aftercare marriage counseling and Sex Addicts Anonymous: poses no threat to my survival; is very important for my relationship success and; presents only minor personal embarrassment consequences. I need to push past my embarrassment and do this."

Treatment Exercise: Change Impact Analysis

Facilitate individual and/or group treatment session in Change Impact Analysis in three steps. First have clients discuss and suggest possible positive changes that could help them avoid relapse and achieve healthy body, relationship and life direction goals. Than have them weigh the impact of accepting those changes on the Reality Scales. Finally, have them share their conclusions about the changes being considered.

"If you can change your mind, you can change your life"-- William James (1842- 1910)

Decisional Balance Theory and Research Support Summary: Decisional balance theory is historically based on the decision-making conflict model of Janis and Mann (1977). This conflict model assumes that sound decision-making comes from entering all of the conflicting pros/benefits and cons/drawbacks of the decision to be made into a decisional balance sheet. Since there are always unexpected benefits and drawbacks, the decisional balance sheet allows resolution of the decision conflict by comparing the expected benefits and expected drawbacks (Mann, 1972). This comparative approach to decision-making by weighing out the pros and cons was first supported in the study of the decision to quit smoking and has been used as a structured discovery component in Motivational Interviewing to help patients through their stages of change in letting go of unhealthy harmful behavior for over 25 years (Velicer et. al. 1985).

Decisional balance techniques including development of pros and cons checklists have received support across a wide range of problem including drinking, smoking, cocaine, prescription drug abuse, criminal activity, weight control, healthy eating, exercise, adolescent delinquent behaviors, driving behavior, safer sex/condom use, sunscreen use, radon gas exposure, ear protection, mammography, pap testing, birth control pills, STD testing, HIV and cardiac treatment adherence (e.g., Braun, Bischof & Rumpf, 2012; Collens et. al. 2013; 2014; Elliot et. al. 2011; Foster et.al. 2015; Jordon et. al. 2013; Mainvil et. al 2010; Prat et. al. 2012; Prochaska et. al. 1994; Santiago-Rivas, Velicer & Redding, 2015; Steele, Steele & Cushing, 2012; Velicer et. al. 1985).

Decisional Balance Summary

In summary, the following basic SRT Decisional Balance tools are used to help clients "Think it through", make responsible decisions, avoid unhealthy, harmful behavior and approach healthy lifestyle goals.

- The "Reality Check"- Having the client ask themselves, "Is what I'm thinking about doing helpful or harmful to myself or others?"
- The Fork in the Road "Pros and Cons" Decision List- A list of all the benefits and drawbacks of the action being considered.
- The Reality Scales (0 to 10 scales):
  1. Survival scale- How necessary for my survival is it for me to… ? ("Do I need to do this to survive?", "Could this threaten my safety?")
  2. Success scale- How important for my success is it for me to…? ("Will this decision change my life forever?", "In 10 years will I probably look back and say doing this made a positive change in my life that I will never forget?)
  3. Severity scale- How severe would the consequences be if I...? (Could this endanger the safety or security of myself or other? Could this jeopardize my freedom or violate the rights of others?)
- The Decisional Balance Sheet- Weighs the benefits and drawbacks of doing and not doing the target behavior on in a 2 X 2 matrix.

Integrate Decisional Balance into the Relapse Prevention Plan

In high risk situations for relapse first Avoid Trouble with the "3 G's".

1. Get out (Remove yourself)
2. Get honest (Block the thought)- Use Decisional Balance. Ask yourself "Is what I'm thinking about doing going to be helpful or harmful?" (to self/others) and weigh your decision on the "Reality Scales"
3. Get Responsible (Substitute a more responsible thought)- Go to the opposite extreme, a non-stressful place where you are not likely to do the harmful behavior and use Emotional Regulation (i.e., the ABC's of letting feelings go or holding on to feelings) to calm down and avoid justifying actions based on feelings.
   - Note: Decisional Balance is not a subset of Relapse Prevention, it's a separate skill that supports Relapse Prevention and is best used after leaving stressful situations.

"A human being is a deciding being"-- Viktor Frankl (1905- 1997)

Chapter 7
Internal Control- Healthy Behavior Success Skill #4:
Helping Clients "Solve the Problem"
with Social Problem Solving

Helping clients "Solve the problem" with Social Problem Solving

"If you're not working on the solution, you're part of the problem"-- Eldridge Cleaver (1935- 1998) [1]

Social problem solving is the cognitive-affective-behavioral process by which people attempt to resolve real-life problems in a social environment (Siu & Shek, 2010). This process of generating options and evaluating them to select the best solution is what clinicians do so regularly that they probably take this skill for granted. Social Problem Solving can help with problems relating to unhealthy, harmful behavior as well as barriers to healthy, positive lifestyle development. Problems interfere with achievement of our life goals and create stress buildup which increases tension, physical complications and acting out through unhealthy, harmful behaviors. Social problem solving was designed to resolve life problems and help us: get what we want; do as well as we want and; be treated the way we want in life. In resolving life problems, social problem solving decreases stress below the threshold of physical manifestation or behavioral acting out.

Good social problem solving has been associated with positive self-esteem, life satisfaction, decreased stress and better family functioning. Achieving positive lifestyle change requires the ability to solve problems that are barriers to healthy body, relationship and life direction goals. Many clients with unhealthy, harmful behavior habits share a common problem solving deficit. Social problem-solving deficits have been linked to depression, suicide attempts, anxiety, chronic fatigue and chest pain. Stress buildup from not being able to solve life problems and overcome barriers to achieving positive goals sets the occasion for relapse into unhealthy, harmful behavior and giving up on healthy lifestyle goals.

Social Problem Solving: "Straight to the Point"

The point of this section is to help clients become aware of what they need to know, develop the skills they need and the tolerance they need to solve life problems that are barriers to life goals and can result in relapse or relationship problems.

Social Problem Solving Goals and Objectives

Awareness Training Goal: Increase client awareness of the goal behind their problem.

Objectives: Clients will be able to differentiate between the surface desire to vent feelings about the problem and the real goal which requires understanding self-motivation and solving the problem.

Responsibility Training Goal: Develop a responsible social problem solving strategy.

Objectives: Clients will be able to explain how to use the "SET" social problem solving skill to: 1) Set their goal; 2) Evaluate their progress and options; 3) Take responsible action in order to decrease stress buildup that can result in relapse and overcome barriers to achieving positive goals.

Tolerance Training Goal: Improve tolerance for setbacks and acceptance of the need to try multiple options.

Objectives: Clients will practice the "SET" social problem solving skill implementing one option after another to help them develop tolerance for setback disappointment and avoid giving up.

Common barriers to achieving healthy body, relationship and life direction goals that require Social Problem Solving include: external barriers (e.g., physical illness/limitations; work/academic obligations; financial limitations; legal issues; environmental relapse triggers); internal barriers (e.g., self-defeating habits, low frustration/distress tolerance, unmet or exaggerated needs for attention, acceptance and excitement, low self-efficacy,) and social barriers (e.g., negative or enabling social network, family factors, relationship conflict/sabotage). Given these barriers, social problem solving for many individuals with unhealthy, harmful behavior problems can be an iterative process that establishes the best solution by trying and ruling out prior solution options.

Treatment Exercise: Social Problem Solving Benefits

Desire to achieve long term life goal benefits can provide motivation for learning how to solve life problems that are barriers to goals. Have clients write and discuss examples of how ignoring problems or just venting their feelings about problems without working on the solution has prevented them from developing the healthy body, healthy relationships and healthy life direction that they need to succeed in life.

Since "There is no pill for other people's behavior", social problems will always require social problem solving

The ART of Social Problem Solving

The ART of Social Problem Solving involves: Awareness training to help clients become aware of their real goal (i.e., clarifying- What do I really want?); Responsibility training on evaluating progress and options (e.g., How is what I'm doing working for me? and What else could I try?); and; Tolerance training on learning to tolerate setbacks, disappointment and barriers to success by taking responsible action and continuing to explore new options to goal attainment until a solution is identified (Figure 7.1).

The ART of Social Problem Solving, is also particularly important in managing basic self-defeating characteristics (i.e., ruminating, procrastinating, and giving up) and exaggerated needs (i.e., acceptance, excitement, and attention) that support unhealthy, harmful behavior and are barriers to healthy lifestyle development. For example, rumination over (dwelling on) perceived or expected injustices

Awareness Training
If you're not Aware of the goal behind your problem, any solution you come up with may not meet your goal.

Responsibility Training
If you don't take Responsibility to evaluate your progress, you won't consider options that could get you to your goal.

Figure 7.1 The ART of Social Problem Solving

Tolerance Training
If you can't Tolerate setbacks, you won't be able to keep trying options until you meet your goal.

about something done by others or on the consequences of getting honest about something done by self gets clients stuck in emotions as opposed to looking for solutions. Putting off facing life

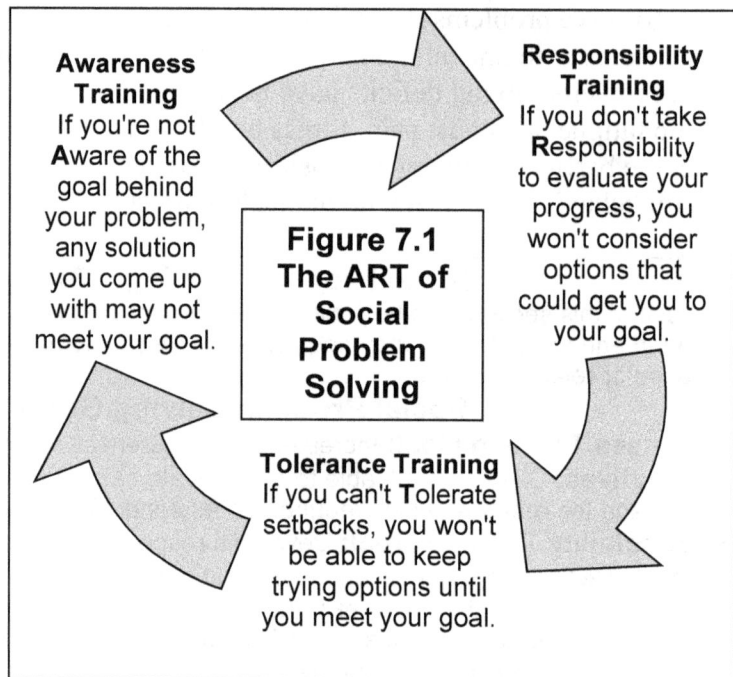

problems and working on solutions to life goal barriers (procrastination) blocks progress towards healthy lifestyle development. Finally, giving up which often relates to low frustration/distress tolerance, prevents any social problem solving at all. Getting caught up in meeting exaggerated needs for attention, acceptance or excitement keeps clients stuck in immediate gratification and pulls the client away from solving the problem and slows their progress in moving on towards their healthy lifestyle goals.

Social Problem Solving is used in SRT for healthy relationship development and positive goal achievement. Social Responsibility Therapy utilizes a simple three step SET Social Problem Solving tool to help clients solve problems: 1) Set your goal; 2) Evaluate your progress and options; 3) Take responsible action.

The SET Social Problem Solving Skill
Set your goal
"Life can be pulled by goals just as surely as it can be pushed by drives"
-- Viktor Frankl (1905- 1997)

Set your real goal is the first step in getting SET to solve the identified problem. The positive impact of goal setting on behavior change has received research support in a number of health-related behaviors, e.g., healthy diet and exercise, alcohol consumption and substance use (Cho, 2007; McEwan et. al. 2016; Spohr, Taxman & Walters, 2015). Setting your real goal involves helping clients identify their real goal by focusing on what they really want in the end, not their feelings about how things are now. Have clients process their goal in sessions and write it down. Put a copy in the client file for future discussion.

Evaluate your progress and options
"Solving the problem requires more research and less reaction"-- SRT Maxim

The second step in getting SET to solve the identified problem is to Evaluate your progress and options. This involves helping clients get honest about how well what they are doing is working and exercising their creativity to "Think outside the box" in generating new solution options. In addition to self-evaluation of goal progress, it is very important for clients to get objective feedback from responsible parents, peers, partners and professionals. This is because the value of feedback and goal setting over goal setting alone has been supported by meta-analytic research (e.g., Neubert, 1998). Behavior goal feedback has been demonstrated effective in promoting a wide range of healthy behaviors including walking, running, weight management, healthy grocery shopping, decreasing alcohol use, child communicable disease inoculation, sun screen use and safety belt use (e.g., Bertz, Pacanowski & Levitsky, 2015; Hagenzieker, Bijleveld & Davidse, 1997; Lombard, Lombard & Winett, 1995; Martens et. al. 2015; Wack, Crosland & Miltenberger, 2014; Winett, Cleaveland, Tate et. al., 1997; Winett, Moore, Wagner et. al., 1991; Yokley & Glenwick, 1984).

Evaluating Progress- Helping clients evaluate their progress involves guiding them to discover answers to the questions, "What have I been doing? How well has it working in getting me what I want? and How will things likely turn out if I continue doing the same thing?" This requires getting honest about their present responses and reactions to the problem along with their past solutions and exactly how well those things have worked in solving the identified problem. In order to get an objective point of view evaluation of goal progress needs to include feedback from others (e.g., clinicians, treatment group members, responsible parents, partners and peers). Have clients discuss their progress in sessions, get feedback from others and <u>write it down</u>. Put a copy in the client file for future discussion.

Evaluating options- Helping clients evaluate their options involves guiding them to discover answers to the questions, "What are my options?", "What can I change?", "What really needs to get done?" Help clients make as long of a list as you can of all possible options and choices that could get them to their your goal. Tell them "You are only limited by your creativity", ask them to be creative and get ideas from others. Have clients discuss all of their options both positive and negative in sessions. Make sure that all options are achievable. Then have clients <u>write out all of their options</u> and have them mark the options that they believe are most likely to solve the problem. Put a copy in the client file for future discussion.

Take responsible action
"The trouble with most therapy is that it helps you feel better. But you don't get better. You have to back it up with action, action, action" -- Albert Ellis (1913- 2007)

<u>T</u>ake responsible action is the third and final step in getting S<u>ET</u> to solve the identified problem. In this step, clients need to get honest about what is the right thing to do to get what they want or the best thing to do to solve the problem. This involves helping clients take responsibility to change by getting honest about what needs to change and correcting their course. This step requires guiding clients to discover answers to the questions, "What do I need to do differently to reach my goal?", "What is the best way to get what I want?" (i.e., the best solution option) and "What option should I try first?" With serious problems and important life goal decisions help clients "Think it through" by weighing out their decision on a "Fork in the Road Pros and Cons" decision list (p. 120), the Reality Scales (p. 120) or on a Decisional Balance Sheet (p. 125) before Taking Responsible Action. Have clients discuss the responsible action they are going to implement and <u>write it down</u>. Put a copy in the client file for future discussion.

Awareness Training in Social Problem Solving
"If you're not **A**ware of the goal behind your problem, your problem solution may not meet your goal"

Awareness Training Goal: Increase client awareness of the goal behind their problem.
   Objectives: Clients will be able to differentiate between the surface desire to vent feelings about the problem and the real goal which requires understanding self-motivation and solving the problem.

Identifying the real goal to solve the real problem- Life always has problems that kick up feelings and require solutions. Problems are only problems when we are not meeting our goals to get what we want in life. Behind every problem there is a goal. If clients are not aware of the real goal behind their problem, any solution they come up with may not meet their goal to solve the problem. In research, this mistake is known as a Type III error or "solving the wrong problem" (Mitroff & Silvers, 2009). For example, suppose the real client goal is to solve unhealthy junk food eating or Vodka drinking relapses that are triggered by <u>external control</u> (i.e., partner always brings it home) and <u>negative social influence</u>, (i.e., friends encouraging it). If the client enters individual therapy because they define the problem as not enough "willpower" (<u>internal control</u>), they are trying to solve the wrong problem. They have identified the entire problem as self-control which resulted in using individual therapy for a couple's therapy and social network problem. In another example, assume that the real client goal is to solve unhealthy, harmful sexual infidelity relapses triggered by continued masturbatory fantasies of sex with strippers and escorts (<u>internal control</u>). If the client blames the relapse problem on <u>negative social influence and external control</u> (i.e., regular peer and email invitations to strip clubs and escort services) and changes their email address instead of seeking help to modify their infidelity fantasies and develop a positive social network, they are trying to solve the wrong problem. They have identified the entire problem as things outside of themselves. As mentioned in Chapter 3 (Figure 3.1, p. 44), Social Responsibility Therapy targets unhealthy, harmful behavior with internal control, external control, and social learning approaches at the same time. This is done to: Help clients Pull themselves towards positive change (with cognitive interventions); Push clients toward positive change (with external reinforcement and consequences) and; Redirect/Motivate clients towards positive change (with positive social modeling/influence).

Self-motivation and real goals- Working with your clients on understanding self-motivation can help them shape their real goal. Use the simple man concept"[2] which holds that the simplest, most obvious, direct (and sometimes embarrassing) basic need (e.g., for attention, acceptance/companionship, excitement, pleasure seeking or pain avoidance) or mood (i.e., justifying actions based on feelings) is often the driving behavior motivation force.

Take the example of an overeater with high blood pressure who enters a weight loss program stating that their goal is "I want to lose weight and get healthy." If they are unaware of the fact that they also want to improve their appearance in hopes of: 1) meeting needs for acceptance and companionship by developing a dating social life and; 2) developing the self-esteem needed to interview for and obtain a better job, their goal will fall short of what they want in life. As a result, this client will probably not be satisfied with their progress after they achieve their weight loss goal and their blood pressure improves. This is likely because while decreasing weight will improve weight-related health problems, it will not automatically increase the self-esteem or dating social skills that were suppressed from years of weight-related rejection. Helping the client set their real goal in this case would involve helping them look at the big picture of getting what they want in life (Chapter 2). This involves doing a Five-Year Future Introduction to become aware of their healthy body, healthy relationship and healthy life direction goals (Figure 2.1. p. 25). Looking at what they need to succeed in getting what they want in life will allow them to examine all of the contributing factors to their weight loss motivation. Becoming aware of their self-motivation will in turn allow them to expand their goal from "I want to lose weight and get healthy" to "I want to lose weight, get healthy and develop the social skills needed for a fulfilling social life and career."

Consider the drunk driving client who enters treatment with a stated goal of "I want to stop drinking and get my driver's license back" but is unaware of (or leaves out) the fact that they have a strong need to avoid the painful thoughts and feelings associated with their history of sexual abuse. Achieving their goal of alcohol abstinence and getting their driver's license back is not likely to help them let go of the unwanted thoughts and feelings that have resulted in drinking themselves to sleep at night. Helping this client set their real goal would involve helping them look at their motivation to drink and expand their goal from "I want to stop drinking and get my driver's license back" to "I want to stop drinking, get my driver's license back and learn to cope with my past painful memories."

Think about the youth charged with sexual abuse of younger children who enters sex offender treatment telling themselves and others that their goal is "I want to avoid re-offense and stay out of trouble." If they leave out the fact that they want to feel comfortable around others their own age and fit in at school, their goal will not reflect everything that they want. Meeting their goal of developing a track record of avoiding re-offense will keep them out of trouble but will not help them fit in with peers. While avoiding re-offense by following their treatment rules to stay away from the high-risk situations is a social responsibility that they need to assume, it will not help them deal with their insecurity, shyness and social anxiety. In this case it is important for the client to understand that part of their relapse prevention responsibility is to learn the social skills needed to fit in with peers in order to avoid continually gravitating back towards younger children who are typically very accepting and not anxiety provoking. Helping the client set their goal in this case would involve helping them expand "I want to avoid re-offense and stay out of trouble" to "I want to avoid re-offense, stay out of trouble and develop age appropriate positive relationships."

Setting your goal vs venting your feelings- That being said, the first step towards solving problems is helping clients set their goal. This requires helping the client get honest about their real goal, what they really want. They need to ask themselves, "What is my goal? and What do I really want?" This involves learning to look at actual problem-solving goals, not feelings about the problem. There is a big difference between venting feelings and solving problems. When clients keep complaining about reality and the way things are, we know they just want to vent their feelings. When clients get honest about their real goal, we know they want to solve the problem. Clients need to ask themselves, "Is my real goal to solve the problem or just vent my feelings?" "If I'm angry about something I think was not right, will getting my feelings off by getting even get me what I want or will it just result in further problems?

Many if not most Social Problem Solving involving relatively minor life goal issues and barriers are easily solved by clients the first time through. However, with more serious long standing problems, clients who have long term Self-Defeating habits, foresight deficits and difficulty taking the advice of others can also have difficulty selecting the best solution option first. This tendency to follow feelings and needs is easily confused with purposeful resistance to treatment. These problems with rational decision-making cause them to have to learn by experience in a trial and error fashion.

Professional publications typically provide descriptions of cases where the intervention was highly successful without modification and at the first attempt. Unfortunately presenting the best case scenario leaves clinicians unprepared for more difficult, challenging cases. The following three case examples illustrate the Social Problem Solving struggles of more challenging clients.

Practical Application Example: Unhealthy Eating- Diana
Consider the weight management case of Diana (p. 58), the 43-year-old obese female weight-

management client whose entire social network consisted of her four Friday night restaurant binge eating "food gang" members. She had known these ladies for years. They accepted her for who she was and their friendship met the strong needs for acceptance. She had developed this need for acceptance historical risk factor (see p. 231) as a result of early parent abandonment and later weight-related rejection including being dumped by boyfriends for more attractive women since junior high school. Given this situation, her relapse prevention announcement that, "I guess I have to give up the food gang" was quickly followed by "What if I just go out with them to socialize, not eat and just have a salad while we visit?" Diana had to clarify her real goal and what she really wanted. She had to weigh the benefits of continuing to meet her social acceptance needs against the risk of gaining more weight by associating with unhealthy eaters. She had to answer the question, "Is my real goal to maintain my 'food gang' social acceptance needs or is my real goal to lose weight?"

S̲et your goal. What is my goal? What do I really want?
Diana had to clarify her real goal. Despite considerable group discussion on "Problem Priorities" (see p. 115), the need to take care of herself, she maintained her goal of wanting to lose weight but not wanting to let go of any of her "food gang" social life.

Practical Application Example: Unhealthy, Harmful Substance Use- Jeff

Jeff was a 17-year-old, male in court ordered residential drug treatment. He developed an authority problem and an exaggerated need for attention as a reaction to being ignored by his family. These historical risk factors (see p. 231) set him up for having the last word with authorities, school behavior problems and becoming psychologically addicted to dealing marijuana. This along with his renown stoner image made him the center of negative peer attention. Jeff claimed that he didn't need treatment since he was "only smoking weed, not crack" and was "just selling it to have it on hand to smoke, not dealing for profit." This attitude left him feeling held back by staff and believing that he could "make it on my own" if staff would just get off his back about the rules and release him from treatment. He based this claim on the fact that he had successfully run away from home a number of times in the past and "I always made it on my own." Brief questioning revealed that after running away, Jeff would typically go "couch surfing" spending several nights on the couch at one friend's house until their parents got sick of him, then wear out his welcome at another friend's house and so on. Sometimes when he had exhausted living off of his friends, he would break into an empty building and sleep there. Basically Jeff never really supported himself on his own. His negative attention seeking combined with his authority problem was reflected in ongoing attempts to unite youth against program rules and staff decisions. He kept himself locked in staff conflicts over whether he could ever make it on his own: 1) without finishing treatment (i.e., learning enough relapse prevention to avoid another drug-related arrest); 2) without finishing high school and; 3) without getting a job to support himself in his own apartment. Jeff had to clarify his real goal and what he really wanted. He had to weigh his short-term needs for autonomy against what it takes for long-term achievement of self-sufficiency. Jeff had to answer the question, "Is my real goal to just get out from under my residential treatment rules or is my real goal to develop the skills needed to support myself in my own place?

Set your goal. What is my goal? What do I really want?

Jeff had to clarify his real goal. He decided that what he really wanted was to be able to support himself in his own place. This required completing treatment, getting off of probation and getting a job. Using the Reality Scales helped him realize that while he really enjoyed getting high with friends, he didn't need it to survive, it was interfering with his success and it would not be too severe to give up.

Practical Application Example: Harmful Sexual Behavior- Dirk

Dirk was a 28-year-old male on probation after a county jail sentence for molesting Amber, the 7th grade daughter of Brandy, an exotic dancer that he moved in with 6 months earlier. Brandy was from a dysfunctional family and leaned on Dirk for support. Dirk had his own problems. He liked excitement and had a history of petty thrill crimes. His historical risk factors (see p. 231) included shoplifting with his alcoholic father. He also valued looks over loyalty. Brandy was exciting and made him look good, a two for one ego deal for Dirk. The conditions of his probation included no contact with Amber (or any other minors), no drugs and alcohol and a midnight curfew. Dirk's cool dude image was everything to him and he was a popular regular at local rock band after parties. His sex offense conviction and having to move back in with his mother dealt a serious blow to his image and he was desperate to restore it. About a month after Dirk moved in with his mother, he received a text from Brandy stating that she missed him and wanted to see him again. Dirk met Brandy at an after party that weekend. They started seeing each other regularly and getting asked to parties as a couple again. Brandy was cool like him and fit in with his friends who took notice of their relationship. His self-esteem was starting to improve and he advanced things rapidly to the point where Brandy asked him to move back in with her. Dirk really liked Brandy and couldn't stand living with his mother but knew that if he moved back in while Amber was still living there, it would violate his probation. He brought his invitation to move back in to the attention of his treatment group hoping to win their support. He pointed out that he was "only" caught by Brandy making out with Amber and fondling her breasts while he still had his clothes on so he was "just" charged with sexual imposition, not rape. He added that his program polygraph examinations would show if he had any sexual contact with minors. The discussion that followed put Dirk on the spot. He was confronted about minimizing his sex offense, lacking empathy, taking advantage of Brandy's dependency issues, not considering Amber's feelings or his sexual re-offense risk in addition to the probation violation issue. Dirk had to clarify his real goal. He had to look at his need to rekindle his romance with Brandy, get out of his mother's house, restore his image and self-esteem versus his need to preserve his freedom, consider his own re-offense risk and respect Amber's feelings. He had to answer the question, "Is my real goal to move out of my mother's house and back in with Brandy or is my real goal to get off probation and stay out of jail?"

Set your goal. What is my goal? What do I really want?

Dirk had to clarify his real goal. As bad as he wanted to move out of his mother's house and in with Brandy, Dirk decided that what he really wanted was to get off of probation and stay out of jail.

Treatment Exercise: Setting Your Real Goals

Review the goal setting issues and examples of Diana, Jeff and Dirk. Then have your clients discuss a recent problem in their life that they need to solve and their problem solving goal. Have them identify the barrier to their goal. Identify the area or intervention path that they need to target to address that barrier (e.g., internal control, external control, social learning/influence) to help them solve the whole problem and not the wrong problem. Help them get honest about their self-motivation to achieve the goal using "The simple man concept" [2] to discuss any basic needs which may be in play. Don't forget to discuss feelings about the problem and help separate wanting to vent feelings versus solve the problem. After this short term goal setting practice. Have the same discussion to help set long term healthy body, healthy relationship and healthy life direction goals.

Responsibility Training in Social Problem Solving
"If you don't take **Responsibility** to evaluate your progress,
you won't consider options that could get you to your goal"

Responsibility Training Goal: Develop a responsible social problem solving strategy.
Objectives: Clients will be able to explain the "SET" social problem solving skill, evaluate their progress and options and take responsible action.

While Awareness training to help clients clarify the real goal behind their problem is a necessary first step, if they don't take responsibility to evaluate their progress, they won't consider options that could get them to their goal. Thus, after clients clarify the real goal behind their problem, they need to evaluate their progress, their options and take responsible action. This involves clients learning to show real concern for self by taking the time to look at how they are really doing, what they need to change and in many cases having the courage to try something new. This also requires the client to get honest about ALL of their options are which means letting go of unhealthy pride, getting constructive feedback from others, looking at what they may not want to do and asking others for options.

Evaluating Progress
Involves helping clients consider...
- "Is what I am doing helping me achieve my goal?" Look at real feelings and motivations (e.g., justifying actions based on feelings).
- "What have I been doing?"
- "How well is what I am doing working in getting me what I want?"
- "How will things likely to turn out for me if I continue doing the same thing?" Use fantasy fast-forward to look ahead to play the story all of the way through to the real end including all of the likely consequences. Most planning problems result from only thinking about the beginning or middle action portion of the story and not fast-forwarding all the way to the end results portion of the story. Play the story all the way through to its end in order to discover reality of goal achievement by continuing the present method.

Evaluating Options
If the client determines that what they are doing is not helping them achieve their goal, they need to consider...
- "What are my options?"
- "What can I change?"

- "What really needs to get done?"
- "What do I need to do differently to reach my goal?"
- "How do I need to adjust my course to reach my goal?"

Clients need to be creative ask others for ideas, use individual and group therapy support to make as long of a list as they can of possible options/choices that could attain their goal.

The Options Test: Separating Obligations from Excuses

In life there a certain situations you can't get out of and certain obligations that have to be met. One way to determine if a client has an obligation that puts them in a high-risk situation or is making an excuse to enter a high-risk situation for relapse (in order to blame doing their unhealthy, harmful behavior on circumstances) is to evaluate options with them.

Obligation = Patient has looked, asked others and no other options exist.

Excuse = Patient hasn't even looked for alternative options.

Practical application example: Unhealthy Eating- Jean, an overweight young female adult client states they "must" go to a wedding with a lavish reception buffet as company for one of her friends will be there without a date. Start by siding with the negative[3], then introduce possible consequences and finally test the client for options. For example...

"Perhaps going to the wedding reception is so important to you that you won't give it up, even if is likely to trigger an unhealthy eating relapse. Sounds like an impossible situation anyway so why not just go? What could go wrong? What's the worst that could happen? Maybe you should just accept that you have to do what your friends bride want, unless there's some way you can solve the problem for them. What are your options?"

When Jean listed all of the options available to her, she realized that her self-imposed "people pleaser" feelings of responsibility to support her friend could end with sitting with her friend during the ceremony. Since the reception does not have assigned seating with prepaid catered meals there is no obligation to stay for it. Jean got honest and told her friend that staying for the food fest reception after the ceremony would be too difficult for her.

"You are only limited by your creativity" -- SRT Maxim

Practical application example: Unhealthy, Harmful Drinking- Bob, an employee referred for alcohol treatment who has three months sobriety received an invitation "plus one" to the annual Christmas party after work on Friday with "open bar" listed on it. They stated that they are obligated to go because the invitation came directly from the boss. Start by siding with the negative[3], then introduce possible consequences and finally test the client for options. For example...

"Perhaps going to the boss's party is so important to you that you won't give it up, even if is likely to trigger a drinking relapse. Sounds like an impossible situation anyway so why not just go? What could go wrong? What's the worst that could happen? Maybe you should just accept that you have to do what the boss wants, unless there's some way you can solve the problem for him. What are your options?"

Bob listed all of his options and decided on honesty. He told his boss that he was in alcohol treatment with 3 months sobriety. They made arrangements for the bar to stock sparkling cider for them to drink during the traditional champagne office toast and Bob invited his AA sponsor to come as his "plus one" guest.

"Where there's a will, there's a way" -- Samuel Smiles (1812- 1904)

Practical application example: Harmful Sexual Behavior- Kevin, a high school dropout on parole referred for gross sexual imposition of a minor (i.e., fondling a child) received a call from his single parent neighbor across the hall pleading with him to watch her 6-year-old daughter three times a week so she can take her father to physical therapy for a knee injury. She regularly fed, watered and walked his dog during days when Kevin volunteered to work a second custodian shift to make extra money. Now he feels strongly obligated to return the favor. Start by siding with the negative[3], then introduce possible consequences and finally test the client for options.. For example...

"Perhaps babysitting for your neighbor is so important to you that you won't refuse, even if is likely to violate your parole or result in a sexual re-offense. Sounds like an impossible situation anyway so why not just do it? What could go wrong? What's the worst that could happen? Maybe you should just accept that you owe her and have to do what she asks, unless there's some way you can solve the problem for her. What are your options?"

Kevin discussed all of his options and decided to tell his single parent neighbor that he will be glad to take her father to physical therapy for her.

"It is our choices... that show what we truly are, far more than our abilities"-- J. K. Rowling

The Options Test: Youth Example- The options test may be particularly useful in youth cases where it appears that youth options are limited by parental wishes and behavior. Take the case of Shontell, an overweight teenage girl that became so tired of feeling self-conscious about her weight around peers, sick of the disapproving looks and feed up with mean girl comments, that she asked her physician for help during her back to school physical. After her referral to weight management, she stopped asking her mother to bring home her favorite unhealthy foods from the grocery. However, old habits die hard and her obese single parent mother continued unhealthy grocery shopping. Her mother viewed this situation as a youth self-control "will power" problem, not a parent grocery shopping problem. As a result Shontell's food logs continued to reflect the unhealthy food that is being brought into the house. She was not losing weight, felt that she just didn't have the "willpower" to do it and was considering quitting weight management. She stated, "There's nothing I can do, I can't eat healthy meals if there's nothing healthy to eat in the house." Start by siding with the negative[3], then introduce possible consequences and finally test the client for options. For example...

"Perhaps continuing to eat your favorite junk food is so important to you that you won't give it up, even if it means not losing weight. Sounds like an impossible situation anyway so why not just keep eating your favorite junk food? What could go wrong? What's the worst that could happen? Maybe you should just accept that you have to eat what your mother brings home, unless there's some way you can solve the problem for her. What are your options?"

Shontell discussed all of her options with her weight management staff and decided that she needed to stop doing individual therapy for a family therapy problem and get her mother involved. Her weight management staff pulled her mother aside at her next appointment and convinced her that as the head of the household, it was most important for her to stay healthy. Her mother agreed and was scheduled for a physical exam. The results of that physical exam revealed a diagnosis of morbid obesity along with pre-diabetes, high blood pressure and high cholesterol. A referral to pulmonary clinic for an evaluation of sleep apnea was made along with a referral to weight management for treatment of weight-related health problems. A brutally honest physician discussion of the expected debilitating weight-related health consequences helped shift her mother's view from "It's your problem" to "It's our problem." In addition, her first few food logs and weigh ins without planning a healthy grocery list taught her that "Planning power beats will power." Both Shontell and her mother now meet with the dietitian regularly to plan a healthy grocery lists and both are beginning to lose weight.
"Think outside the box"-- (Derived from the 9 dot box puzzle, Sam Loyd, 1914)

A Brief Note on Social Problem Solving with Children
If younger children can't generate alternatives/options, then they will act on their only solution. Thus, the problem solving focus with younger children may need to stay on ability to generate alternative options/solutions. Repeatedly ask, "What else could you do?" Adolescents on the other hand may benefit from traditional problem-solving training on both generating alternatives/options and evaluation of the best coping strategies/solutions. This may be particularly important when dealing with aggression (e.g., Takahashi, Koseki & Shimada, 2009).

Taking Responsible Action
Clients need to take responsibility to choose the best option and implement it.
- What is the right thing to do that would best benefit both myself and others?
- What is the best method to use or choice to make?
- Which will most likely help me reach my goal?
- Which option, choice or course of action should I try first?
- Use the reality scales to weigh out the benefits and drawbacks of all of the options.
  - How much will each option benefit my goal success?
  - How much is each option needed for the survival of my goal?
  - How severe will the consequences of doing each option be?

Practical Application Example: Unhealthy Eating- Diana
Evaluate your Progress and Options- Regarding progress towards her weight loss goals, Diana got honest about continuing to gain weight as a member of the restaurant "food gang" but also stated that "since we *only* go out once a week, it *should* not really matter all that much." The options she listed included:
1. Keep the same friends but try harder- Continue to go out to restaurants with the food gang but start appetite suppressant medication so that she wouldn't overeat;
2. Avoid high-risk situations for relapse (places) but keep the same friends and try to change them- Stop going out to restaurants with the food gang and see if she could get any of the food gang to join weight management with her;

3. Avoid high-risk situations for relapse (people and places) and develop positive support- Stop going out to restaurants with the food gang. Start exercise class and make some new friends to hang out with at weight management and exercise class.

Take responsible action- The biggest thing that Diana initially believed that she needed to do differently to reach her weight goal was to try harder and build up her willpower. As a result she said, "I'll just go out with them to socialize, not eat and just have a salad while we visit." She selected option #1 and got a prescription for appetite suppressants. This worked fairly well for her the first Friday night out with the food gang as she explained her weight loss goal to her friends who supported her choice to *only* taste of a few things. However, since taste was the issue, even though her appetite suppressants worked and she wasn't really hungry, continuing to taste everything took its toll. She gained 8 pounds over the next month. In summary, Diana justified choosing option #1 based on her feelings and put her needs for acceptance before her healthy body goal. As a result, Diana ended up feeling like a failure had to re-evaluate her progress look at her real goal and consider another option.

"To succeed in your mission, you must have single-minded devotion to your goal"
-- A. P. J. Abdul Kalam (1931- 2015)

Practical Application Example: Unhealthy, Harmful Substance use- Jeff
Evaluate your Progress and Options- Regarding progress towards his self-sufficiency goals, Jeff got honest about the fact that his drug use held him back. He accepted that smoking marijuana decreased his motivation to study which held him back from getting his high school diploma and the job that he needed to get his own place. However, since he only sold marijuana to friends that he knew, he did not accept that his dealing jeopardized his freedom. The options Jeff listed included:
1. Tell staff what they want to hear- Stop having the last word and arguing with staff so they will get off his back, he can graduate the program and run away to a state where smoking marijuana is legal.
2. Stop temporarily- Avoid smoking marijuana until he graduates high school, gets a job and his own place, then do it if he still feels like it.
3. Stop permanently- Make a relapse prevention plan that will maintain his independence goals. Develop a sober support network, get a sponsor or counselor to help him stay with the plan after completing treatment and getting off probation .

Take responsible action- The biggest two things that Jeff said he needed to do differently to reach his self-sufficiency goal was to accept the facts that: 1) living off others is not making it on his own and; 2) marijuana decreases his motivation to succeed in school which is needed to get a job and make it on his own. He used his acceptance of these facts to select option #2 above in order to pass all of his home pass urine tests, get him through treatment and off probation. Unfortunately for Jeff, he neglected to consider the fact that while he was in treatment considering his life goals, his stoner friends were not. They knew when he was returning home from treatment and organized a party for him which got out of control and became so large that it included many invitations to persons of interest to the police. Fast forwarding to the end, Jeff knew that he shouldn't go but his exaggerated need for attention prevented him from turning down his invitation. The party was a huge success for the stoner crowd but a colossal failure for

Jeff's independence goals. Disturbing the peace and noise violations brought the police who arrested Jeff and 15 of his stoner friends the weekend after he was released from treatment.
"The truth of the matter is that you always know the right thing to do, the hard part is doing it"
--- Gen. H. Norman Schwartzkopf

Practical Application Example: Harmful Sexual Behavior- Dirk

Evaluate your Progress and Options- Regarding progress towards his probation completion goal, Dirk got honest about the fact that he was always extremely self-conscious about how others looked at him but he left out how Brandy's exotic dancer occupation fueled his need for excitement and sexual fantasies. He admitted that he was considering violating his probation by moving back in with Brandy. The options Dirk listed included:

1. Move in now- Move in with Brandy and ask his mother to cover for him by not telling his probation officer.
2. Move in later- Keep living with his mother and don't do any more activities with Brandy when Amber is around. Move in with Brandy after he completes treatment and gets off probation.
3. Don't move in, move on- Keep living with his mother while working on the sexual behavior problems that resulted in his court ordered treatment. Take time to develop healthy relationship success skills in treatment. Then move on towards developing a new, positive, healthy relationship.

Take responsible action- The biggest thing that Dirk said he needed to do differently to avoid probation violation was not to move in with Brandy. He told his treatment group that he needed to move on. Unfortunately, Dirk relapsed back into following his feelings and justified moving back in with Brandy based on his sexually charged romantic feelings for her. He convinced Brandy to move Amber in with her uncle so that he could move back in with her. He told Brandy that it was "no big deal" since Amber really liked her uncle, would be in the same school and was at the age where friends were more important than family.

Treatment Exercise: Social Problem Solving Practice

Review the SET social problem solving skills with your clients. Then have them discuss their Healthy Body goal (e.g., unhealthy eating, drinking, drug use, smoking, gambling and risky sexual behavior) and the top three barriers to their goal. Have them use the SET social problem solving skill to solve those problems and write out each step in the same format as presented in the prior case examples of Diana, Jeff and Dirk. Review and discuss each SET step. If in a group setting get creative options from the group.

Tolerance Training in Social Problem Solving
If you can't Tolerate setbacks, you won't be able to keep trying options until you meet your goal"

Tolerance Training Goal: Improve tolerance for setbacks and acceptance of the need to try multiple options.
   Objectives: Clients will practice the "SET" social problem solving skill implementing one option after another to help them develop tolerance for setback disappointment and avoid giving up.

Improving Tolerance for Setbacks

"If at first you don't succeed, try, try again"-- Thomas H. Palmer (1782- 1861)

As illustrated by the case examples in this chapter, humans make mistakes and don't always make rational choices when selecting the best option to solve their problems. Social problem solving is often an iterative trial and error process for clients: who are guided by exaggerated needs for attention, acceptance or excitement; have foresight deficits; have difficulty taking the advice of others or; "have to see things for themselves". If clients can't tolerate setbacks and disappointment, they won't be able to keep trying one solution after another until they "solve the problem." The case examples in this chapter illustrate that even if clients are aware of their real goal, evaluate their progress and make a comprehensive list of options, if the solution that they implement is not socially responsible, things are not likely to work out for them. In these situations it is important for clients to identify and accept the barriers and self-defeating habits that are getting in the way of their goals and try again. This requires learning to accept their situation and tolerate disappointment by trying one option after another until a socially responsible solution is found for the problem.

Clients have to be able to tolerate disappointment and frustration in order to keep from falling into self-defeating giving up. Self-defeating giving up is described earlier in Chapter 4 on "Recovery Perfectionism" (Relapse Prevention Issue #3) which involves giving up after one mistake. The three basic ways that humans give up when they fail to solve their problems, fall short of life goals and become overwhelmed with feelings is summarized on p. 76. Tolerating disappointment requires reinforcing client tenacity or "stick-to-itiveness." this is important because the road to recovery by changing unhealthy, harmful behavior and achieving life goals has barriers that can be difficult to overcome. Clients have to accept that progress on unhealthy, harmful behavior recovery and towards healthy lifestyle goals involves two steps up, one back, two up, one back and so on until they finally get there. The bottom line is that setbacks are part of goal attainment which requires tenacity.

"Winners never quit and quitters never win"-- Vince Lombardi (1913- 1970)

Practical Application Example: Unhealthy Eating- Diana

Tolerating Setbacks- Diana was very upset about gaining weight while on appetite suppressants. She got little relief from the fact that her weight management staff helped her understand how that was possible. She viewed her food gang's decision to send the restaurant leftovers home with her because Diana didn't eat as much and they all split the check as "just being fair." She was confusing enabling with purposeful diet sabotage. Since these were her longtime friends, she had a hard time accepting that they were "enabling" her unhealthy eating. In addition, since she was still convinced that her Friday night restaurant binging was the sole reason for her weight problem, she was very lax about recording her food logs the rest of the week. After some responsible "Confrontation with Concern", Diana agreed to snap a cell phone picture of each meal for the next week. As expected the photo review showed considerable unhealthy eating on Friday night and again on Saturday when Diana polished off all of the restaurant leftovers. What wasn't expected was the Sunday night fried chicken, mashed potatoes, biscuits and gravy with corn on the cob. Diana later disclosed that this church dinner was a weekly event with her best friend Latisha who sang with her in the choir and was one of her food gang members. She also disclosed that they went to Wednesday night bible study together, which explained the Dunkin Donuts and coffee after dinner. In summary, Diana's strong need for acceptance, confusing sabotage with enabling and not wanting to view her close friends as "enablers" of unhealthy eating, kept her from addressing the serious negative social influence that was preventing her from losing weight.

"Denial is not a river in Egypt"-- Sandi Bachom

Revaluate your Progress and Reconsider your Options- On the positive side, Diana was able to implement option #2, talk Latisha into joining weight management with her, lost 35lbs and was able to buy clothes off the rack. Latisha also lost over 30lbs and they began to enjoy clothes shopping at places they avoided in the past. On the negative side, as Diana began to fit into flattering clothes, her then boyfriend became jealous. He "love bombed" her with compliments, dinners and desserts. He went on about how she was beautiful just the way she was and didn't need to lose any weight at all. As a result, Diana gained 15lbs back, could no longer fit in the flattering clothes she had bought with Latisha and stopped shopping with her and started skipping weight management class to avoid the weigh in at the beginning. Latisha was angry at seeing her best friend who helped her lose her weight get conned by this "chubby chaser" who put his insecurity before her health. Latisha was known for saying just what was on her mind. She told Diana not to let this "junk in the trunk punk" ruin everything she worked for. She reminded Diana that her [four letter words removed] boyfriend doesn't live with her, support her or care about her goal and if she ever wants to make her goal she better start hanging around people want her to succeed. Diana reevaluated her progress. She got honest about the fact that her need to be accepted by others was running her life. She began to accept that it was about time she started running her own life instead of always trying to please others by going along to get along. Diana reconsidered her options, and selected option #3 (p. 157). She attended her weight management class religiously, added Jazzercise class with Latisha, lost the 15 pounds she had regained, started shopping with Latisha again. Diane lost another 15 pounds and achieved her healthy body goal of losing 50 pounds. In the process she let go of her boyfriend and gained three other Jazzercise friends who make up her new positive healthy lifestyle support network.

"To get something you have to give something away" – SRT Maxim

Practical Application Example: Unhealthy, Harmful Substance use- Jeff

Tolerating Setbacks- Jeff's arrest forced him to accept that his stoner party lifestyle jeopardized his freedom even when he wasn't smoking and dealing. He received a suspended sentence to the state youth authority (Juvenile prison) until age 21 which was contingent on completion of his extended probation with random urinalysis and court-ordered outpatient treatment. Initially, his need for attention kept him hanging out with his old stoner friends. He was forced to pass blunts, joints and pipes along to the next stoner while repeatedly explaining his random urinalysis and suspended sentence. He was getting invited to fewer and fewer parties. At the same time, his 90 Twelve-Step meetings in 90 days was developing the sober support network that he had earlier refused.

Revaluate your Progress and Reconsider your Options- In reevaluating his progress, Jeff had to accept that he was getting just as much positive attention from his sober support network as he was rejection from his stoner friends since he could no longer smoke with them.

He also had to accept that he did much better in school without his stoner friends. Jeff was finally ready to accept option three (p. 157). He got a sponsor to help him stick with his relapse prevention plan after he got off probation. Jeff and his new best friend both got accepted into a Job Corps program to learn how to trim trees from around city power lines. Upon graduation, all of his tools were paid for and he received a job interview at a large city public works department. He got the job, his own apartment and a brand new red Dodge Ram pickup truck. He no longer smokes marijuana and this has been confirmed by the city random drug screening requirement for operating heavy equipment.

"People grow up when they have to"-- SRT Maxim

Practical Application Example: Harmful Sexual Behavior- Dirk

Tolerating Setbacks- As a result of moving in with Brandy after getting her to move her daughter Amber out, things did not work out well for Dirk. When Brandy told Amber that she had to go live with her uncle so Dirk could move back in with her, Amber did not go quietly. She was crying and screaming until Brandy made the mistake of telling her that she could come by any time, she just couldn't stay overnight. That was the beginning of the end for Dirk who was back in jail in less than 4 weeks. Dirk stated that Amber set him up by dropping in to visit with her mother every day after school and slowly sneaking items of clothing back into her bedroom dresser until it was full. Dirk states that after Amber was basically moved back in, she waited until she saw his probation officer's car in the driveway and used that opportunity to drop in to tell her mother that she was getting some of her clothes to say over at a friend's house. This resulted in the probation officer following Amber into her bedroom to observe her removing a few items from drawers that were full of her clothes. When the probation officer asked Brandy if Amber was still living there, he was told that she only comes over after school when Dirk is not home. The probation officer called human services who went to her uncle's house and found her room empty. When the social worker asked her uncle if Amber lived there he said, "Not really, she just comes and goes". A probation violation was filed on Dirk for not complying with his no contact order with Amber and a warrant for his arrest was issued.

Revaluate your Progress and Reconsider your Options- After 6 months in jail, Dirk was released to a halfway house where his community behavior could be more closely monitored while he continued his outpatient treatment. His group revisited the options that he had listed and he got honest about the need to be responsible to both self and others when choosing options to social problems. After considerable work on his Maladaptive Self-Image (p. 256), empathy and healthy relationship success skills, Dirk accepted and made progress on option #3 (p. 158). He transitioned from the halfway house to living with his mother and developed a relationship with Vera, a 28-year-old hospital clerk with no children that he met in night community college class where they are both now working on their Associates Degrees. Dirk is in the beginning stages of treatment and needs considerable work on developing social responsibility. However, jail was apparently therapeutic for him as at this point he has stopped blaming Amber for his probation violation and started taking responsibility for his offense against her.

"Don't find fault, find a remedy"-- Henry Ford (1863- 1947)

Tolerating Barriers to Change

Recognition Disappointment

Since many unhealthy, harmful behaviors are self-reinforcing, difficult to stop and involve a number of setbacks prior to achieving a track record of healthy behavior maintenance, friends and family are not always ready to believe that clients have changed. Clients need to be stress-inoculated against giving up as a result of their efforts towards change not being recognized. It is important for clients to understand that trust is not something that is given but must be earned using the "Pendulum concept" of going to the opposite extreme to build a long track record of responsible behavior. A client workbook example of Social Problem Solving with this change recognition issues is provided on pages 154- 158 in Yokley (2012).

Setback Rumination- In order to help clients tolerate change and maintain focus on solving the problem, clients also need to stay mindful of negative emotional rumination (e.g., on unwanted feelings and perceived injustices) and when detected, shift to positive contemplation of viable solutions. Specifically, clients need to be aware that Recovery Perfectionism can trigger a version of the Slip Give-up Trigger during setbacks. In this situation, justifying the action of giving up can be based on the feeling of disappointment that the solution option didn't work and "assuming" that since one option didn't work, no options will work. In this situation, it is important to use the ABC's of letting feelings go that interfere with healthy life goals (e.g., frustration, self-disappointment) in order to dissipate feelings of disappointment below the threshold of emotional acting out and giving up. For example...

- Action that occurred- The solution option of [enrolling in aerobics class to help with weight-management; stopping smoking to help with alcohol abstinence; avoiding places where potential victims are present to help decrease sexual abuse fantasies] is proving too difficult to achieve.
- Belief problem- "I should be able to do this and because I can't, this must mean that nothing will work so I might as well just give up"- triggers frustration, self-disappointment and giving up on recovery.
- Challenging the Belief problem- "Where is the evidence that just because I am struggling with this solution option (or this option didn't work for me) that no options will work for me?" Maybe I need to try another option or get some support for this option like [building up my stamina for aerobics with regular walking; getting help through Smokenders; seeing a psychiatrist for medication to decrease my arousal level] before giving up.

Treatment Exercise: Tolerating Setbacks and Barriers to Change

Review the Social Problem Solving barriers to change and setback problem examples of Diana, Jeff and Dirk. Then have your clients (or group) discuss a real life problem where they had difficulty solving the problem, experienced setbacks and had to reevaluate their progress and options. If your clients state that they have never had difficulty solving a real life problem, then hold a "devil's advocate" discussion on the barriers and issues that could be encountered in their life goal (i.e., either their healthy body, healthy relationship or healthy life direction goals) and challenge them to tolerate the setbacks that you describe by re-evaluating their progress and options.

Integrate Social Problem Solving into the Relapse Prevention Plan

In high risk situations for relapse first Avoid Trouble with the "3 G's".

1. Get out (Remove yourself)
2. Get honest (Block the thought)- Use Decisional Balance. Ask yourself "Is what I'm thinking about doing going to be helpful or harmful?" (to self/others) and weigh your decision on the "Reality Scales"
3. Get Responsible (Substitute a more responsible thought)- Go to the opposite extreme, a non-stressful place where you are not likely to do the harmful behavior and use Emotional Regulation (i.e., the ABC's of letting feelings go or holding on to feelings) to calm down. Then solve the problem with the SET <u>Social Problem Solving</u> skill.
   - Note: Social Problem Solving is not a subset of Relapse Prevention, it's a separate skill that is best used after leaving stressful situations.

Social Problem Solving Skills Practice: The Situation Response Analysis Log

Have clients journal their progress in making responsible decisions using any of the SET Social Problem Solving skill that they learned (i.e., Set your goal, Evaluate your progress and options, Take responsible action) on their Situation Response Analysis log. These daily logs that document their high-risk situations, their response to those situations and their analysis of their response need to be reviewed and discussed in each treatment session. Basic client log instructions are listed in Table 4.7 on p. 61 and several Situation Response Analysis Log formats are presented in Appendix B, p. 263.

Social Problem Solving Research Support Summary: Social problem-solving has a clinical and research literature base dating back over 30 years (e.g., Chang, D'Zurilla & Sanna, 2009; D'Zurilla & Nezu, 1980). Social problem-solving deficits have been linked to depression, suicide attempts, anxiety, chronic fatigue and chest pain (e.g., Becker-Weidman et al., 2010; Christopher & Thomas, 2009; Howat & Davidson, 2002; McMurran & Christopher, 2009). Good social problem solving has been associated with positive self-esteem, life satisfaction, decreased stress and better family functioning (e.g., Chang, D'Zurilla & Sanna, 2009; Hamarta, 2009; Siu & Shek, 2010).

With adults, poor problem-solving has been linked to depression across age groups in: College students (e.g., Anderson, Goddard & Powell, 2009); Adults over 21 and under 65 (e.g., Marx, Williams & Claridge, 1992) and; Older adults age 65+ (e.g., Howat & Davidson, 2002). Poor problem-solving has been linked with suicide attempts in older adults (e.g., Howat & Davidson, 2002). In addition, a social problem-solving deficit was the sole predictor of anxiety and depression in adult male prisoners (McMurran & Christopher, 2009).

In the medical setting, social problem solving deficits were found in chronic fatigue syndrome patients (Christopher & Thomas, 2009). Dysfunctional problem-solving abilities have been associated with caregiver depression among the family of stroke survivors (Shanmugham et al., 2009). Social problem solving can mediate the relationship between perceived stress and noncardiac chest pain in adults undergoing stress myocardial perfusion imaging (MPI) to determine if cardiovascular disease is related to chest pain, (Nezu, Nezu & Jain, 2008).

On the positive side, rational problem solving has been positively correlated with self-esteem and life satisfaction in university students (Hamarta, 2009). Path analysis has indicated that social problem solving partially mediates the link between stress and psychological well-being of middle-aged adults (Chang, D'Zurilla & Sanna, 2009). In addition, problem solving has been effectively applied to the treatment of depression and sexual offending (Bell & D'Zurilla, 2009; Nezu, D'Zurilla & Nezu, 2005).

With adolescents and children, social problem-solving deficits have been associated with depression, anxiety and suicide ideation (Becker-Weidman et al., 2010; Lai Kwok & Shek, 2009; Siu & Shek, 2010). Higher parental social problem solving has been related to indicators of family well-being, including better overall family functioning, and fewer parent–adolescent conflicts (Siu & Shek, 2010). Finally, problem-solving style is a predictor of bullying victimization in school children (Cassidy, 2009).

Healthy Behavior Success Skills Summary

In summary, help clients remember the ACTS Healthy Behavior Success skills: **A**void trouble; **C**alm down; **T**hink it through and; **S**olve the problem by remembering that "Your ACTS speak louder than words." Brief Healthy Behavior Success Skill exercises to "Avoid Trouble, Calm Down, think it through and Solve the problem" are provided at the beginning of Social Responsibility Therapy Workbook 1 "How did I get this problem" p. 12- 16, Workbook 2 "Why do I keep doing this?" p. 19- 27 and Workbook 3 "How did my problem spread?" p. 18- 27 (Yokley, 2010b; 2011a; 2012).

Make sure that clients carry their ACTS skills card (Table 3.2), complete their daily Situation Response Analysis log, help themselves by discussing their progress/setbacks using ACTS skills for healthy lifestyle development and help others by pulling them up to their level of awareness.

"The only person who is educated is the one who has learned how to learn and change"
-- Carl Rogers (1902- 1987)

Chapter 8
External Control: Setting Clients up to Succeed

External Control: Behavior Modification and Prosocial Healthcare
Setting Clients up to Succeed

"The environment shapes people's actions" -- B. F. Skinner (1904- 1990)

"Strong Medicine for Strong Problems" in Review

In review, unhealthy, harmful behaviors are often self-reinforcing and highly resistant to change. These strong problems require a strong treatment response with multiple intervention methods across multiple intervention pathways. The Multimethod-Multipath Behavior Therapy utilized in SRT targets these strong problems with: Internal Control interventions to help clients pull themselves towards positive change; External Control interventions to push them towards positive change and; Social Learning interventions to motivate and redirect them towards positive change (See Figure 3.1, p. 44). In terms of who is the agent of change, internal control interventions are implemented by clients, external control interventions are implemented by others and social learning interventions occur as a result of the social environment (i.e., what we see others around us doing). Chapters 4- 7 in this text covered four Internal Control interventions involving cognitive coping, reasoning and restructuring. These SRT "Healthy Behavior Success Skills" help clients Avoid trouble; Calm down; Think it Through and Solve the problem when confronted with psychosocial stressors that would typically result in unhealthy, harmful behavior relapse. The present chapter will describe External Control methods and procedures used in SRT by agents of change (e.g., clinicians, partners, parents, peers and probation officers) to help push clients towards positive change and redirect them towards positive behavior.

External control interventions are an important part of Multimethod-Multipath Behavior Therapy. While SRT Internal Control interventions are implemented by clients, External Control interventions are implemented by others with client consent (unless there is a danger to self or others). The agents of change for external control interventions can include mental health professionals, case managers, physicians, probation officers, employers, relatives, custodians, parents, partners and peers. External control methods and procedures are typically implemented to help modify and avoid behavior that could be harmful to the client or others.

External Control: "Straight to the Point"
The point of this section is to help clinicians support client relapse prevention efforts and healthy lifestyle change goals by adding external control interventions (e.g., reinforcement and consequences) to help push clients towards positive change and away from unhealthy, harmful behavior.
External Control Goals and Objectives
Goal: Review basic external control interventions and increase clinician awareness of how to support relapse prevention efforts and treatment program rules with external control interventions.
Objectives: Clinicians will be able to: 1) Support relapse prevention efforts and treatment program rules with external control interventions and; 2) Develop appropriate treatment program protocols that increase the types and frequency of external intervention as the severity of unhealthy, harmful behavior increases.

The Most Basic Form of External Control: Social Rules

The most basic External Control methods in place in our society are our system of rules that are supported by rewards for adherence and consequences for non-compliance. This rule system includes Federal laws, State laws, Municipal ordinances, company policies and residual rules.

Social Responsibility Rules- Since Federal Laws, State laws and Municipal ordinances govern our conduct on the community and protect the rights of others, these are Social Responsibility Rules. Violation of Federal/State laws, and Municipal ordinances have legal consequences typically involving incarceration (banishment) for more serious felony offenses and lesser consequences such as probation supervision and/or fines for misdemeanors. City crime stoppers reward tip lines are probably the best example of reinforcement provided to citizens for upholding laws.[1] Reinforcement for upholding laws is also provided through media broadcasting of heroic behavior by police, firemen and citizens that protect others from the perils of lawbreakers. Citizen medals of honor or plaques of recognition often accompany media reinforcement of heroic behavior.

Social Organization Rules- State and private employment organizations (e.g., state departments of public health and privately owned companies) along with schools, colleges and universities all have their own organization rules. Externally controlled reinforcement and consequences help maintain organization rules. Violation of more serious, cardinal rules of organizations can result in expulsion. Common examples of externally controlled organizational consequences for cardinal rule violation are: expulsion from college as a student for exam cheating or fraternity hazing; getting fired from a newspaper as a journalist for plagiarism or; a drug treatment program client being removed for getting high during drug treatment. Common examples of externally controlled organizational reinforcement include: college academic achievement awards (e.g., designation of "Summa Cum Laude" for graduation with 3.95 or above grade point average); the $10,000 Pulitzer Prize for journalism achievement or; a treatment program completion certificate that allows a drug treatment client to get off of probation (which enables a return to work and child visitation). Company consequences for policy violations can involve fines in terms of being placed on leave without pay or employment termination. Companies reinforce productivity policies and goals with employee of the month plaques on the wall, productivity incentive programs and end of the year bonus checks.

Social Interaction Rules- These are the residual rules or unwritten rules of respect, common courtesy and conduct that govern how we interact with each other. They reflect community cultural norms that are expected and have consequences. For example, a verbally reinforcing "Thank you" is typically received when you hold the door for someone and a scowling look or negative comment is likely if you let the door close on them. Letting someone know about a sensitive issue with others or feedback about self, with "I need to make you aware of..." is often reinforced with, "Thanks for the heads up" while not "being your brother's keeper" and remaining silent typically results in a verbal admonishment like, "Why didn't you tell me about that?" When given an incorrect assignment by a supervisor, the social interaction rule is to, "Keep your praise public and your criticism private." This involves "earning the right to complain" by doing the responsibility that was incorrectly assigned, then privately telling the supervisor that the task was completed but was someone else's responsibility. Refusing a supervisor directive in front of others is likely to receive the consequence of an insubordination write up while "earning the right to complain" by doing the assignment and bringing the error to the supervisor's attention in private is likely to earn the employee a favor from their boss and possibly an apology. Finally, there are many unwritten social interaction rules for apology. That being said, in general, when someone comes to us and lets us know that we have hurt their feelings, the proper social interaction rule is "If you can't make it better, don't make it worse." This involves an apology if we recognize the mistake. If we don't recognize the mistake an apology for the feelings may help, "I am sorry you feel that way." In either case, apology is likely to be verbally rewarded while bringing a mistake that the person made in the past and confronting them about how that hurt your feelings is likely to result in consequences.

When combined, the behavior of citizens is managed by these multiple sets of laws, policies, rules and associated positive or negative consequences. Unfortunately, since many unhealthy, harmful behaviors are self-reinforcing, continuing to do them can develop a habit or dependency that is stronger than the consequences of society laws regulating those behaviors (e.g., unhealthy, harmful substance use and sexual behavior). Finally, some unhealthy, harmful behaviors such as overeating, overspending and gambling are not regulated at all.

External Control Intervention #1: Treatment Program Rules
In order to help clients learn to manage unhealthy, harmful behaviors that are self-reinforcing, treatment programs need to establish rules. These rules need to focus on helping clients avoid unhealthy, harmful behavior relapse and developing a track record of appropriate behavior control through reinforcement and consequences.

As mentioned in Chapter 2, recovery from unhealthy, harmful behavior often involves two steps up, one back, two up and so on until the recovery goal is reached. Relapse is the typical step back in recovery and life goal attainment. Relapse is a barrier that slows progress towards achieving a healthy body, relationship and life direction. In order to help clients achieve their healthy lifestyle, conditions that set the occasion for relapse needs to be targeted with external control interventions. Put another way, since "It is much easier to avoid trouble than escape it once it starts", external control interventions need to target exposure to high-risk situations for relapse. This needs to begin by including avoidance of high-risk situations for relapse in treatment program rules.

Support Harmful Behavior Recovery Through Treatment Program Rules
Awareness Training on becoming aware of high-risk situations is needed prior to Responsibility Training on making plans to avoid those situations (See Chapter 4, p. 50- 57). However, the self-reinforcing nature of unhealthy, harmful behavior coupled with human "I can handle this" grandiosity[2] or "Testing self-control"[3] curiosity requires more than just making plans to avoid high-risk situations. Treatment programs need to include avoidance of certain high-risk situations in their program rules and support those rules with external control interventions (e.g., reinforcement of adherence and consequences for non-compliance).

High-risk situations for relapse are typically divided into two categories, static and dynamic. Static risk factors are predictors of relapse that are fixed and unchanging such as onset, frequency and duration of the unhealthy, harmful behavior. Dynamic risk factors are predictors of relapse that are not fixed and can be changed. Examples include: associating with others who have the unhealthy, harmful behavior problem; attitudes that normalize or accept the unhealthy, harmful behavior and; direct access or opportunity to commit the behavior. External control interventions that support avoidance of these dynamic risk factors include: sex offender programs that have an approved associates list; Therapeutic Community substance abuse programs that ban "bad rapping" the program or negative talk that glorifies drug abuse and; weight management programs that require participants to "clean house" by removing all unhealthy food. A number of dynamic high-risk situations for relapse are fairly common across unhealthy harmful behaviors. Dynamic high-risk situations for relapse that can be changed and therefore warrant inclusion in program rules for external control intervention include: Enabling Environments; Negative Social Influence; Problem Behavior Access and; Mood Triggers.

Enabling Environments

Enabling environments are high-risk places that set the occasion for, allow, encourage or trigger unhealthy, harmful behavior. These environments are often places where there the client has typically engaged in their unhealthy, harmful behavior and are likely to trigger cravings/urges and relapse thoughts. For example, "All you can eat" buffets are enabling environments for weight management patients as overeating is allowed, encouraged through modeling by others and the wide variety of enticing food and associated smells are likely to trigger an overeating relapse. Fast food restaurants can set the occasion for overeating with "supersize" portion offers. The negative impact of enabling fast food environments on the spread of obesity has reached an "epidemic" level (see McAllister et. al. 2009). The 2004 documentary film "Supersize Me" [8] documents the adverse impact of constant exposure to this enabling environment that encourages unhealthy eating for profit. Vacations, particularly on cruise ships are known enabling environments for overeating and weight gain.[9] There's an old joke in the cruise ship industry that, "People come aboard as passengers and leave as cargo." In addition, home can be an enabling environment for clients if they don't "clean house" by removing all of the unhealthy foods that they used to eat and replacing it with the healthy foods recommended by their treatment program. Clients referred for substance use problems have similar enabling environments involving past favorite bars or frequented drug houses (AKA, "trap house", "crack house"), parties and being at home if they still have alcohol or drug stashes in the house. Gambling clients also have similar enabling environments including race tracks, casinos, internet gambling cafes and houses that hold poker games.

Enabling environments for clients with a history of harmful sexual behavior are places that can trigger re-offense thoughts. For clients with a history of child sexual abuse, this may be their own back yard of they have set it up with children's swing sets and other "child attractor" play equipment that enables them to get children into their home when no one else is present. Along this line, that section of the client's local park where the child play equipment is located (especially during weekends when children are out playing) is a high risk environment as is the elementary school yard during recess when the children are out. Going to parties late in the evening where there are highly intoxicated women is an enabling environment for clients with a history of peer rape offenses. Enabling environments for clients with a history of peer sexual abuse include places where there are disinhibitors to appropriate social behavior control (e.g., drugs or alcohol), acceptance of rape myths (e.g., "Women say no when they really mean yes"), isolation (no witnesses) or abuse normalization through group criminal collusion. In this context, "Date rape" has often been associated with drunken college fraternity parties where macho sexual behavior is reinforced and offender judgment is impaired by alcohol.

Make "Avoid High-Risk Places" a Treatment Program Rule

Since it is far easier to avoid trouble than escape it when it starts, help clients make a relapse prevention plan that lists all of the places to avoid that are high-risk for relapse. Help them develop their relapse prevention plan to avoid high-risk places and decrease stress that can set the occasion for unhealthy, harmful behavior. Do a step-by-step review of using their "SET Social Problem Solving skill" (in Chapter 7) to improve their avoidance plan for high-risk places. If the client is self-referred, implement external control relapse prevention plans that include positive parent, peer or professional high risk place supervision. If the client is court-referred, have this treatment program rule written into the conditions of their probation or parole.

> **Research Identifying Enabling Environments as High-Risk Situations for Relapse:** The need to target enabling environments with external control interventions is supported by research identifying enabling environments for unhealthy, harmful eating, drinking and sexual behavior relapse. For example, unhealthy eating habits occur more by heavier restaurant patrons at all you can eat buffets (e.g., Wansink & Payne, 2016), fast food restaurant eating was associated with increased odds of being obese (Fraser et. al. 2012) and a consistent weight gain occurs during vacations (e.g., Cooper & Tokar, 2016). With respect to drinking, as expected, increased alcohol consumption has been related to length of time spent in bars and extended late-night bar hours lead to further increased drinking and related harms (Stockwell & Chikritzhs, 2009; Sykes, Rowley & Schaefer, 1990). Regarding harmful sexual behavior, the adolescent offender's home, when no one else is there is an enabling environment for sexual offense initiation (e.g., Leclerc, Beauregard & Proulx, 2008) and bars tend to be enabling environments for sexual aggression by college males (Thompson & Cracco, 2008).

Negative Social Influence

"Example is not the main thing in influencing others. It is the only thing" -- Albert Schweitzer (1875- 1965)

Negative Social Influence involves people who engage in, encourage, promote, enable or trigger unhealthy, harmful behavior. In the case of weight management clients, this includes associating with other unhealthy eaters (e.g., family, friends or coworkers) who encourage the client to overeat with them. For example, offering to take them out to dinner or making their favorite unhealthy dish. Similarly, when clients referred for substance abuse treatment look up, run into or are approached by old drinking or drug using peers who offer to buy drinks or share drugs, they are at high risk for relapse. Negative social influence can occur for clients in treatment for harmful sexual behavior against children when they receive e-mail from past members of internet chat rooms that normalize, justify and promote sexually abusive behavior. For example, online pedophile networks such as DanPedro, BoyChat and Annabelleigh. The impact of negative social influence on peer sexual assault has been described in campus rape cases where a "campus rape culture" has been cited as a contributor to sexual assault.

The most direct example of early negative social influence is being taught to do the behavior by someone else in the home. For example being fed too much by an obese parent, being introduced to drugs or alcohol by a parent or being sexually molested by a parent or parental figure. Other fairly early negative social influences that can result in adopting unhealthy, harmful behavior are adolescent peer group associates who overeat, drink, use drugs or act out sexually. The finding that and delinquent peers are powerful reinforcers of youth antisocial behavior has clinical and research literature support dating back over 30 years (e.g., Hanson et. al. 1984) and negative peer involvement has been significantly related to youth treatment failure, particularly when negative peer involvement is comprised of gang affiliation (e.g., Boxer, 2011). Negative social influence can be longstanding if passed down through generations in families or adopted by groups as an aspect of their cultural attitude. Examples include the intergenerational transmission of substance abuse (e.g., Orford & Velleman, 1991) and physical abuse in the form of domestic violence (e.g., Simons & Johnson, 1998). Longstanding patterns of sexual abuse have also been related to negative social influence. For example, despite the fact that a fraternity rape culture was identified some 20 years ago (e.g., Boswell & Spade, 1996), fraternity rape accusations continue to be reported in the news media[4] resulting in a well-publicized campus rape documentary film entitled "The Hunting Ground".[5] Similarly, despite the fact that a military culture of secrecy enabling rape also came to light with scandals reported for over 20 years (see review in Turchik & Wilson, 2010), sexual assaults in the military continue to be reported in the news media[6] and have resulted in a documentary film entitled "Invisible War ".[7]

"Given appropriate social conditions, decent, ordinary people
can be led to do extraordinarily cruel things" -- Albert Bandura

Make "Avoid High-Risk People" a Treatment Program Rule

Help clients make complete a list of individuals to avoid who: 1) have (or will) enable or encourage the unhealthy, harmful behavior that they need to stop and; 2) have (or will) sabotage their efforts to stop their unhealthy, harmful behavior. When around others, help clients learn to "Make your own decisions, don't let others make them for you." Do a review of decisional balance with them on how to do a quick "Reality Check" and if needed use "The Reality Scales" (Chapter 6) to weigh out whether what you are about to do (or say) will be healthy/helpful or unhealthy/harmful. If the client is self-referred, implement external control relapse prevention plans that include positive parent, peer or professional supervision. If the client is court-referred, have this treatment program rule written into the conditions of their probation or parole.

Research Identifying Negative Social Influence as a High-Risk Situation for Relapse: Research identifying negative social influence as a high-risk situation for unhealthy, harmful behavior relapse that warrant external control intervention includes the following. With respect to unhealthy eating, one meta-analytic study revealed that both peers and family influence adolescent eating (Marcos et. al. 2013). Negative social influence by family and friends has been known as a strong contributing factor to unhealthy, harmful substance use particularly with adolescents for over 20 years (e.g.. Bates & Labouvie,1995; Gainey et. al, 1997; Neighbors et al 2016). Initial relapse prevention research has revealed that 18% to 36% of substance abusers report relapses associated with social pressure (Marlatt, 1985). Regarding harmful sexual behavior, negative social influence in the form of a college campus rape culture (Burnett et. al. 2009) particularly in fraternities (Neuman, 2006) has resulted in campus sexual assault reaching epidemic levels (Carey et. al. 2015; Lisak & Miller, 2002) and requiring national prevention programs (Lu, 2015). Negative social influence in the family is reflected in a number of unhealthy, harmful behavior risk factor studies. Parental obesity is a risk factor for becoming overweight (e.g., Martin & Ferris, 2007; Reilly et. al. 2005), parent alcoholism or drug addiction is a risk factor for engaging in substance use (e.g., Hussong et. al. 2012; Kaplow et. al. 2002) and being sexually molested is a risk factor for sexual offending (e.g., Perillo et. al. 2008; Starzyk & Marshall, 2003).

Problem Behavior Access

Problem behavior access is a high-risk situation for relapse where there is direct access to the unhealthy, harmful behavior that the client needs to control. Problem behavior access provides an immediate opportunity to engage in unhealthy, harmful behavior. In real estate, the key to home sales is "Location, Location and Location." In unhealthy, harmful behavior treatment, the key to relapse is "Access, Access and Access" to high-risk situations that provide an immediate opportunity to repeat the unhealthy, harmful behavior.

In legal cases, it is common knowledge that in order for a crime to occur, the perpetrator needs to have the "means" (necessary tools, weapons, etc.), the "motive" (the idea, plan, desire, motivation) and the "opportunity" (the access and chance to commit the crime without interference or detection). In unhealthy, harmful behavior relapse "opportunity" involves both an enabling environment and access. For example, relapse "opportunity" for a weight management client would be attending a wedding reception where all of their favorite desserts were being served (enabling environment) with nothing to stop them from trying everything (unobstructed problem behavior access). Attending a wedding reception where all of their favorite desserts were being served (enabling environment) with their dietitian to help them avoid unhealthy eating would obstruct unhealthy eating access and block opportunity despite the enabling environment. Likewise, relapse "opportunity" for an alcohol treatment client would be attending an after work office party at a local bar (enabling environment) with nothing to stop them from drinking (unobstructed problem behavior access). Attending that party with their AA sponsor to help them through would obstruct drinking access and block opportunity. For clients with a history of child sexual abuse, relapse "opportunity" would be created by renting a house in a neighborhood heavily populated with children, setting up a children's swing set and other elaborate "child attractor" play equipment in the back yard (enabling environment) and volunteering to babysit for neighbors (unobstructed problem behavior access). Treatment program rules (included in conditions of probation/parole) requiring individuals referred for child sexual imposition or abuse to move into an adults only apartment complex blocks this relapse opportunity. Relapse "opportunity" for clients with a history of peer sexual abuse would be bar hopping near closing time (enabling environment) and climbing into a cab that a vulnerable young woman called with no one to stop him from following her home to sexually assault her (unobstructed problem behavior access). Hopping into a cab with a vulnerable young woman leaving a bar at closing time (enabling environment) only to feel his electronic ankle bracelet buzzing while receiving a cell phone call from his probation officer telling him that if he didn't return to his apartment right now, a warrant for his arrest would be issued blocks opportunity. In all three cases involving unhealthy, harmful eating, substance use and sexual behavior, external control intervention by others involved in the client's case helps the client avoid relapse by blocking problem behavior access. The ramifications here involve the need to implement external control "blockers" of problem behavior access for relapse prevention. "Clean House" by removing unhealthy harmful behavior items and triggers in the home. Limit access and "Win the war in the store" by not purchasing unhealthy foods, alcohol or pornography if in treatment for unhealthy harmful eating, drinking or sexual behavior. Regardless of whether clients purchase junk food for the kids, beer or adult movies for their partner, "If you buy it you'll try it" and trigger a relapse.

Make "Avoid/Escape Access to Relapse Opportunities" a Treatment Program Rule
Help clients make a complete list of the past problem behavior access situations to avoid that provided an immediate opportunity for repeating their unhealthy, harmful behavior. Help clients get in touch with the fact that when they are in a high-risk place for relapse or are around high-risk people and have access to their unhealthy, harmful behavior, they are at highest risk for relapse and need to escape that high-risk relapse opportunity without hesitation. Review using "the 3 G's" (Chapter 4) for high-risk opportunity escape. If the client is self-referred, implement external control relapse prevention plans that include positive parent, peer or professional supervision. If the client is court-referred, have this treatment program rule written into the conditions of their probation or parole.

> **Research Identifying Problem Behavior Access as a High-Risk Situation for Relapse:** The need to target problem behavior access with external control interventions is supported by research identifying enabling environments for unhealthy, harmful eating, drinking and sexual behavior relapse. Regarding access to unhealthy food, a study of students with fast-food restaurants near (within one half mile of) their schools consumed fewer servings of fruits and vegetables, more servings of soda, and were more likely to be overweight than were youths whose schools were not near fast-food restaurants (Davis & Carpenter, 2009). A similar access finding was revealed with adults where increased density of neighborhood fast food outlets was associated with unhealthy lifestyles, poorer psychosocial profiles, and increased risk of obesity among older adults (Li et. al. 2009). Access to alcohol at the ages of 15 and 18 years has been shown to be significantly predictive of the quantities of alcohol they consumed during a drinking occasion both then and in subsequent years (Casswell & Zhang, 1997). Density of alcohol outlets was associated with increased risk of drinking alcohol at levels associated with harm (Kavanagh et. al. 2011). Conversely, limiting alcohol access through higher minimum legal drinking ages, greater controls over alcohol sales, lower outlet numbers, reduced outlet densities and limited hours and days of sale can effectively reduce alcohol sales, use, and problems (Gruenewald, 2011). A census tract study in three counties in California revealed areas with greater densities of bars had higher rates of child maltreatment (Freisthler, 2004). Alcohol-related disruptive behavior and physical altercations has been found to be lower among students living off-campus with parents which tends to indicate that even partial external control contact has a positive impact (Harford, Wechsler & Muthen, 2003). As expected, substance-using healthcare patients in Colorado with access to state legalized medical marijuana had higher frequency of marijuana use than those without a medical marijuana card (Richmond et. al, 2015). Neighborhood access to gambling opportunities is related to gambling and problem gambling (Pearce et. al. 2008). With respect to risk factors for sexual offending, access involving working with children has been significantly associated with a self-reported sexual offense against children (Turner et. al. 2016).

Mood Triggers

Mood triggers are unwanted feelings (which include urges and cravings) often associated with enabling thoughts. Since humans tend to avoid pain and pursue pleasure, it is not unusual for clinicians to encounter client reports of stress-related emotional eating, drinking or drugs (i.e., "self-medicating") and sexual behavior (e.g., "rebound relationships"). It is also not uncommon for clinicians to encounter client reports of excessive celebration eating (e.g., over-eating during holidays, vacations, etc), celebration drinking/drugs (i.e., "partying") and celebration sexual behavior (e.g., "make up sex" after an argument or getting back together after a break up). The biological factor of inherited negative emotional state, mood instability or reactivity increases the risk of situational factors triggering acting emotions out or self-regulating them through unhealthy, harmful behavior. Negative emotional states have been related to relapse in individuals with multiple forms of unhealthy, harmful behavior across the harmful behavior continuum from behaviors that are primarily harmful to self (e.g., overeating) to those that are harmful to self and others (e.g., drug/alcohol abuse) to behaviors that are primarily harmful to others (e.g., physical & sexual abuse). Although some individual substance abuse clients maintain that they do not use drugs to relieve negative emotional states or numb unwanted feelings, once an individual uses long enough to develop a tolerance, their use shifts from pursuit pleasure to avoidance of pain. Excitement and arousal can also be mood triggers.

When confronted with stressful life events, overeaters take comfort in thoughts of eating, substance abusers are comforted by thoughts of drug or alcohol use and sexual abusers take comfort in sexual behavior thoughts. Ruminating on these unhealthy, harmful behavior thoughts results in cravings or urges that set the occasion for unhealthy, harmful behavior relapse. Thus, cravings and urges can be viewed as simply feelings with a behavior motivation attached. With respect to mood trigger motivation, "The self-medication hypotheses" that humans use drugs and alcohol to relieve emotional suffering can be applied to using food and sex for comfort and self-soothing as is seen in emotional eating and sexual addiction. Physical and sexual aggression motivation can include the need to feel in control and powerful (sometimes to relieve feelings of helplessness, inadequacy) or to vent anger. Working self up over conflicts can create unwanted feelings, which trigger cravings and urges to relieve those feelings through unhealthy, harmful behavior. In some cases, clients report starting an argument to create the unwanted feelings and stress needed to excuse indulging in the unhealthy behavior. When cravings and urges are involved, there are many sources for this mood trigger including visual (e.g., food, alcohol and lingerie advertisements), auditory (e.g., discussions of favorite food recipes, favorite bars, getting high, attractive people or having sex) or olfactory (e.g., smell of fresh baked pie, smell of marijuana, smell of partners perfume or cologne). At this point a brief word about disinhibitors is warranted because they can be "the straw that broke the camel's back" in the client's struggle to maintain appropriate self-control over their unhealthy, harmful behavior when experiencing unwanted feelings or during a stressful event. Being under the influence of alcohol or other drugs of abuse can disinhibit emotional regulation and enable an existing emotional state to rise to a level that exceeds the threshold of self-control. This results in justifying unhealthy, harmful actions based on those unwanted feelings. Using substances, food or sex to elevate mood, relieve mood states or manage stress involves justifying actions based on feelings. Justifying actions based on feelings is a form of irresponsible thinking that links the client's unwanted feelings to their unhealthy, harmful behavior typically after a stressful event. Table 8.1 provides several client population examples.

Make "Avoid Mood Triggers & Let Go of High-Risk Feelings"
a Treatment Program Rule
Help clients make a complete list of unwanted feelings and conflicts to avoid that resulted in unhealthy, harmful behavior relapse. Include disinhibitors of feelings that justify unhealthy harmful behavior (e.g., drugs and alcohol). Help clients justify their actions based on facts not feelings. Review using "The ABC's of letting feelings go" (Chapter 5) or other client preferred emotional regulation skill (e.g., mindfulness meditation for distress tolerance, p. 95) to help them avoid following feelings back into unhealthy, harmful behavior. If the client is self-referred, implement external control relapse prevention plans that include positive parent, peer or professional supervision. If the client is court-referred, have this treatment program rule written into the conditions of their probation or parole.

Table 8.1

Justifying Actions Based on Feelings After a Stressful Event: Selected Examples

Client Population and Stressful Event	Justifying Actions Based on Feelings
Weight management client has taken on too much but got it all done and feels stressed out.	"I was really stressed out so I treated myself to the Cheesecake Factory for getting it all done"
Drug and alcohol treatment client finds out her partner was cheating and leaving her.	"I got really depressed after we broke up so I got high"
Gambling client in a retirement community experiences loneliness and can't pay utility bills	"I was lonely and desperate so I went to the Casino"
Sexual behavior problem treatment client becomes aroused speaking to a woman at a party.	"They got me really excited talking to them, so I got them alone and did what I wanted"

Source: Adapted from Table 13, p. 128 in SRT Workbook 3 "How did my problem Spread?" (Yokley, 2012)

Research Identifying Negative Emotional States as High-Risk Situations for Relapse: Research identifying unwanted feelings as high risk-situations for unhealthy, harmful behavior relapse that warrant external control intervention includes the following. Negative emotional states have been related to relapse in individuals with multiple forms of unhealthy, harmful behavior including alcoholics, smokers, heroin addicts, gamblers and overeaters (Marlatt, 1985; Shiffman et al., 1996; Schotte, Cools & McNally, 1990). One study revealed that anger and self-criticism fully mediate the relationship between unhealthy binge eating and childhood emotional abuse where 53% of women with serious binge eating reported a history of childhood emotional abuse (Feinson & Hornik-Lurie, 2016). Depressive symptoms have been related to higher emotional eating which has predicted greater increases in weight gain independently of depression (van Strien et. al. 2016). Conversely, decreased emotional eating has been associated with greater odds of weight loss success (Braden et. al. 2016). While carbohydrate craving remains somewhat controversial, there is some evidence that consuming carbohydrates improves mildly dysphoric mood in females with carbohydrate craving (Corsica & Spring, 2008).

The "self-medication hypotheses" of emotional drug and alcohol use holds that substances are used to relieve emotional suffering in susceptible individuals and specific substances are preferred to relieve specific unwanted feelings (Khantzian, 2003). For example, a depressed client may elevate their mood with cocaine, an anxious client may numb nervousness with alcohol or an angry client may calm themselves with marijuana. While all individuals with a specific type of unwanted feelings may not always use a certain substance to relieve that unwanted feeling (e.g., Lembke, 2012), evidence that humans in emotional pain use substances to relieve their emotional pain in general, continues to receive research support. For example, the link between sexual victimization and alcohol use has been well documented. Specifically, having a history of sexual assault has been associated with increased psychological distress, which in turn has contributed to alcohol use to relieve that distress in women (Miranda et. al. 2002). In addition, increased emotional distress has been related to more heavy episodic drinking in the transition from adolescence to early adulthood (Pape & Norstrom, 2016). The use of alcohol as a strategy to regulate emotional distress has been widely considered as a core risk factor for problem drinking and continuing to think/talk about drinking is a risk factor for transition from social to problem drinking (Caselli et. al. 2015). Even during treatment, changes in negative mood have been significantly associated with changes in heavy drinking (e.g., Witkiewitz, Bowen & Donovan, 2011). 19- 38% of substance abusers report relapses associated with negative emotional states (Marlatt, 1985; Shiffman et al., 1996). The "self-medication hypothesis" that drugs and alcohol are used to relieve emotional suffering (Khantzian, 2003) can be applied to emotional eating and sexual addiction both of which can also be used to relieve feelings of depression, anxiety or other unwanted feelings (e.g., Corsica & Spring, 2008; Opitz, Tsytsarev & Froh, 2009). Working self up over interpersonal conflicts and stressful life events creates another negative emotional state that is high risk for substance abuse and 14% to 18% of substance abusers report relapses associated with interpersonal conflict (Marlatt, 1985).

Young adults gamble for both positive mood enhancement and negative mood reduction (Goldstein et. al 2014). Gambling can alleviate the under-arousal associated with boredom (Mercer & Eastwood, 2010) and loneliness is an important predictor of problem gambling in older adults (Botterill et. al. 2016). While the consequences of problem gambling are certainly depressing, a literature review by O'Brein (2011) suggests that depression is more of a cause than a consequence. Gamblers who play slots to self-regulate negative emotional states are at elevated risk for pathological gambling (MacLaren, Harrigan, & Dixon. 2012).

When confronted with stressful life events, sexual abusers often report taking comfort in sexual thoughts and behavior (Cortoni, Heil, & Marshall, 1996). Ruminating on and masturbating to deviant sexual fantasies builds a deviant sexual arousal pattern that creates another high-risk situation for abusive sexual behavior. With respect to arousal as a mood trigger, deviant content pornography has been found to add significantly to the prediction of sexual aggression recidivism in child molesters (Kingston et. al. 2008). Deviant sexual arousal is one of the most consistent predictors of sexually coercive behavior in adults and college students (Prentky & Knight, 1991). Another high-risk situation for sexual abuse involves stressful life events with 80% of convicted rapists reporting an antecedent event involving an upsetting life problem, 76% of which involved anger over an incident with a girlfriend or wife (Scully & Marolla, 1984).

In conclusion, relapse risk is cumulative where various combinations of being in an enabling environment, exposure to negative social influence, mood triggers (unwanted feelings, stress, cravings or urges) interact with unobstructed problem behavior to result in a high risk for relapse. Enabling Environments; Negative Social Influence; Problem Behavior Access and; Mood Triggers are dynamic high-risk situations for relapse that can be changed and therefore warrant inclusion in program rules for external control intervention.

Treatment Program Rule Examples
Basic Program Rule Examples: Unhealthy Eating

Examples of basic SRT treatment program Social Responsibility, Social Organization and Social Interaction rules for unhealthy eating are provided in Table 8.2.

Table 8.2
Ten Basic SRT Weight Management Treatment Program Rule Examples

Social Responsibility Rules
1. **Make healthy decisions-** Do not eat fast food or other forms of unhealthy food. Do not hang out with overeaters, avoid individuals who encourage or enable unhealthy eating or that sabotage healthy eating plans. Do not drink alcohol, smoke cigarettes or marijuana. When others offer you anything unhealthy, remove yourself and use your decisional balance skills to weight the benefits against the drawbacks of eating it.
2. **Help yourself and others-** If you gained weight, hold yourself accountable and get honest about what you ate. If you lost, help others by sharing what worked for you. Accept feedback and suggestions from others and "be your brother's keeper" by giving feedback and suggestions to others. Do not bring food to group, offer unhealthy food (or coupons) to others and do not pull others into "glory stories" of delicious meals you have enjoyed in the past. Do not disclose the identity of any participants or information revealed in group to anyone outside of the group.

Table 8.2   Ten Weight Management Treatment Rules (continued)

Social Organization (SRT Program) Rules

3. **Stick to your program-** Attend and participate in all treatment sessions. Show up before each session and weigh in. Follow all diet and medication prescriptions and keep all appointments. Arrive on time in order to give yourself time to discuss important issues. "If you want your program to work, you have to work your program." Block direct access and opportunities for unhealthy eating. "Clean house" of all unhealthy food. If you have an obligation to attend wedding receptions, funeral repast dinners, or office parties where you have direct access to unhealthy food, bring a support person who will help avoid trouble. Do not go to places that can trigger unhealthy eating like all you can eat buffets, bakeries, cruises or all-expense paid vacations.

4. **Complete all of your assignments-** Do all SRT workbook assignments prior to group discussion on the topic assigned. Stay consistent with on your food and activity log- "If you bite it, you write it." "If you jog you log." Record it when you do it. Don't rely on memory to complete your log later.

5. **Use distraction for activity, not eating-** Listen to upbeat motivating music while walking, jogging or biking. Don't eat in front of the television, while on the computer, reading, driving or other distraction.

6. **Deal with your feelings as they come up-** "Walk it off and talk it off", take your cell phone on a walk and talk to a responsible support person about what you are going through. Let go of high-risk feelings- Use "The ABC's of letting feelings go" when you are by yourself and get hit with cravings.

7. **Avoid high-risk situations for unhealthy eating-** Since it is much easier to avoid trouble than escape it once it starts, stay out of your high-risk situations for relapse. Avoid the high-risk people (other unhealthy eaters), places (e.g., all you can eat buffets, bakeries), and things (e.g., dwelling on negative thoughts or unwanted feelings) that set you up for unhealthy eating (e.g., "I feel so bad and I've been so good, I'll just have one bite." Limit unhealthy food access, don't buy it for others, accept it from others or bring it into the house. Associate with others who encourage you to stay active, eat healthy and sit next to supportive people during holiday and other celebration meals. "If you can't change the people around you, change the people around you." Don't create emotional stress buildup, which can trigger stress-related eating (e.g., feeding anxiety by always saying yes to people and getting overwhelmed by taking on more than you can do as opposed to being assertive, drawing the line and not taking on too much).

8. **Escape high-risk situations for unhealthy eating-** If you find yourself in a high-risk situation where there is opportunity for unhealthy eating relapse, use "the 3 G's" to Get out, Get honest (about what will happen if you return) and Get responsible (by going to a no risk situation, for example the Library where food is not allowed).

Social Interaction Rules

9. **Stay on topic-** Since "There is no recipe solution for a self-control problem", don't get yourself or others side tracked with the latest "foodie" recipes.

10. **Solve problems, don't avoid issues-** Develop and maintain a positive support network of individuals who you can bounce problem issues off of and get positive solutions from. When someone offers a positive solution, don't avoid trying it by "hole-punching" through reasons it won't work, thank the person for their concern and it. Use your SET Social Problem Solving Skills to decrease stress that can trigger stress eating, "If you're not working on the solution, you're part of the problem".

Since "We do our best when we are prepared and our worst when we are caught off guard", client adherence to weight management program rules requires education on the weight loss process. To maximize success, in addition to consulting with a weight management physician or dilatation, make sure that your clients understand and accept the following basic weight-management points.

- **Accept the healthy lifestyle facts** that :1) "There is no recipe solution for a self-control problem" and; 2) "Planning power beats willpower" to stay focused on planning a healthy eating and activity schedule. Get ready for a weight loss plateau. Be aware of the fact that as you lose weight, your body releases less of the fullness hormone. This tells your body that you need more food and to burn less fat calories which keeps your weight the same and requires increased planning power to overcome. Let go of the idea that weight-management is like suffering through a hard study course, when it's over you're done forever. Accept that weight-management involves a healthy eating and activity lifestyle, which takes time to develop by working on it day in and day out until it becomes part of your daily routine. Just like "Old habits die hard" adopting new ones is hard also and cannot be done with a simple time limited diet. Stop skipping meals and diet shopping.

- **Jump-start your weight loss efforts**. Since seeing immediate results motivates us to continue, when you begin, make a one-month weight loss goal that you can make (e.g., about 1500 calories/day for women and 2000/day for men should result in one pound weight loss per week). At first cut sugar, drinking alcohol while doubling protein (from the recommended 46- 56 grams/day) and avoiding carbohydrates.

- **Get back to the basics**. Accept that your body was designed to run on the natural foods that existed for thousands of years before food processing plants began injecting additives to preserve food. Get back to eating what you can get by hunting (e.g., lean meats) and gathering (e.g., fruits and nuts). Let go of the processed foods that are high in saturated fats, refined starch and sugar which can disrupt your hormonal "full" signals and result in eating too much. Accept that the Lays potato chip advertisement "I bet you can't eat just one" is really true, that junk food is addictive and creates a tolerance that requires more and more to feel satisfied. Start eating unprocessed foods (e.g., vegetables, lean meat, and healthy fats like salmon, almonds, walnuts, eggs and cheese).

- **If you bite it, you write it**. Keeping a food log of everything you eat helps decrease overeating. If you use a cell phone app, make sure that you can print out the entire week so you can see eating patterns that are not visible one day at a time. Don't leave anything out and do the math. For example, if you chew Wrigley's Juicy Fruit Gum all day at your 9- 5 desk job, and your food log shows that you chew another piece every 10 minutes after it has completely lost its flavor, do the math. Six pieces of Wrigley's 8 calorie gum per hour is 48 calories per hour minus 11 calories/hour burned by chewing leaves 37calories/hour times 8 hours is 296 calories. Since the average 150lb person can burn 100 calories in 15 minutes walking, you will need to walk about 45 minutes after work to burn off the calories from chewing gum at your desk job all day. Add a daily weight in to your log.

- **When eating, eat**. Stop distraction eating. If you're watching late night TV while eating, your eyes are on the tube, not the table and you won't be able to accurately log what you ate. If your food logs are not accurate, you can't make responsible decisions on what you need to change the following week to manage your weight. Slow down and let yourself be mindful of what you are eating. Chew slowly and be mindful of the taste and smell of your food. Don't take another bite until after you have swallowed. Mindful eating results in eating less compared to distraction eating.

- **Get a physical exam** and clearance for an exercise routine. Alternate between cardio exercises (e.g., jog, run, bike, swim) and strength training (e.g., weights) every other day.

- **Accept that your body is a highly efficient machine**. If it were a car it would get 500 miles per gallon of gas. This means that it can run for a very long time on very little food. Start eating only when you are really hungry. Use your body's natural gas gauge (i.e., growling stomach) to let you know if you need a snack. Check your body signals when you have an urge to eat. The saying "If you can't sleep right, eat right and if you can't eat right, sleep right" teaches you that your body needs both food and sleep to function. According to this saying, when your body is fatigued, it calls for fuel to keep going (i.e., not enough sleep increases ghrelin a hormone associated with hunger and decreases leptin a hormone that signals fullness) so get enough sleep to prevent eating urges. People who sleep at least 8 hours/night lose more fat and are less hungry than those who sleep less than 6 hours/night. Getting over 7 hours sleep/night helps lower stress which in turn can decrease stress-related eating. When you get an urge or craving be sure to "HALT" and check your body signals by asking yourself "Am I really <u>H</u>ungry or am I <u>A</u>ngry (or anxious), <u>L</u>onely (or bored), or <u>T</u>ired? If you are really hungry then a healthy snack (e.g., fruit) should be acceptable. If it's anger, loneliness or fatigue, a healthy snack won't seem acceptable. Food is supposed to be the fuel that runs your body from dawn to dusk. Identify when you need fuel and get back to using food as fuel, not as comfort, entertainment or a social activity.

Basic Program Rule Examples: Unhealthy/Harmful Substance Use

Examples of basic SRT treatment program Social Responsibility, Social Organization and Social Interaction rules for unhealthy/harmful substance use are provided in Table 8.3.

Table 8.3
Ten Basic SRT Substance Abuse Treatment Program Rule Examples

Social Responsibility Rules
1. **Stay clean and sober-** Do not use intoxicating substances or drink alcohol and don't associate with drug/alcohol users or those who enable using by offering it to you or doing it in front of you. <u>Avoid high-risk places and people-</u> "If you can't change the people around you, change the people around you." <u>Let go of high-risk feelings-</u> Don't create emotional stress buildup which can trigger stress-related eating drinking or drug use (e.g., kicking feelings of helplessness by ruminating on the past or other people's behavior, often guilt, shame or sadness from past substance-related mistakes and relationship loss). When you get hit with unwanted feelings use "The ABC's" to let them go.
2. **No abusive behavior-** Respect human rights for safety and security. No sexual abuse, harassment or sexual contact with another treatment program member. No physical abuse (to self or others). No violence, no threats of violence and stay in your seat (or in control) at all times. No property abuse (arson, theft or vandalism). No substance abuse (including tobacco products and bringing substances of abuse into treatment). No trust abuse (including false allegations of criminal behavior and unauthorized use of telephones or computers). Do not disclose the identity of any participants or information revealed in group to anyone outside of the group. Use "The Reality Scales" to help you avoid trouble by weighing out the impact of your decisions before taking action.

Table 8.3   Ten Substance Abuse Treatment Rules (continued)

Social Organization (SRT Program) Rules

3. **Abide by your program rules** (i.e., your Treatment Behavior Contract, your Community Behavior Contract and your probation/parole rules)- <u>Don't test yourself, stay out of places that can trigger relapse</u> (e.g., bars, drug houses, streets where dealers hang out, baseball games where you have to pass beer down the aisle to other fans). Attend and participate all scheduled treatment sessions each week. Come on time and call if you can't come. Respect the group by coming back on time from breaks and not interrupting group. Attend your required number of AA meetings each week and have your Twelve Step Attendance Sheet stamped. "Keep your eyes on the prize"- Use your "SET social problem solving skill" to help keep you on track with your treatment and life goals. <u>Block direct access to alcohol and drug use</u>. Remove all alcohol and drugs from your home. If having money is a drug/alcohol access trigger for you, don't carry cash. Get a legal payee to handle your money. Have all money transactions handled automatically by direct deposit and electronic bill payment. If you have an obligation to attend a funeral wake, wedding reception or office party where you will have direct access to alcohol or drugs, bring your sponsor to help you avoid relapse.

4. **Complete all assignments**- Complete all SRT workbook assignments prior to group discussion on the topic assigned.

5. **Respect other's personal space**- Complete and total hands off policy, No touching. Arms length personal space.

6. **No intimidation**- No gang representations. No "selling wolf tickets", i.e., wolfing or barking out idle threats.

7. **No negative contracts** (i.e., covering up negative behavior for others who in turn agree to do the same for you) and no negative associates (i.e., individuals who are still getting high, drunk and/or engaging in criminal behavior). Escape high-risk opportunities- If someone approaches you about getting drunk or high, use "the 3 G's" to get out of trouble.

Social Interaction Rules

8. **Get honest- "Dishonesty is disrespect"**
- Get honest with yourself about high-risk situations (i.e., problem people, places and things that can trigger relapse) and hold yourself accountable for slips (slip = "sobriety lost its priority"). For example entering high-risk situations or starting to use. Open the group on yourself and talk about your slips.
- Get honest with yourself when you are defensive and block out others feedback. Correct your automatic negative responses. When you find yourself "hole punching" (i.e., punching a hole in a solution offered to you) telling someone, "I already tried that and it didn't work", correct yourself. Go through what you did and see if there is something you could change to make it work.
- Get honest with others about high-risk behavior. Use Confrontation with Concern. If you think something others are doing could result in relapse, tell them. "Be your brother's keeper".

9. **Show Concern- Be supportive, constructive and positive**
- **Supportive**- "Identification is an obligation." If someone brings up something that you have gone through yourself, don't leave them hanging out there all by themselves, tell them. The only thing worse than being stuck with an upsetting problem is thinking you're the only one that has it. That leaves you both upset and lonely. Be supportive, identify with others. No group incest. Being supportive does not mean being seductive. You are here to support each other not date each other.
- **Constructive**- "If you're not working on the solution, you're part of the problem." If you see a problem, come up with a couple of solutions to the problem and talk about both the problem and the possible solutions. When someone gives you a solution, don't fall into "Hole punching" by giving reasons why the solution won't work. "Earn the right to complain" by trying it before denying it.

Table 8.3   Ten Substance Abuse Treatment Rules (continued)

- **Positive**- "If your words are no better than silence, silence is far better than words." Human beings are far better at knowing how to plan a perfectly bad day than they are at planning a perfectly good one. Making further negative comments about someone or something that a group member is talking about just to let them know you are on their side doesn't help. Concern means telling people what you think they need to hear, not what you think they want to hear. Stay positive or stay quiet until you have something positive to say.

10. **Be Responsible- "Our biggest social responsibility is self-control"**

- **"No red-crossing"**- don't rescue others when they are being confronted about a behavior problem or issue. Respect the ability of others to speak for themselves and don't enable or support denial. "Be your brother's keeper" and if you think they are heading for trouble tell them.

- **Respect others opinions and feelings**. Don't: walk out of groups; talk over others; have side conversations (No cross-talking) or; call names (natural language is acceptable but don't make fun of something that is not the other persons fault or choice (e.g., race, gender, religion). No disrespect to staff. The only acceptable response to feedback is "Thank you, I'll take care of that."

- **Pay attention**. Don't devalue what someone is saying by doing anything that may be disruptive or distracting. For example knitting, flossing teeth, filing nails, eating, playing video games, checking Facebook or e-mail, taking cell phone calls (phones must be off).

- **Use feedback to change**. Accept "the mirror concept" that others may see you better than you see yourself and use their feedback as a mirror to get a better view of yourself.

Since "We do better when we know better", client adherence to substance abuse treatment program rules requires education on the drug and alcohol recovery process, the philosophy of recovery and recovery wisdom. There are many recovery maxims or "words to live by" on the path to developing a clean and sober, healthy, positive lifestyle. In the Therapeutic Community, which is considered the predominant residential addiction treatment model from Chile to China (Waters et al., 2002), the start of every treatment day begins with a maxim. Maxims have been used successfully to help people succeed in therapeutic community addiction treatment and maximize their chances of getting what they want in life by building group identity, cohesion and to define the group behavioral code (e.g., Bassin, 1984). Maxims center on maintaining personal balance in daily effort to achieve recovery and positive life goals. The following combination of Therapeutic Community, Twelve Step and Social Responsibility Therapy maxims help correct and counteract typical addiction characteristics such as problems with honesty, concern, responsibility, unrealistic goal setting, impatience, low frustration tolerance and fears of failure. To maximize recovery success, make sure that your clients understand and accept the following 10 basic recovery maxims.[10]

1. "Act as if"- is the lifestyle change responsibility to consistently behave as the person you want to be (or should be) rather than the person you have been in the past. "Acting as if" is one of the most important tools in positive behavior change because according to ancient Greek philosopher Aristotle, "We are what we repeatedly do." In other words when someone acts in a certain way long enough, the thoughts and feelings that support that behavior will strengthen. For example, if out of control, rebellious, irresponsible addicts "act as if" they have self-control and are responsible by repeatedly following treatment program rules, doing what they should, when they should for the reason they should, their new responsible behavior habits will eventually replace their old irresponsible ones. [11]

2. "Guilt kills"- Reminds clients that "You are only as sick as the secrets you keep" and that holding guilt kills recovery. This typically happens after a rule violation mistake when the client uses negative coping and covers it up. Cover-up of mistakes requires holding guilt for doing the wrong thing along with worry about getting caught and having to remember all of the details of the cover story. This creates stress buildup which eventually results in a slip typically involving entering a high-risk situation for relapse and starting to drink/drug (Note: slip = "sobriety lost its priority"). The slip then sets the occasion for a fall through the Rule Violation Effect, telling self, "Since I already had a sip/hit, I blew my sobriety and might as well get drunk/high."

4. "When you're looking bad you're looking good"- When you think you are looking bad by admitting rule violations, slips (entering high-risk situations) or falls (relapse), you are looking good in terms of getting honest and holding yourself accountable. When you "blow your image" of being perfect or cool, feel ashamed from looking bad by being wrong and admit a mistake or apologize, you are looking good in terms of being honest and responsible.

5. "One day at a time"- along with "Take care of today and tomorrow will take care of itself" helps clients stay focused on dealing with what's going on right now and not get overwhelmed with all of the addiction-related life problems yet to be resolved. Staying focused on doing the right thing each hour, each day, decreases anxiety and relapse risk while supporting healthy life goals.

6. "To be aware is to be alive"- Becoming aware of your thoughts, feelings and "where you are coming from" (i.e., your motivations for why you do what you do) allows you to lead a much more fulfilled life. Awareness training allows addicts to plan around trigger thoughts, feelings and motivations which improves relapse prevention because "Planning power beats willpower."

7. "You get out of it, what you put into it"- Points out that what you get out of treatment depends on what you put into it in terms of following the program rules and doing the program work in the program (i.e., attendance, participation, honesty, holding self and others accountable, accepting feedback). Put another way, "If you want the program to work, you have to work the program." Accept that full participation is required for full recovery and view your recovery like money. Don't let anyone take it from you and use it to get what you want in life. "

8. There are only two things that you can't change in life- The past and other people's behavior are the only two things we can't change in life. Spending all day focusing on the things we can't change (i.e., the past and other people's behavior), creates feelings of helplessness. On the other hand, shifting your focus from the past and other people's behavior to the present and your behavior (i.e., the things you can change) will leave you feeling empowered and in control. In summary, we control whether we set ourselves up for relapse by staying focused on the past and other people's behavior or whether we set ourselves up for success by staying focused on the present and our behavior in order to get what we want in life. This is where the Serenity Prayer applies... "God, grant me the serenity to accept the things I cannot change, the courage to change the things I can and wisdom to know the difference."

9. "If you forget where you came from you're doomed to return there"- Remembering the substance-related problems, pains and negative identity of the past helps us "keep our eyes on the prize", stay focused on present recovery and build a track record of responsible living that will support future healthy lifestyle goals. To build a track record, you need a starting point. Mark your sobriety date where you can see it and watch the track record you are building.

10. "You have to go to the opposite extreme in order to meet the median"- Before treatment, the unhealthy, harmful lifestyle basically involved doing what you want, when you want for the reason you want. During treatment clients need to use the "Pendulum Concept" and go to the opposite extreme by consistently doing what they should when they should for the reason they should. This is needed so that after treatment when self-control naturally swings back to the median they have developed enough positive lifestyle practice to meet the acceptable community behavior standards and avoid relapse. Put another way, setting your treatment sights high protects your recovery after treatment, "Aim for the stars, hit the trees, aim for the trees, hit the ground."

Basic Program Rule Examples: Harmful Sexual Behavior

Examples of basic SRT treatment program rules for harmful sexual behavior are provided in Table 8.4.

Table 8.4
Ten Basic SRT Sex Offender Treatment Program Rule Examples
Social Responsibility Rules

1. **Do not break the law**- Including probation/parole rules banning possession of weapons, use alcohol or other psychoactive drugs, associating with known criminals and saying out past curfew.
2. **Do not abuse others**- This includes interpersonal abuse (sexually, physically, emotionally) sexual exploitation (i.e. deception, conning, coercion or manipulation in order to use someone or take advantage of them) or sexually objectifying others. Do not force, trick or talk anyone into sexual contact. Do not use aggressive, sexual or verbally abusive language designed to get even or build myself up by putting others down and hurting their feelings. Do not have any pornographic material in my possession or view any pornographic material including, adult sexual videos, sexually explicit TV channels or movies. Do not disclose the identity of any participants or information revealed in group to anyone outside of the group. "Hesitation kills your recovery"= Use "the 3 G's" to escape high-risk opportunities for relapse immediately. Avoid high risk people and places- Don't make decisions about others when you are angry or upset. Use "The ABC's of letting feelings go" and put off your decision until tomorrow. Use "The Reality Scales" to weigh out your decision when you have calmed down.
3. **Do not abuse yourself**- Including all forms of self-destructive behavior such as masturbation to deviant fantasies or porno use, gambling, smoking drinking/drugs, or creating emotional stress buildup which can trigger sexually abusive acting out. Let go of high-risk feelings- Use the ABC's of letting feelings go to stay out of drama, avoid working yourself up and keeping conflicts going by having the last word. Don't fuel anger by blaming others for problems or ruminating on what you feel are injustices. "If you blame other people for your problems, you give them control over your life".

Table 8.4   Ten Sex Offender Treatment Rules (continued)

4. **Avoid high-risk situations for sexual re-offense-** Do not put yourself at risk for taking advantage of another person. <u>Block relapse opportunities where you have direct access to potential victims</u>. If you are in treatment for child sexual imposition or abuse, move into an adult only apartment complex. If you are in treatment for peer sexual imposition or abuse, do not go to bars or attend parties where potential victims are under the influence of alcohol or drugs. Adhere to the following program safety rules. Complete and total hands off policy with potential victims. 24-hour line of sight supervision by an adult who is aware of your problem when around potential victims. No association with or attempt to make friends with anyone who resembles a past victim. No contact (physical, visual, written, phone, pictures, tapes or videos) with any past victims. Do not encourage anyone else to have any contact with past victims on your behalf. Do not be in the vicinity of any place where a past or potential a victim lives or frequents. If dating is approved by staff, do not date any person who has or is frequently involved with potential victims. No discussion about sexual behavior with anyone unless in the presence of a mental health professional or authorities directly involved with your case.

Social Organization (SRT Program) Rules
5. **Do not abuse your treatment** (therapy rules, principles or therapist)- Including all forms of treatment sabotage such as denial and forming negative contracts; division or splitting (playing people or concepts against each other); resistance to change (a. behavioral- missed sessions, not bringing up own issues or confronting others, not doing treatment assignments; b. verbal- punching holes in treatment concepts with reasons why what is being presented to or requested of you does not apply, or cannot be done) or; passive aggression (a. behavioral- late for sessions, attending but not participating, treatment assignments incomplete or haphazard without attention to issues; b. verbal- diversions such as "throwing out a bone" by confessing to a minor problem to avoid discussing a major one, changing the subject with topic "hop-over's" or "what if" questions and Problem Priorities that place discussion of non-treatment issues before treatment issues, before speaking ask yourself, "How does this relate to your recovery?"). Use your SET Social Problem Solving skill to deal with problems in treatment and keep your eyes on positive goals instead of avoiding problems, letting stress build up and blocking your treatment and positive life goal progress.
6. **Respect others' rights of privacy-** Do not impose yourself on others. Knock on all closed doors before entering and do not enter unless invited in or you are sure the room is empty. Do not enter bathrooms for any reason when they are occupied. Bathe and dress out of view of others and do not view others bathe and dress. Always close bathroom doors when using it. Do not borrow items without asking and do without it if others are not around to ask.
7. **Attend and participate in all treatment sessions-** Unless excused and notify staff in advance of missing sessions.
8. **Complete all SRT workbook assignments-** Turn in assignments on time (i.e., prior to the next group where they will be discussed).

Social Interaction Rules
9. **Use Confrontation with Concern-** Confrontation is done to pull someone up to your level of awareness. It is to be motivated by concern for another person's welfare, i.e., that they may be slipping or approaching relapse. It is "Being your brother's keeper" to help them change. It is not putting someone down to build yourself up and it is not "winning by intimidation."
10. **Do not form negative contracts-** Do not cover up negative behavior for others with the agreement that they will cover up for you. Again, "Be your brother's keeper" and develop positive contracts to hold each other accountable in order to avoid the rule violation effect and falling back into the Stress-Relapse Cycle.

Unlike basic treatment program rules for unhealthy eating which are primarily harmful to self (e.g., weight-related health problems) and unhealthy substance use which can be both harmful to self (e.g., overdose) and others (e.g., drunk driving), treatment program rules for behavior that is primarily harmful to others such as harmful sexual behavior need to include both program rules and home/community safeguards which are typically implemented as signed contracts between the client and those who will monitor their behavior. Examples of 12 basic home and community safeguards for sex offender treatment are provided in Yokley (2008) Tables 3.3 and 3.4

Since many of these typical social responsibility rule examples can be applied to multiple forms of unhealthy, harmful behavior, the example rules listed for unhealthy eating on Table 8.2, unhealthy, harmful substance use on Table 8.3 and harmful sexual behavior on Table 8.4 can be substituted or exchanged between these types of unhealthy, harmful behavior programs to best meet the individual treatment program focus.

Treatment Exercise: Program Rule Development

Use the external control information provided to develop a set of treatment program rules that cover basic Social Responsibility Rules, Social Organization Rules and Social Interaction Rules tailored to provide the structure needed for your unhealthy, harmful treatment population.

Support Treatment Program Rules with External Control Interventions
Program Rule Support: Unhealthy Eating Examples

Monitoring improves rule adherence, in other words "Trust but Verify" (Ronald Reagan 1911-2004). Regarding unhealthy eating, external control methods to help weight-management clients adhere to treatment rules include weigh ins at the beginning of each treatment session to validate healthy eating recorded on the daily food log assignment. Healthy eating can also be supported with cell phone pictures of meals sent to weight-management program staff. In addition, serum cholesterol lab tests and blood pressure checks can be implemented to support healthy eating rules regarding fatty foods and salt intake. Since "three can keep a secret if two of them are dead" (Benjamin Franklin), set up buddy systems to help each other through social obligations where unhealthy food is prevalent. This can support healthy eating rules by increasing monitoring and holding each other accountable. Monitoring walking steps objectively with pedometers or cell phone step counters and recording those steps to the daily food log can help support healthy activity. Like health eating, implementing small group buddy systems that meet for regularly agreed upon walking, swimming or gym workouts can act to support healthy exercise. Finally, recording weight from the weekly group weigh in on a graph that is reviewed with weight management staff can also support healthy eating and activity rule adherence.

Program Rule Support: Unhealthy/Harmful Substance Use Examples

Monitoring of substance use recovery rules to improve adherence includes breathalyzer and urine screening along with AA/NA attendance sheets, signed by meeting secretaries with verification phone numbers. Monitoring needs to be a treatment admission requirement. At admission, clients need to sign releases that allow contact calls to the referral source (e.g., probation/parole officers, human services case workers, family) along with individuals in close contact with the client to discuss attendance, participation and breathalyzer/urine screen results. Monitoring consent needs to include unannounced home visits if indicated by failed breathalyzer or urine screenings. Consequences improve rule adherence, "People grow up when they have to" (SRT maxim). Adding over-correction consequences (i.e., "Do it right once or do it right twice") can improve

184

rule adherence. Here are several examples:

- "Each time that you don't come to a treatment session and don't call, two treatment days will be added to your treatment plan in addition to whatever other consequence you receive";
- "Each time you come back late from your ten minute break between sessions, you will receive a 20 minute recovery exercise to complete at the end of the treatment day"
- "Each time that you do not turn in your weekly signed AA attendance sheet, two more meetings will be added to your required number of AA meetings that week. You will be asked to attend meetings with your sponsor who will be contacted about your attendance."

Since relapse is always a possible reason for missing treatment it is important to implement breathalyzer and urine screening after any missed session.

Since the consequence of increasing treatment is better than letting clients get out of treatment, over-correction and increased length of treatment is always a better consequence than suspension or expulsion from treatment. However, clients need to be informed that serious rule violations, which threaten or violate the rights of others, can result in suspension or expulsion with a letter to the referral source.

A good summary of residential Therapeutic Community substance abuse treatment program rules with support through appropriate external monitoring and consequences are provided on pages 224- 233 in DeLeon (2000). The Therapeutic Community model of residential treatment strives to "make the inside of the house like the outside world" in order to promote transfer of training from the treatment environment to the community. Thus, the Therapeutic Community model has a rule violation severity hierarchy for Cardinal rules, Major rules and House rules that parallel societies felony, misdemeanor and organization rule violations. Violations of Cardinal rules like "no violence, no threats of violence, no drug use" can result in removal from the community at the first violation but most often permanent removal involves "three strikes" similar to laws for violent offenders in many states that result in permanent removal from society (i.e., a life sentence) after three violent felonies. Violations of Major rules involve criminal addict behaviors that are not crimes against persons like stealing, contraband possession and other non-violent criminal behaviors. Finally, House rules address the norms and values of the treatment program, like listening, behaving, being on time, proper manners and other typical socialization problems that need to be improved. The take away message with the Therapeutic Community Cardinal, Major and House Rules and the SRT Social responsibility, Social organization and Social interaction rules are the need to have a hierarchy of rule violations with the most serious being a danger to self and/or others and the least serious being socialization problems.

Program Rule Support: Harmful Sexual Behavior Examples

With serious behaviors that are harmful to others, an advanced directive contract signed at treatment admission may be helpful in supporting program rules on client avoidance of high-risk situations for relapse (e.g., sexual re-offense). Unlike a general waiver of confidentiality (which may not be legal in some states), advanced directives detail relapse prevention actions to take in specific high-risk situations. Releases of information for the specific high risk-situations listed on the client's treatment plan will still be needed for situations that are not covered by duty to warn statutes. Since rules on advanced directives and confidentiality vary between states, it is important to review your state law and write your contract to comply with that law. The following is a general example.

Example of Advanced Directive and Conditional Request for Protective Supervision
I understand that if I begin to lose control of my sexual impulses that I may not be able to make myself cooperate with treatment approaches designed to help me avoid planning or committing a sexual offense and thereby could become a danger to others. As a demonstration of my commitment to maintaining appropriate social behavior control and in order to assist my program staff in helping me avoid sexual re-offense, I hereby request protective supervision including the contact of others in the community during these conditions to help me avoid relapse during the course of my treatment. If, at any time, I violate my behavior contract by not fully cooperating with my treatment program rules, I request that my staff to take the necessary precautions to help me avoid a sexual offense by:

- Contacting [list specific person(s)] who are in [list specific situations] that I need to avoid and having them tell me to leave;
- Contacting my [intended/potential victims, list names] and warning them to stay away from me ;
- Reporting any information regarding the occurrence or potential occurrence of a sexual offense on my part to the appropriate legal authorities including child protective service agencies.

I understand that information regarding the potential occurrence of a sexual offense on my part includes a professional opinion by my program staff about my capacity for committing a sexual offense. Where a second opinion may be necessary, I authorize my treatment staff to obtain professional consultation from any qualified outside source.

In order to prevent "doctor shopping" for programs with less restrictive treatment rules, adding a "Hotel California" clause, i.e., "You can check out (of this program) but you can never leave" (treatment for dangerous behavior) to harmful behavior contracts may be needed. For example…

I have been offered the opportunity to ask questions about my behavior contract and request for protective supervision. I understand that this contract will remain in force until such time that my case is closed or transferred to another treatment provider with a written, dated and signed summary by current treatment staff. I understand that my case will not be considered closed without a significant increase in my Awareness of high-risk situations for relapse, Responsibility in leaning how to "Avoid trouble, calm down, think it though and solve the problem" along with basic Tolerance for frustration and delay of gratification. I further understand that the appropriate legal and child protective service authorities will be informed in writing if I terminate treatment prematurely without a transfer to another treatment provider. I understand that my case will not be considered transferred without the written acceptance of my case by another treatment provider after they receive all of my current treatment program records.

Summary of Interventions to Support Treatment Program Rules
In summary, it is important to include general dynamic high-risk situations in treatment program rules along with specific high-risk situations identified by clients in behavior contracts along with any identified protective factors or relapse safeguards that are supported by reinforcement

and consequences. External control interventions are needed to help clients avoid high-risk situations outlined in their treatment program rules. For example: contact with people who promote, enable or trigger unhealthy, harmful behavior; entering places that are high risk for relapse and; retaining possession or things needed for unhealthy, harmful behavior relapse. A summary of basic treatment program external control rules, monitoring and interventions addressing common dynamic risk factors is provided in Table 8.5 for selected unhealthy, harmful behaviors.

Table 8.5.	Basic Treatment Program External Control Rules, Monitoring and Intervention Examples		
Type of Treatment Program	Program Rule Examples: 1) Avoid high-risk places & people & feelings; 2) Remove problem behavior access; 3) Attend positive support activities.	External Monitoring Examples	External Control Intervention Examples (Reinforcement & Consequences)
Weight Management Program	1) Avoid dining with overeaters. Avoid all you can eat buffets, fast food and going to the grocery without a dietitian approved list, holding on to negative feelings; 2) Remove all junk food from the house; 3) Walk daily, stock healthy food.	Weigh in verification of daily food logs. Cell phone step counter review. Serum cholesterol labs.	Group applause for weight loss and group discussion of weight gain. Treatment progress increases social reinforcement (peer, parent and partner complements about personal appearance).
Drug and Alcohol Program	1) Avoid hanging out with old using friends. Avoid going to bars, parties and places where people are getting drunk or high, working self up; 2) Remove drugs and alcohol along with paraphernalia from the house. Delete negative cell phone numbers; 3) Go to AA/NA meetings 3X/week and get a sponsor.	Breathalyzer and Urine screening along with AA/NA attendance sheets, signed by meeting secretaries with verification phone numbers. Collateral contact calls.	Positive drug and alcohol screening results are reported to the referral source (e.g, court, human services). Client AA/NA sponsors are invited to client treatment sessions. Consistent treatment progress can earn more community freedom and less supervision.
Sex Offender Program	1) No contact with potential victims or substance use; 2) Remove all pornography and other trigger objects from the house; 3) Go to "Circles of Support and Accountability" groups and age-appropriate positive social activity (e.g., sports, clubs, etc.) as prescribed.	Collateral contact calls and community visits, attendance of client positive activities or probation/parole officer home visits. Pager supervision. Polygraph examination on adherence to treatment program rules.	Inability to find client at the location on their schedule and deceptive polygraph results are reported to the referral source (e.g, court, human services). Consistent treatment progress can earn more community freedom and less supervision.

Basic External Control Methods and Procedures

As mentioned in Chapter 3, External Control methods and procedures include: relapse risk assessment; behavior modification; behavior monitoring; physiological/electronic monitoring and; medication prescriptions.

Assessment before Treatment: The first external control procedure that needs to be implemented with clients who have unhealthy, harmful behavior problems is evaluation of the severity of their condition in order to provide more intense treatment on higher levels of care for clients with higher levels of problem severity and relapse risk.

Relapse Risk Assessment

External Control Intervention: Relapse Risk Assessment is an important external control tool in the management of unhealthy, harmful behavior. Relapse Risk Assessment evaluates relapse risk in order to help determine appropriate treatment intensity (i.e., number and type of treatment sessions per day or week) and level of care (i.e., outpatient, intensive outpatient/partial hospitalization or residential treatment). Conduct a Relapse Risk Assessment of negative affective states and other psychosocial factors that can set the occasion for relapse or has triggered relapse in the past. Whenever possible, include specific relapse risk assessments designed for your client's particular type of unhealthy, harmful behavior. Implement more intense treatment on higher levels of care for clients with higher levels of emotional disturbance and relapse risk.

Emotional eating, drinking and sexual behavior- Eating to regulate mood has been associated with relapse in the form of weight regain, national survey data reveals a positive association between most substance use disorders, mood and anxiety disorders and there is a very high lifetime prevalence of mood disorders in individuals with sexual behavior problems (See "Research Support...", p. 188). Thus, identifying elevated levels of unwanted feelings that can set the occasion for relapse (See "Research Identifying Mood Triggers...", p. 167) and need to be reduced below the threshold of acting those feeling out through unhealthy, harmful behavior is part of this assessment. There are quite a few psychological tests that measure levels of depression, anxiety, anger, mood and mood swings. Commonly used psychological measures of: depression include the Beck Depression Inventory-II and the PHQ-9 (Patient Health Questionnaire); anxiety include the Beck Anxiety Inventory and the GAD-7 (Generalized Anxiety Disorder); anger include the State-Trait Anger Expression Inventory-2 and the Novaco Anger Scale and; mood swings include the Mood Disorders Questionnaire for bipolar spectrum disorder screening.

Research Support for the Reliability and Validity of Selected Basic Tests of Affective State
Meta-analytic studies of the Beck Depression Inventory-II have revealed good internal consistency and test-retest reliability with a two factor model comprising Cognitive and Somatic-Affective factors but the existence of a general depression factor supported by the good fit of the one factor model (Erford et. al 2016; Huang & Chen 2015). When the BDI-II and PHQ-7 these depression measures were closely correlated (r= .77), particularly in outpatients (r= .81) making them essentially interchangeable (Kung et. el. 2013). A meta-analysis of the Beck Anxiety Inventory has revealed good internal consistency and test-retest reliability and validity of the two factor model (Bardhoshi, Duncan & Erford, 2016). The reliability and validity of the State-Trait Anger Expression Inventory-2 has been substantiated along with concurrent

---

validity in both clinical and non-clinical populations (Lievaart, Franken & Hovens, 2016). A review of studies on the Mood Disorder Questionnaire found that general population had a much lower sensitivity (i.e., ability to correctly identify those with the condition) and higher specificity (i.e., ability to correctly identify those without the disease) than psychiatric outpatient studies and was much better at detecting bipolar I than bipolar II disorder (Zimmerman & Galione, 2011).

Relapse risk assessment was originally developed to identify psychosocial relapse risk factors for more severe behaviors on the harmful behavior continuum (See Table 1.1, p. 2) that are primarily harmful to others (i.e., criminal behavior and sex offender re-offense). Those assessments have traditionally been referred to as "re-offense risk assessment." With less severe behaviors like substance abuse that can be either unhealthy to self or harmful to others, relapse risk assessment has focused on determining what level of care would best help the client avoid relapse and has typically been referred to as "level of care assessment."

While a specific relapse risk protocol for clients with unhealthy eating has yet to be developed, a number of risk factors for relapse have been identified that can be assessed. Evaluation of current psychosocial stressors is important as stress is a key risk factor in the development of addiction and in addiction relapse which also changes eating patterns (e.g., eating faster and therefore more) and has been associated with obesity (Sinha & Jastreboff, 2013). Poor coping or problem-solving skills, low self-efficacy and tendency to evaluate self-worth in terms of weight and shape are factors to assess that have been associated with weight regain (Byrne, 2002; Byrne, Cooper & Fairburn, 2003). Unrealistic expectations for weight loss, "all or nothing thinking" and ability to establish a "reasonable weight" to avoid failure to achieve weight goals or dissatisfaction with weight loss achieved and establish an individual "best fit" appears to be important in eating relapse assessment (e.g., Brownell & Wadden, 1992; Byrne, 2002; Byrne, Cooper & Fairburn, 2003). In the most severe unhealthy eating clients with morbid obesity, recommendations for the psychological evaluation and psychosocial assessment for clients seeking weight loss surgery have been established by the American Board of Metabolic and Bariatric Surgery (LeMont et. al. 2004; Sogg, Lauretti & West-Smith, 2016).

An important function of risk assessment is to help determine how much external control in the form of treatment intensity is recommended to help clients avoid unhealthy, harmful behavior relapse. Levels of treatment care control the amount of client contact with positive agents of change and the external environment (i.e., negative exposure to high-risk situations for relapse). Outpatient treatment provides the lowest level of external control with the client treatment environment typically limited to one or two brief treatment sessions per week. Day treatment programs often referred to as "partial hospitalization" or "intensive outpatient", provide a moderate level of external control through treatment half a day. Open (unlocked) residential treatment programs provide a high level of external control through treatment 24 hours/day, 7 days/week. The highest level of external control is provided by secure (locked) residential treatment. It should be noted that the amount of staff supervision and staff-client interaction can vary considerably even between programs that treat the same unhealthy, harmful behavior. That being said, psychological evaluation of factors associated with unhealthy, harmful behavior relapse are used to recommend a higher level of treatment care (external control) for clients with a higher risk of relapse.

In the area of unhealthy, harmful substance use, various forms of the American Society of Addiction Medicine (ASAM) level of care criteria are the most widely used. The ASAM criteria evaluates substance abuse referrals on 6 dimensions: 1) Acute Intoxication and/or Withdrawal potential; 2) Biomedical Conditions and Complications; 3) Emotional, Behavioral or Cognitive Conditions and Complications; 4) Readiness to change; 5) Relapse, Continued use, or Continued Problem Potential and; 6) Recovery/Living Environment. The results are used to recommend client placement on: Level I (Outpatient Services); Level II (Intensive Outpatient/Partial Hospitalization Services); Level III (Residential/Inpatient Services) or; Level IV (Medically-Managed Intensive Inpatient Services). A complete description of ASAM level of care criteria and assessment process is provided in (Mee-Lee, 2013).

Regarding the risk assessment of criminal offenders, the Level of Service Inventory-Revised is a validated tool which identifies problem areas in an offender's life and predicts recidivism (Campbell et. al. 2014; Vose, Cullen & Smith, 2008). This assessment tool was designed to assist in classifying offenders (age 16 and older) based upon risk of re-offending (low, moderate, high). It is useful in helping probation/parole officers, correctional workers in jails, detention facilities, and halfway houses make decisions about probation and placement, security level classifications, and assess treatment progress.

With behaviors that are primarily harmful to others, the general rehabilitation principles of risk, need and responsivity have been found effective in the control, management and relapse prevention of unhealthy, harmful criminal behavior including violent offending and sexual offences (Dowden & Andrews, 2000; Dowden, Antonowicz & Andrews, 2003; Hanson et. al. 2009). The Risk principle involves matching the level of program intensity to the offender risk level and providing more intensive levels of treatment for higher risk offenders). The Need principle requires targeting criminogenic needs that are functionally related to criminal behavior. Dynamic factors related to criminal behavior that can be changed like present antisocial attitudes and criminal associates are selected over static factors that can't be changed. The Responsivity principle involves matching the style and mode of intervention to the offender's learning style and abilities. These three principles require the psychological evaluation of offender risk, need and responsivity. Reoffense risk assessment for harmful sexual behavior evaluates both static risk and dynamic risk factors. Adolescent sex offender reoffense risk assessment protocols that are frequently used are the J-SOAP-II and the ERASOR-II (Chu et. al. 2012; Viljoen, Mordell & Beneteau, 2012). Common established adult sex offender reoffense risk assessment protocols are the Static-99R (and 2002R) and the Vermont Assessment of Sex Offender Risk (Helmus et. al. 2012; McGrath et. al 2014).

Behavior Modification

"The consequences of an act affect the probability of its occurring again"
--- B. F. Skinner (1904- 1990)

External Control Intervention: Add behavior modification to support program rules with more types and/or increased frequency of behavior modification techniques for clients with higher levels of relapse risk.

Brief Review: Behavior modification is a set of therapy techniques based on Operant

Conditioning, a type of behavior learning where behavior is modified by consequences and different schedules of reinforcement for behavior modification are employed to achieve the desired results (Ferster & Skinner, 1957). Behavior modification relies on: Positive reinforcement (i.e., positive reward after a healthy/helpful behavior); Negative reinforcement (i.e., negative consequence until healthy/helpful behavior starts); Consequences (e.g., loss of privileges after unhealthy/harmful behavior); Extinction (i.e., consistently not rewarding or ignoring unhealthy/harmful behavior until that behavior extinguishes); Shaping (i.e., reward of successive approximations "baby steps" toward a target healthy/helpful behavior) and; Contingency management, a type of applied behavior analysis that manages rewards and consequences (e.g., token economies, voucher programs, privilege level systems) for treatment adherence. Behavior modification through reinforcement, consequences, behavior feedback and monitoring has been found to exert a powerful influence on managing and decreasing unhealthy harmful behavior along with maintaining and increasing positive, healthy behavior. Behavior modification is referred to as Applied Behavior Analysis when the functional relationship between the target behavior and the environment is analyzed prior to intervention.

Behavior modification procedures are typically used in SRT treatment program behavior contracts after violations of important rules that can or have resulted in unhealthy, harmful behavior relapse. These contracts specify consequences for the unhealthy, harmful behavior along with reinforcement for prosocial alternatives. Important elements of behavior therapy contracts include the:
- Client's name and date of the behavior contract;
- Specific target behaviors that are expected to increase, decrease, start or stop;
- Time frame for target behavior change and the amount of change expected;
- Reinforcement/rewards that will be received for upholding parts of the contract;
- Consequences that will be received for failure to carry out parts of the contract;
- Signatures of the client, staff and involved parties (e.g., parents, probation officers)

Positive Behavior Achievement Contract: A Case Example
Bart was a 14-year-old African American male admitted for Social Responsibility Therapy in forensic foster care. He presented with five types of unhealthy, harmful behavior, eight sex offense victims, regular restraint for violence in prior residential treatment and eight foster home failures (sex offenses in four). Bart had a big, muscular, athletic, intimidating presence. His cognitive ability limitations, anger management problems and poor grades kept him in SBH classes (i.e., Severely Behaviorally Handicapped) despite his repeated requests to be transitioned to mainstream classes. Given his athletic ability, varsity football was one positive outlet option for his anger that would expose him to positive modeling of teamwork, following rules, goal achievement and would require passing grades for participation. This intervention proved quite successful. During one community behavior observation of Bart on the playing field, his staff witnessed him sprinting about 10 yards ahead of his teammates towards the opposing team during their kickoff. Bart hit the receiver so hard his helmet came off and that player had to be taken off the field on a stretcher. The coach loved him, opposing players feared him, his teammates supported him and he elevated his grades to passing levels in order to continue receiving this positive reinforcement. Channeling Bart's aggression into football basically

eliminated threats and physical violence in his foster home although his foster mother continued to report that when angry he was involved in breaking things "by accident".

Since his football teammates where in mainstream classes, Bart's desire to get out of SBH classes increased. For the first time he asked his treatment providers for help in achieving a positive goal. Bart was placed on a positive behavior achievement contract that targeted his uncooperative, unruly and disruptive classroom rule infractions. His school counselor provided weekly behavior feedback from his teachers every Friday. On his contract, every week that he received a positive behavior report (i.e., no rule infractions of any kind, he would receive a program Achievement Award copied to his foster parents. A second (deidentified) copy was posted on his group room wall after review and positive social reinforcement (i.e., peer acknowledgement and applause) by his treatment group and foster parents who sat in the first five minutes of his groups to discuss home behavior. The "three strikes rule" on his contract required that he start over again after three consecutive weeks where rule infractions were listed on his Friday school behavior report. He was told that when he lined the entire group room wall from one side to another with behavior Accomplishment Awards, his program staff would take all of his school counselor positive behavior reports to his principal and advocate for transitioning him into mainstream classes. Given the length of the wall, this would take 25 positive accomplishment awards. These criteria were listed on Bart's contract which he signed along with his staff, foster parents and school counselor all of whom received copies. Bart lined the group room wall behavior Accomplishment Awards in a little over six months. His positive school behavior track record allowed his staff to advocate for him and he was transitioned to mainstream classes. Bart was discharged to regular foster care after 36 months with no need for physical restraint and no sexual or physical violence.

Integration and Incorporation of Behavior Modification
Behavior modification is built into response-cost token economy interventions. In the token economy, clients typically receive tokens or points that they can redeem for items, activities or privileges that are rewarding to them. In response-cost token economies, clients receive reinforcement points for positive target behaviors and lose points for exhibiting negative target behaviors. In SRT, the token economy is primarily used with preteen children but is also applicable to clients who require a high degree of structure to maintain appropriate social behavior control. For further information, see Yokley (2008), p. 229- 230.

Behavior modification is also commonly incorporated into treatment program rules. For example, regarding unhealthy eating, having weigh ins at the beginning of each weight management groups allows for both verbal praise and group applause for weight loss (i.e., following healthy eating rules). On the other hand weigh ins allow accountability consequences for weight gain (i.e., not following rules). This would typically occur through Confrontation with Concern (See p. 67) as follows. "What do you think resulted in your gain this week?", "Let's look at your food log and circle the items that could have resulted in your weight gain this week" or "Let's review the week and see if we can find anything that you forgot to log that could have resulted in your weight gain this week." In substance abuse treatment, violating the sobriety rule through failed urine toxicology screening may result in probation violation and a house arrest ankle bracelet while consistently passing drug screenings could result in more treatment program privileges. Clients in treatment for sexually abusive behavior who violate their community supervision rules and cannot be located at work or in school, may have to pay for a polygraph examination on the question of whether they have committed a sexual re-offense while consistent treatment progress could earn less community supervision.

"Immature people need rigid structure" (SRT Maxim)- Meeting the client's developmental needs requires providing more behavioral intervention structure for younger clients and those who are developmentally immature or emotionally insecure. The treatment model is matched to developmental level and needs in SRT. This is accomplished by shifting from a highly structured behavioral modification model (i.e., Token Economy reinforcement and consequences) to a therapeutic community social learning model and finally a cognitive behavioral mental health model across the developmental age continuum as illustrated in Table 8.6. For further description of this SRT group program delivery system see p. 227- 240 in Yokley (2008).

Table 8.6
Matching Intervention Structure to Client Developmental Needs

Child (age 6- 9)	**Preteen** (age 10- 12)	**Teen** (age 13- 17)	**Adult** (age 18+)
Target multiple forms of unhealthy, harmful (i.e., sexual abuse, physical abuse, property abuse, substance abuse & trust abuse) in group, family & individual therapy			
Develop Honesty, Concern & Responsibility as competing factors to unhealthy, harmful behavior			
Focus on how abuse behavior was acquired	Focus on how abuse behavior was acquired & maintained	Focus on how abuse behavior was acquired, maintained & generalized to other forms of abuse	
Token Economy Model	Transition from Token Economy Model to Social Learning Model (behavior feedback slips)	Social Learning Model with treatment with community behavior contracts	Transition from Social Learning Model to Modified Mental Health Model

Behavior Monitoring: Collateral Contacts and Community Supervision
"Trust but verify" – Ronald Reagan (1911- 2004)

External Control Intervention: Add collateral contacts and community supervision to support program rules and verify self-report measures of client unhealthy, harmful behavior with more types and/or increased frequency of collateral contacts and community supervision for clients with higher levels of relapse risk. With youth, external control intervention needs to include supervision/monitoring in the home (including parent behavior reports during the first part of youth treatment sessions), at school (e.g., arranging Friday school counselor feedback slips or calls) and in the community (e.g., making the home the place where the youth bring their friends). Parents who befriend the girlfriends of male youth gain access to important behavior assessment data and external control influence. Strong research support for implementing external control interventions across all client environments is provided by the Multisystemic Therapy literature. This highly effective delinquent behavior treatment provides problem-focused intervention with the individual youth and their family members in the home, school and neighborhood settings. Multisystemic therapy has demonstrated significant effects on the criminal activity of serious and violent juvenile offenders in more than a dozen clinical trials

(Wagner, Sawyer & Dopp, 2014). A behavior feedback slip system is implemented within residential and foster-family based treatment programs for behavior monitoring that allow clients to "drop a slip" (write accomplishment awards or incident reports) on others who are doing well or having problems with social-emotional maturity (See Appendix D, p. 269). Dropping a slip is also typically used in the residential therapeutic community to identify interpersonal conflicts and put individuals in the same group encounter session to address those issues (See DeLeon, 2000, p. 291- 292). Staff review of behavior self-monitoring logs along with collateral contacts with those who interact with the client in the community and community supervision by probation/parole officers are important external control behavior monitoring tools. Self-monitoring is a standard component in behavior modification that has an advantage of creating a "reactive effect" which typically decreases unhealthy/harmful behavior while increasing healthy/helpful behavior (Hawtol et. al. 2000). Part of SRT Awareness Training is self-monitoring of triggers for unhealthy, harmful behavior using Situation Response Analysis Logs (See p. 63- 64). Behavioral self-monitoring through food and activity logs are included for unhealthy eating clients. With adults add partners to couples/family therapy interventions along with peers and Twelve-Step program sponsors, probation/parole officers and Human Services workers to collateral contacts for effective community monitoring. Releases of information from clients for collateral contacts (i.e., community outreach calls to those in close contact with the client) need to be obtained at treatment intake and releases for regular contact with probation/parole officers need to be obtained for clients referred for harmful substance use or sexual behavior.

Physiological/Electronic Monitoring
External Control Intervention: Add physiological and electronic monitoring to support program rules and verify self-report measures of client unhealthy, harmful behavior with more types and/or increased frequency of physiological/electronic monitoring for clients with higher levels of relapse risk.

Physiological testing is an important support tool in behavior monitoring. Physiological testing for unhealthy eating behavior includes regular weight monitoring at the beginning of each treatment group session. Cell phone snap shots of meals can be used to verify food logs. Serum cholesterol testing may reveal continued unhealthy eating and consumption of fatty foods. Pedometers and step counters on cell phones are helpful in monitoring walking recorded on food and activity logs. In addition, regular aerobic exercise (e.g., walking, jogging, biking, swimming, dancing) and healthy eating (e.g., low salt, low sugar, low fat, less than 2 alcoholic drinks/day) should result in decreased blood pressure readings. Physiological monitoring for unhealthy, harmful drug and alcohol use includes random broadband urine toxicology screens (typically covering 10 classes of substances) and blood alcohol level breathalyzer tests. Penile plethysmograph (PPG) examination can be helpful in relapse prevention for clients with sexually abusive behavior. The PPG measures blood flow to the penis while the client is exposed to sexually suggestive content, such as pictures, movies or audio. PPG testing can help to validate client self-report on the age and gender of potential victims, which is needed to develop effective community monitoring for relapse prevention. PPG testing can also be used to determine if arousal to potential victims has decreased at the end of treatment. The Abel Assessment avoids the invasive nature of having a band monitor on the clients penis to measure arousal by measuring visual reaction time to potentially arousing pictures. Finally, polygraph examination can be useful in verifying client self-report on their sexual offense history as well as adherence to their home and community safety safeguard rules which were developed after identifying the client's high-risk situations for relapse. It should also be noted that polygraph examination may also be of use for monitoring sex offenders who are permitted supervised child visitation. For example, one polygraph study of child molesters who received court-ordered supervised visitation with minors (and victims), revealed a statistically significant 59.5% increase in deviant fantasies and masturbation while thinking about a known minor compared to 3% of offenders who were not permitted any contact with minors (Davis, Williams & Yokley, 1996).

Behavior Monitoring Research Support

Self-Monitoring- Support for self-monitoring of unhealthy, harmful behavior (Table 8.5) includes the following research findings. Self-monitoring through client use of daily food logs has resulted in increased weight loss (e.g., Bellack, Rozensky & Schwartz, 1974; Hollis et. al., 2008; Johnson & Wardle, 2011) and self-monitoring cigarette smoking has decreased number of cigarettes smoked per day (e.g., Chasse & Ladouceur, 1980; McFall & Hammen,1971). In contrast, while self-monitoring of alcohol consumption has been found to be in agreement with collateral monitoring (Samo, Tucker & Vuchinich, 1989) and may decrease drinking in college students (Cho, 2007), the positive reactive effect of self-monitoring on alcohol has been generally weak (Korotisch & Nelson-Gray, 1999).

External Monitoring- Adherence to social rules requires external monitoring. Support for External Monitoring by staff and others of unhealthy, harmful eating, substance use and sexual behavior (Table 8.5) includes the following research findings. Increases in parental monitoring across home, school and neighborhood settings during Multisystemic Therapy has predicted decreases in delinquent peer affiliation and delinquent behaviors (Huey, Henggeler, Brondino, & Pickrel, 2000). Community supervision and monitoring by probation/parole officers which has been in effect since the establishment of probation over 100 years ago can decrease re-arrest rates considerably, particularly with probation officer training on the principles of risk, need and responsivity (e.g., Andrews et. al. 1990; Cary, 2011; Bonita et. al. 2011). Probation/parole supervision is an important component in collaboration with risk assessment and treatment in maintaining sex offenders in the community (e.g., Buttars, Huss & Brack, 2016; Wilson et. al. 2000). Intensive probation/parole supervision can have a positive impact on alcoholic probationers (e.g., Latessa & Travis, 1988), is an important adjunct treatment service in decreasing re-arrest of drug court clients (e.g., Banks & Gottfredson, 2003) and can significantly decrease arrest rates in serious and violent offenders (e.g., Veysey, Ostermann & Lanterman, 2014).

Physiological Testing/Monitoring- Implementation of regular breathalyzer testing after alcohol-related offenses has decreased impaired driving and domestic violence relapse (e.g., Kilmer et. al. 2013). While client self-report of drug use is typically poor (e.g., Chermack et. al. 2000; Kilpatrick et. al. 2000), external monitoring (i.e., conducting urine tests before an interview) can increase the accuracy of self-report (e.g., Hamid et. al. 1999).The penile plethysmograph (PPG) has demonstrated predictive validity in adolescent sex offenders where post-treatment arousal and inability to suppress deviant arousal to male and female children was significantly related to sexual re-offense and over a 6 year follow-up period (Clift, Rajlic & Gretton, 2009). It should be noted that in addition to the invasive nature of the PPG test, there are problems with generalization where the PPG measure have shown decreased deviant sexual in the laboratory but not in the natural environment when a portable PPG was used (Rea et. al. (2003). Finally, the Able Assessment avoids having a band monitor of the client's penis by measuring visual reaction time to potentially arousing pictures (Able et. al. 2004) which may be more acceptable for juvenile sex offender assessment. Research evidence for the use of polygraph examination has been provided for verifying client self-report on their sexual offense history (e.g., Wilcox & Sosnowski, 2005) as well as adherence to their post-conviction home and community safety safeguard rules (e.g., Kokish, Levenson & Blasingame, 2005).

Medication Prescriptions

External Control Intervention: Add physician referrals for prescription medications as needed to decrease negative mood states that can increase the risk of relapse along with prescription medications that target cravings/urges likely to trigger relapse. Increase the frequency of medication review on clients with higher levels of relapse risk.

Medication prescriptions can help clients with unhealthy, harmful behavior relapse prevention by targeting emotional states that set the occasion for or trigger relapse. Specifically, prescribing medications can help with two basic emotional motivations for engaging in unhealthy/harmful behavior, i.e., the avoidance pain and pursuit of pleasure. Avoiding the pain of unwanted feelings provides mood-related relapse motivation (e.g., falling into comfort eating, drinking or a rebound relationship sex during a period of loneliness and depression). The pursuit of pleasure also provides mood-related relapse motivation by gratifying cravings and urges (e.g., falling into unhealthy, harmful eating, drinking or sexual behavior during after ruminating on how good it can make you feel).

Prescriptions for unwanted feelings that can trigger relapse- The high prevalence of unwanted feelings (often depression and anxiety) in many individuals with unhealthy, harmful behavior problems warrants treatment with prescription medications to decrease emotional pain below the relapse trigger threshold. Regarding the avoidance of pain, unwanted feelings have been related to relapse with multiple forms of unhealthy, harmful behavior (See "Mood Triggers", p. 166). The "self-medication hypothesis" of using drugs and alcohol use to relieve emotional suffering can be applied to emotional eating and sexual addiction both of which can also be used to relieve unwanted feelings (See "Research Identifying Mood Triggers..." p. 167).

Adding psychiatric medication prescriptions to cognitive behavior therapy can improve emotional treatment outcome which addresses the goal of lowering unwanted feelings below the threshold of acting emotions out through unhealthy, harmful behavior. For example, a three group treatment study of chronically depressed patients with antidepressant medication, CBT or both revealed that 85% in the combined group responded favorably to treatment compared to 55% in the psychotherapy only group and 52% in the medication only group (Keller et. al. 2000). A nine-month treatment study of anxious patients (panic disorder) with medication (SSRI), CBT or both revealed that treatment completers who received both had a better outcome than those who received medication or CBT alone (van Apeldoorn et. al. 2008). In SRT, it is important to remember that "Pills don't teach skills" and reducing unwanted feelings with medications is recommended when indicted as an addition to ACTS skills training.

Research Support for the High Prevalence of Unwanted Feelings in Clients with Unhealthy/Harmful Behavior: Selected Examples

Individuals with obesity have a higher prevalence of binge eating which in turn is associated with higher depressive symptomatology (Smith et. al. 1998) and eating to regulate mood has been associated with relapse in the form of weight regain (Byrne, Cooper & Fairburn, 2003). Obesity appears higher in women with mood disturbance which has been related to higher emotional eating and increased weight (e.g., Baskaran et. al. 2014; van Strien et. al. 2016) and decreased emotional eating has been associated with greater weight loss success (Braden et. al. 2016). Morbidly obese individuals who are bariatric surgery candidates may have an increased risk of drug and alcohol use (Donnadieu-Rigole et. al. 2016) and the relationship between depression and obesity appears to be bidirectional. Specifically, a meta-

---

analysis exploring the bi-directional relationship between depression and obesity by Mannan et. al. (2016) involving 226,063 participants (33.7% men) revealed that those who were depressed had a 37% increased risk of being obese and those who were obese had an 18% increased risk of being depressed.

A range of alcohol consumption, not just heavy drinking or alcohol use disorders has been associated with major depression (Goldstein & Levitt, 2006) and a large scale study of 6,355 clients (14–66+ yrs of age) in inpatient and outpatient addiction treatment programs at 41 sites revealed a lifetime diagnosis of major depression of 43.7% (Miller at. al. 1996). In general, national survey data reveals a positive association between most substance use disorders, mood and anxiety disorders (e.g., Grant et. al 2006). Meta-analysis of the prevalence of depression and anxiety in prescription opiate clients in substance abuse treatment has revealed a 43% prevalence of "any" mental health problems, 27% prevalence of a depression diagnosis and 29% prevalence of an anxiety diagnosis (Goldner et. al. 2006).

Sexual behavior problem studies of the lifetime prevalence of mood disorder in individuals with paraphilias and paraphilia-related disorders (including pedophilic sex offenders) reveal a very high lifetime prevalence of mood disorder ranging between 67%- 76.7% (e.g., Raymond et. al. 1999; Kafka & Hennen 2002; Kafka & Prentky, 1994; 1998). Regarding the presence of depression in this population, one study reported early onset dysthymic disorder at 55% and major depression at 39% lifetime prevalence (Kafka & Hennen 2002). The lifetime prevalence of anxiety has also been reported as high with anxiety disorders at 38.3%- 46.7% and a 21.6% social phobia prevalence (Kafka & Hennen 2002; Kafka & Prentky, 1994; 1998). The lifetime prevalence of psychoactive substance use disorder in this population has been reported as 40.8% - 60% with alcohol abuse at 30%- 40% (e.g., Raymond et. al. 1999; Kafka & Hennen 2002; Kafka & Prentky, 1994; 1998). Incarcerated sex offenders were found to have more affective psychopathology such as anxiety, dysthymia, PTSD and major depression than other general population prison inmates (Ahlmeyer et. al. 2003). The prevalence of unwanted feelings in sex offenders may be elevated as a result of their own history of being abused. Specifically, a study of youth sex offenders revealed that 42% had depression (i.e., elevated Beck Depression Inventory scores) and youth sex offenders with a history of physical or sexual abuse had higher levels of depression (Becker et. al 1991).

Prescriptions for urges/cravings that can trigger relapse- Prescribing medications to suppress unhealthy, harmful behavior urges/cravings is another useful external control intervention for physicians and other agents of change with prescription privileges. In obesity treatment, the number of over the counter advertised "diet pills" and weight loss supplements have always continued to expand particularly around the holidays when New Year's resolutions to lose weight increase the demand for these products. While traditional appetite suppressants such as amphetamine and phenmetrazine are no longer recommended because of their stimulant properties and addictive potential, FDA approved prescription medications for obesity treatment have made new advances. A number of drugs have been FDA approved that target parts of the brain involved with appetite and hunger signals which reduce the chances of overeating. For example, in 2015 Vyvanse (Lisdexamfetamine) a central nervous system stimulant used in the treatment of Attention Deficit Hyperactivity Disorder was approved as the first U.S. drug to treat binge eating disorder. In 2014 Contrave was approved as a weight-loss medicine for adults with obesity. Contrave, a combination of naltrexone, used to combat drug and alcohol addiction, and bupropion, prescribed as Wellbutrin for depression and as Zyban for smoking cessation. Saxenda, a drug that works like a hormone the body produces that naturally regulates appetite was also FDA approved in 2014. Belviq (Lorcaserin), approved in 2012 is an appetite suppressant that activates brain receptors for serotonin, triggering feelings of satiety and satisfaction. Qsymia, also approved in 2012 is a combination of two older drugs, phentermine (an amphetamine substitute) and topiramate (an anti-seizure medication). Prescription medications to suppress appetite or cravings are recommended for use with a reduced-calorie diet and increased physical activity.

In alcohol and drug treatment, prescription medications to support staying sober include Antabuse (disulfiram) which blocks an enzyme that is involved in metabolizing alcohol intake and helps prevent drinking as a result of unpleasant side effects of nausea and vomiting that will occur if alcohol is consumed. Campral (Acamprosate) helps avoid alcohol relapse by restoring the chemical balance in the brain that may be unbalanced in clients who are addicted to alcohol. Naltrexone is prescribed to reduce cravings, control or abstain from drinking alcohol or taking opiates. Naltrexone belongs to a class of drugs known as opiate antagonists. It works in the brain to prevent opiate effects (e.g., feelings of well-being, pain relief). Vivitrol (extended-release injectable naltrexone) blocks the effects of opiates and interferes with drinking pleasure which can be used as part of a treatment program for opiate or alcohol dependence. Monthly Vivitrol injections are used to help prevent relapse. In the treatment of heroin and other opiates, methadone maintenance therapy is prescribed to individuals who want to stop heroin but have been unable to maintain abstinence. Methadone reduction programs are suitable for addicted persons who wish to stop using drugs altogether. Buprenorphine (Subutex) like methadone is used in opioid detoxification but has the advantage over methadone of less potential of life threatening respiratory depression in cases of abuse. Suboxone for opioid dependence combines buprenorphine (Subutex) and naloxone which blocks or reverses the effects of opioid medication and is used in the form of a nasal spray (Narcan) for emergency treatment of opioid overdose. Buprenorphine alone and the combination of buprenorphine and naloxone prevent opioid withdrawal symptoms by producing similar effects to these drugs. The observation that one unhealthy, harmful behavior can trigger another may make it advisable to help individuals with drug and alcohol problems quit smoking. Bupropion (marketed as Welbutrin and Zyban) can help reduce nicotine withdrawal and the urge to smoke. Varenicline (Chantix) can help reduce nicotine withdrawal and the urge to smoke and also blocks the effects of nicotine from cigarettes if the user starts smoking again. Prescription medications to suppress drug and alcohol cravings are recommended for use with counseling for relapse prevention.

In the treatment of harmful sexual behavior, prescribing medications to reduce sexual arousal is implemented to reduce the motivation for sexually re-offending in individuals with harmful sexual behavior problems. Antiandrogen medications which decrease sexual drive include medroxyprogesterone acetate (MPA) or Depo Provera in shot form, leuprolide acetate (Lupron) and cyproterone acetate. Since antiandrogen treatment is equated with "chemical castration" and can have medical side effects (e.g. breast enlargement, weight gain, blood clots, depression, gallstones, diabetes mellitus, osteoporosis, hot flushes), this approach is often directed towards the more harmful or violent sexual behaviors such as child molestation or rape. Another approach of prescription medications for unhealthy, harmful sexual behavior is to reduce the conditions that can set the occasion for relapse. For example, the goal of prescribing medications that target the mood disorders that have a high prevalence in this population is to lower the level of unwanted feelings below the threshold of acting those feelings out sexually. This approach is more often implemented with nonviolent, compulsive unhealthy sexual behaviors. Prescription medications to suppress harmful sexual urges are recommended for use with counseling for relapse prevention.

> **Research Support for Prescription Medication Treatment of Sexually Harmful Behavior**
> A meta-analysis by Losel and Schmucker (2005) examining the effectiveness of various treatment interventions for adult sex offenders indicated that testosterone-lowering hormonal treatments may be linked to greater reductions in recidivism for some offenders than the use of psychosocial treatments alone. While antiandrogen treatment outcome data is limited, there is some evidence that offenders receiving this treatment have lower rates of recidivism (e.g., Maletzky, Tolan, & McFarland, 2006). Regarding prescribing medications to target mood disorders that can trigger sexual re-offense, there is a large research data base supporting the efficacy of these medications for reducing unwanted mood states. However, few studies have reported on the impact of reducing unwanted feelings on sexual behavior problem relapse. One retrospective study reported significant reduction in paraphilic activity among participants who received Selective Serotonin Reuptake Inhibitor (SSRI) medications and psychotherapy. (Kraus, Strom, Hill, et al., 2007). Another study of SSRI treatment reported significant reduction in men with depressive symptoms, paraphilia and nonparaphilic sexual addiction without affecting conventional sexual interest and associated behaviors (Kafka & Prentky, 1992). A study of SSRI augmentation with psychostimulants in men assessed for mood disorder, ADHD and paraphilia revealed SSRI treatment had statistically significant effects in diminishing paraphilia and paraphilia-related disorders and addition of methylphenidate SR had additional statistically significant effects on paraphilia (Kafka & Hennen, 2000b). Finally, a case study of an adolescent male with multiple paraphilias and mood disorder responded to SSRI treatment after failing to respond to long term residential treatment (Galli et. al 1998).

Treatment Exercise: Program Rule Support

Use the external control information provided to support your set of treatment program rules with the assessment; behavior modification; behavior monitoring; physiological/electronic monitoring and; medication prescription procedures to provide the external control support needed for relapse prevention in your unhealthy, harmful treatment population. Match the intensity of external control intervention to behavior problem severity as illustrated in Table 8.7.

One last point to consider: Severity vs Frequency of Unhealthy, Harmful Behavior

While it is important to add more external control interventions to more severe behavior problems, less severe problems with a high frequency need external control intervention as well. "The more severe the problem, the harder it is to change" may not always be the case. Less severe harmful behaviors on the harmful behavior continuum (Table 1.1, p. 2) can be just as difficult if not more difficult to change because of…

- Impact Rationalization- It's low on the social impact continuum, e.g., Smoking, overeating and overspending "Only hurts me. It doesn't hurt others."
- Normalization - "Everyone does it" or "Lots of people do it." Negative social modeling, more people around the client doing it. "It's normal to overeat sometimes. What about family reunions, Thanksgiving Dinner, Fourth of July picnics".
- Comparison and contrast thinking- This occurs when the client compares their problem to a more severe one. For example, "I just eat a little too much, I don't drink too much. I just spend too much, I don't gamble. I just drink, I don't do drugs. I just smoke cigarettes not marijuana. I just smoke marijuana, not crack."
- Severity Minimization- It's the least on the harmful behavior severity continuum and "It's not illegal." You can get arrested for drinking and driving but you can't get arrested for overeating and driving. You can get arrested for smoking crack but not for smoking cigarettes.

Table 8.7
Matching External Control to Behavior Problem Severity

Behavior Problem Severity: Unhealthy, Harmful Behavior Continuum
(See Table 1.1)

Primarily Harmful to Self	Harmful to self & others	Primarily harmful to others
(e.g., Unhealthy eating)	(e.g., Substance abuse)	(e.g., Sexual offenses)

Behavior Problem Severity and Intervention Intensity
(Number of Intervention Pathways, See Figure 3.2)

Primarily Harmful to Self	Harmful to self & others	Primarily harmful to others
Mild (Less interventions)	Moderate	Severe (More interventions)
Internal Control	Internal Control	Internal Control
	+ Social Learning	+ Social learning
		+ External Control

Behavior Problem Severity and Treatment Methods/Procedures

Primarily Harmful to Self	Harmful to self & others	Primarily harmful to others
More Internal Control Tools		More External Control Tools
(e.g., Cognitive restructuring)		(e.g., Behavior modification)

Behavior Problem Severity and Behavior Monitoring Locus of Control

Primarily Harmful to Self	Harmful to self & others	Primarily harmful to others
More Self-Monitoring		More External Monitoring
(e.g., thought & behavior logs)		(e.g., staff, probation/parole officers)

The bottom line here is that while it is important to add more external control interventions to more severe behavior problems, it is also important to add external control interventions to certain higher frequency unhealthy behaviors that are relatively common and easy to normalize.

Summary and Conclusion

In general, more types and increased frequency of external intervention needs to be implemented as the severity of unhealthy, harmful behavior increases and the type of unhealthy, harmful behavior shifts from primarily harmful to self to primarily harmful to others.

"The ideal of behaviorism is to eliminate coercion: to apply controls by changing the environment in such a way as to reinforce the kind of behavior that benefits everyone" -- B. F. Skinner (1904- 1990)

Chapter Focus

In review, Chapters 4- 7 covered the SRT Internal Control interventions referred to as "Healthy Behavior Success Skills" used by clients to pull themselves towards positive change and Chapter 8 described the SRT External Control interventions used by others to help push clients towards positive change. The present chapter describes SRT social learning procedures that have a strong focus on modeling the "Healthy Relationship Success Skills" that can help redirect and motivate clients towards positive behavior change (See Figure 3.1, p. 44).

Social Learning Theory and Behavior Modeling

"Most human behavior is learned observationally through modeling from others" -- Albert Bandura

Social Learning Theory advanced behavioral and cognitive learning theories with an observational learning theory asserting that humans also learn by observation of others and modeling their behavior (Bandura, 1977b). In social learning, reinforcement of a behavior occurs indirectly (vicarious reinforcement) when an observed behavior is rewarded. Social learning requires attention to the behavior being modeled, retention/remembering the behavior, reproduction of the behavior and motivation to do the behavior (e.g., seeing someone else get praise for doing it). An important aspect of social learning theory is the concept of reciprocal determinism which states that modeling between a person and their social environment goes both ways. For example, a person overeating, drinking or sex texting will likely influence their peers to overeat, drink or sex text which then encourages that person to do more eating, drinking or sexting. In other words, when clients model the "Healthy Relationship Success Skills" that motivate them towards positive behavior change, this influences their treatment peers to move in that positive direction which in turn encourages them to make more positive changes. That being said, "A treatment program is only as strong as its number of positive role models".

Healthy social learning requires healthy social modeling in healthy social relationships. Referring back to our human psychological needs for healthy positive social relationships (See Figure 2.1, p. 25), people with healthy relationships are happier and more likely to receive positive support towards achieving healthy lifestyle goals. On the other hand, there is considerable research indicating that unhealthy relationships involving negative social influence

Social Learning: "Straight to the Point"

The point of this section is to help clinicians support client relapse prevention efforts and healthy lifestyle change goals by developing the "Healthy Relationship Success Skills" needed to initiate and maintain healthy relationships that model positive behavior and redirect/motivate clients towards positive change.

Social Learning Goals and Objectives

Goal: Review developing "Healthy Relationship Success Skills" by putting multicultural prosocial values into action and learn the PRAISE multicultural group unity and participation motivation skills.

Objectives: Clinicians will be able to: 1) Help clients put multicultural prosocial values into action as "Healthy Relationship Success Skills" and; 2) Utilize PRAISE multicultural group skills to develop group unity and participation motivation.

and unhealthy peer pressure are important contributing factors to multiple forms of unhealthy, harmful behavior. A research literature summary of social learning theory is provided below.

> **Social Learning Theory Summary:**
> Social learning involves behavior modeling by others and imitation of behavior models making social influence an important factor for both healthy or harmful behavior acquisition and maintenance. Albert Bandura's original social learning theory (Bandura, 1962) has been advanced by Ronald Akers (Akers & Jensen, 2006) to explain unhealthy harmful behavior (crime and deviance) and may subsume intergenerational transmission theory along with peer support theory, i.e., the social influence model (Sellers, Cochran & Branch, 2005). According to Akers' theory, association with individuals doing the harmful behavior, reinforcement of the harmful behavior, favorable definitions/attitudes towards the harmful behavior and harmful behavior role models (imitation) can explain how harmful behavior is acquired and maintained.

What are Healthy Relationships?

Probably the most pervasive social learning experience that we as a society receive on a regular basis is constant exposure to news of confidence schemes, drug overdose, robbery, domestic violence, rape and mass shootings. The perpetrators of this trust abuse, substance abuse, property abuse, physical abuse and sexual abuse are continually on display in the nightly news. In short, we are constantly exposed to media modeling of <u>what we DO NOT want</u> in others. Social modeling of <u>what we DO want</u> in others is scarce in the media and teachings on what we want in others is close to non-existent in our school, college and university curriculums. This social learning deficit may help explain our high divorce rate. It could be argued from the huge volume of beauty, grooming and hygiene products sold in our society that we believe attracting others is all that is necessary and nothing is needed to maintain relationships after they are started.

Healthy relationships can involve good positive friendships, romantic partnerships, relationships with teachers and bosses, classmates, coworkers and employer relationships along with family relationships. Healthy, positive relationships involve people who care as much about us as we care about them. Healthy relationship partners help each other move towards healthy lifestyle goals and support each other during stressful times. They do not enable each other to relapse or hold each other back from achieving positive goals. Instead, both partners feed reciprocal determinism by modeling positive behavior for each other. Since a relationship can't be healthy or successful if we do not value the other person, the first question to answer is "What do we value in others?" or put another way "What do we want in others?"

Treatment Exercise: What Do We Want in Others?

The first step towards developing healthy relationships is clarifying relationship values. This awareness training exercise is structured to help clients discover what they want in others. In the visual flip chart version of this exercise, six poster sheets are taped to the wall, one for each multicultural prosocial value category (i.e., honesty, trust, loyalty, concern, and responsibility) and one for miscellaneous descriptors like looks, money, etc., that are not multicultural prosocial values. The poster sheets are numbered one to five without value category titles, just the numbers. The awareness training staff starts by stating, "Let's take a minute and think about what we want from others in our life. If we were looking for a best friend in the whole world, and were able to get online at www.relationships.com to select the ideal best friend, what characteristics would we select?" As the group gives characteristics describing what they want from others, the trainer writes these descriptors on the appropriate poster sheets one to six with a blue marker (i.e., descriptors of honesty characteristics go on the first sheet, trust descriptors go on the second sheet and so on). When participants have run out of comments for what they want in a best friend, the process is repeated with a red marker for what participants want in a life partner (if participants are adults) or girlfriend/boyfriend (if participants are youth). When participants have run out of comments for what they want in a life partner, the process is repeated with a green marker for what they want in a child (if participants are adults) or parent (if participants are youth).

At the end of this exercise, the title of each multicultural value category (i.e., honesty, trust, loyalty, concern, responsibility, miscellaneous) is written after each number at the top of each poster sheet to illustrate that almost all of the descriptors given fall under the five multicultural prosocial value categories with a few exceptions.

After this is illustrated, the last question that clients need to answer in this exercise is, "If honesty, trust, loyalty, concern and responsibility are the things that we want from others in our life, what do others want from us?" The response to this question is almost always, "The same thing." This solidifies client awareness of the need to learn, demonstrate and practice these characteristics if they want to develop healthy relationships. If the group is made up of parents, also ask, "What should we be teaching our children?" If the audience receiving this exercise is staff, they discover the answer to the question, "What should we be teaching the youth in our treatment programs?" Developing client awareness of the multicultural prosocial characteristics needed to get the acceptance they want from others provides motivation for change along with a foundation to bridge the generation gap, culture clash with authorities and develop the therapeutic relationship.

Table 9.1 provides a summary example of the results of conducting the "What do we want in others?" exercise with 437 participants in 38 SRT training sessions with clients and staff from outpatient and residential weight management, substance abuse and sex offender treatment programs. This version (also described on in Yokley, 2008) is recommended. However, the same exercise can be conducted in a group therapy session structured to help clients discover important relationship values. Guided discovery questions can be used in group therapy to help clients arrive at the conclusion that they want: honesty (i.e., no one wants to be lied to); trust (i.e., no one wants to be back-stabbed); loyalty (i.e., no one wants to be cheated on); concern (i.e., no one wants to be disrespected) and; responsibility (i.e., no one wants to have to have to do all of the work in a relationship) from others. The top five miscellaneous descriptors that did not fit in any of the multicultural values categories were: Sense of humor; Good Looks; Intelligence; Shared interests and; Fun. Unlike honesty, trust, loyalty, concern and responsibility, these characteristics are "icing on the cake", not relationship deal breakers. Thus, it is important to point out that in relationships if you pick...

- Humor over honesty, don't be surprised if you get lied to.
- Charming over trustworthy, don't be surprised, if you get manipulated.
- Looks over loyalty, don't be surprised if you get cheated on or dumped.
- Cool over concern, don't be surprised if you get disrespected
- Fun over responsibility, don't be surprised if you end up doing all the work.

Table 9.1   Summary of What Humans Want from Other Humans

(i.e., What clients, parents and treatment staff want from best friends, life partners and close family)

Honesty	Trust	Loyalty	Concern	Responsibility
Honest Truthful Expressive Sincere Straightforward Doesn't steal, not a thief	Trustworthy Reliable Obedient Respects boundaries Trust their judgment Can confide in them Trusting	Loyal Dependable Faithful Sticks with you Has family loyalty Doesn't cheat Loyal to what is right Has my back Not a back stabber Keeps confidences	Caring, kind Supportive Understanding Loving person Good listener Accepting Tolerant Considerate Compassionate Tries to get along Patient Nice, pleasant Gives as much as takes Friendly Empathy Unconditional love (6) Generous Forgiving Not hurtful	Responsible Respectful Good work ethic Good hygiene Positive role model Employed Takes initiative Holds self accountable Sober, drug & alcohol free Good money management Completes tasks Self-sufficient Neat, tidy Financially stabile Good morals Stays organized, Puts things back Helpful Pulls own weight Resolves conflicts Educated Common sense Good manners Cooperative

Note: Descriptors of "What we want in others" are rank ordered by number of exercises in which they were disclosed. Descriptors disclosed in less than 5 exercises were not included. Descriptor categories include synonyms. The top 5 descriptors that participants wanted in others that were not multicultural prosocial values were: Sense of humor; Attractive; Intelligent; Shared interests and; Fun.

Discuss the fact that in life "pain is inevitable but suffering is optional." There will always be painful experiences in life but you can avoid suffering by avoiding those who make you suffer as a result of their problems with honesty, trust, loyalty, concern and responsibility. Help clients admit that they don't like people who are socially immature, lie, backstab, cheat and don't come through for them. Structure a discussion summary to help clients discover that honesty, trust, loyalty, concern and responsibility are what makes up *social maturity* by discussing the fact that whether someone is considered "immature" or "mature" almost always relates to these multicultural values. For example, when you call someone an "Immature jerk" who just…

- Lied to you, what you really mean is "Immature *dishonest* jerk."
- Talked about you behind your back, what you really mean is "Immature *untrustworthy* jerk."
- Left you for someone else, what you really mean is "Immature cheating *(disloyal)* jerk."
- Forgot your birthday, what you really mean is "Immature, selfish *(unconcerned)* jerk."
- Quit their job without first getting another one leaving you to pay the bills, what you really mean is "Immature *irresponsible* jerk."

Some clients may need further values clarification discussion that is structured to help them discover how the five multicultural prosocial values characteristics are relationship "must haves". Discuss the fact that in terms of what we want in others, basic *social maturity* (i.e., honesty, trust, loyalty, concern and responsibility) are "must have" characteristics and if a friend or partner does not have basic *social maturity* it's typically a relationship "deal breaker". No one wants to be with a liar, a gossip, a cheater, a selfish person or someone who doesn't do their share of work. Being extremely good-looking, very rich or highly intelligent are just added extras. These miscellaneous characteristics that clients listed are just "icing on the cake". It may be helpful to point out that, "If money and looks were all it took to have healthy relationships, there would be no divorce in Hollywood". Yet, one nasty Hollywood break-up after another continues to appear in the news media. Bringing in a copy of the latest tabloid with the latest TV, movie or rock star break up may help underscore this point.

A final point to discuss is accepting that unhealthy, harmful behavior develops social immaturity. For example, unhealthy pride and not wanting to admit having a problem typically results in dishonesty about that problem. Worrying about possible consequences often results in trust abuse deception tactics designed to cover-up the problem in order to avoid consequences. Stress buildup from covering up the problem typically results in letting go of loyalty to positive people and associating with others who have the same problem. This negative social influence often results in a "don't care" attitude, not showing concern for self, not being loyal to own sense of right and wrong and not being responsible by staying in high-risk situations with negative associates. This perfect storm of irresponsible decisions often results in relapse.

Developing Healthy Relationships
"Wherever you are, it is your friends who make your world" -- William James (1842- 1910)

Helping clients discover what they want in relationships is step one. Step two is how to get it. This is easy to see but hard to do and has been summarized over the ages as "The Golden Rule", i.e., "Do unto others as you would have them do unto you." Getting what we want in relationships involves breaking the stress-relapse cycle that involves dishonesty, not being trustworthy, disloyalty, selfishness and irresponsibility. This means starting to "do unto others as we would have them do unto us", going to the opposite extreme and acting socially mature (i.e., honest, trustworthy, loyal, concerned and responsible). In summary, who we get in terms of relationships depends on who we are and according to Greek Philosopher Aristotle, who we are is what we repeatedly do. Thus, getting the healthy relationships we want means learning to "act as if" we are who we want to be and practicing that behavior until it becomes automatic.

It is not possible to develop healthy, socially mature relationships while continuing the dishonesty, cover-up trust abuse, shifting loyalty, "Don't care" attitude and irresponsible decision-making that has been reinforced by unhealthy, harmful behavior. In order to develop healthy, socially mature relationships, clients with unhealthy, harmful behavior need to reclaim their dignity through their honesty, trust, loyalty, concern and responsibility. This requires learning to put those multicultural values into action.

Let's break this down and clear up "what's in it for me" to be honest, trustworthy, loyal, concerned and responsible. When it comes to honesty, the first thing that comes to most people's mind is that honesty brings consequences. If we are standing in front of the judge when they ask, "How do you plead?" and answer, "Guilty your honor", we know that our honesty will bring consequences. So here's the drill, we need to accept that the reason people value honesty so much is the tremendous consequences attached to it. If it were easy and carried no consequences, everybody would be honest all of the time. We have to get real with ourselves, admit that we look up to people who are honest, not only because we can trust what they say but because. "Honesty has its price, the good news is you don't have to pay twice." On the flip side of honesty, "dishonesty is disrespect." The people who lie to you are disrespecting you by treating you like a know nothing chump who will never figure it out or a nobody who just doesn't deserve the truth. If you keep disrespecting people by being dishonest, you lose every friend who values honesty and end up surrounded by liars who disrespect you through their dishonesty.

Why Reinforce Multicultural Prosocial Values?

Developing and maintaining positive supportive relationships requires Honesty, Trust, Loyalty, Concern and Responsibility (social maturity). These prosocial values are multicultural. Honesty tends to be valued across cultural groups with multicultural recognition even in children (Fu et al., 2007). Trust is central to human relations of all kinds and is a public culture shared value in democratic communities (Lenard, 2012). Loyalty has a long history of being valued dating back to the beginning of written history, e.g., "Consider loyalty and faithfulness to be fundamental." (Confucius, c. 551-c. 479 BC). Concern and doing for others is valued across cultures (Vakoch, 2013) and appears to actually have health benefits in a diverse sample of older adults (Brown & Magai, 2005). Finally, responsibility is valued by parents, partners, peers and employers worldwide and our responsibility to each other is accepted across cultures (Miller, 1991). A complete description of multicultural prosocial values in SRT is provided in Yokley (2008) p. 31- 39.

Reinforcing these multicultural prosocial values helps clients develop supportive relationships that act as protective factors against giving up on positive change. These prosocial values are needed for a therapeutic alliance. Specifically, unless clients are: Honest with you about their symptoms; Trust you enough to tell you all their problem details; Loyal to your therapeutic alliance and mutual treatment plan (adherence); Concerned enough to hold self accountable and confront slips in others before they take a fall and; Responsible enough to call you when unwanted thoughts, urges, and cravings begin to break through, relapse will occur. Regarding concern, clients often struggle with holding others accountable and mistake "being their brother's keeper" for being a snitch or hypocrite. When this occurs, it is important to point out that since "It takes one to know one", a hypocrite is actually an expert witness. Thus, they can start out their Confrontation with Concern in group with, "As an expert witness by having made the same mistake myself before I need to make you aware that..."

Reinforcing honesty, trust, loyalty, concern and responsibility can inoculate clients against feeling helpless and giving up on change because these multicultural prosocial values "Hold" in the face of adversity (i.e., are present on good days and bad). Help clients become aware that typical life stressors can't take their...
- Honesty away, clients have to give it away by saying "I'm fine".
- Concern away, the people that clients care about stays the same on good days and bad (which

can help keep them from giving up).

- Responsibility away, clients have to give it away by giving up on their #1 responsibility of self-control, giving up on their healthy lifestyle goals (see below) by acting too selfish or too selfless (doing so much more for others and putting self-care last). Clients need to stay responsible to self and others by staying balanced, i.e., "You're #1 but there are other numbers".

Healthy Relationship Success Skills
"Beauty is only skin deep"-- Thomas Overbury, 1581- 1613)

In order to develop healthy relationships, clients need Healthy Relationship Success Skills. "Actualizing" values is a Logotherapy (i.e., finding a meaning in life) concept involving putting prosocial values into action (Frankl, 1963). For example, actualizing the prosocial value of honesty would involve consistently telling the truth. In order to let go of automatic denial and cover-up tactics due to fear of consequences, teach clients to delay their response. Help clients develop the automatic habit of using the Reality Check to consider whether lying will be helpful or harmful to self or others. Review using the Reality Scales (Chapter 6) to help clients determine that in almost all cases, telling the truth will not threaten their survival or success and will not be so severe that they can't handle it. Putting the multicultural prosocial values honesty, trust, loyalty, concern and responsibility into action are Healthy Relationship Success Skills.

Make a Healthy Relationship Success Skills card like the one shown in Table 9.2 for clients to keep with them at all times as a pocket reminder to show the honesty, trust, loyalty, concern and responsibility to others that they would like from them.

As discussed in Chapter 3, honesty, trust, loyalty, concern and responsibility are multicultural prosocial values that are consistent with multicultural values theory in being accepted by many culturally different groups that span both eastern and western cultures. Further information on "Multicultural Prosocial values in Social Responsibility Therapy" is provided in Yokley (2008), p. 31- 39. Putting these multicultural prosocial values into action provides competing responses to unhealthy, harmful behavior. For example...

- being honest on food logs, developing staff trust by showing consistent weight loss on group weight ins and being responsible by attending and participating in all treatment groups are competing responses to unhealthy eating.
- being honest about going to AA meetings, developing staff trust by bringing in all signed AA attendance sheets and passing all random breathalyzer tests are competing responses to unhealthy, harmful drinking.
- getting honest about inability to manage money, developing trust by allowing someone else to manage accounts and being responsible by avoiding casinos, race tracks and lottery tickets are competing responses to problem gambling.
- getting honest about shoplifting, developing trust by following probation rules and showing responsibility by staying out of shopping malls are competing responses property abuse.
- being honest about avoiding high risk places, being responsible by sticking to approved associates list and developing staff trust by passing all polygraph examinations are competing responses to harmful sexual behavior.

See Figure 1.2, p. 28 of Yokley (2008) for illustration of Healthy Relationship Success Skills as competing responses to unhealthy, harmful behavior..

Table 9.2 Healthy Relationship Success Skills Card
Keep your Skill Cards with you at all times

Social Responsibility Therapy- Healthy <u>Relationship</u> Success Skills [a]
What do we want from others in our life and what do they want from us?
Developing the relationships we want in life requires <u>mutual</u>...

Honesty- Involves getting honest <u>with yourself and others</u> by taking responsibility for mistakes along with getting honest about other's mistakes to keep them from getting in worse trouble later.

Trust- Involves <u>building trust</u> in others by keeping your word and respecting their feelings along with <u>learning to trust</u> others by opening up about problems and picking the right people to trust.

Loyalty- Involves <u>standing up for what you know is right</u> and who you know is right when there is peer pressure to keep quiet, "If you don't stand for something, you'll fall for anything."

Concern- Involves <u>helping self</u> by keeping personal problems "up front" so they don't get out of control again and <u>helping others</u> by treating others the way they want to be treated.

Responsibility- <u>Our number one responsibility is self-control</u>. Three others are emotional restitution (making things right), pulling our own weight and learning to accept feedback.

a. "Act as if" we are who we want to be and practice these healthy relationship success skills until they become automatic.

Note: Make a skills card for clients to carry with Healthy Behavior Success Skills on one side (Table 3.2) and Healthy Relationship Success skills on the other side. Honesty, trust, loyalty, concern and responsibility are easily remembered by the mnemonic phrase "there is no TLC in Human Resources"

Treatment Exercise: Healthy Relationship Benefits
Discuss the benefits of having healthy relationships (i.e., best friends, girlfriends, boyfriends, marriage partners or life partners). "You can never have enough friends" is definitely true particularly during hard times when things are not going well and client life problems are blocking their progress towards getting what they want in life. Help clients accept the importance of developing healthy, positive relationships as recovery support people who can redirect and motivate them during times when they are struggling and are at risk for relapse. The bottom line here is that healthy relationships support recovery and healthy life goals. A research summary of the positive social influence benefits of healthy relationships is provided below.

Positive Social Influence and Healthy Relationship Research Support:
Since the social influence model predicts that as a social influence group increases in size, its impact increases (Tanford & Penrod, 1984), the number of models of healthy or harmful behavior in the client's social network can help predict harmful behavior recovery or relapse. For example, adolescent cigarette smoking, marijuana use, heavy episodic drinking, weapon carrying, physical fighting, suicidal ideation and attempts has been related to their friends' behaviors in these areas of concern (Prinstein, Boergers & Spirito, 2001). With respect to healthy behavior, a meta-analysis on social influence and exercise revealed a moderate to large effect of family support (Carron, Hausenblas & Mack, 1996) and peer role models have been found to increase mammogram use in minority females (Suarez, Nichols & Brady, 1993). While peer and adult models are known to exert strong influences on the initiation of adolescent drug use, there is some indication that during high school the perceived number of peer models was more

---

related to usage rates than the perceived number of adult models (Huba & Bentler, 1980). On the positive side, just like negative social influence can initiate substance use in adolescents, positive social influence can protect adolescents from risk activities including smoking, alcohol consumption, marijuana use and tobacco chewing (Maxwell, 2002). Making parents both the source of authority and a role model has resulted in improved weight loss for obese children at 7 year follow up (Golan & Crow, 2004). In drug and alcohol treatment these social influence findings have resulted in the treatment saying, "A therapeutic community is only as strong as it's number of positive role models" and program evaluation results underscore the importance of identifying with a positive role model peer who is further along in recovery (e.g., Sowards, O'Boyle & Weissman, 2006). The Therapeutic Community is probably the strongest, most established social learning model treatment program for harmful, addictive behavior. The SRT social learning components were based on this evidence-based model, described on p. 21- 22 of the SRT treatment manual (Yokley, 2008).

Using Healthy Relationship Success Skills to Improve Relationships

Developing healthy relationships requires learning how to argue in the present without bringing up the past. If you are in a disagreement with a partner, peer or parent and you or the other party are bringing up similar mistake from the past, that is an admission that you never resolved it in the past. When someone does this or gets so upset that they fall into calling names, even though you want to defend yourself, it is very important to use "the 3 G's." Get out (excuse yourself to the bathroom and shut the door or leave the house). Get honest (admit that if you go back in there upset, you will have the last word which will make it go on further). Get responsible (use the Reality scales "Think it through" before going back and having the last word) as indicated on Table 9.3.

Table 9.3 Using the Reality Scales to "Think Through" the Decision to have the last word			
Behavior (Self-medicating social anxiety)	**Reality Scales** 0 = not at all necessary or important/no impact; 10= absolutely necessary or important/very severe impact		
	Survival Scale How necessary for my survival is it for me to...	**Success Scale** How important for my success is it for me to...	**Severity Scale** How severe could the consequences be if I...
Verbal Abuse (Acting out anger)	...have the last word after what they called me? 0- not necessary for survival (I only want to do it to vent feelings. I don't need to do it to survive)	...have the last word after what they called me? 0- not important for success (saying hurtful things won't get me the healthy relationship I want)	...have the last word after what they called me? 5- moderate (It will make things worse & could result in another physical fight)

Weeding your Relationship Garden: Thinking through who you want close to you
"Life is partly what we make it, and partly what it is made by the friends we choose"
-- Tennessee Williams (1911- 1983)

In the residential therapeutic community, "A group is only as strong as it's number of positive role models." In outpatient treatment for unhealthy, harmful behavior a client's recovery is threatened by negative social influence and strengthened by healthy relationships. The important point here is that client decisions on who they associate with can weaken or strengthen their healthy lifestyle development.

In terms of "What we need to succeed" (Figure 2.1, p. 25), after developing a healthy body and healthy behaviors through a track record of Healthy Behavior Success Skills to "Avoid trouble, calm down, think it through and solve the problem" it is time to help clients focus on developing healthy relationships. This means letting go of unhealthy relationships that get in the way of healthy lifestyle goals. In gardening, this involves pulling the weeds that are sapping nutrients and stunting healthy plant growth. In human growth, this means letting go of the unhealthy relationships that stunt personal growth and hold clients back from achieving positive life goals.

Positive Social Influence: A Case Example
Wayne was a 17-year-old Euro-American male admitted for Social Responsibility Therapy in forensic foster care. He presented with five types of unhealthy, harmful behavior, six sex offense victims, gang involvement, frequent fights and serious peer violence. Wayne failed four prior residential treatments. Wayne was removed for sexual aggression (offenses) in two of his four prior residential treatment programs and physical aggression in his other two (i.e., peer assault requiring physical restraint in one and assault on staff in the other). Prior to residential placement he had an adoptive home failure due to sex offenses in the home and community along with arson and violence. Although his above average intelligence would allow him to succeed in almost any subject, his academic success was always sabotaged by his behavior. His treatment staff were able to contain his unhealthy, harmful behavior in the home with line of sight supervision and ongoing intervention. He was not on a program phase level that allowed him out in the community after school. Thus, acting out at home and the community were effectively blocked. However, the school setting where line of sight supervision was not in force remained vulnerable to his unhealthy, harmful behavior which was fueled by negative peer influence. At school, he associated with other negative, unruly, immature youth continuously reinforced his disruptive behavior. As a result, he was expelled from both high schools in his community.

In order to complete his senior year, Wayne needed to be in an academic environment where there were no other negative peers to reinforce his negative, unruly, disruptive behavior. He needed to be in an environment where mature, positive role models would redirect him towards mature, positive behavior and achievement. Fortunately, his school district had a partner agreement with the local community college. This agreement allowed advanced students to complete their senior year in the community college earning both college credits and a high school diploma at the end of the year. Wayne was attracted by the idea of being granted this special student status and being able to view himself as a "college student". He was not aware that he would be surrounded by an entirely different group of motivated, positive, mature students. Wayne easily passed the entrance testing, was admitted and found himself without any negative, unruly, immature youth to encourage his disruptive classroom behavior. As opposed to being able to find a seat between individuals that would laugh at his disruptive remarks and behavior he found himself surrounded by two groups. The first were high school senior AP (Advanced Placement) students in the top third of their class and highly motivated to succeed as young professionals. The second group was adult blue-collar workers with families and full-time jobs coming to class to complete their high school educations and get a start in college to advance their job prospects. According to his foster mother, Wayne was "a fish out of water". Not only was he being redirected with "be quiet" prompts by his AP classmates, he was also receiving much stronger encouragement to stop distracting others by his blue-collar classmates. This included being pulled aside to after class and warned about continuing to distract others. Wayne paid no attention to these warnings and as a result his foster mother reported him returning to his foster home one evening with a black eye.

His new positive social influence environment produced a significant decrease in talking and disruption along with a pronounced increase in test grade scores. He wanted out. He wanted to be back with his negative high school peers who reinforced his negative, unruly, immature behavior. Wayne begged his foster parents and staff to get him another chance at one of the local high schools. He was told that if he wanted his treatment staff to try and get him back in public high school, he would have to earn his way back through his grades. His foster parents, staff and treatment group regularly praised the good test grades he brought home and reinforced his positive "college student" status. Wayne began to respond appropriately to the increased positive social influence and structure he was receiving. He was introduced to a Marine Corps recruiter when he turned 18 and stopped requesting a transfer back to public high school shortly thereafter. Wayne was discharged to the Marine Corps after 18 months of SRT in forensic foster care with no need for physical restraint and no sexual or physical offenses.

"Birds of a feather fail together"- Employers, teachers, parents and people you like often believe that "You are who you hang with". Thus, another reason it can be important for clients to decide who they need to weed out of their relationship garden is so that they are not judged by the company they keep. This can trigger an emotional reaction to continue to hang with socially immature people. Being judged by the company we keep is where a lot of people get side tracked and caught up in pointing out the injustice of getting judged because of other people's behavior.

Ruminating on the injustice of being judged by the company we keep can block the client's ability to be a "dedicated pragmatist" and just look at the benefits and drawbacks of keeping a relationship. It is important to help clients stay focused on honesty, trust, loyalty, concern and responsibility. People with these Healthy Relationship Success Skills can support healthy lifestyle goals and those who have problems in these areas will cause problems that hold others back. It is important to help clients sort out the flowers who will support their positive change from the weeds who will choke out their personal growth. Have clients discuss real friends vs failure friends.
- Real Friends- Help you avoid trouble (have concern). Tell you to do the right thing (are responsible). Talk you out of relapsing (are loyal to your goals).
- Failure Friends- Help you approach trouble (instigate). Tell you what they want you to do, "Come on, let's..." (what's good for them). Enable relapse, "Just this once", (sabotage goals).

Discuss the fact that we don't live on a desert island so it's not possible to totally avoid contact with others especially family. The definition of family seems to be changing over time. If we define family as the people that we let into your life and heart, decide to care about and trust, then we actually have three families (a home family, a school or work family and a community or treatment family). Deciding who should be included in our three families involves clients asking themselves, "Do I want to let someone into my life and heart that is likely to pull me down, turn on me or disappoint me?" Hold a discussion on reasons to: stop expecting loyalty from people who can't even give you honesty and; stop giving trust to people who are not responsible and can't even show you concern. Review the positive social influence case example of Wayne and discuss the idea that "Birds of a feather fail or succeed together".

Treatment Exercise: Relationship Traffic Signal

Have clients draw "My Social Network" in paper with them in the center and a line to each person that they are in regular contact with along with a "Traffic Signal" green, yellow or red comment. If their social contact absolutely will help redirect them away from their unhealthy, harmful behavior and motivate them towards meeting their healthy life goals, this is a "Green light" social family person. If the social contact sometimes models positive behavior (like encouragement to do the right thing or modeling healthy avoidance of unhealthy habits) that redirects away from unhealthy, harmful behavior and towards meeting your healthy life goals, but sometimes is a negative influence (like encouragement to do the wrong thing or modeling unhealthy habits) this is a "Yellow light" person. If the social contact will likely pull them back unto their unhealthy, harmful behavior and away from meeting their healthy life goals, this is a "Red light" person. Discuss the benefits of letting go of unhealthy relationships and pulling in healthy ones. Help clients use their Decisional Balance skills (see Chapter 5) to decide who the need to spend more time with (Green light), less time with (Yellow light) and stop seeing altogether (Red light). A research summary of the social learning effect of negative social influence on several types of unhealthy, harmful behavior is provided below.

Negative Social Influence Research Support: Selected Problem Examples

Social influence/modeling is major determinant of human eating behavior and a literature review by Cruwys, Bevelander, & Hermans (2015) found a statistically significant modeling effect in 93% (64 of 69) of identified published studies. Social learning theory has been recommended as a factor in the explanation of unhealthy eating and childhood obesity (e.g., Golan, 2007) and one study reported that obese children with one or more obese parents were significantly more overweight than those with parents who are not obese 5 yrs after beginning a family-based behavioral weight control program (Epstein et. al. 1987). Teenage girls appear to follow unhealthy food purchases of a peer during supermarket shopping (Bevelander, Anschütz & Engels, 2011). On the positive side, young women appear to eat more vegetables in the presence of peers eating more vegetables (Hermans et. al. 2009). Obviously hunger also plays a part in amount of food consumed and hungry young men follow the snack intake of eating models (Hermans et. al. 2010).

Regarding social learning and substance abuse, support for a social learning component in adolescent marijuana has been evident for over 30 years (e.g., Winfree & Griffiths, 1983). Regarding social influence, associates and housemates are drug and alcohol risk factors. For example, in one study of college students both student living arrangement and social-norm variables were significant predictors of heavy episodic drinking (Ward & Gryczynski, 2009). A study of social modeling on freshman college students revealed that affiliations with alcohol-consuming peer groups was significantly associated with increased alcohol consumption (Talbott, Moore & Usdan, 2012). Alcohol abuse by both adolescents and older adults is associated with number of peers who drink (Preston & Goodfellow, 2006). In a test of factors discriminating stopping drinking among adolescents, peer associations was the biggest factor (Lanza-Kaduce et. al. 1984). Drinking among the elderly is also related to the norms and behavior of one's peer group (Akers et. al. 1989). The risk of non-medical prescription stimulant use for academic reasons was increased in college student study for those who reported more of their friends used (Ford & Ong, 2014). Social learning theory has also been applied to the explanation of adolescent smoking (e.g., Akers & Lee, 1996; Krohn et. al. 1985; Monroe, 2004).

Gambling is also affected by social learning (from parents, peers and in the neighborhood) and a college student study found that the role of social factors appears to be larger than that of cognitive factors (Sarti & Triventi, 2017). Offspring who have a problem gambling parent are at greater risk of developing a gambling problem (Dowling et. al. 2018) and one study found that those endorsing paternal problem gambling were 4.3 times more likely to be classified as at-risk/problem gamblers than their peers (Dowling et. al. (2017). Family and peer gambling individually contribute to adolescent at-risk/problem gambling (Zhai et. al. 2017) and friend models have been positively related to gambling frequency in high school students (Wickwire et. al. 2007).

   With respect to social learning and sexual behavior problems, adult male offenders who were sexually abused as a child are more likely to commit sexual offenses, particularly sexual offenses against children, than nonsexual offenses (e.g., Felson & Lane, 2009). In adolescents, a closer relationship with the deviant model (perpetrator), longer periods of deviant social learning (victimization) with more severe victimization predicted adopting sex offender behavior (Burton, Miller & Shill, 2002). In the college student population, fraternity members were significantly more likely to engage in nonphysical coercion and use drugs and alcohol as a sexual strategy (Boeringer et. al. 1991). This social learning finding appears to hold true for the general high school population as well where peer association (influence) was found to be the best predictor of adolescent intercourse frequency (e.g., DiBlasio & Benda, 1990).

Social Learning in Action: Group Therapeutic Factors
"You alone must do it but you can't do it alone" – TC Maxim

The therapeutic social learning that occurs in group therapy has eleven primary factors (Yalom & Lesczc, 2005) which are summarized as follows.

1. **Instillation of hope**: Group members develop optimism that treatment will be helpful by learning about group effectiveness and other group members success. [Prosocial Modeling]
2. **Imparting information**: Group members learn new information through facilitator instruction and group member advice [Awareness Training]
3. **Universality**: Group members realize that their problems are not unique and others are struggling with similar difficulties. [Identification].
4. **Altruism**: When group members help each other, a sense of self-worth and value is derived (a competing factor to worthlessness). [Prosocial Development- "Helping helps the helper"]
5. **Imitative behavior**: Occurs when group members model positive characteristics and skills learned by observing the behaviors of other group members and of the facilitator(s). [Social Learning]
6. **Development of socializing techniques**: Group members acquire and practice social skills. [Social maturity]
7. **Interpersonal learning**: Group members learn about their interpersonal style and impact they have on others through feedback which is used to change. [Insight].
8. **Group cohesiveness**: Group members experience acceptance, trust, belongingness and support. [Therapeutic Unity]
9. **Existential factors**: Group members deal with human condition issues including isolation, mortality, freedom, responsibility and the search for meaning. [Realize what they want from others and in life].
10. **Catharsis**: Group members share painful experiences and emotional reactions. [Emotional expression]
11. **The corrective recapitulation of the primary family group**: Group members repeat the same interpersonal behaviors which they engaged in with primary family members and have the opportunity for corrective experiences that resolve long-standing issues related to the family. [Mirror concept- Using others feedback as a mirror to better see yourself]

Social Learning in Group: Awareness Training
"Whenever two people meet, there are really six people present. There is each man as he sees himself, each man as the other person sees him, and each man as he really is"-- William James (1842- 1910)

Group therapy has the potential for self-awareness development if clients are able to use the feedback of others as a mirror to better see self (i.e., move clients from the #2 blind Johari window to the #1 open window pane (Table 9.4). However, in order to use others feedback and

Table 9.4 Group: Awareness Training	
The Johari Window (4 panes) Luft, J. (1969).	
1. "Open" windowpane represents information known by self and others. "I'm overweight, I got a drunk driving or sexual imposition charge"	**2. "Blind"** windowpane represents information known by others but not self. "They eat too fast, smell like alcohol" Need to use mirror concept (1, 2)
3. "Private" windowpane represents information known by self but not others. "I have a candy stash, drug stash, porno stash".	**4. "Undiscovered"** windowpane represents information unknown by self or others. "Why do I eat, drink, have risky sex?" Need to accept feedback
1. Involves accepting- "Other people see you better than you see yourself" and 2. "If 10 people say you're a horse, you're a horse" to let go of "You don't know me!"	

benefit from the group social learning environment, clients have to let go of "You don't know me!" accept group consensus, i.e., "If 10 people say you're a horse, you're a horse" and group feedback, i.e., "Other people see you better than you see yourself." Facilitators may need to be concrete about other people seeing us better than we see ourselves with a statement like, "If rushed in here today and was in such a hurry that I forgot to brush my hair, I couldn't see that but you could. We don't walk around all day looking at ourselves from the top down, other people look at us. We're busy living our lives and we need to count on others to help us out with their feedback. In this case that means let us know that we forgot to brush our hair so we can duck in the bathroom real quick and take care of that before the next group."

The Johari window is different than the therapeutic community "Window Concept." The Johari window illustrates types of awareness while the "Window Concept" helps keep clients benefit from feedback by avoiding becoming defensive and shutting down without considering it. According to the "Window Concept", in order to benefit from group clients need to keep an open channel, listen to everyone and take in everything they have to offer. Then they need to evaluate the benefit of that feedback. If it is helpful to self and others, clients need to hold it close to their heart and apply it to their life. If it isn't they need to "open the window and shovel it out."

PRAISE Group Unity and Participation Motivation Skills
Since unhealthy, harmful behavior is multicultural, the demographic makeup of Social Responsibility Therapy groups is often diverse. Given this situation a set of SRT multicultural group unity development "PRAISE" skills was designed for motivational enhancement of client participation in the diverse group setting. These skills need to be modeled for clients by therapists during all group sessions including all SRT workbook section discussions (Yokley, 2010b; 2011a; 2012) to enhance the social learning experience by developing multicultural group unity and therapeutic participation. All occasions of clients modeling these skills in group

need to be verbally reinforced by therapists.

PRAISE group unity and participation motivation skills are grounded in classic group process theory and supported by a contemporary multicultural treatment focus. PRAISE stands for: Pulling People In; Responsible Reinforcement; Acknowledgement; Instant Identification; Social Mathematics and; Enabling Responsibility. PRAISE skills are designed to enhance the group social learning experience by: encouraging participation; reinforcing multicultural prosocial values; recognizing client input and strengths; validating shared experience; developing group unity and; client responsibility. Make a PRAISE group process skills card like the one on Table 9.5 as a reminder group for new group facilitators, interns and residents in training to refer to during group.

Table 9.5

PRAISE Multicultural Group Process Skills Card
Keep your Skill Cards with you at all times
Helping clients get the most out of their group learning experience requires...

Pulling people in- "Can I borrow that from you? That's a really good point we need to discuss" (Making them a part/Integration).

Responsible reinforcement- "That [took a lot of courage, was impressive, etc] let's give him a hand for his... [honesty, trust, loyalty, concern, responsibility]" or "Thank you for your honesty"

Acknowledgement - "What they are teaching us is..." or "An important thing that I got from of what you said was..."

Instant identification- "Please raise your hand if you have also..." followed by head count "one, two, three... people here also..." for awareness development (rapid identification/validation of shared experience).

Social mathematics by finding the least common denominator between group members, during group introductions and when two or more members disclose similar issues- "These two/three have a couple things in common, what are they?/did you notice?" or after introductions, "What does this group have in common?" (Cumulative Identification).

Enabling responsibility- "It's not pick on John time or Let's not put John in the hot seat or Help me take John off the spot, please raise your hand if like John, you have ever (been accused of/made the mistake of)..." Setting the occasion for accepting responsibility and the "no more secrets policy" by getting honest.

Note: Make a skills card for training interns and residents with ACTS Healthy Behavior Success Skills on one side and PRAISE group process skills on the other side.

PRAISE Group Skill 1: Pulling people in
"Tell me and I forget. Teach me and I remember. Involve me and I learn"
-- Benjamin Franklin (1706- 1790)

If clients don't talk, clinicians can't help so group therapy job #1 is to develop group participation. Pulling people in encourages Imparting Information (Group Therapeutic Factor #2- Yalom & Lesczc, 2005). See also p. 38, Yokley (2008). "Pulling people in" is used when a group member makes a therapeutic comment or brings up a positive topic relevant to the group as a whole. "Pulling people in" increases client participation and involvement through integration and inclusion efforts to help make group members feel a part of the group. For example, "Can I borrow that from you? That's a really good point we need to discuss."

"Pulling People in" Alternatives:

- "Can I use that for a minute? I think the whole group could benefit from talking about this."
- "OK, John said _____, which I really think is important. Let's talk about…"
- "Can I share that topic with the group? It's an important one."
- "I think the point you just made was a good one – can I bring that to the group?"
- "Use ownership shifting: "Sometimes I tend to ramble on and not really make sense. Tell me what you think I said, so I know I said it right"

P̲RAISE Group Skill 2: Responsible reinforcement
"Properly used, positive reinforcement is extremely powerful" -- B. F. Skinner

"Responsible reinforcement" involves verbal reinforcement (praise) of clients for positive modeling, particularly of multicultural prosocial values (i.e., social maturity- honesty, trust, loyalty, concern, responsibility). Responsible reinforcement develops Healthy Relationship Success Skills and healthy Imitative Behavior (Group Therapeutic Factor #5- Yalom & Lesczc, 2005). See also p. 38, 105 Yokley (2008). Responsible reinforcement should occur whenever a client has made a positive contribution to the group discussion. Responsible reinforcement allows group members to feel that their contributions are helpful to others. Members are more willing to contribute when their positive contributions are reinforced. In general, "Responsible reinforcement" is used to encourage and support group members after they make positive, therapeutic contributions to the group process or do a socially responsible behavior. Clinicians need to use responsible reinforcement in sessions when clients are honest about problems on their Situation Response Analysis behavior logs (p. 63- 64) and in group when clients model Healthy Relationship Success Skills (i.e., put multicultural prosocial values into action). For example…

- Responsible reinforcement of honesty- "Thank you for your honesty about slipping up". Clinician question to the group: "Who would you rather spend your time with, someone who makes mistakes but tries to correct them or someone who won't tell you the truth? Let's give them a hand for their honesty."
- Responsible reinforcement of trust- "I appreciate your trust with this problem, that took a lot of courage to say. Let's give them a hand for their courage."
- Responsible reinforcement of loyalty- "Holding yourself accountable on your behavior log shows your loyalty to what you believe is right. Let's give them a hand for doing the right thing."
- Responsible reinforcement of concern- "Your Confrontation with Concern of [group member] shows that you care about what could happen to them if they continue on the same path. Let's give them a hand for showing concern."
- Reinforcement of responsibility- "Your social responsibility to help yourself and others shows in your regular group participation. Let's give them a hand for taking care of business."

Responsible Reinforcement Alternatives:

- "You certainly demonstrated [honesty, trust loyalty, concern, responsibility] in that story. Let's give him a hand!"

- "That [took a lot of courage, was impressive, etc.]. I want to make sure it doesn't go unnoticed – let's hear it for John! (model applause, start clapping)"
- "High 9 for your [honesty, trust loyalty, concern, responsibility]. Let's give him a hand!"
- "It can be hard for people to share personal stories. Let's give John a hand for his courage."

PRAISE Group Skill 3: Acknowledgement
"Acknowledgement rewards participation" – SRT Maxim

"Acknowledgement" involves recognizing of the importance of client opinions, feelings and positive behavior accomplishments. Acknowledgement fosters participation & Instillation of Hope (Group Therapeutic Factor #1- Yalom & Lesczc, 2005). See also p. 38, Yokley (2008). This skill is often used to reinforce emotional maturity strengths (i.e., self-awareness, self-efficacy & self-control) in the form of life lessons and important learning experiences shared. After a group member discloses being a high-risk situation for relapse (awareness), having enough confidence to try a new response (self-efficacy) and using "the 3 G's" to escape that situation (self-control), their accomplishment is acknowledged by the group leader. The group leader acknowledges their insight or positive role modeling. For example, "What they are teaching us is…" or "An important thing that I got from of what you said was..."

Acknowledgement Alternatives:
- "What they are showing us is…"
- "What they are bringing to light is…"
- "There's an important life lesson in what John is saying here that we need to pay attention to..." (summarize lesson)
- "You guys understand what they are saying? What can we all learn from this?"
- "There is an important lesson here that we all need to pay attention to. What we can learn from this is..." (summarize)

PRAISE Group Skill 4: Instant identification
"Identification is an obligation" – TC Maxim

"Instant identification" helps clients get validation and realize that their feelings and opinions are shared by other group members. Instant identification fosters group unity & Group Cohesiveness (Group Therapeutic Factor #8- Yalom & Lesczc, 2005). See also p. 192, Yokley (2008). This skill involves rapid identification and validation of shared thoughts, feelings experiences, most often by a show of hands followed by a head count. For example, "Please raise your hand if like John/Jane you have also experienced/felt..." It is important for the group leader to model "Please raise your hand if..." by raising their own hand to increase group member involvement. Additionally, when group members have raised their hands, the group leader need to further reinforce identification through a verbal and visual head count pointing to those who have raised their hands, i.e., "one, two, three, four" It looks like four people here also appear to have [experienced that situation/felt that way] and know what you're talking about." Since "Identification is an obligation" in group, instant identification is always done by the clinician when no one identifies with a client disclosure.

Instant Identification Alternatives:

- "How many of you like John have ever_____?" (Model raising your hand so they will follow)
- "How many of you have had the same or similar experience?" (head count)
- "I see some heads nodding. Has anyone else felt (done / said) this? Please raise your hand."
- "Oh, this looks like something others have done - who else has..."
- "How many here have felt... like John? Please raise your hand if you have..." (followed by head count for awareness development).

PRAISE Group Skill 5: Social Mathematics
"The similarities that unite are far greater than the differences that divide"
– Nelson Mandela (1918- 2013)

The only thing worse than struggling with a difficult problem is believing that you're the only one with it. That adds loneliness to the problem. Social mathematics involves developing group unity by finding common denominators between group members. Social mathematics fosters group unity and sense of Universality (Group Therapeutic Factor #3- Yalom & Lesczc, 2005). See also p. 192, Yokley (2008). This is done during successive group introductions for "cumulative identification" where common issues with the earlier members who introduced themselves are identified after each successive member speaks and later when two or more members disclose similar issues. For example, after introductions, "What does this group have in common?" or later during group... "These two/three have several things in common, what are they? What did you notice?"

Social Mathematics Alternatives:

- "I'm hearing some similar things here, what are they?"
- "What have you noticed that people have in common here?"
- "It seems to me there are some common [problems, situations, etc.]. What are they?"
- "What is the common ground that we have heard so far in group today?"
- "That sounds a lot like what he/she said, did you notice that?"

Finding the common denominator in Social mathematics requires doing the exact opposite of diagnostic training which instills narrowing down characteristics to separate conditions. In photography terms, instead of "zooming in" on more and more specific conditions and narrowing your view by ruling other conditions out, Social mathematics requires that you "zoom out" and broaden your view to be more inclusive of general common characteristics. Social mathematics is similar to the "diversity within unity" approach discussed in Chapter 3 (p.40) where cultural individuality is preserved while seeking unity by taking an approach that all humans adopt when they actually want to make a new friend- looking for similarities. Although "Retraining is harder than training", once clinicians start using this skill and looking for similarities instead of differences it gets easier. Social mathematics needs to be implemented and continued until unity is developed when new groups are started and every time a new member joins the group. Social mathematics should be continued throughout treatment focusing on common issues during regular sessions.

Practical application example: Social Mathematics in the initial group session
The following is a summary of the first three introductions in an outpatient weight management group of clients with different diagnoses, age, race, types of eating problems and concerns meeting for the first time.

- Client #1:Vera introduces herself as an older unemployed Asian woman struggling with weight all of her life, eating when bored/lonely with residual mild depression since the loss of her daughter and having to take in her grandchildren. She has reached a weight loss plateau, cannot break through her emotional eating and feels like giving up on dieting.
- Client #2: Sharese a mid-30's African-American professional introduces herself as struggling with weight for 5 years since a promotion increased her responsibilities without being provided with staff to complete those responsibilities. This resulted in performance anxiety comfort eating, continual weight gain and feeling like giving up on her job.
- Client #3: Stacy a young Euro-American single parent introduces herself as having multiple forms of psychological stress including, financial, parenting and ongoing relationship conflict. Since entering rehab and stopping smoking, her weight increased dramatically as a result of stress eating, being overwhelmed and wanting to give up on her relationship.

The group facilitator needs to stop the introductions each time they identify client similarities and state, "These three have several things in common, what are they? What did you notice?" Using Social Mathematics to "zoom out" reveals allows the clinician to unite the group with a summary of the similarities between these three overweight adult females who share the courage to get honest about the similar misery of unwanted feelings, unhealthy eating and feeling like giving up.

Practical application example: Social Mathematics when a new member joins
The following is a summary of the first three introductions in a 6 member outpatient drug and alcohol treatment group of clients with different diagnoses, age, race, types of substance use problems and concerns with a new member joining. The group facilitator asks the group to introduce themselves to the new member (modeling appropriate problem ownership) first.

- Client #1: Bernard introduces himself as a mid-50's Hispanic male bricklayer by trade with a history of social anxiety, multiple job losses, three drunk driving arrests, recent loss of his home and divorce all related to his drinking. He has a court order to complete residential treatment.
- Client #2 Billy introduces himself as a mid-20's unemployed African-American client on parole for drug trafficking with ongoing girlfriend conflicts and chronic marijuana smoking which he states helps him manage his anger.

The group facilitator needs to stop the introductions each time they identify client similarities. "These two have several things in common, both have employment problems, legal problems, unwanted feelings and relationship problems." The new member goes last, "Now that you know who you are sitting with please introduce yourself to the group".

- Client #6: Jerry introduces himself as a late 30's professional recently fired from his job for unannounced absences and hospitalized for detoxification during his incarceration for cocaine possession. He has situational depression, sleep disturbance, massive legal fees and another upcoming court hearing. This is his first group session.

Using Social Mathematics to "zoom out" reveals allows the clinician to unite the group with a summary of the similarities between these three substance addicted adult males who share the substance-related consequences of employment problems, legal problems, unwanted feelings and relationship problems.

Practical application example: Social Mathematics with regular session issues
The following is a summary of the first three introductions in a residential sex offender treatment group where all members have been attending for the past year.

- Client #1 Craig is mid-50's home TV repair man on parole for an incest conviction involving his teenage daughter who states that his issues this week involve not making enough money to keep up on his child support payments despite working two jobs. He knows that he is encapsulating himself in his work as a manic defense against depression and says that he is anxious about a parole violation as a result of repairing televisions in people's homes who sometimes have children present but he needs the money.
- Client #2 Dirk is a late 20's musician in a rock band on probation for sexual contact with his girlfriend's daughter. He discloses that his band's inconsistent bookings have kept him financially strapped and unable to move out of his mother's basement. He states that his issue this week is about beginning to see his ex-girlfriend again and being nervous about probation violation because she is the mother of his victim.
- Client #3 Dilbert is an early 30's professional referred by a local psychiatrist, He works in a social service agency for children and has a history of child molestation fantasies. He disclosed starting to interview some of these children outside of the agency at a local park and is afraid of his own impulses if he continues to work directly with children.

Setting the legal and moral issues aside for a minute, using Social Mathematics to "zoom out" reveals allows the clinician to unite the group in helping each other make relapse prevention plans with a summary of the similarities between these three sex offender treatment clients who are exposing themselves to high-risk situations for sexually offensive behavior. It goes without saying that if these clients do not form relapse prevention plans that absolutely prevent them from becoming a danger to others, a duty to report their dangerous behavior exists and those with probation/parole officers need to need to share this information with them.

PRAISE Group Skill 6: Enabling Responsibility
"Do unto others as you would have others do unto you" – Matthew 7:12 & Luke 6:31

Enabling responsibility involves setting the occasion for clients to take responsibility for their behavior by creating an environment where clients feel safe enough to hold themselves accountable. This allows them to "reclaim their dignity through honesty" and supports the "no more secrets" policy. Enabling responsibility fosters group unity & Altruism (Group Therapeutic Factor #4- Yalom & Lesczc, 2005). See also p. 176, Yokley (2008). Clinicians need to enlist the aid of the group to take the pressure off of group members when they disclose problems. For example by stating, "It's not pick on John time", "Let's not put John in the hot seat", "Help me take John off the spot" and then "Please raise your hand if like John, you have ever (been accused of/made the mistake of)..." this needs to be followed by a verbal and visual head count to promote identification along with, "Those of you who raised your hands, please tell John about your problem and what you did to cope with that situation."

Enabling Responsibility Alternatives:
- "Help me take the heat off of John. Please raise your hand if..."
- We don't want to put John on the spot. Please raise your hand if..."
- "Let's take John off the hot seat here. Has anyone else..."
- "Don't let John feel singled out here. Let me see a show of hands if you have ever had this happen to you."
- "I don't think John is alone in this. Has anyone else..."

Develop a Core Group of Positive Role Models

While a core group of positive role models is likely to spontaneously develop in a healthy therapy group over time, use PRAISE multicultural group unity and participation motivation skills to expedite a core group development by reinforcing every instance of positive modeling.

> **Core Group Development Research Support Summary:** The importance of developing a "core group" of positive role models within a larger group is strongly supported by modeling theory research. Core group development in residential group treatment through the use of positive role models (See p. 156, DeLeon, 2000) can be traced back over 60 years to the Therapeutic Community model in the 1950's. Today, these social learning programs still utilize an "Each one Teach One" prosocial modeling approach (e.g., Delancy Street in San Francisco) where "a therapeutic community is only as strong as it's number of positive role models." In outpatient group therapy, the importance of developing a core group of several positive role models within the larger group has been documented in the literature for over 30 years (e.g., de Bosset, 1982). "The strength and success of the work... has been due to this working alliance with a... core group within each group, around which the larger group can function" (p. 65, de Bosset, 1991).

Social Learning in SRT: Basic Group Format

Social learning requires a social learning environment. The main social learning environment in SRT is group therapy. Depending on the severity of the population, SRT outpatient groups with 5- 8 clients run for 60 minutes while groups with 9- 12 are typically extended to 90 minutes. Specially called encounter groups and relapse prevention crisis intervention groups for severely harmful behavior are not time limited. All SRT Healthy Behavior Success skills didactic training groups are 60 minutes regardless of size. Brief SRT inpatient groups where length of stay is short are 60 minutes. These groups use a cumulative identification format that makes each group self-contained and does not rely on members to know each other from a previous group. SRT outpatient group members complete a brief "check in" sheet that gives an overview of their past week. The group format includes introductions where each client gives their name what they experienced too much of (e.g., eating, drinking, smoking, spending, sexual issues), where they are with that problem now (listed on their "check in" sheet) and what is going on with them now (i.e., issues this week, also listed on a check in sheet). Treatment program rules (See Chapter 8) are signed by all participants who receive copies.

Conduct brief SRT post group discussions. After each group ask interns and trainees to identify which PRAISE skills they observed the facilitator use, which ones they used and the observed group impact. Be sure to discuss and document how group members helped self (e.g., getting honest about feelings, slips) and others (e.g., identification with others, Confrontation with Concern).

SRT Social Learning Group Facilitation: Outpatient and Residential

How to Start SRT Group

First, all members first complete a brief sign in sheet covering basic mental status, emotional state, life issues and a question about what they need to discuss in group. Then a group confidentiality agreement (i.e., "Vegas rules, what's said in group stays in group") is made. The group is asked to, "Please raise your hand if you agree that everything we say in here stays in here" This is followed by a privacy agreement, i.e., "Please raise your hand of you agree to keep your cell phones off." After that, the group facilitator makes sure that everyone knows each other, "Please raise your hand if you know everyone in this group" and welcomes any new members, e.g., "Please raise your hand if you are new to this group." This is followed by responsible reinforcement, "Let's give them a hand for their motivation to join us in making a change!" and a "we don't pick on the new guy" reminder that new members have the option to listen their first group if they choose not to speak. In groups with clients who were not referred for behavior that was harmful to others if that are no new members, the facilitator asks, "Who wants to talk first?" In groups with clients referred for behavior that has been harmful to others, a brief review of the Social Responsibility rules, e.g.," No violence, no threats of violence and stay in your seat at all times" is given. With this population the client who speaks first is determined by the "check in" sheets where the most serious issues listed are discussed first.

Introductions

If there are new members, the group does brief introductions covering first name, problem ownership and consequences. Traditional drug and alcohol addiction groups self-label for problem ownership and acceptance, e.g., "Hi, my name is Bill and I'm an alcoholic." While problem ownership and acceptance is important in treatment, it may be too difficult for some of the behavioral addictions. For example, the introduction, "Hi my name is Billy and I'm a child molester" could be overwhelming for a teenager with sexual behavior problems and may be counterproductive since we want youth to shed negative labels and adopt positive behaviors, a positive self-image and a positive lifestyle. Another, less overwhelming way to get at behavior ownership and acceptance would be, "Hi my name is Billy and I'm responsible for my harmful behavior." Introductions in SRT briefly cover the three basic healthy needs that humans need to succeed illustrated in Figure 2.1. First there is a brief statement about the condition that is interfering basic physical needs to be healthy and safe (e.g., unhealthy eating, drinking, sexual behavior, etc). This is followed by a brief psychological needs statement on healthy relationships and finally by a brief comment on healthy life direction. Use Instant Identification after each introduction to develop group unity. For example...

- Unhealthy eating group introduction- Client: "Hi my name is Jane and I'm responsible for my unhealthy behavior. My overeating has resulted in type-2 diabetes, stopping dating because of my body image shame and having to give up my job because I can no longer stand for long periods of time."
- Unhealthy (or harmful) Substance use group introduction- Client: "Hi my name is Dick and I'm responsible for my unhealthy, harmful behavior. My drinking has resulted in liver disease, divorce and getting fired for missing too many days when I was hung over".

- Harmful sexual behavior group introduction- Client: "Hi my name is Bill and I'm responsible for my harmful behavior. My sexual behavior has resulted in genital herpes, my wife leaving me and getting fired after my registration as a sex offender was made public."

Instant identification is used during introductions to build group unity. For example, "Please raise your hands, if like [Jane/Dick/Bill], you also experienced health, relationship or employment problems as a result of your unhealthy, harmful behavior" followed by an out loud head count for validation and a unity/support statement. "One, two, three, four. Well [Jane/Dick/Bill], it looks like four other people here have also have experienced these problems." This is important as mentioned earlier, the only thing worse than having a problem is thinking that you're the only one with it. That adds loneliness to the already existing self-disappointment about having the problem.

Life experience tally

In establishing the value of the group to new members discussing difficult issues, a life experience tally can help. This accomplished by the group facilitator asking each member how long they have been dealing with their referral problem (e.g., eating, drinking/drugs, sexual behavior problems). "How many years have you struggled with eating/drinking/sexual issues?" The facilitator does a cumulative tally out loud, "10 years and you? that's 25 and you?..." and then announces the total. "We have a total of 100 years experience dealing with (eating, drinking, sexual) issues in this group so if you're willing to ask and people are willing to share, there's a good chance you'll get help." The life experience tally reminds group members that, "two heads are better than one, three are better than two, etc." and fosters Instillation of Hope (Group Therapeutic Factor #1, Yalom & Lesczc, 2005).

SRT Group Social Interaction Rules

Four basic SRT group social interaction rules are: Identification is an obligation; No cross talking; No red crossing and; No side-tracking. The group social interaction rule that "Identification is an obligation" is in place to develop group unity. Facilitators tell clients that, "If someone discloses a thought, feeling or issue that you have experienced, don't leave them hanging out there by themselves, tell them that you have had the same (or similar) experience and describe it" (Group Therapeutic Factor #3, Yalom & Lesczc, 2005). The "No cross talking" rule involves respecting the speaker and the topic by not talking across others and not starting side conversations with the group member sitting next to you. Facilitators may at times have to remind cross-talking members to have "one group." Accept that, "When your words are no better than silence, silence is far better than words." The "No red crossing" rule means not to act like the "Red Cross." Don't rescue or take up for others. Let everyone speak for themselves. The "No side-tracking" rule instructs clients to stay on relevant recovery topics and not get sidetracked with issues that are not treatment-related. This is easy to detect and redirect when clients with less severe unhealthy behaviors divert the group into superficial small talk. It is harder to detect when clients with more severe behaviors bring up a minor mistake (or problem) to avoid confessing to (or discussing) a major one. This diversion tactic is referred to as "Throwing out a bone." Imagine for a moment that you are cooking a T-bone steak on the back yard grill, a large growling dog smells it and is running straight toward you. You rip the bone out of the steak and toss it as far as you can. The dog runs after the bone and you still have the meat. Similarly, when clients confess to or bring up a minor mistake (or problem) to avoid discussing a major one, this sends those confronting the client (or attempting to help them) after the bone while the real meat of the problem remains covered up. That being said, it is always important to ask clients, "Is there anything more serious going on" after they finish discussing a relatively minor mistake or problem. See SRT Workbook 2, p. 42 (Yokley, 2011a) for a description of other diversion techniques.

Staying on Topic: "The Salad Bar Technique"

The salad bar technique is a topic redirection method that is less intrusive than cutting someone off, changing the subject or Confrontation with Concern. In individual therapy, the clinician works to develop a therapeutic alliance with the client through non-judgmental reflective listening. In group therapy, the clinician works to help each client develop a therapeutic alliance with the group by facilitating their disclosure and redirecting it as needed. The direct method of redirecting high functioning clients who divert the treatment topic into non-therapeutic territory is to simply confront them with, "How does this relate to your recovery?" A non-confrontational method that is good for redirecting group members with co-occurring mental health or behavioral issues is "The salad bar technique." These group members are typically not as focused as higher functioning clients and may ramble off onto non-therapeutic topics. The salad bar technique requires the group leader/facilitator to pick out something therapeutically relevant to the group from an individual's monologue and bring that salient point to the forefront of the group. This technique helps manage and regulate group member disclosure. The salad bar technique encourages participation by reinforcing social-emotional maturity and re-directs non-therapeutic, off topic disclosure without direct confrontation. It is implemented as follows. Imagine you are at a salad bar. If you start with iceberg lettuce, as you move along the salad bar, you select things to put on your plate (like tomatoes and cucumbers) that go with iceberg lettuce. If you start with spinach, as you go along you put things on your plate that go with spinach (like bacon bits and orange wedges or nuts). In the salad bar technique, the group facilitator has a therapeutic group topic plate and follows the off topic client along until they mention something that can be used or tied into a group therapeutic topic. As soon as the client says something that can fit on the group topic plate the facilitator uses the PRAISE skill "Pulling people in" and states "can I borrow that from you, that's a really important issue I think we need to discuss." The off topic client is pulled into the group by selecting that portion of their disclosure that can go on the group therapeutic topic plate and be used in the group learning experience. The facilitation ties the off-topic client back into therapeutic dialogue by immediately implementing the PRAISE "Instant identification" skill, "please raise your hand if you also have…" This serves the multiple purpose of redirecting their disclosure while still validating the importance of their participation and allows the leader transition into a relevant intervention if indicated.

This approach can also be used to regulate disclosure of highly sensitive, past trauma, humiliating events or shameful behavior. These situations require clinical judgment by the group leader to act in the best interest of the client. The leader has to determine whether to facilitate full disclosure for cathartic relief or regulate disclosure to allow desensitization to take effect in order to prevent information overload and disclosure trauma as a result of bringing up too much too quickly. "Pulling people in" combined with "Instant identification" can be used with the Salad Bar Technique if the group leader believes that the sensitive information that is being brought up needs to be regulated to prevent traumatic memory flooding or stimulus-overload and anxiety attack. Other applications include when a group member is heading towards over-disclosure which may trigger stress-overload and scare them away from coming back or inappropriate disclosure which may trigger information overload and alienate them from the group. In these situations, the group leader can step in with instant identification of a positive, benign aspect of the group members disclosure to stop it after the first step, leaving the other steps for later. For example, "Can I borrow that from you, that's a really important issue. Who else has experienced/felt...? It looks like three other people have [been through that/made that mistake]. Thank you for your courage to take this first step. Lets discuss this further in individual sessions and bring it back to the group when you feel ready." This serves the dual purpose of ending the disclosure on a positive note while validating the importance of their participation.

The salad bar technique is also helpful in redirecting group dominators. The nice thing about the long-winded speech of the group dominator client, like the tangential ramblings of the manic client or word salad ramblings of the psychotic client, there is plenty of content to select from. Like manic and psychotic clients, you just have to make sure that you don't let the group dominator run on so long that they alienate themselves from the group. Remember that "pulling people in" isn't cutting them off and "borrowing" a relevant statement is beneficial to both the off-topic client (reinforces something they said) and the group (keeps it on a therapeutic topic). This involves a balancing act in group leader clinical judgment. If the group leader uses the salad bar technique too soon, there may have been a better information nugget to "borrow" down the road and they run the risk of the individual feeling that they haven't been heard. On the other hand, using the salad bar technique too late can result in the individual alienating others by something they said or getting tuned out from off topic rambling. The trick is to listen to the off-topic group member just long enough to identify a relevant thought, feeling or disclosure that can be pulled into a therapeutic group discussion. The important point here is that there is a significant difference between cutting someone off and listening just long enough to identify a portion of their dialogue to borrow and validate as important for therapeutic purposes. Listening just long enough to identify a relevant phrase or issue to "borrow" and use is key here because if you listen too long and let client stay off topic too long, the therapeutic purpose of the group is sabotaged. Finally, the salad bar technique is a useful substitute for "Confrontation with Concern" in redirecting group enablers who reinforce and glorify unhealthy, harmful behavior and set the leader up to confront their negative behavior and use that confrontation to play the group against the leader with complaints that the leader will not let them speak.

Practical application example: "The Salad Bar Technique" Tyler was a 16-year-old street smart male in residential drug and alcohol treatment as a condition of his parole on a drug trafficking conviction which he states was unjust. He was using a group on developing a healthy life direction to complain about the government, the system, how everyone is out to get him and boasting about his own prowess. At one point, he drifted into glorifying the criminal lifestyle. Tyler said, "Why not just sell crack anyway? It's faster and makes more money than a real job!" At this point the group leader intervened with "Pulling people in" by stating, "That's a good point you just brought up. Can I borrow that from you?" Then turning to the group, the facilitator implements "Instant identification" stating, "Please raise your hand if, like Tyler, you believe that selling drugs is easier and more profitable than getting a real job" and after a head count states, "It looks like four other people feel the same way". This served the multiple purpose of ending the non-therapeutic disclosure on a positive note, validating the importance of member participation and allowing the leader to transition into a group adaptation of the SRT "Do the Math" intervention. Group adaptation of "Do the Math" is a Decisional Balance Sheet (e.g., Table 6.8, p. 126) turned into a group discussion that allows group members to challenge their beliefs by finding facts. The substance abuse group "Do the Math" intervention in Appendix E was adapted from the individual session format by substance abuse counselor Stephen Kerestes. The individual "Do the Math" format is provided in Yokley (2012) on p. 145- 146 and Appendix H of that workbook contains unhealthy eating, drug dealing and sexual abuse case examples.

Holding others accountable and making suggestions
"You are your brother's keeper"-- Derived from Genesis 4:9

It is a social responsibility for SRT clients to "be your brother's keeper", show concern and make other group members aware of things that could result in relapse and hold them accountable to avoid high-risk situations for relapse. When discussing others behavior, clients need to use the simple man concept" [2] of human motivation, avoid leaps of logic, speculation and "mind reading". In order to avoid triggering a defensive shut down, it is important to balance confrontation with concern. In addition, since "people don't appreciate anything they don't ask for", using "you" statements to give strong opinions on what another client "should" do is discouraged. However, people do tend to appreciate questions with concern, e.g., "Have you considered...?" particularly with explanations attached, e.g., "The reason I asked is because..." (breaks down defensiveness with openness about where the question was coming from). In addition, direct "I" statements that identify with the client and what worked for them is encouraged., e.g., "I experienced a similar problem and this is what worked for me..." The bottom line here is that there is a big difference in between telling others what to do and telling others what worked for you.

In the case of clients who are very defensive, sometimes it is important to use a "carom shot." In billiards a carom shot is when the cue ball hits an object ball which then hits another object ball before going into a pocket. In group a carom shot is when the facilitator speaks to a less defensive group member about a topic that another group member is very sensitive about. This allows the sensitive group member to be "a fly on the wall" and benefit by less threatening listening as opposed to more threatening discussion.

"Peer pressure and social norms are powerful influences on behavior, and they are classic excuses"-- Andrew Lansley

---

Chapter 10
The Problem Development Triad Section 1
Understanding How Unhealthy, Harmful Behavior was Acquired

"Modern Man is the victim of the very instruments he values most. Every gain in power, every mastery of natural forces, every scientific addition to knowledge, has proved potentially dangerous, because it has not been accompanied by equal gains in self-understanding and self-discipline"
-- Lewis Mumford (1895-1990)

Understanding Unhealthy, Harmful Behavior: Introduction

In order to help clients: 1) develop resiliency from risk factors; 2) support relapse prevention efforts and; 3) develop resistance to new forms of unhealthy, harmful behavior, it is important for them to understand the basic factors involved in the etiology and development of their unhealthy, harmful behavior. In SRT, the "case conceptualization" model of primary contributing factors to unhealthy, harmful behavior is "The Problem Development Triad." Among other things, a well-formulated case conceptualization model identifies developmental, precipitating and maintaining factors that contribute to maladaptive behaviors and adjustment difficulties and that reduce quality of life (Meichenbaum, 2014).

There are three basic types of case conceptualizations (Sperry, 2005). A symptom-focused case conceptualization identifies symptoms (i.e., what is occurring) and then specifies treatment interventions for reducing symptoms (e.g., the DSM-5 approach). A theory-focused case conceptualization identifies symptoms and then provides an explanation (i.e., why it is occurring) from the clinician's theoretical orientation (e.g., the psychodynamic approach). A client-focused case conceptualization elicits the client's conceptualization of their condition and negotiates a common conceptualization with the clinician (i.e., A client and clinician therapeutic alliance towards understanding etiology and development of their unhealthy, harmful behavior).

The Problem Development Triad: "Straight to the Point"

The point of Chapters 10, 11 and 12 covering The Problem Development Triad is to help clinicians and their clients develop a therapeutic alliance in understanding the etiology and development of the clients unhealthy, harmful behavior through structured discovery workbooks.

The Problem Development Triad: Goals and Objectives

Goal: Explore and gain knowledge on how unhealthy, harmful behavior was acquired, maintained and generalized to (or substituted with) other problem areas along with practice the healthy behavior and relationship success skills needed to avoid developing new unhealthy, harmful behaviors, manage present ones and block the spread of current problems into other problem areas.

Objectives: Clients will: 1) Complete SRT assignments on understanding how unhealthy, harmful behavior was acquired, maintained and generalized to (or substituted with) other problem areas and be able to explain this to their clinical staff in a presentation; 2) Be able to implement the ACTS healthy behavior success skills address unhealthy, harmful behavior risk factors, the stress-relapse cycle and the harmful behavior anatomy.

The SRT "Problem Development Triad" provides a client-focused case conceptualization through workbooks that are structured to help clients discover how their unhealthy harmful behavior was acquired, maintained and generalized to other problem areas (See Figure 10.1).

Workbook 1, "How did I get this problem?" focuses on understanding how unhealthy, harmful behavior was acquired through "The Risk Factor Chain" (Yokley, 2010b). Workbook 2, "Why do I keep doing this?" focuses on understanding how unhealthy, harmful behavior problems were maintained by "The Stress-Relapse Cycle" (Yokley, 2011a). Finally, workbook 3 "How did my problem spread?" focuses on understanding how unhealthy, harmful behavior problems were generalized to (or substituted with) other problems through "The Harmful Behavior Anatomy" (Yokley, 2012). The Problem Development Triad is a conceptual model for multiple forms of unhealthy, harmful behavior on the Harmful Behavior Continuum (Table 1.1, p. 2). Three basic research-supported observations need to be understood for effective case conceptualization and treatment of unhealthy, harmful behavior.

The first thing to understand about unhealthy, harmful behavior is that humans can get addicted to compulsively doing anything that brings them pleasure or helps them avoid pain. Diminished control is a common core defining concept of substance addiction (e.g., alcohol, cocaine or heroin addiction) shared by non-substance or "behavioral" addictions (e.g., gambling, kleptomania, compulsive sexual behavior) associated with the same set of neural adaptations in the brains reward system (Grant et. al. 2010). Drug addicts chase their chemical high. Gamblers chase their losses in search of their next big win high. Sex addicts chase their orgasm high. Shoplifters (kleptomaniacs) chase their thrill crime high and so on. Conversely, each can also commit their unhealthy, harmful behavior to elevate an unwanted mood or distract self from unwanted feelings. Finally, common components that support multiple forms of unhealthy, harmful behavior allow the referral problem to be substituted with other problems during treatment through "Harmful Behavior Migration" which blocks self-control development.

The second important thing to understand about unhealthy harmful behavior is that the referral form of unhealthy, harmful behavior is rarely the only form of unhealthy, harmful behavior that has been a client problem in the past. While there are many co-occurring harmful behaviors, substance abuse is a relatively prevalent co-occurring problem across harmful behaviors including sexual abuse, physical abuse, property abuse and food abuse/overeating. The relationship between substance abuse and other unhealthy, harmful behaviors appears to be bidirectional. Smokers drink and drinkers smoke. Drinkers gamble and gamblers drink. Wife beaters abuse alcohol and alcoholics beat their wives. Sex addicts abuse cocaine and cocaine abusers have impulsive, risky sex. Like those with substance addictions, clients with behavioral addictions, will frequently commit illegal acts, such as theft, embezzlement and writing bad checks to fund their addictive behavior or cope with the consequences (Grant et. al. 2010). Youth referred to SRT for sexually abusive behavior typically have over four other types of harmful detected at admission. Males in batterer intervention programs exhibit higher rates of problem gambling, hazardous drinking and sexual aggression. Research support for this unhealthy, harmful behavior is provided on p. 46 of this text, under "Harmful behavior comorbidity" in Yokley (2010a) and "The Target Behavior Problem", p. 10- 13 in Yokley (2008).

The third important thing to understand about unhealthy harmful behavior has to do with case conceptualization. The fact that humans can get addicted to many unhealthy, harmful behaviors and the referral behavior is rarely the only unhealthy, harmful behavior points to a common path for developing unhealthy, harmful behavior. These factors warrant the development of case

Figure 10.1 The Problem Development Triad

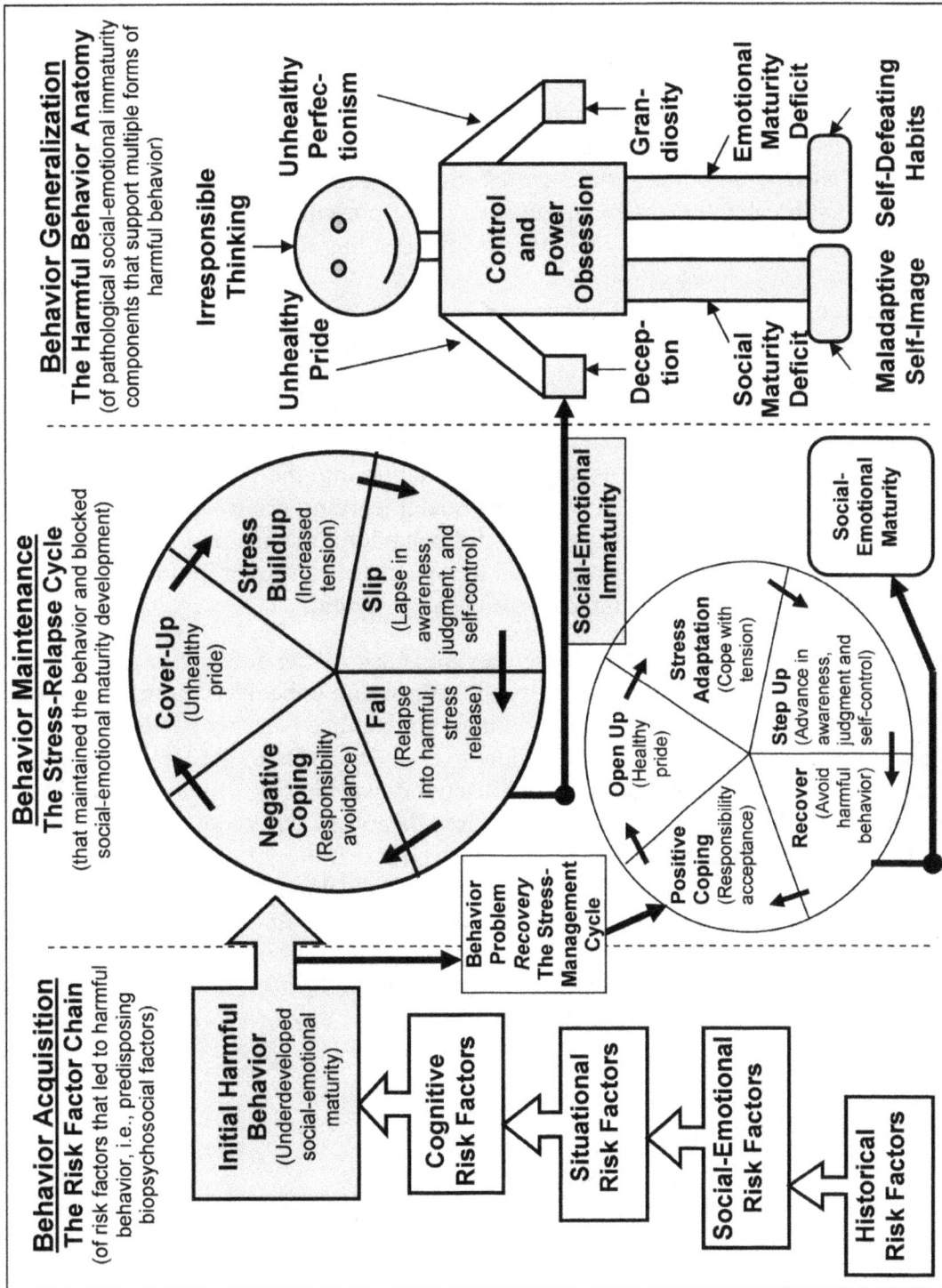

Figure 1. The Problem Development Triad: How Harmful Behavior Was Acquired, Maintained & Generalized Referred to as "The Abuse Development Triad" in cases of sexually and/or physically abusive behavior. Source: Yokley, 2008.

conceptualization models like "The Problem Development Triad" which focus on common contributing factors for the etiology and development of multiple forms of unhealthy, harmful behavior.

Problem Development Triad Focus

Chapters 10, 11 and 12 guides clinicians through each section of each SRT workbook in their therapeutic alliance towards developing an understanding of their behavior. At the same time, instructions are provided on implementing the healthy behavior and relationship success skills. These skills are needed to help the client address their risk factors for developing new unhealthy, harmful behaviors, break the maintenance cycle of their present unhealthy, harmful behaviors and prevent their unhealthy harmful, behavior from spreading to other life areas.

The Importance of Structured Discovery

Guided discovery involves a therapeutic dialogue where the clinician guides the client to discover an understanding of their behavior or a solution to their problem (Overholser, 2013). Since clients are active in this process in a collaboration with the clinician, autonomy is promoted and clients are more open and accepting of understandings they arrive at and solutions they discover. Structured Discovery incorporates structure into the workbook, individual and group learning experience. Structured Discovery social learning groups are structured to help clients discover self-efficacy in managing harmful behavior and engaging in prosocial behavior. Structured discovery workbooks are structured to help clients discover important aspects of their behavior problem development, maintenance and generalization.

Typically, "People don't appreciate anything they don't ask for" and behavior feedback is rarely requested, particularly by those with a history of covering up unhealthy, harmful behavior. Despite being low on the confrontation continuum, guided discovery may trigger clients with very embarrassing unhealthy, harmful behaviors to shut down due to the fact that another person is listening. This cannot occur with structured discovery workbooks where therapeutic disclosure does not require another person listening. Structured discovery workbooks provide the least intrusive intervention on the confrontation continuum (See Table 10.1) and a first step towards problem development understanding discussions in individual guided discovery or group treatment sessions. When deciding how much to confront disclosure of unhealthy, harmful behavior that has been recorded in the SRT workbooks (or mentioned in a session), use the "Kite Analogy" of balancing Confrontation with Concern (See p. 67- 68). Further information on "Confrontation with Concern" is provided on p. 147- 152 in Yokley (2008).

Table 10.1
The Confrontation Continuum

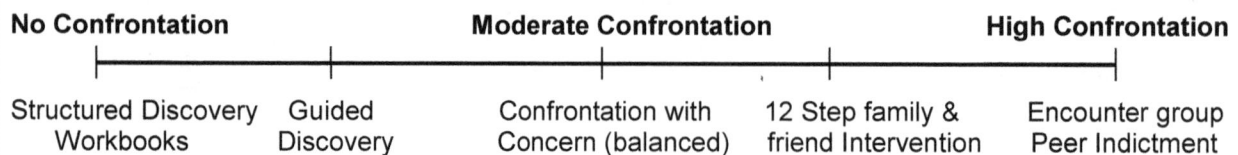

No Confrontation		Moderate Confrontation		High Confrontation
Structured Discovery Workbooks	Guided Discovery	Confrontation with Concern (balanced)	12 Step family & friend Intervention	Encounter group Peer Indictment

General Problem Development Triad Group Agenda and Preparation

General Agenda for all Problem Development Triad Topic Groups

1. If you are using the SRT Understanding Harmful Behavior workbooks, check each workbook assignment at the beginning of each session for completion. If you are not using the workbooks have your clients journal what they learned in each group as an assignment and do a journal check at the beginning of each session. Then have a brief client check in on issues that clients need to discuss.
2. Have a discussion of the Problem Development Triad section introduced in the last group.
3. Describe the Problem Development Triad section to be discussed in the next group and give the next workbook assignment (or journal assignment of you are not using the workbooks) for discussion at the next group.

When to conduct groups with and without workbook support is discussed in the footnotes.[1]

Preparation

Decide on a treatment format that fits your setting, time frame and population. Complete a brief SRT orientation before beginning Problem Development Triad work on understanding how unhealthy, harmful behavior was acquired, maintained and generalized to other problem areas. At a minimum, orientation needs to include unhealthy, harmful behavior assessment (i.e., of problem behavior severity, frequency and relapse risk), behavior contracting; appropriate external controls (e.g., program rules, supervision and community safety standards- see Chapter 8) for behavior that can be harmful to others and; basic relapse prevention (See Chapter 4).

If you are a professional in an outpatient setting or a specific time limited program focusing on helping your clients with...

- Understanding how Harmful Behavior was Acquired, use Workbook 1 (Yokley, 2010b). If you are not using Workbook 1, then cover the Risk Factor Chain material in this chapter.
- Understanding how Harmful Behavior was Maintained and how to break the unhealthy, harmful behavior cycle, use Workbook 2 (Yokley, 2011a). If you are not using Workbook 2, then cover the Stress-Relapse Cycle material in Chapter 11.
- Understanding how Harmful Behavior was Generalized to other problem areas and addressing factors that support multiple forms of unhealthy, harmful behavior, use Workbook 3 (Yokley, 2012). If you are not using Workbook 3, then cover the Problem Development Triad in Chapter 12.

Residential treatment programs typically move through all three workbooks in sequential order (or cover all three sections in this chapter if the workbooks are not being used). Outpatient treatment programs and residential programs that have shorter lengths of stay or that use the cycle model as the focus of their relapse prevention approach often start with Workbook 2 "Understanding how Harmful Behavior was Maintained through the Stress-Relapse Cycle" (or section 2 in this chapter if they are not using the workbook). In this approach, after clinicians develop client understanding on what maintained their unhealthy, harmful behavior (and how to break their relapse cycle), they then move on to Understanding how Harmful Behavior was Acquired through the Risk Factor Chain and finally to Understanding how Harmful Behavior was Generalized to other problem areas through the Harmful Behavior Anatomy. If you **are** using the SRT workbooks review each section of the workbook to understand what your clients will be completing and help you with your group discussion the following week. Administer the SRT Learning Experience Questionnaire pretest (Appendix B, p. 270) before starting treatment.

Problem Development Triad Case Examples

Three case examples were selected for understanding behavior considered primarily harmful to self (e.g., food abuse/overeating), both self and others (e.g., substance abuse) and primarily harmful to others (e.g., sexual abuse) on the Harmful Behavior Continuum (Table 1.1, p. 2).

Outpatient Treatment Referral for Unhealthy Eating/Obesity
Ted was a 40-year-old single Euro-American male referred for outpatient treatment of unhealthy eating/obesity and four other types of harmful behavior requiring treatment. His unhealthy, harmful behavior included: Abuse of food and other substances- emotional eating and smoking marijuana during his Burger King day job and Ben and Jerry's evening job after loss of his mother resulted in a 100lb weight gain. He also drank heavily after work and smoked cigarettes; Physical abuse- verbal intimidation and physical assaults; Property abuse- on the job theft (regularly taking large quantities food without paying); Trust abuse- relationship cheating and invasion of privacy; Sexual Behavior Problems- sexual acting out, unprotected sex, destructive sexual relationships, statutory rape conviction (later recanted). A female case example of a client with multiple forms of unhealthy, harmful behavior referred for weight management/obesity treatment is provided in Chapter 2 of Yokley (2008).

Residential Treatment Referral for Unhealthy, Harmful Substance Use
Ray was a 35-year-old, African-American single male incarcerated for drug trafficking. On parole he was referred for residential substance abuse treatment and four other types of harmful behavior. His unhealthy, harmful behavior included: Substance abuse- started drinking in elementary school, smoking marijuana daily by age 16 and crack cocaine by age 24 resulting in job loss and drug trafficking to support his crack habit; Physical abuse- ongoing fights dating as far back as age 13 and he was expelled from 11th grade for assaulting a teacher; Property abuse- vandalism and theft, which advanced to stealing from family as his drug abuse got out of control; Trust abuse- constant lying to cover up his stealing, dealing womanizing and drug abuse; Sexual Abuse- sexually inappropriate, sometimes abusive behavior typically involving sexual exploitation of women, "I know their weak points and can manipulate them into getting what I want." A youth case example of a client with multiple forms of unhealthy, harmful behavior referred for residential substance abuse treatment is provided in Chapter 2 of Yokley (2008).

Residential Treatment Referral for Harmful Sexual Behavior
Dan was a 16-year-old Euro-American male referred for community-based residential treatment of sexually abusive behavior and four other types of unhealthy harmful behavior after discharge from secure residential treatment. His multiple forms of unhealthy, harmful behavior included: Sexual abuse- molested 6-year-old step sister repeatedly for 2 years; Physical abuse- Fighting and anger-based peer assaults; Property abuse- thrill crime breaking and entering, stealing, fire setting; Substance abuse- Drinking and; Trust abuse- Chronic lying to avoid consequences. A foster family-based (i.e., forensic foster care) case example of a youth with multiple forms of unhealthy, harmful behavior referred for sex offender treatment with a serious history of physical

violence is provided in Chapter 2 of Yokley (2008). In addition, a foster family-based case example of a youth with multiple forms of unhealthy, harmful behavior referred for youth sex offender treatment with a serious, chronic weight management problem is provided in Chapter 54 of Yokley (2011b).

How did I get this problem?
Understanding How Harmful Behavior was Acquired: The Risk Factor Chain
"Those who cannot remember the past are condemned to repeat it" -- George Santayana

In SRT, understanding how unhealthy, harmful behavior was acquired involves helping clients explore and gain knowledge of the Risk Factor Chain links that led to unhealthy, harmful behavior. The primary contributing risk factors that cumulatively set the occasion to acquire an unhealthy, harmful behavior that will be covered are: 1) Historical Risk Factors; 2) Social-Emotional Risk Factors; 3) Situational Risk Factors; 4) Cognitive Risk Factors and; 5) Initial Harmful behavior.

If you are using the SRT workbook #1 "How did I get this Problem?", a series of structured client exercises and assignments to help clients discover their unhealthy, harmful behavior risk factors is provided. If you are not using the workbook, you will need to process each of the risk factors described in this section in group sessions while writing the common factors that the group discloses on a dry erase board or flip chart and having clients journal their risk factors as an assignment after each session.

Each link in the risk factor chain has a key understanding question to help clients establish their own client-focused case conceptualization of "How did I get this problem?" Case study examples and interventions used in each link of the Risk Factor Chain are provided in this chapter. The client goal for this section is to explore and gain knowledge on how unhealthy, harmful behavior was acquired. The objectives are to complete all assignments on all risk factor chain sections and be able to implement the ACTS healthy behavior success skills to address unhealthy, harmful behavior risk factors.

The Risk Factor Chain: Introduction Group
Definition: The risk factor chain is a structured procedure to help clients discover their risk factors for harmful, abusive behavior so that effective treatment plans can be established. The risk factor chain starts with having problems and ends up with acting out the feelings associated with those problems through behavior that is harmful to self and others. Further information is provided in "How harmful behavior was acquired: The risk factor chain", p. 60, Yokley (2008).

Group session work: Hold group member introductions. Pass out SRT Healthy Behavior and Relationship Success skills cards (Table 3.2 and Table 9.2). Explain the group agenda that will occur each week as summarized on p. 227. Overview the Risk Factor Chain that led to unhealthy, harmful behavior. Review the SRT Healthy Behavior Success skills on the skills card and key examples (in Chapters 4- 7). If you are using SRT Workbook 1, review page 17 of SRT Workbook #1 "How did I get this problem." If you are not using Workbook 1, review the following basic summary with clients... No one just got up one morning and said "It's raining outside, I think I'll stay inside and start developing a harmful behavior problem." It wasn't a snap decision and maybe not a decision at all. It developed over a period of time through a Risk Factor Chain that led up to that harmful behavior problem which involved the following five links. This first workbook in the Social Responsibility Therapy series focuses on developing an understanding how harmful behavior was acquired through the Risk Factor Chain (i.e., Section 1 of The Problem Development Triad).

In the Risk Factor Chain, Link 1 Historical Risk Factors consists of stressful life experiences such as toxic parenting, abuse, neglect or other traumatic events that lead to feeling ineffective, powerless or helpless which stunts personal growth. This sets the occasion for Link 2 Social-Emotional Risk Factors such as lying to avoid consequences and emotional maturity problems such as dwelling on or always thinking about past injustices or mistreatment which creates unwanted feelings. Social-emotional problems leave a person feeling one down and gravitates them towards Link 3 Situational Risk Factors (i.e., high-risk situations where they have access to relapse activities such as smoking, drinking, drugging or overeating) and feel less insecure (e.g., are around negative peers) or more in control (e.g., are around those they can influence). Link 4 Cognitive Risk Factors is the last link to relapse which involves Irresponsible Thinking excuses to do what you want and reasons why it is OK. Being in Link 3 high-risk situations for relapse with a Link 1 life stress history and Link 2 social-emotional problems requires only minimal Link 4 irresponsible thinking to trigger Link 5 unhealthy, behavior.

The Risk Factor Chain which starts with having problems and ends up with acting those problems out, can stunt social-emotional growth to the point where serious self-control problems and difficulty with all forms of relationships are created. This portion of your Social Responsibility Therapy will help you understand the Risk Factor Chain that helped you acquire or start your harmful behavior. Understanding how you got your problem to begin with is very important if you want to avoid repeating it or developing a new type of harmful behavior after you have completed your treatment for your present one. Understanding the links in the chain which led up to your harmful behavior, you will help you identify issues that need to be dealt with in order to help maintain your recovery. An illustration of the Risk Factor Chain that led to unhealthy, harmful behavior is provided on the left-hand column of Figure 10.1, p.217).

Structured Discovery for stable recovery- Introduce staff and the Structured Discovery approach used to help clients understand: how they got their problem behavior; why they kept doing it and; how it spread. Explain that… Social Responsibility Therapy uses a Structured Discovery approach to help you look at yourself through structured exercises that help you discover important thoughts and feelings that are connected to unhealthy, harmful behavior. This process increases your self-awareness which develops your self-efficacy (confidence) and helps you maintain your self-control responsibility. Self-control is needed to achieve your personal goals and maintain successful relationships. The social responsibility of self-control tends to get overlooked in our school systems which teach effective control of baseballs, basketballs and footballs but leave it up to you to develop effective control of thoughts, feelings and behaviors.

Conduct the "What do we want in others" Treatment Exercise described in Chapter 9. Conclude with "SRT helps us reclaim the dignity we lost through our unhealthy, harmful behavior by developing our honesty, trust, loyalty, concern and responsibility." An important purpose of discussing the social responsibility issues in this chapter is to help clients develop the characteristics needed for healthy relationships through group practice in: getting honest with self and others; building trust, learning to trust; standing up for what is right, helping self and others by maintaining self-control and; treating others the way they want to be treated. Pass out the SRT cue cards on "Healthy Relationship Success Skills" again at each session for those who have lost them. At every opportunity, use PRAISE skills to develop group Honesty, Trust, Loyalty, Concern and Responsibility. Experienced SRT therapists have developed these skills to the point where they are a fluid part of their group discussion and do not even notice themselves making PRAISE statements such as "Thank you John for your honesty, let's give him a hand for his courage to trust the group!" If you are using SRT Workbook1, review all SRT introduction material on page 1- 10 and have group members complete their harmful behavior history (pages 4- 6). If you are not using Workbook 1, have clients journal their harmful behavior history (i.e., all of the types of unhealthy, harmful behavior that they have engaged in prior to admission).

Note: In all of the following assignments, if you are not using SRT Workbook 1, give your clients the assignment of writing their experience, comments, thoughts and feelings on the topic being covered in a journal to be reviewed and discussed at the next session.

Introduce the next group topic. Describe Link 1 in the Risk Factor Chain (see definition below). Record group personal responsibility ratings on how much each member "helped self" (e.g., workbook effort, honest disclosure) and social responsibility ratings on how much each member "helped others" (e.g., holding self and others accountable, helpful use of ACTS skills) in your progress notes.

Client assignment: Journal your group experience or if you are using SRT Workbook 1, complete the "Risk Factor Chain Link 1: Historical Risk Factors" section for discussion at the next session. Explain and pass out blank Situation Response Analysis (SRA) Logs to be completed for next group (Seep. 63 & Appendix B). If you are using Workbook 1, review Appendix D "Summary of Situation Response Analysis" with your clients.

Next session: Help clients disclose and discuss their Historical Risk Factors. Remind clients to bring their workbooks (or journals) to all groups.

Risk Factor Chain, Link #1: Historical Risk Factors
"That which does not kill us makes us stronger."-- Friedrich Nietzsche (1844- 1900)

Definition: Historical Risk Factors involve past personal problems (i.e., past traumatic events or things that created permanent problems) that increase the risk of unhealthy, harmful behavior. Biological factors include being small, large, short, tall, thin, overweight, unattractive, having a physical disability or learning disability. Psychological factors include the 10 Adverse Childhood Experiences (Felitti et. al. 1998) of abuse (physical, emotional, sexual), neglect (physical, emotional) and household dysfunction (divorce, mother treated violently, substance abuse, mental illness, incarcerated relative) along with loss and unwanted feelings (e.g., anger, anxiety, depression, helplessness) or thoughts. Social factors include being shy, having no friends, having negative influence friends, having no supportive family or negative influence family.

>**Risk Factor Question #1:** What difficult times and harmful situations you have experienced in the past?

Historical Risk Factors Group Session Work

Do a Historical Risk Factors assignment and SRA log check. Then have a brief client check in on issues clients need to discuss. Hold a discussion on the Historical Risk Factors for unhealthy, harmful behavior development that were introduced (see definition above). Allow members to use their workbooks (or journals) in their discussion of risk factors. Group discussion needs to focus first on honest disclosure of risk factors and then on coping topics, methods and skills to address those risk factors. Use the PRAISE group process skills described in Chapter 9 of this guide to build group unity during the initial group focus on honest disclosure of Historical Risk Factors and also during the discussion of interventions to address the risk factors. Refer to the SRT skills cards and integrate Healthy Behavior Success (ACTS) skills into a discussion on how to manage the Historical Risk Factors that clients disclose. Remember to use PRAISE skills to develop Honesty, Trust, Loyalty, Concern and Responsibility at every opportunity. Basic suggestions for helping clients manage their Historical Risk Factors are provided in Exhibit 1 on p. 84 of Workbook 1 (Yokley, 2010b). The Awareness, Responsibility and Tolerance Training focus of this group session work is outlined in the "Treatment Notes" of the SRT treatment manual (Yokley, 2008, p. 63- 64).

Group Treatment Exercise: Discuss client Historical Risk Factors, review case examples in Exhibit 10.1 and discuss the following question with the group. What ACTS skill(s) might help [Ted, Ray or Dan] cope with their Historical Risk Factors?

Introduce the next group topic. Describe Link 2, Social-Emotional Risk factors in the Risk Factor Chain (see following definition). Record group personal responsibility ratings on how much each member "helped self" (e.g., workbook effort, honest disclosure) and social responsibility ratings on how much each member "helped others" (e.g., holding self and others accountable, helpful use of ACTS skills) in your progress notes.

Client assignment: Write the first draft of "My Life Story" that covers all of your past

Exhibit 10.1
Historical Risk Factor Case Examples
Unhealthy Eating/Obesity- Ted
Parent divorce; Death of mother; Absent father (jail); Witnessed physical abuse by father; Rejected, bullied by step-father; Found out oldest daughter was not mine; Feeling bad about weight; Rejected by opposite sex; prison for rape charge (recanted); negative peer & family influence- sister on drugs; Problem relationships, divorce.
Harmful Substance Use- Ray
Abandoned and rejected by father; Neglected by mother; Sister was favorite did better than him in school; Not feeling like fit in at home or school; Physically abused by mother and male relative.
Harmful Sexual Behavior- Dan
Bullied and picked on by older kids who had better things. Physically abused, by mom's husband who threatened me into fighting others. Sisters took attention away from me. Many home moves, never finished a school year after age seven. Absent mother- in prison for escort business conviction.

Note: For more case examples, see p. 63 in Yokley (2008).

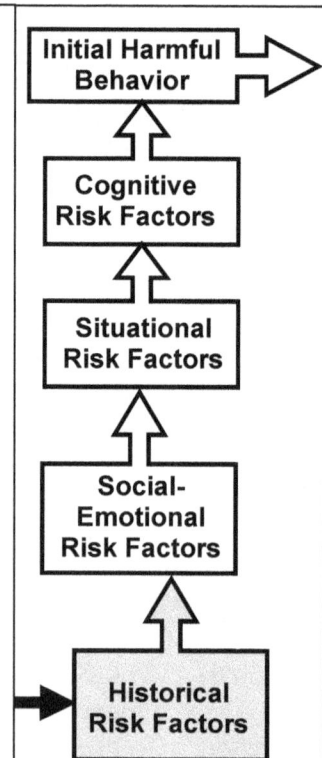

personal/family problems Start at the beginning with where you were born and lived. Include all of the upsetting things and Adverse Childhood Experiences (p. 231) that you have had to deal with during your life. Journal your Historical Risk Factors or if you are using SRT Workbook 1, complete the "Risk Factor Chain Link 2: Social-Emotional Risk Factors" section for discussion at the next session. Answer risk factor question #1. Complete your SRA Log (See Appendix B).

Next session: Help clients disclose and discuss their Social-Emotional Risk Factors.

Risk Factor Chain, Link #2: Social-Emotional Risk Factors
"Maturity is achieved when a person postpones immediate pleasures for long-term values"
-- Joshua L. Liebman

Definition: Social-Emotional Risk Factors involve problems with both Social and Emotional Maturity. Social Maturity involves the healthy development of honesty, trust, loyalty, concern and responsibility. Many Social Maturity Problems may have a connection to Historical Risk Factors. For example, learning that dishonesty works in avoiding abusive consequences interferes with learning to value honesty. Individuals with behavior that is primarily harmful to self may be overly trustworthy and loyal, getting involved too quickly and remaining in relationships with others who are not dependable. They may have more concern for others than they do for themselves, take on too much responsibility and blame themselves unnecessarily. Individuals with behavior that is primarily harmful to others may have problems being trustworthy since they don't feel others can be trusted. This may result in attachment problems and a lack of relationship commitment or loyalty. They may care more about themselves, be less responsible to others and blame them for their problems. In all cases, the need to address honesty, trust, loyalty, concern, and responsibility is clear, though the direction of development (e.g., increase versus decrease or toward self versus others) may be different.

Emotional Maturity involves the healthy development of self-awareness, self-efficacy (confidence) and self-control. Emotional maturity issues also often have connections to Historical Risk Factors. For example, automatic denial feelings for fear of exposing weakness in the past can become a habit leading to total lack of emotional awareness. Self-efficacy or confidence in feeling able to do or master things can't be developed in an environment where the client is always put down and told they will never amount to anything. Lastly, self-control cannot be developed in an environment where caretakers, parents and/or older siblings are continually modeling out-of-control behavior.

Risk Factor Question #2: What about your past experiences may have affected your social and emotional maturity?

Social-Emotional Risk Factors Group Session Work
Do a Social-Emotional Risk Factors assignment and SRA log check. Then have a brief client check in on issues clients need to discuss. Hold a discussion on the Social-Emotional Factors for unhealthy, harmful behavior development that were introduced (see earlier definition). Allow members to use their workbooks (or journals) in their discussion of risk factors. Group discussion needs to focus first on honest disclosure of risk factors and then on coping topics, methods and skills to address those risk factors. Use the PRAISE group process skills to build group unity during the initial group focus on honest disclosure of Social-Emotional Risk Factors

and also during the discussion of interventions to address those risk factors. Refer to the SRT skills cards and integrate Healthy Behavior Success (ACTS) skills into a discussion on how to manage the Social-Emotional Risk Factors that clients disclose. Remember to use PRAISE skills to develop Honesty, Trust, Loyalty, Concern and Responsibility at every opportunity. Basic suggestions for helping clients manage their Social-Emotional Risk Factors are provided in Exhibit 1 on p. 84 of Workbook 1 (Yokley, 2010b). The Awareness, Responsibility and Tolerance Training focus of this group session work is outlined in the "Treatment Notes" of the SRT treatment manual (Yokley, 2008, p. 64- 65).

Group Treatment Exercise: Discuss client Social-Emotional Risk Factors, review the case examples in Exhibit 10.2 and discuss the following question with the group. What ACTS skill(s) might help [Ted, Ray or Dan] cope with their Social-Emotional Risk Factors?

Introduce the next group topic. Describe Link 3, Situational Risk factors in the Risk Factor Chain (see definition below). Record group personal responsibility ratings on how much each member "helped self" (e.g., workbook effort, honest disclosure) and social responsibility ratings on how much each member "helped others" (e.g., holding self and others accountable, helpful use of ACTS skills) in your progress notes.

Exhibit 10.2 Social-Emotional Risk Factor Case Examples

Unhealthy Eating/Obesity- Ted
Lied to get even; Distrustful of others, prejudice against adolescent females; Loyalty issues- Feeling rejected & betrayed; Concern issues- "Have to look out for #1" and use size to advantage (winning by intimidation, learned in bill collecting); Responsibility issues- "Its every man for himself"; Not confident in asking peers out; Angry, resentful, bitter and unhappy, depressed, disgusted with self.

Harmful Substance Use- Ray
Feeling lonely, angry and inadequate, "less than others"; Afraid of failure so stopped trying; Got don't care attitude, "I built a wall around myself", withdrew, not honest with others or concerned about them.

Harmful Sexual Behavior- Dan
Dishonest to avoid consequences. Trusted women more than men. Cared more about image than others- Acted differently (tough) in front of others to be cool/accepted. Not responsible, didn't put forth all effort. Not confident- Shy of girls. Felt less than & jealous of others who had more. Told myself I'd never be popular. Had "Poor me" feelings, felt lonely, kept to myself.

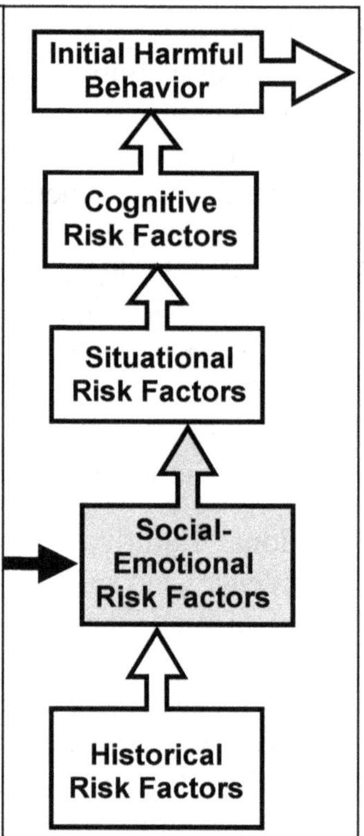

Note: For more case examples, see p. 65 in Yokley (2008).

[Diagram: Risk Factor Chain with boxes connected by arrows — Initial Harmful Behavior ← Cognitive Risk Factors ← Situational Risk Factors ← Social-Emotional Risk Factors ← Historical Risk Factors]

Client assignment: Journal your Social-Emotional Risk Factors or if you are using SRT Workbook 1, complete the "Risk Factor Chain Link 3: Situational Risk Factors" section for discussion at the next session. Answer risk factor question #2. Complete your SRA Log (See Appendix B).

Next session: Help clients disclose and discuss their Situational Risk Factors.

Risk Factor Chain, Link #3: Situational Risk Factors
"Situational variables can exert powerful influences over human behavior,
more so that we recognize or acknowledge" -- Philip Zimbardo

Definition: Situational Risk Factors include "High-risk situations" that put clients at risk for relapse. High-risk situations involve people, places, circumstances, thoughts or feelings that can trigger falling back into unhealthy, harmful behavior. These situations include triggers such as getting very upset or angry, being around others who are encouraging the behavior and being in places where the behavior is being done by others or is not likely to result in consequences. What we see, hear or smell can also put us at risk for relapse. High-risk situations provide clients with motive or opportunity for relapse. Some basic examples are listed in Table 10.2.

Risk Factor Question #3: What situations seem to precede the harmful behavior?

Table 10.2	Situational Risk Factor Examples		
Unhealthy, Harmful Behavior	High risk places	High Risk Feeling	High Risk Thoughts or People
Unhealthy eating	All you can eat buffet	Depressed	"You have to try this"
Drinking	Bar	Anxious	"Have a drink to relax "
Sexual abuse	Intoxicated party girl	Arousal	"Go ahead, she wants it"

Situational Risk Factors Group Session Work

Do a Situational Risk Factors assignment and SRA log check. Then have a brief client check in on issues clients need to discuss. Hold a discussion on the Situational Risk Factors for unhealthy, harmful behavior development that were introduced (see earlier definition). Allow members to use their workbooks (or journals) in their discussion of risk factors. Group discussion needs to focus first on honest disclosure of risk factors and then on coping topics, methods and skills to address those risk factors. Use the PRAISE group process skills to build group unity during the initial group focus on honest disclosure of Situational Risk Factors and also during the discussion of interventions to address the risk factors being discussed. Refer to the SRT skills cards and integrate Healthy Behavior Success (ACTS) skills into a discussion on how to manage the Social-Emotional Risk Factors that clients disclose. Remember to use PRAISE skills to develop Honesty, Trust, Loyalty, Concern and Responsibility at every opportunity. Basic suggestions for helping clients manage their Situational Risk Factors are provided in Exhibit 1 on p. 84 of Workbook 1 (Yokley, 2010b). The Awareness, Responsibility and Tolerance Training focus of this group session work is outlined in the "Treatment Notes" of the SRT treatment manual (Yokley, 2008, p. 67).

Group Treatment Exercise: Discuss client Situational Risk Factors, review the case examples in Exhibit 10.3 and discuss the following question with the group. What ACTS skill(s) might help [Ted, Ray or Dan] cope with their Situational Risk Factors?

Introduce the next group topic. Describe Link 4, Cognitive Risk factors in the Risk Factor Chain (see definition below). Record group personal responsibility ratings on how much each member "helped self" (e.g., workbook effort, honest disclosure) and social responsibility ratings on how much each member "helped others" (e.g., holding self and others accountable, helpful use of ACTS skills) in your progress notes.

Client assignment: Journal your Situational Risk Factors or if you are using SRT Workbook 1, complete the "Risk Factor Chain Link 4: Cognitive Risk Factors" section for discussion at the next session. Answer risk factor question #3. Complete your SRA Log (See Appendix B).

Next session: Help clients disclose and discuss their Cognitive Risk Factors.

Risk Factor Chain, Link #4 Cognitive Risk Factors
"We cannot solve our problems with the same thinking we used when we created them."--Albert Einstein

Definition: Cognitive Risk Factors involve Irresponsible Thinking that supports and allows irresponsible behavior that is unhealthy or harmful. Awareness of Irresponsible thinking is needed in order to substitute more appropriate, responsible thinking. Irresponsible thinking increases the risk of harmful behavior by justifying or minimizing dwelling on harmful behavior thoughts or plans, entering or staying in high-risk situations for harmful behavior, or pushing back the line on what is wrong, bending the rules and heading for trouble.

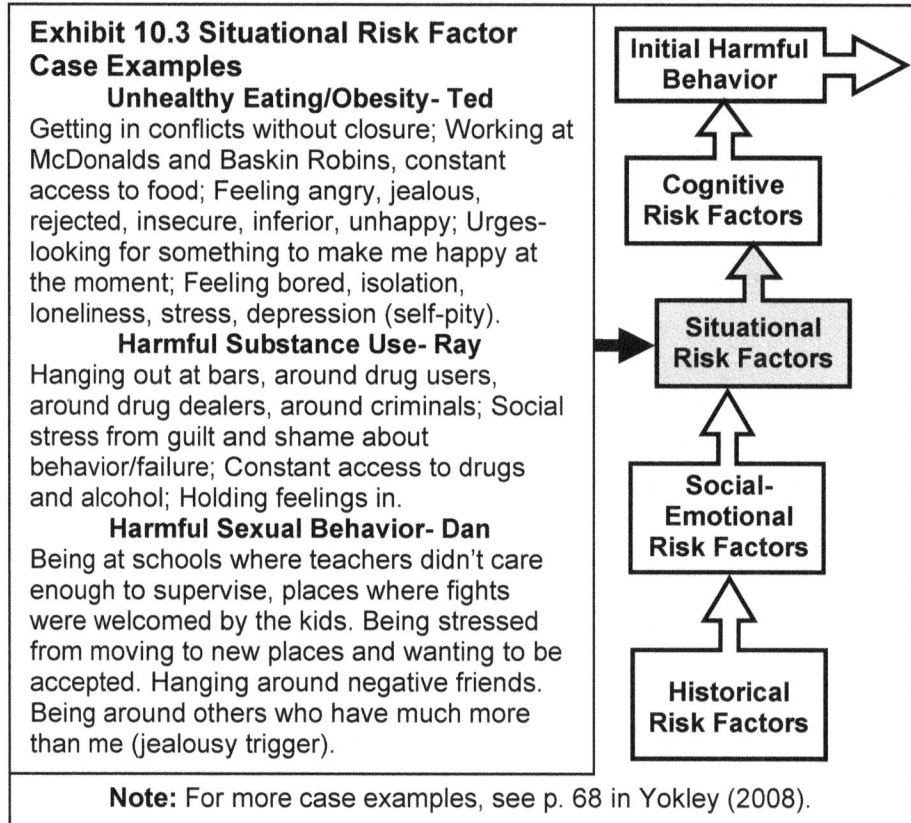

Exhibit 10.3 Situational Risk Factor Case Examples

Unhealthy Eating/Obesity- Ted
Getting in conflicts without closure; Working at McDonalds and Baskin Robins, constant access to food; Feeling angry, jealous, rejected, insecure, inferior, unhappy; Urges-looking for something to make me happy at the moment; Feeling bored, isolation, loneliness, stress, depression (self-pity).

Harmful Substance Use- Ray
Hanging out at bars, around drug users, around drug dealers, around criminals; Social stress from guilt and shame about behavior/failure; Constant access to drugs and alcohol; Holding feelings in.

Harmful Sexual Behavior- Dan
Being at schools where teachers didn't care enough to supervise, places where fights were welcomed by the kids. Being stressed from moving to new places and wanting to be accepted. Hanging around negative friends. Being around others who have much more than me (jealousy trigger).

Note: For more case examples, see p. 68 in Yokley (2008).

Initial Harmful Behavior → Cognitive Risk Factors → Situational Risk Factors → Social-Emotional Risk Factors → Historical Risk Factors

Risk Factor Question #4: What did you say to yourself before, during and after the harmful behavior?

Cognitive Risk Factors Group Session Work
Do a Cognitive Risk Factors assignment and SRA log check. Then have a brief client check in on issues clients need to discuss. Hold a discussion on the Cognitive Factors for unhealthy, harmful behavior development that were introduced (see earlier definition). Allow members to use their workbooks (or journals) in their discussion of risk factors. Group discussion needs to focus first on honest disclosure of risk factors and then on coping topics, methods and skills to address those risk factors. Use the PRAISE group process skills to build group unity during the initial group focus on honest disclosure of Cognitive Risk Factors and also during the discussion of interventions to address those risk factors. Refer to the SRT skills cards and integrate Healthy Behavior Success (ACTS) skills into a discussion on how to manage the Cognitive Risk Factors

that clients disclose. Remember to use PRAISE skills to develop Honesty, Trust, Loyalty, Concern and Responsibility at every opportunity. Basic suggestions for helping clients manage their Cognitive Risk Factors are provided in Exhibit 1 on p. 84 of Workbook 1 (Yokley, 2010b). The Awareness, Responsibility and Tolerance Training focus of this group session work is outlined in the "Treatment Notes" of the SRT treatment manual (Yokley, 2008, p. 69- 70).

Group Treatment Exercise: Discuss client Cognitive Risk Factors, review the case examples in Exhibit 10.4 and discuss the following question with the group. What ACTS skill(s) might help [Ted, Ray or Dan] cope with their Cognitive Risk Factors?

Introduce the next group topic. Describe Link 5, Initial Harmful Behavior in the Risk Factor Chain (see definition below). Record group personal responsibility ratings on how much each member "helped self" (e.g., workbook effort, honest disclosure) and social responsibility ratings on how much each member "helped others" (e.g., holding self and others accountable, helpful use of ACTS skills) in your progress notes.

Client assignment: Journal your Cognitive Risk Factors or if you are using SRT Workbook 1, complete

> **Exhibit 10.4 Cognitive Risk Factor Case Examples**
> **Unhealthy Eating/Obesity- Ted**
> Ruminating on injustices and lack of closure; Food comforts, soothes, decreases anger, doesn't hurt anyone but me and isn't illegal; Perception problems- mistaking stress or hurt for hunger; Awfulizing- "This must get worked out right now!" Justifying- "Since I was lied to/bullied/mistreated, it's OK for me to do it."
> **Harmful Substance Use- Ray**
> Minimized wrongdoing- It wasn't that bad; Blaming- They got me started, I give up, there's no use trying; It's OK because I want to do it; If they don't do what I want, then I get to do what I want (intimidate them); You're either a hero or a zero; Who cares what happens.
> **Harmful Sexual Behavior- Dan**
> "If I get her to trust me, I can do almost anything and she won't tell", Felt like "I always have to be right." Feeling challenged, "I must have the last word and can't let anyone get over on me" (must get even). Felt I was always a victim. Felt I couldn't be put down or look like a punk.
>
> **Note:** For more case examples, see p. 71 in Yokley (2008).

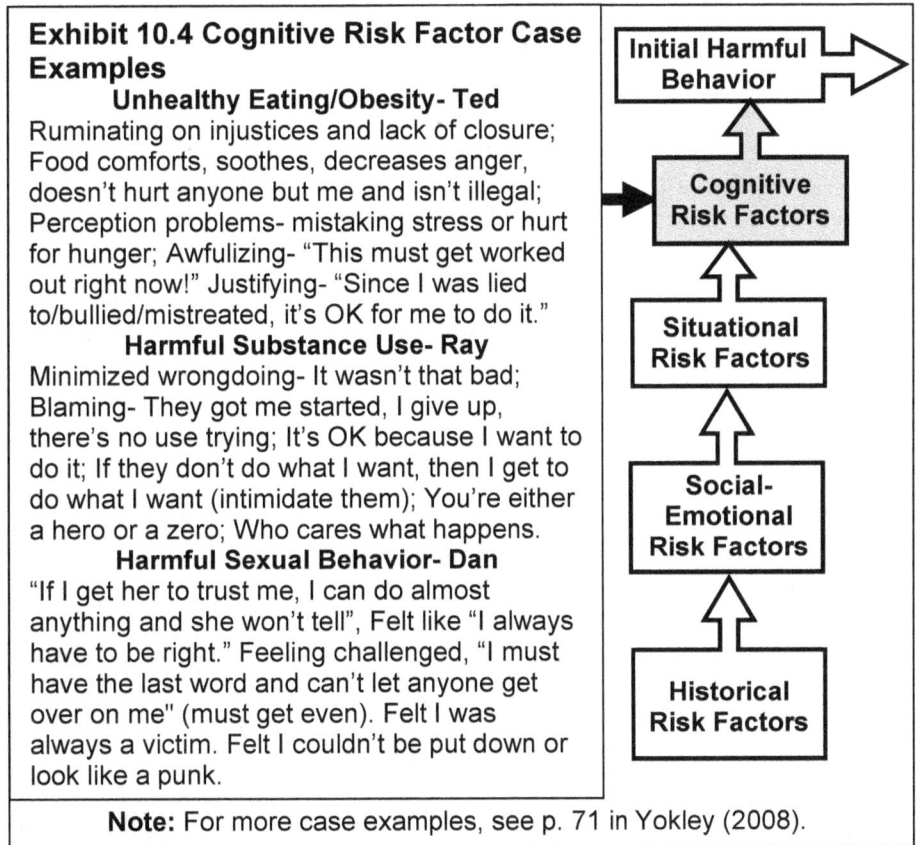

the "Risk Factor Chain Link 5: Initial Harmful Behavior" section for discussion at the next session. Answer risk factor question #4. Complete your SRA Log (See Appendix B).

Next session: Help clients disclose and discuss the cumulative impact of risk factors resulting in their Initial Harmful Behavior. Facilitate the first The Risk Factor Chain practice presentation.

Risk Factor Chain, Link #5: Initial Harmful Behavior
"Having the tools to change your life and succeed in recovery means nothing if you don't choose to use those tools. Using those tools is tough, but the alternative is tougher" -- Edward Flowers (1934- 2008)

Definition: The Initial Harmful Behavior occurs in Link #5 where all of the risk factors interact and combine to set the occasion for an unhealthy, harmful behavior or episode. Typically, though not always, this initial harmful behavior is the referral behavior. Harmful behavior occurs when irresponsible thinking (e.g., minimizing, justifying, assuming) is used in high-risk situations (e.g., exposure to trigger feelings, people or places) before the client has developed the emotional maturity to deal with it (i.e., awareness of trouble brewing, confidence in handling the situation and self-control to do the right thing) which results in poor judgment, uncontrolled feelings, urges and actions that are harmful to self or others. The motivation behind this socially irresponsible behavior typically involves trying to feel better (i.e., elevate mood, feel in control, confident) or get relief (decrease negative feelings of helplessness, anxiety, anger).

> **Risk Factor Question #5:** What links do you see between the risk factors we have discussed and your harmful behavior?

Initial Harmful Behavior Group Session Work

Do an Initial Harmful Behavior assignment and SRA log check. Then have a brief client check in on issues clients need to discuss. Hold a discussion on the Initial Harmful Behavior (cumulative impact of risk factors) topic that was introduced (see earlier definition). Allow members to use their workbooks (or journals) in their discussion of risk factors leading to Initial Harmful Behavior. Group discussion needs to focus first on honest disclosure of the risk factors and resulting Initial Harmful Behavior. Use the PRAISE group process skills to build group unity during the initial group focus on honest disclosure of Initial Harmful Behavior and also during the discussion of interventions to address the risk factors being discussed. Refer to the SRT skills cards and integrate Healthy Behavior Success (ACTS) skills into a discussion on how to manage the risk factor chain that led to unhealthy, harmful behavior disclosed by clients. Remember to use PRAISE skills to develop Honesty, Trust, Loyalty, Concern and Responsibility at every opportunity. Basic suggestions for helping clients manage their Initial Harmful Behavior issues are provided in Exhibit 1 on p. 84 of Workbook 1 (Yokley, 2010b). The Awareness, Responsibility and Tolerance Training focus of this group session work is outlined in the "Treatment Notes" of the SRT treatment manual (Yokley, 2008, p. 71-72).

Exhibit 10.5 Initial Harmful Behavior Case Examples

Unhealthy Eating/Obesity- Ted
Unhealthy, overeating- was 400lbs at age 30. The loss of his mother and emotional eating during resulted in a 120lb weight gain to 520lbs. Angry at world and self- "No date fat ass"; depression & self-pity.

Harmful Substance Use- Ray
Smoking cigarettes and drinking by age 14, smoking marijuana daily by age 16 smoking crack cocaine daily by age 24.

Harmful Sexual Behavior- Dan
Sexual abuse of 6-year-old step sister fondled her, committed cunnilingus, had her fondle me and commit felatio. Started at 12 and continued for around 2 years.

Note: For more case examples, see p. 72 in Yokley (2008).

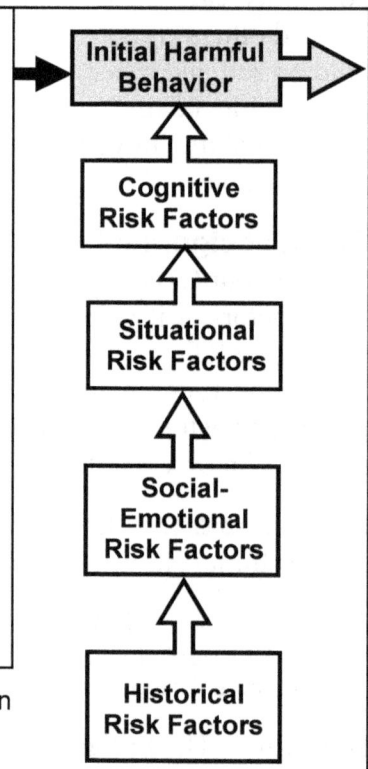

Initial Harmful Behavior → Cognitive Risk Factors → Situational Risk Factors → Social-Emotional Risk Factors → Historical Risk Factors

Group Treatment Exercise: Discuss client unhealthy, harmful behavior, review the Initial Harmful Behavior case examples in Exhibit 10.5 and discuss the following question with the group. What ACTS skill(s) might help [Ted, Ray or Dan] cope with their Initial Harmful Behavior?

Introduce the next group topic. Describe the Harmful Behavior Timeline (see following instructions) and the Stress-Relapse Cycle (see following introduction). Record group personal responsibility ratings on how much each member "helped self" (e.g., workbook effort, honest disclosure) and social responsibility ratings on how much each member "helped others" (e.g., holding self and others accountable, helpful use of ACTS skills) in your progress notes.

Client assignment: Journal your group experience and complete the Harmful Behavior Timeline. If you are using SRT Workbook 2, read the introduction material on the Stress-Relapse Cycle for discussion at the next session and stop at "The Stress-Relapse Cycle, Phase 1: Negative Coping." Answer risk factor question #5. Complete your SRA Log (See Appendix B).

Next session: Review and complete the Harmful Behavior Timeline and "My Life Story".

The Harmful Behavior Timeline

Instructions- Review the Harmful Behavior Timeline case examples (Exhibits 10.6, 10.7 & 10.8), select the one that best represents the clients in your treatment group and review it with them to help them get in the mind frame of connecting their past experiences with the development of their unhealthy, harmful behavior. If one or more clients are too sensitive about their referral problem, review one of the case examples that has a different referral problem with them first to get their focus on connecting past experience with later unhealthy, harmful behavior. If you are using SRT Workbook 1 "How did I get this problem", have your clients complete their Harmful Behavior Time Line following the instructions provided in Workbook 1, Appendix F.

If you are not using the workbook, have your clients complete a Harmful Behavior Time Line worksheet by dividing a blank sheet of paper in half and drawing a time line across the middle. First, have your clients put their birth date at the beginning of the time line and their current age at the end. Then have them write age numbers on the top of the time line as is illustrated in the case examples (Exhibits 10.6, 10.7 & 10.8). Second, have them write the types of unhealthy, harmful behavior (and treatment for that behavior) that they have experienced on the top portion of the time line. Then have clients record the types of unhealthy, harmful behavior that they did to self and others at the bottom of the time line. It goes without saying that clients need to include their referral behavior problem on the bottom part of their time line.

Harmful Behavior Timeline Treatment Exercise: Hold a group discussion where all group members help each other make connections between past experiences and later unhealthy, harmful behavior. Have each client take notes on the connections that were discussed that they believe apply to them.

Client assignment: Have your clients use their notes on the connections between their past experiences and present unhealthy, harmful behavior to write a summary of what they became aware of as is illustrated in the case examples (Exhibits 10.6, 10.7 & 10.8). Complete your SRA Log (See Appendix B).

"My Life Story" Have clients review the first draft of their life story that they wrote for their Historical Risk Factors client assignment (p. 232) and update it to include the connections that they made between their past experiences and later unhealthy, harmful behavior. If you are using the SRT Workbook 1, have clients review the Risk Factor Chain worksheet that they completed (p. 81, Yokley, 2010b) and add the knowledge that they gained about themselves to their life story. If you are not using the workbook have your clients add the knowledge gained from their risk factor chain work that they wrote in their journal

"My Life Story" Treatment Exercise: Have your clients present and discuss the life story that they wrote in group.

Next session: If you will not be moving on to use SRT Workbook 2, administer the SRT Learning Experience Questionnaire posttest (Appendix A). Otherwise review the Stress-Relapse Cycle and discuss positive vs negative coping.

Exhibit 10.6   Harmful Behavior Time Line- Ted (ages are in parentheses)

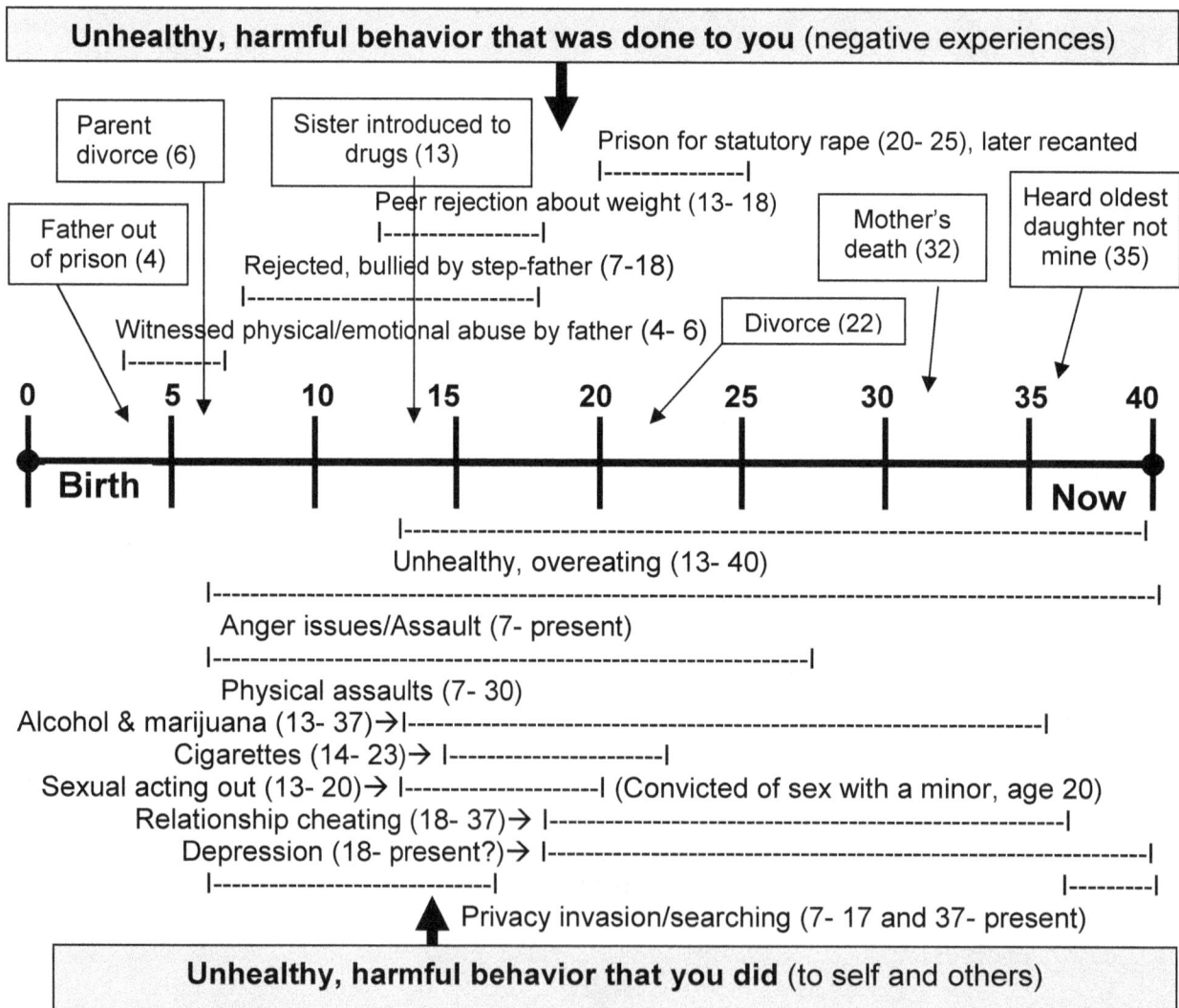

Ted's Summary: Self-awareness connections made by Ted included awareness of his "Vampire Syndrome" repetition compulsion, involving: 1) being bullied, witnessing his father beat his mother and mentally abuse her and later becoming physically and verbally abusive himself; 2) having a father in prison and later going to prison; 3) having an overeating mother and becoming an overeater; 4) being cheated on and cheating on others; 5) his father's wife divorcing his father in prison and his wife divorcing him in prison. He was able to trace his emotional eating back to his childhood and developing a "don't care" attitude. "It started at about age 13. I loved eating, it blocked out pain and rejection. I had a bad attitude and didn't care about anyone or anything. I did what I wanted, when I wanted and whatever, wherever."

Exhibit 10.7   Harmful Behavior Time Line- Ray (ages are in parentheses)

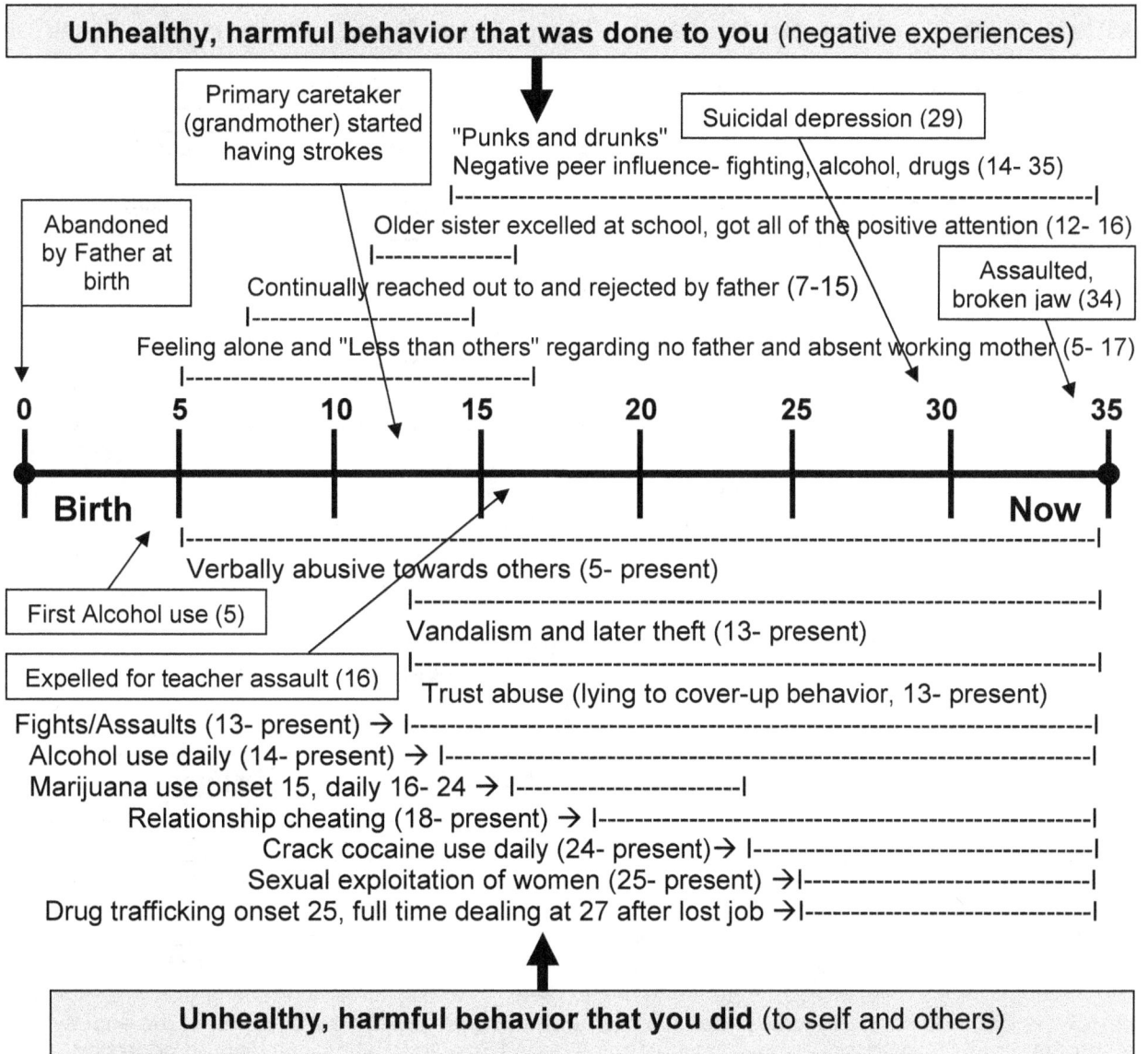

Unhealthy, harmful behavior that was done to you (negative experiences)

Primary caretaker (grandmother) started having strokes

"Punks and drunks"
Negative peer influence- fighting, alcohol, drugs (14- 35)

Suicidal depression (29)

Older sister excelled at school, got all of the positive attention (12- 16)

Assaulted, broken jaw (34)

Abandoned by Father at birth

Continually reached out to and rejected by father (7-15)

Feeling alone and "Less than others" regarding no father and absent working mother (5- 17)

0   5   10   15   20   25   30   35

Birth   **Now**

First Alcohol use (5)

Verbally abusive towards others (5- present)

Expelled for teacher assault (16)

Vandalism and later theft (13- present)

Trust abuse (lying to cover-up behavior, 13- present)

Fights/Assaults (13- present) →
Alcohol use daily (14- present) →
Marijuana use onset 15, daily 16- 24 →
Relationship cheating (18- present) →
Crack cocaine use daily (24- present)→
Sexual exploitation of women (25- present) →
Drug trafficking onset 25, full time dealing at 27 after lost job →

Unhealthy, harmful behavior that you did (to self and others)

Ray's Summary: Self-awareness connections made by Ray included a version of the "Vampire Syndrome" involving seeing his father abandon his mother and then exploiting and abandoning women himself. He connected feeling "less than" others with putting women down to build himself up. He was able to trace his feelings of inadequacy to comparing himself to his sister and feeling "less than" peers who knew their fathers and connect compensating for this feelings with "chemical courage" (drugs and alcohol) to help him interact with others. He also made the connection between his own hurt from being repeatedly rejected when reaching out to his father as a youth and initially acting out his feelings through vandalism and later theft from family to both get even for his hurt and support his drug habit. He realized this rejection left him with exaggerated needs for acceptance and when he was unable to gain the positive acceptance at home that his sister received, he began hanging out with and following drug using peers who accepted him. He concluded that, "My chemical dependency resulted in my loss of values and dignity."

Exhibit 10.8   Harmful Behavior Time Line- Dan (ages are in parentheses)

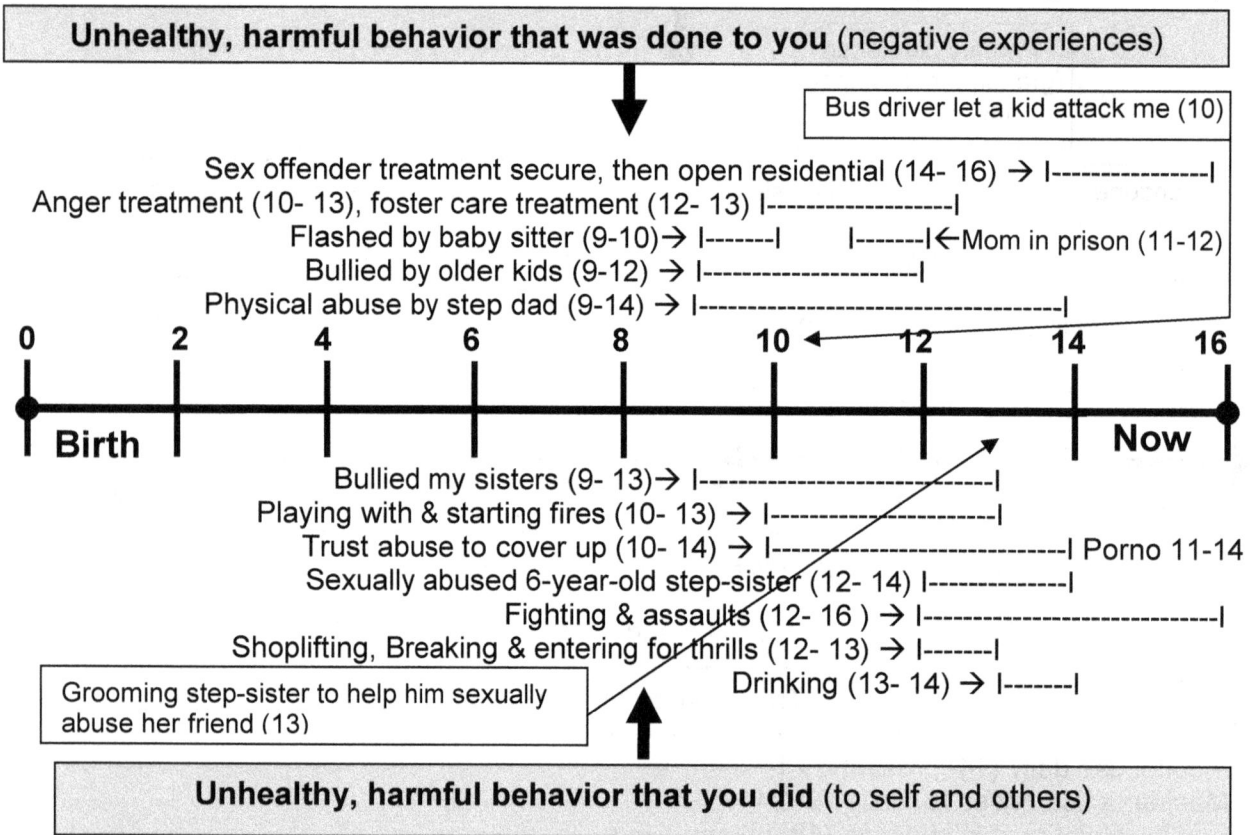

Unhealthy, harmful behavior that was done to you (negative experiences)

Bus driver let a kid attack me (10)

Sex offender treatment secure, then open residential (14- 16) → I----------------I
Anger treatment (10- 13), foster care treatment (12- 13) I-------------------I
Flashed by baby sitter (9-10)→ I-------I   I-------I←Mom in prison (11-12)
Bullied by older kids (9-12) → I----------------------I
Physical abuse by step dad (9-14) → I-----------------------------------I

| 0 | 2 | 4 | 6 | 8 | 10 | 12 | 14 | 16 |

Birth   **Now**

Bullied my sisters (9- 13)→ I----------------------------I
Playing with & starting fires (10- 13) → I--------------------I
Trust abuse to cover up (10- 14) → I-----------------------------I Porno 11-14
Sexually abused 6-year-old step-sister (12- 14) I--------------I
Fighting & assaults (12- 16) → I-----------------------------I
Shoplifting, Breaking & entering for thrills (12- 13) → I-------I
Drinking (13- 14) → I-------I

Grooming step-sister to help him sexually abuse her friend (13)

Unhealthy, harmful behavior that you did (to self and others)

Dan's Summary: Self-awareness connections made in Dan's case included awareness of his "Vampire Syndrome" repetition compulsion, involving being bullied and bullying others along with being physically abused and abusing others. He adopted the attitude of "If I can't hurt you, I'll hurt someone close to you" and justified his actions of sexual abuse to his step sister based on his feelings of hatred of his step father. His thrill seeking generalized from fire to sex to breaking and entering to drinking over time. Other connections Dan made were the babysitter flashing her breasts while saying it was OK for me and my step brother to touch them and me becoming very interested in sexual things including pornography.

Chapter 11
The Problem Development Triad Section 2
Understanding How Unhealthy, Harmful Behavior was Maintained

"We are what we repeatedly do"- Aristotle (384 BC-322 BC)

Positive vs Negative Coping, Recovery or Relapse?

After committing an abusive behavior, clients use positive coping, accept and work on the problem, don't make excuses and get honest, two things are likely. First, they are more likely to get help to avoid doing it again and second there is likely to be consequences. In short, "Honesty has its price but the good news is you don't have to pay twice." If clients use negative coping, they are likely to fall into a Stress-Relapse Cycle that maintains unhealthy, harmful behavior. If they use positive coping they can enter a Stress Management Cycle (Table 11.3)

Cycles, Cycles and More Cycles

Unhealthy, harmful behavior relapse cycles have been documented in the literature for over 50 years (e.g., Ray, 1961). These relapse cycles are have been observed across a number of unhealthy, harmful behaviors including: unhealthy eating relapse; unhealthy/harmful drinking and drug abuse relapse; harmful, compulsive gambling relapse and; harmful sexual behavior relapse. The transtheoretical model of behavior change stages includes relapse making this widely accepted model of behavior change a cycle of recovery and relapse as well. With respect to unhealthy, harmful emotions an anger-relapse cycle and depression-rumination relapse cycle have been described. The point is that unhealthy, harmful behavior habits occur in repeating cycles that humans fall into and need to learn to break.

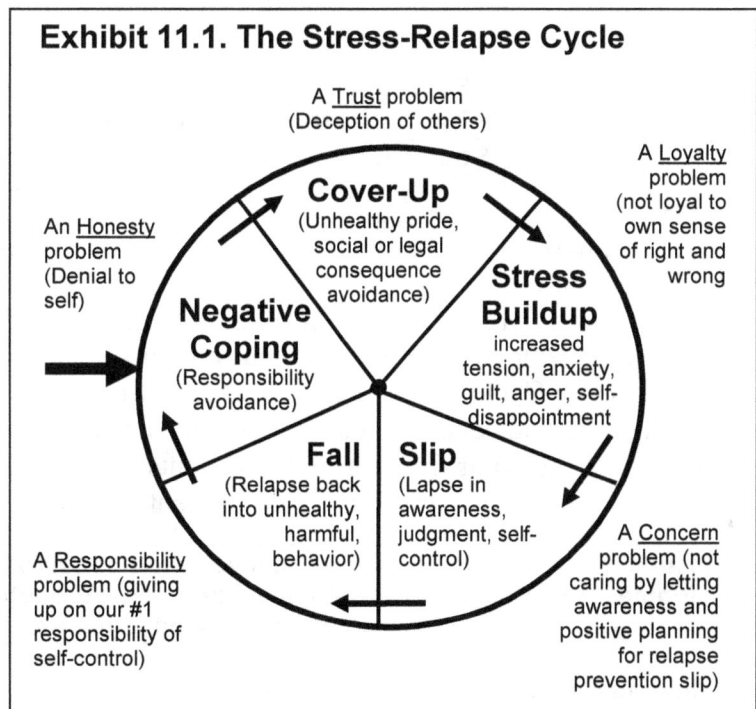

Exhibit 11.1. The Stress-Relapse Cycle

A Trust problem (Deception of others)

A Loyalty problem (not loyal to own sense of right and wrong

An Honesty problem (Denial to self)

Cover-Up (Unhealthy pride, social or legal consequence avoidance)

Negative Coping (Responsibility avoidance)

Stress Buildup increased tension, anxiety, guilt, anger, self-disappointment

Fall (Relapse back into unhealthy, harmful, behavior)

Slip (Lapse in awareness, judgment, self-control)

A Responsibility problem (giving up on our #1 responsibility of self-control)

A Concern problem (not caring by letting awareness and positive planning for relapse prevention slip)

The Stress-Relapse Cycle is used in SRT to help clients address multiple forms of unhealthy harmful behavior (See Exhibit 11.1). The Stress-Relapse Cycle plays an important part in relapse prevention because it: 1) describes the cycle that maintains unhealthy, harmful behavior; 2) summarizes the basic factors in each phase of the cycle that increase relapse risk and; 3) provides the skills needed in each phase to break the cycle.

Relapse Cycle Research Support- Unhealthy, harmful behavior relapse cycles have been documented in the literature over the past 50 years with a number of problem behaviors and conditions. Regarding, unhealthy eating, binge-diet and binge-purge cycles have been reported (e.g., Schulherr, 1998; 2005; Swirsky & Mitchell, 1996; Ward, Hudson & Bulik, 1993). A relapse-recovery cycle has been documented in drug and alcohol treatment (Ray, 1961; Scott, Dennis & Foss, 2005; Scott, Foss & Dennis, 2005). In the treatment of interpersonal and partner violence, a cycle of violence has been described (e.g., Dutton, 2007; Smith, 2000). A gambling cycle has been documented (e.g., Nower and Blaszczynski, 2006). In the treatment of harmful sexual behavior a number of sexual behavior problem relapse cycles have been described (e.g., Bays & Longo, 1989; Kahn, 1996; Lane, 1997; Longo, 2002; Salter, 1995). The transtheoretical model behavior change stages includes relapse, making this popular behavior change model a cycle of recovery and relapse (Passmore, 2012). With respect to harmful emotions an anger-relapse cycle (Clancy, 1996; 1997) and depression-rumination cycle (Law, 2005; Nolen-Hoeksema and Davis, 1999) have been documented in the literature. A Stress-Relapse Cycle for multiple forms of unhealthy, harmful behavior has been described (Yokley, 2008; 2011a). The Transtheoretical Stages of Change model can also be viewed as a cycle because, "individuals typically recycle through these stages several times before termination of the addiction" (p. 63, Prochaska, DiClemente & Norcross, 2003).

Why do I keep doing this?
How Unhealthy, Harmful Behavior was Maintained: The Stress-Relapse Cycle

In SRT, understanding how unhealthy, harmful behavior was maintained involves helping clients develop an understanding of the Stress Relapse Cycle. In the Stress-Relapse Cycle, unhealthy, harmful behavior relapse typically occurs through the following steps or cycle phases listed in the left hand column of Table 11.3).

If you are using SRT Workbook #2 "Why do I keep doing this?", a series of structured client exercises and assignments are

Table 11.3.
Phases in the Stress-Relapse and Stress Management Cycle

Stress Relapse Cycle	Stress Management Cycle
1. Negative Coping	1. Positive Coping (Get honest)
2. Cover Up	2. Open Up (Do the right thing)
3. Stress Build Up	3. Stress Adaptation (Manage feelings)
4. Slip (or lapse)	4. Step Up (Avoid a Slip)
5. Fall (or relapse)	5. Recover (Take responsible action)

provided to help your clients discover their thoughts feelings and behaviors during each phase of the Stress-Relapse Cycle. If you are not using the workbook, you will need to process the thoughts, feelings and behaviors that your clients had during each phase of the cycle with them using a dry erase board or flip chart to help clients see what they have in common and having clients journal what they learned as an assignment after each session.

Note: In all of the following assignments, if you are not using SRT Workbook 2, give your clients the assignment of writing their experience, comments, thoughts and feelings on the topic being covered in a journal to be reviewed and discussed at the next session.

Each phase in the Stress-Relapse Cycle has a key understanding question to help clients establish their own client-focused case conceptualization of "Why do I keep doing this?" Case study examples and interventions used in each phase of the Stress-Relapse Cycle are provided in this chapter. The client goal for this section is to explore and gain knowledge on how unhealthy, harmful behavior was maintained. The objectives are to complete all assignments on all Stress-Relapse Cycle sections and be able to implement the ACTS healthy behavior success skills address unhealthy, harmful behavior during each phase of the cycle.

Stress-Relapse Cycle Introduction Group

Introduction group session work: Hold group member introductions. Pass out SRT Workbook 2 (Yokley, 2011) and have members complete (or repeat) their harmful behavior history (pages 4- 6). Pass out SRT Healthy Behavior and Relationship Success skills cards (Table 3.2 & Table 9.2). Explain the group agenda that will occur each week as summarized on p. 227. Overview the Stress Relapse Cycle that maintains unhealthy, harmful behavior. Review the SRT Healthy Behavior Success skills on the skills card and key examples (in Chapters 4- 7). If you are using SRT Workbook 2, have clients review page 7- 27 and briefly review the SRT Healthy Behavior Success skills. Then briefly introduce the Stress Relapse Cycle covering Workbook 2 material on p. 29. If you are not using the Workbook 2, review the following basic summary with clients... After the first episode of behavior that resulted in your treatment referral, no one sat themselves down and said, "This is the life for me, I need to figure out a way to convince myself to continue this unhealthy, harmful behavior so that I can hurt myself or others to the point where I get in some serious trouble and need treatment." What really happened was that they fell into a Stress-Relapse Cycle. After a unhealthy, harmful behavior there is a crossroads where you must choose to deal with the situation by using negative coping or positive coping. This choice results in: Covering-up or opening-up; Letting Stress Build-Up or using stress management; Slipping up or stepping up; Falling back into or recovering from your harmful behavior. Thus, whether you use positive or negative coping after a harmful behavior episode determines whether you will avoid or continue problems by entering a Stress-Relapse Cycle. In this section we will help you identify the phases of the Stress-Relapse Cycle and how to break out of them. Then describe Phase 1 in the Stress Relapse Cycle (see definition below) and allow brief time during the group for members to make notes on the Negative Coping methods they have used.

Client assignment: Journal your group experience or if you are using SRT Workbook 2, complete the "Stress Relapse Cycle Phase 1: Negative Coping". Explain the Situation Response Analysis (SRA) Logs to be completed for next group (See p. 63 & Appendix B). If you are using Workbook 2, review Appendix D "Summary of Situation Response Analysis" with your clients.

Next session: Help clients disclose and discuss their Negative Coping. Remind members to bring their workbooks (or journals) to all groups.

Stress-Relapse Cycle, Phase 1: Negative Coping
"To thine own self be true" -- William Shakespere (1564- 1616)

Definition: Negative Coping is an *honesty problem* involving denial to self, avoiding responsibility, not working on the problem, using excuses, justify actions, shifting blame to situations/others or minimizing the unhealthy, harmful behavior. Three basic types of Negative Coping are: 1) Minimizing/normalizing; 2) Justifying actions and; 3) the Victim view/blaming. Other examples include: avoiding getting honest and dealing with problems; lying and denial of problems; justifying actions based on feelings; blaming others or; minimizing the impact of the unhealthy, harmful behavior. Continued Negative Coping prevents getting honest with self and taking responsibility for unhealthy, harmful behavior.

> **Relapse Cycle Question # 1:** After making a mistake and falling back into harmful behavior, what did you tell yourself to deal with it?

Negative Coping group session work

Do a Negative Coping assignment and SRA log check. Then have a brief client check in on issues clients need to discuss. Hold a discussion on the Negative Coping tactics that were introduced (see definition above). Allow members to use their workbooks (or journals) in their discussion of Negative Coping. Group discussion needs to focus first on honest disclosure of Negative Coping and then on coping topics, methods and skills to address it. Use the PRAISE group process skills described in Chapter 9 of this guide to build group unity during the initial focus on honest disclosure of Negative Coping and also during the discussion of interventions to address it. Refer to the SRT skills cards and integrate Healthy Behavior Success (ACTS) skills into a discussion on how to manage the Negative Coping that clients disclose. Remember to use PRAISE skills to develop Honesty, Trust, Loyalty, Concern and Responsibility at every opportunity. Basic stress management "Positive Coping" suggestions are provided in Exhibit 2 on p. 105 of Workbook 2 (Yokley, 2011a). The Awareness, Responsibility and Tolerance Training focus of this group session work is outlined in the "Treatment Notes" of the SRT treatment manual (Yokley, 2008, p. 77- 78).

Group Treatment Exercise: Discuss client Negative Coping. Then review the case examples in Exhibit 11.2 and discuss the ACTS skill(s) might help clients with their Negative Coping.

Introduce the next group topic. Describe Phase 2, Cover-Up (see following definition). Record group personal responsibility ratings on how much each member "helped self" (e.g., workbook effort, honest disclosure) and social responsibility ratings on how much each member "helped others" (e.g., holding self and others accountable, helpful use of ACTS skills) in your progress notes.

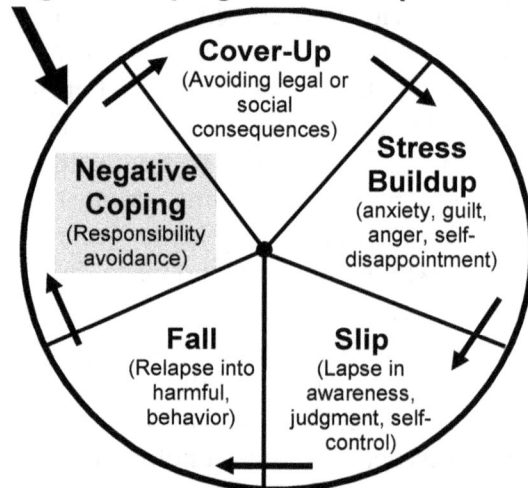

Exhibit 11.2
Negative Coping Case Examples

Cover-Up (Avoiding legal or social consequences)

Negative Coping (Responsibility avoidance)

Stress Buildup (anxiety, guilt, anger, self-disappointment)

Fall (Relapse into harmful, behavior)

Slip (Lapse in awareness, judgment, self-control)

Unhealthy Eating/Obesity- Ted
Ted justifying overeating based on feelings- (I'll show you); Used comparison & contrast excuse- "I didn't eat as much as before"; Minimizing- "It was only one." Excusing unhealthy weight as "Just more to love" or unhealthy eating as earned, a reward.

Harmful Substance Use- Ray
Ray used avoidance- Best way to deal with problems is forget about it; Excuses to use- not my fault; Denial of problem- everybody does it, lied to self (getting high was an exception), this is not really a problem; Victim view- they got me into it; Compared self to others who do worse.

Harmful Sexual Behavior- Dan
Dan minimized- "It only happened twice." Victim stance- "I was getting back at step dad for physical abusing & picking on me. Stirring it up, purposefully making others upset, yelling at people when I was in the wrong.

Note: For more case examples, see p. 77 in Yokley (2008).

Client assignment: Journal your Negative Coping or if you are using SRT Workbook 2, complete the "Stress Relapse Cycle Phase 2: Cover-Up" section for discussion at the next session. Answer relapse cycle question #1. Complete your SRA Log (See Appendix B).

Next session: Help clients disclose and discuss their unhealthy, harmful behavior Cover-Up tactics.

The Stress-Relapse Cycle, Phase 2: Cover-Up
"Three can keep a secret if two of them are dead"-- Benjamin Franklin (1706-1790)

Definition: Covering-up unhealthy, harmful behavior to avoid consequences creates *trust problems*. Threats bribery, intimidation, coercion and blackmail are not the only methods used to Cover Up problems. Three basic Cover Up methods are: Deception, Diversion and Division. Cover up tactics can involve: Lying; Misleading others; Pretending everything's normal; Confessing to a misdemeanor to avoid discussion of a felony; Confronting others problems to avoid looking at self; Division or splitting; Diversion tactics and; Negative contracts (covering for others so they will cover for you). Cover Up tactics destroy ability to be trusted and tendency to trust others.

> **Relapse Cycle Question # 2:** What did you do to keep your harmful behavior from being detected or to avoid consequences?

Cover-Up group session work

Do a Cover-up assignment and SRA log check. Then have a brief client check in on issues clients need to discuss. Hold a discussion on the Cover-up tactics that were introduced (see definition above). Allow members to use their workbooks (or journals) in their discussion of Cover-up tactics. Group discussion needs to focus first on honest disclosure of Cover-up tactics and then on coping topics, methods and skills to address them. Use the PRAISE group process skills described in Chapter 9 of this guide to build group unity during the group focus on honest disclosure of Cover-up tactics and also during the discussion of interventions to address them. Integrate Healthy Behavior Success (ACTS) skills into a discussion on how to let go of the Cover-up tactics that clients disclose. Use PRAISE skills to develop Honesty, Trust, Loyalty, Concern and Responsibility at every opportunity. Basic stress management "Open Up" suggestions are provided in Exhibit 2 on p. 105 of Workbook 2 (Yokley, 2011a). The Awareness, Responsibility

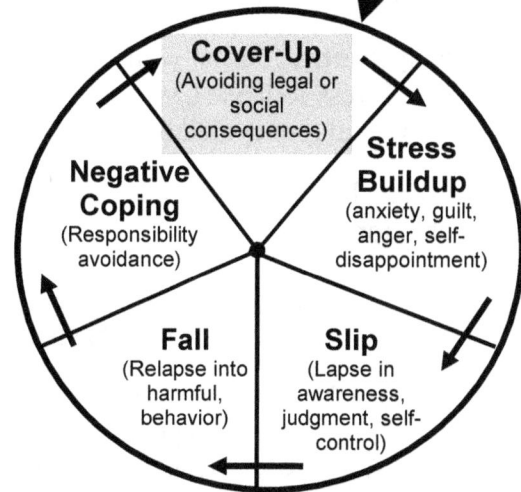

Exhibit 11.3 Cover-Up Case Examples

Cover-Up (Avoiding legal or social consequences)

Stress Buildup (anxiety, guilt, anger, self-disappointment)

Negative Coping (Responsibility avoidance)

Fall (Relapse into harmful, behavior)

Slip (Lapse in awareness, judgment, self-control)

Unhealthy Eating/Obesity- Ted
Ted would hide evidence, put food wrappers in outside trash cans, eat out, secret-keeping, denying, changing subject, stir up confusion to pull wool over their eyes, divert into blaming others for something, black mail & bribery (treats to kids for their silence)

Harmful Substance Use- Ray
Ray would avoid thinking about it, put on a false mask & pretend everything is OK, hide my problem from others. Had negative contracts- covered for others who cover for me. Diversion- focused on accomplishments to avoid looking at mistakes.

Harmful Sexual Behavior- Dan
Dan avoided consequences by splitting mom against step dad. Took victim stance with mom. Acting dumb, walking away, lying, acting innocent/good, keeping low profile/staying away, manipulation, changing the story, forming negative contracts.

Note: For more case examples, see p. 80 in Yokley (2008).

and Tolerance Training focus of this group work is outlined in the "Treatment Notes" of the SRT treatment manual (Yokley, 2008, p. 79).

Group Treatment Exercise: Discuss client Cover-up tactics. Then review the case examples in Exhibit 11.3 and discuss the ACTS skill(s) might help clients let go of their Cover-up tactics.

Introduce the next group topic. Describe Phase 3, Stress Buildup (see definition below). Record group personal responsibility ratings on how much each member "helped self" (e.g., workbook effort, honest disclosure) and social responsibility ratings on how much each member "helped others" (e.g., holding self and others accountable, helpful use of ACTS skills) in your progress notes.

Client assignment: Journal your Cover-up tactics or if you are using SRT Workbook 2, complete the "Stress Relapse Cycle Phase 3: Stress Buildup " section for discussion at the next session. Answer relapse cycle question #2. Complete your SRA Log (See Appendix B).

Next session: Help clients disclose and discuss their Stress Buildup related to unhealthy, harmful behavior.

The Stress-Relapse Cycle, Phase 3: Stress Buildup
"If you tell the truth, you don't have to remember anything"-- Mark Twain (1835- 1910)

Definition: Stress buildup from covering up problems is particularly *damaging to loyalty* when it results in shifting loyalty from positive family and true friends who say what you need to hear to negative peers who just say what you want to hear. Three basic contributors to Stress Buildup are: 1) Refusal to Accept Responsibility; 2) Lack of Effort and; 3) Not Dealing with Feelings. Refusal to Accept Responsibility and maintaining Cover Up tactics requires a great deal of mental concentration and emotional energy. In order to maintain a cover up, you have to remember what you said to who, when you said it and why. This creates "lookout fatigue." The more you lie the more you have to remember. When you stop relying on truth, you have to rely on your memory. In addition, refusal to accept responsibility means isolation or loyalty shift from positive people who will confront your behavior to negative people who won't. Keeping up this energy draining front, eventually is too much and the mental Stress Build Up eventually results in a behavior slip.

Relapse Cycle Question # 3: What stressful thoughts, feelings and situations are you experiencing?

Stress Buildup group session work
Do a Stress Buildup assignment and SRA log check. Then have a brief client check in on issues clients need to discuss. Hold a discussion on the Stress Buildup topics that were introduced (see definition above). Allow members to use their workbooks (or journals) in their discussion of Stress Buildup topics. Group discussion needs to focus first on honest disclosure of Stress Buildup and then on coping methods and skills to address it. Use the PRAISE group process skills described in Chapter 9 of this guide to build group unity during the group focus on honest disclosure of Stress Buildup and also during the discussion of interventions to address them.

Integrate Healthy Behavior Success (ACTS) skills into a discussion on how to let go of the Stress Buildup that clients disclose. Use PRAISE skills to develop Honesty, Trust, Loyalty, Concern and Responsibility at every opportunity. Basic "Stress Adaptation" suggestions are provided in Exhibit 2 on p. 105 of Workbook 2 (Yokley, 2011a). The Awareness, Responsibility and Tolerance Training focus of this group session work is outlined in the "Treatment Notes" of the SRT treatment manual (Yokley, 2008, p. 83).

Group Treatment Exercise: Discuss client Stress Buildup. Then review the case examples in Exhibit 11.4 and discuss the ACTS skill(s) might help decrease client Stress Buildup.

Introduce the next group topic. Describe Phase 4, Slip (or lapse)- see following definition. Record group personal responsibility ratings on how much each member "helped self" (e.g., workbook effort, honest disclosure) and social responsibility ratings on how much each member "helped others" (e.g., holding self and others accountable, helpful use of ACTS skills) in your progress notes.

Client assignment: Journal your Stress Buildup symptoms or if you are using SRT Workbook 2, complete the "Stress Relapse Cycle Phase 4: Slip (lapse)" section for discussion at the next session. Answer relapse cycle question #3. Complete your SRA Log (See Appendix B).

Next session: Help clients disclose and discuss their Slip (lapse) mistakes that set them up for unhealthy, harmful behavior relapse.

Exhibit 11.4
Stress Buildup Case Examples

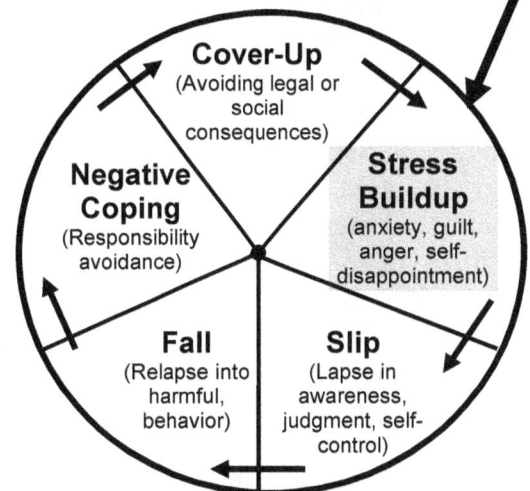

Unhealthy Eating/Obesity- Ted
Ted ruminated on the past, triggering anger and guilt "I failed mom before she died." He created chaos, over-reacting, then felt out of control. He let himself get bored. He would create his own resentment from people pleasing and get frustrated from lack of cooperation or support. Creating cravings.

Harmful Substance Use- Ray
Ray avoided dealing with problems. He could not identify feelings and would not discuss them or vent them; He stuffed his feelings (burying them) and problems would dwell on past negative events creating tension, frustration, stress, guilt, shame and crisis.

Harmful Sexual Behavior- Dan
Dan ruminated on injustices feeling betrayed by mom when she took step-dad's side when he lied about physically abusing or picking on me. Get worked up when, people disagree with me, criticize me, I don't get "my way." Feel worthless when I can't complete something on my own.

Note: For more case examples, see p. 82 in Yokley (2008).

The Stress-Relapse Cycle, Phase 4: Slip (lapse)
"An error doesn't become a mistake until you refuse to correct it."-- Orlando A. Battista

Definition: A slip (or lapse) is a *concern problem* that sets the occasion for relapse by not caring enough to "keep your problem up front" as a priority and letting awareness along with positive planning for relapse prevention slip. In AA a SLIP is when "Sobriety Loses Its Priority". Three basic types are Slips in awareness, judgment and self-control. Awareness slips include not noticing trigger thoughts, feelings or situations that can lead to relapse or a client not noticing that they have entered a high-risk situation for relapse. Poor judgment slips can come from over-confidence in abilities. This "No problem, I can handle it" attitude often results in testing self-control by entering high-risk situations for relapse on purpose or staying in them if entered by accident. Self-control Slips include slipping into a "Don't care attitude", compromising self and leaking feelings. A "Don't care attitude" allows getting lax about self-control in terms of

avoiding high risk people, places and things that can set the occasion for relapse. Compromising self is a social pressure assertiveness slip that often involves compromising self to be accepted by going along with others and doing things that can result in relapse. Self-control slips that involve feelings leaking out on others include aggressive, suggestive or hurtful comments, verbal power struggles, having the last word and inappropriate actions such as aggressive middle finger body language, invasion of personal space or borrowing without asking.

Relapse Cycle Question # 4: What slips have you noticed that can lead you to fall back into your harmful behavior?

Slip (lapse) group session work

Do a Slip assignment and SRA log check. Then have a brief client check in on issues clients need to discuss. Hold a discussion on the Slip topics that were introduced (see definition above). Allow members to use their workbooks (or journals) in their discussion of Slip topics. Group discussion needs to focus first on honest disclosure of Slips and then on coping methods and skills to address them. Use the PRAISE group process skills described in Chapter 9 of this guide to build group unity during the group focus on honest disclosure of Slips and also during the discussion of interventions to address them. Integrate Healthy Behavior Success (ACTS) skills into a discussion on how to manage the Slips that clients disclose. Use PRAISE skills to develop Honesty, Trust, Loyalty, Concern and Responsibility at every opportunity. Basic "Step Up" suggestions are provided in Exhibit 2 on p. 105 of Workbook 2 (Yokley, 2011a). The Awareness, Responsibility and Tolerance Training focus of this group

**Exhibit 11.5
Slip (lapse) Case Examples**

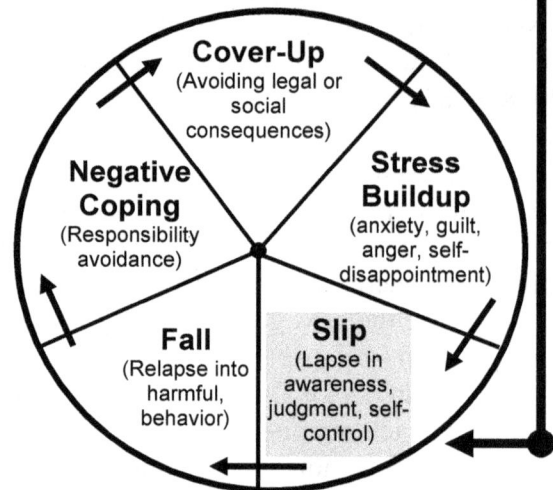

Unhealthy Eating/Obesity- Ted
Ted had slips in Awareness- "I deserve a reward, I'll do this to unwind", Judgment - "I must eat fast food, I'm out of time to make a healthy meal, 2 big ones is less than 4 little ones, Food's not illegal so it's OK" and Self-control- "I was wrongly accused so I'll just do it, one last time, I already ate too many so I might as well finish."
Harmful Substance Use- Ray
Ray had slips in Judgment - Compromised self to be accepted- "Went to places I shouldn't (bar to play pool), hung with people I shouldn't, thought I had to fit in" and Self-control- Temper tantrums; Shopaholic- Irresponsible with money.
Harmful Sexual Behavior- Dan
Dan had slips in Awareness- Taking the victim stance & making self feel controlled & helpless. Judgment- Being around his victim. Assuming "She'll like it, once I get her into it", Not finding something to do, allowing boredom, looking to others to entertain me. and Self-control- Arguing, challenging others.
Note: For more case examples, see p. 86 in Yokley (2008).

session work is outlined in the "Treatment Notes" of the SRT treatment manual (Yokley, 2008, p. 85- 86).

Group Treatment Exercise: Discuss client Slips (lapses). Then review the case examples in Exhibit 11.5 and discuss the ACTS skill(s) that might help manage client Slips in order to avoid heading towards a Fall (relapse).

Introduce the next group topic. Describe Phase 5, Fall (or relapse)- see definition below. Record group personal responsibility ratings on how much each member "helped self" (e.g., workbook effort, honest disclosure) and social responsibility ratings on how much each member "helped others" (e.g., holding self and others accountable, helpful use of ACTS skills) in progress notes.

Client assignment: Journal your Slips (lapses) or if you are using SRT Workbook 2, complete the "Stress Relapse Cycle Phase 5: Fall (relapse)" section for discussion at the next session. Answer cycle question #4. Complete your SRA Log (See Appendix B).

Next session: Help clients disclose and discuss their Fall (relapse) episodes back into unhealthy, harmful behavior.

The Stress-Relapse Cycle, Phase 5: Fall (Relapse)
"Failure is simply the opportunity to begin again, this time more intelligently"-- Henry Ford (1863- 1947)

Definition: A fall (or relapse) is a basic *responsibility problem* that involves giving up on our #1 social responsibility of self-control. A fall involves indulging self, giving up on abstinence, goals or following rules and falling back into unhealthy, harmful behavior. There are many different ways that people Fall (relapse) back into harmful behavior. Three basic contributors to a Fall are: 1) Recovery Perfectionism; 2) Failure to Consider Consequences and; 3) Emotional Rumination. As discussed in Chapter 4, A Recovery Perfectionism relapse through "Slip Give Up Trigger" occurs when a client slips, makes a mistake, falls into "all or nothing" recovery perfectionism and tells themselves that since they blew their perfect track record, they might as well just give up and indulge in or continue their unhealthy, harmful behavior. Failure to consider consequences includes a role-reversal deficit along with minimizing (e.g., "It's not so bad"), normalizing" (e.g., "lots of people do it"), justifying (e.g., "I deserve it, I've earned it" or "They deserve it after what they did") and grandiosity (e.g., "No one will catch on"). Emotional rumination involves going over and over a negative event, dwelling on it and not letting it go until worked up into a need to vent it through unhealthy, harmful behavior. Rumination can also involve dwelling on the good taste or feeling that the client gets from the food, drugs, sex until a craving for the unhealthy, harmful behavior becomes overwhelming.

Relapse Cycle Question # 5: What do you believe led you to fall back into your harmful behavior this last time?

Fall (relapse) group session work
Do a Fall assignment and SRA log check. Then have a brief client check in on issues clients need to discuss. Hold a discussion on the contributing factors that often result in taking a Fall (relapse) that were introduced (see definition above). Allow members to use their workbooks (or journals)

in their discussion of Fall topics. Group discussion needs to focus first on honest disclosure of Falls back into unhealthy, harmful behavior and then on coping methods and skills to address the contributing factors to a Fall. Use the PRAISE group process skills described in Chapter 9 of this guide to build group unity during the group focus on honest disclosure and discussion of

interventions to avoid taking a Fall. Integrate Healthy Behavior Success (ACTS) skills into a discussion on how to manage the contributing factors to a Fall (relapse) that clients disclose. Use PRAISE skills to develop Honesty, Trust, Loyalty, Concern and Responsibility. Basic "Recover" suggestions are provided in Exhibit 2 on p. 105 of Workbook 2 (Yokley, 2011a). The Awareness, Responsibility and Tolerance Training focus of this group session work is outlined in the "Treatment Notes" of the SRT treatment manual (Yokley, 2008, p. 89- 90).

Group Treatment Exercise: Discuss client Falls (relapses). Then review the case examples in Exhibit 11.6 and discuss the ACTS skill(s) that might help manage the contributing factors that often result in taking a Fall (relapse) back into unhealthy, harmful behavior.

Introduce the next group topic. Describe the Harmful Behavior Anatomy (see following description). Record group personal responsibility ratings on how much each member "helped self" (e.g., workbook effort, honest disclosure) and social responsibility ratings on how much each member "helped others" (e.g., holding self and others accountable, helpful use of ACTS skills) in progress notes.

Client assignment: Journal your Falls (relapses) or if you are using SRT Workbook 3, complete the "Harmful Behavior Anatomy Component 1: Irresponsible thinking" section for discussion at the next session. Answer Anatomy question #1. Complete your SRA Log (See Appendix B).

Next session: If you will not be moving on to use SRT Workbook 3, give the SRT Learning Experience Questionnaire posttest (Appendix A). Otherwise review the Harmful Behavior Anatomy and instruction process.

Exhibit 11.6
Fall (relapse) Case Examples

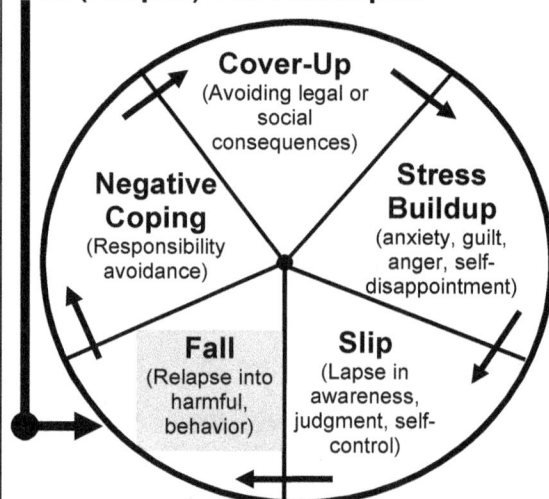

Unhealthy Eating/Obesity- Ted
Ted regularly relapsed on 4 different major diet programs (e.g., Weight watchers) along with supplements and discontinued gym memberships. He failed to succeed in weight management after 30 treatment programs. In almost every case an emotional event would result in him slipping and then giving up.

Harmful Substance Use- Ray
Ray always ran into old using friends, fell into the Slip Give up Trigger and binged after smoking one crack rock or taking one sip of beer. Then he abused others trust borrowing money, taking loans, saying "I love you to get what I want" and continue using.

Harmful Sexual Behavior- Dan
Dan would fall back into molesting his step-sister time and again. His Slip Give Up Trigger often started by violating a rule, fighting to act tough, stealing to look cool, threatening others and negative contracting. Once he thought he was going to get in any kind of trouble he used that as an excuse to give up on self-control entirely and do anything he felt like doing.

Note: For more case examples, see p. 89 in Yokley (2008).

Chapter 12
The Problem Development Triad Section 3
Understanding How Unhealthy, Harmful Behavior was Generalized

"Maturity comes not with age but with the acceptance of responsibility.
You are only young once but immaturity can last a lifetime!" -- Edwin Louis Cole

How did my problem spread?
Understanding How Harmful Behavior Generalized to other Areas:
The Harmful Behavior Anatomy

Pathological Social-Emotional Immaturity and the Harmful Behavior Anatomy- Continuing the Stress-Relapse Cycle of unhealthy, harmful behavior requires negative coping (lying/dishonesty) and covering it up (deception and abuse of others trust). This creates stress buildup (and shifting loyalty away from positive people who try to help to negative people that enable the behavior) until a slip occurs (usually from lack of concern about avoiding high-risk situations). This slip often results in giving up on the responsibility of self-control (i.e., the slip give-up trigger) and falling back into unhealthy, harmful behavior. With each repetition of the Stress-Relapse Cycle, problems with social maturity (i.e., honesty, trust, loyalty, concern and responsibility) increase. Similar problems occur with emotional maturity where, self-awareness of unwanted thoughts and feelings gets avoided by distracting self with the unhealthy, harmful behavior while self-efficacy or confidence to change and self-control is eroded by continuing the unhealthy, harmful behavior. In summary, continuing to fall back into the Stress-Relapse Cycle, develops a pathological level of social emotional immaturity which allows unhealthy, harmful behaviors to generalize or spread to other life problems in the Harmful Behavior Anatomy.

In SRT, the Harmful Behavior Anatomy consists of 10 basic pathological social-emotional immaturity components that support multiple forms of unhealthy, harmful behavior (See Figure 12.1). The Harmful Behavior Anatomy is a treatment framework that helps clients develop an understanding of ten components that work together to support and spread their unhealthy, harmful behavior to other problem areas. The client goal for this section is to explore and gain knowledge on how unhealthy, harmful behavior was generalized or spread to other problem areas. The objectives are twofold. First, complete all assignments on the 10 components that support multiple forms of unhealthy, harmful behavior. Second, be able to implement the ACTS healthy behavior success skills to decrease the unhealthy, harmful behavior support from each component in the Harmful Behavior Anatomy.

Harmful Behavior Anatomy Introduction Group
Introduction group session work
Hold group member introductions. Have members discuss their harmful behavior history. If you are using SRT Workbook 3 have members complete (or repeat) their harmful behavior history in the "Introduction to SRT" section. Pass out SRT Healthy Behavior and Relationship Success skills cards (Table 3.2 & Table 9.2). Review the SRT Healthy Behavior Success skills and discuss examples (provided in Chapters 4- 7) in group.

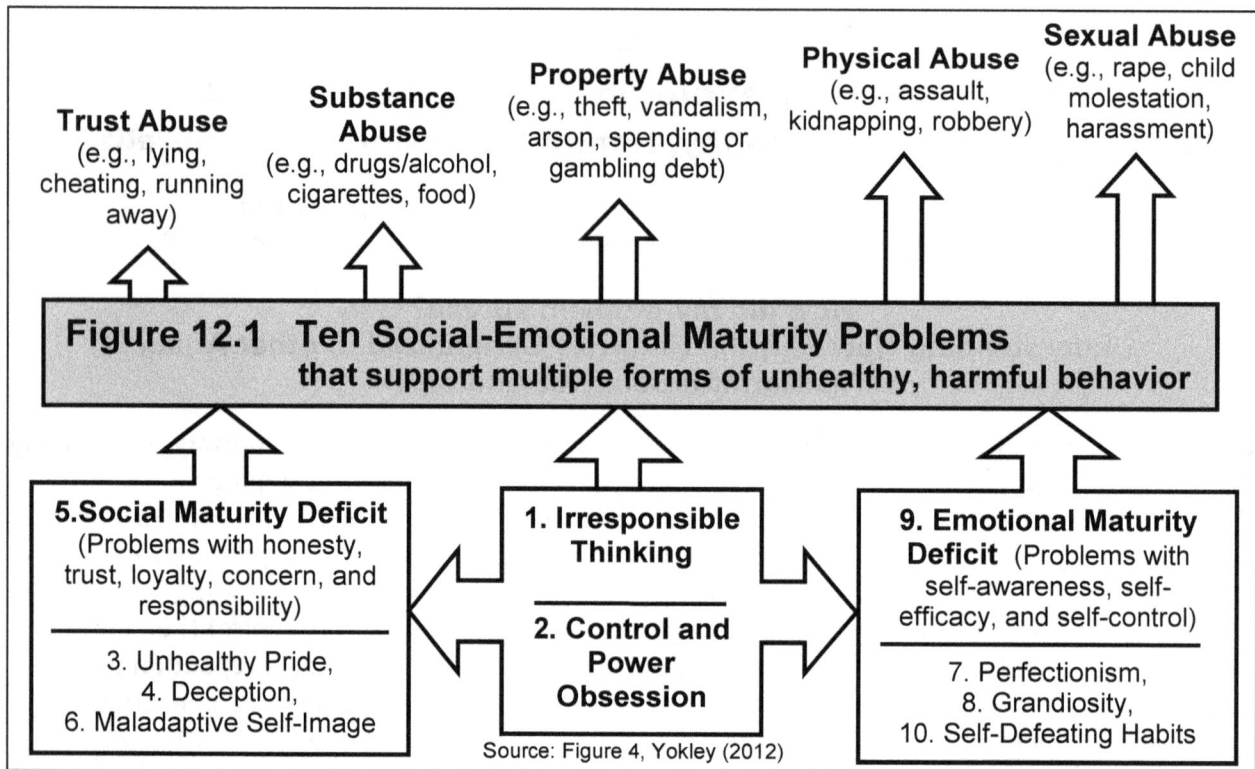

Figure 12.1 Ten Social-Emotional Maturity Problems that support multiple forms of unhealthy, harmful behavior

Source: Figure 4, Yokley (2012)

Explain the group topic that will occur each week as summarized in the following agenda section. If you are using SRT Workbook 3, have clients review the "Introduction to SRT" section and briefly introduce Component 1: Irresponsible Thinking. If you are not using Workbook 3, give a brief overview from the previous section on "Pathological Social-Emotional Immaturity and the Harmful Behavior Anatomy" using definition and case examples from the Anatomy model Exhibits 12.1- 12.5. Then go over the group agenda for all Anatomy groups listed below.

Agenda for all Ten Harmful Behavior Anatomy Topic Groups

The Harmful Behavior Anatomy, Component 1- 10
Start each group with a general description of the Anatomy component being covered that is consistent with the summary found in Exhibit 12.1. If you are using Workbook 3 (Yokley, 2012), introduce each Anatomy component as described on the first page of each component section.

Group Session Work
At the beginning of group, do an SRA log and assignment check. Then have a brief client "check in" on issues clients need to discuss. Hold a separate discussion group on each Harmful Behavior Anatomy Component that supports multiple forms of unhealthy, harmful behavior. Allow members to use their workbooks (or journals) in their discussion. Group discussion needs to focus on honest disclosure of Harmful Behavior Anatomy characteristics first and then on coping methods and skills to address those characteristics. Use the PRAISE group process skills described in Chapter 9 of this guide to build group member unity during the discussions of client Harmful Behavior Anatomy characteristics. Also use PRAISE skills to reinforce and develop

Honesty, Trust, Loyalty, Concern and Responsibility at every opportunity. Integrate Healthy Behavior Success (ACTS) skills into a discussion on how to manage the Anatomy factors clients disclose that contribute to a Fall (relapse). Suggestions for addressing the characteristics if each Harmful Behavior Anatomy component are provided in Exhibit 12.2. Further information on the Awareness, Responsibility and Tolerance Training focus of Harmful Behavior Anatomy group session work is outlined in the "Treatment Notes" of the SRT treatment manual (Yokley, 2008).

Group Treatment Exercise

Review the Harmful Behavior Anatomy component definitions below. Then review the definitions in Exhibit 12.1 and the general examples in Table 12.1 at the end of this section. If you are using SRT workbook 3 review the descriptions at the beginning of each Anatomy component and Tables 9- 13. During each group discussion use PRAISE skills to help clients disclose personal examples of their Anatomy characteristics. Review the Harmful Behavior Anatomy examples of Ted referred for weight management, Ray for substance abuse and Dan for sexual behavior problems in Exhibit 12.3, 12.4 and 12.5. Then discuss the following questions with the group for each Harmful Behavior Anatomy component. What ACTS skill(s) might help [Ted, Ray or Dan] manage the characteristics that they listed in Harmful Behavior Anatomy component [1, 2, 3... 10]? Introduce the next Harmful Behavior Anatomy component group topic. Record group personal responsibility ratings on how much each member "helped self" (e.g., honest self-disclosure) and social responsibility ratings on how much each member "helped others" (e.g., identification, holding self and others accountable, helpful use of ACTS skills) in progress notes. Pass out blank Situation Response Analysis (SRA) Logs to be completed for the next group.

Client assignment: After discussion of each Harmful Behavior Anatomy component, journal your experience, comments, thoughts, feelings and answer the Harmful Behavior Anatomy question. Discuss your journal assignment during each session. If you are using SRT Workbook 3, complete the Harmful Behavior Anatomy component before each session discussion of that component. Complete your SRA Log (See Appendix B) for each session.

Harmful Behavior Anatomy Component 1: Irresponsible Thinking
"Change your thoughts and you change your world" -- Norman Vincent Peale (1898- 1993)

Irresponsible Thinking involves cognitive distortions that support unhealthy, harmful behavior including automatic negative thoughts, thinking errors, irrational beliefs, false perceptions and misattributions. These distortions interfere with social-emotional maturity, break down inhibitions and interfere with self-control which sets the occasion for relapse.

> **Irresponsible Thinking Question:** What type of things can people tell themselves that enable or justify unhealthy, harmful behavior?

Harmful Behavior Anatomy Component 2: Control and Power Obsession
"The greatest power that a person possesses is the power to choose" -- J. Martin Kohe

A Control and Power Obsession (CAPO) can be expressed through: controlling/manipulating people with lies and deceit (i.e., Trust abuse); controlling/decreasing unwanted feelings with drugs, alcohol or food (i.e., Substance Abuse); controlling/elevating excitement with gambling, vandalism, shoplifting or arson (i.e., Property Abuse); controlling/venting anger with harassment, bullying or assault (i.e., physical abuse) and; controlling people while elevating sexual excitement with molestation or rape (i.e., sexual abuse).

Control and Power Obsession Question: What past experiences have you had that could result in a need to keep things under control?

Harmful Behavior Anatomy Component 3: Unhealthy Pride
"Pride goes before a fall" -- Late 14th Century English adaptation of Proverbs 16:18

Unhealthy pride involves an exaggerated need to look good (acceptance) and/or fear of looking bad (rejection). Unhealthy pride symptoms include denial, minimizing, covering up problems and suppressing (stuffing) feelings along with difficulty admitting mistakes and apologizing. Criminal pride involves acting tough, taking pride in criminal activity and the criminal code of not "snitching" on peers. Criminal pride goes before a fall because not snitching means having to take a fall for others when trouble comes down. Unhealthy pride goes before a fall because denial and stuffing feelings creates Stress Build-Up, slipping up and falling back into acting feelings out through unhealthy, harmful behavior.

Unhealthy Pride Question: What could happen if you were to admit a mistake or back down in a conflict?

Harmful Behavior Anatomy Component 4: Deception
"The truth shall set you free" -- John 8:32

Basic types of deception include: *lying* to cover up unhealthy, harmful behavior and avoid consequences; telling people what they want to hear (*appeasing*); purposefully leaving out part of the truth (*dishonesty by omission*) and; agreeing with no intent to comply (*assenting*). Deception also includes various forms of *diversion* such as changing the subject (diverting the conversation) to avoid discussing problems. Other deceptions include *misleading* others with exaggerated/inaccurate information or *stacking the facts* to minimize your part (usually by telling the other persons part first), using *vagueness* to avoid the truth and *attempting to confuse* the truth by bringing up a lot of irrelevant issues. Deception maintains unhealthy, harmful behavior by preventing detection.

Deception Question: What types of things do people do to avoid detection, cover up or deceive others about their harmful behavior and what have you done?

Harmful Behavior Anatomy Component 5: Social Maturity Deficit
"Character, not circumstances, makes the man" -- Booker T. Washington (1856-1915)

In SRT, a Social Maturity Deficit is defined as problems with honesty, trust, loyalty, concern and responsibility. Repeating the Stress-Relapse Cycle of Negative Coping (not being *honest* with self), Cover-up (abusing the *trust* of others), Stress Buildup (stuffing feelings and not being *loyal* to own sense of right and wrong), Slip (letting *concern* about relapse prevention lapse) and Fall (giving up on the #1 *responsibility* of self-control) advances social maturity problems to a pathological level. Pathological social immaturity supports multiple forms of unhealthy, harmful behavior and developing social maturity characteristics provides competing responses. In SRT...
* Honesty involves admitting the truth to ourselves, accepting that we have problems, not

covering them up and getting honest with others in treatment; dishonesty is disrespect.
- Trust isn't given to you, trust is earned through a track record of being trustworthy.
- Loyalty means being loyal to your own sense of right and wrong, not going along to get along, covering for others or making excuses for their behavior.
- Concern involves a healthy balance of caring for self and others.
- Responsibility involves self-control, holding self accountable, being reliable and doing what's right for self and others.
    Social Maturity Deficit Question: How could your past experiences have affected your honesty, trust, loyalty, concern & responsibility?

Harmful Behavior Anatomy Component 6: Maladaptive Self-Image
"Great beauty, great strength and great riches are really and truly of no use.
 The right heart exceeds all" -- Benjamin Franklin (1706-1790)

There are many types of maladaptive self-images. The motivation behind each varies and includes but is not limited to a need to present self in a manner to command respect, gain status, take control or get needs met without considering the welfare of others.
    Maladaptive Self-Image Question: How could your past experiences have affected your self-image and how you want others to view you?

Harmful Behavior Anatomy Component 7: Unhealthy Perfectionism
"When you aim for perfection, you discover it's a moving target" -- Geoffrey F. Fisher (1887-1972)

Perfectionism comes in several forms. *Self-oriented perfectionism* can result in trying to compensate for feelings of inadequacy through career overachievement to the extent of family and child neglect. *Other-oriented perfectionism* has been associated with arrogant, vindictive, control and power obsession characteristics that set the occasion for interpersonal conflict and domestic violence. *Socially prescribed perfectionism* involving trying to live up to exaggerated social expectations can result in "excel at any cost" blind ambition violating the rights of others to get ahead along with a "conceal at any cost" effort to protect the perfect public image. Unhealthy perfectionism typically involves all-or-nothing thinking along with overly high standards, unrealistic expectations and procrastination. *Recovery perfectionism* results in falling back into the Stress-Relapse Cycle after a single slip as a result of all-or-nothing thinking and giving up on recovery (see Yokley, 2011a). When *Recovery Perfectionism* results in giving up on sobriety it is referred to as "the abstinence violation effect". When it results in diet or exercise relapse it is known as "the goal violation effect" and when it results in a rule-breaking relapse of any self-imposed rule (e.g., "I won't go to the casino/back to them again") or other imposed rule (e.g., home, probation, parole or treatment) it is called "the rule violation effect" (Yokley, 2008).
    Unhealthy Perfectionism Question: How has high standards, high expectations and needing things to be perfect caused problems in your life?

Harmful Behavior Anatomy Component 8: Grandiosity
"The worst disease which can afflict executives in their work is not, as popularly supposed, alcoholism; it's egotism" -- Robert Frost (1874- 1963)

Grandiosity has been referred to as egotism (i.e., inflated self-esteem), meglomania (i.e., overestimation of their power) and super-optimism. It is a central component of malignant narcissism where grandiosity includes a thirst for power and in reactive narcissism where grandiosity is a defense against feelings of inadequacy or inferiority. Common threads in conditions that share grandiosity symptoms are over-confidence and unrealistic optimism. Grandiose over-confidence in self-control results in entering or staying in high-risk situations which sets the occasion for relapse. Grandiose optimism enables relapse by telling self that the behavior is not that harmful, won't be detected or if detected won't result in very serious consequences.

Grandiosity Question: How has your strong confidence and "I can handle it" attitude gotten you in trouble or put you at risk for relapse?

Harmful Behavior Anatomy Component 9: Emotional Maturity Deficit
"To be angry is to revenge the faults of others on ourselves" -- Alexander Pope (1688-1744)

In SRT, an Emotional Maturity Deficit is defined as problems with self-awareness, self-efficacy and self-control. Problems with awareness of high-risk situations and processes that reduce self-awareness like blocking out warnings from others set the occasion for relapse. In general, low self-efficacy involves problems with confidence in abilities and can result in giving up on recovery in the face of difficulties. Self- control is impaired when unhealthy, harmful behavior is justified by feelings or needs and justifying actions based on feelings is a primary contributing factor to multiple forms of unhealthy, harmful behavior.

Emotional Maturity Deficit Question: How could your past experiences have affected your self-awareness, self-efficacy & self-control?

Harmful Behavior Anatomy Component 10: Self-Defeating Habits
"Look before you leap" -- Aesop (620-560 BC)

There are too many self-defeating habits that support unhealthy, harmful to cover in any one text. That being said we will only cover several basic self-defeating characteristics (i.e., ruminating, procrastinating, and giving up) and exaggerated needs (i.e., acceptance, excitement, and attention) that support unhealthy, harmful behavior. Ruminating by going over and over something particularly that is unjust, unfair or difficult to handle is a self-defeating habit that can result in falling back into the Stress-Relapse Cycle. Procrastinating getting help allows unhealthy, harmful behavior to get worse. Giving up on recovery is easily done by compromising self to meet exaggerated needs or recovery perfectionism. As mentioned in the Unhealthy Perfectionism section above, the all-or-nothing thinking in recovery perfectionism often results in giving up on recovery after a single mistake. Exaggerated needs for attention, acceptance or excitement often involves following others, feelings or urges which can result in giving up and falling back into unhealthy, harmful behavior.

Self-Defeating Habits Question: How could your past experiences have left you with unmet needs or habits that hold you back?

Final Harmful Behavior Anatomy session: Help clients disclose and discuss their Harmful Behavior Anatomy characteristics. Administer the SRT Learning Experience Questionnaire posttest (Appendix A) after completion of Component 10.

Table 12.1	Examples of Harmful Behavior Anatomy Characteristics for Selected Problem Behaviors		
Anatomy Component	Selected Unhealthy, Harmful Behaviors		
	Unhealthy, Harmful Eating	Unhealthy, Harmful Drug/Alcohol Use	Unhealthy, Harmful Sexual Behavior
1. Irresponsible Thinking (See also Table 4.2)	"I'm just eating and driving, not drinking and driving"	"I'll only have one drink and then go home"	"She said she would do anything to get the job so I'm not taking advantage"
2. Control and Power Obsession	Obsessive comfort eating (controlling mood with food).	Compulsive control of social anxiety with alcohol.	Forcing, manipulating someone into sex to feed control & power needs.
3. Unhealthy Pride	Secret eating or wearing black baggie clothes to coverup overeating.	Denying a drug/alcohol problem. Covering drinking with mouthwash.	Denying a problem or refusing help because of what others will think.
4. Deception	Changing the subject when asked about food logs and telling others what they want to hear.	Lying about getting high and assenting by agreeing to stay clean with no intent to do so.	Using diversion- admitting a less serious problem to avoid discussing a more serious one.
5. Social Maturity Deficit	In denial, trusts too much, too loyal- stays in problem relationships, too concerned and responsible doing more for others than get in return.	Not honest or trustworthy. Has shifting loyalties, can't commit. Selfish, too focused on own feelings. Irresponsible, can't be depended on, doesn't finish what they start.	Acts honest to win others trust. No family loyalty. Does things to act concerned but has selfish obsession with gratifying own needs. Acts responsible to look good.
6. Maladaptive Self-Image	Has social status self-image. Is an over-achiever. Helping others fulfills needs to be accepted.	Acts tough, confident. Streetwise belief that can handle anything and make it on own covers feeling inadequate.	Views self as a good person because of positive deeds or achievements that cover up negative behavior.
7. Unhealthy Perfectionism	Has self-oriented perfectionism, overly high standards sets self up for disappointment.	Has other-oriented perfectionism, unrealistic expectations support impatience.	Has recovery perfectionism, all or nothing recovery thinking with slip give up trigger.
8. Grandiosity	Has grandiose fantasies as defense against feelings of inadequacy, inferiority.	Has grandiosity over-confidence in ability, "I'm not addicted, I can quit any time I want to".	Has grandiose thirst for power & super-optimism under-estimate of getting caught.
9. Emotional Maturity Deficit	Impaired awareness of eating damage to self. Justifying comfort eating based on feelings of loneliness, depression impairs self-control.	Impaired awareness of substance damage to self & others. Justifying social drinking based on need for acceptance impairs self-control.	Impaired awareness of damage to others, "they liked it, will grow to like it". Justifying actions based on power/sexual needs impairs self-control.
10. Self-Defeating Habits	Feeling valued by doing everything for others, making them dependent on you to keep it up which keeps you worn out & eating for energy.	Ruminating on perceived injustices to the point of using to relieve unbearable feelings that were created by ruminating.	Procrastinating on getting help to put off having to admit a problem resulting in the problem getting worse and having to admit it.

Exhibit 12.1
How Unhealthy, Harmful Behavior was Generalized

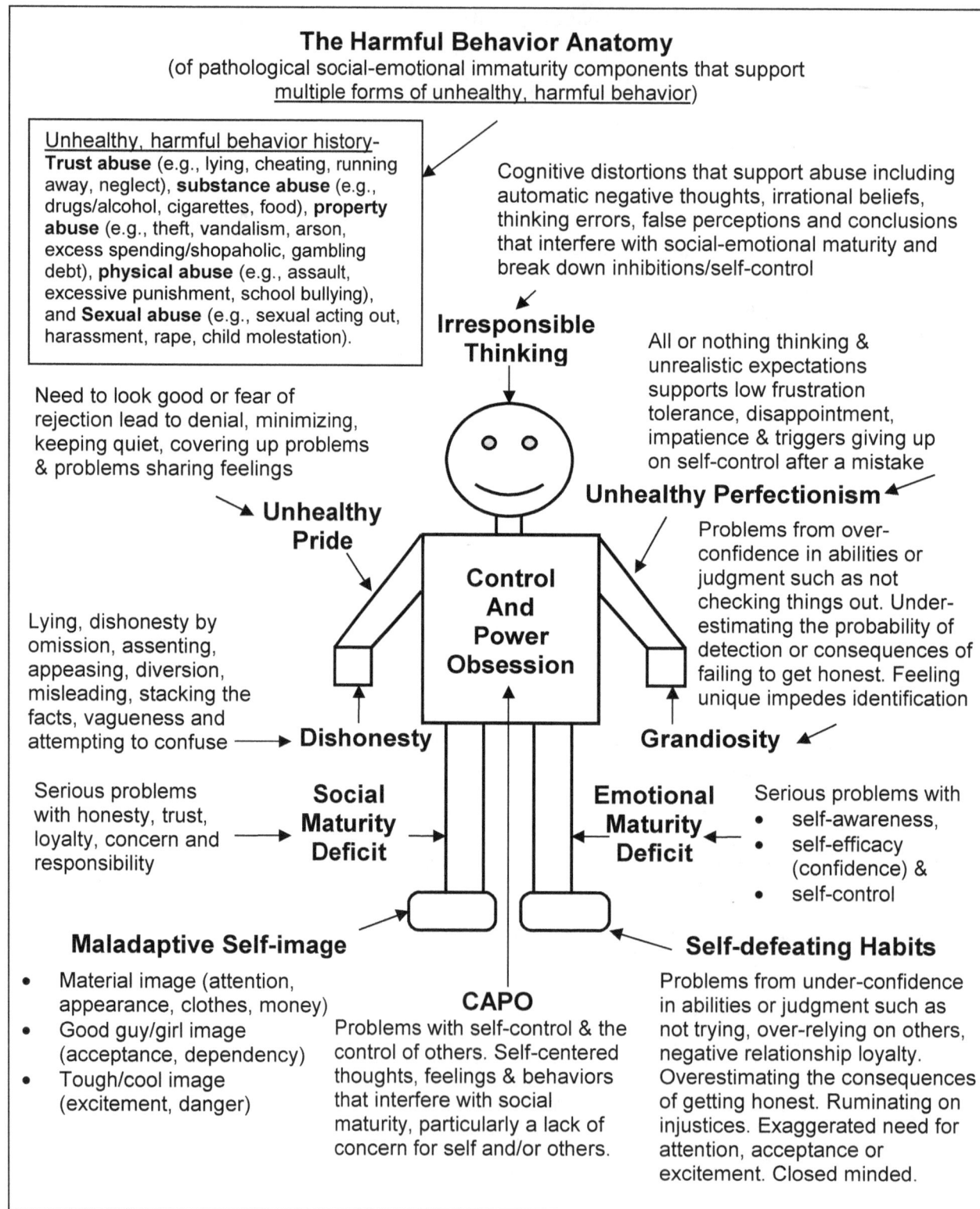

The Harmful Behavior Anatomy
(of pathological social-emotional immaturity components that support
multiple forms of unhealthy, harmful behavior)

<u>Unhealthy, harmful behavior history-</u>
Trust abuse (e.g., lying, cheating, running away, neglect), **substance abuse** (e.g., drugs/alcohol, cigarettes, food), **property abuse** (e.g., theft, vandalism, arson, excess spending/shopaholic, gambling debt), **physical abuse** (e.g., assault, excessive punishment, school bullying), and **Sexual abuse** (e.g., sexual acting out, harassment, rape, child molestation).

Cognitive distortions that support abuse including automatic negative thoughts, irrational beliefs, thinking errors, false perceptions and conclusions that interfere with social-emotional maturity and break down inhibitions/self-control

Irresponsible Thinking

All or nothing thinking & unrealistic expectations supports low frustration tolerance, disappointment, impatience & triggers giving up on self-control after a mistake

Need to look good or fear of rejection lead to denial, minimizing, keeping quiet, covering up problems & problems sharing feelings

Unhealthy Pride

Unhealthy Perfectionism

Problems from over-confidence in abilities or judgment such as not checking things out. Under-estimating the probability of detection or consequences of failing to get honest. Feeling unique impedes identification

Control And Power Obsession

Lying, dishonesty by omission, assenting, appeasing, diversion, misleading, stacking the facts, vagueness and attempting to confuse → **Dishonesty**

Grandiosity

Serious problems with honesty, trust, loyalty, concern and responsibility → **Social Maturity Deficit**

Emotional Maturity Deficit

Serious problems with
- self-awareness,
- self-efficacy (confidence) &
- self-control

Maladaptive Self-image

- Material image (attention, appearance, clothes, money)
- Good guy/girl image (acceptance, dependency)
- Tough/cool image (excitement, danger)

CAPO
Problems with self-control & the control of others. Self-centered thoughts, feelings & behaviors that interfere with social maturity, particularly a lack of concern for self and/or others.

Self-defeating Habits
Problems from under-confidence in abilities or judgment such as not trying, over-relying on others, negative relationship loyalty. Overestimating the consequences of getting honest. Ruminating on injustices. Exaggerated need for attention, acceptance or excitement. Closed minded.

Exhibit 12.2
Addressing Factors that Support Multiple forms of Harmful Behavior

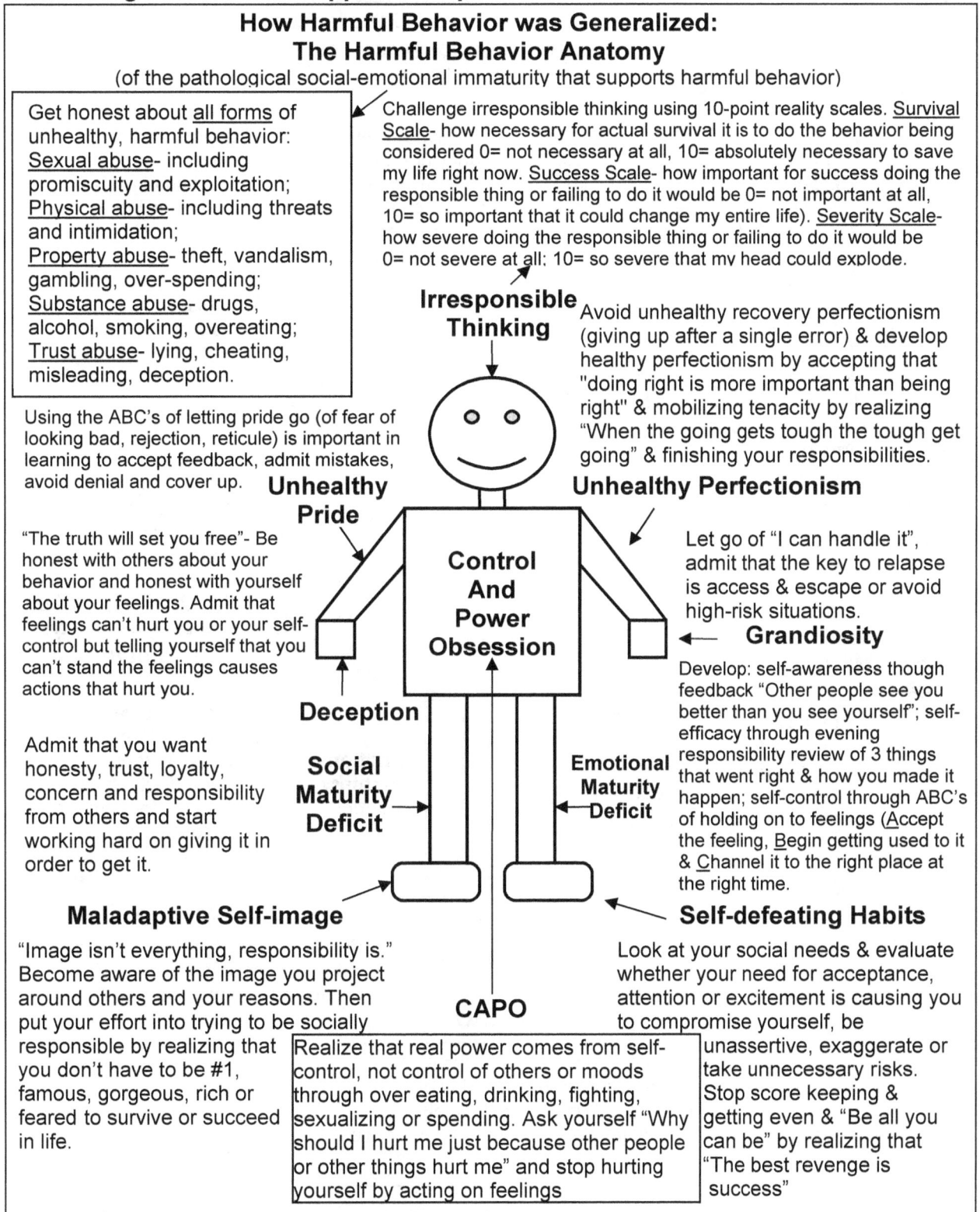

How Harmful Behavior was Generalized:
The Harmful Behavior Anatomy
(of the pathological social-emotional immaturity that supports harmful behavior)

Get honest about all forms of unhealthy, harmful behavior: Sexual abuse- including promiscuity and exploitation; Physical abuse- including threats and intimidation; Property abuse- theft, vandalism, gambling, over-spending; Substance abuse- drugs, alcohol, smoking, overeating; Trust abuse- lying, cheating, misleading, deception.

Challenge irresponsible thinking using 10-point reality scales. Survival Scale- how necessary for actual survival it is to do the behavior being considered 0= not necessary at all, 10= absolutely necessary to save my life right now. Success Scale- how important for success doing the responsible thing or failing to do it would be 0= not important at all, 10= so important that it could change my entire life). Severity Scale- how severe doing the responsible thing or failing to do it would be 0= not severe at all: 10= so severe that my head could explode.

Irresponsible Thinking

Avoid unhealthy recovery perfectionism (giving up after a single error) & develop healthy perfectionism by accepting that "doing right is more important than being right" & mobilizing tenacity by realizing "When the going gets tough the tough get going" & finishing your responsibilities.

Using the ABC's of letting pride go (of fear of looking bad, rejection, reticule) is important in learning to accept feedback, admit mistakes, avoid denial and cover up.

Unhealthy Pride

Unhealthy Perfectionism

"The truth will set you free"- Be honest with others about your behavior and honest with yourself about your feelings. Admit that feelings can't hurt you or your self-control but telling yourself that you can't stand the feelings causes actions that hurt you.

Control And Power Obsession

Let go of "I can handle it", admit that the key to relapse is access & escape or avoid high-risk situations.

Grandiosity

Deception

Social Maturity Deficit

Emotional Maturity Deficit

Develop: self-awareness though feedback "Other people see you better than you see yourself"; self-efficacy through evening responsibility review of 3 things that went right & how you made it happen; self-control through ABC's of holding on to feelings (Accept the feeling, Begin getting used to it & Channel it to the right place at the right time.

Admit that you want honesty, trust, loyalty, concern and responsibility from others and start working hard on giving it in order to get it.

Maladaptive Self-image

CAPO

Self-defeating Habits

"Image isn't everything, responsibility is." Become aware of the image you project around others and your reasons. Then put your effort into trying to be socially responsible by realizing that you don't have to be #1, famous, gorgeous, rich or feared to survive or succeed in life.

Realize that real power comes from self-control, not control of others or moods through over eating, drinking, fighting, sexualizing or spending. Ask yourself "Why should I hurt me just because other people or other things hurt me" and stop hurting yourself by acting on feelings

Look at your social needs & evaluate whether your need for acceptance, attention or excitement is causing you to compromise yourself, be unassertive, exaggerate or take unnecessary risks. Stop score keeping & getting even & "Be all you can be" by realizing that "The best revenge is success"

Exhibit 12.3
Harmful Behavior Anatomy Case Example- Ted (Weight management referral)

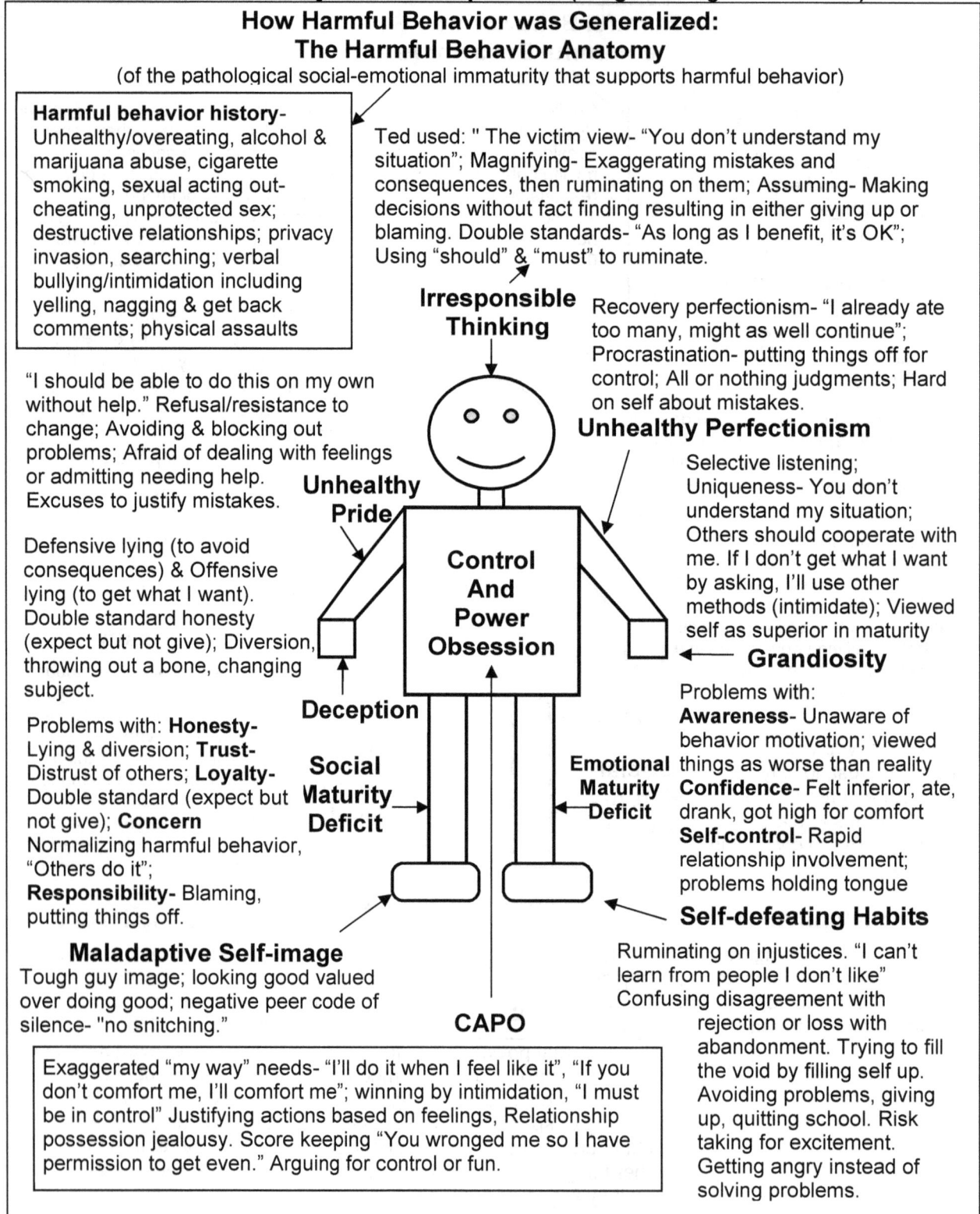

How Harmful Behavior was Generalized:
The Harmful Behavior Anatomy
(of the pathological social-emotional immaturity that supports harmful behavior)

Harmful behavior history-
Unhealthy/overeating, alcohol & marijuana abuse, cigarette smoking, sexual acting out- cheating, unprotected sex; destructive relationships; privacy invasion, searching; verbal bullying/intimidation including yelling, nagging & get back comments; physical assaults

Ted used: " The victim view- "You don't understand my situation"; Magnifying- Exaggerating mistakes and consequences, then ruminating on them; Assuming- Making decisions without fact finding resulting in either giving up or blaming. Double standards- "As long as I benefit, it's OK"; Using "should" & "must" to ruminate.

Irresponsible Thinking

Recovery perfectionism- "I already ate too many, might as well continue"; Procrastination- putting things off for control; All or nothing judgments; Hard on self about mistakes.

Unhealthy Perfectionism

"I should be able to do this on my own without help." Refusal/resistance to change; Avoiding & blocking out problems; Afraid of dealing with feelings or admitting needing help. Excuses to justify mistakes.

Unhealthy Pride

Defensive lying (to avoid consequences) & Offensive lying (to get what I want). Double standard honesty (expect but not give); Diversion, throwing out a bone, changing subject.

Selective listening; Uniqueness- You don't understand my situation; Others should cooperate with me. If I don't get what I want by asking, I'll use other methods (intimidate); Viewed self as superior in maturity

Control And Power Obsession

Grandiosity

Problems with: **Honesty-** Lying & diversion; **Trust-** Distrust of others; **Loyalty-** Double standard (expect but not give); **Concern** Normalizing harmful behavior, "Others do it"; **Responsibility-** Blaming, putting things off.

Deception

Social Maturity Deficit

Emotional Maturity Deficit

Problems with: **Awareness-** Unaware of behavior motivation; viewed things as worse than reality **Confidence-** Felt inferior, ate, drank, got high for comfort **Self-control-** Rapid relationship involvement; problems holding tongue

Self-defeating Habits

Maladaptive Self-image
Tough guy image; looking good valued over doing good; negative peer code of silence- "no snitching."

CAPO

Exaggerated "my way" needs- "I'll do it when I feel like it", "If you don't comfort me, I'll comfort me"; winning by intimidation, "I must be in control" Justifying actions based on feelings, Relationship possession jealousy. Score keeping "You wronged me so I have permission to get even." Arguing for control or fun.

Ruminating on injustices. "I can't learn from people I don't like" Confusing disagreement with rejection or loss with abandonment. Trying to fill the void by filling self up. Avoiding problems, giving up, quitting school. Risk taking for excitement. Getting angry instead of solving problems.

Exhibit 12.4
Harmful Behavior Anatomy Case Example- Ray (Substance abuse referral)

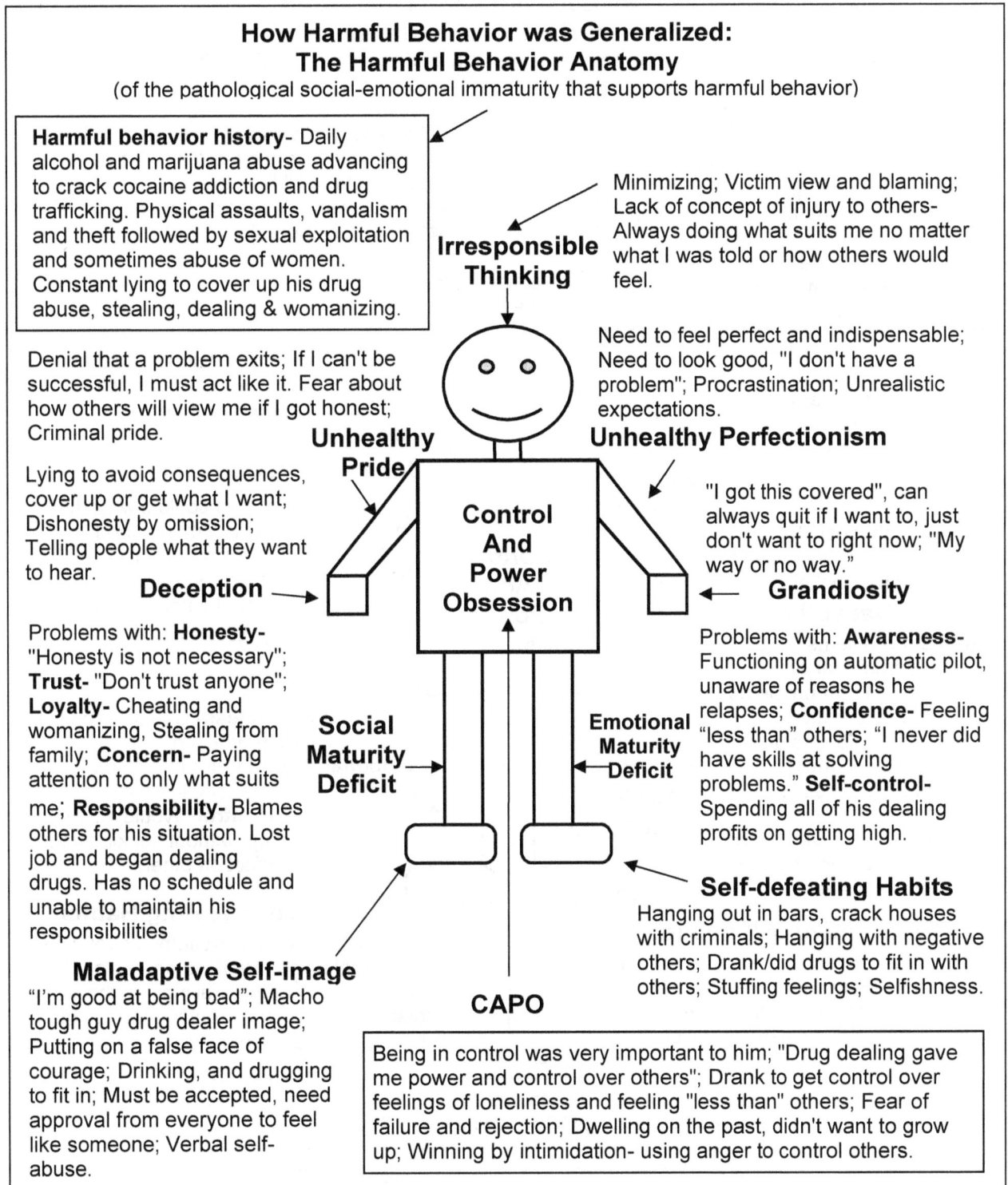

How Harmful Behavior was Generalized:
The Harmful Behavior Anatomy
(of the pathological social-emotional immaturity that supports harmful behavior)

Harmful behavior history- Daily alcohol and marijuana abuse advancing to crack cocaine addiction and drug trafficking. Physical assaults, vandalism and theft followed by sexual exploitation and sometimes abuse of women. Constant lying to cover up his drug abuse, stealing, dealing & womanizing.

Denial that a problem exits; If I can't be successful, I must act like it. Fear about how others will view me if I got honest; Criminal pride.

Lying to avoid consequences, cover up or get what I want; Dishonesty by omission; Telling people what they want to hear.

Deception

Problems with: **Honesty-** "Honesty is not necessary"; **Trust-** "Don't trust anyone"; **Loyalty-** Cheating and womanizing, Stealing from family; **Concern-** Paying attention to only what suits me; **Responsibility-** Blames others for his situation. Lost job and began dealing drugs. Has no schedule and unable to maintain his responsibilities

Maladaptive Self-image
"I'm good at being bad"; Macho tough guy drug dealer image; Putting on a false face of courage; Drinking, and drugging to fit in; Must be accepted, need approval from everyone to feel like someone; Verbal self-abuse.

Irresponsible Thinking

Minimizing; Victim view and blaming; Lack of concept of injury to others- Always doing what suits me no matter what I was told or how others would feel.

Need to feel perfect and indispensable; Need to look good, "I don't have a problem"; Procrastination; Unrealistic expectations.

Unhealthy Perfectionism

Unhealthy Pride

Control And Power Obsession

"I got this covered", can always quit if I want to, just don't want to right now; "My way or no way."

Grandiosity

Problems with: **Awareness-** Functioning on automatic pilot, unaware of reasons he relapses; **Confidence-** Feeling "less than" others; "I never did have skills at solving problems." **Self-control-** Spending all of his dealing profits on getting high.

Social Maturity Deficit

Emotional Maturity Deficit

Self-defeating Habits
Hanging out in bars, crack houses with criminals; Hanging with negative others; Drank/did drugs to fit in with others; Stuffing feelings; Selfishness.

CAPO

Being in control was very important to him; "Drug dealing gave me power and control over others"; Drank to get control over feelings of loneliness and feeling "less than" others; Fear of failure and rejection; Dwelling on the past, didn't want to grow up; Winning by intimidation- using anger to control others.

Exhibit 12.5
Harmful Behavior Anatomy Case Example- Dan (Sexual behavior problem referral)

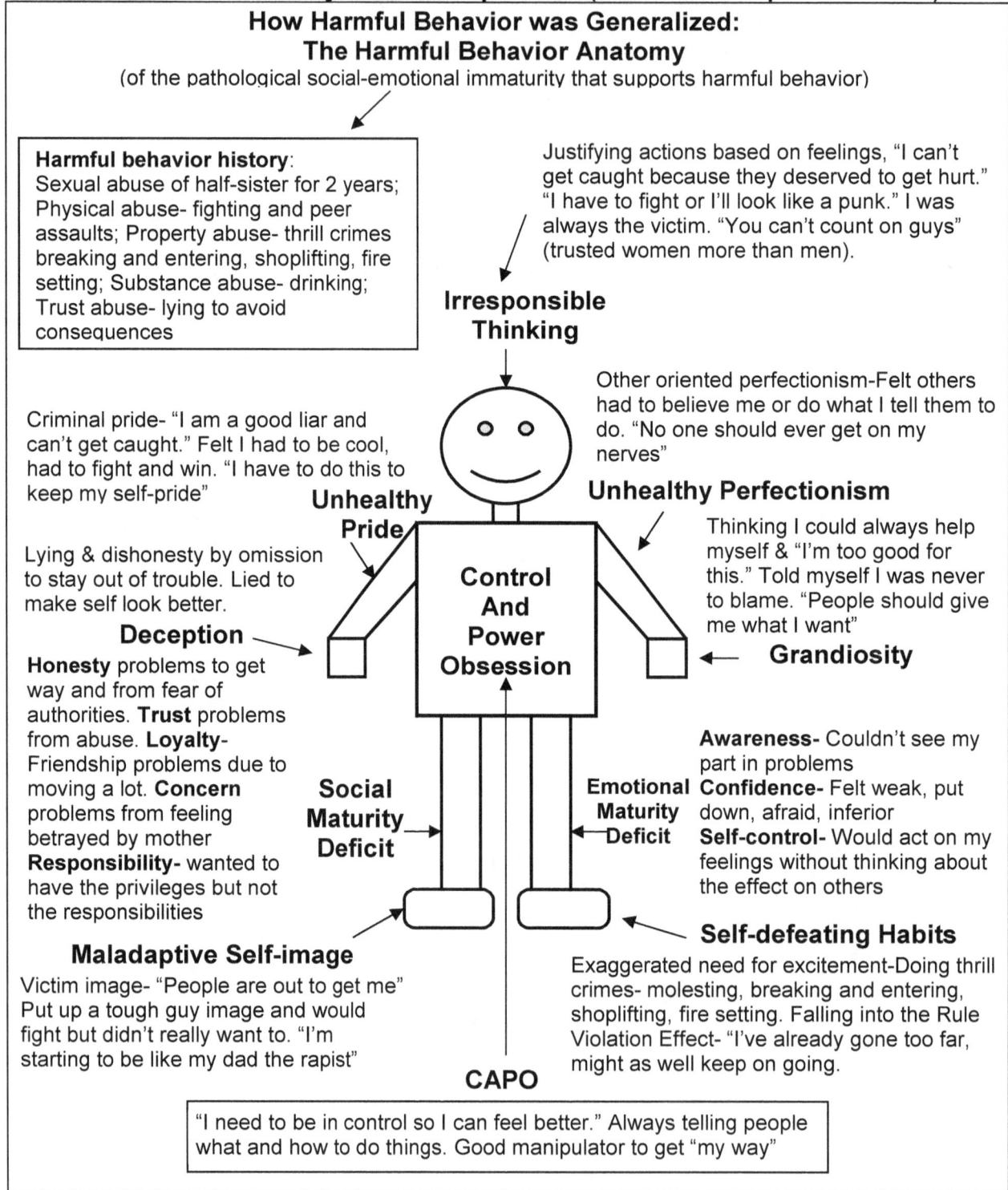

How Harmful Behavior was Generalized:
The Harmful Behavior Anatomy
(of the pathological social-emotional immaturity that supports harmful behavior)

Harmful behavior history:
Sexual abuse of half-sister for 2 years; Physical abuse- fighting and peer assaults; Property abuse- thrill crimes breaking and entering, shoplifting, fire setting; Substance abuse- drinking; Trust abuse- lying to avoid consequences

Justifying actions based on feelings, "I can't get caught because they deserved to get hurt." "I have to fight or I'll look like a punk." I was always the victim. "You can't count on guys" (trusted women more than men).

Irresponsible Thinking

Criminal pride- "I am a good liar and can't get caught." Felt I had to be cool, had to fight and win. "I have to do this to keep my self-pride"

Other oriented perfectionism-Felt others had to believe me or do what I tell them to do. "No one should ever get on my nerves"

Unhealthy Pride

Unhealthy Perfectionism

Lying & dishonesty by omission to stay out of trouble. Lied to make self look better.

Control And Power Obsession

Thinking I could always help myself & "I'm too good for this." Told myself I was never to blame. "People should give me what I want"

Deception

Grandiosity

Honesty problems to get way and from fear of authorities. **Trust** problems from abuse. **Loyalty-** Friendship problems due to moving a lot. **Concern** problems from feeling betrayed by mother **Responsibility-** wanted to have the privileges but not the responsibilities

Social Maturity Deficit

Emotional Maturity Deficit

Awareness- Couldn't see my part in problems
Confidence- Felt weak, put down, afraid, inferior
Self-control- Would act on my feelings without thinking about the effect on others

Self-defeating Habits

Maladaptive Self-image
Victim image- "People are out to get me" Put up a tough guy image and would fight but didn't really want to. "I'm starting to be like my dad the rapist"

CAPO

Exaggerated need for excitement-Doing thrill crimes- molesting, breaking and entering, shoplifting, fire setting. Falling into the Rule Violation Effect- "I've already gone too far, might as well keep on going.

"I need to be in control so I can feel better." Always telling people what and how to do things. Good manipulator to get "my way"

Implementation Options for SRT Workbooks 1- 3 on Understanding Harmful Behavior

Good teaching is one-fourth preparation and three-fourths pure theatre-- Gail Godwin

Social Responsibility Therapy Implementation Options for Clinicians

The three SRT Problem Development Triad workbooks on understanding how unhealthy, harmful behavior was acquired, maintained and generalized were developed for client use with clinician guidance. However, these workbooks provide the high level of structure needed for clients to discover how their unhealthy, harmful behavior was acquired, maintained and generalized in institutions or residential care where more self-directed workbook learning is needed. These three structured discovery workbooks also provide self-awareness homework assignments for session discussion with outpatient clients in need of structure and relapse prevention support between sessions. The vocabulary bar has been set relatively high for self-help workbooks to encourage cognitive as well as social-emotional growth. This allows clinicians to encourage clients whose unhealthy, harmful behavior has interfered with their education to improve their vocabulary by looking up definitions of words that they never learned and sharing them in sessions with clinician prompting. This promotes autonomy, develops "learning how to learn" self-efficacy and gives the client practice asking for help on less emotionally charged issues.

The Problem Development Triad: Three "Stand Alone" Sections

Figure 10.1 on page 217, illustrates the three sections in The Problem Development Triad. The first section has five structured discovery learning experience links on understanding of how harmful behavior was acquired. The second has five learning experience phases on how harmful behavior was maintained, The third section covers 10 learning experience components that allow harmful behavior to generalize or be substituted for other problem behavior. This makes a total of 20 structured discovery units to cover in the Problem Development Triad on understanding how unhealthy, harmful behavior was acquired, maintained and generalized. These three Problem Development Triad sections are covered in three "stand alone" workbooks that can be integrated into existing treatments individually. Clinicians seeking to develop client understanding and insight into how they acquired their unhealthy, harmful behavior, can use workbook one on, "How did I get this problem?" in their treatment. Clinicians who wish to focus on relapse prevention and developing client understanding of how they maintained their problem behavior, can use workbook two on, "Why do I keep doing this?" Some clinicians have clients who exhibit multiple forms of unhealthy, harmful behavior at the same time or who have substituted one harmful behavior for another over time (e.g., stopping overeating and starting excess drinking; stopping compulsive substance use and starting compulsive sexual behavior or; stopping thrill crime sexual behavior and starting thrill crime shoplifting). These clinicians can address their concerns about client harmful behavior generalizing (or harmful behavior migration to another problem during treatment), by using workbook three on, "How did my problem spread?" in their treatment. However, solid recovery support from a thorough understanding of how unhealthy, harmful behavior was acquired, maintained and generalized requires Structured

Discovery learning during the completion of all three workbooks along with the successful completion of the Problem Development Triad presentation (See Workbook 3, p. 169, "Putting it all together"). In residential, institutional or foster-family based treatment where the client will be in care for six months or more, completion of all three SRT workbooks is strongly recommended. Secure residential or correctional settings may require clinicians to sign off at the end of each section under the "Discussed with" heading in order to get required completion certificates.

Experienced clinicians with a treatment focus on insight into how clients acquired their unhealthy, harmful behavior over time, can complete SRT Workbook one in 6- 8 sessions. Those with a focus on relapse prevention of unhealthy, harmful behavior can complete SRT Workbook two in 6- 8 sessions. Clinicians who are treating co-occurring unhealthy, harmful behaviors, can complete SRT Workbook 3 in 11- 12 sessions. Client Problem Development Triad presentations take between one and two hours per person depending on the extent of the unhealthy, harmful behavior history. Whether implemented individually or in group, all three workbooks can be completed in 27- 28 weekly outpatient sessions or an eight week intensive outpatient program with sessions Monday, Wednesday and Friday. As with all treatments, doing it the first time may take longer and working with lower functioning clients may take longer.

SRT Workbook Group Sessions

For clinicians running a treatment group or program where individuals start treatment at different times, the three SRT workbooks can be completed in any order but require an introduction session before each which has an overview of the Problem Development Triad. As in individual/family therapy a summary of what has been learned is needed at the end of each section along with one presentation session per person in treatment. In group therapy sessions that are time limited (e.g., 1 ½ hours per session for 6- 8 members), it may not be possible to cover all issues for all clients so clinicians will need to prioritize by making sure they cover the top three issues first. This can be done easily by asking each group member to list several section descriptors (i.e., link section in workbook 1, phase section in workbook 2 or component section n workbook 3) that they rated highest and most important to their recovery. Hold one session for each section where the topic of discussion is the characteristics that were rated highest by clients in that section. Reinforce the Healthy Relationship Success Skills (Chapter 9) and teach the ACTS healthy behavior success skills (Chapters 4- 7) as indicated. Foster multicultural group unity and participation motivation with PRAISE skills (p. 214- 221). Create "Instant Identification" by pulling together similarities with a show of hands, e.g., "Who else rated this characteristic as a 2 or above?" discuss those common characteristics (see). Then move on to the next person asking for three that haven't been discussed. Usually after several people have talked in a group of 6- 8, the top symptom of that component has been covered for each group member and the group can be moved to processing how that problem affected their life and to generating one positive ACTS healthy behavior success skill to use for each problem characteristic discussed. Give an assignment for the next session of using those ACTS skills on their Situation Response Analysis Logs (Appendix B). A simplified log may have to be implemented by the clinician for low functioning groups.

SRT Individual/Family Sessions

Since some unhealthy, harmful behavior problems are difficult to share, individual sessions in SRT are considered practice for group. Many individuals with unhealthy, harmful behavior problems have relationship issues in need of repair. A set of SRT individual therapy "REPAIR" collaboration skills was designed for motivational enhancement in individual sessions. These six skills were derived from two client-centered skills and four SRT participation motivation skills. The "REPAIR" acronym helps SRT clinicians remember the following relationship collaboration skills: **R**eflection, **E**ncouraging, **P**ulling the client in, **A**cknowledgement, **I**dentification and **R**esponsible Reinforcement (See Table 12.1). These motivational enhancement skills develop the therapeutic alliance by conveying positive regard, acceptance and respect for client thoughts, feelings and opinions.

"People only seriously consider change when they feel accepted for exactly who they are"
-- Carl Rogers (1902- 1987)

Table 12.2   Individual Therapy Problem Collaboration REPAIR Skills
Combined from two Person-Centered therapy and four PRAISE participation motivation skills

Reflection- "It sounds like you are feeling...", "What I hear you saying is..." (reflecting feelings & message)

Encouraging- "mm-hm," "oh", "yes", "and...", "OK", "go on" and nod acknowledging understanding or repeating a key word (e.g., "upset?") or "Can you talk/say more about that?" [Shows willingness to listen without interrupting, judging or giving advice and tolerate clinical silence].

Pulling the client in- "Can I borrow that from you? That's a really good point we need to discuss" (Making them a part/Integration), p. 210. [Allows you to interrupt & re-direct without offending client.]

Acknowledgement - "What you are teaching us is...", "That's an important lesson to remember" [e.g., "having the last word, continues arguments"], p.212. [Acknowledges important life learning experiences. Allows awareness training with client ownership- insight development without directive interpretation]

Identification- "I can see/buy/understand that", "Makes sense to me" (Validation/Recognition), p. 192.

Responsible reinforcement- "Thank you for your honesty" or "What you did showed a lot of [trust, loyalty, concern, responsibility]" (p. 211). [Reinforces multicultural prosocial values.]

Repetition

Implement three repetitions in each workbook section to reinforce learning. For example: 1) have client read and complete exercises marking areas that need clarification; 2) review each section with the client, translating material, clarifying areas as needed and asking key concept questions; 3) "Each one teach one"- Have the client teach the concepts learned and share personal information/discoveries with their group or appropriate others in family sessions.

Adjustment for Special Needs

Reading level can be ahead of math simply because reading is used more in the everyday life of many people. Thus, it is not uncommon to see clients do well in rating all of the characteristics in a section and transcribing their top three characteristics to their worksheet correctly but getting the math wrong and showing low average scores next to severe behavior statements with high statement ratings in sections where ratings are required. If you have individuals like this, handle it by focusing your discussion on the top three rated characteristics in each component which does not require calculating average rating scores.

SRT Progress Evaluations

Treatment programs addressing unhealthy, harmful behavior often have their participants review their self-evaluations at the end of each Problem Development Triad section in a group treatment setting with their peers and staff. This is compared with clinician/staff evaluations. Promotion to the next program phase or requests for increases in program privileges are typically linked to successful progress in social-emotional maturity development (i.e., honesty, trust, loyalty, concern, responsibility, self-awareness, self-efficacy and self-control) which is documented on program progress notes and behavior incident reports. The same process can be used in foster family or family therapy meetings where youth privileges are based on social-emotional maturity progress.

Client Reinforcement

Accomplishment awards (e.g., certificates of completion for adults which included tangible reinforcement for youth) after the completion of each workbook, helps maintain a high level of client participation. A presentation discussion by clients of their understanding of how their acquired, maintained or generalized their unhealthy, harmful behavior, keeps them in touch with their past which helps them avoid returning there and helps dissipate resentment in mandated treatment cases.

Abbreviated Versions

Social Responsibility Therapy can accommodate an abbreviated version for treatment session limitations that are sometimes imposed by program length or funding source session limitations. In general, for all three workbooks, introduce the topic of each section (i.e., workbook 1 link, workbook 2 phase or workbook 3 component) and start with a writing assignment on "What I know about this topic." Then cover the top three key characteristics or concepts to cover and move on to the nest section topic. This allows covering more than one section in each treatment session. Since both SRT Workbooks one and two on harmful behavior acquisition and maintenance have five learning experience units that can easily be completed in 6- 8 sessions, they did not have abbreviated instructions included. However, since workbook three (the Harmful Behavior Anatomy) has 10 learning experience components that can take 11- 12 sessions; methods to abbreviate this section were provided. There are five basic ways that mental health professionals can abbreviate section three of The Problem Development Triad covered in Workbook 3. If you do Appendix D Candy Bar exercise, discuss the risk in all cases.

Using Workbook 3, The Harmful Behavior Anatomy in Time Limited Treatments

A "basic form" of Workbook 3 can be used with less severe cases in time limited treatment programs or where number of sessions the client can attend is limited. The "basic form" allows the client to skip portions in 8 of the 10 structured discovery learning experience components (i.e., all but Component 1- Irresponsible Thinking and Component 5- Social Maturity Deficit). Clients completing this workbook are instructed to ask their clinical staff whether they should complete the "basic form" or the complete version of each component. Since clients can't achieve behavior change without awareness of what they need to change, Awareness Training is central to unhealthy, harmful behavior treatment. Some clients require more Awareness Training than others and the complete version includes more Structured Discovery work on awareness in each component of the Harmful Behavior Anatomy. Although treatment completion time is always a practical factor to consider, other indicators of the need to assign the complete version of each component include clients who: have not completed workbooks 1 and 2; are placed in a residential/institutional treatment setting; exhibit more severe behavior and; need to increase their awareness of personal symptoms that support harmful behavior. In addition, to the "basic form", a "focused treatment plan" can be developed by selecting certain components in Workbook 3 that fit the individual needs of certain clients.

In Workbook 3, focusing treatment on one Harmful Behavior Anatomy component requires three section assignments. It is important to always include assignment of the Introduction to Social Responsibility Therapy & Understanding Harmful Behavior along with Harmful Behavior Anatomy Component 1- Irresponsible Thinking. This is needed so that the SRT healthy behavior and relationship success skills along with the irresponsible thinking that interferes with behavior change and achieving personal goals will always be covered. For example, if you want to focus your treatment on your client's problem perfectionism, you would assign the Introduction that covers healthy behavior and relationship success skills and Component 1 on Irresponsible Thinking along with Component 7 on Unhealthy Perfectionism. If you only want to focus your treatment on your client's control and power problem, assign the Introduction, Component 1 and Component 2- Control and Power Obsession and so on.

Workbook 3 Recommendations for clients with multiple harmful behaviors

Review the client intake assessment on frequency and severity of their unhealthy, harmful behavior (See p. 4- 6 in Workbook 3) and verify that information through collateral contacts (parents, partners, peers, probation/parole officers). If your client has exhibited multiple behaviors that are primarily harmful to others (e.g., physical and sexual abuse), they need to complete all of Workbook 3. If you are using this workbook for clients with multiple forms of less severe behaviors on the Harmful Behavior Continuum that are not primarily harmful to others, a minimum of five components is recommended as follows.

1. **Component 1**- Irresponsible Thinking (Includes the ART of avoiding trouble)
2. **Component 3**- Unhealthy Pride (Includes the ART of thinking it through)
3. **Component 5**- Social Maturity Deficit
4. **Component 9**- Emotional Maturity Deficit (Includes the ART of calming down)
5. **Component 10**- Self-Defeating Habits (Includes the ART of social problem solving)

The "focused treatment plan" listed above is generic and should be modified to meet individual client or program needs. For example...

- Clients whose behavior imposes on others need to have Control and Power problems (Component 2) included as part of their treatment plan;
- Clients with a criminal behavior history or who were not honest about their referral problem need to have Deception (Component 4) included as part of their treatment plan.
- Clients with image problems need to have Maladaptive Self-Image (Component 6) included as part of their treatment plan;
- Clients with denial issues who minimize or cover up problems need to have Unhealthy Perfectionism (Component 7) included as part of their treatment plan and;
- Clients with inflated self-esteem need to have Grandiosity (Component 8) included as part of their treatment plan.

A third abbreviated Workbook 3 alternative with high functioning clients who are not likely to get overwhelmed by information overload is to hold five combination sessions covering two sections each. This involves assigning the 10 Anatomy components in five pairs of topics covering: 1) Irresponsible thinking and Control and power Obsession;2) Unhealthy Pride and Deception; 3) Social Maturity Deficit and Maladaptive Self-Image; 4) Unhealthy Perfectionism and Grandiosity; 5) Emotional Maturity Deficit and Self-Defeating Habits. Discuss the Irresponsible Thinking used in all of those areas.

If your client needs some work on all of these issues but treatment time is limited, start with a writing assignment on "What I know about this topic." Then cover the top three key characteristics or concepts to cover and move on to the next section topic. This allows covering more than one section in each treatment session. You can use this time management approach with any of the three workbooks if needed. If you do the Candy Bar exercise in Workbook 3, Appendix D, discuss the risk in all cases.

Time limited treatment is not recommended for clients with multiple forms of more severe behaviors on the Harmful Behavior Continuum that are primarily harmful to others (i.e., abuse of power, property and people). Those clients will require completion of all 10 components in the present workbook (i.e., the complete form not the basic form) and all three SRT workbooks in addition to successful completion of their Problem Development Triad presentation and a strong external control focus in their treatment (See Chapter 8). The amount of learning experience abbreviation (i.e., material skipped) is a clinical judgment that must be made by the individual mental health professional based on the extent and severity of the harmful behavior being treated.

Narrative Version
There are some cases, typically in high functioning young adults with well-developed self-awareness where their insight makes them capable of writing a clear, detailed narrative of each factor (i.e., link, phase, component) in their Problem Development Triad after hearing the description of that section. In these cases, some clinicians prefer to have their client write a detailed narrative summary in their "Life Story" on how they acquired, maintained and generalized their unhealthy, harmful behavior from their journal assignments after Problem Development Triad discussion sessions. However, the SRT Workbook assignments may still needed to revive memories, add to and complete their narrative life story. Although some clinicians may prefer a narrative life story for their high functioning clients, it is recommended that these narratives be used in conjunction with, not in place of SRT workbook assignments and in addition to completion of the worksheets at the end of each workbook along with completion of the Problem Development Triad presentation. The SRT workbook assignments are considered important therapeutic activities that help summarize and solidify harmful behavior development understanding and should not be skipped.

The ART of SRT: Awareness, Responsibility & Tolerance Training
Throughout the implementation of SRT, a consistent focus on basic Awareness, Responsibility and Tolerance Training is needed to deal with the primary contributing factors to acquiring,

maintaining and generalizing unhealthy, harmful behavior. The basic ART of Social Responsibility Therapy includes the following.

- Awareness Training focus on the antecedents/triggers, consequences/reinforces and social modeling of unhealthy, harmful behavior;
- Responsibility Training focus on learning the Healthy Relationship and Behavior success Skills needed to manage unhealthy, harmful behavior and;
- Tolerance Training focus on: learning how to tolerate the feedback needed to change; developing the frustration tolerance needed to overcome barriers to goals; tolerating conflict that triggers relapse and; tolerating mistakes that activate the slip give up trigger.

Building an SRT "Core Team"

The saying, "A group only goes as fast as its slowest member", applies directly to how fast group members are able to get honest about their unhealthy, harmful behavior, accept the need to change it and redirect their focus from covering it up or playing it down to changing it. The saying "A group is only as strong as its number of positive role models" (i.e., a "Core Team") determines how fast change will occur in group through social learning.

An SRT group core consists of several positive group members willing to help self and others through role modeling social responsibility and blocking negative peer influence through Confrontation with Concern. A Core Team can generally be built through the normal course of early group development by putting every client in individual therapy first and gradually beginning to work with clients together, selecting those most responsive to SRT in individual treatment to begin working in group together. This generally works because in the beginning of placement, client energy is channeled into adjusting to the group environment, leaving less energy to be devoted to power struggles with authorities or ambivalence about the need to change. Put another way, clients are caught off guard in the beginning making acceptance of the group rules, agenda and expectations possible. Ideally, every group member should be a positive contributor but this is not always the case and thus it is important to always develop a Core Team of several members to keep the group stable, productive and therapeutic through positive role modeling and Confrontation with Concern as a competing factor to negative peer influence, enabling, resistance to change and associated negative contracts (covering up for each other).

Core Team Rebuilding

Since negative attitudes can be contagious, (i.e., "One bad apple can spoil the whole bunch"), group treatment programs must have interventions to address the issue of negative peer influence if/when it is detected. One negative peer influence intervention is core team rebuilding with is particularly important in residential and foster-family based treatment.

In cases where a negative contract has been developed (i.e., 2 or more members are involved in joining together in overt treatment resistance), sometimes clinicians have to take things apart to be able to see what is wrong in order to repair the damages. Core team rebuilding is a "divide and conquer" strategy where the group is disbanded and everyone assigned to individual "booster sessions" on program orientation with no privileges to determine the best core team dyad to start a new group. Since self-centered clients with immature needs prefer to be the center of attention in individual sessions as opposed to having to share time with others in group, program privileges and advancement must be tied to success in group. Thus, the two clients selected to start the new group get their privileges back at the first group session. After a Core Team dyad has been functioning together, select another addition from the pool of members still in individual therapy to create a core team triad. After the Core Team triad has been functioning well for several sessions, others can be added slowly with the understanding that core team members are responsible to "be their brother's keeper" and address the negative behavior of new clients added to the group.

It is critically important to the stability of the group that the Core Teams efforts to help themselves and others in group treatment not be allowed to be frustrated by treatment resistance from negative peers who join the group and vent their rebelliousness into group sabotage. Thus, the three strikes rule is in effect. Each group significant disruption incident report results in removal of the negative peer influence and return to individual therapy with no privileges on orientation. Three strikes (i.e., incident reports and removals) results in a treatment team meeting to determine whether the negative peer trying to disrupt others treatment should be allowed to remain in a group therapy setting or whether their negative peer influence calls for intervention.

> **Core Team Summary and "Booster Session" Research Support:** While a Core Team can and is likely to spontaneously develop in a healthy therapy group over time, the development of a Core Team in time limited groups requires encouragement if unity is to be developed before the group ends. PRAISE multicultural group unity and participation motivation skills are often effective in rapid development of a Core Team. Probably the closest thing to a positive Core Team influence in time limited groups are the positive effects that can occur when clients who have completed the time limited group are referred back for booster sessions and end up solidifying their own learning experience through positive modeling to others. Booster sessions have been shown to produce varying degrees of client benefit in the treatment of a number of health-related problems including exercise, child and adolescent mood disorders, binge eating, chronic back pain, smoking and drinking (e.g., Fleg et. al., 2013; Gearing et. al., 2013; Schlup et. al. 2009; Mangels et. al., 2009; Metz et. al., 2007 and; Connors & Walitzer, 2001).

Summary and Conclusion

In summary, the Problem Development Triad is a collaborative case conceptualization model. This approach to understanding harmful behavior is implemented in SRT through three structured discovery workbooks. These SRT workbooks help clients and clinicians work together to understand the basic contributing factors that set the occasion for clients to acquire their unhealthy, harmful behavior, maintain it and generalize it to other problem areas. At the same time, this case conceptualization model provides a framework that allows clients to practice the Healthy Behavior Success Skills needed to manage their problem behavior. The Problem Development Triad was not designed to be an intervention tool. Although providing a case conceptualization approach that promotes the practice of intervention skills may improve outcome, it is still a case conceptualization tool and was not designed to be evaluated as a treatment intervention. The logic behind this approach is simple. If you don't teach clients the skills that they need to manage their unhealthy, harmful behavior at the same time you are helping them understand it, you put them at risk for relapse. In serious cases this can result in very damaging consequences to both self and others.

We make a living by what we get, but we make a life by what we give" -- Winston Churchill (1874- 1965)

SRT Learning Experience Questionnaire

Name: _____   Date: _____

Note: This questionnaire is given at the beginning and end of your treatment to let the staff know how well we have done in teaching you the basic recovery skills needed to manage your unhealthy, harmful behavior in order to get the healthy body, relationships and life direction that you want. You are not expected to know any of the recovery skills listed below before your treatment. We will give this questionnaire again at the end to see how much you have learned during your treatment.

Life Long Recovery Skills

Please check <u>how much you know about</u> the following skills needed to get what you want in life.

Getting What You Want In Life	Never thought about it	Very little	Some	A fair amount	Quite a bit
Knowing the basic human needs that must be met before you can get what you want in life.					
Knowing what you want in life- Goals.					
Knowing what is holding you back from getting what you want in life.					
Knowing the steps it takes to get what you want in life.					
Connections between your thoughts, feelings and behavior.					

Healthy Relationship Success Skills

I am using the scales below to rate <u>How often I have worked on improving the following healthy relationship success skills</u>:
__ DURING MY WHOLE LIFE (check this if you are just starting treatment)
__ SINCE I ENTERED TREATMENT (check this if you just finished treatment)

Healthy Relationship Success Skills	Never thought about it	Not very often	Some-times	Fairly often	Very Often
Honesty- <u>with yourself and others</u> (e.g., about your mistakes and problems)					
Trust- <u>being trustworthy</u> and picking the right people to trust (e.g., positive, responsible people)					
Loyalty- Involves <u>standing up for what you know is right</u> and who you know is right					
Concern- for self and others involves keeping a good balance between <u>helping self</u> and <u>helping others</u> (e.g., not being selfish and forgetting about others but also not putting self last and doing too much for others)					
Responsibility- <u>self-control</u> of what you say and do; pulling your own weight, avoiding trigger people, places and things.					

Healthy Behavior Success Skills

Please check <u>how much you know about</u> the following skills needed to manage unhealthy, harmful behavior.

Healthy Behavior Success Skills Knowledge	Never taught this skill	Very little	Some	A fair amount	Quite a bit
Relapse Prevention (Avoid trouble) How to keep from falling back into unhealthy, harmful behavior.					
Emotional Regulation (Calm down) How to calm down and avoid justifying actions based on feelings.					
Decisional Balance (Think it through) Skills on how to make responsible decisions.					
Social Problem Solving (Solve the problem) Skills on how to solve life problems that get in the way of goals.					

If you checked "A fair amount" or "Quite a bit" for any of these skills, use the space below to list the skills that you have learned and where your learned them (name of program or therapist)

_____

_____

_____

Now use the scales below to rate <u>How often I have used these healthy behavior success skills</u>:
__ DURING MY WHOLE LIFE (check this if you are just starting treatment)
__ SINCE I ENTERED TREATMENT (check this if you just finished treatment)

Using Healthy Behavior Success Skills	Never really used it	Not very often	Some-times	Fairly often	Very Often
Relapse Prevention (Avoid trouble)					
Emotional Regulation (Calm down)					
Decisional Balance (Think it through)					
Social Problem Solving (Solve the problem)					

Knowledge About How you Developed your Problem

Please check <u>how much you understand about</u> how you got, maintained and spread your unhealthy, harmful behavior into other life areas.

Understanding How Unhealthy, Harmful Behavior was Developed	Never taught this	Very little	Some	A fair amount	Quite a bit
The Risk Factor Chain that led to your unhealthy, harmful behavior					
The Stress-Relapse Cycle that kept your unhealthy, harmful behavior going.					
The Harmful Behavior Anatomy that allowed your unhealthy, harmful behavior to spread.					

Situation Response Analysis Log Example #1

Social Responsibility Therapy **Situation Response Analysis Log**   Name: _____

Situation	Response	Analysis
Date & Description (What actually happened)	**My Thoughts, Feelings and Behavior**	1. Was my response positive/helpful or negative/harmful? 2. What do I need to do in this situation next time?
	Thoughts- Feelings*- Behavior-	**Thoughts:** _Positive Coping; _Negative Coping **Feelings:** _Tolerable; _Stressful; _Unbearable **Behavior:** _Healthy/helpful; _Unhealthy/harmful **My positive plan for next time is...**
	Thoughts- Feelings*- Behavior-	**Thoughts:** _Positive Coping; _Negative Coping **Feelings:** _Tolerable; _Stressful; _Unbearable **Behavior:** _Healthy/helpful; _Unhealthy/harmful **My positive plan for next time is...**
	Thoughts- Feelings*- Behavior-	**Thoughts:** _Positive Coping; _Negative Coping **Feelings:** _Tolerable; _Stressful; _Unbearable **Behavior:** _Healthy/helpful; _Unhealthy/harmful **My positive plan for next time is...**
	Thoughts- Feelings*- Behavior-	**Thoughts:** _Positive Coping; _Negative Coping **Feelings:** _Tolerable; _Stressful; _Unbearable **Behavior:** _Healthy/helpful; _Unhealthy/harmful **My positive plan for next time is...**

* Rate any cravings/urges to eat, drink, drug, smoke, gamble, fight, get sex (1-10: 1=mild urge, 5=moderate urge, 10=very strong urge)

Situation Response Analysis Log Example #2

Social Responsibility Therapy **Situation Response Analysis Log** Name: _____

Situation	Response			Analysis
Date & Description (What actually happened)	**My Thoughts**	**My Feelings**	**My Behavior**	Was my response positive coping or negative coping? What do I need to do in this situation next time?
				I used: ___ Positive Coping; ___ Negative Coping — My positive plan for next time is...
				I used: ___ Positive Coping; ___ Negative Coping — My positive plan for next time is...
				I used: ___ Positive Coping; ___ Negative Coping — My positive plan for next time is...
				I used: ___ Positive Coping; ___ Negative Coping — My positive plan for next time is...

Situation Response Analysis Log Example #3

Social Responsibility Therapy   Situation Response Analysis Log   Name: _____

Situation		Response		Analysis	
Date	Description (What actually happened)	Triggers Thoughts & Feelings	Behavior (What you did and whether it was responsible or not)	Positive or Negative Coping (Check & list your responsible or irresponsible thinking/plans)	

SOBER Breathing Summary

SOBER breathing is an exercise developed by Bowen, Chawla & Marlatt (2011) that can be done almost anywhere, anytime and can be used in the midst of a high-risk situation when you are upset or are experiencing trigger feelings or urges. The purpose is to focus on breathing in order to pull out of "automatic pilot", become less reactive, and more aware of your response. A way to help remember this exercise is the acronym SOBER.

Stop. When you are in a stressful or risky situation, stop and step out of automatic pilot, take a break and check in with yourself. Slow down and let yourself feel.

Observe. Observe the sensations that are happening in your body. Also observe any emotions, moods or thoughts you are having. Just notice as much as you can about your experience. Assess what is going on with you right now in the moment.

Bring your attention to your breath. Take three (or more) slow, deep breaths and focus all of your awareness on the experience of breathing.

Expand your awareness to include the rest of your body, your surroundings, your experience, situation, be mindful of all of these things.

Respond mindfully with awareness of the healthy, responsible options that you can take. Accept what is truly needed to best care for yourself in this moment and make a healthy choice as opposed to reacting emotionally. Then take the problem issue to the right place at the right time.

> **Note:** The above snippet is from the complete treatment description provided in "Mindfulness-based Relapse Prevention for Addiction Behaviors" (Bowen, Chawla & Marlatt, 2011). If you are working with clients who have unhealthy substance use problems, this book is highly recommended. An online search of "SOBER breathing" will provide many examples of this approach. If you prefer the video version of this approach, search "Mindfulness-based relapse prevention " on www.YouTube.com. Unless you are an experienced clinician in the use of mindfulness with addictions, training in mindfulness-based relapse prevention is recommended and can be found at http://www.mindfulrp.com.

Mindful Breathing Summary

Probably the best known mindful breathing clinician and teacher is Jon Kabat-Zinn, the developer of Mindfulness-based Stress Reduction. This treatment approach has a solid evidence base extending back over its 20+ years of development (Kabat-Zinn, 1991). This guided meditation on the breath helps clients learn to simply be and to look within themselves. It shifts the client out of the usual mode of doing and into simply being. A short description follows.

Sitting in an erect posture, either on a straight back chair or on a cushion. As you allow your body to become still, bring your attention to the fact that you are breathing. Become aware of the movement of your breath as it comes into your body and as it leaves your body. Not manipulating the breath in any way or trying to change it. Simply being aware of it and of the feelings associated with breathing. And observing the breath deep down in your belly. Feeling the abdomen as it expands gently on the in-breath, and as it falls back towards your spine on the out-breath. Being totally here in each moment with each breath. Not trying to do anything, not trying to get any place, simply being with your breath. Giving full care and attention to each in-breath and to each out-breath. As they follow one after the other in a never ending cycle and flow. You will find that from time to time your mind will wander off into thoughts. When you notice that your attention is no longer here and no longer with your breathing, and without judging yourself, bring your attention back to your breathing and ride the waves of your breathing, fully conscious of the duration of each breath from moment to moment. Every time you find your mind wandering off the breath, gently bringing it back to the present, back to the moment-to-moment observing of the flow of your breathing. Using your breath as an anchor to focus your attention, to bring you back to the present whenever you notice that your mind is becoming absorbed or reactive. Using your breath to help you tune into a state of relaxed awareness and stillness.

Note: The above snippet is from an online script from http://mindfulnesshamilton.ca/meditation-scripts retrieved on 3/26/16 (source unidentified). An online search of "mindfulness breathing script" or "Jon Kabat Zinn scripts" will provide many scripts and examples of this approach. If you prefer the video version of this intervention, search "Jon Kabat Zinn the breathing space" on www.YouTube.com.Unless you are an experienced clinician in the use of mindfulness with stress reactive behavior, training in mindfulness-based stress reduction is recommended and can be found at http://www.umassmed.edu/cfm/stress-reduction. Additional, free resources can be found at www.palousemindfulness.org.

Urge Surfing Summary

Urge Surfing is an emotional accommodation/urge reduction intervention utilized in Mindfulness-based Relapse Prevention (e.g., Bowen, Chawla & Marlatt 2011; Bowen & Marlatt, 2009) and Dialectical Behavior Therapy (e.g., Gratz & Chapman, 2009). Urge Surfing is best done in a quiet place relatively free from distractions and interruptions. Some versions take client ratings on severity of the urge, confidence in managing the urge or desire to act on the urge before and after the exercise. A short description follows.

Sit in a comfortable position. Then, imagine that you're sitting a surfboard floating in the ocean in a warm, tropical place. You can see the white, sandy shore in front of you, there's a slight breeze and you can smell the salt of the ocean. Imagine that your unwanted mood or harmful urge is the ocean wave that that you have decided to paddle onto and are now riding. Use your breath to steady yourself on your surfboard. Your goal is to ride the emotional wave from its beginning as it grows, staying right with it, through its peak. Imagine that you're surfing the mood or urge wave, riding it rather than giving into it and being wiped out by it. Really notice what the mood or urge feels like in your body. Imagine that you're an excellent surfer who can handle any wave that comes your way. As the mood or urge gets stronger and stronger and the wave gets higher and higher until it crests, imagine that you're riding the wave to shore. When it starts to build again, imagine that you're back out there on the wave, just riding it. Notice how you can simply stay present with the wave of emotion instead of immediately acting on it, reacting to it, fighting it or trying to make it go away. Accept that like ocean waves, moods and urges always pass. When you feel that it has subsided, gently let go of your surfing scenario and bring you attention back to where you are, taking a deep breath or moving your body to pick up your mental surf board and move on.

Note: To decrease the danger to others, individuals with severely harmful behavior should not remain in high risk situations to practice urge surfing. Simply put, a compulsive overeater remaining in an all-you-can-eat buffet to practice craving tolerance (e.g., "urge surfing")[1] does not present a danger to others but a compulsive child molester remaining in an amusement park for the same practice does present a danger to others. As the severity of the unhealthy, harmful behavior increases, the focus on planning to avoid high risk situations for relapse needs to increase.

The above Mindfulness-based Relapse Prevention snippet was retrieved on 3/26/16 from http://www.selfgrowth.com/articles/ Freedom_from_Self-Harm_Urge_Surfing_-_A_Mindfulness_Skill_to_Cope_with_Urges.html. An online search of "Urge Surfing" will provide many scripts and examples of this approach. Unless you are an experienced clinician in the use of mindfulness with addictions, training in Mindfulness-based Relapse Prevention is recommended and can be found at http://www.mindfulrp.com. If you prefer the video version of this approach, go to the Mindfulness-based relapse prevention website (http://www.mindfulrp.com/) and click on Urge Surfing or go to *YouTube at... https://www.youtube.com/watch?v=WrvB7GVj67o.*

Mindfulness Meditation Summary

Mindfulness meditation keeps the clients focus on being mindful of themselves and the environment. The focus is on awareness of sensations and observing thoughts come and go without following them into emotion or action. There are many online scripts and descriptions of this approach, a brief summary follows.

As you allow your body to become still, bring your attention to the fact that you are breathing. Become aware of the movement of your breath as it comes into your body and as it leaves your body. Being totally here in each moment with each breath. Every time you find your mind wandering off the breath, gently bringing it back to the present, back to the moment-to-moment observing of the flow of your breathing. As you maintain awareness of your breathing, see if it is possible to expand the field of your awareness so that it includes a sense of your body as a whole as you sit here. Feeling your body, from head to toe, and becoming aware of all the sensations in your body. Being here with whatever feelings and sensations come up in any moment without judging them, without reacting to them, just being fully here, fully aware of whatever you're experiencing. Now as you sit here once again allowing the field of your awareness to expand. This time, expanding your awareness to include thoughts as they move through your mind. So letting your breathing and sense of your body be in the background and allowing the thinking process itself to be the focus of your awareness. And rather than following individual thoughts and getting involved in the content and going from one thought to the next, simply seeing each thought as it comes up in your mind as a thought and letting the thoughts just come and go as you sit and dwell in stillness, witnessing them and observing them. Whatever they are…just observing them as events in the field of your consciousness…as they come into your awareness and they linger and as they dissolve. Noticing that from moment to moment, new thoughts will come and go. As the meditation ends, you might give yourself credit for having spent this time nourishing yourself in a deep way by dwelling in this state of non-doing, in this state of being. For having intentionally made time for yourself to simply be who you are. As you move back into the world, allow the benefits of this practice to expand into every aspect of your life.

Note: The above snippet is from an online script of mindfulness meditation retrieved on 3/26/16 from http://mindfulnesshamilton.ca/meditation-scripts (source unidentified). An online search of "mindfulness meditation" will provide many scripts and examples of this approach.
If you prefer the video version of this approach, search "Jon Kabat Zinn Mindfulness Meditation" on *YouTube.* Go to the Mindfulness-based relapse prevention website (http://www.mindfulrp.com/) and click on "Brief sitting meditation."

Behavior Incident Report and Accomplishment Award Examples

Transfer of training is said to be best when the training environment is similar to the application environment. Thus, in order to promote positive community adjustment, it is important to "Make the inside of your house (i.e., treatment program) like the outside world." SRT in foster-family based and residential treatment settings employs incident report and accomplishment award slips to provide a behavior awareness guidance system that is similar to the real world. Best practice behavior change programs provide consequences for negative behavior while rewarding positive/prosocial alternatives. The SRT slip system targets negative unhealthy, harmful behavior with Incident Reports while reinforcing positive, prosocial, helpful behavior with Accomplishment awards. Two brief examples are provided below.

Incident Report

Name of person with the problem behavior: _____

Date Observed: _____ **Reported by** (your name): _____

Area of problem behavior (please check): __Honesty; __Trust; __Loyalty; __Concern; __Responsibility; __Self-Awareness; __Self-Control

Severity of violation: __ **Social Interaction Rule Violation** (Inappropriate behavior) __ **Social Organization Rule Violation** (Program, probation or parole rule violation); __ **Social Responsibility Rule Violation** (Illegal behavior or self-control problem with unhealthy, harmful behavior- in sexual, physical, property, substance or trust abuse categories)

Description of the problem behavior: _____

_____

Learning Experience Assigned: _____

_____

Date completed: _____ Staff Signature: _____

Accomplishment Award

Name of person who made the accomplishment: _____

Date achieved: _____ **Reported by** (your name): _____

Area of Accomplishment (please check): __Honesty; __Trust; __Loyalty; __Concern; __Responsibility; __Self-Awareness; __Self-Control

Description of the Accomplishment **behavior:** _____

_____

Date presented in treatment group or family meeting _____

Comments/Reward/Privilege presented _____

Individual Service Plan- Greg
Behavior Report Summary   Total incident reports in past quarter (90 days) = <u>33</u>

Type of Behavior Problem		Problem Severity		Problem Area	
Sexual	0	Program rule violation	19	Honesty	0
Physical	0	Probation/Parole violation	7	Trust	3
Property	0	Legal violation	7	Loyalty	7
Substance	7			Concern	5
Trust/verbal	26			Responsibility	18

Note: Greg went AWOL 17 days after this report. This outcome was consistent with research indicating that over 20 incident reports per quarter is a risk factor for not completing treatment in this foster-family based treatment population (Yokley & Boettner, 1999).

Decisional Balance Group Exercise- Doing the math on drug dealing

1. Engage the group in discussion about "stealing and dealing" and whether it is easier/more profitable than a "real job." Discuss issues involved with drug dealing including...
   - How important is drug dealing for: supporting using drugs; things you can buy; party invitations/peer attention; excitement/street reputation; ability to set your own hours and work when you want?
   - How necessary is dealing drugs to: succeed in life, get what you want and survive in life, make it on your own?
   - How severe will it be to give up dealing?
   - How does drug dealing compare to a legal job in pay, difficulty, risks of arrest/injury?
   - How many have been arrested, robbed, injured as a result of dealing?
   - How much would a legal job have to pay for you to give up dealing?
   - How much money is needed for a person to be happy with what they can buy?
   - What keeps you from working a regular job?
   - How much would you deal if you had a regular job?
2. Make a Decisional Balance flip chart. Brainstorm the benefits of dealing drugs (e.g., fast money, make own hours, attention, no boss) and drawbacks (e.g., always have to watch your back, could get arrested, robbed, shot). List everything that the group discussion generates.
3. With the list up, discuss full time benefits that often go along with legal jobs (vacation, sick time, medical and dental coverage, 401K, stock options, overtime and bonus pay, etc.) and discuss the lack of these benefits when dealing drugs.
4. Ask group members how much they typically would make in a week selling drugs. After several examples are shared, choose one on the higher side as the example to use.
5. Start to "Do the Math" by subtracting the costs to "re-up" (resupply) along with costs of own personal drugs use.
6. Ask how many hours a day are typically spent in dealing and dealing related activities. Include "on call" time where they have to drop everything to make a sale. Typically, this ends up close to 24 hours a day, but take a conservative estimate for the example.
7. Divide the weekly profits from the weekly hours worked to determine the hourly wage.
8. Get a group consensus/average on how much time they have been incarcerated due to dealing related issues (drug possession, curfew violation, probation violation, etc., not just drug trafficking). Then ask how long they have been dealing all together. Determine the percentage of time they have lost due to being incarcerated and take off that percentage from the hourly wage. Compare it to the wages of full time work. The result will almost always be significantly less than minimum wage. In cases where dealing pays higher than minimum wage, it is almost always less than the amount they said that a legal job would have to pay for them to give up dealing and less than the amount they said they would need to be happy with what they could buy.
9. Discuss jobs that allow you to set your own hours, have no boss, make as much as you want through commissions, etc.
10. Review the issues involved with drug dealing covered in step #1 to reinforce the fact that working a legal job is more beneficial not only in pay but other important issues.

Note: Stephen Kerestes adapted this group "Do the Math" exercise from their original individual therapy format. Individual therapy examples are provided in Appendix H of Yokley (2012).

Notes

Chapter 1

1. Evidence-based practice in psychology (EBPP) is the integration of the best available research with clinical expertise in the context of patient characteristics, culture, and preferences (APA Task Force on Evidence Based Practice, 2006, p. 273).
2. Closed Channel- In a "channel" of communication, a clear two-way passage is mandatory. An open channel has three components: disclosure, receptivity, and self-criticism. For a channel to be open, *both* parties must be open and receptive. In addition, a constructive self-critical attitude enhances each person's functioning. A closed channel is secretive, closed minded and self-righteous. A closed channel present formidable barriers in the change process. An open channel is fundamental to the change process. Without it, change is impossible. **Source:** Thinking Errors Characteristic of the Criminal: II. Automatic Errors of Thinking. Chapter 5 in The Criminal Personality (Yochelson & Samenow, 1976).
3. See "The Importance of Structured Discovery p. 218 and p. 3 in Yokley, 2010b for further description.
4. See p. 27- 47 in Yokley 2008 for further information.
5. For a more detailed description, see Table 1.1, p.7 in Yokley (2008) or Table 1, p. in Yokley 2010b; 2011; 2012.
6. Further description is provided on p. 67- 70 and 93- 99 along with Table 3.5 in Yokley (2008) with clinical application on p. 43, 53- 68 in Yokley (2010b) and p. 37- 44 in Yokley (2012).
7. Instructions for situation, response, analysis and copies of the Situation Response Analysis Log are provided in Appendix D of Yokley (2010b; 2011; 2012).
8. Further description is provided on p. 121- 125 in Yokley (2008) with clinical application on p. 143- 159 in Yokley (2012)
9. The Problem Development Triad is depicted in Figure 2.1, p. 58 of Yokley (2008) and reproduced with permission in Figure 1, p.8 (Yokley, 2010b; 2011; 2012). Described in Chapter 2 of Yokley (2008) with clinical workbook application in Yokley (2010b; 2011; 2012)
10. For further information see "Multicultural values in Social Responsibility Therapy" (p. 31- 39 in Yokley, 2008) and "Top Three Social Responsibilities in Social Responsibility Therapy (p. 49- 52 in Yokley, 2008).
11. Retrieved from Top 101 cities with the highest number of police officers in 2006 per 1000 residents (population 50,000+). http://www.city-data.com/top2/c423.html
12. Low frustration tolerance has been associated with anger and hostility in youth (Mahon et. al., 2006) which is the fuel for justifying unhealthy, harmful behavior. Albert Ellis has pointed to low frustration tolerance as an important factor underlying substance abuse and other self-defeating behavior (e.g., Ellis & Dryden, 1997). The very serious problem of immediate gratification or PIG that wants what it wants when it wants it is a concept from relapse prevention developed by G. Alan Marlatt and is dealt with by viewing the PIG craving/urge as separate from self in order to look at it and recognize that once you feed the PIG, it will want more and the more you will have to feed it (Marlatt, 1989).
13. For further information see "Self-defeating Exaggerated Needs", p. 123- 125 in Yokley (2008).
14. See "Tolerance Training" section in De Leon (1990-91).
15. For further information see "Justifying actions", p. 104 in Yokley (2010b), p. 124 in Yokley (2011) or p. 198- 199 in Yokley (2012).
16. See p. 31- 39 in Yokley (2008) for complete description.
17. See p. 25- 26 in Yokley (2008) for further information.
18. Renowned Social Psychologist researcher on self-control, need to belong, human sexuality, free will and self-defeating behavior.
19. 1899 March 6, The Johnstown Daily Republican, (Freestanding quotation), Quote Page 7, Johnstown, New York. (Old Fulton).

Chapter 2

1. "Give me liberty, or give me death!" a quotation attributed to Patrick Henry from his speech to the Virginia Convention in 1775 urging them to join the Revolutionary War.
2. The Harmful Behavior Continuum is described in Yokley (2008) on p. 6- 8 and illustrated in Table 1.1.

Notes

3. "Keep Your Eyes on the Prize" was originally the title to a folk song that became influential during American civil rights movement of the 1950's and 1960's often attributed to Alice Wine from Johns Island, South Carolina.

Chapter 3
1. The "Diversity within unity" project was developed and advocated by renowned sociologist, Brookings Institution Scholar and Senior White House advisor Amitai Etzioni (2001) with funding from The Atlantic Foundation, the Robert Bosch Stiftung, and the Carnegie Corporation of New York.
2. Yokley, J. (2009, August). Multicultural Recognition in Treatment Program Design: Another Path to Explore. 117th Annual Convention of the American Psychological Association, Toronto, Ontario, Canada. Division 45- Society for the Psychological Study of Ethnic Minority Issues.
3. Behavioral addictions that indirectly affect the neurotransmitter systems of the brain can serve as reinforcers comparable to chemical substances that directly affect these systems (Alvi, et. al. 2012).

Chapter 4
1. See Footnote 1, Chapter 1.

Chapter 5
1. Rational Emotive Behavior Therapy(REBT) is structured for clients to discover (A) Activating events, (B) irrational Beliefs, (C) emotional Consequences, (D) Disputing irrational beliefs, and (E) Effective response substitution. The ABC's of REBT where our emotional and behavioral responses (C) to activating events lie our beliefs (B) about these activating events (A) has been summarized by Dryden (2003) as "people are disturbed not by things, but by their irrational beliefs about things." REBT which was developed by Dr. Albert Ellis and originally described in "A New Guide to Rational Living" (Ellis and Harper, 1975), has been applied to many common psychological problems (e.g., Yankura and Dryden, 1997). The advantages of integrating REBT into unhealthy, harmful behavior treatment are well worth the time spent in training at the Albert Ellis Institute (www. rebt.org). Therapists who are trained in REBT can easily blend it into SRT by teaching clients to identify social maturity problems (e.g., problems with honesty, concern, and responsibility) as irrational belief consequences and to use socially mature responses (e.g., honesty, concern, and responsibility) as their effective responses (the "E" portion of the ABCDE model). On p. 83.
2. "You have to stop musturbating and shoulding all over yourself" is a saying by Dr. Albert Ellis that addicts like to use to help them identify self-statements with "should" and "must" in them that enable relapse. On p. 86.
3. Source: Adapted from, "Emotional Accommodation", p. 23- 24, in Yokley (2011). Emotional accommodation through acceptance and mindfulness may be more useful than "the ABC's of letting feelings go" in helping clients overcome grief without worrying that that they are letting go of their loved ones.

Chapter 6
1. See Prochaska, J., Velicer, W., Rossi, J. et. al. (1994).
2. Practicing going to the opposite extreme of negative attitudes and irresponsible behaviors by modeling positive attitudes and responsible behaviors is a key therapeutic community training method for positive change towards " right living" (Chapter 5, DeLeon, 2000) dating back to the early therapeutic community development period in the United States (1958- 1971). "You have to go to the opposite extreme [in treatment through the primary values of right living] to meet the median [after treatment]" is a time honored therapeutic community recovery maxim from Second Genesis founded in 1970 by Psychiatrist Sidney Shankman and evaluated by Nemes, Wish, Messina, (1999).
3. "Not to make a decision, is to make a decision." This insight was pointed out by Harvard Medical School professor and philosopher William James (1842- 1910). Often referred to as the father of American psychology, James stated, "When you have to make a choice and don't make it, that is in itself a choice." Thus, not to make a decision to "Get out" of a high-risk situation for relapse, is to make a decision to set yourself up for relapse.

Notes

Chapter 7

1. Adapted from, "You are either part of the solution or part of the problem", by Eldridge Cleaver, This American writer and political activist, wrote the book "Soul on Ice" while in prison and became an early Black Panther Party leader after his release. In the book "Soul on Ice", Cleaver is honest about his sexual offenses and the irresponsible thinking that enabled his felony crimes.
2. "The simple man concept" is a term coined by Eve Wolf, Ph.D., Wright State University School of Professional Psychology Associate Dean for Academic Affairs and eating disorders treatment expert. This concept applies the scientific principle of parsimony (i.e., that one should always choose the simplest explanation of a phenomenon, that requires the fewest leaps of logic, AKA Occam's Razor) to human behavior motivation.
3. To "side with the negative" and take up the negative voice in the discussion is a Motivational Interviewing strategy for eliciting positive change talk from the client (Miller & Rollnick, 2013). For example, "Perhaps [the unhealthy, harmful behavior or entering a high-risk situation that could trigger the behavior] is so important to you that you won't give it up, no matter what the cost." If your client is ambivalent, when you take the negative (status quo) side of the argument, it can evoke a "Yes, but..." from the client, who then expresses the other (positive) side.

Chapter 8

1. Crime Stoppers of Houston has operated the famed tip line, 713-222-TIPS since1981. Known as a world leader in crime prevention, the Crime Stoppers of Houston tip line program has paid over $10 million in cash rewards, solved over 33,000 felony cases, and arrested nearly 25,000 felony fugitives. The tip Line is open 24 hours a day, seven days a week, and receives over 6,500 tips per year. Crime Stoppers publicizes crimes and offers cash rewards up to $5,000 for information leading to the charging or arrest of felony suspects to anonymous citizens who provide tips through the Tip Line Program. See 2015 Crime Stoppers Annual Report at http://crime-stoppers.org/media/123930/Crime-Stoppers-Annual-Report-2015.pdf, retrieved 9/10/16.
2. A description of grandiosity with case examples is provided on p. 115- 118 in Yokley, 2008 and workbook exercises are provided on p. 115- 126, Yokley, 2012.
3. Testing self-control by entering a high-risk situation for unhealthy, harmful behavior relapse has been an observed immediate antecedent to eating, drinking, gambling and substance abuse problem relapse (e.g., Marlatt, 1985; Schonfeld, et al., 1989; Waters, Hill & Waller, 2001).
4. A typical example was a report from a female student attending a Delta Tau Delta fraternity party who was drinking, went to the house to look for a bathroom and found herself in a room with an unknown male having sex with her, despite her telling him "no" repeatedly and trying to push him away (Schmidt 2016).
5. Campus rape has been documented in the film "The Hunting Ground" which premiered at the 2015 Sundance Film Festival and aired on CNN (edited version) on November 22, 2015. The film focuses on two former University of North Carolina at Chapel Hill students who filed a Title IX complaint against the university in response to their rapes while enrolled. The use of Title IX in campus sexual assault cases became a model for universities across the country. See http://thehuntinggroundfilm.com/.
6. A good example is the Frontline news coverage of a young female Air Force recruit that provides a description of how sexual assault is kept secret through culture of retaliation against those who come forward (Childress, 2015).
7. Military sexual assault has been documented in the film "Invisible War" which premiered at the 2012 Sundance Film Festival. The film provides narratives of the survivors which reveal a cover up culture of secrecy including lack of recourse to an impartial justice system, retaliation against survivors, the absence of adequate survivor's emotional and physical care, forced expulsion of survivors from service in contrast with the unjust career advancement of perpetrators. See http://invisiblewarmovie.com/index.php

8. The unhealthy eating enabling environment of fast food restaurants was documented in the 2004 documentary film "Supersize Me" in which the subject of the documentary ate only McDonalds food. Frequenting this enabling environment for 30 consecutive days resulted in a 24 pound weight gain, increased cholesterol to an unhealthy level, mood swings and sexual dysfunction. See https://www.amazon.com/Super-Size-DVD-John-Banzhaf/dp/B0002OXVBO
9. According to Holland America spokesman John Primeau, the typical cruise passenger gains about one pound a day on a 7- 10 day cruise (http://www.cnn.com/2010/TRAVEL/08/26/healthy.cruises/, Retrieved 9/5/16).
10. References for recovery maxims include Bassin (1984), Center for substance abuse treatment (2006), Resource sheet #1-1, page PM 1- 4 and DeLeon (2000), p. 79- 83.
11. "Act as if" is a positive behavior change method used in the Therapeutic Community model in the United States since the 1960's. However, the notion that continuing to "Act as if" will eventually result in adopting the imitated trait, skill or behavior can be traced back to William James in the 1800's. "We need only in cold blood 'act as if' the thing in question were real, and keep acting as if it were real, and it will infallibly end by growing into such a connection with our life that it will become real" -- William James (1842- 1910).

Chapter 10

1. Chapter 10 has a key question to be processed with clients and answered in each link of the Risk Factor Chain that set the occasion for unhealthy, harmful behavior. The Clinician's Guide instructions in Chapter 10 for using the SRT Understanding Harmful Behavior workbooks in group therapy sessions has two sets of instructions. One is for using the SRT workbooks and the other is for group topic processing of each key risk factor question without workbook support or assignments. This is needed for groups where the reading level is low and there is no available staff time to help clients process workbook material and complete their workbook assignments.

While understanding how unhealthy, harmful behavior was acquired, maintained and generalized through The Problem Development Tried can be implemented without SRT workbook support, having clients complete workbook assignments has five basic treatment benefits: 1) Personal time investment in their treatment; 2) Increased honesty- Writing is usually less threatening than open verbal disclosure; 3) Preparation- "We do our best when we are prepared and our worst when caught off guard"- In settings where there is no staff time to provide individual sessions to process the topics that will be covered in group (i.e., get clients ready to disclose difficult issues), the workbook covers that material and helps prepare them; 4) Reinforcing the learning experience- Going over important treatment issues twice (once in workbooks and once in group) reinforces learning and in residential/correctional settings; 5) Channeling emotional energy- "Idle hands are the devils workshop"- Staying busy and channeling emotional energy into working on treatment assignments (own issues) helps avoid getting pulled into unnecessary residential setting drama (others issues) which if too frequent or too intense can block discharge.

References

Abel, G.G., Jordan, A., Rouleau, J.L., Emerick, R., Barboza-Whitehead, S. & Osborn, C. (2004). Use of Visual Reaction Time to assess male adolescents who molest children. Sexual Abuse: A Journal of Research and Treatment, Vol. 16, No. 3, 255-265.

Abraham, S. F. & Beumont, P. J. V. (1982). How patients describe bulimia or binge eating. *Psychological Medicine, 12,* 625-635.

Ahlmeyer, S., Kleinsasser, D., Stoner, J., & Retzlaff, P. (2003). Psychopathology of incarcerated sex offenders. *Journal of Personality Disorders, 17*(4), 306-318.

Akers, R. L., & Jensen, G. F. (2006). The Empirical Status of Social Learning Theory of Crime and Deviance: The Past, Present, and Future. In F. T. Cullen, J. P. Wright, & K. R. Blevins (Eds.), *Advances in criminological theory: Vol. 15. Taking stock: The status of criminological theory* (pp. 37-76). Piscataway, NJ: Transaction.

Akers, R. L., la Greca, A. J., Cochran, J., & Sellers, C. (1989). Social learning theory and alcohol behavior among the elderly. *The Sociological Quarterly, 30*(4), 625-638.

Akers, R. L., & Lee, G. (1996). A longitudinal test of social learning theory: Adolescent smoking. *Journal of Drug Issues, 26*(2), 317-343.

Akiba, D. & Klug, W. (1999). The different and the same: Reexamining east and west in a cross-cultural analysis of values. *Social Behavior & Personality,* 27(5), 467-473.

Alberts, H. J.E.M., Martijn, C., & de Vries, N. K. (2011). Fighting self-control failure: Overcoming ego depletion by increasing self-awareness. *Journal of Experimental Social Psychology, 47*(1), 58-62.

Ali, B., Seitz-Brown, C. J., & Daughters, S. B. (2015). The interacting effect of depressive symptoms, gender, and distress tolerance on substance use problems among residential treatment-seeking substance users. *Drug and Alcohol Dependence, 148,* 21-26.

Alavi, S., Ferdosi, M., Jannatifard, F. et. al. (2012). Behavioral Addiction versus Substance Addiction: Correspondence of Psychiatric and Psychological Views, *International Journal of Preventive Medicine,* 3(4): 290–294.

Anderson, C. (2003). Evolving Out of Violence: An Application of the Transtheoretical Model of Behavioral Change. *Research and Theory for Nursing Practice: An International Journal,* 17, 225-240.

Andrews, D. A., Zinger, I., Hoge, R. D., Bonta, J., Gendreau, P., & Cullen, F. T. (1990). Does correctional treatment work? A clinically relevant and psychologically informed meta-analysis. *Criminology, 28,* 369–404.

Angelillo, J. C. (2001). Rational-emotive behavioral therapy in the treatment of pathological gambling. In L. VandeCreek & T. L. Jackson (Eds.), *Innovations in clinical practice: A source book,* Vol. 19, pp. 141-158). Sarasota, FL: Professional Resource Press/Professional Resource Exchange.

APA Task Force- American Psychological Association, Presidential Task Force on Evidence-Based Practice (2006). Evidence-based practice in psychology. *American Psychologist, 61*(4), 271-285.

Aquino, K., & Reed, A. II, (2002). The self-importance of moral identity. *Journal of Personality and Social Psychology,* 83, 1423–1440.

Armitage, C. J., Wright, C. L., Parfitt, G., Pegington, M., Donnelly, L. S., & Harvie, M. N. (2014). Self efficacy for temptations is a better predictor of weight loss than motivation and global self-efficacy: Evidence from two prospective studies among overweight/obese women at high risk of breast cancer. *Patient Education and Counseling, 95*(2), 254-258.

A-Tjak, J. G. L., Davis, M. L., Morina, N., Powers, M. B., Smits, J. A. J., & Emmelkamp, P. M. G. (2015). A meta-analysis of the efficacy of acceptance and commitment therapy for clinically relevant mental and physical health problems. *Psychotherapy and Psychosomatics, 84*(1), 30-36.

Babcock, J. C., Canady, B. E., Senior, A., Eckhardt, C. I. (2005). Applying the Transtheoretical Model to Female and Male Perpetrators of Intimate Partner Violence: Gender Differences in Stages and Processes of Change. *Violence and Victims,* 20, 235-250.

Baker, T. B., Piper, M. E., McCarthy, D. E., Majeskie, M. R., Fiore, M. C. (2004) Addiction motivation reformulated: An affective processing model of negative reinforcement. -Psychological Review 111: 33-51.

Baldacci, A. N., Hoffman, E. M., Lejuez, C. W., & Koenen, K. C. (2014). The impact of childhood abuse on inpatient substance users: Specific links with risky sex, aggression, and emotion dysregulation. *Child Abuse & Neglect, 38*(5), 928-938.

Bandura, A. (1962). Social learning through imitation. In M. R. Jones (Ed.), *Nebraska Symposium on Motivation, 1962* (pp. 211-274). Oxford, England: Univer. Nebraska Press.

References

Bandura, A. (1973). *Aggression: A Social Learning Analysis*. Englewood Cliffs, NJ: Prentice-Hall.

Bandura, A. (1977). Self-efficacy: Toward a unifying theory of behavior change. *Psychological Review*, 84, 191-215.

Bandura, Albert (1977b). *Social Learning Theory. Oxford, England: Prentice-Hall.*

Bandura, Albert (1982). Self-efficacy mechanism in human agency. *American Psychologist.* 37 (2): 122–147.

Bandura, A. (1993). Perceived self-efficacy in cognitive development and functioning. *Educational Psychologist*, 28, 117-148.

Bandura, A. (2001). Social cognitive theory: An agentic perspective. *Annual Review of Psychology*, 52, 1-26.

Banks, D., & Gottfredson, D. C. (2003). The effects of drug treatment and supervision on time to rearrest among drug treatment court participants. *Journal of Drug Issues, 33*(2), 385-412.

Bardhoshi, G., Duncan, K., & Erford, B. T. (2016). Psychometric meta-analysis of the English version of the Beck Anxiety Inventory. *Journal of Counseling & Development, 94*(3), 356-373.

Baron, S. W. (2003). Self-Control, Social Consequences, And Criminal Behavior: Street Youth And The General Theory Of Crime. *Journal of Research in Crime and Delinquency*, 40, 403-425.

Baskaran, A., Cha, D. S., Powell, A. M., Jalil, D., & McIntyre, R. S. (2014). Sex differences in rates of obesity in bipolar disorder: Postulated mechanisms. *Bipolar Disorders, 16*(1), 83-92.

Bassin, A. (1984). Proverbs, slogans and folk sayings in the therapeutic community: A neglected therapeutic tool. *Journal of Psychoactive Drugs, 16*(1), 51-56.

Bates, M and Labouvie, E. (1995). Personality-environment constellations and alcohol use: A process-oriented study of intraindividual change during adolescence, *Psychology of Addictive Behaviors*, 9(1), 23-35.

Basu, A., Paltiel, A. D., & Pollack, H. A. (2008). Social costs of robbery and the cost-effectiveness of substance abuse treatment. *Health Economics, 17*, 927-946.

Baumeister, R. F., Bratslavsky, E., Muraven, M., & Tice, D. M. (1998). Ego-depletion: Is the active self a limited resource? *Journal of Personality and Social Psychology, 74,* 1252–1265.

Baumeister, R. F., Heatherton, T. F., & Tice, D. M. (1994). *Losing control: How and why people fail at self-regulation.* San Jamar, CA: Academic Press.

Baumeister, R. F., & Vonasch, A. J. (2014). Uses of self-regulation to facilitate and restrain addictive behavior. *Addictive Behaviors.* Advance online publication.

Becker, J. V., Kaplan, M. S., Tenke, C. E., & Tartaglini, A. (1991). The incidence of depressive symptomatology in juvenile sex offenders with a history of abuse. *Child Abuse & Neglect, 15*(4), 531-536.

Beck, A. T., Rush, A. J., Shaw, B. F., and Emery, G. (1979). *Cognitive Therapy of Depression.* New York: Guilford Press.

Becker, J. V., & Stein, R. M. (1991). Is sexual erotica associated with sexual deviance in adolescent males? *International Journal of Law and Psychiatry, 14*(1-2), 85-95

Becker-Weidman, E. G., Jacobs, R. H., Reinecke, M. A., Silva, S. G., & March, J. S. (2010). Social problem-solving among adolescents treated for depression. *Behaviour Research and Therapy, 48(1),* 11-18.

Bell, A. C., & D'Zurilla, T. J. (2009). Problem-solving therapy for depression: A meta-analysis. *Clinical Psychology Review, 29*(4), 348-353.

Bellack, A. S., Rozensky, R., & Schwartz, J. (1974). A comparison of two forms of self-monitoring in a behavioral weight reduction program. Behavior Therapy, 5, 523- 530.

Benishek, L. A., Dugosh, K. L., Kirby, K. C., Matejkowski, J., Clements, N. T., Seymour, B. L., & Festinger, D. S. (2014). Prize-based contingency management for the treatment of substance abusers: A meta-analysis. *Addiction, 109*(9), 1426-1436.

Berne, Eric (1964). *Games People Play- The Basic Hand Book of Transactional Analysis.* New York: Ballantine Books.

Bertz, F., Pacanowski, C. R., & Levitsky, D. A. (2015). Frequent self-weighing with electronic graphic feedback to prevent age-related weight gain in young adults. *Obesity, 23*(10), 2009-2014.

Bevelander, K. E., Anschütz, D. J., & Engels, R. C. M. E. (2011). Social modeling of food purchases at supermarkets in teenage girls. Appetite, 57(1), 99-104.

Biase, D. V., and Sullivan, A. P. (1986). Emerging cross-cultural therapeutic community research. *Journal of Psychoactive Drugs, 18*, 199-201.

Bishop, F. M. (2000). Helping clients manage addictions with REBT. *Journal of Rational-Emotive & Cognitive-Behavior Therapy, 18*(3), 127-151.

References

Bishop, S.R., Lau, M., Shapiro, S., Carlson, L., et al. (2004). "Mindfulness: A Proposed Operational Definition", *Clinical Psychology Science & Practice.* 11, 230–241.

Bingham, R. P., Porché-Burke, L., James, S., Sue, D. W., and Vasquez, M. J. T. (2002). Introduction: A report on the National Multicultural Conference and Summit II. Cultural Diversity and Ethnic Minority Psychology, 8, 75-87.

Black, D. W., Shaw, M., McCormick, B., & Allen, J. (2013). Pathological gambling: Relationship to obesity, self-reported chronic medical conditions, poor lifestyle choices, and impaired quality of life. *Comprehensive Psychiatry, 54*(2), 97-104.

Black, D. W., Shaw, M. C., McCormick, B. A., & Alien, J. (2012). Marital status, childhood maltreatment, and family dysfunction: A controlled study of pathological gambling. *Journal of Clinical Psychiatry, 73*(10), 1293-1297.

Blow, A., & Hartnett, K. (2005). Infidelity in committed relationships II: A substantive review. *Journal of Marital and Family Therapy*, 31, 217–233.

Boeringer, S. B., Shehan, C. L., & Akers, R. L. (1991). Social contexts and social learning in sexual coercion and aggression: Assessing the contribution of fraternity membership. *Family Relations: An Interdisciplinary Journal of Applied Family Studies, 40*(1), 58-64.

Bolton, J. M., Robinson, J., & Sareen, J. (2009). Self-medication of mood disorders with alcohol and drugs in the National Epidemiologic Survey on Alcohol and Related Conditions. *Journal of Affective Disorders, 115*(3), 367-375.

Bonta, J., Bourgon, G., Rugge, T., Scott, T.-L., Yessine, A. K., Gutierrez, L., & Li, J. (2011). An experimental demonstration of training probation officers in evidence-based community supervision. *Criminal Justice and Behavior, 38*(11), 1127-1148.

Bornovalova, M. A., Gratz, K. L., Daughters, S. B., Hunt, E. D., & Lejuez, C. W. (2012). Initial RCT of a distress tolerance treatment for individuals with substance use disorders. *Drug and Alcohol Dependence, 122*, 70–76.

Bond, M. (1988). Finding universal dimensions of individual variation in multicultural studies of values: The Rokeach and Chinese Value Surveys, *Journal of Personality and Social Psychology*, 55(6), 1009-1015.

Boswell, A. A., & Spade, J. Z. (1996). Fraternities and collegiate rape culture: Why are some fraternities more dangerous places for women? *Gender & Society, 10*(2), 133-147.

Boswell, G., and Wedge, P. (2003). A pilot evaluation of a therapeutic community for adolescent male sexual abusers. *Therapeutic Communities: International Journal for Therapeutic and Supportive Organizations*, 24, 259- 276.

Botterill, E., Gill, P. R., McLaren, S., & Gomez, R. (2016). Marital status and problem gambling among Australian older adults: The mediating role of loneliness. *Journal of Gambling Studies, 32*(3), 1027-1038.

Bowen, S., Chawla, N., & Marlatt, G. A. (2011). Mindfulness-based relapse prevention for addictive behaviors: A clinician's guide. New York: Guilford Press.

Bowen S, Marlatt A (2009). Surfing the urge: brief mindfulness-based intervention for college student smokers. *Psychol Addict Behav*, 23(4):666-71.

Bowen, S., Witkiewitz, K., Clifasefi, S. L., Grow, J., Chawla, N., Hsu, S. H., . . . Larimer, M. E. (2014). Relative efficacy of mindfulness-based relapse prevention, standard relapse prevention, and treatment as usual for substance use disorders: A randomized clinical trial. *JAMA Psychiatry, 71*(5), 547-556.

Boxer, P. (2011). Negative peer involvement in multisystemic therapy for the treatment of youth problem behavior: Exploring outcome and process variables in "real-world" practice. Journal of Clinical Child and Adolescent Psychology, 40(6), 848-854.

Braden, A., Flatt, S. W., Boutelle, K. N., Strong, D., Sherwood, N. E., & Rock, C. L. (2016). Emotional eating is associated with weight loss success among adults enrolled in a weight loss program. *Journal of Behavioral Medicine, 39*(4), 727-732.

Bradizza, C. M., & Stasiewicz, P. R. (2003). Qualitative analysis of high-risk and alcohol use situations among severely mentally ill substance abusers. *Addictive Behaviors, 28*(1), 157-169.

Brasfield, H., Febres, J., Shorey, R., Strong, D., Ninnemann, A., Elmquist, J., . . . Stuart, G. L. (2012). Male batterers' alcohol use and gambling behavior. *Journal of Gambling Studies, 28*(1), 77-88.

Braun, S. I., Bischof, G., & Rumpf, H.-J. (2012). Development and validation of the Decisional Balance Scale for problematic prescription drug use (DBS-PD)-20. *Addictive Behaviors, 37*(4), 444-448.

References

Brown, W. M., Consedine, N. S., & Magai, C. (2005). Altruism relates to health in an ethnically diverse sample of older adults. *The Journals of Gerontology: Series B: Psychological Sciences & Social Sciences, 60*(3), 143-152.

Brownell, K. D., Marlatt, G. A., Lichtenstein, E., & Wilson, G. T. (1986). Understanding and preventing relapse. *American Psychologist, 41*(7), 765-782.

Brownell, K. D., & Wadden, T. A. (1992). Etiology and treatment of obesity: Understanding a serious, prevalent, and refractory disorder. *Journal of Consulting and Clinical Psychology, 60*(4), 505-517.

Burke, J. G., Gielen, A. C., McDonnell, K. A., O'Campo, P., Maman, S. (2001). The process of ending abuse in intimate relationships: A qualitative exploration of the transtheoretical model. Violence Against Women, 7, 1144-1163.

Burnett, A., Mattern, J. L., Herakova, L. L., Kahl, D. H., Jr., Tobola, C., & Bornsen, S. E. (2009). Communicating/muting date rape: A co-cultural theoretical analysis of communication factors related to rape culture on a college campus. *Journal of Applied Communication Research, 37*(4), 465-485.

Burns, D. (1980). *Feeling Good: The New Mood Therapy.* Avon Books: New York.

Burton, D. (2008, October). Trauma and subsequent nonsexual criminality amongst juvenile sexual offenders and nonsexual offending incarcerated youth. 27th Annual Research and Treatment Conference of the Association for the Treatment of Sexual Abusers, Atlanta, Georgia.

Burton, D. L., Miller, D. L., & Shill, C. T. (2002). A social learning theory comparison of the sexual victimization of adolescent sexual offenders & nonsexual offending male delinquents. *Child Abuse & Neglect*, 26(9), 893-907.

Burton, V. S. Jr., Evans, T. D., Cullen, F. T., Olivares, K. M., & Dunaway, R. G. (1999). Age, self-control, and adults' offending behaviors: A research note assessing A General Theory of Crime. *Journal of Criminal Justice*, 27, 45-54.

Buttars, A., Huss, M. T., & Brack, C. (2016). An analysis of an intensive supervision program for sex offenders using propensity scores. *Journal of Offender Rehabilitation, 55*(1), 51-68.

Byrne, S. M. (2002). Psychological aspects of weight maintenance and relapse in obesity. *Journal of Psychosomatic Research, 53*(5), 1029-1036.

Byrne, S., Barry, D., & Petry, N. M. (2012). Predictors of weight loss success. Exercise vs. dietary self-efficacy and treatment attendance. *Appetite, 58*(2), 695-698.

Byrne, S., Cooper, Z., & Fairburn, C. (2003). Weight maintenance and relapse in obesity: A qualitative study. *International Journal of Obesity, 27*(8), 955-962.

Campbell, C., Onifade, E., Barnes, A., Peterson, J., Anderson, V., Davidson, W., & Gordon, D. (2014). Screening offenders: The exploration of a Youth Level of Service/Case Management Inventory (YLS/CMI) Brief Screener. *Journal of Offender Rehabilitation, 53*(1), 19-34.

Carey, M. (2011). Probation. In C. Leukefeld, T. P. Gullotta, J. Gregrich (Eds.) & J. M. Ramos (Collaborator), *Issues in children's and families' lives. Handbook of evidence-based substance abuse treatment in criminal justice settings* (pp. 143-171).

Carey, K. B., Durney, S. E., Shepardson, R. L., & Carey, M. P. (2015). Incapacitated and forcible rape of college women: Prevalence across the first year. *Journal of Adolescent Health, 56*(6), 678-680.

Carich, M. S., & Stone, M. H. (2001). Using relapse intervention strategies to treat sexual offenders. *Journal of Individual Psychology*, 57, 26-36.

Carron, A. V., Hausenblas, H. A., & Mack, D. (1996). Social influence and exercise: A meta-analysis. *Journal of Sport & Exercise Psychology, 18*(1), 1-16.

Caselli, G., Canfora, F., Ruggiero, G. M., Sassaroli, S., Albery, I. P., & Spada, M. M. (2015). Desire thinking mediates the relationship between emotional intolerance and problem drinking. *International Journal of Mental Health and Addiction, 13*(2), 185-193.

Cassidy, T. (2009). Bullying and victimisation in school children: The role of social identity, problem-solving style, and family and school context. *Social Psychology of Education*, 12(1), 63-76.

Casswell, S., & Zhang, J.-F. (1997). Access to alcohol from licensed premises during adolescence: A longitudinal study. *Addiction, 92*(6), 737-745.

Cauffman, E., Espelage, D. L., Mazerolle, P., & Piquero, A. (2003). Sex differences in empathy and its relation to juvenile offending. *Violence and Victims*, 18, 503-516.

References

Center for Substance Abuse Treatment (2006). *Therapeutic Community Curriculum: Participant's Manual.* DHHS Publication No. (SMA) 06-4122. Rockville, MD: Substance Abuse and Mental Health Services Administration.

Chang, E. C., D'Zurilla, T. J., & Sanna, L. J. (2004), *Social problem solving: Theory, research, and training.* Washington, DC, US: American Psychological Association. (2004). xvi, 276 pp..

Chang, E. C., D'Zurilla, T. J., & Sanna, L. J. (2009). Social problem solving as a mediator of the link between stress and psychological well-being in middle-adulthood. *Cognitive Therapy and Research, 33(1),* 33-49.

Chase, C., Chin, D., Oppezzo, M. & Schwartz, D. (2009). Teachable Agents and the Protege Effect: Increasing the Effort towards Learning, *Journal of Science Education and Technology,* 18(4), 334-352.

Chassé, F., & Ladouceur, R. (1980). Temporal order of self-monitoring in cigarette smoking. *Psychological Reports, 47*(3, *Pt 2*), 1115-1118.

Chermack, S. T., Roll, J., Reilly, M., Davis, L., Kilaru, U., & Grabowski, J. (2000). Comparison of patient self-reports and urinalysis results obtained under naturalistic methadone treatment conditions. *Drug and Alcohol Dependence, 59*(1), 43-49.

Childress, S. (2015, May 18). How the military retaliates against sexual assault victims, *FRONTLINE* Enterprise Journalism Group. Retrieved from www.pbs.org/wgbh/ frontline/article/how-the-military-retaliates-against-sexual-assault-victims/

Cho, H. (2007). Influences of self-monitoring and goal-setting on drinking refusal self-efficacy and drinking behavior. *Alcoholism Treatment Quarterly, 25*(3), 53-65.

Chu, C. M., Ng, K., Fong, J., & Teoh, J. (2012). Assessing youth who sexually offended: The predictive validity of the ERASOR, J-SOAP-II, and YLS/CMI in a non- Western context. *Sexual Abuse: Journal of Research and Treatment, 24*(2), 153-174.

Christopher, G., & Thomas, M. (2009). Social problem solving in chronic fatigue syndrome: Preliminary findings. *Stress and Health: Journal of the International Society for the Investigation of Stress,* 25(2), 161-169.

Clift, R. J. W., Rajlic, G., & Gretton, H. M. (2009). Discriminative and predictive validity of the penile plethysmograph in adolescent sex offenders. *Sexual Abuse: Journal of Research and Treatment, 21*(3), 335-362.

Coid, J. (1984). Relief of diazepam-withdrawal syndrome by shoplifting. *The British Journal of Psychiatry, 145,* 552-554.

Collins, R. L., & Lapp, W. M. (1991). Restraint and attributions: Evidence of the abstinence violation effect in alcohol consumption. *Cognitive Therapy and Research, 15,* 69-84.

Connors, G. J., & Walitzer, K. S. (2001). Reducing alcohol consumption among heavily drinking women: Evaluating the contributions of life-skills training and booster sessions. *Journal of Consulting and Clinical Psychology, 69*(3), 447-456.

Cooper, J. A., & Tokar, T. (2016). A prospective study on vacation weight gain in adults. *Physiology & Behavior, 156,* 43-47.

Corcoran, J. (2002). The Transtheoretical Stages of Change model and Motivational Interviewing for building maternal supportiveness in cases of sexual abuse. *Journal of Child Sexual Abuse: Research, Treatment, & Program Innovations for Victims, Survivors, & Offenders, 11*(3), 1-17.

Corsica, J. A., & Spring, B. J. (2008). Carbohydrate craving: A double-blind, plecebo-controlled test of the self-medication hypothesis. *Eating Behaviors, 9*(4), 447-454.

Cameron, A. Y., Palm Reed, K., & Gaudiano, B. A. (2014). Addressing treatment motivation in borderline personality disorder: Rationale for incorporating values-based exercises into dialectical behavior therapy. *Journal of Contemporary Psychotherapy, 44*(2), 109-116.

Carbonari, J. P., & DiClemente, C. C. (2000). Using transtheoretical model profiles to differentiate levels of alcohol abstinence success. *Journal of Consulting and Clinical Psychology, 68,* 810–817.

Carano, Alessandro, De Berardis, Domenico, Campanella, Daniela, et. al. (2012). Alexithymia and suicide ideation in a sample of patients with binge eating disorder. *Journal of Psychiatric Practice,* Vol 18(1),   5 11.

Carton, S., Bayard, S., Paget, V., Jouanne, C., Varescon, I., Edel, Y., & Detilleux, M. (2010). Emotional awareness in substance-dependent patients. *Journal of Clinical Psychology, 66*(6), 599-610.

Chapple, C. L. (1999). Testing the boundaries: Dating violence and the general theory of crime. (crime, violence, intimacy, victimization). *Dissertation Abstracts International Section A: Humanities and Social Sciences.* 60(4), 1999, 1337A.

References

Chapple, C. L., & Hope, T. L. (2003). An Analysis of the Self-Control and Criminal Versatility of Gang and Dating Violence Offenders. *Violence and Victims*, 18, 671-690.

Clarke, P. (2002). Therapeutic communities: A model for effective intervention with teenagers known to have perpetrated sexual abuse (Chapter 6, pp. 102-111). In M. Calder (Ed.), Young People Who Sexually Abuse: Building the Evidence Base for Your Practice. Dorset, UK: Russell House Publishing.

Cochran, J. K., Wood, P. B., Sellers, C. S., Wilkerson, W., & Chamlin, M. B. (1998). Academic dishonesty and low self-control: An empirical test of a general theory of crime. *Deviant Behavior*, 19, 227-255.

Collins, S. E., Eck, S., Torchalla, I., Schröter, M., & Batra, A. (2013). Understanding treatment-seeking smokers' motivation to change: Content analysis of the decisional balance worksheet. *Addictive Behaviors, 38*(1), 1472-1480.

Collins, S. E., Kirouac, M., Taylor, E., Spelman, P. J., Grazioli, V., Hoffman, G., . . . Hicks, J. (2014). Advantages and disadvantages of college drinking in students' own words: Content analysis of the decisional balance worksheet. *Psychology of Addictive Behaviors, 28*(3), 727-733.

Connolly, E. J., & Beaver, K. M. (2014). Examining the genetic and environmental influences on self-control and delinquency: Results from a genetically informative analysis of sibling pairs. *Journal of Interpersonal Violence, 29*(4), 707-735.

Cooperman, N. A., Falkin, G. P., and Cleland, C. (2005). Changes in women's sexual risk behaviors after therapeutic community treatment. *AIDS Education and Prevention*, 17, 157-169.

Crane, R. (2009). *The CBT distinctive features series. Mindfulness-based cognitive therapy: Distinctive features.* New York: Routledge/Taylor & Francis Group, 176pp.

Crescioni, A. W., Ehrlinger, J., Alquist, J. L., Conlon, K. E., Baumeister, R. F., Schatschneider, C., & Dutton, G. R. (2011). High trait self-control predicts positive health behaviors and success in weight loss. *Journal of Health Psychology*, 16(5), 750–759.

Cruwys, T., Bevelander, K. E., & Hermans, R. C. J. (2015). Social modeling of eating: A review of when and why social influence affects food intake and choice. *Appetite*, 86, 3-18.

Cunningham, T. (1992). King Baby. Center City, MN: Hazelden Publishing and Educational Services.

Curry, S., Marlatt, G. A., & Gordon, J. R. (1987). Abstinence violation effect: Validation of an attributional construct with smoking cessation. *Journal of Consulting and Clinical Psychology*, 55, 145-149.

Da Ros, A., Vinai, P., Gentile, N., Forza, G., Cardetti, S. (2011). Evaluation of alexithymia and depression in severe obese patients not affected by eating disorders. *Eating and Weight Disorders*, 16(1), e24-e29.

Daughters, S. B., Lejuez, C. W., Bornovalova, M. A., Kahler, C. W., Strong, D. R., & Brown, R. A. (2005). Distress tolerance as a predictor of early treatment dropout in a residential substance abuse treatment facility. *Journal of Abnormal Psychology, 114*(4), 729-734

Daughters, S. B., Sargeant, M. N., Bornovalova, M. A., Gratz, K. L., & Lejuez, C. W. (2008). The relationship between distress tolerance and antisocial personality disorder among male inner-city treatment seeking substance users. *Journal of Personality Disorders, 22*(5), 509-524.

Davis, B., & Carpenter, C. (2009). Proximity of fast-food restaurants to schools and adolescent obesity. *American Journal of Public Health, 99*(3), 505-510.

Davis, G., Williams, L. and Yokley, J. (1996, November). An Evaluation of Court-Ordered Contact Between Child Molesters and Children: Polygraph Examination as a Child Protective Service. 15th Annual Research and Treatment Conference of the Association for the Treatment of Sexual Abusers, Chicago, Illinois.

Day, A. (2009). Offender emotion and self-regulation: Implications for offender rehabilitation programming. *Psychology, Crime & Law, 15*(2-3), 119-130.

de Bosset, F. (1982). Core group: A psychotherapeutic model in an outpatient clinic. *The Canadian Journal of Psychiatry / La Revue canadienne de psychiatrie, 27*(2), 123-126.

de Bosset, F. (1991). Group psychotherapy in chronic psychiatric outpatients: A Toronto model. *International Journal of Group Psychotherapy, 41*(1), 65-78.

De Leon, George (1990-91). The Therapeutic Community and Behavioral Science. *The International Journal of the Addictions*, 25(12A), 1537-1557.

De Leon, G. (2000). *The Therapeutic Community: Theory, Model and Method.* New York: Springer Publishing Company.

De Leon, G., Melnick, G., Schoket, D., and Jainchill, N. (1993). Is the therapeutic community culturally relevant? Findings on race/ethnic differences in retention in treatment. *Journal of Psychoactive Drugs*, 25(1), 77- 86.

References

De Leon, G., Sacks, S., Staines, G., McKendrick, K. (2000). Modified therapeutic community for homeless mentally ill chemical abusers: Treatment outcomes. *American Journal of Drug & Alcohol Abuse*. 26(3) 461-480.

Delude, C. (2005). Researchers explain why old habits die hard. MIT Tech Talk, Volume 50, Number 8, Wednesday, November 9, 2005, p. 5

de Ridder, D., Lensvelt-Mulders, G., Finkenauer, C. F., Stok, M., & Baumeister, R. F. (2011). Taking stock of self-control: A meta-analysis of how trait self-control relates to a wide range of behaviors. *Personality and Social Psychology Review*. Advance online publication.

de Zubicaray, G., & Clair, A. (1998). An evaluation of differential reinforcement of other behavior, differential reinforcement of incompatible behavior, and restitution for the management of aggressive behaviors. *Behavioral Interventions, 13*(3), 157-168.

DiBlasio, F. A., & Benda, B. B. (1990). Adolescent sexual behavior: Multivariate analysis of a social learning model. *Journal of Adolescent Research, 5*(4), 449-466.

DiGiuseppe, R. A., Ford, P., Esposito, M. A. (2010). Meta-analytic review of efficacy studies of REBT. 118th Annual Convention of the American Psychological Association, San Diego, California.

DiGiuseppe, R., & Kelter, J. (2006). Treating Aggressive Children: A Rational-Emotive Behavior Systems Approach. In A. Ellis & M. E. Bernard (Eds.), *Rational emotive behavioral approaches to childhood disorders: Theory, practice and research* (pp. 257-280).

DiGiuseppe, R., & McInerney, J. (1990). Patterns of addiction: A rational-emotive perspective. *Journal of Cognitive Psychotherapy, 4*(2), 121-134.

Dimeff, L., Rizvi, S. L., Brown, M., & Linehan, M. M. (2000). Dialectical behavior therapy for substance abuse: A pilot application to methamphetamine-dependent women with borderline personality disorder. *Cognitive and Behavioral Practice, 7*(4), 457-468.

Dingfelder, S. (2005). Closing the gap for Latino patients, *Monitor on Psychology*, 36(1), p. 58-61)

Dinwiddie, S. H. (1992). Psychiatric disorders among wife batterers. *Comprehensive Psychiatry, 33*(6), 411-416.

Dolan, S. L., Martin, R. A., & Rohsenow, D. J. (2008). Self-efficacy for cocaine abstinence: Pretreatment correlates and relationship to outcomes. *Addictive Behaviors, 33,* 675–688.

Donnadieu-Rigole, H., Olive, L., Nalpas, B., Duny, Y., Nocca, D., & Perney, P. (2016). Prevalence of psychoactive substance consumption in people with obesity. *Substance Use & Misuse, 51*(12), 1649-1654.

Dowden, C., & Andrews, D. A. (2000). Effective correctional treatment and violent reoffending: A meta-analysis. *Canadian Journal of Criminology, 42*(4), 449-467.

Dowden, C., Antonowicz, D., & Andrews, D. A. (2003). The effectiveness of relapse prevention with offenders: A meta-analysis. *International Journal of Offender Therapy and Comparative Criminology, 47*(5), 516-528.

Dowling, N. A., Oldenhof, E., Shandley, K., Youssef, G. J., Vasiliadis, S., Thomas, S. A., . . . Jackson, A. C. (2018). The intergenerational transmission of problem gambling: The mediating role of offspring gambling expectancies and motives. *Addictive Behaviors, 77,* 16-20.

Dowling, N. A., Shandley, K. A., Oldenhof, E., Affleck, J. M., Youssef, G. J., Frydenberg, E., . . . Jackson, A. C. (2017). The intergenerational transmission of at-risk/problem gambling: The moderating role of parenting practices. *The American Journal on Addictions.* Advance online publication.

Dryden, W. (2003). 'The cream cake made me eat it': An introduction to the ABC theory of REBT. In W. Dryden (Ed.), *Advancing theory in therapy. Rational emotive behaviour therapy: Theoretical developments* (pp. 1-21). New York: Brunner-Routledge.

Dudeck, M., Spitzer, C., Stopsack, M., Freyberger, H. J., & Barnow, S. (2007). Forensic inpatient male sexual offenders: The impact of personality disorder and childhood sexual abuse. *Journal of Forensic Psychiatry & Psychology, 18*(4), 494-506.

Duwe, G. (2013). Can circles of support and accountability (COSA) work in the United States? Preliminary results from a randomized experiment in Minnesota. *Sexual Abuse: Journal of Research and Treatment, 25*(2), 143-165.

D'Zurilla, T. J., & Nezu, A. (1980). A study of the generation-of-alternatives process in social problem solving. *Cognitive Therapy and Research, 4*(1), 67-72.

D'Zurilla, T. and Netzu, A. (2007), *Problem-Solving Therapy: A Positive Approach to Clinical Intervention*, Third Edition. New York: Springer Publishing

Echeburúa, E., Fernández-Montalvo, J., & Báez, C. (2000). Relapse prevention in the treatment of slot-machine pathological gambling: Long-term outcome. *Behavior Therapy, 31*(2), 351-364.

References

Eckhardt, C. I., Babcock, J., Homack, S. (2004). Partner Assaultive Men and the Stages and Processes of Change. *Journal of Family Violence*, 19, 81-93.

Edwards, K. M., Dixon, K. J., Gidycz, C. A., & Desai, A. D. (2014). Family-of-origin violence and college men's reports of intimate partner violence perpetration in adolescence and young adulthood: The role of maladaptive interpersonal patterns. *Psychology of Men & Masculinity, 15*(2), 234-240.

Edwards, C., & Hendrix, R. (2001). Traumagenic dynamics in adult women survivors of childhood sexual abuse vs. adolescent male sex offenders with similar histories. *Journal of Offender Rehabilitation, 33*(2), 33-45

Eisenberg, N., & Miller, P. A. (1987). The relation of empathy to prosocial and related behaviors. Psychological Bulletin, 101, 91-119.

Ekers D., Richards D., Gilbody S., Ekers D., Richards D., Gilbody S. (2008). A meta-analysis of randomized trials of behavioural treatment of depression. *Psychological Medicine*, 38(5), 611-23.

Elliott, I. A., & Beech, A. R. (2013). A U.K. cost-benefit analysis of circles of support and accountability interventions. *Sexual Abuse: Journal of Research and Treatment, 25*(3), 211-229.

Elliott, J. C., Carey, K. B., & Scott-Sheldon, L. A. J. (2011). Development of a decisional balance scale for young adult marijuana use. *Psychology of Addictive Behaviors, 25*(1), 90-100.

Ellis, A. (1994). *Reason and Emotion in Psychotherapy*, NY: Birch Lane Press

Ellis, A. & Dryden, W. (1997). *The practice of rational emotive behavior therapy* (2nd ed.). New York: Springer.

Ellis, A. & Ellis, D. (2011). *Rational Emotive Behavior Therapy: Theories of Psychotherapy*. Washington, DC, US: American Psychological Association. xvi, 154 pp.

Ellis, A., and Harper, R. A. (1961). *A Guide to Rational Living*. Oxford, England: Prentice Hall.

Ellis, A., and Harper, R. A. (1975). *A New Guide to Rational Living*. Oxford, England: Prentice Hall.

Ellis, A., McInerney, J., Di Giuseppe, R. & Yeager R. (1988). A Rational-Emotive Theory of Addiction. Chapter 3 in *Rational-Emotive Therapy with Alcoholics and Substance Abusers*, New York: Pergamon Press, p. 22- 37.

Ellis, A., McInerney, J. F., DiGiuseppe, R., & Yeager, R. J. (1988). *Rational-emotive therapy with alcoholics and substance abusers*. Elmsford, NY, US: Pergamon Press.

Ellis, A., & Velten, E. (1992). *When AA doesn't work for you: Rational steps to quitting alcohol*. New York: Barricade Books.

El Sheikh, S. E., G., & Bashir, T. Z. (2004). High-risk relapse situations and self-efficacy: Comparison between alcoholics and heroin addicts. *Addictive Behaviors, 29*(4), 753-758.

Engels, G. I., Garnefski, N., and Diekstra, R. F.W. (1993). Efficacy of rational-emotive therapy: A quantitative analysis. *Journal of Consulting and Clinical Psychology, 61*, 1083-1090.

Ent, M. R., Baumeister, R. F., & Tice, D. M. (2015). Trait self-control and the avoidance of temptation. *Personality and Individual Differences, 74*, 12-15.

Epstein, L. H., Wing, R. R., Valoski, A., & Gooding, W. (1987). Long-term effects of parent weight on child weight loss. *Behavior Therapy*, 18(3), 219-226.

Erford, B. T., Johnson, E., & Bardoshi, G. (2016). Meta-analysis of the English version of the Beck Depression Inventory–Second Edition. *Measurement and Evaluation in Counseling and Development, 49*(1), 3-33.

Etzioni, A. (2001). *The Diversity Within Unity Platform*. Available online at http://www.gwu.edu/%7Eccps/dwu_positionpaper.html.

Etzioni (2004). Diversity within unity: Immigrants can belong and be themselves *New York Times* Opinion section available at http://www.nytimes.com/2004/01/02/opinion/02iht-edetzioni_ed3_.html

Etzioni (2006) The rights and responsibilities of immigrants. *Quadrant*. Vol L No. 6, p. 9- 13 Quadrant Magazine Company, Inc.

Exum, M. L. (2006). Alcohol and aggression: An integration of findings from experimental studies. *Journal of Criminal Justice, 34*, 131-145.

Feldman, C. and Ridley, C. (1995). The etiology and treatment of domestic violence between adult partners, *Clinical Psychology, Science and Practice*, 2, 317-348.

Felson, R. B., & Lane, K. J. (2009). Social learning, sexual and physical abuse, and adult crime. *Aggressive Behavior, 35*(6), 489-501.

Feinson, M. C., & Hornik-Lurie, T. (2016). Binge eating & childhood emotional abuse: The mediating role of anger. *Appetite, 105,* 487-493.

References

Felitti, V., Anda, R., Nordenberg, D. (1998). Relationship of Childhood Abuse and Household Dysfunction to Many of the Leading Causes of Death in Adults: The Adverse Childhood Experiences (ACE) Study. *American Journal of Preventative Medicine*,14(4), 245- 258.

Ferster, C. B., & Skinner, B. F. (1957). *Schedules of reinforcement*. East Norwalk, CT, US: Appleton-Century-Crofts.

Fisher, D. G., Lankford, B. A., and Galea, R. P. (1996). Therapeutic community retention among Alaska Natives: Akeela house. *Journal of Substance Abuse Treatment,* 13, 265-271.

Fleig, L., Pomp, S., Schwarzer, R., & Lippke, S. (2013). Promoting exercise maintenance: How interventions with booster sessions improve long-term rehabilitation outcomes. *Rehabilitation Psychology, 58*(4), 323-333.

Ford, J. A., & Ong, J. (2014). Non-medical use of prescription stimulants for academic purposes among college students: A test of social learning theory. *Drug and Alcohol Dependence*, 144, 279-282.

Foster, S. L., & Mash, E. J. (1999). Assessing social validity in clinical treatment research: Issues and procedures. *Journal of Consulting and Clinical Psychology, 67, 308-319.*

Foster, D. W., Neighbors, C., & Pai, A. (2015). Decisional balance: Alcohol decisional balance intervention for heavy drinking undergraduates. *Substance Use & Misuse, 50*(13), 1717-1727.

Foubert, J. D., & Newberry, J. T. (2006). Effects of two versions of an empathy-based rape prevention program on fraternity men's survivor empathy, attitudes, and behavioral intent to commit rape or sexual assault. *Journal of College Student Development*, 47, 133-148.

Foxx, R., & Azrin, N. (1972). Restitution: A method of eliminating aggressive disruptive behavior of retarded and brain-damaged patients. *Behavior Research and Therapy*, 10, 15- 27.

Frankl, V. (1963). *Man's Search for Meaning*. New York: Pocket Books, a division of Simon and Schuster.

Fraser, L. K., Clarke, G. P., Cade, J. E., & Edwards, K. L. (2012). Fast food and obesity: A spatial analysis in a large United Kingdom population of children aged 13–15. *American Journal of Preventive Medicine, 42*(5), e77-e85.

Freeman, A., Pretzer, J., Fleming, B., & Simon, K. (2004). *Clinical applications of cognitive therapy*, Second Edition. New York: Kluwer Academic/Plenum Publishers.

Freisthler, B. (2004). A spatial analysis of social disorganization, alcohol access, and rates of child maltreatment in neighborhoods. *Children and Youth Services Review, 26*(9), 803-819.

Friend, K. B. & Pagano, M. E. (2005). Changes in cigarette consumption and drinking outcomes: Findings from project MATCH. *Journal of Substance Abuse Treatment,* 29, 221-229.

Fu, G., Xu, F., Cameron, C., Heyman, G., and Lee, K. (2007). Cross-cultural differences in children's choices, categorizations, and evaluations of truths and lies. *Developmental Psychology, 43*(2), 278-293.

Gailliot, M. T., Gitter, S. A., Baker, M. D., & Baumeister, R. F. (2012). Breaking the rules: Low trait or state self-control increases social norm violations. *Psychology, 3*(12), 1074-1083.

Gainey, R., Catalano, R., Haggerty, K. & Hoppe, M. (1997). Deviance among the children of heroin addicts in treatment: Impact of parents and peers. *Deviant Behavior*, 18(2) 143-159.

Galante, J., Iribarren, S. J., & Pearce, P. F. (2013). Effects of mindfulness-based cognitive therapy on mental disorders: A systematic review and meta-analysis of randomised controlled trials. *Journal of Research in Nursing, 18*(2), 133-155.

Galli, V., Raute, N. J., McConville, B. J., & McElroy, S. L. (1998). An adolescent male with multiple paraphilias successfully treated with fluoxetine. *Journal of Child and Adolescent Psychopharmacology, 8*(3), 195-197.

Gearing, R. E., Schwalbe, C. S. J., Lee, R., & Hoagwood, K. E. (2013). The effectiveness of booster sessions in CBT treatment for child and adolescent mood and anxiety disorders. *Depression and Anxiety, 30*(9), 800-808.

Gery, I., Miljkovitch, R., Berthoz, S., & Soussignan, R. (2009). Empathy and recognition of facial expressions of emotion in sex offenders, non-sex offenders and normal controls. *Psychiatry Research, 165*(3), 252-262.

Gilbert, L., El-Bassel, N., Manuel, J., Wu, E., Go, H., Golder, S., . . . Sanders, G. (2006). An integrated relapse prevention and relationship safety intervention for women on methadone: Testing short-term effects on intimate partner violence and substance use. *Violence and Victims, 21*(5), 657-672.

Gino, F., Schweitzer, M. E., Mead, N. L., & Ariely, D. (2011). Unable to resist temptation: How self-control depletion promotes unethical behavior. *Organizational Behavior and Human Decision Processes, 115*(2), 191-203.

Golan, M. (2007). Social learning and weight-related problems. In O. N. Saracho & B. Spodek (Eds.), *Contemporary perspectives on early childhood education. Contemporary perspectives on socialization and social development in early childhood education* (pp. 241-266). Charlotte, NC: IAP Information Age Publishing.

References

Golan, M., & Crow, S. (2004). Targeting parents exclusively in the treatment of childhood obesity: Long-term results. *Obesity Research, 12*(2), 357-361.

Goldner, E. M., Lusted, A., Roerecke, M., Rehm, J., & Fischer, B. (2014). Prevalence of Axis-1 psychiatric (with focus on depression and anxiety) disorder and symptomatology among non-medical prescription opioid users in substance use treatment: Systematic review and meta-analyses. *Addictive Behaviors, 39*(3), 520-531.

Goldstein, B. I., & Levitt, A. J. (2006). Is current alcohol consumption associated with increased lifetime prevalence of major depression and suicidality? Results from a pilot community survey. *Comprehensive Psychiatry, 47*(5), 330-333.

Goldstein, A. L., Stewart, S. H., Hoaken, P. N. S., & Flett, G. L. (2014). Mood, motives, and gambling in young adults: An examination of within- and between-person variations using experience sampling. *Psychology of Addictive Behaviors, 28*(1), 217-228.

Gonzalez, J., Nelson, J., Gutkin, T., Saunders, A., Galloway, A., & Shwery, C. (2004). Rational emotive therapy with children and adolescents: A meta-analysis. *Journal of Emotional and Behavioral Disorders, 12*, 222-235.

Gowell, E. C. (1975). Transactional analysis and the body: Sensory stimulation techniques. *Transactional Analysis Journal, 5*(2), 148-151.

Gorka, S. M., Ali, B., & Daughters, S. B. (2012). The role of distress tolerance in the relationship between depressive symptoms and problematic alcohol use. *Psychology of Addictive Behaviors, 26*(3), 621-626.

Gottfredson, M. R., & Hirschi, T. (1990). *A general theory of crime.* Stanford, CA: Stanford University Press.

Grant, J. E., Potenza, M. N., Weinstein, A., & Gorelick, D. A. (2010). Introduction to Behavioral Addictions. *The American Journal of Drug and Alcohol Abuse, 36*(5), 233–241.

Grant, B. F., Stinson, F. S., Dawson, D. A., Chou, S. P., Dufour, M. C., Compton, W., . . . Kaplan, K. (2006). Prevalence and co-occurrence of substance use disorders and independent mood and anxiety disorders: Results from the National Epidemiologic Survey on Alcohol and Related Conditions. *Alcohol Research & Health, 29*(2), 107-120.

Gratz, K. & Chapman, A. (2009) *Freedom from Self-Harm: Overcoming Self-Injury with Skills from DBT and Other Treatments.* Oakland CA: New Harbinger Publications

Greenfield, S. F., Gordon, S. M., Cohen, L., & Trucco, E. (2010). Eating disorders in patients with substance use disorders: Bulimia, anorexia, overeating disorder, and obesity. In E. V. Nunes, J. Selzer, P. Levounis, & C. A. Davies (Eds.), *Substance dependence and co-occurring psychiatric disorders: Best practices for diagnosis and treatment* (pp. 1-34). Kingston, NJ, US: Civic Research Institute.

Griffith, J. D., Rowan-Szal, G. A., Roark, R. R., & Simpson, D. D. (2000). Contingency management in outpatient methadone treatment: A meta-analysis. *Drug and Alcohol Dependence, 58*(1-2), 55-66.

Griffiths, M., Wardle, H., Orford, J., Sproston, K., & Erens, B. (2011). Internet gambling, health, smoking and alcohol use: Findings from the 2007 British gambling prevalence survey. *International Journal of Mental Health and Addiction, 9*(1), 1-11.

Grilo, C. M., & Shiffman, S. (1994). Longitudinal investigation of the abstinence violation effect in binge eaters. *Journal of Consulting and Clinical Psychology, 62*, 611-619.

Gruenewald, P. J. (2011). Regulating availability: How access to alcohol affects drinking and problems in youth and adults. *Alcohol Research: Current Reviews, 34*(2), 248-256.

Gruszczyńska, E., Kaczmarek, M., & Chodkiewicz, J. (2016). Hitting rock bottom? Resource loss as a predictor of alcoholism treatment completion. *Nordic Journal of Psychiatry, 70*(5), 351-357.

Hagenzieker, M. P., Bijleveld, F. D., & Davidse, R. J. (1997). Effects of incentive programs to stimulate safety belt use: A meta-analysis. *Accident Analysis & Prevention, 29*, 759-777

Hall, G. W., Carriero, N. J., Takushi, R. Y., Montoya, I. D., Preston, K. L., & Gorelick, D. A. (2000). Pathological gambling among cocaine-dependent outpatients. *The American Journal of Psychiatry, 157*(7), 1127-1133.

Hamid, R., Deren, S., Beardsley, M., & Tortu, S. (1999). Agreement between urinalysis and self-reported drug use. *Substance Use & Misuse, 34*(11), 1585-1592.

Hamarta, E. (2009). A prediction of self-esteem and life satisfaction by social problem solving. *Social Behavior and Personality, 37(1)*, 73-82.

Hanson, R. K., Bourgon, G., Helmus, L., & Hodgson, S. (2009). The principles of effective correctional treatment also apply to sexual offenders: A meta-analysis. *Criminal Justice and Behavior, 36*(9), 865-891.

References

Hanson, C. L., Henggeler, S. W., Haefele, W. F., & Rodick, J. D. (1984). Demographic, individual, and family relationship correlates of serious and repeated crime among adolescents and their siblings. *Journal of Consulting and Clinical Psychology, 52*(4), 528-538.

Harris, T. A. (1969). *I'm ok you're ok: A practical guide to transactional analysis.* Oxford, England: Harper & Row.

Harford, T., Wechsler, H., & Muthén, B. (2003). Alcohol-Related Aggression and Drinking at Off-Campus Parties and Bars: A National Study of Current Drinkers in College. *Journal of Studies on Alcohol, 64*(5), 704-711.

Hawton, K., Salkovskis, P. M., Kirk, J., & Clark, D. M. (2000). *Cognitive behavior therapy for psychiatric problems: A practical guide.* Oxford: Oxford University Press (Oxford Medical Publications).

Hayatbakhsh, M. R., Clavarino, A. M., Williams, G. M., Bor, W., & Najman, J. M. (2013). Early life course predictors of young adults' gambling. *International Gambling Studies, 13*(1), 19-36.

Hayes, S. C., and Toarmino, D. (1995). If behavioral principles are generally applicable, why is it necessary to understand cultural diversity? *Behavior Therapist, 18*, 21-23.

Hays, R. D., & Ellickson, P. L. (1990). How generalizable are adolescents' beliefs about pro-drug pressures and resistance self-efficacy? *Journal of Applied Social Psychology, 20*(4, Pt 1), 321-340.

Hearn, M. & Evans, D. (1972). Anger and reciprocal inhibition therapy. *Psychological Reports*, 30, 943-948.

Helmus, L., Hanson, R. K., Thornton, D., Babchishin, K. M., & Harris, A. J. R. (2012). Absolute recidivism rates predicted by Static-99R and Static-2002R sex offender risk assessment tools vary across samples: A meta-analysis. *Criminal Justice and Behavior, 39*(9), 1148-1171.

Hendershot, C. S., Marlatt, G. A., & George, W. H. (2009). Relapse prevention and the maintenance of optimal health. In S. A. Shumaker, J. K. Ockene, & K. A. Riekert (Eds.), *The handbook of health behavior change (3rd ed.)* (pp. 127-149). New York: Springer.

Heriot, S. A., & Pritchard, M. (2004). 'Reciprocal Inhibition as the Main Basis of Psychotherapeutic Effects' by Joseph Wolpe (1954). *Clinical Child Psychology and Psychiatry, 9*(2), 297-307

Hermans, R. C. J., Herman, C. P., Larsen, J. K., & Engels, R. C. M. E. (2010). Social modeling effects on snack intake among young men. The role of hunger. Appetite, 54(2), 378-383.

Hermans, R. C. J., Larsen, J. K., Herman, C. P., & Engels, R. C. M. E. (2009). Effects of social modeling on young women's nutrient-dense food intake. Appetite, 53(1), 135-138.

Higgins, G. E. (2005). Can low self-control help with the understanding of the software piracy problem? *Deviant Behavior, 26*(1), 1-24.

Hodgins, D. C., Peden, N., & Makarchuk, K. (2004). Self-efficacy in pathological gambling treatment outcome: development of a gambling abstinence self-efficacy scale (GASS). *International Gambling Studies, 4*(2), 99-108.

Höing, M., Bogaerts, S., & Vogelvang, B. (2013). Circles of support and accountability: How and why they work for sex offenders. *Journal of Forensic Psychology Practice, 13*(4), 267-295.

Hollis, J. F., Gullion, C. M., Stevens, V. J., Brantley, P. J., Appel, L. J., Ard, J. D., . . . Weight Loss Maintenance Trial Research Group. (2008). Weight loss during the intensive intervention phase of the weight-loss maintenance trial. *American Journal of Preventive Medicine, 35*(2), 118-126.

Holmes, T. & Rahe, R. (1967). The Social Readjustment Rating Scale. *Journal of Psychosomatic Research, 11*(2), 213-218.

Howat, S., & Davidson, K. (2002). Parasuicidal behaviour and interpersonal problem solving performance in older adults. *British Journal of Clinical Psychology*, *41(4)*, 375-386.

Huang, C., & Chen, J.-H. (2015). Meta-analysis of the factor structures of the Beck Depression Inventory–II. *Assessment, 22*(4), 459-472.

Huba, G. J., & Bentler, P. M. (1980). The role of peer and adult models for drug taking at different stages in adolescence. *Journal of Youth and Adolescence, 9*(5), 449-465.

Hudson, S. M., Ward, T., & France, K. G. (1992). The abstinence violation effect in regressed and fixated child molesters. *Annals of Sex Research, 5*, 199-213.

Hudson, S. M., Ward, T., & Marshall, W. L. (1992). The abstinence violation effect in sex offenders: A reformulation. *Behaviour Research and Therapy, 30*, 435-441.

Huey, S. J., Jr., Henggeler, S. W., Brondino, M. J., & Pickrel, S. G. (2000). Mechanisms of change in multisystemic therapy: Reducing delinquent behavior through therapist adherence and improved family and peer functioning. Journal of Consulting and Clinical Psychology, 68(3), 451-467.

References

Hussong, A. M., Huang, W., Serrano, D., Curran, P. J., & Chassin, L. (2012). Testing whether and when parent alcoholism uniquely affects various forms of adolescent substance use. *Journal of Abnormal Child Psychology, 40*(8), 1265-1276.

Jacobson, Neil S. (Ed), (1987). Psychotherapists in clinical practice: Cognitive and behavioral perspectives. , (pp. 190-231). New York, NY, US: Guilford Press, ix, 451 pp.

Jacobson N., Dobson K., Truax P., Addis M., Koerner K., Gollan J., et al. (1996). A component analysis of cognitive-behavioral treatment for depression. *Journal of Consulting and Clinical Psychology*, 64(2), 295-304.

Jainchill, N., Hawke, J., and Messina, M. (2005). Post-treatment outcomes among adjudicated adolescent males and females in modified therapeutic community treatment. *Substance Use and Misuse*, 40, 975-996.

Jeglic, E. L., Mercado, C. C., & Levenson, J. S. (2012). The prevalence and correlates of depression and hopelessness among sex offenders subject to community notification and residence restriction legislation. *American Journal of Criminal Justice, 37*(1), 46-59.

Jenkins-Hall, K. D., & Marlatt, G. A. (1989). Apparently irrelevant decisions in the relapse process. In D. R. Laws (Ed.), *Relapse prevention with sex offenders* (pp. 47-55). New York: Guilford Press.

Johnson, W. G., Schlundt, D. G., Barclay, D. R., Carr-Nangle, R. E., & et al (1995). A naturalistic functional analysis of binge eating. *Behavior Therapy, 26*, 101-118.

Johnson, F., & Wardle, J. (2011). The association between weight loss and engagement with a web-based food and exercise diary in a commercial weight loss programme: A retrospective analysis. *The International Journal of Behavioral Nutrition and Physical Activity, 8,* Article ID 83.

Jones, R. S., & Baker, L. J. (1990). Differential reinforcement and challenging behaviour: A critical review of the DRI schedule. *Behavioural Psychotherapy, 18*(1), 35-47.

Jones, S. & Quisenberry, N. (2004). The general theory of crime: How general is it? *Deviant Behavior*, 25, 401-426.

Jordan, M. J., Rogers, R., Neumann, C. S., & Norlander, B. (2013). Evaluating the positive and negative benefits of crime: Development and validation of the Decisional Balance Scale for Adolescent Offenders (DBS-AO). *Journal of Criminal Justice, 41*(2), 108-114.

Kabat-Zinn, Jon (1991) *Full catastrophe living: using the wisdom of your body and mind to face stress, pain, and illness*, Delta Trade Paperbacks.

Kafka, M. P., & Hennen, J. (2002). A DSM-IV Axis I Comorbidity Study of Males (n = 120) With Paraphilias and Paraphilia-Related Disorders. *Sexual Abuse: Journal of Research and Treatment, 14*(4), 349-366.

Kafka, M. P., & Hennen, J. (2000b). Psychostimulant augmentation during treatment with selective serotonin reuptake inhibitors in men with paraphilia-related disorders: A case series. *The Journal of Clinical Psychiatry, 61*(9), 664-670.

Kafka, M. P., & Prentky, R. A. (1998). Attention-deficit/hyperactivity disorder in males with paraphilias and paraphilia-related disorders: A comorbidity study. *The Journal of Clinical Psychiatry, 59*(7), 388-396.

Kafka, M. P., & Prentky, R. A. (1994). Preliminary observations of DSM-III—R Axis I comorbidity in men with paraphilias and paraphilia-related disorders. *The Journal of Clinical Psychiatry, 55*(11), 481-487.

Kafka, M. P., & Prentky, R. (1992). Fluoxetine treatment of nonparaphilic sexual addictions and paraphilias in men. *The Journal of Clinical Psychiatry, 53*(10), 351-358.

Kaplow, J. B., Curran, P. J., Dodge, K. A., & Conduct Problems Prevention Research Group. (2002). Child, parent, and peer predictors of early-onset substance use: A multisite longitudinal study. *Journal of Abnormal Child Psychology, 30*(3), 199-216.

Kaskutas, L. A. (2009). Alcoholics Anonymous effectiveness: Faith meets science. *Journal of Addictive Diseases, 28*(2), 145-157.

Kavanagh, A. M., Kelly, M. T., Krnjacki, L., Thornton, L., Jolley, D., Subramanian, S. V., . . . Bentley, R. J. (2011). Access to alcohol outlets and harmful alcohol consumption: A multi-level study in Melbourne, Australia. *Addiction, 106*(10), 1772-1779.

Kazdin, A. E. (1982). Symptom substitution, generalization, and response covariation: Implications for psychotherapy outcome. *Psychological Bulletin, 91*(2), 349-365.

Kazdin (2008, March). Culturally Informed Treatment: Desperately Needed Research Directions to Optimize Impact. Culturally Informed Evidence Based Practices: Translating Research and Policy for the Real World. National Conference. Bethesda, Maryland.

Keane, C., Maxim, P. S., & Teevan, J. J. (1993). Drinking and driving, self-control, and gender: Testing a general theory of crime. *Journal of Research in Crime and Delinquency*, 30, 30-46.

References

Keller M., McCullough J., Klein D., et. al. (2000). A comparison of nefazodone, the cognitive behavioral-analysis system of psychotherapy, and their combination for the treatment of chronic depression. *New England J Med.* 342(20), 1462-70.

Kenrick, D. T., Griskevicius, V., Neuberg, S. L., & Schaller, M. (2010). Renovating the pyramid of needs: Contemporary extensions built upon ancient foundations. *Perspectives on Psychological Science, 5*(3), 292-314.

Khantzian, E. J. (2003). The Self-Medication Hypothesis Revisited: The Dually Diagnosed Patient. *Primary Psychiatry, 10*(9), *47-48*, 53-54.

Khoury, B., Sharma, M., Rush, S. E., & Fournier, C. (2015). Mindfulness-based stress reduction for healthy individuals: A meta-analysis. *Journal of Psychosomatic Research, 78*(6), 519-528.

Kilmer, B., Nicosia, N., Heaton, P., & Midgette, G. (2013). Efficacy of frequent monitoring with swift, certain, and modest sanctions for violations: Insights from South Dakota's 24/7 Sobriety Project. *American Journal of Public Health, 103*(1), e37-e43.

Kilpatrick, B., Howlett, M., Sedgwick, P., & Ghodse, A. H. (2000). Drug use, self report and urinalysis. *Drug and Alcohol Dependence, 58*(1-2), 111-116.

King, L. L., & Polaschek, D. L. L. (2003). The Abstinence Violation Effect: Investigating lapse and relapse phenomena using the relapse prevention model with domestically violent men. *New Zealand Journal of Psychology*, 32, 67-75.

Kingston, D. A., Fedoroff, P., Firestone, P., Curry, S., & Bradford, J. M. (2008). Pornography use and sexual aggression: The impact of frequency and type of pornography use on recidivism among sexual offenders. *Aggressive Behavior, 34*(4), 341-351.

Klostermann, K., Kelley, M. L., Mignone, T., Pusateri, L., & Fals-Stewart, W. (2010). Partner violence and substance abuse: Treatment interventions. *Aggression and Violent Behavior, 15*(3), 162-166.

Kodl, M. M., Fu, S. S., Willenbring, M. L., Gravely, A., Nelson, D. B., & Joseph, A. M. (2008). The impact of depressive symptoms on alcohol and cigarette consumption following treatment for alcohol and nicotine dependence. *Alcoholism: Clinical and Experimental Research*, 32, 92–99.

Korotisch, W. J., & Nelson-Gray, R. O. (1999). An overview of self-monitoring research in assessment and treatment. *Psychological Assessment*, 11, 415- 425.

Kownacki, R. J., & Shadish, W. R. (1999). Does Alcoholics Anonymous work? The results from a meta-analysis of controlled experiments. *Substance Use & Misuse, 34*(13), 1897-1916.

Kozak, A. T., & Fought, A. (2011). Beyond alcohol and drug addiction. Does the negative trait of low distress tolerance have an association with overeating? *Appetite, 57*(3), 578-581.

Kraus, C., Strohm, K., Hill, A., et al. (2007). Selective serotonin reuptake inhibitors (SSRI) in the treatment of paraphilia: a retrospective study [in German]. *Fortschr Neurol Psychiat.* 75(6). 351–356.

Krohn, M. D., Skinner, W. F., Massey, J. L., & Akers, R. L. (1985). Social learning theory and adolescent cigarette smoking: A longitudinal study. *Social Problems, 32*(5), 455-473.

Kung, S., Alarcon, R. D., Williams, M. D., Poppe, K. A., Jo Moore, M., & Frye, M. A. (2013). Comparing the Beck Depression Inventory-II (BDI-II) and Patient Health Questionnaire (PHQ-9) depression measures in an integrated mood disorders practice. *Journal of Affective Disorders, 145*(3), 341-343.

Kuusisto, K., Knuuttila, V., & Saarnio, P. (2011). Clients' self-efficacy and outcome expectations: Impact on retention and effectiveness in outpatient substance abuse treatment. *Addictive Disorders & Their Treatment, 10*(4), 157-168.

Lai Kwok, S. Y. C., & Shek, D. T. L. (2009). Social problem solving, family functioning, and suicidal ideation among Chinese adolescents in Hong Kong. *Adolescence, 44(174)*, 391-406.

Langlands, R. L., Ward, T., & Gilchrist, E. (2009). Applying the good lives model to male perpetrators of domestic violence. *Behaviour Change, 26*(2), 113-129.

Langton, L., Piquero, N. L., & Hollinger, R. C. (2006). An empirical test of the relationship between employee theft and low self-control. *Deviant Behavior, 27*(5), 537-565.

Lanza-Kaduce, L., Akers, R. L., Krohn, M. D., & Radosevich, M. (1984). Cessation of alcohol and drug use among adolescents: A social learning model. *Deviant Behavior, 5*(1-4), 79-96.

Larimer, M. & Marlatt, G. A. (1990). Applications of relapse prevention with moderation goals. Journal of Psychoactive Drugs, 22, 189- 195.

Larimer, M., Palmer, R., & Marlatt, G. (1999). Relapse prevention: An overview of Marlatt's cognitive- behavioral model. *Alcohol Research & Health, 23*(2), 151-160.

References

Latessa, E. J., & Travis, L. F. (1988). The effects of intensive supervision with alcoholic probationers. *Journal of Offender Counseling, Services & Rehabilitation, 12*(2), 175-190.

Latner, J. (2000) The Theory of Gestalt Therapy, in *Gestalt therapy: Perspectives and Applications*, Edwin Nevis (ed.) Cambridge, MA: Gestalt Press.

Lavender, J. M., Happel, K., Anestis, M. D., Tull, M. T., & Gratz, K. L. (2015). The interactive role of distress tolerance and eating expectancies in bulimic symptoms among substance abusers. *Eating Behaviors, 16,* 88-91.

Law, B. (2005) Probing the depression-rumination cycle: Why chewing on problems just makes them harder to swallow. *Monitor on Psychology*, (36), 38- 39.

Leclerc, B., Beauregard, E., & Proulx, J. (2008). Modus operandi and situational aspects in adolescent sexual offenses against children: A further examination. *International Journal of Offender Therapy and Comparative Criminology, 52*(1), 46-61.

Lee, E. B., An, W., Levin, M. E., & Twohig, M. P. (2015). An initial meta-analysis of acceptance and commitment therapy for treating substance use disorders. *Drug and Alcohol Dependence.* Advance online publication.

Lee, N. K., Oei, T. P. S., & Greeley, J. D. (1999). The interaction of alcohol expectancies and drinking refusal self-efficacy in high and low risk drinkers. *Addiction Research, 7*(2), 91-102.

Lees, J., Manning, N., & Rawlings, B. (2004). A culture of enquiry: Research evidence and the therapeutic community . *Psychiatric Quarterly, 75, 279-293.*

Lega, L. I., and Ellis, A. (2001). Rational Emotive Behavior Therapy (REBT) in the new millennium: A cross-cultural approach. *Journal of Rational-Emotive and Cognitive Behavior Therapy,* 19, 201-222.

LeGray, M. W., Dufrene, B. A., Mercer, S., Olmi, D. J., & Sterling, H. (2013). Differential reinforcement of alternative behavior in center-based classrooms: Evaluation of pre-teaching the alternative behavior. *Journal of Behavioral Education, 22*(2), 85-102.

Lembke, A. (2012). Time to abandon the self-medication hypothesis in patients with psychiatric disorders. *The American Journal of Drug and Alcohol Abuse, 38*(6), 524-529

LeMont, D., Moorehead, M., Parish, M., Reto, C. & Ritz, S. (2004). Suggestion for the Pre-Surgical Psychological Assessment of Bariatric Surgery Candidates ASMBS Allies Health Science Section Ad-Hoc Behavioral Health Committee. Retrieved from https://asmbs.org/resources/pre-surgical-psychological-assessment

Lenard, P. T.(2012). *Trust, Democracy, and Multicultural Challenges*. University Park: Penn State University Press. Retrieved December 1, 2016, from Project MUSE database.

Lenz, A. S., Taylor, R., Fleming, M., & Serman, N. (2014). Effectiveness of dialectical behavior therapy for treating eating disorders. *Journal of Counseling & Development, 92*(1), 26-35.

Levenson, J. (2016). Adverse childhood experiences and subsequent substance abuse in a sample of sexual offenders: Implications for treatment and prevention. *Victims & Offenders, 11*(2), 199-224.

Li, F., Harmer, P., Cardinal, B. J., Bosworth, M., & Johnson-Shelton, D. (2009). Obesity and the built environment: Does the density of neighborhood fast-food outlets matter? *American Journal of Health Promotion, 23*(3), 203-209.

Lievaart, M., Franken, I. H. A., & Hovens, J. E. (2016). Anger assessment in clinical and nonclinical populations: Further validation of the State–Trait Anger Expression Inventory-2. *Journal of Clinical Psychology, 72*(3), 263-278.

Lisak, D., & Miller, P. M. (2002). Repeat rape and multiple offending among undetected rapists. *Violence and Victims, 17*(1), 73-84.

Lombard, D. N., Lombard, T. N., & Winett, R. A. (1995). Walking to meet health guidelines: The effect of prompting frequency and prompt structure. *Health Psychology, 14*, 164-170.

Linehan, Marsha M. (1987). Dialectical behavior therapy for borderline personality disorder. Theory and method. Bulletin of the Menninger Clinic, 51(3), 261- 76.

Linehan M. M. (1993). *Skills Training Manual for Treating Borderline Personality Disorder.* New York: The Guilford Press.

Linehan, Marsha (2015). DBT Skills Training Manual, Second Edition. By New York, US: The Guilford Press.

Longshore, D. (1998). Self-control and criminal opportunity: A prospective test of the general theory of crime. *Social Problems*, 45, 102-113.

Losel, F, & Schmucker, M. (2005). The effectiveness of treatment for sexual offenders: a comprehensive meta-analysis. *Journal of Experimental Criminology*, 1, 117–146.

References

Lovegrove, P. J., Henry, K. L., & Slater, M. D. (2012). Examination of the predictors of latent class typologies of bullying involvement among middle school students. *Journal of School Violence, 11*(1), 75-93.

Lowenstein, L. (1973). A case of exhibitionism treated by counter-conditioning. *Adolescence,* 8, 213-218.

Lu, S (2105). White House taps psychologists to study sexual violence on campus. *Monitor on Psychology*, Feb 2015, Vol 46(2).

Luft, J. (1969). *Of Human Interaction.* Palo Alto, CA: Mayfield.

Lyons, L. C., and Woods, P. J. (1991). The efficacy of rational-emotive therapy: A quantitative review of the outcome research. *Clinical Psychology Review,* 11, 357-369.

Luszczynska, A., Mazurkiewicz, M., Ziegelmann, J. P., & Schwarzer, R. (2007). Recovery self-efficacy and intention as predictors of running or jogging behavior: A cross-lagged panel analysis over a two-year period. *Psychology of Sport and Exercise, 8*(2), 247-260.

MacLaren, V. V., Harrigan, K. A., & Dixon, M. (2012). Gambling motives and symptoms of problem gambling in frequent slots players. *Journal of Gambling Issues, 27,* 1-13.

MacPherson, L. Stipelman, B. A. Duplinsky, M. Brown, R. A. Lejuez, C. W. (2008). Distress tolerance and pre-smoking treatment attrition: Examination of moderating relationships. *Addictive Behaviors,* 33, 1385-1393.

Mahon, N. E., Yarcheski, A., Yarcheski, T. J., & Hanks, M. M. (2006). Correlates of low frustration tolerance in young adolescents. *Psychological Reports, 99*(1), 230.

Mainvil, L. A., Lawson, R., Horwath, C. C., McKenzie, J. E., & Hart, I. (2010). Validated scales to assess adult decisional balance to eat more fruits and vegetables. *Appetite, 55*(3), 454-465.

Maisto, S. A., & Connors, G. J. (2006). Relapse in the addictive behaviors: Integration and future directions. *Clinical Psychology Review, 26*(2), 229-231.

Maletzky, B.M., Tolan, A., & McFarland, B. (2006). The Oregon Depo-Provera program: a five-year follow-up. *Sexual Abuse: A Journal of Research and Treatment*, 18, 303–316.

Mangels, M., Schwarz, S., Worringen, U., Holme, M., & Rief, W. (2009). Evaluation of a behavioral-medical inpatient rehabilitation treatment including booster sessions: A randomized controlled study. *The Clinical Journal of Pain, 25*(5), 356-364.

Mannan, M., Mamun, A., Doi, S., & Clavarino, A. (2016). Is there a bi-directional relationship between depression and obesity among adult men and women? Systematic review and bias-adjusted meta-analysis. *Asian Journal of Psychiatry, 21,* 51-66.

Maramba, G. G., and Hall, G. C. N. (2002). Meta-analyses of ethnic match as a predictor of dropout, utilization, and level of functioning. *Cultural Diversity and Ethnic Minority Psychology,* 8, 290-297.

Marcos, Y. Q., Sebastián, M. J. Q., Aubalat, L. P., Ausina, J. B., & Treasure, J. (2013). Peer and family influence in eating disorders: A meta-analysis. *European Psychiatry, 28*(4), 199-206.

Marlatt, G. (1985) Relapse prevention: Theoretical rationale and overview of the model. In Marlatt, G. & Gordan, J. (Eds.) *Relapse Prevention: Maintenance Strategies in Addictive Behavior Change* (pp. 3- 70). New York/London: The Guilford Press.

Marlatt, G. A. (1989). Feeding the PIG: The problem of immediate gratification. In D. R. Laws (Ed.), *Relapse prevention with sex offenders* (pp. 56-62). New York: Guilford Press.

Marlatt, G. A., & Donovan, D. M. (Eds.). (2005). *Relapse prevention: Maintenance strategies in the treatment of addictive behaviors* (2nd ed.). New York: Guilford Press.

Marlatt, G.A. & Gordon (1985). *Relapse prevention: Maintenance strategies in addictive behavior change.* New York: Guilford.

Marlatt, G. A., & George, W. H. (1984). Relapse prevention: Introduction and overview of the model. *British Journal of Addiction, 79*(3), 261-273.

Marshall, I. H., & Enzmann, D. (2012). The generalizability of self-control theory. In J. Junger-Tas, I. H. Marshall, D. Enzmann, M. Killias, M. Steketee, & B. Gruszczyńska (Eds.), *The many faces of youth crime: Contrasting theoretical perspectives on juvenile delinquency across countries and cultures* (pp. 285-325).

Martin, K. S., & Ferris, A. M. (2007). Food insecurity and gender are risk factors for obesity. *Journal of Nutrition Education and Behavior, 39*(1), 31-36.

Martens, M. P., Cadigan, J. M., Rogers, R. E., & Osborn, Z. H. (2015). Personalized drinking feedback intervention for veterans of the wars in Iraq and Afghanistan: A randomized controlled trial. *Journal of Studies on Alcohol and Drugs, 76*(3), 355-359

References

Masicampo, E. J., & Baumeister, R. F. (2011). Consider it done! Plan making can eliminate the cognitive effects of unfulfilled goals. *Journal of Personality and Social Psychology, 101*(4), 667-683.

Maslow, A. H. (1943). A theory of human motivation. *Psychological Review, 50*(4), 370–396.

May, R. K., Whelan, J. P., Steenbergh, T. A., & Meyers, A. W. (2003). The Gambling Self-Efficacy Questionnaire: An initial psychometric evaluation. *Journal of Gambling Studies, 19,* 339 –357.

Maxwell, K. A. (2002). Friends: The role of peer influence across adolescent risk behaviors. *Journal of Youth and Adolescence, 31*(4), 267-277.

McAllister, E., Dhurandhar, N. & Keith S., et. al. (2009). Ten Putative Contributors to the Obesity Epidemic, *Critical Reviews in Food Science and Nutrition,* 49(10), 868-913

McCormick, J., Delfabbro, P., & Denson, L. A. (2012). Psychological vulnerability and problem gambling: An application of Durand Jacobs' general theory of addictions to electronic gaming machine playing in Australia. *Journal of Gambling Studies, 28*(4), 665-690.

McEwan, D., Harden, S. M., Zumbo, B. D., Sylvester, B. D., Kaulius, M., Ruissen, G. R., . . . Beauchamp, M. R. (2016). The effectiveness of multi-component goal setting interventions for changing physical activity behaviour: A systematic review and meta-analysis. *Health Psychology Review, 10*(1), 67-88.

McGinn, L. K., & Young, J. E. (1996). Schema-focused therapy. In P. M. Salkovskis (Ed.), *Frontiers of cognitive therapy* (pp. 182-207). New York: Guilford Press.

McGrath, R. J., Lasher, M. P., Cumming, G. F., Langton, C. M., & Hoke, S. E. (2014). Development of Vermont Assessment of Sex Offender Risk (VASOR) Reoffense Risk Scale. *Sexual Abuse: Journal of Research and Treatment, 26*(3), 271-290.

McIntyre, J. C., Barlow, F. K., & Hayward, L. E. (2014). Stronger sexual desires only predict bold romantic intentions and reported infidelity when self-control is low. *Australian Journal of Psychology.* Advance online publication.

McKeel, A. N., & Dixon, M. R. (2014). Furthering a behavior analytic account of self-control using relational frame theory. *Behavioral Development Bulletin, 19*(2), 111-118.

McMackin, R. A., Leisen, M. B., Cusack, J. F., LaFratta, J., & Litwin, P. (2002). The relationship of trauma exposure to sex offending behavior among male juvenile offenders. *Journal of Child Sexual Abuse: Research, Treatment, & Program Innovations for Victims, Survivors, & Offenders, 11*(2), 25-40.

McMurran, M., & Christopher, G. (2009). Social problem solving, anxiety, and depression in adult male prisoners. *Legal and Criminological Psychology*, 14(1), 101-107.

Mee-Lee, D. [Ed] (2013). *The ASAM Criteria: Treatment Criteria for Addictive, Substance-Related, and Co-Occurring Conditions*, American Society of Addiction Medicine: Chevy Chase Md.

Meichenbaum, D. (2014, May). The role of case conceptualization model and core tasks of intervention. 18th Melissa Institute Conference "Ways to Improve Community-based, Educational and Psychotherapeutic Interventions: Lessons Learned, Miami, Florida.

Mercer, K. B., & Eastwood, J. D. (2010). Is boredom associated with problem gambling behaviour? It depends on what you mean by 'boredom.' *International Gambling Studies, 10*(1), 91-104.

Merrill, L. L., Thomsen, C. J., Crouch, J. L., May, P., Gold, S. R., & Milner, J. S. (2005). Predicting adult risk of child physical abuse from childhood exposure to violence: Can interpersonal schemata explain the association? *Journal of Social and Clinical Psychology, 24*(7), 981-1002

Messina, N. P., Wish, E. D., Hoffman, J. A., and Nemes, S. (2002). Antisocial personality disorder and TC treatment outcomes. *American Journal of Drug and Alcohol Abuse, 28,* 197-212.

Metz, K., Flöter, S., Kröger, C., Donath, C., Piontek, D., & Gradl, S. (2007). Telephone booster sessions for optimizing smoking cessation for patients in rehabilitation centers. *Nicotine & Tobacco Research, 9*(8), 853-863.

Miller, J. G. (1991). A cultural perspective on the morality of beneficence and interpersonal responsibility. In S. Ting-Toomey & F. Korzenny (Eds.), *International and intercultural communication annual, Vol. 15. Cross-cultural interpersonal communication* (pp. 11-27). Thousand Oaks, CA: Sage Publications.

Miller, P. A., & Eisenberg, N. (1988). The relation of empathy to aggressive and externalizing/antisocial behavior. *Psychological Bulletin*, 103, 324-344.

Miller, N. S., Klamen, D., Hoffmann, N. G., & Flaherty, J. A. (1996). Prevalence of depression and alcohol and other drug dependence in addictions treatment populations. *Journal of Psychoactive Drugs, 28*(2), 111-124.

Miller, W. R., & Rollnick, S. (1991). *Motivational interviewing: Preparing people to change addictive behavior.* New York: Guilford Press.

References

Miller, W., & Rollnick, S. (2013). *Motivational Interviewing: Helping people change* (3rd ed.). New York: Guilford Press.

Mitchell, C., & Stuart, R. B. (1984). Effect of self-efficacy on dropout from obesity treatment. *Journal of Consulting and Clinical Psychology, 52*(6), 1100-1101.

Miranda, R., Jr., Meyerson, L. A., Long, P. J., Marx, B. P., & Simpson, S. M. (2002). Sexual assault and alcohol use: Exploring the self-medication hypothesis. *Violence and Victims, 17*(2), 205-217.

Miranda, J., Nakamura, R., and Bernal, G. (2003). Including ethnic minorities in mental health intervention research: A practical approach to a long-standing problem. *Culture, Medicine and Psychiatry,* 27, 467-486.

Mischke-Reeds, M. (2015). *8 keys to mental health. 8 keys to practicing mindfulness: Practical strategies for emotional health and well-being.* New York: W W Norton & Co.

Mitroff & Silvers (2009). *Dirty rotten strategies: How We Trick Ourselves and Others into Solving the Wrong Problems Precisely,* Stanford Business Press.

Mooney, J. P., Burling, T. A., Hartman, W. M., & Brenner-Liss, D. (1992). The Abstinence Violation Effect and very low calorie diet success. *Addictive Behaviors, 17,* 319-324.

Monroe, J. (2004). Getting a puff: A social learning test of adolescents smoking. *Journal of Child & Adolescent Substance Abuse, 13*(3), 71-83.

Muraven, M., & Baumeister, R. F. (2000). Self-regulation and depletion of limited resources: Does self-control resemble a muscle? *Psychological Bulletin, 126,* 247–259.

Muraven, M., Collins, R. L., Morsheimer, E. T., Shiffman, S., & Paty, J. A. (2005). The morning after: Limit violations and the self-regulation of alcohol consumption. *Psychology of Addictive Behaviors, 19*(3), 253-262.

Muraven, M., Collins, R. L., Shiffman, S., & Paty, J. A. (2005). Daily Fluctuations in Self-Control Demands and Alcohol Intake. *Psychology of Addictive Behaviors, 19*(2), 140-147.

Muraven, M., Pogarsky, G., & Shmueli, D. (2006). Self-control depletion and the General Theory of Crime. *Journal of Quantitative Criminology, 22*(3), 263-277.

Neighbors, C., Young, C. M., Krieger, H., & Tackett, J. L. (2016). Social influence, pressure, and norms: Vulnerability for substance use in adolescents. In C. E. Kopetz & C. W. Lejuez (Eds.), *Frontiers of social psychology. Addictions: A social psychological perspective* (pp. 170-198). New York: Routledge/Taylor & Francis Group.

Nemes, S., Wish, E., Messina, N. (1999). Comparing the impact of standard and abbreviated treatment in a therapeutic community: Findings from the District of Columbia Treatment Initiative experiment. *Journal of Substance Abuse Treatment.* Dec Vol 17(4) 339-347.

Neubert, M. J. (1998). The value of feedback and goal setting over goal setting alone and potential moderators of this effect: A meta-analysis. *Human Performance, 11*(4), 321-335

Neumann, S., (2006). "Gang Rape: Examining Peer Support and Alcohol in Fraternities" in Hickey, E.W. (ed.), *Sex Crimes and Paraphilia* Pearson Education, 2006, pp. 397–407.

Newring, K. A. B., Loverich, T. M., Harris, C. D., & Wheeler, J. (2008). Relapse prevention. In W. T. O'Donohue & J. E. Fisher (Eds.), *Cognitive behavior therapy: Applying empirically supported techniques in your practice (2nd ed.)* (pp. 422-433). Hoboken, NJ: John Wiley.

Nezu, C. M., D'Zurilla, T. J., & Nezu, A. M. (2005). Problem-Solving Therapy: Theory, Practice, and Application to Sex Offenders. In M. McMurran & J. McGuire (Eds.), *Wiley series in forensic clinical psychology. Social problem solving and offending: Evidence, evaluation and evolution* (pp. 103-123).

Nezu, A. M., Nezu, C. M., & Jain, D. (2008). Social problem solving as a mediator of the stress-pain relationship among individuals with noncardiac chest pain. *Health Psychology, 27(6),* 829-832.

NIDA Archives (1998).The National Institute on Drug Abuse (NIDA) Archives, A Cognitive-Behavioral Approach: Treating Cocaine Addiction (Therapy Manuals for Drug Abuse: Manual 1) (Printed April, 1998), Topic 4: Seemingly Irrelevant Decisions. Retrieved July 9, 2016 from http://archives.drugabuse.gov/TXManuals/CBT/CBT11.html

Nigg, C. R., Burbank, P. M., Padula, C., Dufresne, R., Rossi, J. S., Velicer, W. F.,... Prochaska, J. O. (1999). Stages of change across ten health risk behaviors for older adults. *The Gerontologist, 39*(4), 473-482.

Nolen-Hoeksema, S. & Davis, C. (1999). "Thanks for Sharing That" Ruminators and their social support networks, *Journal of Personality and Social Psychology*, 77(4), 801-814

Nower, L. & Blaszczynski, A. (2006). Impulsivity and pathological gambling: A descriptive model. *International Gambling Studies,* 6(1), 61-75.

References

O'Brien, C. (2011). Depression, cause or consequence of pathological gambling and its implications for treatment. *Counselling Psychology Review, 26*(1), 53-61.

Okunna, N. C., Rodriguez-Monguio, R., Smelson, D. A., & Volberg, R. A. (2016). An evaluation of substance abuse, mental health disorders, and gambling correlations: An opportunity for early public health interventions. *International Journal of Mental Health and Addiction*, 14(4), 618-633.

Opitz, D. M., Tsytsarev, S. V., & Froh, J. (2009). Women's sexual addiction and family dynamics, depression and substance abuse. *Sexual Addiction & Compulsivity, 16*(4), 324-340.

Orford, J., & Velleman, R. (1991). The environmental intergenerational transmission of alcohol problems: A comparison of two hypotheses. *British Journal of Medical Psychology, 64*(2), 189-200.

Overholser, J. (1993). Elements of the Socratic method: I. Systematic questioning, *Psychotherapy Theory Research & Practice* 30(1), 67-74.

Overholser, J. (2005). Contemporary psychotherapy: Promoting personal responsibility for therapeutic change. *Journal of Contemporary Psychotherapy*, 35, 369- 376.

Overholser, J. C. (2013). Guided discovery: Problem-solving therapy integrated within the Socratic method. *Journal of Contemporary Psychotherapy, 43*(2), 73-82.

Panos, P. T., Jackson, J. W., Hasan, O., & Panos, A. (2014). Meta-analysis and systematic review assessing the efficacy of Dialectical Behavior Therapy (DBT). *Research on Social Work Practice, 24*(2), 213-223.

Pape, H., & Norström, T. (2016). Associations between emotional distress and heavy drinking among young people: A longitudinal study. *Drug and Alcohol Review, 35*(2), 170-176.

Pardeck, J. T., Callahan, D., Allgier, P., Fernandez, N., et al. (1991). Family dysfunction and the potential for alcoholism in college students. *College Student Journal, 25*(1), 556-559.

Passmore, J. (2011). Motivational interviewing: A model for coaching psychology practice. *The Coaching Psychologist, 7*(1), 36-40.

Pastorelli, C., Caprara, G.V., Barbaranelli, C., Rola, J., Rozsa, S., Bandura, A. (2001). The structure of children's perceived self-efficacy: A cross-national study, *European Journal of Psychological Assessment.* 17(2), 87-97.

Pearce, J., Mason, K., Hiscock, R., & Day, P. (2008). A national study of neighbourhood access to gambling opportunities and individual gambling behaviour. *J. of Epidemiology and Community Health, 62*(10), 862-868.

Pearson, F. S., and Lipton, D. S. (1999). A meta-analytic review of the effectiveness of corrections-based treatments for drug abuse. Prison Journal, 79, 384-410.

Perillo, A. D., Mercado, C. C., & Terry, K. J. (2008). Repeat offending, victim gender, and extent of victim relationship in Catholic Church sexual abusers: Implications for risk assessment. *Criminal Justice and Behavior, 35*(5), 600-614.

Perls, F., Hefferline, R. F., & Goodman, P. (1965). *Gestalt therapy*. Oxford, England: Dell.

Peters, E. N., & Hughes, J. R. (2010). Daily marijuana users with past alcohol problems increase alcohol consumption during marijuana abstinence. *Drug and Alcohol Dependence, 106*(2-3), 111-118.

Petscher, E. S., Rey, C., & Bailey, J. S. (2009). A review of empirical support for differential reinforcement of alternative behavior. *Research in Developmental Disabilities, 30*(3), 409-425.

Pieterse, A. L., Lee, M., Ritmeester, A., & Collins, N. M. (2013). Towards a model of self-awareness development for counselling and psychotherapy training. *Counselling Psychology Quarterly, 26*(2), 190-207.

Pinheiro, R. T., Pinheiro, K. A. T., Da Silva Magalhães, P. V., Horta, B. L., Da Silva, R. A., Sousa, P. L. R., & Fleming, M. (2006). Cocaine addiction and family dysfunction: A case-control study in Southern Brazil. *Substance Use & Misuse, 41*(3), 307-316.

Polakowski, M. (1994). Linking self- and social control with deviance: Illuminating the structure underlying a general theory of crime and its relation to deviant activity. *Journal of Quantitative Criminology*, 10, 41-78.

Pratt, T. C., & Cullen F. T. (2000). The empirical status of Gottfredson and Hirschi's general theory of crime: A meta-analysis. *Criminology, 38*, 931-964.

Prat, F., Planes, M., Gras, M. E., & Sullman, M. J. M. (2012). Stages of change and decisional balance for condom use with a romantic partner. *Journal of Health Psychology, 17*(8), 1193-1202.

Prendergast, M., Podus, D., Finney, J., Greenwell, L., & Roll, J. (2006). Contingency management for treatment of substance use disorders: A meta-analysis. *Addiction, 101*(11), 1546-1560.

Preston, P., & Goodfellow, M. (2006). Cohort comparisons: Social learning explanations for alcohol use among adolescents and older adults. *Addictive Behaviors, 31*(12), 2268-2283.

References

Prinstein, M. J., Boergers, J., & Spirito, A. (2001). Adolescents' and their friends' health-risk behavior: Factors that alter or add to peer influence. *Journal of Pediatric Psychology, 26*(5),

Prochaska, J. O., & DiClemente, C. C. (2005). The Transtheoretical Approach. In Norcross, John C. (Ed), Goldfried, Marvin R. (Ed). *Handbook of psychotherapy integration* (2nd ed.). (pp. 147-171). New York, NY, US: Oxford University Press.

Prochaska, J. O., DiClemente, C. C., & Norcross, J. C. (2003). In search of how people change: Applications to addictive behaviors. In Salovey, Peter (Ed), Rothman, Alexander J. (Ed). Social psychology of health. (pp. 63-77). New York, NY, US: Psychology Press.

Prochaska, J. M., Prochaska, J. O., Cohen, F. C., Gomes, S. O., Laforge, R. G., Eastwood, A. L. (2004). The transtheoretical model of change for mutli-level interventions for alcohol abuse on campus. *Journal of Alcohol and Drug Education, 47*, 34-50.

Prochaska, J., Velicer, W., Rossi, J. et. al. (1994). Stages of change and decisional balance for 12 problem behaviors. *Health Psychology, 13*, 39-46.

Ray, M. B. (1961). The cycle of abstinence and relapse among heroin addicts. *Social Problems, 9*(2), 132-140.

Raymond, N. C., Coleman, E., Ohlerking, F., Christenson, G. A., & Miner, M. (1999). Psychiatric comorbidity in pedophilic sex offenders. *The American Journal of Psychiatry, 156*(5), 786-788.

Rea, J. A., Williams, D., Saunders, K. J., Dixon, M., Wright, K., & Spradlin, J. E. (2003). Covert sensitization: A generalization analysis in the laboratory and natural environment through the use of a portable-penile plethysmograph. *The Behavior Analyst Today, 4*(2), 192-201.

Reilly, J. J., Armstrong, J., Dorosty, A. R., Emmett, P. M., Ness, A., Rogers, I., . . . Avon Longitudinal Study of Parents and Children Study Team. (2005). Early life risk factors for obesity in childhood: Cohort study. *BMJ: British Medical Journal, 330*(7504), 1357.

Reinecke, M. A. (1995). Comorbidity of conduct disorder and depression among adolescents: Implications for assessment and treatment. *Cognitive and Behavioral Practice, 2*(2), 299-326.

Resnick, Stella (1974). Gestalt therapy: The hot seat of personal responsibility, *Psyc Today*, Vol 8(6), 110-117.

Richmond, M. K., Pampel, F. C., Rivera, L. S., Broderick, K. B., Reimann, B., & Fischer, L. (2015). Frequency and risk of marijuana use among substance-using health care patients in Colorado with and without access to state legalized medical marijuana. *Journal of Psychoactive Drugs, 47*(1), 1-9.

Rich, G. J. (2013). Finding flow: The history and future of a positive psychology concept. In J. D. Sinnott (Ed.), *Positive psychology: Advances in understanding adult motivation* (pp. 43-60).

Robb, H. (2007). Values as leading principles in Acceptance and Commitment Therapy. *International Journal of Behavioral Consultation and Therapy, 3*(1), 118-122.

Rommel, D., Nandrino, J.-L., Ducro, C., Andrieux, S., Delecourt, F., & Antoine, P. (2012). Impact of emotional awareness and parental bonding on emotional eating in obese women. *Appetite, 59*(1), 21-26.

Ross, A. A., Filstead, W. J., Parrella, D. P., & Rossi, J. J. (1994). A comparison of high-risk situations for alcohol and other drugs. *The American Journal on Addictions, 3*(3), 241-253.

Ruedy, N. E., Moore, C., Gino, F., & Schweitzer, M. E. (2013). The cheater's high: The unexpected affective benefits of unethical behavior. *Journal of Personality and Social Psychology, 105*(4), 531-548.

Russell, K., Sturgeon, V. H., Miner, M. H., & Nelson, C. (1989). Determinants of the abstinence violation effect in sexual fantasies. In Laws, D. Richard (Ed), *Relapse prevention with sex offenders.* (pp. 63-72). New York, NY, US: Guilford Press.

Rychtarik, R. G., Prue, D. M., Rapp, S. R., & King, A. C. (1992). Self-efficacy, aftercare and relapse in a treatment program for alcoholics. *Journal of Studies on Alcohol, 53*, 435–440.

Salter, A. (1995). *Transforming Trauma: A guide to understanding and treating adult survivors of child sexual abuse.* Thousand Oaks CA: Sage Publications.

Salwen, J. K., Hymowitz, G. F., Vivian, D., & O'Leary, K. D. (2014). Childhood abuse, adult interpersonal abuse, and depression in individuals with extreme obesity. *Child Abuse & Neglect, 38*(3), 425-433.

Samenow, S. E. (1996). The criminal personality. In *The Hatherleigh Guide to Psychiatric Disorders* (pp. 137-152). New York: Hatherleigh Press.

Samenow, S. E. (2001). Understanding the criminal mind: A phenomenological approach. *Journal of Psychiatry and Law, 29*, 275-293.

Samo, J. A., Tucker, J. A., & Vuchinich, R. E. (1989). Agreement between self-monitoring, recall, and collateral observation measures of alcohol consumption in older adults. *Behavioral Assessment, 11*(4), 391-409.

References

Sams, D. P., & Truscott, S. D. (2004). Empathy, exposure to community violence, and use of violence among urban, at-risk adolescents. *Child & Youth Care Forum*, 33, 33-50.

Santiago-Rivas, M., Velicer, W. F., & Redding, C. (2015). Mediation analysis of decisional balance, sun avoidance and sunscreen use in the precontemplation and preparation stages for sun protection. *Psychology & Health, 30*(12), 1433-1449.

Sargeant, M., Daughters, S., Curtin, J., Schuster, R. & Lejuez, C. (2011). Unique roles of antisocial personality disorder and psychopathic traits in distress tolerance. *Journal of Abnormal Psychology, 120*(4), 987-992.

Sarti, S., & Triventi, M. (2017). The role of social and cognitive factors in individual gambling: An empirical study on college students. *Social Science Research, 62,* 219-237.

Satre, D. D., Kohn, C. S., & Weisner, C. (2007). Cigarette smoking and long-term alcohol and drug treatment outcomes: A telephone follow-up at five years. *The American Journal on Addictions, 16,* 32- 37.

Schlup, B., Munsch, S., Meyer, A. H., Margraf, J., & Wilhelm, F. H. (2009). The efficacy of a short version of a cognitive-behavioral treatment followed by booster sessions for binge eating disorder. *Behaviour Research and Therapy, 47*(7), 628-635.

Schmidt, S. (2016, June 28). Former Indiana University Student Accused of Two Rapes Avoids Prison in Plea Deal. *The New York Times*, U.S. Section, p. A11. Online version can be retrieved from http://www.nytimes.com/2016/06/28/us/indiana-rape-plea-deal.html.

Schnoll, R. A., Martinez, E., Tatum, K. L., Glass, M., Bernath, A., Ferris, D., & Reynolds, P. (2011). Increased self-efficacy to quit and perceived control over withdrawal symptoms predict smoking cessation following nicotine dependence treatment. *Addictive Behaviors, 36,* 144–147

Schonfeld, L., Rohrer, G. E., Dupree, L. W., Thomas, M. (1989). Antecedents of relapse and recent substance use. Community Mental Health Journal, 25, 245-249.

Schotte, D. E., Cools, J. & McNally, R. J. (1990). Induced anxiety triggers overeating in restrained eaters. *Journal of Abnormal Psychology*, 99, 317-320.

Schulherr, S. (2005). Exiting the Binge-Diet Cycle. In Shapiro, Robin (Ed), *EMDR solutions: Pathways to healing.* (pp. 241-262). New York, NY, US: W W Norton & Co.

Schulherr, S. (1998). The binge-diet cycle: Shedding new light, finding new exits. *Eating Disorders: The Journal of Treatment & Prevention, 6,* 267-271.

Schwartz, S. H. & Bilsky, W. (1987). Toward a universal psychological structure of human values. Journal of *Personality and Social Psychology*, 53, 550-562.

Schwartz, S. H. & Bilsky, W. (1990). Toward a theory of the universal content and structure of values: Extensions and cross-cultural replications. *Journal of Personality and Social Psychology*, 58, 878-891.

Schwartz, S. H., Melech, G., Lehmann, A., Burgess, S., Harris, M., and Owens, V. (2001). Extending the cross-cultural validity of the theory of basic human values with a different method of measurement. *Journal of Cross-Cultural Psychology, 32*(5), 519-542.

Schwartz, J. P., Waldo, M., & Daniel, D. (2005). Gender-role conflict and self-esteem: Factors associated with partner abuse in court-referred men. *Psychology of Men & Masculinity*, 6, 109-113.

Scott, C. K., Dennis, M. L., & Foss, M. A. (2005). Utilizing recovery management checkups to shorten the cycle of relapse, treatment reentry, and recovery. *Drug and Alcohol Dependence*, 78, 325-338.

Scott, C. K., Foss, M. A., & Dennis, M. L. (2005). Pathways in the relapse--treatment--recovery cycle over 3 years. *Journal of Substance Abuse Treatment*, 28, S63-S72.

Scully, D., & Marolla, J. (2003). Interviewing in a difficult situation: "Riding the bull at Gilley's": Convicted rapists describe the rewards of rape. In J. M. Henslin (Ed.), *Down to earth sociology: Introductory readings (12th ed.)* (pp. 48-64). New York: Free Press.

Seiden, D. (1999). The effect of research on practice in cross-cultural behavior therapy: A single case study (You're the case). *The Behavior Therapist*, 22, 200-201.

Sellers, C. S., Cochran, J. K., & Branch, K. A. (2005). Social learning theory and partner violence: A research note. *Deviant Behavior, 26*(4), 379-395.

Shaffer, H. J., and Hall, M. N. (2002). The natural history of gambling and drinking problems among casino employees. *Journal of Social Psychology, 142,* 405-424.

Shanmugham, K., Cano, M. A., Elliott, T. R., & Davis, M. (2009). Social problem-solving abilities, relationship satisfaction and depression among family caregivers of stroke survivors. *Brain Injury, 23(2)*, 92-100.

References

Sharp, W., Schulenberg, S. E., Wilson, K. G., & Murrell, A. R. (2004). Logotherapy and Acceptance and Commitment Therapy (ACT): An initial comparison of values-centered approaches. *International Forum for Logotherapy, 27*(2), 98-105.

Shiffman. S., Hickcox, M., Paty, J., Gnys, M., Kassel, J. & Richards, T. (1996). Progression from a smoking lapse to relapse: Prediction from abstinence violation effects, nicotine dependence, and lapse characteristics, *Journal of Consulting and Clinical Psychology*, 64(5), 993-1002.

Shiffman, S., Hickcox, M., Paty, J. A., Gnys, M., Kassel, J. D., & Richards, T. J. (1997). The abstinence violation effect following smoking lapses and temptations. *Cognitive Therapy and Research, 21*, 497-523.

Shiffman, S., Paty, J. A., Gnys, M., Kassel, J. A., and Hickcox, M. (1996). First lapses to smoking: Within-subjects analysis of real-time reports. *Journal of Consulting and Clinical Psychology,* 64, 366-379.

Shorey, R. C., Larson, E. E., & Cornelius, T. L. (2014). An initial investigation of the relation between mindfulness and female-perpetrated dating violence. *Partner Abuse, 5*(1), 3-20.

Simons, R. L., & Johnson, C. (1998). An examination of competing explanations for the intergenerational transmission of domestic violence. In Y. Danieli (Ed.), *The Plenum series on stress and coping. International handbook of multigenerational legacies of trauma* (pp. 553-570).

Sinha, R., & Jastreboff, A. M. (2013). Stress as a common risk factor for obesity and addiction. *Biological Psychiatry, 73*(9), 827-835.

Siu, A. M. H., & Shek, D. T. L. (2010). Social problem solving as a predictor of well-being in adolescents and young adults. *Social Indicators Research*, 95(3), 393-406.

Smith, R. (2002). The biopsychosocial revolution: Interviewing and provider-patient relationships becoming key issues for primary care, *Journal of General Internal Medicine*, 17(4), 309–310.

Smith, D. E., Marcus, M. D., Lewis, C., Fitzgibbon, M., & Schreiner, P. (1998). Prevalence of binge eating disorder, obesity, and depression in a biracial cohort of young adults. *Annals of Behavioral Medicine, 20*(3), 227-232.

Smith, S., Wampler, R., Jones, J. & Reifman, A. (2005). Differences in self-report measures by adolescent sex offender risk group. *International Journal of Offender Therapy and Comparative Criminology*, 49, 82-106.

Shmueli, D., & Prochaska, J. J. (2009). Resisting tempting foods and smoking behavior: Implications from a self-control theory perspective. *Health Psychology, 28*(3), 300-306.

Soberay, A. D., Grimsley, P., Faragher, J. M., Barbash, M., & Berger, B. (2014). Stages of change, clinical presentation, retention, and treatment outcomes in treatment-seeking outpatient problem gambling clients. *Psychology of Addictive Behaviors, 28*(2), 414-419.

Sogg, S., Lauretti, J. & West-Smith, L. (2016). ASMBS Guidelines/Statements: Recommendations for the presurgical psychosocial evaluation of bariatric surgery patients. *Surgery for Obesity and Related Diseases,* (12) 731–749.

Solomon, G. S., & Ray, J. B. (1984). Irrational beliefs of shoplifters. *Journal of Clinical Psychology, 40*(4), 1075-1077.

Sorenson, A. M., & Brownfield, D. (1995). Adolescent drug use and a general theory of crime: An analysis of a theoretical integration. *Canadian Journal of Criminology*, 37, 19-37.

Sowards, K. A., O'Boyle, K., & Weissman, M. (2006). Inspiring hope, envisioning alternatives: The importance of peer role models in a mandated treatment program for women. *Journal of Social Work Practice in the Addictions*, 6(4), 55-70.

Sperry, L. (2005). Case conceptualization: A strategy for incorporating individual, couple and family dynamics in the treatment process. *American Journal of Family Therapy, 33*(5), 353-364.

Spohr, S. A., Taxman, F. S., & Walters, S. T. (2015). The relationship between electronic goal reminders and subsequent drug use and treatment initiation in a criminal justice setting. *Addictive Behaviors, 51,* 51-56.

Stasiewicz, P. R., Bradizza, C. M., Gudleski, G. D., Coffey, S. F., Schlauch, R. C., Bailey, S. T., . . . Gulliver, S. B. (2012). The relationship of alexithymia to emotional dysregulation within an alcohol dependent treatment sample. *Addictive Behaviors, 37*(4), 469-476.

Starzyk, K. B., & Marshall, W. L. (2003). Childhood family and personological risk factors for sexual offending. *Aggression and Violent Behavior, 8*(1), 93-105.

Stockwell, T., & Chikritzhs, T. (2009). Do relaxed trading hours for bars and clubs mean more relaxed drinking? A review of international research on the impacts of changes to permitted hours of drinking. *Crime Prevention and Community Safety, 11*(3), 153-170.

References

Steele, M. M., Steele, R. G., & Cushing, C. C. (2012). Weighing the pros and cons in family-based pediatric obesity intervention: Parent and child decisional balance as a predictor of child outcomes. *Children's Health Care, 41*(1), 43-55.

Steen, C. (1995). *The relapse prevention workbook for youth in treatment.* Safer Society Press: Brandon VT.

Stein, J. A., Zane, J. I., & Grella, C. E. (2012). Impact of abstinence self-efficacy and treatment services on physical health-related behaviors and problems among dually diagnosed patients. *Journal of Dual Diagnosis, 8*(1), 64-73.

Stephens, R. S., Curtin, L., Simpson, E. E., & Roffman, R. A. (1994). Testing the abstinence violation effect construct with marijuana cessation. *Addictive Behaviors, 19,* 23-32.

Stephens, R. S., Wertz, J. S., & Roffman, R. A. (1995). Self-efficacy and marijuana cessation: A construct validity analysis. *Journal of Consulting and Clinical Psychology, 63,* 1022–1031.

Stetson, B., Beacham, A., Frommelt, S., Boutelle, K., Cole, J., Ziegler, C. & Looney, S. (2005). Exercise slips in high-risk situations and activity patterns in long-term exercisers: An application of the relapse prevention model. *Annals of Behavioral Medicine, 30*(1), 25-35.

Stevens, J. O. (1971). *Awareness: Exploring, experimenting, experiencing.* Moab, UT: Real People Press.

Stith, S., Crossman, R., and Bischof, G. (1991). Alcoholism and marital violence: A comparative study of men in alcohol treatment programs and batterer treatment programs. *Alcoholism Treatment Quarterly, 8*(2), 3-20.

Stoop, D. (2012). Helping couples deal with betrayal and affairs. In A. Vernon (Ed.), *Cognitive and rational-emotive behavior therapy with couples: Theory and practice* (pp. 117-132).

Stylianou, S. (2002). The relationship between elements and manifestations of low self-control in a general theory of crime: Two comments and a test. *Deviant Behavior, 23,* 531-557.

Suarez, L., Nichols, D. C., & Brady, C. A. (1993). Use of peer role models to increase Pap smear and mammogram screening in Mexican-American and Black women. *American Journal of Preventive Medicine, 9*(5), 290-296.

Sue, S. (2003). In defense of cultural competency in psychotherapy and treatment. *American Psychologist, 58,* 964-970.

Swick, K. (2005). Preventing Violence through Empathy Development in Families. *Early Childhood Education Journal, 33,* 53-59.

Swirsky, D., & Mitchell, V. (1996). The binge-purge cycle as a means of dissociation: Somatic trauma and somatic defense in sexual abuse and bulimia. *Dissociation: Progress in the Dissociative Disorders, 9,* 18-27.

Sykes, R. E., Rowley, R. D., & Schaefer, J. M. (1990). Effects of group participation on drinking behaviors in public bars: An observational survey. *Journal of Social Behavior & Personality, 5*(4), 385-402.

Symbaluk, D. G. (1998). An application of the general theory of crime to sex offenders. *Dissertation Abstracts International Section A: Humanities and Social Sciences.* 58(10), 1998, 4076A.

Tanford, S., & Penrod, S. (1984). Social Influence Model: A formal integration of research on majority and minority influence processes. *Psychological Bulletin, 95*(2), 189-225.

Taormina, R. J., & Gao, J. H. (2013). Maslow and the motivation hierarchy: Measuring satisfaction of the needs. *The American Journal of Psychology, 126*(2), 155-177.

Takahashi, F., Koseki, S., & Shimada, H. (2009). Developmental trends in children's aggression and social problem-solving. *Journal of Applied Developmental Psychology, 30*(3), 265-272.

Talbott, L. L., Moore, C. G., & Usdan, S. L. (2012). Social modeling influences and alcohol consumption during the first semester of college: A natural history study. Substance Abuse, 33(2), 146-155.

Tate, S. R., Wu, J., McQuaid, J. R., Cummins, K., Shriver, C., Krenek, M., & Brown, S. A. (2008). Comorbidity of substance dependence and depression: Role of life stress and self-efficacy in sustaining abstinence. *Psychology of Addictive Behaviors, 22*(1), 47-57.

Tejero, A., Trujols, J., Hernández, E., de los Cobos, J. P., Casas, M. (1997). Processes of change assessment in heroin addicts following the Prochaska and DiClemente transtheoretical model. *Drug and Alcohol Dependence, 47,* 31-37.

Thompson, E. H., Jr., & Cracco, E. J. (2008). Sexual aggression in bars: What college men can normalize. *The Journal of Men's Studies, 16*(1), 82-96.

Tierney, D. W., & McCabe, M. P. (2004). The assessment of motivation for behaviour change among sex offenders against children: An investigation of the utility of the Stages of Change Questionnaire. *Journal of Sexual Aggression, 10*(2), 237-249.

Tinklenberg, J. A., Steiner, H., Huckaby, W. J., & Tinklenberg, J. R. (1996). Criminal recidivism predicted from narratives of violent juvenile delinquents. *Child Psychiatry & Human Development, 27,* 69-79.

References

Toneatto, T., Pillai, S., & Courtice, E. L. (2014). Mindfulness-enhanced cognitive behavior therapy for problem gambling: A controlled pilot study. *International Journal of Mental Health and Addiction, 12*(2), 197-205.

Tonigan, J. S., & Rice, S. L. (2010). Is it beneficial to have an Alcoholics Anonymous sponsor? *Psychology of Addictive Behaviors, 24*(3), 397-403.

Tonigan, J. S., Toscova, R., & Miller, W. R. (1995). Meta-analysis of the literature on Alcoholics Anonymous: Sample and study characteristics moderate findings. *Journal of Studies on Alcohol, 57*(1), 65-72.

Turchik, J. A., & Wilson, S. M. (2010). Sexual assault in the U.S. military: A review of the literature and recommendations for the future. *Aggression and Violent Behavior, 15*(4), 267-277

Turner, C. B., & Cashdan, S. (1988). Perception of college students' motives for shoplifting. *Psychological Reports, 62*(3), 855-862.

Turner, D., Hoyer, J., Schmidt, A. F., Klein, V., & Briken, P. (2016). Risk factors for sexual offending in men working with children: A community-based survey. *Archives of Sexual Behavior.* Advance online publication.

Turner, N. E., Preston, D. L., Saunders, C., McAvoy, S., & Jain, U. (2009). The relationship of problem gambling to criminal behavior in a sample of Canadian male federal offenders. *Journal of Gambling Studies, 25*(2), 153-169.

Vakoch, D. A. (Ed.). (2013). *International and cultural psychology. Altruism in cross-cultural perspective.* NY: Springer.

van Apeldoorn, F. J., van Hout, W. J. P. J., Mersch, P. P. et. al. (2008). Is a combined therapy more effective than either CBT or SSRI alone? Results of a multicenter trial on panic disorder with or without agoraphobia. *Acta Psychiatrica Scandinavica, 117*(4), 260-270.

van Strien, T., Konttinen, H., Homberg, J. R., Engels, R. C. M. E., & Winkens, L. H. H. (2016). Emotional eating as a mediator between depression and weight gain. *Appetite, 100,* 216-224.

Vaziri, S., & Azimi, A. L. (2012). The effect of empathy training in decreasing adolescents' aggression. *Journal of Iranian Psychologists, 8*(30), 167-176.

Vazsonyi, A. T., & Crosswhite, J. M. (2004). A test of Gottfredson and Hirschi's general theory of crime in African American adolescents. *Journal of Research in Crime and Delinquency*, 41, 407-432.

Vazsonyi, A. T., Pickering, L. E., Junger, M., & Hessing, D. (2001). An empirical test of a general theory of crime: A four-nation comparative study of self-control and the prediction of deviance. *Journal of Research in Crime and Delinquency*, 38, 91-131.

Vazsonyi, A. T., Wittekind, J. E. C., Belliston, L. M., & Van Loh, T. D. (2004). Extending the general theory of crime to "The East:" Low self-control in Japanese late adolescents. *J Quantitative Criminology*, 20, 189-216.

Velasquez, M. M., von Sternberg, K., Johnson, D. H., Green, C., Carbonari, J. P., & Parsons, J. T. (2009). Reducing sexual risk behaviors and alcohol use among HIV-positive men who have sex with men: A randomized clinical trial. *Journal of Consulting and Clinical Psychology, 77*(4), 657-667.

Velicer, W. F., DiClemente, C. C., Prochaska, J. O., & Brandenburg, N. (1985). Decisional balance measure for assessing and predicting smoking status. *Journal of Personality and Social Psychology, 48*(5), 1279-1289.

Veysey, B. M., Ostermann, M., & Lanterman, J. L. (2014). The effectiveness of enhanced parole supervision and community services: New Jersey's serious and violent offender reentry initiative. *The Prison Journal, 94*(4), 435-453.

Viljoen, J. L., Mordell, S., & Beneteau, J. L. (2012). Prediction of adolescent sexual reoffending: A meta-analysis of the J-SOAP-II, ERASOR, J-SORRAT-II, and Static-99. *Law and Human Behavior, 36*(5), 423-438.

Vohs, K. D., Baumeister, R. F., Schmeichel, B. J., Twenge, J. M., Nelson, N. M., & Tice, D. M. (2014). Making choices impairs subsequent self-control: A limited-resource account of decision making, self-regulation, and active initiative. *Motivation Science, 1*(S), 19-42.

Vose, B., Cullen, F. T., & Smith, P. (2008). The empirical status of the Level of Service Inventory. *Federal Probation, 72*(3), 22-29.

Wack, S. R., Crosland, K. A., & Miltenberger, R. G. (2014). Using goal setting and feedback to increase weekly running distance. *Journal of Applied Behavior Analysis, 47*(1), 181-185.

Wagers, S. M. (2015). Deconstructing the "power and control motive": moving beyond a unidimensional view of power in domestic violence theory. *Partner Abuse, 6*(2), 230-242.

Wagner, D. V., Borduin, C. M., Sawyer, A. M., & Dopp, A. R. (2014). Long-term prevention of criminality in siblings of serious and violent juvenile offenders: A 25-year follow-up to a randomized clinical trial of multisystemic therapy. Journal of Consulting and Clinical Psychology, 82(3), 492-499

References

Walker, D. M., Clark, C., & Folk, J. (2010). The relationship between gambling behavior and binge drinking, hard drug use, and paying for sex. *UNLV Gaming Research & Review Journal, 14*(1), 15-26.

Walker, L. & Pitts, R. (1998). Naturalistic conceptions of moral maturity. *Developmental Psychology*, 34(3), 403-419.

Ward, T. & Fortune, C. (2013). The Good Lives Model: Aligning risk reduction with promoting offenders' personal goals. *European Journal of Probation*. University of Bucharest, 5(2), 29- 46.

Ward, B. W., & Gryczynski, J. (2009). Social learning theory and the effects of living arrangement on heavy alcohol use: Results from a national study of college students. *Journal of Studies on Alcohol and Drugs, 70*(3), 364-372.

Ward, T., Hudson, S. M., & Bulik, C. M. (1993). The abstinence violation effect in bulimia nervosa. *Addictive Behaviors, 18*, 671-680.

Ward, T., Hudson, S. M., & Marshall, W. L. (1994). The abstinence violation effect in child molesters. *Behaviour Research and Therapy, 32*, 431-437.

Wansink, B., & Payne, C. R. (2008). Eating behavior and obesity at Chinese buffets. *Obesity, 16*(8), 1957-1960.

Warziski, M. T., Sereika, S. M., Styn, M. A., Music, E., & Burke, L. E. (2008). Changes in self-efficacy and dietary adherence: The impact on weight loss in the PREFER study. *Journal of Behavioral Medicine, 31*(1), 81-92.

Wasson, D. H., & Jackson, M. (2004). An Analysis of the Role of Overeaters Anonymous in Women's Recovery from Bulimia Nervosa. *Eating Disorders: The Journal of Treatment & Prevention, 12*(4), 337-356.

Wastell, C. A., Cairns, D., & Haywood, H. (2009). Empathy training, sex offenders and re-offending. *Journal of Sexual Aggression, 15*(2), 149-159.

Waters, A., Hill, A., Waller, G. (2001). Internal and external antecedents of binge eating episodes in a group of women with bulimia nervosa. *International Journal of Eating Disorders*, 29, 17-22.

Waters, J. A., Fazio, S. L., Hernandez, L., and Segarra, J. (2002). The story of CURA, a Hispanic/Latino drug therapeutic community. *Journal of Ethnicity in Substance Abuse*, 1, 113-134.

Weinstock, J., Whelan, J. P., Meyers, A. W., & McCausland, C. (2009). The performance of two pathological gambling screens in college students. *Assessment, 14,* 399–407.

Wheeler, G., & Axelsson, L. (2015). *Theories of psychotherapy series. Gestalt therapy.* Washington, DC, US: American Psychological Association.

Wheeler, J. G., George, W. H., & Marlatt, G. A. (2006). Relapse Prevention for Sexual Offenders: Considerations for the "Abstinence Violation Effect". *Sexual Abuse: Journal of Research and Treatment, 18*(3), 233-248.

White, W. L., Campbell, M. D., Spencer, R. A., Hoffman, H. A., Crissman, B., & DuPont, R. L. (2014). Participation in narcotics anonymous and alcoholics anonymous and abstinence outcomes of 322 methadone maintenance patients. *Journal of Groups in Addiction & Recovery, 9*(1), 14-30.

Whitford, R., & Parr, V. (1995). Uses of rational emotive behavior therapy with juvenile sex offenders. *Journal of Rational-Emotive & Cognitive-Behavior Therapy, 13*(4), 273-282.

Wickwire, E. M., Whelan, J. P., Meyers, A. W., & Murray, D. M. (2007). Environmental correlates of gambling behavior in urban adolescents. *Journal of Abnormal Child Psychology, 35*(2), 179-190.

Williams, A. D., Grisham, J. R., Erskine, A., & Cassedy, E. (2012). Deficits in emotion regulation associated with pathological gambling. *British Journal of Clinical Psychology, 51*(2), 223-238.

Williamson, D. (1990). *Assessment of Eating Disorders: Obesity, Anorexia, and Bulimia Nervosa.* New York: Pergamon Press.

Williamson, D. F., Thompson, T. J., Anda, R. F., Dietz, W. H., & Felitti, V. (2002). Body weight and obesity in adults and self-reported abuse in childhood. *International Journal of Obesity, 26*(8), 1075-1082.

Wills, T. A., & Hirky, A. E. (1996). Coping and substance abuse: A theoretical model and review of the evidence. In M. Zeidner & N. S. Endler (Eds.), *Handbook of coping: Theory, research, applications* (pp. 279-302). Oxford, England: John Wiley.

Wilson, R. J., Stewart, L., Stirpe, T., Barrett, M., & Cripps, J. E. (2000). Community-based sexual offender management: Combining parole supervision and treatment to reduce recidivism. *Canadian Journal of Criminology, 42*(2), 177-188.

Winett, R., Cleveland, B., Tate, D., Lombard, D., Lombard, T., Russ, C. & Galper, D. (1997). The Effects of the safe-sun program on patrons' and lifeguards' skin cancer risk-reduction behaviors at swimming pools. *Journal of Health Psychology, 2*, 85-95.

Winett, R. A., Moore, J. F., Wagner, J. L., Hite, L. A., & et al (1991). Altering shoppers' supermarket purchases to fit nutritional guidelines: An interactive information system. *Journal of Applied Behavior Analysis, 24*, 95-105.

References

Winfree, L. T., & Griffiths, C. T. (1983). Social learning and adolescent marijuana use: A trend study of deviant behavior in a rural middle school. *Rural Sociology, 48*(2), 219-239.

Wing, R. R., & Jeffery, R. W. (1999). Benefits of recruiting participants with friends and increasing social support for weight loss and maintenance. *Journal of Consulting and Clinical Psychology, 67*(1), 132-138.

Wisner, B. L., & Starzec, J. J. (2015). The process of personal transformation for adolescents practicing mindfulness skills in an alternative school setting. *Child & Adolescent Social Work Journal. p. 1- 13,* Advance online publication. *http://dx.doi.org/10.1007/s10560-015-0418-0*

Witkiewitz, K., Bowen, S., & Donovan, D. M. (2011). Moderating effects of a craving intervention on the relation between negative mood and heavy drinking following treatment for alcohol dependence. *Journal of Consulting and Clinical Psychology, 79*(1), 54-63.

Witkiewitz, K., Donavan, D. M., & Hartzler, B. (2012). Drink refusal training as part of comorbid behavioral intervention: Effectiveness and mechanisms of change. *J of Consulting and Clinical Psychology, 80,* 440- 449.

Witkiewitz, K. A., & Marlatt, G. A. (Eds.). (2007). *Practical resources for the mental health professional. Therapist's guide to evidence-based relapse prevention.* San Diego, CA: Elsevier Academic Press.

Witkiewitz, K., & Marlatt, G. A. (2009). Relapse prevention for alcohol and drug problems: That was Zen, this is Tao. In G. A. Marlatt & K. Witkiewitz (Eds.), *Addictive behaviors: New readings on etiology, prevention, and treatment* (pp. 403-427).

Witkiewitz, K., Warner, K., Sully, B., Barricks, A., Stauffer, C., Thompson, B. L., & Luoma, J. B. (2014). Randomized trial comparing mindfulness-based relapse prevention with relapse prevention for women offenders at a residential addiction treatment center. *Substance Use & Misuse, 49*(5), 536-546.

Wolpe, J. (1958). *Psychotherapy by reciprocal inhibition.* Oxford, England: Stanford University Press.

Wolpe, J. (1995). Reciprocal inhibition: Major agent of behavior change. In O'Donohue, William T. (Ed), Krasner, Leonard (Ed). *Theories of behavior therapy: Exploring behavior change.* (pp. 23-57). Washington, DC, US: American Psychological Association.

Wood, P. B., Wilson, J. A., & Thorne, D. P. (2015). Offending patterns, control balance, and affective rewards among convicted sex offenders. *Deviant Behavior, 36*(5), 368-387.

Wros, P. L., Doutrich, D., and Izumi, S. (2004). Ethical concerns: Comparison of values from two cultures. *Nursing and Health Sciences*, 6, 131-140.

Yancey, J. R., Venables, N. C., Hicks, B. M., & Patrick, C. J. (2013). Evidence for a heritable brain basis to deviance-promoting deficits in self-control. *Journal of Criminal Justice, 41*(5), 309-317.

Yankura, J., & Dryden, W. (Eds.). (1997). *Using REBT with common psychological problems: A therapist's casebook.* New York: Springer.

Yalom, I. D., & Leszcz, M. (Collaborator). (2005). *The theory and practice of group psychotherapy.* New York: Basic Books.

Yates, P. M., & Ward, T. (2007). Treatment of sexual offenders: Relapse prevention and beyond. In K. A. Witkiewitz & G. A. Marlatt (Eds.), *Practical resources for the mental health professional. Therapist's guide to evidence-based relapse prevention* (pp. 215-234).

Yochelson, S., and Samenow, S. E. (1976). *The Criminal Personality, Volume 1: A Profile for Change.* New York: Jason Aronson. [Note: Thinking Errors are described in Chapter 5].

Yoder, V. C., Virden, T. B. III, & Amin, K. (2005). Internet pornography and loneliness: An association? *Sexual Addiction & Compulsivity, 12*(1), 19-44.

Yokley, J. (2008). *Social Responsibility Therapy for Adolescents & Young Adults: A Multicultural Treatment Manual for Harmful Behavior*, New York, NY, US: Routledge/Taylor & Francis Group., 357 pp. **ISBN: 978-0-7890- 3121-1.**

Yokley, J. (2010a). Social Responsibility Therapy for Harmful, Abusive Behavior, *Journal of Contemporary Psychotherapy,* 40(2), p. 105- 113.

Yokley, J. (2010b). *How did I get this problem? Social Responsibility Therapy: Understanding Harmful Behavior Workbook 1.* Social Solutions Press. ISBN: 978-0-9832449-0-5, 123 pp.

Yokley, J. (2011a). *Why do I keep doing this? Social Responsibility Therapy: Understanding Harmful Behavior Workbook 2.* Social Solutions Press. ISBN: 978-0-9832449-1-2, 143 pp.

Yokley, J. (2011b). The treatment of youth referred for sexual behavior problems in Forensic Foster Care: A Social Responsibility Therapy program description. In B. Schwartz (Ed.), *Handbook of Sex Offender Treatment* (Chapter 54). Kingston, NJ: Civic Research Institute.

References

Yokley, J. (2012). *How did my problem Spread? Social Responsibility Therapy: Understanding Harmful Behavior Workbook 3.* Social Solutions Press. ISBN: 978-0-9832449-2-9, 233 pp.

Yokley, J. & Boettner, S. (1999, September). Behavior Norms for Outpatient Youth Sex Offenders: Constructing A Database for Treatment Intervention Decisions. 18th Annual Research & Treatment Conference of the Association for the Treatment of Sexual Abusers, Lake Buena Vista, Florida.

Yokley, J., and Boettner, S. (2002). Forensic foster care for young people who sexually abuse: Lessons from treatment. In M. Calder (Ed.), *Young People who Sexually Abuse: Building the Evidence Base for Your Practice,* Chapter 20. Dorset, UK: Russell House Publishing.

Yokley, J. & Glenwick, D. (1984). Increasing the immunization of preschool children: An evaluation of applied community interventions. *Journal of Applied Behavior Analysis,* 17(3), 313-325. Reprinted in Behavior Analysis in the Community 1968-1986, JABA Reprint Series Volume 2.

Yong, A. D., Williams, M. W. M., Provan, H., Clarke, D., & Sinclair, G. (2015). How do offenders move through the stages of change? *Psychology, Crime & Law, 21*(4), 375-397.

Young, J. (1990). *Cognitive therapy for personality disorders: A schema-focused approach.* Sarasota, FL: Professional Resource Exchange.

Xiao, J. J., O'Neill, B., Prochaska, J. M., Kerbel, C. M., Brennan, P., & Bristow, B. J. (2004). A consumer education programme based on the Transtheoretical Model of Change. *International Journal of Consumer Studies, 28*(1), 55-65.

Zhai, Z. W., Yip, S. W., Steinberg, M. A., Wampler, J., Hoff, R. A., Krishnan-Sarin, S., & Potenza, M. N. (2017). Relationships between perceived family gambling and peer gambling and adolescent problem gambling and binge-drinking. *Journal of Gambling Studies, 33*(4), 1169-1185.

Zimmerman, M., & Galione, J. N. (2011). Screening for bipolar disorder with the mood disorders questionnaire: A review. *Harvard Review of Psychiatry, 19*(5), 219-228.

Zmuda, N. (2014). Assessment and treatment of co-occurring substance use disorders and process addictions: Eating disorders, pathological gambling, and sexual addiction. In S. L. A. Straussner (Ed.), *Clinical work with substance-abusing clients* (pp. 520-536). New York, NY, US: Guilford Press.

Žvelc, G., Černetič, M., & Košak, M. (2011). Mindfulness-based transactional analysis. *Transactional Analysis Journal, 41*(3), 241-254.

Index

Social Responsibility Therapy for Adolescents and Young Adults: A Multicultural Treatment Manual for Harmful Behavior provides a comprehensive explanation of Social Responsibility Therapy, its advantages, and the intervention evidence-base for multiple forms of harmful behavior. This text discusses in detail the multicultural intervention approach, its rationale, and content. Implementation methods and treatment protocol are explored. The book includes illustrated case studies, tables, figures, and references to additional available readings.

Topics discussed in Social Responsibility Therapy for Adolescents and Young Adults: A Multicultural Treatment Manual for Harmful Behavior include:

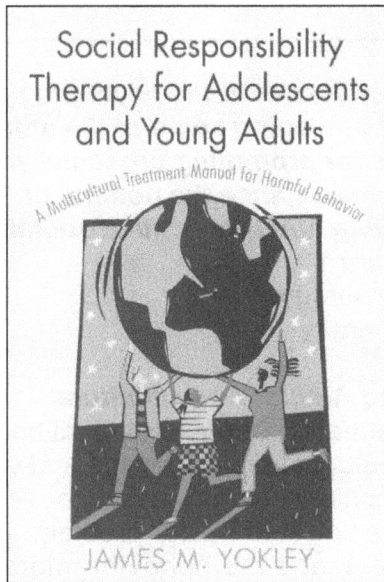

- evidence-based procedures used in Structured Discovery learning experiences to target harmful behavior
- helping clients discover how they acquired, maintained, and generalized a broad range of harmful behavior
- addressing target behavior problems, negative social influence problems, and the dose-response problem
- five areas of human functioning that are critical to the wellbeing of self and others which can only be addressed through psychotherapy and forensic parenting
- developing prosocial behavior alternatives which contribute to both relapse prevention and personal development and much more!

Social Responsibility Therapy for Adolescents and Young Adults: A Multicultural Treatment Manual for Harmful Behavior is an essential resource for social workers, counselors, psychologists, and psychiatrists whose caseloads include a multicultural population of young people who exhibit multiple forms of unhealthy, harmful behavior.

Order online through
www.socialsolutionspress.com

Table of Contents

About the Author

James M. Yokley, Ph.D., **is a Clinical Psychologist on the medical staff in the Department of Psychiatry at MetroHealth Medical Center in Cleveland, Ohio, as well as an Assistant Professor at Case Western Reserve University School of Medicine and Department of Psychology. He has expertise in cognitive-behavior therapy with multiple forms of unhealthy, harmful behavior, has authored over 50 research publications, book chapters, and professional presentations, and is a regular conference speaker on this topic.**

Paperback: 978-0-7890-3121-1. $49.95 • May 2008, 357pp

Social Responsibility Therapy for Adolescents and Young Adults
A Multicultural Treatment Manual for Harmful Behavior
James M. Yokley, Ph.D.

"*A valuable contribution to the field, confronting important issues at the psychological and societal levels. Provides a comprehensive framework for managing some of the most challenging clinical problems. Provides useful guidelines for promoting prosocial values and behaviors in delinquent youth. The treatment strategies balance the notions of therapeutic structure with client discovery. Many interesting and provocative quotations are laced throughout the text. A valuable addition to any library.*"
   —James C. Overholser, PhD, ABPP, professor of psychology, director of clinical training, Case Western Reserve University

Social Responsibility Therapy for Adolescents and Young Adults: A Multicultural Treatment Manual for Harmful Behavior is a crucial treatment manual for mental health professionals whose caseloads include a multicultural population of adolescents and young adults who exhibit multiple forms of harmful behavior. This unique therapy enhances relapse prevention in harmful behavior treatment by addressing the target behavior problem, negative social influence problem, dose-response problem, and the behavior migration problem. It also acknowledges that harmful behavior is multicultural, and it addresses the key criticisms of multicultural therapy through a theory-driven treatment approach that utilizes methods and procedures from existing evidence-based treatments with known multicultural applications.

This text provides a comprehensive explanation of Social Responsibility Therapy, its advantages, and the intervention evidence-base for multiple forms of harmful behavior. It discusses in detail the multicultural intervention approach, its rationale, and content; describes the implementation methods and treatment protocol; and includes illustrated case studies, tables, figures, and references to additional readings. This book is an essential resource for mental health professionals from all disciplines, including social workers, counselors, psychologists, and psychiatrists who are involved in the treatment of multiple forms of harmful behavior.

James M. Yokley, PhD, is a clinical psychologist in the Department of Psychiatry at MetroHealth Medical Center in Cleveland, Ohio, and is an assistant professor at Case Western University School of Medicine and Department of Psychology.

Routledge
Taylor & Francis Group

www.routledgementalhealth.com

Printed in the U.S.A.
Cover design: Elise Weinger Halprin

ISBN: 978-0-7890-3121-1
90000

9 780789 031211

an **informa** business

The Social Responsibility Therapy:
Understanding Harmful Behavior Workbook Series

The Social Responsibility Therapy workbook series on Understanding Harmful Behavior was structured to help individuals with unhealthy, harmful behavior discover how they got their problem, what kept it going and how it spread to other areas through "The Problem Development Triad."

Workbook 1- "How did I get this problem?" focuses on understanding how unhealthy, harmful behavior was acquired through "The Risk Factor Chain." ISBN: 978-0-9832449-0-5.

Workbook 2- "Why do I keep doing this?" focuses on understanding how unhealthy, harmful behavior problems were maintained by "The Stress-Relapse Cycle." ISBN: 978-0-9832449-1-2.

Workbook 3- "How did my problem spread?" focuses on understanding how unhealthy, harmful behavior problems were generalized to other areas using "The Harmful Behavior Anatomy." ISBN: 978-0-9832449-2-9.

Further description is available at www.socialsolutionspress.com

Order information for Social Responsibility Therapy:
Understanding Harmful Behavior Workbooks 1-3

Volume order discounts are available. Discounts are also available for non-profit or faith-based organizations and professionals caring for underserved populations.

For volume or special discounts, e-mail order information (Name, zip code and number of workbooks, organization and population served) to...
info@socialsolutionspress.com

Note:

Social Responsibility Therapy is a
Social Solutions Healthy Behavior Lifestyle Project
www.socialsolutionspress.com

www.ingramcontent.com/pod-product-compliance
Lightning Source LLC
Chambersburg PA
CBHW080325270326
41927CB00014B/3102